LEGAL
ETHICS

The West Legal Studies Series

Your options keep growing with West Legal Studies

Each year our list continues to offer you more options for every area of the law to meet your course or on-the-job reference requirements. We now have over 140 titles from which to choose in the following areas:

Administrative Law

Alternative Dispute Resolution

Bankruptcy

Business Organizations/Corporations

Civil Litigation and Procedure

CLA Exam Preparation

Client Accounting

Computer in the Law Office

Constitutional Law

Contract Law

Criminal Law and Procedure

Document Preparation

Environmental Law

Ethics

Family Law

Federal Taxation

Intellectual Property

Introduction to Law

Introduction to Paralegalism

Law Office Management

Law Office Procedures

Legal Research, Writing, and Analysis

Legal Terminology

Paralegal Employment

Real Estate Law

Reference Materials

Torts and Personal Injury Law

Will, Trusts, and Estate Administration

You will find unparalleled, practical support

Each book is augmented by instructor and student supplements to ensure the best learning experience possible. We also offer custom publishing and other benefits such as West's Student Achievement Award. In addition, our sales representatives are ready to provide you with dependable service.

We want to hear from you

Our best contributions for improving the quality of our books and instructional materials is feedback from the people who use them. If you have a question, concern, or observation about any of our materials, or you have a product proposal or manuscript, we want to hear from you. Please contact your local representative or write us at the following address:

West Legal Studies, 5 Maxwell Drive, P. O. Box 8007, Clifton Park, New York 12065

For additional information point your browser at

www.westlegalstudies.com

THOMSON

™

DELMAR LEARNING

LEGAL
ETHICS

Kent D. Kauffman

THOMSON

DELMAR LEARNING

Australia   Canada   Mexico   Singapore   Spain   United Kingdom   United States

THOMSON

DELMAR LEARNING

WEST LEGAL STUDIES

LEGAL ETHICS
Kent D. Kauffman

Career Education Strategic Business Unit:

Vice President:
Dawn Gerrain

Director of Editorial:
Sherry Gomoll

Acquisitions Editor:
Pamela Fuller

Developmental Editor:
Melissa Riveglia

Editorial Assistant:
Sarah Duncan

Director of Production:
Wendy A. Troeger

Production Manager:
Carolyn Miller

Production Editor:
Betty L. Dickson

Technology Project Manager:
Joseph Saba

Director of Marketing:
Donna J. Lewis

Channel Manager:
Wendy Mapstone

Cover Design:
Dutton and Sherman Design

Library of Congress Cataloging-in-Publication Data
Kauffman, Kent D.
   Legal ethics / Kent D. Kauffman.
      p. cm.— (The West Legal Studies series)
   Includes index.
   ISBN 0-7668-4255-X
   1. Legal ethics—United States. 2. Legal assistants—United States—Handbooks, manuals, etc.   I. Title. II. Series.

KF306.Z9K38 2003
174'.3'0973—dc21   2002041725

NOTICE TO THE READER

This is dedicated to Karen, my wife.
The very thought of you makes me smile.

Contents

Table of Cases   xv

Preface   xxi

Acknowledgments   xxvii

About the Author   xxix

Chapter 1   Lawyers, Legal Assistants, and the Regulation of the Legal Profession   1
Introduction   1
Who Regulates Lawyers and the Practice of Law?   3
What Are Rules of Ethics?   3
A Summary of the Disciplinary Process   6
Why Doesn't the Legislature Regulate the Practice of Law?   7
How to Brief a Case   9
   The Facts   9
   The Issue   10
   The Holding   10
   The Reasoning   10
   The Decision   10
A Case Study in Lawyer Discipline: The Disbarment Proceedings against
   William Jefferson Clinton   13
   The Background to the Disciplinary Charges   14
   The Nature of the Disciplinary Charges   14
   The Debate over Disbarment   15
Final Thoughts on the ABA's Role in Regulating Lawyers   20
Summary   21
Points to Ponder   21
Key Concepts   22
Key Terms   22

Chapter 2   Paralegals and Their Profession   23
Introduction   23
A Short History of Legal Assisting   24
Paralegal Associations   26
   The National Federation of Paralegal Associations   26

The National Association of Legal Assistants   27
Paralegal Compensation   28
The Great Debate: Licensure versus Certification   29
   Minimum Qualifications: When Does One Become a Paralegal?   30
   The Licensing of Paralegals: Not Yet   33
   Is Certification the Alternative to Licensure?   34
Paralegal Discipline: Is It Possible to Sanction a Paralegal?   36
   Paralegal Associations Can Sanction Their Members   37
   The Lawyer's Duty of Supervision: The Stick, Not the Carrot   37
   Can a Legal Assistant Be Directly Sanctioned by a Court?   45
Miscellaneous Issues for the Paralegal Profession   49
   Salary versus Overtime Pay: Does That Make One a "Professional"?   49
   Disbarred or Suspended Lawyers Working as Paralegals   51
   Legal Assistants Joining State Bar Associations   55
Ethics 2000 and the Duty to Supervise Non-Lawyer Employees or Assistants   56
   Proposal by the Ethics 2000 Commission   56
   Action Taken by the ABA House of Delegates   56
Summary   57
Points to Ponder   58
Key Concepts   59
Key Terms   59

Chapter 3   The Unauthorized Practice of Law   60

Introduction   60
What Is the Practice of Law?   61
Exisiting Rules That Prohibit the Unauthorized Practice of Law   70
   Statutes Prohibit UPL   70
   Attorney Rules of Professional Conduct Prohibit UPL   71
   Paralegal Codes of Conduct Prohibit UPL   72
What Activities Are Paralegals Prohibited from Performing?   74
   Giving Legal Advice   74
   Establishing the Attorney-Client Relationship   76
   Establishing Legal Fees   76
   Miscellaneous Prohibitions   76
What Activities Are Paralegals Permitted to Perform?   83
   What Do the Paralegal Ethics Rules Authorize?   83
   Paralegals and the Representation of Others before Administrative Agencies   85
   Local Rules of Court   92
Independent Paralegal Services and UPL   93
   Legal Services Rendered by Non-Lawyers Serving the Public: Treading on Thin Ice   94
   Legal Services Rendered by Non-Lawyers as Independent Contractors to Lawyers   100
Ethics 2000 and the Unauthorized Practice of Law   106
   Proposed by the Ethics 2000 Commission   106
   Action Taken by the ABA House of Delegates   107
Summary   107

Points to Ponder   108
Key Concepts   109
Key Terms   109

Chapter 4   Confidentiality   110
Introduction   110
The Duty of Confidentiality   111
 Distinctions between the Confidentiality Rules of the Model Rules and Those of the Model Code   111
 When Does the Duty of Confidentiality Arise?   114
 For How Long Does the Duty of Confidentiality Apply?   115
 Do the Principles of Confidentiality Apply to the Lawyer's Employees?   115
 How Is Confidentiality Affected When the Client Is an Organization?   116
 Are Certain Kinds of Client Information Considered Not Confidential?   117
Exceptions to the Duty of Confidentiality   123
 Implied Authorizations   123
 The Prevention of Client Criminal Conduct or Fraud   124
 The Defense of a Claim against the Lawyer   125
 The Collection of Fees   126
Technology and Client Confidentiality   127
 E-Mail Messages and Client Confidentiality   129
 Fax Machines and Client Confidentiality   129
 Mobile Phones and Client Confidentiality   130
Ethics 2000 and the Duty of Confidentiality   130
 Proposal by the Ethics 2000 Commission   130
 Action Taken by the ABA House of Delegates   131
The Attorney-Client Privilege: Related to the Duty of Confidentiality   131
 The Basics of Discovery   135
 The Basics of the Work Product Rule   136
 Inadvertent Disclosure: What to Do When Mistakes Occur   138
The Legal Assistant and Confidentiality   148
 How Does the Attorney-Client Privilege Cover the Legal Assistant?   148
 Tips to Protect Confidentiality and the Attorney-Client Privilege   149
Summary   151
Points to Ponder   152
Key Concepts   153
Key Terms   153

Chapter 5   Conflicts of Interest   154
Introduction   154
 The Model Rules' Starting Point for Conflicts of Interest   156
 The Model Code and General Conflicts of Interest   156
Common Conflicts of Interest   157
 Double Representation: One Lawyer Representing the Plaintiff and the Defendant   157
 Simultaneous Representation of Clients in Different, but Related, Matters   160

Suing an Existing Client in an Unrelated Suit   160
Joint Representation: Two Clients with the Same Lawyer   162
Conflicts Caused by the Lawyer's Own Interests   167
Conflicts between Present and Former Clients   174
Special Circumstances: Prohibited Transactions   177
Business Transactions with Clients   177
Using Client Information to the Client's Detriment   178
Gifts from Clients   178
Media Rights for the Client's Story   180
Helping the Client Financially   180
Someone Other Than the Client Paying the Legal Expenses   181
Settlement of Combined Claims   182
Agreements Limiting the Lawyer's Liability   182
Related Lawyers Opposing Each Other   183
The Lawyer's Ownership of the Client's Case   183
The Model Code and Prohibited Transactions   184
Conflicts When the Client Is a Corporation or Other Organization   184
Who Is the Client?   184
What If the Organization Is Engaging in Illegal Activity?   185
The Model Code and the Corporate Entity   187
Imputed Disqualification: One Lawyer's Conflict Affecting the Firm   187
The General Policy: Disqualification   187
Imputed Disqualification: Formerly Associated Lawyers   188
Imputed Disqualification and Client Consent   189
Imputed Disqualification: The Use of Screens for the Tainted Employee   190
The Use of Screens for Tainted Lawyers   190
Screens for Non-Lawyer Employees: The News Is Pretty Good   191
The Legal Assistant and Conflicts of Interest Rules   203
Tips on Avoiding Conflicts of Interest   203
Protecting the Interests of Present and Former Clients   203
Protecting Oneself When Seeking Different Employment   204
Ethics 2000 and Conflicts of Interest   204
MR 1.7 and Current Client Conflicts   204
MR 1.8 and Specific Prohibitions   205
MR 1.9 and Former Client Conflicts   206
MR 1.10 and Imputed Disqualification   206
MR 1.11 and Conflicts of Former and Current Government Employees   207
MR 1.13 and Corporate Attorneys   207
Summary   207
Points to Ponder   209
Key Concepts   210
Key Terms   210

Chapter 6   **Advertising and Solicitation**   **211**
Introduction   211

A Short History of Lawyer Advertising   211
    From the Nineteenth Century to the 1950s   212
    The Supreme Court's View Shifts from the 1940s through the 1970s   213
An Overview of the Rules on Advertising   219
    Information about Legal Services Shall Not Be False or Misleading   219
    Lawyer Advertising: The Nuts and Bolts   223
Advertising and the Paralegal   231
    The Paralegal as Part of the Law Firm's Advertising   231
    Direct Advertising by Independent Paralegals: Be Careful   232
Solicitation   233
    The Rules against Direct Contact with Prospective Clients   233
    Permissible Solicitation   242
    Solicitation and the Legal Assistant   243
    A Case Study in Illegal Solicitation   244
Ethics 2000 and Advertising and Solicitation   248
    MR 7.1 and Communications Concerning a Lawyer's Services   248
    MR 7.2 and Advertising   249
    MR 7.3 and Solicitation   249
    MR 7.4 and Communication of Fields of Practice   249
    MR 7.5 and Firm Names and Letterheads   250
Summary   250
Points to Ponder   252
Key Concepts   253
Key Terms   253

Chapter 7   Fees and Fee Sharing   254
Introduction   254
Types of Legal Fees   255
    Hourly Rate   255
    Contingent Fee   255
    Fixed Fee   256
The Rules on Legal Fees   257
    A Lawyer's Fee Shall Be Reasonable   257
    Legal Fees Need to Be Clearly Explained to the Client   260
    Where Is the Client's Money to Be Kept?   264
    Special Rules Regarding Contingent Fees   273
    Fee Sharing between Lawyers of Different Firms   275
Prohibition against Fee Sharing between Lawyers and Non-Lawyers   275
    Why Is Sharing Fees with a Non-Lawyer Prohibited?   275
    When Is a Compensation Scheme Not Fee Sharing and What Is the Difference?   279
Recovery of Legal Fees from the Opposing Party in Litigation   280
    Separate Recovery of Legal Assistant Fees in Federal Cases   281
    Separate Recovery of Legal Assistant Fees in State Cases   286
Ethical Considerations for the Legal Assistant   291
    The Legal Assistant May Not Establish Legal Fees   291

The Legal Assistant Must Report Accurate Hours   292
Ethics 2000 and Fees   293
    MR 1.5 and Fees   293
    MR 5.4 and the Sharing of Fees with Non-Lawyers   294
Summary   294
Points to Ponder   296
Key Concepts   297
Key Terms   298

Chapter 8   Miscellaneous Ethics Issues   299

Introduction   299
Competence   300
    Preparation   300
    Diligence   301
    Communication   301
    Competence and the Legal Assistant   302
Truthfulness   310
    The General Rule on Truth   310
    Clients and Truthfulness   311
    Represented Persons and Truthfulness   315
    Unrepresented Persons and Truthfulness   318
    Ex Parte Communication and Truthfulness   320
    Legal Research and Truthfulness   322
Malpractice Liability for the Non-Lawyer   325
    What Constitutes Malpractice?   325
    The Theory behind Non-Lawyer Malpractice   326
    Non-Lawyer Malpractice Is Not a Universal View   331
Pro Bono Services   332
    The Evolution of the Pro Bono Rules   332
    Should Lawyers be Required to Perform Pro Bono Services?   333
    Pro Bono and the Paralegal   335
Summary   336
Points to Ponder   338
Key Concepts   339
Key Terms   340

Appendix A   ABA Model Guidelines for the Utilization of Legal Assistant Services   340

Appendix B   NFPA Model Code of Ethics and Professional Responsibility and Guidelines for Enforcement   351

Appendix C   NALA Model Standards and Guidelines for Utilization of Legal Assistants   360

Appendix D   NALA Code of Ethics and Professional Responsibility   368

Appendix E   Legal Ethics and Related Web Sites   371

Appendix F   Legal Ethics Movie Guide   374

Glossary   381

Index   389

Table of Cases

Main cases in the text are indicated by boldface.

Chapter 1
Grievance Administrator v. Lopatin   20
In re Conduct of Wittemyer   20
In the Matter of Anonymous   11
In the Matter of Hein   17
Marbury v. Madison   7
Shochet v. Arkansas Board of Law Examiners   15

Chapter 2
Attorney Grievance Commission of Maryland v. Ficker   43
In re Elkins   53
In re Ethics Opinion No. 24 of the Committee on the Unauthorized Practice of Law   34
In re Petition to Amend Code of Professional Responsibility   25
Iowa Supreme Court Bd. of Professional Ethics and Conduct v. Ackerman   38
Kentucky Bar Ass'n v. Legal Alternatives, Inc.   49
Matter of Frabizzio   52
Matter of Wilkinson   52
Musselman v. Willoughby Corporation   39
State v. Robinson   47
Statewide Grievance Committee v. Pinciaro   43

Chapter 3
Doe v. Condon   81
Farretta v. California   77
Fink v. Peden   62
The Florida Bar re Advisory Opinion on Nonlawyer Representation in Securities Arbitration   89
Florida Bar v. Catarcio   95
Greenwell v. State Bar of Nevada   80
In re Disciplinary Action against Tatone   87
In re Ethics Opinion No. 24 of the Committee on the Unauthorized Practice of Law   102
In re Flint   62
In re Harris   99
In re Thonert   65

Johnson v. Avery 76
Johnson v. Ivimey 77
Matter of Bright 99
Osei-Afriyie by Osei-Afriyie v. Medical College of Pennsylvania 77
State ex rel. Pearson v. Gould 68
Turner v. Kentucky Bar Association 87

Chapter 4

A. v. B. 125
Baird v. Koerner 122
Bloss v. Ford Motor Co. 139
Brett v. Barques 114
Corey v. Norman, Hanson & DeTroy 145
Gilmore v. Goedecke 114
Goldsborough v. Eagle Crest Partners, Ltd. 145
In re Anonymous 112
In re Grand Jury Investigation of Ocean Transportation 145
In re Grand Jury Subpoena 122
In re Grand Jury Subpoena Duces Tecum 137
In re Mandelman 124
In re Marick 114
In re Sealed Case 115
In re Subpoena to Testify before Grand Jury 121
International Digital Systems Corp. v. Digital Equipment Corp. 145
Lawyer Disciplinary Bd. v. McGraw 124
Liggett Group v. Brown & Williamson Tobacco Corp. 145
Lipin v. Bender 142
Mayberry v. State 132
Palomba v. Sullivan 120
People v. Harris 118
Pennsylvania v. Mrozek 116
Purcell v. District Attorney for Suffolk County 124
Samaritan Foundation v. Goodfarb 148
Samaritan Foundation v. Superior Court 148
State v. Post 149
State v. Rhodes 117
United States v. Microsoft 127
Upjohn v. United States 117
Weil v. Investment/Indicators, Research & Management, Inc. 145

Chapter 5

Alex Munoz Gen. Contractor, Inc. v. MC3D, Inc. 157
Baldasarre v. Butler 165
Balla v. Gambro, Inc. 186
Burkhart v. Semitool, Inc. 186

Ciaffone v. District Court 199
Cole v. Ruidoso Mun. Schools 185
Crews v. Buckman Laboratories Intern., Inc. 186
Damron v. Herzog 175
Davis v. York International Corp. 176
Elan Transdermal Ltd. v. Cygnus Therapeutic Sys. 189
Employers Ins. of Wausau v. Albert D. Seeno Cont. Co. 190
Evans v. Jeff D. 168
Florida Bar v. Belleville 166
Florida Bar v. Clark 166
Florida Bar v. Jordan 183
Florida Bar v. Mastrilli 164
Florida Bar v. Milin 160
Florida Bar v. Sofo 159
Fox Searchlight Pictures v. Paladino, Inc. 186
General Dynamics Corporation v. Superior Court 186
Glasser v. United States 163
Glover Bottled Gas Corp. v. Circle M. Beverage Barn, Inc. 199
Green v. Toledo Hospital 198
Hayes v. Central States Orthopedic Specialists, Inc. 192
Harrison v. Fisons Corp. 161
Henriksen v. Great American Savings & Loan 191
Holloway v. Arkansas 163
Hyman Cos., v. Brozost 175
In re Adoption of Vincent 167
In re Advisory Committee 188
In re Berg 169
In re Charlton 168
In re Complex Asbestos Litigation 193
In re Dalto 178
In re DiSandro 170
In re Estate of Divine 180
In re Gillinghamn 179
In re Horine 160
In re Marriage of Carter 189
In re Michelman 167
In re Ober 178
In re Pohlman 165
In re Rinella 169
In re Shannon 163
Kapoo Mfg. Co., Inc. v. C & O Enterprises, Inc. 198
Lawyer Disciplinary Bd. v. Frame 158
Lee v. Aiu 184
Matter of Lively 159
Memphis & Shelby County Bar Ass'n v. Sanderson 161

Mississippi Bar v. Attorney HH   181
Munoz Gen. Contractor, Inc., v. MC3d, Inc.   157
Pacific Employers Ins. Co. v. P.B. Hoidale Co.   189
Peters v. Hyatt Legal Services   159
Richardson v. Griffiths   176
Rowland v. Rowland   165
Schiessle v. Stephens   190
Shongutsie v. State   163
Smart Industries v. Superior Court   200
State ex rel. FirsTIER Bank v. Buckley   189
State ex rel. Oklahoma Bar Ass'n v. Watson   182
United States v. Hearst   180
Vallinoto v. DiSandro   170
Walden v. Hoke   158
Wheat v. United States   162
Williams v. Trans World Airlines   199
Zimmerman v. Mahaska Bottling Co.   199

Chapter 6

Attorney Grievance Commission of Maryland v. Wills   228
Bates v. State Bar of Arizona   234
Committee on Professional Ethics & Conduct v. Humphrey   228
Ficker v. Curran   241
Florida Bar v. Doe   226
Florida Bar v. Gudish   221
Florida Bar v. Went For It, Inc.   238
Grievance Comm. for Hartford–New Britain Judicial Dist. v. Trantolo   228
Gulf Oil Co. v. Bernard   243
In re Anonymous   223
In re Charges of Unprofessional Conduct against 95–30   220
In re Frank   222
In re Petition for Rule of Court Governing Lawyer Advertising   228
In re Primus   243
In re R.M.J.   224
Leoni v. State Bar   221
Matter of Pavilick   222
Matter of Zang   222
Medina County Bar Ass'n v. Grieselhuber   220
Ohralik v. Ohio State Bar Association   234
Peel v. Attorney Registration and Disciplinary Commission   226
People ex rel. Attorney General v. MacCabe   212
People v. Roehl   221
Petition of Felmeister and Isaacs   228
Shapero v. Kentucky Bar Asssociation   238
Spencer v. Honorable Justices of the Superior Court   223

State v. Robinson   232
Texans Against Censorship, Inc. v. State Bar of Texas   226
Valentine v. Chrestensen   213
Virginia State Board of Pharmacy v. Virginia Citizens Consumer Council   213
Zauderer v. Office of Disciplinary Counsel   221

Chapter 7

Absher Const. Co. v. Kent School Dist. No. 415   287
Atkins v. Tinning   278
Attorney Grievance Commission of Maryland v. Brennan   276
Baranowski v. State Bar   263
Columbus Bar Association v. Brooks   263
Committee on Legal Ethics of West Virginia State Bar v. Burdette   299
Committee on Professional Ethics and Conduct of Iowa State Bar Association v. Lawler   277
Cuyahoga County Bar Association v. Petrancek   264
Davis v. City and County of San Francisco   260
Elliot v. Joyce   262
The Florida Bar v. Bailey   265
Gallagher v. Weiner   276
Infante v. Gottesman   276
In re Baltimore   263
In re Bass   277
In re Estate of Larson   260
In re Gerard   259
In re Lawyers Responsibility Board Panel No. 94-17   258
In re Marriage of Pitulla   262
In re Maruko Inc.   292
In re Struthers   276
In the Matter of Comstock   260
Iowa Supreme Court Bd. of Professional Ethics and Conduct v. Apland   271
Joel R. Brandes, P.C. v. Zingmond   264
Joerger v. Gordon Food Service, Inc.   288
Jones v. Armstrong Cork Co.   286
Keith v. Volpe   258
Mahoney v. Pataki   286
Matter of Brown   274
Missouri v. Jenkins   281
Opperud v. Bussey   274
People v. Easley   276
Phillips v. Washington Legal Foundation   272
State ex rel. Oklahoma Bar Ass'n v. Hatcher   299
Trotter v. Nelson   278
Washington Legal Foundation v. Legal Foundation of Washington   272
Washington Legal Foundation v. Texas Equal Access to Justice Foundation   272

Wright v. U-Let-Us Skycap Services, Inc. 258
Wylie v. Coxe 256

Chapter 8

Biakanja v. Irving 327
Bland v. Reed 332
Bowers v. Transamerica Title Ins. Co. 326
Busch v. Flangas 329
Crane v. State Bar 317
Florida Bar v. Newhouse 320
Geter v. State 323
Hill-Rom Co. v. Kinetic Concepts 321
In re Air Crash Disaster 319
In re Bard 312
In re Conduct of Smith 317
In re Deardorff 301
In re Estate of Divine 331
In re Farmer 304
In re Kovitz 301
In re Morris 315
In re Shannon 315
In re Two Anonymous Members of the South Carolina Bar 321
In re Watkins 314
Jorgenson v. Volusia County 323
Lewis v. State Bar 300
L.S. Mississippi Bar 320
Matter of Roberts 321
Mays v. Neal 304
Nix v. Whiteside 314
Office of Disciplinary Counsel v. Slodov 320
Omaha Bank for Cooperatives v. Siouxland Cattle Cooperative 320
Palmer v. Westmeyer 331
People v. Crist 301
People v. Johnson 314
Public Administrator of County of New York v. Cohen 312
Runsvold v. Idaho State Bar 317
Sandstrom v. Sandstrom 317
Trumball County Bar Association v. Makridis 317
United Steelworkers of America, AFL-CIO v. Craig 331
Webb v. Pomeroy 326
Wolfgram v. Wells Fargo Bank 313

Preface

Legal Ethics is a new textbook for two- and four-year college students, and is also valuable for working paralegals and legal assistants. *Legal Ethics* springs from the author's experiences starting from the time when he first offered a legal ethics course at his college and discussed with his students what they liked and did not like about their class.

ORGANIZATION

The chapter topics in the book logically progress in the following order: an examination of how lawyers are regulated; a history and overview of the paralegal profession; the unauthorized practice of law; confidentiality; conflicts of interest; advertising and solicitation; legal fees and fee sharing; and miscellaneous ethics issues, much of which has to do with litigation, including competence, truthfulness, malpractice liability for the non-lawyer, and pro bono. Special attention is paid to particularly thorny issues, such as whether paralegals and legal assistants should be licensed, whether independent contracting paralegals and legal assistants engage in the unauthorized practice of law, the relationship between confidentiality and the attorney-client privilege, the work product rule as it applies to non-lawyer employees, imputed disqualification and screening for non-lawyer employees, fee sharing between lawyers and non-lawyer employees, and the recovery of paralegal fees under statutes that explicitly provide for the recovery of lawyer's fees.

PEDAGOGY

Legal Ethics provides a fresh approach to the study of the significant professional responsibility issues facing the legal profession. Starting with the premise that students should not be "talked down to," and because non-lawyer employees are required to act with the same professional care as if they are lawyers, the book provides a thorough and substantive analysis of the major principles that affect how the practice of law is regulated. And since lawyers are responsible for the conduct of their non-lawyer employees, the text then applies those principles to this group. Supporting citations to federal and state statutes and case law, as well as national, state, and local ethics opinions, are provided in-text.

But, recognizing that studying ethics rules can be tedious (and lacks the panache of studying other subjects, such as criminal law), *Legal Ethics* provides a variety of methods designed to improve the reader's understanding and interest. It begins by explaining how one becomes licensed to practice law, how the American Bar Association affects the practice of law, and how the behavior of lawyers is regulated. To provide an example of how the lawyer-disciplinary process works, a thorough and provocative look at the disbarment proceedings against former President Bill Clinton is presented in the first chapter. Other real-world examples and hypotheticals are provided throughout the chapters in order to facilitate a better grasp on the technical material. Visual aids are provided where needed most, so that critical and difficult concepts can be better retained. Case law is provided immediately following the material it is designed to amplify, and the case questions are framed to promote both the understanding of the legal analysis, as well as the cultivation of the reader's own opinions. Review questions at the end of each chapter, called "Points to Ponder," will, if studied, force the student to get an outstanding grade on any quiz or test and serve as a springboard for further, independent study, if desired. A fascinating news article is provided in full on the illegal solicitation of clients by a lawyer thought to be one of America's richest. Two high-ranking officials of the national paralegal and legal assistant associations have each written an essay specifically for the book, found in the last chapter, on the subject of what makes a paralegal or a legal assistant professional and competent. And there is a legal ethics movie guide at the book's end, where the author discusses more than a dozen entertaining movies that have a connection to legal ethics or the practice of law. Readers from any jurisdiction will benefit by reading and relying on *Legal Ethics* in their own practice.

FEATURES

This book has many features that distinguish it from other legal ethics books, including the following:

- A discussion of the latest trends affecting the paralegal/legal assistant profession, including the controversial subjects of the licensing and certification of paralegals, the application of federal overtime pay requirements, as well as recent paralegal/legal assistant compensation information.
- A current analysis of Ethics 2000, providing explanations in each substantive chapter on the correlative proposals for changing the ABA Model Rules of Professional Conduct *and* their final versions, as accepted or rejected by the ABA House of Delegates.
- Explanations of the important distinctions between the ABA Model Rules of Professional Conduct and the ABA Model Code of Professional Responsibility.

- Exhibits designed to help explain some of the more difficult concepts in the book, including conflicts of interest, lawyer and non-lawyer screening, the unauthorized practice of law, and lawyer-client confidentiality.
- Dozens of real-life examples of lawyer and non-lawyer misbehaviors—including bizarre misbehaviors—provided throughout the chapters, which help breathe life into the ethics rules.
- A discussion of the disbarment proceedings against President Clinton and F. Lee Bailey.
- A discussion of news events of famous and infamous people, which relate to the chapter topics, including Hillary Clinton, Bill Gates, Newt Gingrich, Patty Hearst, and Timothy McVeigh.
- A *Wall Street Journal* article on illegal client-solicitation, commonly called "accident running," provided in Chapter 6.
- Essays by the current president of the National Association of Legal Assistants and by the vice president of positions and issues of the National Federation of Paralegal Associations.
- The latest versions of the significant ethics codes designed for paralegals and legal assistants.
- Inclusion of current and classic case law, which help the reader see how courts interpret and apply the ethics rules to lawyers and their non-lawyer employees.
- Definitions of key legal words used in the text, and a complete glossary.
- A legal ethics Web site directory that provides over seventy Web site addresses.
- A legal ethics movie guide that reviews such movies as *Erin Brockovich, To Kill a Mockingbird,* and *The Rainmaker.*

Ancillary Materials

- **Instructor's Manual**—There is also an accompanying instructor's manual, written by the author and completed after he used it in his legal ethics classes for two semesters. The instructor's manual will significantly assist in class preparation since it has features such as chapter outlines, teaching suggestions, and full case briefs for all the case law in the text. It includes answers for the questions that follow the case law, as well as the chapter review questions, called "Points to Ponder." The instructor's manual also includes complete test banks for each chapter, including essay questions and accompanying answers. Because of the book's organization and chapter sequence, professors and instructors will be able to logically divide the material into either a traditional sixteen-week semester or a shorter semester.
- **Web page**—come visit our website at www.westlegalstudies.com, where you will find valuable information such as hot links and sample materials to download, as well as other West Legal Studies products.
- **WESTLAW®**—West's on-line computerized legal research system offers students "hands-on" experience with a system commonly used in law offices. Qualified adopters can receive ten free hours of WESTLAW®.

WESTLAW® can be accessed with Macintosh and IBM PC and compatibles. A modem is required.

- **WestLegalEdCenter**—Chapters 3 and 4 are available on audiotape for continuing education credits, and can be accessed at www.westlegaledcenter.com.
- **Strategies and Tips for Paralegal Educators**, a pamphlet by Anita Tebbe of Johnson County Community College, provides teaching strategies specifically designed for paralegal educators. A copy of this pamphlet is available to each adopter. Quantities for distribution to adjunct instructors are available for purchase at a minimal price. A coupon on the pamphlet provides ordering information.
- **Survival Guide for Paralegal Students**, a pamphlet by Kathleen Mercer Reed and Bradene Moore covers practical and basic information to help students make the most of their paralegal courses. Topics covered include choosing courses of study and note-taking skills.
- **West's Paralegal Video Library**—West Legal Studies is pleased to offer the following videos at no charge to qualified adopters:
  - *The Drama of the Law II: Paralegal Issues Video*
    ISBN: 0-314-07088-5
  - *The Making of a Case Video*
    ISBN: 0-314-07300-0
  - *ABA Mock Trial Video—Product Liability*
    ISBN: 0-314-07342-6
  - *Arguments to the United States Supreme Court Video*
    ISBN: 0-314-07070-2
- **Court TV Videos**—West Legal Studies is pleased to offer the following videos from Court TV for a minimal fee:
  - *New York v. Ferguson—Murder on the 5:33: The Trial of Colin Ferguson*
    ISBN: 0-7668-1098-4
  - *Ohio v. Alfieri*
    ISBN: 0-7668-1099-2
  - *Flynn v. Goldman Sachs—Fired on Wall Street: A Case of Sex Discrimination?*
    ISBN: 0-7668-1096-8
  - *Dodd v. Dodd—Religion and Child Custody in Conflict*
    ISBN: 0-7668-1094-1
  - *In Re Custody of Baby Girl Clausen—Child of Mine: The Fight for Baby Jessica*
    ISBN: 0-7668-1097-6
  - *Fentress v. Eli Lilly & Co., et al.—Prozac on Trial*
    ISBN: 0-7668-1095-x
  - *Garcia v. Garcia—Fighting over Jerry's Money*
    ISBN: 0-7668-0264-7
  - *Hall v. Hall—Irretrievably Broken: A Divorce Lawyer Goes to Court*
    ISBN: 0-7668-0196-9

- *Maglica v. Maglica—Broken Hearts, Broken Commitments*
  ISBN: 0-7668-0867-x
- *Northside Partners v. Page and New Kids on the Block—New Kids in Court: Is Their Hit Song a Copy?*
  ISBN: 0-7668-0426-7

Please note the Internet resources are of a time-sensitive nature and URL addresses may often change or be deleted.

Contact us at westlegalstudies@delmar.com

Acknowledgments

This book would not have been possible without the help of many, and I would like to thank a few of them in print. First, my sincerest gratitude goes to Joan Gill and Pamela Fuller, the two acquisitions editors at West Legal Studies, an imprint of Delmar Learning, who took my project and helped shepherd it to completion. As well, developmental editors Alexis Ferraro and Melissa Riveglia provided me with much needed technical assistance. And editorial assistants Lisa Flatley and Sarah Duncan were quite helpful to me with much of what is inaccurately referred to as "the small stuff."

There are certain valuable items in this book that are provided to the reader because of the graciousness of the copyright holders. Thank you to Judy Rodriguez at Dow Jones & Company, Inc., for permitting me to use an excellent article from the *Wall Street Journal* as part of my text. Thank you to those organizations that allowed me to reprint their ethics codes, as appendices in this book: Richard Vittenson, director of copyrights and contracts at the American Bar Association; Lu Hangley, managing director of the National Federation of Paralegal Associations; and Marge Dover, executive director of the National Association of Legal Assistants.

Vicki Kunz, the president of the National Association of Legal Assistants, and Lesley Cox, vice president of positions and issues of the National Federation of Paralegal Associations, provided an essay on professionalism for the book, both of which are located in the last chapter. Thank you for your significant contributions.

Thank you to the following reviewers of the manuscript:

Melody Brown
Eastern Idaho Technical College
Idaho Falls, ID

Lynne D. Dahlborg
Suffolk University
Boston, MA

Leslie Sturdivant Ennis
Samford University
Birmingham, AL

Fernaundra Ferguson
University of West Florida
Pensacola, FL

Kathleen Fisher
National Center for Paralegal Training
Atlanta, GA

Michael F. Krimmel
Harrisburg Area Community College
Lancaster, PA

Cynthia Lauber
Community College of Aurora
Aurora, CO

Patricia E. Lyons
Roger Williams University
Providence, RI

Linda Potter
Saginaw Chippewa Indian Tribe
Mount Pleasant, MI

Nicholas Riggs
Sullivan College
Louisville, KY

Christine Taylor
Volunteer State Community College
Gallatin, TN

Three former students of mine volunteered their time to help me with certain research that was done for the book. They are fine examples of generosity and dedication. Mindy Birely conducted many hours of legal research, searching for case law for me. Rita Mitchell spent much of her free time reading legal magazines and journals for me. And, Michelle Roberts surfed the World Wide Web, helping me find legal ethics Web sites that might be part of an appendix. Thank you to the students from my first legal ethics course, who were a great group, fun to teach, and encouraging of my aspiration at attempting a book such as this.

Last, three friends who are no longer here were instrumental in opening doors for me by giving me a chance: Peter Kutulakis of The Dickinson School of Law; Sue Kahle of Ivy Tech State College; and Mike Downs of Indiana University–Purdue University Fort Wayne. They were taken too soon and are still deeply missed.

About the Author

Kent D. Kauffman is the Paralegal Program Chair at Ivy Tech State College, in Fort Wayne, Indiana, where he teaches legal ethics, legal research and writing, business law, criminal law, and alternative dispute resolution. He is licensed to practice law in Indiana and is a member of the American Bar Association, the Indiana State Bar Association, and the American Association of University Professors. Mr. Kauffman is a *summa cum laude* graduate of Temple University and a graduate of The Dickinson School of Law of The Pennsylvania State University. He also teaches political science at Indiana University–Purdue University Fort Wayne, is a multiple recipient of *Who's Who among America's Teachers*, and is listed in *Who's Who in America*.

Lawyers, Legal Assistants, and the Regulation of the Legal Profession

The first thing we do, let's kill all the lawyers.

—William Shakespeare, *King Henry VI* (1591)

What do you call one thousand lawyers at the bottom of the ocean? A good start.

INTRODUCTION

Admit it. You like lawyer jokes. In fact, if you were paid ten dollars for every lawyer joke you could think of off the top of your head, you could probably make enough money to buy this textbook. Why are lawyer jokes so prevalent, so much a part of our culture, that books and Web sites are dedicated solely to poke fun at lawyers? Is it because lawyer jokes are especially hilarious, better than those jokes about certain religious officials sitting in a bar or stuck on a lifeboat or about mentally challenged, fair-haired women? Or is it because lawyers remain one of the last groups in American society that can still be safely lampooned—the other group being politicians, who just so happen to be mostly lawyers. Generally, jokes or insults about groups have fallen out of favor under the scrutiny of political correctness and a heightened awareness of unkindness, but jokes about lawyers abound.

Unfortunately for the legal profession, the jokes may be born more out of ire than humor. In fact, in April 2002, the Litigation Section of the American Bar Association released the results of two surveys it commissioned from the Chicago research firm of Leo J. Shapiro & Associates, asking non-lawyer respondents to rate various occupations in terms of public confidence. The results from a survey done before the September 11 attacks show that only the news media was held in lower disregard than lawyers, while doctors placed first on the list. When a second survey was taken, a few months after September 11, the news media got out of the public confidence cellar by jumping one place ahead of the legal profession. Sadly, some respondents referred to lawyers as greedy and corrupt and believed that lawyers fail to adequately police themselves. *ABA Journal e-Report*, Volume 1, Issue 16 (April 26, 2002). How interesting it is that doctors—who often get sued by their patients for malpractice and have an average income almost twice that of lawyers—are thought of so highly, while lawyers—a lot of whom represent those patients in their malpractice claims—are thought of so differently.

Many people think that William Shakespeare said, "let's kill all the lawyers." He did not. But he wrote it in 1591 for Dick the Butcher, who said the infamous line in Act IV, Scene II, of the play *King Henry VI, Part II*. That line has aroused controversy concerning whether it was meant as a humorous smear or a sly compliment. Some say Shakespeare was using an evil character like Dick the Butcher to express his own disdain of lawyers. Others, however, believe the line is complimentary: Dick the Butcher wanted to kill all the lawyers because he thought that such murders would guarantee success in the evil plans conspired by Jack Cade, the anarchist leader of the gang to which Dick the Butcher belonged. By getting the lawyers out of the way first, injustice could then be allowed to prevail. How ironic it is that a line that launched a thousand smirks might, in fact, have been intended as a badge of honor for the legal profession.

Does any book about legal ethics need to be longer than a postcard? Is "legal ethics" really an oxymoron? Do lawyers deserve the ill will heaped upon them? Perhaps. But if such a negative stereotype is deserved, then should those who work for lawyers be guilty by association? No, at least not yet. Not until it is earned, which hopefully will be never.

Paralegals and legal assistants continue to become more of an integral part of the legal team. Where once attorneys considered that there was a divide between themselves and everyone else in the firm, a bridge has been built upon which paralegals cross every day. When a paralegal is used effectively, he or she does substantive legal work, not solely clerical tasks. Interviewing, case management, research, and writing are just some of the functions in which legal assistants can engage, thereby allowing attorneys to work on other projects. However, with more responsibility in the law office comes a recognition that paralegals need to be fully acquainted with the same rules of ethics (commonly called rules of professional responsibility or professional conduct) that their supervising attorneys are obligated to follow, or else the belief that paralegals are professionals might prove incorrect.

To put the legal assistant's role and ethical obligations in perspective, it is necessary that we first examine how one becomes a lawyer and then determine what rules of ethics are incumbent on that profession. The subsequent chapters will analyze specific themes of the ethics rules, with emphasis on how they affect paralegals. Throughout this book, the terms *paralegal* and *legal assistant* will be used interchangeably, as they are often considered synonymous, with some regions in the United States preferring one title over the other. (However, not all groups consider the terms equally, as will be discussed in Chapter 2.)

WHO REGULATES LAWYERS AND THE PRACTICE OF LAW?

Once one graduates from law school (having endured years of torture, tedium, and triviality), the next step is to take—and pass—the bar exam. The practice of law is jurisdiction specific; there is no such thing as a national bar exam. An applicant to the bar must take the bar exam of the state (including the District of Columbia) where one wants to be licensed to practice law. There are some exceptions, one of which is an attorney who has passed a **multi-state bar exam**. In that situation, a state, other than the one giving the exam, agrees to license the attorney who passed the former state's exam with a sufficient passing score. In addition, attorneys can seek permission to practice law on a limited basis in another jurisdiction by seeking permission from that jurisdiction's highest court.

Despite the jokes made about lawyer ethics, a premium is placed on ethics as a prerequisite to being admitted to the bar. As part of applying for permission to take the bar exam, an applicant must be found morally fit to practice law, and permission can be refused based on prior conduct, including having a felony conviction. And recently, state bar associations have begun to debate whether members of hate groups who advocate violence toward others should be denied entrance into the bar. Some have argued that one cannot swear to uphold the Constitution—which is part of the lawyer's oath—and, at the same time, seek to deny, by violence or other methods, the constitutional rights of others.

Beyond the bar exam, applicants to practice law must also pass a legal ethics exam, which can be taken before the bar exam. The ethics exam questions the applicant's specific knowledge and application of the rules of professional responsibility. Thus, after having paid one's examination fees, passed the bar exam (which is, in many jurisdictions, a multiday, essay extravaganza), passed the ethics exam, and paid the appropriate court membership fees, the applicant now becomes an attorney and is obligated by the oath of admission to the bar to honor his or her jurisdiction's rules of ethics.

State and local bar associations do not regulate their members' conduct the way the courts do, but bar associations have a role in discipline in several ways. First, a bar association has its own membership bylaws and can sanction its members for bylaws violations. Second, a bar association can contact its jurisdiction's highest court (the regulating court) to make recommendations regarding the regulation of the practice of law, including the unauthorized practice of law. Some jurisdictions have a **unified bar association**, which means that membership is required upon being admitted to practice law. More than thirty states have such associations, which are also known as integrated bar associations. Other jurisdictions make the decision to join the bar association a voluntary one.

multi-state bar exam—A bar exam that allows the successful applicant to be licensed in more than one jurisdiction. Such an exam is a result of a reciprocity agreement between the jurisdictions.

unified bar association—A bar association whose members must join upon being admitted to practice to law in a particular jurisdiction. It is also known as an integrated bar association.

WHAT ARE RULES OF ETHICS?

Rules of ethics, more formally known as rules of professional responsibility or professional conduct, are those rules created by the American Bar Association (ABA), the largest and most powerful national bar association in America. Founded in New York in 1878 and headquartered in Chicago, Illinois, the ABA has over 400,000 members. The ABA's first set of ethics rules was its Canons of Professional Ethics in 1908, which was based in large part on the Alabama Bar Association Code of Ethics, from 1887. The inspiration for Alabama's Code of Ethics can be traced to the lectures of Judge George Sharswood in the 1850s, whose lectures were later published as a book, *Professional Ethics*.

In 1969, the ABA adopted the Model Code of Professional Responsibility. The Model Code was organized by three distinctions: Canons, which were general statements of ethical ideals; Ethical Considerations, which were aspirational statements associated with the Canons and signified as *EC*; and Disciplinary Rules, which were the mandatory portions of the Model Code and signified by *DR*.

In 1983, and after a six-year process, the ABA adopted the Model Rules of Professional Conduct, designed to replace the Model Code of Professional Responsibility. Formated differently and with some substantive changes, the Model Rules consist of mandatory rules, followed by advisory paragraphs, called **comments**.

comments—In this context, a comment is the official commentary of the rules committee that follows specific rules of court. Comments are designed to give meaning to the specific rules.

In 1997, the ABA Commission on Evaluation of the Model Rules of Professional Conduct, more commonly known as the Ethics 2000 Commission, was appointed to put forward a report concerning revising the Model Rules. The Ethics 2000 Commission issued a report in November 2000, and then issued its final report in August 2001. Some of the proposals in the two reports included allowing more discretion for attorneys to disclose client confidences, requiring all fee agreements to be in writing, expressly banning sexual relationships between lawyers and clients, and prohibiting real-time Internet solicitation of clients. None of the Ethics 2000 proposals would go into effect until they were specifically adopted by the governing body of the ABA, known as the ABA House of Delegates.

At the August 2001 meeting of the ABA House of Delegates, and also at the February 2002 mid-year meeting of the ABA House of Delegates, the delegates voted on, and approved, many of the recommendations of the Ethics 2000 Commission. Some of the Ethics 2000 proposals that were rejected by the House of Delegates included a requirement that lawyers put all fee agreements with their clients in writing and expansion of the lawyer's discretion to reveal confidential information to the extent proposed by the Ethics 2000 Commission. Throughout the chapters of this book that concern specific ethics issues, separate sections will discuss how the Ethics 2000 Commission proposed changes to the corresponding parts of the ABA Model Rules and whether those changes were accepted or rejected by the ABA House of Delegates.

It is important to understand that the ABA's various sets of ethics rules are not operative on lawyers, even those who are members of the ABA. This is so because the ABA, being a private organization, does not license attorneys. The rules that apply to a lawyer are the particular ABA version that has been adopted by the highest appellate court in the state where a lawyer is licensed. A state supreme court, having **jurisdiction** over its lawyers and their professional behavior, always has the

jurisdiction—In this context, jurisdiction means a particular place over which a court has authority, usually a state.

authority to change the language of an ABA ethics rule it chooses to adopt or to refuse to adopt certain parts of the ABA ethics rules. For example, although Florida's Rules of Professional Conduct are based on the ABA Model Rules, Florida's rule on the solicitation of clients differs from the ABA Model Rules version in that it prohibits a lawyer from contacting a prospective personal injury client in writing for 30 days after an accident. Florida Rules of Professional Conduct, Rule 4-7.4(b)(1)(A). Once adopted by a jurisdiction, though, a jurisdiction's rules of conduct are the ones that jurisdiction's attorneys must follow, and not the ABA's rules. According to the 2001 edition of the *ABA Compendium of Professional Responsibility Rules and Standards*, forty-two states, the District of Columbia, and the Virgin Islands have ethics codes based on the ABA's Model Rules of Professional Conduct. Iowa, Nebraska, New York, Ohio, Oregon, and Puerto Rico have ethics codes that are based on the ABA's Model Code of Professional Responsibility.

Effective March 1, 2003, Tennessee will have become the latest jurisdiction to adopt a set of ethics rules based on the ABA Model Rules. Formerly—at least for the prior thirty-three years—Tennessee's rules of ethics were based on the ABA Model Code. California and Maine have ethics rules that are distinctly different from either the ABA Model Rules or the ABA Model Code (Exhibit 1–1).

Rules of professional responsibility, being adopted by state supreme courts instead of passed by legislatures, are **rules of court**, rather than statutes. Be advised, though, that some jurisdictions have placed their lawyer ethics codes in their statutory codes. For instance, New York's Code of Professional Responsibility is located in the Appendix of the "Judiciary Law" section of the New York Statutes. The more common kinds of rules of court with which legal and paralegal students are familiar include rules of trial procedure, rules of appellate procedure, and rules of evidence. A student who truly wants to grasp the principles in this textbook must, in addition to reading it, study his or her own state's rules of professional responsibility. The nuances of those rules instruct legal assistants how to protect their professionalism and, most critically, the licenses of their employers because, as discussed in detail in Chapter 2, supervising attorneys are responsible for the conduct of their non-lawyer employees and assistants.

When studying your jurisdiction's rules of court, it is always preferable to use an **annotated** rules of court, as opposed to an official set of rules. Both sets have the same rules in them, but an annotated rules of court (similar to an annotated statutory code), which is published by a company instead of the government, has more in it than just the rules. What follow the rules and comments are case summaries—specific to that jurisdiction—that correspond to the particular rule. For instance, if you are using an annotated version when looking at your state's rule on solicitation (likely to be Rule 7.3 if your state has adopted the ABA Model Rules), you can find summaries of cases in your state, with their citations, that have interpreted the meaning of the rule on solicitation. By measuring all three angles to this triangle—the rules, the official commentary, and any cases interpreting the rules—you will find yourself as capable as any lawyer of understanding the significance of professional ethics.

rules of court—Sets of rules that are adopted by the highest appellate court of a jurisdiction and apply to the practice of law, unlike statutes, which are passed by a legislature and apply to all.

annotated—When a rule of court or statute is annotated, that means it is privately published and comes with research material in addition to the statute or rule.

Rules Based on the ABA Model Rules		Rules Based on the ABA Model Code	Rules Not Based on Either Set
Alabama	Montana	Iowa	California
Alaska	Nevada	Nebraska	Maine
Arizona	New Hampshire	New York	
Arkansas	New Jersey	Ohio	
Colorado	New Mexico	Oregon	
Connecticut	North Carolina	Puerto Rico	
Delaware	North Dakota	Tennessee	
District of Columbia	Oklahoma	(prior to March 1, 2003)	
Florida	Pennsylvania		
Georgia	Rhode Island		
Hawaii	South Carolina		
Idaho	South Dakota		
Illinois	Tennessee		
Indiana	(effective March 1, 2003)		
Kansas	Texas		
Kentucky	Utah		
Louisiana	Vermont		
Maryland	Virgin Islands		
Massachusetts	Virginia		
Michigan	Washington		
Minnesota	West Virginia		
Mississippi	Wisconsin		
Missouri	Wyoming		

Exhibit 1-1   Jurisdictions and Their Sources of Attorney Ethics Rules

A SUMMARY OF THE DISCIPLINARY PROCESS

disciplinary commission—A panel consisting mostly of lawyers and authorized by a state supreme court to investigate and prosecute lawyer misconduct.

Although not identical in every jurisdiction, the disciplinary process generally includes three similar components: investigation, prosecution, and appeal. A complaint can be filed against an attorney by clients, other attorneys, or even a bar association. Once filed, it is usually the task of a state's **disciplinary commission** to investigate the allegation. The disciplinary commission notifies the attorney that he or she is the subject of a grievance and then proceeds to gather the facts necessary to determine if the grievance should go forward or be dismissed. At this stage, the attorney under investigation is given the opportunity to respond in writing to the allegation of misconduct.

If the disciplinary commission finds there is reasonable cause to believe the attorney committed misconduct worthy of discipline, it will fill a formal complaint against the attorney. A special hearing officer, in many instances a retired judge, will be appointed to preside over the disciplinary hearing, at which the trial rules of evidence usually will not apply. If the attorney is found to be in violation of the rules, then a sanction will be recommended. Sanctions can range from a reprimand (private or public) to suspension or disbarment. When an attorney is suspended for a short term (less than six months), reinstatement generally occurs automatically at the conclusion of the suspension. However, in cases where more severe violations result in a long-term suspension, the attorney will need to apply for reinstatement at suspension's end. Disbarment usually means forever, but some jurisdictions, Florida for instance, allow a disbarred attorney to apply for reinstatement to the bar.

Disciplinary sanctions are generally not final until they are approved by the highest court in the jurisdiction (the state supreme court), because that court has authority over the lawyers licensed in its jurisdiction. Furthermore, an attorney has the right to appeal any finding of misconduct and/or sanction issued against him or her. When the appellate court renders its decision, the opinion it authors serves two purposes: first, to explain to the attorney the basis for the court's decision; and, second, to make precedent so that other attorneys in the jurisdiction can better understand how to follow the legal ethics rules.

WHY DOESN'T THE LEGISLATURE REGULATE THE PRACTICE OF LAW?

Much of the law that regulates the daily lives of citizens is statutory, coming from the legislature. Trades and occupations, such as construction, and professions, such as medicine, are regulated by a variety of legislative and administrative rules. But the legal profession is different. With limited exceptions, state supreme courts, rather than legislatures, regulate the practice of law. There are two primary reasons for this. One reason is connected to the fact that courts are composed of lawyers, and the second concerns the principle of **judicial review**.

The first reason seems obvious. Lawyers become judges, and judges work in courts. Even though most lawsuits are settled before trial and many lawyers are not litigators, everything a lawyer does for a client may end up in a court. Since the practice of law is very much like a regulated monopoly (one cannot do legal work for someone else without first being licensed to engage in the practice of law), then tradition dictates that courts will be the most appropriate regulator of the legal profession. In fact, some state constitutions grant their state's highest court the power to set the requirements for the right to practice law. For example, the Indiana constitution, in the fourth section of article seven, grants the Indiana Supreme Court the exclusive right to regulate the practice of law.

That, however, does not explain why legislatures rarely intrude into the regulation of the practice of law. After all, state legislatures are overwhelmingly filled with lawyers, so it would seem that they would also be inherently knowledgeable about the legal profession. Furthermore, nothing requires legislators to have worked in the construction industry, for example, in order to have the right to draft laws concerning the construction industry. This brings us to judicial review, a hallowed doctrine in constitutional law with which all legal students should be acquainted. The doctrine of judicial review comes from *Marbury v. Madison* 5 U.S. 137 (1803), a case whose significance is not to be underestimated and is worthy of background explanation.

judicial review—The doctrine from *Marbury v. Madison* that gives appellate courts the right to review the constitutionality of the acts of the legislative and executive branches, in addition to reviewing the decision of lower courts.

federalist—A founding father who believed in the need for the federal government to have unlimited power, as designed in the Constitution.

antifederalist—A founding father who opposed the design of the Constitution because it provided for an unlimited federal government.

The U.S. Constitution replaced the Articles of Confederation as the first document governing the country. Two camps opposed each other in the constitutional ratification fight: those in the **federalist** camp who believed in the need for a powerful, even unlimited federal government, and those in the **antifederalist** camp who did not. The second president, John Adams, was a federalist who, as he was leaving office, appointed a number of federalist judges. As Thomas Jefferson, an antifederalist, took office as the third president, it was discovered that some of those judges had yet to have their official commissions (documents of employment) delivered to them, an oversight by Adam's secretary of state. President Jefferson ordered his secretary of state to refuse delivery of the seals, thereby keeping some of Adams's federalist judges off the federal bench. William Marbury was one of those judges, and like all good Americans, he sued. But he took his lawsuit to the U.S. Supreme Court, rather than to a federal trial court.

The Supreme Court was led by its federalist chief justice, John Marshall, whose opinion in *Marbury v. Madison* alone makes him, according to some, the most powerful chief justice ever. Justice Marshall decided the case in a most unusual way, first declaring Marbury right in his assertion that he had been wrongfully denied his federal job, but then declaring him the loser under a line of reasoning that we know as "judicial review." Marshall argued that a federal statute authorized Marbury to bring his suit originally to the Supreme Court, whereas the Constitution gives the Supreme Court authority over such a suit only in its appellate function. Setting up such a self-opposing premise allowed Marshall to debate the question of which is superior—the Constitution or an act of Congress that contradicts the Constitution. Marshall argued that since America's new government was based on a written constitution, the Constitution must be higher than a federal statute, whose existence flows from the Constitution. He viewed the Constitution as "superior . . . law, unchangeable by ordinary means." *Marbury*, at 177. Therefore, the statute in question must be invalid since it contradicts the Constitution.

Another question presented in *Marbury* was whether the Supreme Court had the power to declare a statute unconstitutional, since the Supreme Court was given authority in the Constitution over lower courts but not another branch of government like Congress. Marshall resolved this question in favor of the Supreme Court by declaring: "[I]t is emphatically the province and duty of the judicial department to say what the law is. . . . If two laws conflict with each other, the courts must decide on the operation of each. . . . *This is the very essence of judicial duty.*" *Marbury*, at 177, 178 (emphasis added). And that is the doctrine of judicial review. The U.S. Supreme Court, in *Marbury v. Madison*, created a power for itself not granted to it in the Constitution but not questioned since 1803, holding that it had ultimate authority over any law, whatever the source.

How does that apply to the regulation of the practice of law? First, judicial review is a doctrine whose scope extends to state supreme courts, giving them the power to declare state laws void. Second, since the practice of law is regulated on a state level rather than a national level, state supreme courts grant their own lawyers—and perhaps paralegals some day—the right to practice law. Therefore, whenever a state legislature passes a law dealing with lawyers, the right to practice law, or the expansion of the rights of non-lawyers to engage in certain legal transactions, it is likely that the supreme court of that state will strike down the statute as an impermissible intrusion into the supreme court's business. Keep this in mind, and you will better understand how the regulation of the practice of law is unlike that of any other occupation or profession.

In the spirit of Paul Harvey, here is the twist to *Marbury v. Madison*. President Adams's secretary of state, the one who neglected to deliver the judicial commission to William Marbury, was none other than John Marshall, chief justice of the Supreme Court. Perhaps that makes Marbury's decision to go directly to the Supreme Court more logical.

HOW TO BRIEF A CASE

Few things make legal students more annoyed than being assigned cases to brief. That is an understandable reaction because briefing cases is tedious. It requires one to read case law very carefully, often more than once and often using highlighters. Then it requires the reader to analyze the case, making judgment calls in choosing the portions that are relevant for the reader's needs. Finally, it requires the reader to turn those judgment calls into a coherent, summary form that expresses the essence of the judge's opinion. And that is exactly why case briefing is so important. In a **common law** country, such as America, case law will always be the ultimate answer to any legal question. Therefore, appellate cases will always need to be read and understood. And, at a pragmatic level, the better one gets at legal analysis the more valuable one becomes, and nothing sharpens one's legal analysis skills more than briefing cases. As you read the cases in the chapters, understand that they are presented for two reasons: to help you understand how courts interpret the rules of professional responsibility and to help bring those dry rules to life. Be aware that the fact that a case in the text may have come from your jurisdiction does not mean that that case is still followed in its original form or even followed at all.

Like making omelettes, everyone has their own method on how to brief cases. My view is that a case brief should consist of five elements: facts, issue, holding, reasoning, and decision. A sixth element could be the dissent, but not all cases have a dissenting opinion. As these elements are explained, bear in mind that your instructor might have a different view on the format of a case brief.

common law—This phrase has three related definitions. In this context, common law refers to judge-made law, or the process whereby appellate courts make precedent that lower courts must follow. Because of our colonial history with England, America is known as a common law country.

The Facts

Law does not occur in a vacuum. A good case brief starts with its facts section, but in order to be "brief," a facts section should only include the key facts. As a rule of thumb, key facts are those whose existence not only places the case in a context, but also helps to shape the case's outcome. How is that determined? It is done through careful reading. As you examine the facts from a case in order to brief it, ask yourself if the court could have reached its decision without that fact being in existence. If not, that usually indicates a key fact that should be in your brief.

The Issue

The issue is the brain center of a case brief and the hardest part of a brief to grasp. A good issue asks a legal question, not an "outcome" question. An issue is about what the court has to grapple with in the appeal, not about who wins or loses. A good issue also incorporates some of the key facts into its wording. You know you have written a good issue when it stands on its own—when it, by itself, would allow a reader who has not read the case to still get an understanding of it. Write your issue in the form of a question. Do not be alarmed if your issue reads differently than someone else's, since issues can convey the same legal question but be expressed in different ways.

The Holding

For a case brief, the holding should simply answer the question presented in the issue in as short a method as possible. On a formal level, however, a holding is the pronouncement of law issued by the court's majority opinion; it is the precedent. The holding in a case brief, however, should just answer the issue.

The Reasoning

black letter law—Legal principles that have become so accepted and unequivocal that they are cited as truisms

affirm—The decision of an appellate court that maintains the status quo and keeps the lower court's decision in place.

reverse—The opposite of affirm.

remand—A remand occurs when an appellate court sends at least part of an appeal back to a lower court in order to reexamine the evidence or damages in light of the higher court's decision.

vacate—Similar to a remand, but sometimes a higher court vacates a lower court's decision to temporarily set a matter aside with instructions that the lower court rewrite its opinion in light of the higher court's opinion.

The reasoning section is the heart of the brief. A good reasoning section tells the reader why the court did what it did or how it reached its conclusion. Since appellate courts most often reach their conclusions through relying on case law, then a question is often raised concerning whether a reasoning section should include case citations. It generally should not, since citations, by themselves, explain nothing. Instead of citations, a reasoning section should give the principles from the precedent cited in the case. Sometimes courts use prominent legal doctrines, commonly called **black letter law**, as the foundation on which their reasoning is built. A court's reasoning is often in the latter part of the opinion and usually makes reference to the facts in the earlier part of the opinion. Likewise, your reasoning section should revisit integral facts in order to summarize the court's analysis.

The Decision

The decision section is procedural in nature. Appellate courts do one of four things with a case: **affirm**, **reverse**, **remand**, or **vacate**. At times, however, courts do more than one of those options in the same opinion. One can usually find the court's decision at either the beginning or the end of the case. If a disciplinary sanction against an attorney is stated or upheld, it is wise to include that sanction in your decision.

Please read the following case twice. Then, try briefing it along the left half of one or two pages of paper, leaving the right half of the paper open. This visual method will allow you to include on the right half of the same section of the brief any critical elements discussed in class that you may have missed, as well as any class notes associated with that case. When you are done briefing the case, look at the following page in the text, where you will find a sample brief of the case. The sample brief will be in italics, with some instructional comments placed in brackets. Compare your brief to the sample for similarities. On a final note, the more one briefs cases, the faster and better one gets at it, so hang in there.

Case Law

In the Matter of Anonymous, 689 N.E.2d 434 (Ind. 1997)

PER CURIAM.

Lawyers who advertise that they are "specialists" in a particular area of the law must comply with the provisions of Ind.Admission and Discipline Rule 30. The respondent in this disciplinary action failed to comply with those provisions and for that misconduct will receive a private reprimand. Herein, we set forth the facts and circumstances of this case in order to educate the bar with respect to provisions regarding lawyer specialist certification, while preserving the private nature of the admonishment.

The Commission charged the respondent with violating Rule 7.4(a) of the *Rules of Professional Conduct for Attorneys at Law* by claiming, in an advertisement, that he was a specialist in personal injury law when in fact he was not so certified. Pursuant to Ind.Admission and Discipline Rule 23, Section 11, the respondent and the Commission have agreed that the respondent engaged in misconduct and that a private reprimand is an appropriate sanction. That agreement is now before us for approval.

The parties agree that in 1995, the respondent purchased advertising time on a radio station and provided text for an advertisement of his law office.

The text he submitted for the ad was culled from "canned" advertisements the respondent purchased from a legal periodical several years before. The respondent allowed his office manager to send the material to the radio station without first reviewing its contents. On March 15, 1995, the radio station broadcast the advertisement, which stated that the respondent "specialize[d] in personal injury cases." At the time the advertisement aired, the respondent was not certified as a specialist in any area of the law under Ind.Admission and Discipline Rule 30.

Indiana Professional Conduct Rule 7.4(a) provides that lawyers may not express or imply any particular expertise except that authorized by Prof.Cond.R. 7.4(b), which in turn allows certification as a specialist only when authorized by the provisions of Admis.Disc.R. 30. Admission and Discipline Rule 30 provides, in relevant part:

Section 5. Qualification Standards for Certification. (a) To be recognized as certified in a field of law in the State of Indiana, the lawyer must be duly admitted to the bar of this state, in active status, and in good standing, throughout the period for which the certification is granted. (b) The lawyer must be certified by an ICO [independent certifying organization] approved by CLE [Commission for Continuing Legal Education], and must be in full compliance with the Indiana Bar Certification Review Plan, the rules and policies of the ICO and the rules and policies of CLE.

At the time the respondent's radio advertisement aired, he was not certified as a specialist in the area of personal injury law pursuant to Admis.Disc.R. 30. We therefore find that he violated Prof.Cond.R. 7.4(a) by expressing an expertise when he was not certified as a specialist pursuant to Admis.Disc.R.30.

We find that a private reprimand is appropriate in this case largely because the respondent's misconduct was unintentional. The offending content of the advertisement made its way on air due to the respondent's failure to review the material prior to submitting it to the radio station. We therefore view his misconduct as less culpable than if he had knowingly submitted a wrongful advertisement.

It is, therefore, ordered that the tendered *Settlement of Circumstances and Conditional Agreement for Discipline* is approved, and accordingly, the respondent is to be given a private reprimand.

SAMPLE BRIEF

In the Matter of Anonymous, 689 N.E.2d 434 (Ind. 1997)

Facts: The Disciplinary Commission charged an attorney with violating Rule 7.4 of the Indiana Rules of Professional Conduct. In 1995, the attorney paid for a radio commercial to advertise his services. The text for his radio spot came from "canned" advertisements he had previously purchased from a legal periodical. The advertisement was given to the radio station by the attorney's paralegal before the attorney reviewed it. The ad stated that the attorney "specialized in personal injury cases." At the time the commercial aired, the attorney wasn't certified as a specialist under Indiana law.

[Notice that the attorney's name is not listed in this case; this is an example of private discipline. Also, this case is not on appeal to the Indiana Supreme Court since the attorney and the disciplinary commission agreed to the facts and a sanction. The Supreme Court has this case in order to approve the sanction. Your facts should show that the lawyer placed an ad that implied he was a specialist when, at the time of the ad's publication, he was not certified, as required by Rule 7.4. The sample facts section

includes the facts about the paralegal because it is important to know that the lawyer is responsible for the mistake of his employees. Moreover, maybe the paralegal would not have sent the ad at all if he or she had been more aware of the Indiana Rules of Professional Conduct.]

Issue: When an attorney uses an advertisement that states he or she "specializes" in some area of the law, is that equivalent under the rules of professional responsibility to stating he or she is a "specialist"?

[Since this is not a traditional appeal, there is no "legal conflict" as earlier described. That makes the issue a bit harder to find. So, instead, craft an issue that would come out of the case if the attorney here was disputing the findings of the disciplinary commission. What would that be? Namely, that he did not say he was a specialist, but that he was specialized, which might mean that he does a lot of a certain kind of cases. Do not forget to use key facts in your issue so that it can stand securely by itself.]

Holding: Yes.

[Since a reading of the case shows that the attorney did violate the advertising rules, the answer to our issue is yes.]

Reasoning: Rule 7.4 states that one cannot even imply he or she is a specialist unless he or she is certified as a specialist, as allowed by Admission Rule 30. That rule says that in order to be certified as a specialist, an attorney must be certified by an independent certifying organization that has been approved by the Indiana Commission for Legal Education. Since the attorney's ad said he specialized in personal injury law, it implied he was a specialist. And, at the time of the ad's broadcast, he was not certified, as required.

[Since this is a case brief, do not include all of the court's explanation, including copying all of the language from the two rules (MR 7.4, and A&D Rule 30(5)), but include enough to leave you with a definitive explanation. The key to this reasoning section is to close the loop, to show in your brief why the attorney violated the advertising and specialization rules, not to restate that he did violate them, failing to include any of the details.]

Decision: The Court agreed that a private reprimand was sufficient here, since the attorney unintentionally violated the advertising and specialization rules.

[In attorney discipline cases, the decision will usually include a sanction, or approval of a sanction, unless the Court finds that the rules were not violated. Here, your decision should state why a minimal sanction was given because that shows how intent to break the rules affects a court's sanctioning process.]

A CASE STUDY IN LAWYER DISCIPLINE: THE DISBARMENT PROCEEDINGS AGAINST WILLIAM JEFFERSON CLINTON

On January 19, 2001, the day before leaving office, President Clinton reached a written agreement with Robert Ray, the **independent counsel** who succeeded Kenneth Starr and was in charge of the criminal investigation of what has commonly been called the "Whitewater Matter." That agreement involved President Clinton acknowledging that he misled federal judge Susan Webber Wright, the trial judge overseeing the lawsuit of Paula Jones, filed in 1994 and accusing the president of sexually harassing Ms. Jones in a hotel room in Little Rock when he was governor of Arkansas. The agreement reached between the president and the independent counsel called for the president to pay a $25,000 dollar fine and prevented the president from being criminally charged with obstruction of justice and perjury after leaving office. The agreement also allowed the president to bring a conclusion to the disbarment proceeding pending against him in Arkansas. On that same day, a statement, signed by the president and filed in Little Rock, Arkansas, acknowledged that he "knowingly gave evasive and misleading answers" in his **deposition** from the Paula Jones lawsuit and that his behavior was "prejudicial to the administration of justice." In exchange for admitting such behavior, the president agreed to have his law license suspended for five years.

independent counsel—A special prosecutor, authorized by specific statute with a broad scope of authority to investigate and, if necessary, criminally prosecute high government officials.

deposition—A litigation discovery device, similar to testifying at trial, whereby the deponent is put under oath and subject to lawyer questioning. Depositions occur in law offices or conference rooms, but not in courtrooms.

Then, in October 2001, the U.S. Supreme Court suspended President Clinton from practicing before it and gave the president forty days to respond by showing cause why he should not be permanently disbarred by the high court. Although President Clinton had never argued a case before the Supreme Court, membership alone is considered a high honor. Initially, President Clinton's lawyer, David Kendall, promised that a response to the Court would be forthcoming, but on November 9, the president formally resigned from the Supreme Court bar. Although many pundits believed it impossible for the president to have been convicted had he been indicted by the special prosecutor, the issue of whether President Clinton would (or should) have been disbarred from the Arkansas bar—which was the recommendation of the Arkansas disciplinary panel—is also likely to be debated for quite some time.

The Background to the Disciplinary Charges

Part of the discovery process in Paula Jones's sexual harassment lawsuit against the president included depositions. At his January 17, 1998, deposition, when asked about his relationship with Monica Lewinsky, the president declared under oath that he had had no sexual relationship with Lewinsky. Furthermore, Ms. Lewinsky put forward an **affidavit** stating the same. Months later, and after giving testimony to the Whitewater grand jury, President Clinton admitted he had been misleading regarding his relationship with Ms. Lewinsky. In April 1999, Judge Weber Wright then held the president in **contempt** for what she found to be his "intentionally false" testimony, rebuking him sharply in her contempt order, fining him $90,000 dollars in attorneys' fees and court costs, and referring the matter to the Arkansas Supreme Court Committee on Professional Conduct. Although being given the opportunity by the nature of Judge Weber Wright's order, the president did not appeal her sanction. Ironically, one year earlier, on April 1, 1998, the Jones lawsuit came to a conclusion when Judge Weber Wright granted the president's motion for **summary judgment**, dismissing the case. Eventually, the president settled with Ms. Jones in November 1998 (while Ms. Jones's appeal of the summary judgment was with the Eighth Circuit Court of Appeals), paying her $850,000.

The Nature of the Disciplinary Charges

After its investigation, the Arkansas Supreme Court Committee on Professional Conduct recommended to the Arkansas Supreme Court in May 2000 that President Clinton be disbarred. The committee's letter to the Arkansas Supreme Court stated that a majority of the committee found "that certain of the attorney's conduct as demonstrated in the complaints constituted serious misconduct in violation of Rule 8.4(c) and 8.4(d) of the Arkansas Model Rules of Professional Conduct." The rule in question to which the committee made reference states, "It is professional misconduct for a lawyer to: (c) engage in conduct involving dishon-

affidavit—A written statement of declaration made under oath and very often in the course of litigation.

contempt—Also known as contempt of court, this is an act or omission that tends to obstruct the administration of justice or shows disrespect for the court; it can include disobeying the instructions or orders of the court.

summary judgment—A litigation strategy in which a trial is prevented because the judge dismisses the case due to two prerequisites: (a) there are no material facts concerning the case that are in disagreement by both parties; and (b) the law applying to the case is on the side of the party who has asked the judge for a summary judgment.

esty, fraud, deceit or misrepresentation; (d) engage in conduct that is prejudicial to the administration of justice." Since the Model Rules (or state versions of them) have official comments that follow specific rules, it is interesting to notice some of the language in the Comment to Rule 8.4.

Paragraph 1 of that Comment notes that "some matters of personal morality, such as adultery and comparable offenses . . . have no specific connection to the fitness for the practice of law." That paragraph then speaks to the kind of morality with which the Rules are concerned. "Offenses involving violence, dishonesty, breach of trust, or serious interference with the administration of justice are in that category." Ironically, Paragraph 3 of that Comment states, "Lawyers holding public office assume legal responsibilities going beyond those of other citizens. A lawyer's abuse of public office can suggest an inability to fulfill the professional role of an attorney."

The Debate over Disbarment

While it is hard to separate the legal issues from the political issues in a case such as this, the question of whether it would have been appropriate to disbar President Clinton provides a fascinating framework for analyzing lawyer discipline. Those who were in favor of disbarment have made a few key points.

- *A Lawyer Lied under Oath.* Bill Clinton is an attorney, and anything short of disbarment would be an insufficient deterrent to both lawyers and non-lawyers who might also consider lying under oath. If lying under oath is not interferance with the administration of justice, then what is? Those who commit perjury can be charged with a crime, so why should the president not be disbarred?
- *This Lawyer Is Also the President.* President Richard Nixon lost his New York law license due to his deception, even though he was never under oath when he made misleading or false statements. Remember that the Comment to Rule 8.4 states that lawyers holding public office should be held to a higher standard and that no lawyer can hold any higher public office than president of the United States. Before becoming president, Clinton was an Arkansas law professor, Arkansas attorney general, and also governor, and thus should be more than cognizant of the ramifications of lying under oath.
- *The Arkansas Disciplinary Commission Recommended Disbarment.* According to Howard Brill, an ethics professor at the University of Arkansas Law School (and former colleague of the president), the Arkansas Supreme Court very often upholds the recommendation of a disciplinary panel. Furthermore, the Arkansas Supreme Court, in a recent opinion on lawyer ethics, quoted another state supreme court by stating, "There simply is 'no place in the law for a man or woman who cannot tell the truth, even when his or her own interests are involved.'" *Shochet v. Arkansas Board of Law*

Examiners, 979 S.W.2d 888, at 894 (Ark. 1998). And since the president never appealed the contempt sanction of Judge Weber Wright, which was a harsh condemnation against his false testimony, how could he argue that he should not be disbarred because he did not lie?

Those who would oppose the disbarment of the president make arguments that are equally compelling.

- *The President Never Lied.* David Kendall, the president's lawyer in this matter, has always maintained that President Clinton gave evasive answers in that deposition, but not legally false answers. Furthermore, the president did not commit perjury, even assuming he lied. Since the Lewinsky relationship was determined to be irrelevant to the Jones lawsuit—one that was ultimately dismissed—then President Clinton's misleading statements were not material to the case and, therefore, not perjury.
- *The President's Statements in That Deposition Concerned His Private Life.* Although a public figure, President Clinton's consensual relationship with Ms. Lewinsky has no bearing whatsoever on anything related to his law license. In fact, the Comment to Rule 8.4, under which the president was charged, clearly states that personal issues of morality, such as adultery, are not a specific concern of the Arkansas Model Rules of Professional Responsibility. Therefore, even if the president did lie, such a lie had nothing to do with him as a lawyer, but rather concerned him as a man, who would naturally be evasive in these circumstances.
- *The President Was Acting as a Client, Not as a Lawyer.* Beyond the fact that Mr. Clinton's obfuscation was of a personal nature, it was made in his role as a witness, not as a lawyer. Since the president was not representing himself in the lawsuit, then one could not even make the leap of an argument that he, as a lawyer, assisted himself, as a witness, in deceiving the court. The rules of professional responsibility apply to lawyers acting as lawyers, which was not the case here.

If possible, put aside your political ideologies and personal opinions of President Clinton. Now, revisit the issues and choose the disciplinary sanction: disbarment, suspension, or reprimand. While a five-year suspension and disbarment from the U.S. Supreme Court bar are undoubtedly heavy sanctions, those sanction have a practical mootness, since there is no indication that the former president, now living in both Washington, D.C., and the New York City region, will be practicing law in Arkansas or arguing cases before the U.S. Supreme Court. Examine your own state's rules of professional responsibility for its version of Rule 8.4, or DR 1-102(A) for those in a Model Code jurisdiction. If you use an annotated Rules of Court, such as those published by West Publishing, then read the annotations that follow that Rule's Comment to see if there are any cases in your state on lawyers being disbarred for lying, whether or not under oath.

In the following case, the New Jersey Supreme Court disbarred a lawyer for misappropriating his clients' funds. While reading it, notice that the Court is perplexed about how the attorney's alcoholism affected the Court's decision to disbar him.

Case Law

In the Matter of Hein, 516 A.2d 1105 (N.J.1986)

PER CURIAM.

This matter arises from a report of the Disciplinary Review Board (DRB) recommending disbarment of respondent. The recommendation is based upon its finding of multiple instances of misconduct involving neglect of clients' matters, misrepresentation of the status of matters, and, most significantly, two instances of misappropriation of clients' funds. Based upon our independent review of the record, we are clearly convinced that respondent engaged in the described conduct and that the ethical infractions warrant the discipline recommended.

Respondent was admitted to the bar in 1976. He opened an office for the practice of law as a sole practitioner. He practiced without incident until 1979, when the first of these incidents involving neglect arose. The problem matters continued into 1980 and were concluded in August 1981, when respondent closed his office. Various complaints were filed against him, including certain matters that were resolved without a finding of disciplinary infraction. He was suspended on September 28, 1982, for failure to answer the complaints. Respondent made no answer to any of the disciplinary complaints until January 11, 1983, when he appeared at a hearing conducted by the District III Ethics Committee (Ocean/Burlington). At that time, he substantially conceded the matters set forth in the complaints and attributed his failings to very serious drinking problems.

The DRB made detailed findings with respect to the several incidents as to which it sustained the District Ethics Committee's presentment of unethical conduct. Those findings may be summarized as fol-

lows: three clients gave retainers to respondent to represent them in matrimonial matters. Despite receipt of the retainers, respondent failed to file the requested complaints or to prosecute the parties' claims. He misrepresented the status of the file to one client. Another client retained him to handle various tax and commercial matters, to collect rents, and to prepare and file an income tax return. Respondent failed to file the tax return, to respond to inquiries about the matters, and to turn over $174 in rent receipts. In another instance, respondent was found to have aided a non-lawyer in the practice of law by reviewing bankruptcy petitions that the non-lawyer was preparing for filing. The non-lawyer signed respondent's name to the petitions without his consent.

The matter of gravest consequence to us and the ethics panels is a matter in which respondent was given a power-of-attorney, by clients who were in the military service, to collect the proceeds of a second mortgage. The clients had to leave the state before the matter could be resolved. Respondent collected almost $1,400 due on the mortgage but never responded to the clients' inquiries about the status of the matter and never turned the proceeds over to the clients. When the clients learned from the mortgagor that she had paid the mortgage balance to respondent, this complaint ensued.

It is plain that respondent exhibited a pattern of neglect in his handling of legal matters generally, in violation of DR 6–101(A)(2); that he failed to carry out his clients' contracts of employment, in violation of DR 7–101(A)(2); and that he misrepresented the status of various matters to his clients, in violation of

DR 1–102(A)(4). Standing alone, these incidents would probably not warrant disbarment since they occurred during a relatively brief period of respondent's career and were influenced, at least in part, by respondent's dependence upon alcohol during the period. . . . However, we remain gravely troubled by the misappropriation of clients' funds. Respondent acknowledges that he collected about $1,400 on behalf of the clients and that these funds were converted to his own use. This evidence clearly established that respondent unlawfully appropriated clients' funds. Although the amounts involved do not evidence a course of magnitude, there is no suggestion in the proofs that it was an unintentional misuse of clients' funds through neglect, *In re Hennessy,* 93 *N.J.* 358, 461 *A.*2d 156 (1983), or through misunderstanding, *In re Hollendonner,* 102 *N.J.* 21, 504 *A.*2d 1174 (1985).

Respondent, in a quite appealing sense of candor, admitted to the District Ethics Committee that, with certain exceptions not relative to our disposition, the allegations are essentially true. When asked if there was anything he would like to say by way of mitigation, he told the committee that he had "very serious drinking problems" and "that I didn't have enough sense to seek help when I should have. . . . I thought I was succeeding. But it did not succeed. It got progressively worse." His final comments were:

> MR. HEIN: I would like to add for what it is worth, I am sorry for the other members of the Bar. I cast a bad look on lawyers for doing this. But it got out of my control.
> MR. BEGLEY: That is a nice thing to say. But you have to try to think about yourself and straighten your own life out.
> MR. HEIN: That is why I am here today. I just want to get this all resolved and I will never practice law again. But at least I will be able to live with myself again.

How far we should look behind such an uncounseled admission concerns us deeply. Unfortunately, respondent did not appear before the DRB. It acted on his matter on the record before it.

Before us, respondent was represented by counsel who forcefully argued that his misconduct was causally related to his alcohol dependency and that his alcoholism should be a mitigating factor that would avoid the extreme sanction of *In re Wilson,* 81 *N.J.* 451, 409 *A.*2d 1153 (1979). . . .

To some extent a similar effect on perception, cognition and character may be caused by financial reverses, especially when that results in extreme hardship to respondent's family. It is not unusual in these cases to find such hardship, at least as perceived by most respondents. Yet we disbar invariably. It is difficult to rationalize a lesser discipline where alcohol is the cause—especially in view of the often related factors of financial reverses, failure in the profession, family hardship, and ultimately misappropriation.

We recognize, as respondent argues, that alcoholism is indeed not a defect in character. The public policy of the State of New Jersey recognizes alcoholism as a disease and an alcoholic as a sick person. *See, e.g., N.J.S.A.* 26:2B–7 (alcoholics "should be afforded a continuum of treatment" rather than subjected to criminal prosecution). The course that we have pursued in disciplinary matters is premised on the proposition that in our discipline of attorneys our goal is not punishment but protection of the public. *In re Goldstein,* 97 *N.J.* 545, 547-48, 482 *A.*2d 942 (1984); *In re Jacob,* 95 *N.J.* 132, 138, 469 *A.*2d 498 (1984). There may be circumstances in which an attorney's loss of competency, comprehension, or will may be of such magnitude that it would excuse or mitigate conduct that was otherwise knowing and purposeful. *See In re Jacob, supra,* 95 *N.J.* at 137, 469 *A.*2d 498.

We have carefully tested against the *Jacob* standard the proofs submitted by the respondent consisting of evidence of his seeking treatment at a rehabilitation center, expert analysis and expert opinion with respect to his condition, and personal affidavits from himself, his wife, and an employee. These documents do demonstrate an alcohol dependency, but they do not demonstrate to us the kind of loss of competency, comprehension, or will that can excuse the misconduct. Respondent's expert described the normal progression of alcohol dependency to the point where "there is a disruption eventually of the normal critical thinking and in concern and judgment in his perception of daily living and in the accomplishment of skills in his particular profession." He concluded that respondent "has gone through all the expected stages of drug abuse. . . . There is no question, in my opinion, that there is a direct causal relationship between the progressive disease of alcoholism and the loss of critical care and judgment affecting [respondent's] practice of law."

In this case the evidence falls short, however, of suggesting that at the time the mortgage proceeds were converted to respondent's use, he was unable to comprehend the nature of his act or lacked the capacity to form the requisite intent. In addition, it does not appear that he was continually in a dependent state, since he was able to attend to his practice. We must, however, accept, as respondent's expert points out, that the alcoholic becomes skilled at concealing the impairment. Respondent's secretary candidly stated that she was surprised that he could function as he did. These psychological states are extremely difficult for us to resolve. We do not purport here to determine definitively the effect alcohol dependency can have upon the volitional state of an individual. We have only the legal standard to guide us. We wish that we knew more.

Until we know more, perhaps until science and society know more, we shall continue to disbar in these cases. We believe that to do less will inevitably erode the *Wilson* rule and the confidence of the public in the Bar and in this Court. We believe that public attitudes towards alcoholics and addicts have changed, that they are much more compassionate, and almost totally nonpunitive, and that the members of the public have recognized more and more that they are dealing more with a disease than with a crime. Nevertheless we do not believe that that sympathy extends to the point of lowering the barriers to the protection we have attempted to give to that portion of the public who are clients, especially clients who entrust their money to lawyers.

The circumstance of the rehabilitated alcoholic or addict is deeply troubling to us. He has presumably recovered from the condition that contributed to cause his clients harm, and he will probably never again do any harm. But many of the lawyers, nonalcoholic, nonaddicted, disbarred by us for misappropriation would probably never again misappropriate. Indeed the probabilities may be even greater. Yet we disbar. That individual harshness—and so it is in most cases—is justified only if we are right about the devastating effect misappropriation—unless so treated—has on the public's confidence in the Bar and in this Court. Our primary concern must remain protection of the public interest and maintenance of the confidence of the public and the integrity of the Bar.

There may come a time when knowledge of the effect of drugs or alcohol, or other dependency upon the ability of individuals to conform their conduct to a norm, may lead us to alter our current view. Programs may be developed in conjunction with the Bar and the involved professionals that will promise the avoidance of public injury with the concurrent rehabilitation of dependent attorneys. We have seen, as they attest, that dependent attorneys become skilled at deception, not only of others, but of themselves. The best help is self-help, but others may be able to detect the need and help attorneys to take the first step to recovery. Under such programs an attorney could demonstrate commitment to a firm plan of recovery from the disease or condition. That in turn could assure the Court, and therefore the public, of the individual's ability to practice under circumstances or conditions that will assure public confidence until the disease or defect was arrested. For now, we find it difficult to exonerate the conduct influenced by the compulsion of alcohol dependency as contrasted with the compulsion to preserve one's family or assist another in a time of extreme need. . . .

Upon consideration of all the circumstances, we conclude that the appropriate discipline is disbarment. We direct further that respondent reimburse the Ethics Financial Committee for appropriate administrative costs.

Case Questions

1. What were the attorney's acts of misconduct? Which of those acts really bothered the Court?
2. If the attorney originally told the ethics committee that he was never going to practice law again, why did he fight the disbarment? Do you think his change of heart made his original declaration a lie?
3. What makes alcoholism, or other chemical addictions, a mitigating factor in attorney discipline?
4. Do you think addictions should be mitigating factors for surgeons or air traffic controllers who have committed wrongful professional acts? Why or why not?
5. Why did the Court disbar the attorney?

FINAL THOUGHTS ON THE ABA'S ROLE IN REGULATING LAWYERS

The ABA, like state and local bar associations, issues its own ethics opinions. These ethics opinions are meant to interpret the ABA Model Code of Professional Responsibility or the ABA Model Rules of Professional Conduct, depending on the date of the ethics opinion. Because the ABA is a private association and does not license lawyers, these ethics opinions are advisory only and do not have the force of law. In fact, all ethics opinions are advisory in nature, but because of the ABA's significance, its ethics opinions are important and very often other bar associations make references to ABA opinions. ABA ethics opinions come with two possible labels: Formal and Informal. According to the Rules of Procedure of the ABA's Model Rules of Professional Conduct, the distinction between the two is that "[f]ormal Opinions are those upon subjects the [Rules of Procedure] Committee determines to be of widespread interest or unusual importance." Certain ABA ethics opinions are cited throughout the chapters.

The ABA has also issued a document called "The ABA Standards for Imposing Lawyer Sanctions." Those standards consider four factors: (a) the duty violated; (b) the lawyer's mental state; (c) the potential or actual injury caused by the lawyer's misconduct; and (d) the existence of aggravating or mitigating factors. ABA Standards 3.0. The ABA Standards lists possible sanctions and the reasons for giving different levels of sanctions, such as whether there are any aggravating or mitigating circumstances. Included in the aggravating circumstances are selfish or dishonest motives, multiple offenses, a refusal to acknowledge wrongfulness, and substantial experience in the practice of law. ABA Standards 9.22. Included in the mitigating circumstances are the lawyer's reputation for having a good character, recovery from a chemical dependency that caused the misconduct, and a lack of a prior disciplinary record. ABA Standards 9.32. Some sanctioning courts look to the ABA Standards for guidance when disciplining their lawyers, and others direct their disciplinary panels to follow the ABA Standards in their proceedings. *See In re Conduct of Wittemyer*, 980 P.2d 148 (Or. 1999); *Grievance Administrator v. Lopatin*, 612 N.W.2d 120 (Mich. 2000).

Summary

Lawyers are licensed to practice law on a jurisdiction-specific basis by the highest courts in their jurisdictions. Those courts set the prerequisites for those who want to practice law in their jurisdictions, one of which is the requirement that once admitted to the bar, an attorney is obligated to follow the rules of professional conduct that have been adopted. Such rules of conduct originate from the American Bar Association, which created the Model Code of Professional Responsibility and, later, its replacement, the Model Rules of Professional Conduct. The Ethics 2000 Commission of the ABA issued a report concerning revisions recommended for the Model Rules, and many of the commission's recommendations have been adopted by the ABA.

If an attorney violates the rules of conduct in his or her jurisdiction, he or she is subject to discipline by the court that granted that attorney's law license, after an investigation by a disciplinary commission and a hearing. Sanctions can range from a reprimand to disbarment. All findings of misconduct can be appealed to that jurisdiction's highest court. Rules of professional responsibility are given fuller meaning in two primary ways. First, each rule is accompanied by its official commentary. Second, case law interprets the rules by applying them to specific situations.

Paralegals also need to abide by their jurisdictions' rules of lawyer ethics. Because legal assistants do substantive legal work, they face many of the same types of situations lawyers face, which requires legal assistants to have a sufficient understanding of what is appropriate, professional conduct. While not directly responsible to a court for violations of professional ethics rules, paralegals are indirectly responsible, since attorneys are accountable for the misconduct of their legal assistants.

Points to Ponder

1. Generally, how does one become a lawyer?
2. Examine the Rules of Court for your jurisdiction (probably included for purchase with this text) to determine how someone from your jurisdiction is admitted to practice law.
3. Why is it that the ABA's rules of conduct do not apply to lawyers?
4. Are your jurisdiction's rules based on the ABA Model Code or the ABA Model Rules?
5. Does your jurisdiction's rules of lawyer conduct have a section for legal assistants?
6. Do you know if attorneys in your jurisdiction must join the bar association?
7. What sanctions are available to be used against an attorney who is found to be in violation of his or her jurisdiction's rules of conduct?
8. Why do state legislatures usually stay out of the regulation of the legal profession?
9. What is the significance of *Marbury v. Madison*? (Honestly, it really is significant.)
10. Why is it important for all nonlawyer employees in a legal office, especially paralegals, to have a working knowledge of their jurisdiction's rules of lawyer conduct?
11. Do you think President Clinton should have been disbarred? Why or why not?

Key Concepts

ABA House of Delegates

ABA Model Code of Professional Responsibility

ABA Model Rules of Professional Conduct

American Bar Association (ABA)

Case brief

Disbarment

Disciplinary commission

Ethics opinions

Ethics 2000 Commission

Impeachment

Judicial review

Jurisdiction

Rules of court

Key Terms

affidavit	contempt	multi-state bar exam
affirm	deposition	remand
annotated	disciplinary commission	reverse
antifederalist	federalist	rules of court
black letter law	independent counsel	summary judgment
comments	judicial review	unified bar association
common law	jurisdiction	vacate

Paralegals and Their Profession

*It cannot be helped, it is as it should be,
that the law is behind the times.*

—Oliver Wendell Holmes, Jr.,
United States Supreme Court Justice, 1902–1932

*Somewhere, "out there," beyond the walls of the courthouse, run
currents and tides of public opinion which
lap at the courtroom door.*

—William H. Rehnquist,
United States Supreme Court Justice,
Chief Justice, 1972–

INTRODUCTION

What makes an occupation a profession? A professional athlete is one who gets paid to play, but does that make the sport a profession? The clergy, doctors, and lawyers work in what are classically referred to as professions, yet all of those professions involve many aspects that arguably make them businesses. Whatever makes something a profession today, one of the historical, distinguishing features of a profession is that entry into it requires the successful completion of two prerequisites: high levels of education and licensure.

That brings us to the paralegal. Some would say that paralegals are professionals because they engage in substantive legal work on behalf of attorneys, who are professionals. Others would say that even if paralegals are to be distinguished from other support staff, such as secretaries and receptionists, they cannot be considered professionals unless they are licensed. Still others would say that paralegal certification, rather than licensure, is a sufficient benchmark. Concerning the ethical obligations of paralegals, there is some inconsistency (as was discussed in Chapter 1), in the fact that paralegals are obligated to obey the ethics rules of lawyers, even though many legal assistants have yet to be granted traditional membership in state bar associations. This chapter will examine the history of legal assisting, paralegal associations, the debate concerning licensure versus certification, the dynamics of lawyer supervision and paralegal discipline, legal assistants joining state bar associations, and disbarred lawyers working as legal assistants.

A SHORT HISTORY OF LEGAL ASSISTING

Plenty of people, most of them women, were doing paralegal-type work long before the terms *legal assistant* or *paralegal* were coined. Curiously enough, Della Street, who worked so loyally all those years for the television lawyer Perry Mason, might be considered the first legal assistant. Although she may have been thought of as Perry Mason's secretary, she did a lot more than answer the phone: she worked with clients, she engaged in investigation, and, on occasion, she went to court with Perry. As peculiar as that comparison may seem, the fact remains that her depiction on a television show is evidence that the positive changes for legal assistants, including their formal recognition, are a result of an evolution whose initial changes may have gone unnoticed.

The distinguishing feature between a secretary and a paralegal is not the level of their education, but the level of their participation in the services rendered for the client. As the last half of the twentieth century progressed, the realization came that there was a growing number of non-lawyer employees in law offices, as well as the legal departments of corporations and government agencies, who were engaged in substantive legal work for their supervising attorneys. Certainly, a significant reason for such a shift was the fact that legal services could be delivered in a more cost-efficient manner if non-lawyers were trained to do the work of lawyers. The client's bill would then be smaller, since the billing rate of a non-lawyer is less than that of an **associate** or a **partner**. Likewise, the firm could increase its productivity by deploying its lawyers to other billable endeavors while its skilled, non-lawyer employees were being used in their expanded roles. Increased productivity leads to increased profitability, while at the same time clients get smaller bills due to the expanded role of the lower-billing, non-lawyer employees. That is what is known as a classic win-win outcome.

Recognizing this evolution, the American Bar Association (ABA) created a committee in 1968, known as the Special Committee on Lay Assistants for Lawyers. It was organized to encourage the use of non-lawyer employees in legal employment and to develop initiatives that would promote cost-effective methods for the delivery of legal services. The committee's name was changed in 1971 to the Special Committee on Legal Assistants, and its role was expanded to include studying the tasks undertaken by legal assistants, their role in other professions, the training given to them for those tasks, and the education available for legal assistants. By 1975, the ABA gave permanent status to the committee, renaming it the Standing Committee on Legal Assistants (SCOLA) and authorizing it to determine curriculum guidelines appropriate for legal assistant education, as well as grant ABA approval to legal assistant programs, of which there are over 240 in America.

associate—A lawyer in a law firm who has not reached partnership status, but may be on a partnership track. Associates report to their supervising partner or partnership mentor.

partner—A lawyer who has been granted ownership status in a firm, having been voted in as a partner by the other partners. Partners generally share in the firm's profits.

In 1991, SCOLA issued the American Bar Association Model Guidelines for the Utilization of Legal Assistant Services (reprinted in Appendix A). As stated in the Preamble to the ABA Model Guidelines, the purpose of SCOLA's efforts was to assist states that did not yet have guidelines for the use of legal assistants in adopting such guidelines, as well as assisting, for revision purposes, the seventeen states that already had paralegal or legal assistant guidelines. (In fact, Florida had addressed the use of legal assistants in 1976, when its Supreme Court adopted amendments to its Code of Professional Responsibility. *In re Petition to Amend Code of Professional Responsibility*, 327 So.2d 13 (Fla. 1976). That same year, Michigan adopted Guidelines for the Utilization of Legal Assistant Services. SCOLA acknowledged that the ABA Model Guidelines were drafted to conform with the ABA's Model Rules of Professional Conduct, and the Guidelines have a similar format to the model rules in that the model guidelines have declarative statements (the specific guidelines), followed by explanatory paragraphs (the comments to the guidelines). While specifically addressing the use of legal assistants, the ABA Model Guidelines are written to and for lawyers because they address how lawyers can appropriately and ethically utilize legal assistants in their profession.

The ABA's Web site has a Web page specifically dedicated to legal assistants (see Appendix E). There, one can learn about ABA-approved legal assistant education programs, access information concerning the ABA's position on legal assistants, gather career-related information, and order legal assistant–related publications.

The American Association for Paralegal Education (AAfPE), founded in 1981 and headquartered in Longwood, Florida, is a national organization serving the needs of educational institutions that offer paralegal education. Like the ABA, the AAfPE provides guidelines on appropriate paralegal curricula and grants institutional membership status to paralegal programs that are either ABA approved or in substantial compliance with ABA guidelines and also accredited by a nationally recognized accrediting agency. Presently, there are over 300 such programs in America. Legal education programs that fail to qualify for institutional membership can be granted associate membership in the AAfPE, upon providing evidence that their education programs meet six listed objectives, which include providing a well-designed curriculum, sufficient instructor-student interaction, and access to legal research library facilities.

The AAfPE has developed a model paralegal curriculum that it believes qualified paralegal programs should offer, which includes a minimum of eighteen general education credits and electives such as accounting, business or computer classes. An AAfPE membership curriculum should also include a core curriculum of legal research, legal writing, litigation, legal ethics, computer applications in the law, and an internship. The AAfPE recommends a minimum of eighteen credit hours of core courses and also recommends the availability of specialty courses, such as "Wills," "Criminal Law," or "Bankruptcy." All courses in an AAfPE membership curriculum are supposed to develop "Core Competencies for Paralegals," which are specific skills and types of knowledge the AAfPE believes a paralegal graduate should possess. Included in the skills section of the core competencies are the following: critical thinking skills, general communication skills, legal research and writing skills, and interviewing skills. Included in the knowledge section of the Core Competencies are the following: organization and operation of the legal system, the paralegal profession and ethical obligations, torts, and litigation procedures.

The AAfPE publishes *The Paralegal Educator*, a magazine for its members. It also periodically surveys paralegal program directors on their views on issues facing paralegal education. Some of the more recent surveys have concerned whether paralegal programs are considering changing the name of their programs to titles that are more neutral, such as legal studies, and inquiring about the propriety and extent of distance learning courses that are offered in paralegal programs.

The Legal Assistant Management Association (LAMA) is an organization dedicated to serving the needs of those who manage legal assistants, referred to by LAMA as legal assistant management professionals. Founded in 1984 and located in Atlanta, Georgia, part of LAMA's goals include "be[ing] the primary provider of information and educational resources on legal assistant management" and "promot[ing] the value of the legal assistant manager's role in the delivery of legal services." There are LAMA chapters in eighteen metropolitan areas in America and Canada and there are four membership categories, the highest being reserved for those who are responsible for managerial duties specifically related to legal assistants. Among the services provided, LAMA publishes a magazine, *The LAMA Manager*, and conducts surveys related to legal assistant compensation, as well as legal assistant utilization.

PARALEGAL ASSOCIATIONS

Paralegals can get involved in their profession by joining paralegal or legal assistant organizations. These organizations provide various benefits, including employment assistance and networking opportunities, continuing legal education, and professional ethics education. At the national level, there are two leading organizations: the National Federation of Paralegal Associations and the National Association of Legal Assistants.

The National Federation of Paralegal Associations

The National Federation of Paralegal Associations (NFPA), founded in 1974, is headquartered in Kansas City, Missouri. It has approximately 17,000 members, belonging to fifty-six regional NFPA associations. The NFPA publishes its own magazine, *The National Paralegal Reporter*, and has a Web site that provides extensive information on the paralegal profession, as well as legal research options.

The NFPA created its own rules of ethics, the NFPA Model Code of Ethics and Professional Responsibility and Guidelines for Enforcement (reprinted in Appendix B). Within this code is the NFPA Model Disciplinary Rules, adopted in 1997, which replaced its Model Code of Ethics, adopted in 1993, which in turn had replaced its Affirmation of Professional Responsibility, adopted in 1987. The NFPA Model Code of Ethics and Professional Responsibility consists of eight sets of rules, each with its own Ethical Considerations. In addition, the NFPA issues its own Informal Ethics and

Disciplinary Opinions, which have a similar appearance to the kinds of ethics opinions issued by the ABA and various state bar associations. In May 2002, the delegates to the NFPA conference voted to change the NFPA's definition of a paralegal by removing the term "legal assistant" from the definition. The NFPA's removal of legal assistant from its definition was done because the NFPA policy makers believe that too many law firms call their secretaries legal assistants. However, the NFPA's membership policy will still allow those who call themselves legal assistants to join the NFPA.

The NFPA offers its own certification exam, known as the Paralegal Advanced Competency Exam (PACE). Designed to test the competency of experienced paralegals, PACE is a four-hour, computer-generated exam, which is offered in two tiers. Tier I consists of general legal knowledge and legal ethics questions, and Tier II consists of legal specialty questions. In order to be eligible to take Tier I, an applicant must have at least four years of paralegal experience by December 31, 2000 *or* a bachelor's degree and completion of a paralegal program (including an associate degree program) from an institutionally accredited college, as well as two years of paralegal experience. Tier II's prerequisites include successful completion of Tier I *and one of the following:* at least six years of paralegal experience or the same educational requirements for Tier I plus a minimum of four years of paralegal experience. Successful completion of PACE allows a paralegal to use the title PACE-Registered Paralegal (R-P). Continuing legal education is also required to maintain the designation. If, however, an applicant for the PACE certification has a felony conviction (or comparable crime in a jurisdiction where there are no felony classifications), the applicant will be disqualified from eligibility.

Since 1996, close to 1,100 candidates have taken the PACE Tier I exam, and more than 500 have passed it. The Tier II exam has yet to be created, due to the small number of Tier I R-Ps.

The National Association of Legal Assistants

The National Association of Legal Assistants (NALA) was founded in 1975 and is headquartered in Tulsa, Oklahoma. Through its ninety-one affiliated associations, there are approximately 18,000 members. The NALA publishes its own magazine, *Facts and Findings*, and also has a Web site that serves as a clearinghouse for information on legal assisting and provides members with access to the NALA Net Files, a unique research site consisting of legislation, court decisions, and ethics opinions that concern legal assistants.

The NALA has two sources of ethics guidelines. The NALA Code of Ethics and Professional Responsibility (reprinted in Appendix D), first adopted in 1975 and revised on three occasions, consists of nine canons of aspiration-linked statements of professional ethics. The NALA Model Standards and Guidelines for the Utilization of Legal Assistants (reprinted in Appendix C), first adopted in 1984, serves as a declaration concerning how a legal assistant may be used and is written in reference to existing law dealing with legal assistants.

The NALA also has its own certification process available to its members, the NALA Certified Legal Assistant (CLA) Program, which began in 1976. The CLA exam is a two-day, comprehensive exam on federal law and procedure. The exam consists of the following major subject areas: communications; legal research; ethics; human relations and interviewing techniques; judgment and analytical ability; and legal terminology. The seventh subject area consists of five "mini-exams," one of which is on the American Legal System; the remaining four mini-exams are chosen by the applicant from a list of legal specialty areas, which include contracts, criminal law and procedure, family law, and litigation. Less than half of all participants pass all seven sections of the exam in their first sitting. As of December 2000, there were approximately 11,000 Certified Legal Assistants. The NALA also offers an advanced CLA exam for those who have reached CLA status and want to be certified in one of seven specialty areas. Additionally, there are three, state-specific, advanced CLA exams: legal assistants in California, Florida, and Louisiana can sit for certification exams that test the applicant on their state's substantive and procedural law. To be eligible to take the special CLA exams in California and Florida, a legal assistant must first have passed the national CLA exam. Moreover, in Louisiana, the legal assistant must take both the national and state-specific certification exams.

The eligibility requirements for taking the CLA exam provide three alternatives. The first alternative of eligibility involves the applicant for the CLA exam graduating from a legal assistant program that either is institutionally accredited or ABA approved, or has a minimum of sixty semester hours, of which at least fifteen semester hours consist of substantive legal courses. The second alternative involves the applicant having a bachelor's degree in any major plus one year's experience as a legal assistant (however, fifteen semester hours of substantive legal courses are considered equivalent to one year's experience). The third alternative involves the applicant having a high school diploma and seven years of legal assistant experience under the supervision of an attorney, as well as twenty hours of continuing legal education credits completed within two years of the date of the CLA examination.

PARALEGAL COMPENSATION

Once a new occupational category is created, it can then be analyzed in terms of employment trends. It probably comes as no surprise that computer jobs (such as computer engineers and systems analysts) have the highest projections of employment growth, but according to the Bureau of Labor Statistics, an agency of the U.S. Department of Labor, the field of legal assistants is projected to grow 62 percent by 2008, as compared to 1998. Such an increase places paralegalism sixth on the Bureau of Labor Statistics "Table of Fastest Growing Occupations." The Department of Labor's projections for paralegal employment between 2000 and 2010 is that the profession will grow faster than average, which means an employment increase of 21 to 35 percent. Furthermore, those projections concern traditional legal jobs—in law firms and the like. Additionally, students with legal educations are becoming more valuable in alternative careers where their critical thinking skills, communication skills, as well as their understanding of the legal system and legal research, can be quite valuable, such as in business, public relations, politics, education, and human resources.

Paralegal compensation is both a complicated and serious issue. Since the paralegal field is relatively small (as compared to other, more mature occupations), average compensation figures can be less than certain if they come from too small a sample size or if the respondents to a salary survey are not representative of the class of paralegals as a whole, and particularly if a large majority of the respondents have been working as paralegals for many years. Also, wages and other forms of compensation for legal jobs are higher in larger markets and larger firms, and wages for legal jobs in federal agencies are higher than in state and local agencies.

Nevertheless, there are some averages to consider. According to the Bureau of Labor Statistics *2000 National Occupational Employment and Wage Estimates*, the mean annual paralegal wage was $38,790 dollars, while the median annual paralegal wage was $35,360 dollars. The mean hourly paralegal wage was $18.65 per hour, while the median hourly paralegal wage was $17.00 per hour. The Bureau of Labor Statistics's information is a result of calculating data that comes from conducting surveys of employers, both large and small, throughout the country, and the bureau uses the words *paralegal* and *legal assistant* synonymously.

According to the *National Federation of Paralegal Associations 2001 Compensation and Benefits Report Executive Summary*, in 2001 the average paralegal salary was $41,721 and the average annual bonus was $2,468. This information is based on surveying NFPA members and nonmembers. The average respondent to the NFPA survey was a thirty-nine-year-old woman with between seven and ten years of law firm experience. The NFPA study also includes information on other compensation-related and job satisfaction issues, as well as the educational backgrounds of the survey respondents. Moreover, according to the *National Association of Legal Assistants 2002 National Utilization and Compensation Report*, the average legal assistant salary was $43,002 dollars, with an average annual bonus of $2,909. The NALA report is an extensive document that even includes compensation averages within types of legal specialties and is based on the information received from over 2,100 survey respondents, including nonmembers of the NALA. The report also tends to show an increase in the use of legal assistants working at firms whose sizes range from two to sixty lawyers. Compared to prior years, there is a smaller ratio of attorneys per legal assistant in those firms.

The Legal Assistant Management Association, in conjunction with the law firm–consulting group, Altman Weil, Inc., released its survey on legal assistant salaries in May 2002. The LAMA/Altman Weil *2002 Annual Compensation Survey*, based on the responses of 290 law firms, 99 law departments, and 5 other law-related organizations, shows that legal assistants/paralegals earned an average $44,416. Finally, to gain a greater appreciation of the significance of the numbers, you should examine in detail all of the previously mentioned compensation surveys.

THE GREAT DEBATE: LICENSURE VERSUS CERTIFICATION

As explained in Chapter 1, one is not an attorney by virtue of graduating from law school. Future attorneys become attorneys after being licensed in the jurisdiction whose bar exam and ethics exam they pass. Likewise, the certified public accountant and the doctor are required to be licensed. Licensing is mandatory in a profession, and the methods of licensure are determined and managed by government authority. Certification, on the other hand, is a voluntary method of formally standardizing competence and is usually a title granted by private organizations.

Minimum Qualifications: When Does One Become a Paralegal?

The paralegal presently exists in a no-man's-land, where almost nothing prevents anyone from referring to him- or herself as a paralegal or legal assistant. The ABA first adopted a definition of a legal assistant in February 1986, and according to the minutes of its board of governors, the definition is the following:

> A legal assistant is a person, qualified through education, training, or work experience, who is employed or retained by a lawyer, law office, governmental agency, or other entity in a capacity or function which involves the performance under the ultimate direction and supervision of an attorney, or specifically delegated substantive legal work, which work, for the most part, requires a sufficient knowledge of legal concepts that, absent such assistant, the attorney would perform the task.

Then, in 1997, the ABA House of Delegates adopted what is the current ABA definition of a legal assistant or paralegal. The current definition, drafted by the ABA Standing Committee on Legal Assistants (SCOLA), is the following:

> A legal assistant or paralegal is a person, qualified by education, training or work experience, who is employed or retained by a lawyer, law office, corporation, governmental agency or other entity and who performs specifically delegated substantive legal work for which a lawyer is responsible.

Even though the ABA's original definition of a legal assistant included the notion that a legal assistant works under the supervision of an attorney, that idea is not determinate, because every non-lawyer in a law firm—from the receptionist to the secretary to the billing department—ultimately works under the supervision of an attorney.

Does education make one an authentic paralegal? Not necessarily. Although the trend is that legal assistants should have at least some legal education at the college level (ideally a degree), many of the first paralegals were not educated beyond high school, and almost no one working as a paralegal back then had any legal education. Decades ago, there were almost no legal courses offered at the college level, so it would have been nearly impossible to study the law without attending law school. Moreover, where rules of courts or statutes define paralegals, often those definitions do not make a certain level of education, much less a degree, a requisite. Instead, the definitions generally focus on "someone who is qualified through education, training or work experience," as is stated in the ABA definition.

As was discussed in Chapter 1, state legislatures generally defer to their judicial counterparts when it comes to regulating lawyers and the practice of law. Likewise, many state supreme courts include paralegal codes of conduct into their already-created schemes by incorporating into their rules that govern lawyers those ethics rules that concern paralegals. The use of the word *rules* is tricky since—as will be discussed later in the chapter—paralegals, as outsiders, cannot be sanctioned for violating the rules of lawyer conduct. Furthermore, there are no "rules" concerning paralegals or legal assistants in either the ABA Model Code or ABA Model Rules, the sources for the lawyer conduct rules. Very often the word *guidelines*, as in "Guidelines for the Use of Legal Assistants," is used in the rules of professional conduct.

Some state legislatures, however, use their lawmaking power to formally define what it means to be a paralegal. Illinois, Indiana, Maine, and South Dakota are states where the legislative definitions of a legal assistant or paralegal are quite synonymous with the definition created by the ABA Standing Committee on Legal Assistants. 5 Ill. Comp. Stat. 70/1.35; Ind. Code § 1–1–4–6(a); Me. Rev. Stat. tit. 4, § 921; S. D. Codified Laws § 16–18–34. Maine also provides for a fine of $1,000 dollars against anyone who unlawfully uses the title of paralegal or legal assistant. Me. Rev. Stat. tit. 4, § 922(2).

Some states define a paralegal or legal assistant in their supreme court–created rules of court or bar association rules. North Dakota's definition of a legal assistant is found in the "Terms" section of its rules of professional conduct; the definition states

> "Legal Assistant" (or paralegal) means a person who assists lawyers in the delivery of legal services, and who through formal education, training, or experience, has knowledge and expertise regarding the legal system and substantive and procedural law which qualifies the person to do work of a legal nature under the direct supervision of a licensed lawyer.

Other states also define a legal assistant or paralegal in their rules of court. Kentucky defines a paralegal in the Preliminary Statement of Rule 3.700, titled "Rules Relating to Paralegals," located in the Kentucky Rules of the Supreme Court. New Mexico defines a legal assistant in Rule 20–102 in a set of its rules of court entitled "Rules Governing Legal Assistant Services." Rhode Island's definition is located in Provisional Order No. 18—Use of Legal Assistants, which follows the Comment to Rule 5.5 of the Rhode Island Rules of Professional Conduct.

Some state bar associations issue definitions of legal assistant or paralegal. The Oklahoma Bar Association Board of Governors adopted a legal assistant definition in 2000 that is very much like the ABA's current definition. The Virginia State Bar Association's Standing Committee on the Unauthorized Practice of Law issued a formal statement in 1995 that recommended all Virginia lawyers make reasonable efforts that their paralegals conform their conduct to the Educational Standards and Professional Responsibility Guidelines of the Virginia Alliance of Legal Assistant Associations, thereby incorporating the definition of the standards and guidelines. Moreover, West Virginia's governor restated the SCOLA definition of a legal assistant in a proclamation of Legal Assistant Day, on May 19, 2000.

Some states, such as South Dakota, even establish minimum qualifications for a paralegal or legal assistant *See* S. D. Codified Laws § 16–18–34.1. But even when a state provides a definition and minimum qualifications, the minimum qualifications are usually not contingent on one uniform prerequisite, including a legal education. For instance, California defines a paralegal as

> a person who either contracts with or is employed by an attorney, law firm, corporation, governmental agency, or other entity and who performs substantial legal work under the direction and supervision of an active member of the State Bar of California, as defined in Section 6060, or an attorney practicing law in the federal courts of this state, that has been specifically delegated by the attorney to him or her. Cal. Bus & Prof. Code § 6450(a).

A later section within the statute establishes minimum qualifications and requires a paralegal to possess one of four prerequisites: (1) a certificate from an ABA approved paralegal program; (2) a certificate of completion from an accredited paralegal program that requires at least twenty-four legal credits; (3) at least a baccalaureate degree in any subject, with at least one year's experience working for a California attorney who has at least three years of legal experience and a letter from that attorney stating that the person is qualified to perform legal tasks; or (4) a high school diploma or general equivalency diploma (GED), with at least three years of experience working for a California attorney who has at least three years of legal experience and with a letter from that attorney stating that the person is qualified to perform legal tasks. § 6450(c). While the California statute does allow one to be considered a paralegal without any accredited college education, that method is effectively tolled by a required completion date of December 31, 2003. § 6450(c)(4). California paralegals are also required to earn continuing legal education credits, including legal ethics credits. § 6450(d). Since these statutes are the most progressive to date and come close to a licensure requirement, California's paralegal statutes might serve as a blueprint for other jurisdictions that are considering regulating paralegals more directly.

Then does certification make one a paralegal? Logically, it could not, because both the NFPA and NALA certification programs require applicants to have experience; one must first be working as a legal assistant in order to be eligible to be a certified legal assistant. While lack of a certification title may affect one's pay or promotion, it does not prevent one from being a paralegal, because *the root of any paralegal definition, whether legislatively or judicially created, is the employment of one as a paralegal or legal assistant.*

An example of the dilemma faced by bar associations and courts over issues such as state-run certification can be found in Hawaii. Since 2000, Hawaii has been considering the certification of its paralegals, when court staff of the Hawaii Supreme Court, prompted in part by the desire to promote greater competency in the paralegal profession, proposed rules that would require certification of paralegals. The Hawaii Supreme Court then asked the Hawaii State Bar Association (HSBA) for official comments on the proposals, and a special task force was formed. The task force rejected the call for mandatory certification, but asked the Court for time to consider the idea of voluntary certification. More study and reflection was given, and by June 2002, this special committee of the HSBA acknowledged that it had failed to reach a consensus on voluntary certification and recommended that no rule amendments concerning paralegal certification be adopted.

The Licensing of Paralegals: Not Yet

It might seem logical to suppose that paralegals would need to be licensed in the jurisdictions where they work, particularly in light of the fact that the ideal role for paralegals is engaging in substantive legal tasks, limited only by that which would constitute the unauthorized practice of law. That, however, is not the case.

The Standing Committee on Legal Assistants (SCOLA)

It may come as a surprise to realize that no state regulates paralegals to the point of licensing them. It may come as a greater surprise to realize that the ABA's Standing Committee on Legal Assistants is in opposition to paralegal licensure. The Standing Committee on Legal Assistants has twice issued formal policy statements opposing the licensing of paralegals, in 1975 and 1986. On both occasions, SCOLA reached the conclusion that licensure was unnecessary in light of the fact that paralegals are required to work under the direct supervision of attorneys, as well as follow the rules of professional responsibility that govern the attorneys for whom they work. Since lawyers are professionally responsible for the work of their non-lawyer employees, it is believed that regulation of paralegals is unnecessary.

The ABA revisited the issue in the 1990s and, after a lengthy study and investigation, confirmed its earlier position against paralegal licensing. However, the ABA adopted a revised legal assistant/paralegal definition in 1997, using the phrase, "for which a lawyer is responsible" to replace the prior language of "under the ultimate direction and supervision of an attorney." Notice that even though the ABA opposes paralegal licensing, its revised paralegal definition shows a loosening of the historical grip on the role of legal assistants.

The National Association of Legal Assistants

The National Association of Legal Assistants opposes paralegal licensing. The NALA was able to restate its opposition after the New Jersey Supreme Court Committee on Paralegal Education and Regulation issued a report in 1998 concerning the use of paralegals, which included the recommendation of paralegal licensure. That committee was formed as a result of a 1992 New Jersey Supreme Court decision, *In re Ethics Opinion No. 24 of the Committee on the Unauthorized Practice of Law*, 607 A.2d 962 (N.J. 1992), that concerned the use of independent contracting paralegals. (That case is presented in Chapter 3.) The NALA responded by issuing its own response report in 1999, in which it stated its opposition to paralegal licensure. Specifically, the NALA's response stated that licensing of paralegals would be harmful to the expansion of the paralegal profession, as well as anticompetitive. One aspect in the New Jersey report that the NALA found to be unfair was that New Jersey's licensing scheme required a post–high school education. The NALA's response was that a legal education, without any paralegal experience, is an insufficient measure of competence. An overview of the NALA response is as follows: there is no demonstrable evidence of a need for paralegal licensing; paralegal licensing would increase the costs of paralegal services to legal employers; such increased costs would then be passed on to the general public; and licensing would unduly limit the growth and evolution of the paralegal profession. In May 1999, the New Jersey Supreme Court issued an administrative determinations report that rejected its committee's proposal concerning paralegal licensure and regulation, finding that the supervision of paralegals is best left to attorneys.

The National Federation of Paralegal Associations

The National Federation of Paralegal Associations does endorse paralegal licensure. In 1992, the NFPA adopted a regulation that stated it is in favor of state-by-state licensing, particularly licensing that would be consistent with the NFPA's two-tier certification program. Specifically, the NFPA resolution states that it may support paralegal licensing in a state where the majority of voting NFPA members in that state are in support of the licensing, and as long as the criteria for licensing are consistent with NFPA policy. When the New Jersey Supreme Court was considering the licensure and regulation of paralegals, the NFPA issued its own response to the recommendation report stating that it was generally in favor of a paralegal licensing scheme that would provide for an expanded role of paralegals.

Is Certification the Alternative to Licensure?

As one can see, the powers that be seem to oppose paralegal licensure, with the National Federation of Paralegal Associations being the only exception. Why is licensure an idea that has been opposed? Many states require day care providers, as well as those who cut and style hair, to be licensed. Every state requires schoolteachers not only to have at least a bachelor's degree, but to also be licensed in the states in which they teach—people cannot be schoolteachers simply because they have lots of experience with children. And yet, in a peculiar anomaly, while few states require one to meet any prerequisite in order to work as a legal assistant, the two national certification programs originally required years of experience as a prerequisite to certification eligibility. Eventually, after a grandparenting period waned, both certification programs instituted a mandatory educational component in conjunction with paralegal experience.

Herein lies the paradox: (a) there is rarely anything official that one must do to be a legal assistant, other than be employed as a legal assistant; (b) the American Bar Association, the most powerful force for change in the legal profession, opposes the licensing of legal assistants, while at the same time continuing to ask states to consider expanding the roles of legal assistants; and, (c) increasingly, the ability to obtain employment as a legal assistant and also be promoted requires that one have a certain level of formal education and then become certified by one of two private, unregulated organizations that determine the worthiness of legal assistants to be certified for a field where they are working with licensed (i.e., regulated) attorneys (Exhibit 2-1).

The Arguments in Opposition to Paralegal Licensure

The arguments in opposition to paralegal licensure seem to be threefold. First, there is the argument that there has been no demonstrable evidence that licensure is necessary. Since paralegals work under the supervision of lawyers, who are regulated by their jurisdictions' rules of ethics and discipline and are also responsible for the conduct of their non-lawyer employees, it would be redundant to license paralegals. That argument has history on its side, bolstered by the recognition that in the last few decades, improvements in the delivery of legal services have come without the licensing of paralegals.

Second, the licensing of paralegals would cause the costs of legal services to precipitously increase, thereby hurting the very clients who are most benefited by the increased use of paralegals. The use of a paralegal reduces the client's bill because a paralegal is paid less than a lawyer, which allows the law firm to bill the client for the paralegal's work at a rate smaller than if a lawyer had done the work. Therefore, if paralegals were licensed, the increased costs of obtaining licensure (and increased prestige) would be passed along to clients, whose bill would then be higher, not because of increased effort, but increased status.

Third, the licensing of paralegals would unfairly prevent some from entering a field that would pay them a living wage. Access to employment is a critical issue in free-market economy, and even in the area of conflicts of interests (to be discussed in Chapter 5), some states provide more leniency to paralegals, in contrast to lawyers, partly because of the desire to provide them greater access to legal employment.

Licensure	Certification
• Licensure is mandatory.	• Certification is voluntary.
• Licensure is determined and regulated by government.	• Certification is determined and regulated by private groups.
• Applicants must possess law degrees.	• Applicants do not always have to possess four-year degrees.
• Members are held to legally required standards.	• Members are held to internally required standards.
• Licensure is valid only in the jurisdiction granting the license.	• Certification is valid nationally.

Exhibit 2-1   Differences between Law Licensure and Paralegal Certification

The Arguments in Support of Paralegal Licensure

There are those who support paralegal licensure. Those proponents make the following arguments. First, there is a need for real regulation of paralegals by the bar. In the last thirty-five years, the paralegal field has grown from being a laughingstock (at least to those traditionalists who believed that there was no role in a law office for a "para"-legal), to a curiosity, and then to a vibrant segment of the legal profession. As this occupation moves out of its infancy, the next logical step is to institute some licensing mechanism.

Second, a licensing procedure will prevent some people from entering a field for which they are unsuitable. Plenty of people are denied entrance into an employment field because they lack certain proficiencies, and the legal assistant field should scarcely be considered sacred to the point of protecting deficient paralegals at the expense of clients. Some people would say that greater respect for legal assistants would be cultivated if the general public understood that those who call themselves legal assistants have officially earned that privilege, at the risk of failing.

Third, there is no evidence that licensing will prohibitively increase legal costs. Certainly, the ABA has not considered the likelihood of increased costs to the public due to the influx of graduates of paralegal programs that have been ABA approved, an extremely arduous process. Nor has the NALA, when promoting its certification programs, considered this possibility. Not only do certifications cost considerable sums (membership fees, testing fees, continuing legal education fees, and opportunity costs), but also, one of the promoted benefits of any certification program is higher income to the certified legal assistant. And presumably, state-specific certification, in those states that provide for it, would result in even more prestige and accompanying financial benefits.

Furthermore, as earlier stated, some form of a college degree is required in order for someone to sit for either the PACE or CLA certification exam. And, greater than the pursuit of knowledge, the most compelling reason for getting a college degree (and assuming the debt that goes with it) is the presumption of higher starting and continuing wages.

PARALEGAL DISCIPLINE: IS IT POSSIBLE TO SANCTION A PARALEGAL?

A basic question of life in an orderly society concerns what makes something law. Tradition, custom, and ritual may share some of the same ideas as law, but they are not law. All of the aforementioned involve some level of planning, order, and an agreed way of doing things, but law includes an aspect that distinguishes it from all else—penalty. Law is organization plus penalty. Although obeying the law may be virtuous, it is rare that virtue causes people to obey the law. It is the risk of a ticket and higher insurance rates that keeps us driving as close to the speed limit as we dare. It is the risk of an Internal Revenue Service audit that might catch an intentional evasion of taxes that leads us to report our income accurately. While the chances of getting a ticket or getting audited are statistically rare, the fact that they are possibilities is the stick, and not the carrot, that keeps us—at least most of us—in line.

Paralegal Associations Can Sanction Their Members

If a legal assistant belongs to a national, state, or local paralegal association, then failure to abide by the association's sets of rules can result in some form of a sanction. For instance, the NALA Rules for Disciplinary Proceedings lists three, nonexclusive sanctions against its Certified Legal Assistants found to be in violation of NALA ethics standards: a formal caution, a suspension of CLA designation, and a revocation of CLA designation. And Rule 2.7(a) of the NFPA Guidelines for the Enforcement of the Model Code of Ethics and Professional Responsibility lists five possible sanctions that can be issued against its rules violators, including suspension from the NFPA and fines. Furthermore, both the NALA and NFPA will revoke the CLA or PACE certifications of their members who are subsequently convicted of a felony or equivalent crime.

The NFPA issues its own Informal Ethics Opinions, which have a similar appearance to the ethics opinions issued by the disciplinary commissions of the state bar associations. Responding to questions by its members, the NFPA Informal Ethics Opinions interpret the NFPA Model Code of Ethics and Professional Responsibility. However, such opinions do not have the effect of law, and by contacting the NFPA for guidance, the interested party warrants that he or she will refuse to hold the NFPA liable for any consequences resulting from relying on the ethics opinion.

The Lawyer's Duty of Supervision: The Stick, Not the Carrot

As long as paralegals are unlicensed, then their misconduct or **malfeasance** has to be laid at the feet of their employing lawyers, assuming the misconduct is within the scope of their employment. Because legal assistants are not licensed to practice law, they cannot be professionally disciplined for violating the rules of conduct, even though those rules apply to them by virtue of their professional relationship to licensed attorneys. Therefore, lawyers pay the price for the errors of their legal assistants. Such is the scheme in place due to the general principles of **respondeat superior** and the rules of professional responsibility.

The ABA Model Rules make that expressly clear in Rule 5.3, which is titled, "Responsibilities Regarding Nonlawyer Assistants." MR 5.3(a) requires partners to make reasonable efforts to ensure that their law firms have taken steps to ensure that their non-lawyer employees or assistants conduct themselves compatibly with the same obligations as lawyers. This rule is the key to the professional life of the legal assistant because, by implication, it requires legal assistants in ABA Model Rules jurisdictions to learn, understand, and follow the operative rules of attorney conduct. This rule expresses, almost in passing, the need for legal assistants to study their operative attorney rules of conduct; those rules, after all, are the only rules that apply to the supervisors of legal assistants.

malfeasance—A wrongful or unlawful act.

respondeat superior—A Latin phrase that means, "let the superior reply." This is a legal doctrine that makes employers (or principals) liable for the misconduct of their employees (or agents) that is committed within the scope of the employment.

MR 5.3(b) requires supervising lawyers to make reasonable efforts to ensure that their non-lawyer assistants comply with the professional obligations of lawyers. This rule makes it incumbent upon the firm to formally acquaint their legal assistants with those operative rules of professional responsibility. Preferably, such acquaintances would be made at the orientation for a newly hired legal assistant.

Moreover, MR 5.3(c) closes the loop by stating:

> a lawyer shall be responsible for conduct of such a person that would be a violation of the Rules of Professional Conduct if engaged in by a lawyer if:
> (1) the lawyer orders or, with the knowledge of the specific conduct, ratifies the conduct involved; or
> (2) the lawyer is a partner in the law firm in which the person is employed, or has direct supervisory authority over the person, and knows of the conduct at a time when its consequences can be avoided or mitigated but fails to take reasonable remedial action.

Why is it important that a legal assistant know the operative rules of professional responsibility? Because the supervising lawyer of any legal assistant will be sanctioned for the misconduct of that legal assistant, with limited exceptions. Lawyers will even be sanctioned for the clerical errors of their legal assistants. For instance, in an Iowa case, a criminal defense lawyer put forward a motion to dismiss his client's charges because the indictment was not brought within forty-five days of arrest. However, the legal assistant who prepared the motion mistook the date of the alleged crime for the date of arrest, which made the motion misleading, and the lawyer (who failed to read his legal assistant's work) was suspended. *Iowa Supreme Court Bd. of Professional Ethics and Conduct v. Ackerman*, 611 N.W.2d 473 (Iowa 2000).

The older ABA Model Code of Professional Responsibility lacked a general directive like MR 5.3, but it had specific directives. For instance, DR 4-101(D) stated that an attorney "shall exercise reasonable care to prevent his employees, associates, and others whose services are utilized by him from disclosing or using confidences or secrets of a client." And Guideline 1 of the ABA Model Guidelines for the Utilization of Legal Assistant Services puts the burden on lawyers, making them responsible for, "all of the professional actions of a legal assistant performing legal assistant services at the lawyer's direction."

Distinct from the ethics rules, lawyers could be considered responsible for the conduct of their paralegals because of legislation that mandates it. Such is the case in California, where one of the statutes that concerns paralegals states that a lawyer who uses a paralegal "is liable for any harm caused as the result of the paralegal's negligence, misconduct, or violation of [the statutes on paralegals]." Cal. Bus & Prof. Code § 6452(b).

The following case shows the common result of the lack of appropriate supervision of a legal assistant who engages in conduct that hurts the client—namely, that the legal assistant's supervising lawyer will be held accountable.

Case Law

Musselman v. Willoughby Corporation, 337 S.E. 2d 724 (Va. 1985)

This is an attorney malpractice case arising from a real estate transaction. The lawyer represented a corporate client and employed an untrained paralegal who played a significant role in the closing of the transaction.

The relevant facts mainly are undisputed. Appellee Willoughby Corporation, the plaintiff below, was formed in September 1974 by a large number of holders of O'Neill Enterprises, Inc., real estate bonds which had been secured by undeveloped land known as the "Willoughby Tract," lying in the City of Charlottesville and Albemarle County. When O'Neill Enterprises defaulted and went into bankruptcy, the bondholders formed Willoughby Corporation (hereinafter, the Corporation) in order to sell or develop the property to recoup their investments. Appellant Robert M. Musselman, a defendant below, represented the bondholders in formation of the Corporation. He became attorney for the Corporation and also served as its Secretary. He was not a member of the Board of Directors. The daily operations of the Corporation were handled from defendant's law office by defendant's employees. One director testified that Musselman took "a very dominant role in the affairs of the corporation" and that the Board looked to defendant for "guidance and leadership." Upon formation of the Corporation, several tracts of land, residential and commercial, were combined. One of the parcels, an 11.5-acre commercial piece known as Parcel 9, is the subject of this controversy.

In 1976, aware that the Board of Directors wished to sell a portion of the Willoughby Tract, defendant contacted Thomas J. Chandler, Jr., a local real estate broker, who obtained an offer to purchase Parcel 9. The offer was made by Charles W. Hurt, a medical doctor who had been a real estate developer in the Charlottesville and Albemarle County area for a number of years. Initially, Hurt offered to pay $200,000 for the land. The realtor completed a standard form purchase contract dated March 26, 1976 reciting that amount and, as instructed by Hurt, showed the purchaser to be "Charles Wm. Hurt or Assign." The proposal was delivered to defendant who later asked the realtor to attend a special meeting of the Board of Directors, held at Musselman's law office on April 9, 1976.

Among those present at the meeting were the following Board members: Charles J. Frankel, President, a medical doctor who held a law degree; John H. Robinson; and William Massie Smith, an attorney. Defendant attended along with Chandler and consultants in the fields of finance and real estate. The Board minutes of the meeting show that Chandler "presented" Hurt's offer to the Board at the meeting and that the Board fully considered "the advantages and disadvantages" of the proposed sale. The Board decided to accept the offer subject to several modifications, to which Hurt later agreed.

Subsequently, another standard form purchase contract for $215,000 was completed dated May 6, 1976. The purchaser was shown to be "Charles Wm. Hurt or Assigns." The contract provided that the purchaser pay $45,000 cash by the time of closing, scheduled for March 1, 1977, and the balance of $170,000 evidenced by a deferred purchase money note secured by a deed of trust, the terms of which were set forth in an addendum attached to the contract. The contract was executed by Hurt, by Musselman on behalf of the Corporation as corporate Secretary, and by the realtor.

The closing did not occur on March 1, 1977. The delay was attributed, in part, to a disagreement between Hurt's attorney and Musselman about the matter of interest on the debt as it related to the availability of sewer service to the property. The delay in closing was a subject of discussion during a meeting of the Board of Directors on September 1, 1977. Directors present at that meeting were Frankel, Clifford C. Fox, and Lloyd T. Smith, Jr., an attorney with extensive experience in real estate matters. Also present were Musselman and one Stanley K. Joynes, III. Joynes had been employed by Musselman in June 1977. Joynes had just graduated from college but had no formal training either as a lawyer or a paralegal. His main responsibility, under Musselman's direction, was to "shepherd the Willoughby Project along." Joynes attended his first Board meeting in July 1977 and was chosen Assistant Secretary of the Corporation. In the course of the September 1977 Board meeting, defendant was directed to close the Hurt transaction "as soon as possible." Three weeks later, Stuart F. Carwile, Hurt's attorney, notified Musselman by letter dated September 22, 1977 that his client desired to take title to Parcel 9 as follows: "Stuart F. Carwile and David W. Kudravetz, as trustees for the Fifth Street Land Trust, pursuant to the terms of a certain land trust agreement dated 22 September 1977." Carwile advised that after Musselman submitted a draft of the deed, Carwile would forward the proposed deed of trust and note for defendant's approval.

The paralegal then prepared the deed, with "some assistance" from other employees of defendant, in accordance with Carwile's request showing the Land Trust as grantee. Joynes arranged for Frankel to execute the deed, dated October 5, 1977, and on that day participated with Carwile in the closing of the transaction. Musselman was out of town on business on both October 4th and 5th. In the course of the closing on October 5th, the paralegal accepted the deed of trust, and other closing documents prepared by Carwile, which specifically exculpated Hurt from personal liability in the transaction as beneficiary under the land trust.

At this point, we note several important undisputed facts. First, the Board of Directors, upon being advised that Hurt, a man of substantial wealth, was to be the purchaser of Parcel 9, intended to rely on Hurt's potential personal liability as a part of the security for payment of the deferred purchase price. Second, Musselman maintained in his trial testimony that he was authorized by the Board to execute the contract of sale on behalf of the Corporation, and this was not contradicted by any witnesses. In addition, Musselman testified that Joynes, the paralegal, represented the Corporation at the closing, acting within his authority as an employee of defendant. Also, none of the Board members, prior to closing, ever examined either the proposed contract of March 26 or the final contract dated May 6. Moreover, no member of the Board knew before closing that the contract showed the purchaser to be "Hurt or Assigns." In addition, Musselman always was of opinion that the foregoing language in the contract authorized Hurt to escape personal liability under the contract by assigning his rights in the contract to whomever he chose. Also, Musselman never called the language to the Board's attention or explained its meaning to the Board. Finally, the fact that the closing documents exculpated Hurt from personal liability as beneficiary under the land trust was never revealed or explained to the Board of Directors prior to closing.

The Board of Directors met on October 6, the day after closing. Directors present were Frankel, Fox, and Lloyd T. Smith, Jr. Joynes and Musselman were also present, among others. The paralegal reported that the sale of Parcel 9 was complete. When a question arose about the date from which interest was to run, Smith asked to see Musselman's file and discovered that the property had been conveyed to a land trust and not to Hurt. He examined the note, saw that Hurt had not endorsed it, and thought the situation was "just frightening." Smith also examined the other closing documents and saw they specifically provided that Hurt would have no personal liability. Smith next observed the provisions dealing with release of large portions of the property from the lien of the deed of trust upon receipt of the down payment of $45,000 and he was "really concerned." As a result of the discussion at that meeting, "Musselman stated that he would speak with Dr.

Hurt and his attorney . . . in an attempt to clear up these problems." The contract of sale was not exhibited to the Board until the following meeting and no discussion had taken place during the October meeting about the "or Assigns" language . . . .

The Land Trust defaulted under the terms of the $170,000 note in respect to an interest payment due on April 1, 1978. Subsequently, this action to recover the principal sum, plus interest, due under the real estate transaction was filed in September 1978 in numerous counts against Hurt and Musselman. The proceeding against Hurt was severed and he was eventually dismissed by the trial court as a party defendant.

The Corporation's action against Musselman was based on alternative theories. The plaintiff charged that defendant breached certain fiduciary duties in his capacity as an officer of the Corporation. In addition, the Corporation alleged that Musselman, in his capacity as attorney for the Corporation, was negligent and breached his fiduciary duty as counsel to the Corporation. At the March 1982 trial, the jury was permitted, under the instructions, to find against defendant in his capacity either as attorney, or as an officer of the Corporation, or as both attorney and officer. The jury found against defendant in his capacity as attorney only and fixed the damages, which were not in dispute, at $243,722.99. This sum represented the principal amount due on the obligation, plus interest through the last day of trial. The trial court entered judgment on the verdict in June 1982, and we awarded defendant this appeal in July 1983.

On appeal, defendant understandably does not seriously contend that the evidence was insufficient to raise a jury question on the issue of negligence and breach of fiduciary duty in his capacity as an attorney. Under the circumstances, Musselman had a duty to disclose anything known to him which might affect his client's decision "whether or how to act." *Owen v. Shelton*, 221 Va. 1051, 1054, 277 S.E.2d 189, 191 (1981) (applying the rule in the case of a real estate broker). *See Allen Realty v.*

Holbert, 227 Va. 441, 446-47, 318 S.E.2d 592, 595 (1984) (applying the rule in the case of accountants). And, contrary to defendant's assertion, a lawyer is not relieved of such duty owed to a corporate client merely because some members of the board of directors are attorneys. Of course, an attorney acting as counsel for a corporate client is not required to explain to the board of directors every sentence in a standard form land contract. But the attorney has a duty to disclose information necessary to enable the client to understand those contract provisions that have the potential for affecting the client adversely.

In the present case, the evidence showed that defendant failed to advise the Board before closing that the crucial "or Assigns" language was in the contract, and failed to explain the legal effect of the language when, in defendant's opinion, use of the language enabled Hurt to escape personal liability, a consideration of prime importance to the Board in view of the manner in which the deal was structured. In addition, the evidence demonstrated that Musselman permitted an untrained paralegal to accept formulation of final documents that further exculpated Hurt, without bringing such documents to the Board for approval. In sum, the evidence was sufficient to support the jury's finding that defendant breached his duty as an attorney to adequately inform his client and that such breach was a proximate cause of plaintiff's loss.

Inexplicably, defendant's main contentions on appeal are based on the faulty premise that he lacked corporate authority to act in executing the contract containing the "or Assigns" language and in completing the conveyance to a land trust, while, in the process, exculpating Hurt from personal liability. This argument is totally inconsistent with defendant's trial testimony that he did, in fact, have authority to execute the contract. It is also at odds with the uncontroverted evidence about defendant's "dominant role" in acting for the Corporation. This idea relies on the following circular reasoning: Even though specifically empowered to execute the contract, defendant had no authority to permit conveyance to a land trust, because the Board of Directors was unaware of the crucial contract provisions, which Musselman had the duty to disclose to the Board in his capacity as attorney....

There is no merit to this argument. Musselman, being authorized to execute the contract and to close the transaction, had the responsibility as counsel to advise his client, immediately upon discovery of the "problem," that it should attempt to rescind the transaction, if we assume an attempt at rescission would have been successful. Instead, defendant at no time advised the Board of Directors that it should

pursue rescission. At the meeting on October 6, the day after closing, Musselman merely stated that he would "attempt to clear up these problems" by speaking with Hurt and his attorney. At the next Board meeting, Musselman only promised to perform further research on the "or Assigns" question. All the while, the Board justifiably expected that the transaction would be satisfactorily completed and that Hurt would consent to become personally bound in the event of default....

For these reasons, the judgment of the trial court will be Affirmed.

Case Questions

---

1. Why did the court refer to the paralegal, Stanley K. Joynes III, as having no formal training as a paralegal if he had a college degree? If Joynes had been trained, would that have helped in this case?
2. According to the Court, why was the corporation willing to sell the land to Dr. Hurt?
3. What did Musselman do, or not do, that caused the corporation for which he served as attorney and an officer to sue him?
4. What did Musselman's paralegal do that contributed to Musselman's liability?
5. How was it that the paralegal's work was unsupervised?
6. If two members of the corporation's board were also attorneys, why were they not responsible for the losses suffered when the purchaser of Parcel 9 defaulted?

Although lawyers are professionally responsible for the conduct of their non-lawyer assistants, it is not always the case that, for the purpose of professional discipline, lawyers will be liable for any misstep taken by those who work for them. The duty of supervision is not automatically violated when associates, paralegals, or secretaries do that which they knew, or should have known, was not to be done. Instead, courts focus on what methods were in place to ensure appropriate conduct, or what remedial measures were taken once any mistake was discovered. And, on occasion, someone's conduct can be blatantly unethical or even criminal. If such conduct is found to be outside the scope of employment, the supervising lawyer will not be liable. For example, in a Connecticut case, an attorney's investigator took an illegal kickback from a client when transferring the proceeds from a settlement to the client. The attorney was accused of violating the duty of supervision. Rule 5.3(b) and (c). However, the Court ruled in favor of the attorney because, since the attorney had no knowledge of the illegal kickback nor ratified it, there was simply no evidence to show how his supervision, or lack thereof, contributed to his employee's wrongful behavior. *Statewide Grievance Committee v. Pinciaro*, No. CV 970396643S, 1997 WL 155370 (Conn. Super. Ct. Mar. 21, 1997).

In the following case, an attorney ran his law practice like a fast-food restaurant and was then accused of a variety of ethics violations, one of which involved his failure to adequately represent a client after the attorney's paralegal was neglectful.

Case Law

Attorney Grievance Commission of Maryland v. Ficker,
706 A.2d 1045 (Md. 1998)

The complaints against Ficker arise largely from alleged deficiencies in the way he ran his office—principally in the way he kept track of cases and assigned them to associates. In 1990, we reprimanded Ficker for a similar inattention to detail that, as in some of the instant cases, led to a failure to appear in court for two scheduled trials or hearings. *Attorney Griev. Comm'n v. Ficker*, 319 Md. 305, 572 A.2d 501 (1990) (*Ficker I*).

Ficker was admitted to practice in 1973. In 1986, when his earlier troubles surfaced, he was a solo practitioner who operated out of an office in Bethesda and was assisted by a clerk with no legal training. As we pointed out in *Ficker I*, he maintained no diary or tickler system, and his only schedule of court dates was a large desk calendar. *Id.* at 308, 572 A.2d 501. By 1988, when the current charges began to arise, he had three offices—one in Bethesda, one in College Park, and one in Frederick. His practice was a high-volume one that concentrated on serious traffic violations, often alcohol-related. He estimated that, in 1988–91, he handled between 750 and 850 cases a year. He had cases throughout the State but practiced primarily in Montgomery, Prince George's, and Frederick Counties. To assist him in maintaining that practice, Ficker hired various associates, none of whom, according to this record, remained in his employ very long or consistently. Stephen Allen was employed as Ficker's first associate in June, 1988.

In August, 1989, Ficker hired a second associate, Denise Banjavic. Banjavic quit five months later, in January, 1990, and was replaced by B. Edward McClellan and Thomas Mooney. A month later, Allen left, after 19 months; he was replaced, in March, 1990, by David Saslaw and Noreen Nelligan. McClellan left in February, 1991 (13 months); Mooney left in March, 1992 (26 months). Saslaw and Nelligan left for a time but later returned. Ficker apparently did not have a secretary but instead employed one non-lawyer assistant. His first assistant was Art Williams; after Mr. Williams, who was then in his seventies, suffered a stroke in 1989, Ficker employed Alex Burfield, a law student, to replace him.

. . . With this general background, we shall turn to the eight complaints made against Ficker. [The only complaint against Ficker that is relevant here, in this edited version of the case, is one made by Ms. Theo Dylewski.] In October, 1987, Ms. Dylewski met Ficker in the lobby of the Holiday Inn in Frederick and retained him to represent her in connection with a charge of driving while intoxicated. She paid him $100 toward a $650 fee but received neither a receipt nor a written retainer agreement. Trial was scheduled in the District Court in Frederick County for March 2, 1988; Ficker formally entered his appearance in November, 1987.

Ms. Dylewski testified before the AGC Inquiry Panel that she called Ficker's office in late January or early February to advise that she would be in Florida on March 2 and to request that the trial be postponed. She thought that she spoke to Ficker himself and that he told her a postponement would not be a problem, but that, if it were, he would let her know. Ficker said that he had no recollection of speaking with Ms. Dylewski about a postponement. He testified that, a day or two before the trial date, his assistant Art Williams told him that Ms. Dylewski had called and said that she wanted to be in Florida on the day of trial. He had no recollection of speaking with Ms. Dylewski at that point but said that he "probably" tried to reach her. Mr. Williams, who was 81 when he testified in this matter in 1995, said that he had no recollection of Ms. Dylewski but asserted that he would never, on his own, advise a client of Ficker's that a postponement would be granted or that it was all right not to show up for trial. He acknowledged that one of his duties was to answer the telephone and take messages, and that, if a client called and said that she needed a postponement, he would tell Ficker about it.

Ficker appeared in court on the trial date and orally requested a continuance, informing the court that his employee had informed him that his client wanted to be in Florida. He said that he did not file a motion in advance because (1) he had experienced difficulty in getting postponements in the District Court in Frederick, and (2) he had no idea of "why she wasn't going to be in court or indeed if it was a sure thing that she wasn't going to be in court." When the prosecutor objected to a continuance, the court denied the request and issued a bench warrant for Ms. Dylewski. Ficker said that, upon returning to his office, he called the number he had for Ms. Dylewski and left a message with "someone" that a bench warrant had been issued. Ms. Dylewski testified that her first awareness of the warrant was on April 8, after she had returned from Florida, when her husband informed her that the State Police had been to her home to serve the warrant. She called Ficker, who advised her to surrender herself. Upon

the advice of a District Court clerk, she wrote a letter to the judge explaining the circumstances, and, eventually, the warrant was withdrawn. Ms. Dylewski later retained other counsel. Ficker never refunded the $100.

AGC charged Ficker with violations of MLRPC Rules 1.1 (requiring the provision of competent representation), 1.3 (requiring a lawyer to act with reasonable diligence and promptness), 1.4 (requiring a lawyer to keep a client reasonably informed about the status of a matter), 5.3 (requiring a lawyer to provide proper supervision over non-lawyer assistants), and 8.4(d) (engaging in conduct prejudicial to the administration of justice).

On the evidence presented, Judge Ferretti said that he could not find by clear and convincing evidence that Ms. Dylewski spoke personally with Ficker when she called his office in January or February. He did find, however, that Ficker was informed of her request for a continuance at least three or four days before the scheduled trial date. Judge Ferretti concluded that, as "a written request for a continuance might have been consented to by the State," by failing to file a motion for continuance at that time, Ficker did not act with reasonable diligence and promptness in representing Ms. Dylewski, in violation of MLRPC 1.3. He concluded further that, in failing to communicate with his client in a reasonably prompt manner, he also violated MLRPC 1.4(a) and 1.4(b). The court found no violation of MLRPC Rule 1.1 and no violations of MLRPC Rules 5.3 or 8.4(c), by not having a better management system in place or by not properly supervising Mr. Williams. . . .

AGC excepted to the court's failure to find a violation of Rule 5.3. . . . AGC . . . urges that, if Ficker did not know of his client's situation until three or four days before trial, that was because he did not have in place proper measures to assure that Mr. Williams would do his job properly, and that that failure constitutes a violation of Rule 5.3.

. . . We find no merit in AGC's exception with respect to MLRPC Rule 5.3 in this matter. That rule provides, in relevant part, that a lawyer having direct supervisory authority over a non-lawyer shall make reasonable efforts to ensure that the non-lawyer's conduct is compatible with the professional obligations of the lawyer. AGC notes that, if Ms. Dylewski did not talk to Ficker, she spoke with Mr. Williams, among whose duties were answering the telephone and taking messages. Its position is that Ficker should have had in place some procedure to assure that Williams would, in a timely manner, relay any message he received from Ms. Dylewski. Judge Ferretti found that no tickler or calendaring system would have prevented the lapse in question. It was simply a matter of Mr. Williams apparently not

timely relaying a call, which he acknowledged was his duty to do. There is no evidence in this record that that was a persistent problem with respect to Mr. Williams, and we are not prepared to conclude, on this record, that one missed communication, even though significant, constitutes a violation of MLRPC Rule 5.3.

[Ficker was charged with many ethics violations in connection with eight clients, and was found to be in violation of most of the remaining charges not appearing here. As a result of those violations, he was indefinitely suspended from the practice of law with a right to reapply for admission following 120 days after his suspension began.]

Case Questions

1. If Ficker's client was harmed by the communication breakdown, then why did the Court find no violation here?
2. Since Mr. Williams, Ficker's non-lawyer assistant, failed to relay a client message, then if Ficker was not found in violation, why did the Court fail to find Williams in violation and sanction him?
3. Do you think the result would have been different if Ms. Dylewski had been arrested, placed in jail, and then while in jail, been beaten or sexually assaulted?

Can a Legal Assistant Be Directly Sanctioned by a Court?

If a legal assistant misses the statute of limitations by neglecting to file a pleading on time, or if a legal assistant drafts a complaint that fails to state a **cause of action**—thereby resulting in the defendant succeeding in its motion to dismiss—that negligence is the attorney's negligence for two reasons. First, the kind of work that is properly delegated to an attorney must also be properly supervised. If a paralegal fails to draft a complaint competently, it is really the attorney who has failed, since the attorney's signature on the complaint, in compliance with what is commonly Rule 11 of most rules of civil procedure, is evidence that the attorney has "officially" prepared the complaint and is responsible for its contents. Likewise, if a paralegal places an attorney advertisement that violates that jurisdiction's rules on advertising, it is the attorney who is responsible for failure to properly supervise their paralegal. That is the message of Model Rule 5.3. In fact, the end of the official Comments to MR 5.3 states, "The measures employed in supervising nonlawyers should take

cause of action—Facts that are sufficient to entitle a party to claim a legal wrong, entitling the claimant to a remedy. Lawsuits are based on causes of action and can be dismissed if they fail to state a claim of action.

account of the fact that *they do not have legal training and are not subject to professional discipline*" (emphasis added).

The second reason is more subtle. A lawyer is also subject to discipline for the legal assistant's misconduct because it would be quite difficult for a state supreme court to discipline a legal assistant for failing to obey rules that only apply to licensed attorneys. As explained in Chapter 1, any jurisdiction's rules of professional responsibility apply to a person after that jurisdiction's admission and discipline rules have first been met. If a person is subject to professional discipline, that is because he or she has first been admitted to the bar, which then makes the rules of conduct obligatory.

Some jurisdictions do make their rules of conduct applicable to paralegals, at least indirectly. For instance, New Mexico, which has separate rules for the use of legal assistants, requires its lawyers to make sure that their legal assistants do nothing that, if done by lawyers, would be a violation of the New Mexico Rules of Professional Conduct. N.M. Rules Governing Legal Assistant Services, Rule 20–114. Interestingly enough, Indiana's Guidelines on the use of Legal Assistants, found at the end of its Rules of Professional Conduct, require a legal assistant to obey at least three sets of attorney rules. The first two come from Guideline 9.10(j), which states the following: "A legal assistant shall be governed by the American Bar Association Model Code of Professional Responsibility and the American Bar Association Model Rules of Professional Conduct." And, of course, an Indiana legal assistant would have to follow the Indiana Rules of Professional Conduct for two reasons: it is the set of rules that are operative on those who are responsible for the conduct of Indiana legal assistants (not any version from the ABA); and Guideline 9.1 specifically requires Indiana lawyers to impress upon their legal assistants the need for them to obey the Indiana Rules of Professional Conduct (again, the only set of rules that an Indiana attorney is obligated to follow).

This raises two questions: where would such a legal assistant find both sets of ABA rules in order to learn them, and how would that legal assistant handle a situation where there is conflict among the sets of rules? As an example, although the Indiana Rules of Professional Conduct are based on the ABA Model Rules, the Indiana rule on client confidentiality, Rule 1.6, has an exception that is based on the ABA Model Code's exception. Indiana's rule allows a lawyer to disclose otherwise confidential information in order to prevent the client from committing "any criminal act." Ind. Rules of Professional Conduct, Rule 1.6(b)(1). Moreover, it is very similar to the ABA Model Code's exception that allows a lawyer to reveal "[t]he intention of his client to commit a crime and the information necessary to prevent the crime." DR 4-101(C)(3). The ABA Model Rules's exception allows a lawyer to reveal client information to the extent necessary to "prevent the client from committing a criminal act that the lawyer believes is likely to result in imminent death or substantial bodily harm." Model Rule 1.6(b)(1). The three versions are not alike, and two of them are significantly different. Indiana lawyers have no qualms knowing what to do, since they are obligated to obey the Indiana rule on confidentiality. But such is not the case for a legal assistant working for an Indiana lawyer.

There is, however, a two-step method of sanction that can be used directly against non-lawyers, although its use is rare. The first is the issuance of an **injunction**. If, for

injunction—A court order forbidding a party to do something or ordering them to start doing something.

example, a non-lawyer is engaging in the unauthorized practice of law, a court could issue an injunction against that person, ordering them to cease from such unauthorized conduct. And, in the event the non-lawyer disobeys the injunction, a court could hold the non-lawyer in contempt, resulting in a fine or other punishment.

The following case involves a self-styled, independent paralegal in South Carolina who was sued by the state attorney general for the unauthorized practice of law.

Case Law

State v. Robinson, 468 S.E.2d 290 (S.C. 1996)

MOORE, Justice.

This case is before us in our original jurisdiction. The State seeks an injunction prohibiting the unauthorized practice of law and solicitation of clients by defendant Robinson. We grant the injunction as follows.

FACTS

This case was referred to a special master to make findings of fact and conclusions of law. After two evidentiary hearings, the master made findings of fact including the following: 1) Robinson is not licensed or qualified to practice law; 2) he has a business license from Anderson County and advertises in the yellow pages as a "paralegal"; 3) Robinson performs services without attorney supervision; 4) he has represented more than sixteen clients in court; 5) when appearing in family or circuit court, Robinson does not charge a fee to his clients but requires reimbursement for costs; 6) Robinson obtains leave of court to appear pursuant to S.C.Code Ann. § 40–5–80 (1986); and 7) Robinson gives legal advice.

The master concluded as a matter of law that Robinson's appearances in court did not constitute the unauthorized practice of law because he sought and obtained leave of court in each instance. He found, however, that Robinson's solicitation of clients, giving of legal advice, and preparation and

filing of legal documents constituted the unauthorized practice of law and recommended Robinson be enjoined from engaging in these activities. Neither the State nor Robinson takes exception to any of the master's findings of fact.

ISSUES

1. Does Robinson have a first amendment right to advertise himself as a paralegal?
2. Are giving legal advice and preparing legal documents activities authorized under § 40–5–80?

DISCUSSION

The advertisement in question here is a yellow pages listing under "Paralegals" that reads as follows:

Robinson Melvin J "IF YOUR CIVIL RIGHTS HAVE BEEN VIOLATED—CALL ME." 1612 E River St. . . . 224-7800

Robinson also has a business card he distributes with the same message on it. His business card and letterhead refer to him as "Paralegal Consultant."

It is undisputed the First Amendment does not protect commercial speech that is false, deceptive, or misleading. *Zauderer v. The Office of Disciplinary Counsel*, 471 U.S. 626, 105 S.Ct. 2265, 85 L.Ed.2d 652 (1985). Robinson contends, however, that advertising himself as a paralegal is not false since there are no regulations requiring any qualifications to be a paralegal in this State. This Court has addressed the function of a paralegal in *In re: Easler,* 275 S.C. 400, 272 S.E.2d 32 (1980):

> Paralegals are routinely employed by licensed attorneys to assist in the preparation of legal documents such as deeds and mortgages. The activities of a paralegal do not constitute the practice of law as long as they are limited to work of a preparatory nature, such as legal research, investigation, or the composition of legal documents, which enable the licensed attorney-employer to carry a given matter to a conclusion through his own examination, approval or additional effort. *Id.* at 400, 272 S.E.2d at 32–33

While there are no regulations dealing specifically with paralegals, requiring a paralegal to work under the supervision of a licensed attorney ensures control over his or her activities by making the supervising attorney responsible. *See* Rule 5.3 of the Rules of Professional Conduct, Rule 407 SCACR (supervising attorney is responsible for work of nonlawyer employees). Accordingly, to legitimately provide services as a paralegal, one must work in conjunction with a licensed attorney. Robinson's advertisement as a paralegal is false since his work product is admittedly not subject to the supervision of a licensed attorney.

Further, the ad's statement, "If your civil rights have been violated—call me," is an unlawful solicitation. It is unlawful for one who is not a licensed attorney to solicit the cause of another person. S.C.Code Ann. § 40–5–310 (Supp.1994). We find Robinson should be enjoined from advertising himself as a paralegal or soliciting the representation of others.

Next, Robinson contends he should not be enjoined from giving legal advice and preparing legal documents since he obtains the right to represent others by leave of court under § 40–5–80. That section is entitled, "Citizens not prevented from appearing in person or for others without reward" and provides:

> This chapter shall not be construed so as to prevent a citizen from *prosecuting or defending* his own cause, if he so desires, or *the cause of another, with leave of the court first had and obtained; provided,* that he declare on oath, if required, that he neither has accepted nor will accept or take any fee, gratuity or reward on account of such prosecution or defense or for any other matter relating to the cause. (emphasis added)[1]

Robinson argues "defending or prosecuting" necessarily includes giving legal advice and preparing and filing legal papers and therefore the leave granted by the court includes leave to engage in these activities. This Court has defined the practice of law to include the preparation and filing of legal documents involving the giving of advice, consultation, explanation, or recommendations on matters of law. *State v. Despain,* 319 S.C. 317, 460 S.E.2d 576 (1995); *State v. Buyers Service Co.,* 292 S.C. 426, 357 S.E.2d 15 (1987). Clearly, one defending or prosecuting a cause of action must engage in these activities. We note, however, the express language of § 40–5–80 requires that leave be obtained *first.* The record indicates Robinson does not always obtain leave before giving advice and preparing pleadings. Accordingly, we find Robinson should be enjoined from preparing and filing legal documents and giving legal advice unless he first obtains leave of court pursuant to § 40–5–80. Further, we emphasize that it is within the trial judge's sound discretion whether to allow such representation.

INJUNCTION ISSUED.

FINNEY, C.J., and TOAL, WALLER and BURNETT, JJ., concur.

---

[1]This Court has also construed § 40-5-80 to allow a nonlawyer officer, agent, or employee to represent a business in civil magistrate's court for compensation. *In re: Unauthorized Practice of Law Rules,* 309 S.C. 304, 422 S.E.2d 123 (1992).

Case Questions

1. What specific conduct of Robinson was the state trying to stop?
2. Why did the state Supreme Court agree that Robinson was not engaging in the unauthorized practice of law by representing others in state trial courts?
3. What two things were wrong with Robinson's yellow pages advertisement? Could he safely advertise after the Court's decision?
4. In light of the fact that there were no formal requirements about what made someone a paralegal, what did the Court say was conclusive as to whether someone is a paralegal?
5. Did the Court discipline Robinson for his unauthorized practice of law or his false advertising?

Although rare, fines can be issued against a nonlawyer for failing to abide by a court's order to cease and desist. In a Kentucky case, an Oregon corporation called, Legal Alternative, Inc., that advertised its legal document completion services, was ordered to cease and desist from engaging in the unauthorized practice of law in Kentucky. After violating the order (and failing to respond to the contempt motion), Legal Alternatives, Inc., was fined $5,000 dollars (and assessed the court costs). *Kentucky Bar Ass'n v. Legal Alternatives, Inc.*, 792 S.W.2d 368 (Ky. 1990).

MISCELLANEOUS ISSUES FOR THE PARALEGAL PROFESSION

As with any profession, there are certain work-related issues that are peculiar to that profession. Three issues that are relevant to the ever-changing paralegal profession are whether paralegals must be paid overtime, whether suspended or disbarred lawyers should be allowed to work as paralegals, and whether paralegals may join state and local bar associations.

Salary versus Overtime Pay: Does That Make One a "Professional"?

One of the characteristics of professionals is that their pay is not generally tied to their hours worked. Professionals are salaried personnel who are not required to be paid overtime. According to the Fair Labor Standards Act, overtime pay must be paid to employees, unless the employees qualify as being "exempt" from the overtime requirements. *See* 29 U.S.C. §§ 201–219. Lawyers are exempt employees, falling under the professions exemption of the Act. 29 C.F.R. § 541.3 (2001). Part of that definition of a professional includes:

(1) Work requiring knowledge of an advance type in a field of science or learning customarily acquired by a prolonged course of specialized intel-

lectual instruction and study, as distinguished from a general academic education and from an apprenticeship, and from training in the performance of routine mental, manual, or physical processes. *Id.*

Do paralegals qualify as being exempt from overtime pay requirements? That depends on whom you ask. According to 29 C.F.R. § 541.314, the exceptions for the classic professions (medicine, law, and education) do not apply to employees in related professions who "merely serve these professions." And since paralegals are unlicensed and generally unregulated, then it would be difficult to classify them as exempt under the professional exemption classification. A 1986 opinion letter issued by the Department of Labor, considering the question of whether a paralegal with an educational certificate (after six months of study) qualified as nonexempt under the professional employee exception, declared that such an educational level, "would not qualify as a prolonged course of specialized, intellectual instruction as required by . . . § 541.3(a)." FLSA–1035, August 18, 1986.

There is also an administrative exemption for those employees whose office or nonmanual work is directly related to the firm's management policies or business operations, and who regularly exercise independent judgment and discretion. 29 C.F.R. § 541.2(a, b) (2001). In order to qualify for the administrative exemption, the employee must meet certain prerequisites, including that the employee devotes no more than 20 percent of his or her hours worked to non-administrative tasks. *See* 29 C.F.R. 541.2 (a–e) (2001). Some law firms might make the argument that their paralegals qualify as being exempt for administrative reasons. The Department of Labor does not see it that way, however, and according to a 1994 opinion letter issued by the Department of Labor, paralegals do not qualify as being exempt under the administrative exemption because they do not exercise the discretion and independent judgment countenanced by the regulation, and, therefore, must be paid overtime. FLSA–1369, November 10, 1994.

There is also a third exemption category, applying to those who are executives. *See* 29 C.F.R. § 541.1 (2001). There are those who believe the executive exemption applies to *certain* paralegals or legal assistants, because some legal assistants do have supervisory roles over other legal assistants and other non-lawyer personnel. In fact, the Legal Assistant Management Association, discussed earlier in the chapter, was organized to meet the needs of those types of law firm employees. But in order to qualify as an executive under this exemption, the employee must meet six prerequisites listed in the regulations. Included in those prerequisites are the requirements that: the employee's "primary duty consists of the management of the enterprise"; the employee "regularly directs the work of 2 other employees"; the employee has the power to affect the hiring and firing of employees; and, the employee devotes no more than 20 percent of his or her hours worked to nonexecutive work. *See* 29 C.F.R. § 541.1 (a–f) (2001). Later regulations amplify the meaning of terms used in those prerequisites. *See* 29 C.F.R. §§ 541.101–112 (2001).

Employers and employees may not agree to opt out of the overtime pay requirements by waiving the overtime pay rights granted by federal law, and willful violations of the overtime pay requirements can subject the employer to a $10,000 dollar fine and, possibly, incarceration. 29 C.F.R. § 778.102 (2001); 29 U.S.C. § 216(a). But, due to the fact-specific nature of the professional, administrative, or executive exemptions—as well as the ways in which law firms might interpret the federal regulations—it is likely that some law firms might classify at least some of their paralegals as exempt, thereby sidestepping the overtime pay requirement. In a federal case in 1994, the Department of Labor sought the payment of $40,000 dollars in back overtime pay for paralegals from the law firm of Page & Addison. *Reich v. Page & Addison*, No. 91–CV–2655-P (N.D. Tex, March 9, 1994). The jury, however, found that ten paralegals from Page & Addison were exempt from the overtime pay requirements of the Fair Labor Standards Act, agreeing with the law firm's argument that the administrative exemption (independent judgment test) applied to their paralegals. The Department of Labor eventually dropped its appeal, so the decision stood. However, the decision—based on the specific facts presented in the litigation—has no value as precedent because the case got no higher than a trial court.

Philosophically, it might be detrimental to the advancing recognition of paralegals and legal assistants as professionals to treat them as secretaries for overtime purposes, regardless of whether they might make more money being paid overtime. On the other hand, nurses are nonexempt employees who are paid overtime, and that is a fact that does not seem to hinder the nursing reputation in the United States. The NFPA does not take an official position on whether paralegals are exempt from the requirement of overtime pay, but it has issued a variety of reports on the subject. According to the *NFPA 2001 Paralegal Compensation and Benefits Report*, 52 percent of the respondents were considered nonexempt employees. The NALA issued a press release following the Page & Addison decision, summarizing the case and stating that the NALA membership was divided on the issue of exempt vs. nonexempt employment status. After surveying its membership, the NALA found that many members depended upon the overtime pay, while other members believed that being exempt from overtime pay was an appropriate mark of a professional. Based upon its status as an nonprofit corporation (the NALA thinks it inappropriate for it to engage in lobbying activities), and combined with the mixed response of its members, the NALA believes it should limit itself to educating its members and the public about the issues related to overtime pay and nonexempt status for legal assistants. The NALA, however, believes that a change in the federal regulations should be made to clear up the confusion.

Disbarred or Suspended Lawyers Working as Paralegals

An issue of growing concern to paralegals and paralegal associations is whether lawyers who have been disbarred, or are serving a suspension, can be employed as paralegals. As discussed in Chapter 1, disbarment occurs for extreme professional misconduct, certain kinds of criminal conduct, or excessive violations of the rules of professional responsibility, while suspensions can occur for a variety of intentional and unintentional acts of misconduct and can range from a month to a few years. To be disbarred is to receive the scarlet letter of misbehavior. However, that does not necessarily mean that a disbarred attorney is monumentally dumb about the law. Working as a paralegal after having been disbarred, or while serving a suspension, would then seem a natural employment option. Who would know better about substantive legal work—the kind of work legal assistants are educated and trained to do—than those who were at one time lawyers?

Should lawyers, no matter their abilities, be allowed to work in the law in a non-lawyer capacity if they have been found unfit to practice law, even if temporarily? As would be expected, paralegal associations are opposed to sanctioned lawyers working as paralegals. They argue that the reputation of paralegals is severely damaged by allowing unethical lawyers to become paralegals, since paralegals are expected to behave ethically and have their own sets of ethics rules, while those sanctioned lawyers have already proven themselves unethical. In fact, the National Federation of Paralegal Associations has its own character and fitness criteria that precludes disbarred or suspended lawyers from becoming NFPA members. Furthermore, it is contended that clients will be confused about the proper role of the sanctioned lawyer, which is likely to lead to the unauthorized practice of law. There is also a thorny employment opportunity issue at stake—there will be fewer jobs for paralegals if they will have to compete with women and men who have law degrees and practice experience.

Some states expressly prohibit disbarred or suspended lawyers being employed as legal assistants. For example, Indiana and Illinois require lawyers who have been disbarred or suspended for at least six months to make sure they do not give any impression that they work as legal assistants. Indiana Admission and Discipline Rules, Rule 23(26)(b); Illinois Supreme Court Rules, Rule 764(b). Guideline 10 of the Rhode Island Guidelines on the Utilization of Legal Assistants states, "A lawyer shall not use or employ as a legal assistant any attorney who has been suspended or disbarred pursuant to an order of this court, or an attorney who has resigned in this or any other jurisdiction for reasons related to a breach of ethical conduct."

Perhaps surprisingly, there are states that do permit disbarred lawyers to work as paralegals. For instance, an opinion of the General Counsel for the Alabama State Bar not only took the position that disbarred or suspended Alabama lawyers may work as legal assistants, but also stated (without citations) that a majority of states allow the same thing. 58 Ala. Law. 106 (1997). Delaware and Kansas allow disbarred or suspended lawyers to work as paralegals, but in contrast with traditional paralegals, sanctioned lawyers working as paralegals are not allowed to have any client contact. *See Matter of Frabizzio*, 508 A.2d 468 (Del.1986); *Matter of Wilkinson*, 834 P.2d 1356 (Kan.1992). In fact, restrictions on client contact seem to be a common limitation placed on disbarred or suspended lawyers who are allowed to work as paralegals.

Iowa's Rules of Court allow suspended attorneys to work as legal assistants, provided they do not have direct client contact. *See* Iowa Court Rule 35.12(4). The Pennsylvania Supreme Court amended Rule 217 of its Rules of Disciplinary Enforcement in 2000 to allow formerly admitted attorneys to work in law firms and engage in paralegal work, provided that they work under the direct supervision of a member in good standing of the Pennsylvania Bar, who is designated as the supervising attorney of the formerly admitted attorney. There are some limitations placed on such formerly admitted attorneys, including the fact that they may not have any direct contact with or perform any law-related services for any clients who were clients before such attorneys were disbarred. *See* Pa. Rules of Disciplinary Enforcement, Rule 217(j). And, South Dakota initially forbids disbarred or suspended lawyers from working as legal assistants, but then allows them to apply to the South Dakota Supreme Court for permission to work as legal assistants. *See* S. D. Codified Laws §§ 16–18–34.4 and 16–18–34.5.

The following case from Louisiana demonstrates a tacit approval of suspended lawyers acting as paralegals, even though no statute or rule of court explicitly authorizes it.

Case Law

In Re Elkins, 700 S.2d 211 (La. 1997)

PER CURIAM.

This disciplinary proceeding arises from one count of formal charges filed against respondent, Randy D. Elkins, by the Office of Disciplinary Counsel ("ODC"), alleging that he engaged in the unauthorized practice of law in violation of Rule 5.5 of the Rules of Professional Conduct when he initiated plea negotiations with the district attorney's office, while he was under suspension and acting as a paralegal, knowing such negotiations were traditionally performed by licensed attorneys.

A review of the underlying facts indicates that on September 23, 1994, this court suspended respondent for thirty months from the practice of law for convictions on three counts of willfully and knowingly making false statements to a bank for the purposes of influencing a loan decision. The suspension was made retroactive to September 21, 1992, the date of respondent's interim suspension. *In re Elkins*, 94–2070 (La.9/23/94), 644 So.2d 189.

After his suspension, respondent, who had previously practiced criminal law, was hired as a paralegal by Jack Montgomery, an attorney whose practice involved banking law. On or about August 26, 1994, respon-

dent contacted the Webster Parish District Attorney's Office regarding a pending criminal matter, *State v. Randy McEachern,* involving third offense DWI [driving while intoxicated] and expired inspection sticker charges. He spoke with Assistant District Attorney Louis Minifield about the case. On or about December 16, 1994, respondent again contacted Minifield concerning another criminal case, *State v. Stephen Harris,* which dealt with possession of marijuana, simple obstruction of a highway, and driving without a license. Although the testimony is conflicting regarding the substance of the conversation of the two phone calls, the record indicates that respondent asked questions such as: (1) what were the defendants charged with, (2) when were they suppose to go to court, and (3) would they be allowed to plead to only one of the charges or to a lesser charge. Minifield later testified that at the time of the phone calls, he was aware that respondent was suspended and employed by Montgomery as a paralegal. He indicated that as to the *McEachern* matter, he instructed respondent to inform Montgomery that he would accept a plea of DWI, second offense. As to the *Harris* matter, he instructed respondent to inform Montgomery that he would accept a plea of possession of marijuana and drop the other charges. He testified Montgomery later appeared in court on behalf of the two criminal defendants and entered pleas under these terms.

After a formal hearing, the hearing committee rendered its findings, concluding that the ODC failed to prove by clear and convincing evidence that respondent engaged in the unauthorized practice of law. As guidance, it utilized La. R.S. 37:212, which defined the unauthorized practice of law. The committee determined the ODC failed to prove that respondent appeared in a representative capacity on behalf of the defendants, or that he received any consideration, reward or pecuniary benefit as a result of representing the defendants. The disciplinary board filed its recommendation with this court concurring in the decision of the hearing committee recommending dismissal of the charges. One member of the board dissented and would have imposed a one year suspension. The ODC filed an objection in this court to the board's recommendation, alleging that the board applied the incorrect standard of review. It proposed that respondent's suspension be extended for a period of at least one year.

We recognize that the unauthorized practice of law by suspended or disbarred lawyers is a serious breach of ethical rules which should be dealt with harshly. Nevertheless, based on our review of the record, we agree with the findings of the hearing committee and the disciplinary board that the ODC failed to prove the charges by clear and convincing evidence. Given the evidence presented, it does not appear that respondent opened plea negotiations with the district attorney's office, nor did he engage in any other acts which only a licensed attorney could perform. Rather, it seems that respondent's calls to the district attorney's office were made for the purpose of gathering information for Montgomery, a function which could have been performed by a paralegal or legal secretary. The testimony of Montgomery and the criminal defendants could have shed light on whether respondent's conduct crossed the line from information gathering to the practicing of law; however, these witnesses were not called by the ODC. On the basis of this record, therefore, we conclude that a violation of Rule 5.5 of the Rules of Professional Conduct has not been proven by clear and convincing evidence.

DECREE

Upon review of the hearing committee and disciplinary board findings and recommendations, and considering the record, briefs, and oral argument, it is the decision of this court that the recommendation of the disciplinary board be accepted. Accordingly, it is ordered that the charge against respondent, Randy D. Elkins, be dismissed.

Case Questions

1. If Elkins had been disbarred, rather than suspended for 30 months, would that have changed the outcome of this case?
2. On what basis did the Office of Disciplinary Counsel allege that Elkins had engaged in the unauthorized practice of law?
3. On what basis did the Court find that Elkins did not engage in the unauthorized practice of law?
4. Do you think there are any other problems not addressed by the Court concerning having suspended lawyers acting as paralegals during their suspension?

Legal Assistants Joining State Bar Associations

Even though a legal assistant needs to obey the rules of professional conduct in place in the jurisdiction where the legal assistant is employed, the legal assistant is usually on the outside looking in at the organization whose rules they are supposed to follow. Legal assistants have historically been unwelcome as members in state bar associations since admission to a state bar association is generally contingent on being licensed to practice law. Furthermore, since paralegals are unlicensed, there remains an uncertainty as to what prerequisites would determine eligibility and what role paralegals would have in state bar associations. And it must be emphasized that where those jurisdictions allow non-lawyers to join bar associations, that does not make those non-lawyers members of the bar, since bar membership is contingent upon being licensed to practice law.

The American Bar Association allows non-lawyers whose careers are connected to the law—and even those who are simply interested in the law—to become members and affiliate themselves with one of nine associate membership categories. Paralegals and legal assistants may join the ABA as associate members, under the specific membership category of "legal assistant associate." Such a membership provides many of the privileges and benefits that are afforded to ABA members who are attorneys.

Fortunately, more state bar associations have begun to allow legal assistants to join their ranks, usually as part of a section within the bar association or as a division of the bar association. Texas is one of the states that does allow legal assistants entrance into its state bar association, having created its Legal Assistant Division of the Texas State Bar in 1981. The stated purpose of the Legal Assistant Division is "to enhance legal assistants' participation in the administration of justice, professional responsibility and public service in cooperation with the State Bar of Texas." The membership classifications range from active members to student members. In order to qualify as an active member, the legal assistant must be: professionally employed as a legal assistant under the direct supervision of a licensed attorney and also meet one of six options, ranging from being certified (by the Texas Board of Legal Specialization, the NALA, or the NFPA), to having completed varying levels of collegiate-legal study accompanied with corresponding years of legal assistant experience and on to having no legal education but having at least three years of legal assistant experience and ten hours of continuing legal education credits. An active member is entitled to vote on division matters and is subject to professional discipline, including expulsion from the division for a variety of criminal acts, engaging in the unauthorized practice of law, or violating the Canons of the Legal Assistant Division Code of Ethics. The division has a board of directors and holds an annual meeting at the same time the Texas Bar holds its annual meeting, and publishes an official periodical, *The Texas Paralegal Journal.*

Other state bar associations also allow membership for legal assistants. The Illinois State Bar Association has a membership category for law office administrators and legal assistants who may join the bar association with the required sponsorship of an active lawyer-member. The Indiana State Bar Association voted in the fall of

Legal Ethics

2001 to allow legal assistants to become affiliate members, beginning in 2002. Indiana legal assistants must meet certain entrance requirements, including establishing that at least 70 percent of their work is substantive legal work. Maryland's State Bar Association also decided in 2001 to allow paralegals and law firm administrators to join as associate members, provided they are sponsored by an active attorney-member of the association. Michigan's Bar Association Bylaws, Article I, Section 6, allow currently employed or retained legal assistants who meet a combination of educational or experiential prerequisites to become a "Legal Assistant Affiliate Member" of the Michigan State Bar Association. Once inside, legal assistants can join the Legal Assistant Section of the State Bar of Michigan, which has its own set of bylaws. In 1999, the Montana Bar Association created a Paralegal Section and started to allow paralegals to join. Applicants for membership must meet postsecondary educational requirements, and sign a statement promising to follow the Montana Rules of Professional Conduct. After one year in the Paralegal Section, members must then earn ten approved hours of continuing legal education credits. Interestingly, one of the professed reasons for creating the Paralegal Section was to stem the tide of the unauthorized practice of law by independent paralegals in Montana. The New Jersey State Bar Association allows legal assistants to become nonvoting members, provided they are employed as legal assistants, as described by the association's bylaws. Like Texas, New Mexico has a Legal Assistant Division in its state bar association, with its own set of bylaws, a code of ethics, and continuing legal education requirements (fifteen annual hours, one of which must be in ethics). The Ohio State Bar Association also allows paralegals to become members if they are employed by members in good standing of the bar association.

ETHICS 2000 AND THE DUTY TO SUPERVISE NON-LAWYER EMPLOYEES OR ASSISTANTS

Proposal by the Ethics 2000 Commission

The Ethics 2000 version of Model Rule 5.3 has a few changes. Rule 5.3(a) applies the duty of supervision not only to partners, but also to those lawyers who have "comparable managerial authority." Moreover, 5.3(c)(2) also makes lawyers with comparable managerial authority responsible for the conduct of their non-lawyer employees, when those lawyers could have done something to mitigate the unethical conduct of their non-lawyer employees. And there is a new comment to 5.3 that expresses the notion that a firm's lawyers who have managerial authority need to make reasonable efforts to establish internal policies to assure that their non-lawyer employees understand their own obligations to know and follow the rules of professional comment.

Action Taken by the ABA House of Delegates

Approved.

Summary

People have been working as legal assistants for years before such an occupation was formally acknowledged. The American Bar Association first got involved in the late 1960s by creating a committee to study the role and regulation of paralegals. That committee is now known as the Standing Committee of Legal Assistants (SCOLA), and it encourages the use of legal assistants and establishes guidelines for appropriate curricula for colleges that offer paralegal programs. The American Association for Paralegal Education (AAfPE) is a national organization that also promotes educational standards for paralegal programs. According to the Department of Labor, paralegalism is an occupational category that is expected to be the sixth fastest grower for much of the next decade.

There are two significant national paralegal organizations: the National Federation of Paralegal Associations and the National Association of Legal Assistants. Both organizations have thousands of members who are in regional or local associations, and both have their own sets of ethics rules that members are expected to follow. The NFPA has its own certification program, the Paralegal Advanced Certification Examination (PACE), which members are entitled to take if they meet the educational and work experience prerequisites. The NALA also has its own certification program, the Certified Legal Assistant program (CLA), which its members are, similarly, entitled to take if they meet the educational and work experience prerequisites. Members of NFPA and NALA are subject to discipline from their respective organizations for violations of their codes of ethics.

Legal assisting is largely an unregulated profession, and those states that define a legal assistant rarely do so in such a way as to require any education or training. No state licenses paralegals, and with few exceptions, the certification programs in existence are voluntary and unconnected to any state bar. The American Bar Association's Standing Committee of Legal Assistants is opposed to the licensure of paralegals, believing that it is unnecessary since paralegals work under the supervision of lawyers who are licensed. SCOLA also believes that licensure will unduly increase the cost of legal services. The NALA is also opposed to legal assistant licensing, but the NFPA is in favor of it.

Because paralegals work under the supervision—or on the behalf—of lawyers, the ethics rules make supervising lawyers personally responsible for the misconduct of their paralegals. ABA Model Rule 5.3 requires that a supervising lawyer ensure that the actions of his or her non-lawyer assistants be compatible with the lawyer's own professional ethics standards of the lawyer, as well as makes the lawyer responsible for the conduct of their non-lawyer assistants. Since legal assistants are unlicensed by state supreme courts, then it is difficult for such courts or their disciplinary committees to sanction legal assistants for professional misconduct. One possible exception would be if a court were to hold a paralegal in contempt for violating an injunction ordering him or her to stop engaging in the unauthorized practice of law. Moreover, members of legal assistant associations can be sanctioned by the associations for violating association rules, which can include fines and membership suspensions.

According to federal labor law, paralegals are not considered exempt from overtime pay requirements under either the professional or administrative exemptions. Some jurisdictions allow suspended or disbarred attorneys to work as paralegals, although client contact is generally prohibited for those paralegals. Increasingly, state bar associations have begun to allow paralegals to become members, and a few state bar associations have created legal assistant divisions within their state bar associations.

Points to Ponder

1. What distinguishes a legal assistant from other law office personnel, such as secretaries or receptionists?
2. When did paralegalism start to be recognized as a separate legal occupation?
3. What role does the American Bar Association play in the paralegal field?
4. If you are a student in a legal studies department, does your department's curriculum comport with SCOLA or AAfPE guidelines?
5. Does your state define *paralegal* or *legal assistant* in its state code or rules of court? If so, is the definition broad or narrow?
6. Does your state's attorney rules of professional conduct have any rules or guidelines specifically addressed to the use of paralegals?
7. Does your state's rules of professional conduct have the ABA Model Rules version of Rule 5.3?
8. Are you a member, or do you know any members, of either the NFPA or NALA? If so, what benefits derive from being in either organization?
9. If it is necessary that paralegals comply with their state's attorney rules of ethics, why do the national paralegal organizations have their own rules of ethics?
10. What prerequisites must be met in order for a legal assistant to have a certification designation, under the auspices of either the NFPA or NALA?
11. Do you think it is fair that one must have working experience in order to sit for a certification exam?
12. Do you think it is fair that one must, with limited exceptions, have a bachelor's degree in order to sit for a certification exam?
13. Does your state offer any state-specific certifications?
14. What are the pros and cons of paralegal licensure?
15. Are there any other considerations regarding paralegal licensure not mentioned in the chapter?
16. Are you in opposition to, or in favor of, paralegal licensure? Why?
17. Why is it that attorneys are responsible for the misconduct of their non-lawyer assistants, including paralegals?
18. When would a lawyer be excused from either professional discipline or personal liability for the misconduct of the lawyer's non-lawyer assistants?
19. Why is it that courts do not sanction paralegals for violations of their jurisdiction's rules of professional conduct?
20. What, under federal labor law, determines whether someone should be paid overtime?
21. Regardless of the financial benefits of overtime pay, do you think legal assistants should be exempted from overtime pay under either of the federal exemptions?
22. Do you think suspended lawyers should be allowed to work as paralegals? Why or why not?
23. Does your state have any rule or statute that concerns suspended or disbarred lawyers working as paralegals? Should either category of lawyers be allowed to work as paralegals?
24. Does your state or local bar association provide for legal assistant membership? If so, are there any continuing legal education requirements for legal assistants who are members?

Key Concepts

ABA Model Guidelines for the Utilization of Legal Assistant Services

ABA Model Rule 5.3

ABA Standing Committee on Legal Assistants

American Association for Paralegal Education (AAfPE)

Certified Legal Assistant (CLA)

Exempt employee

Legal Assistant Management Association (LAMA)

NALA Code of Ethics and Professional Responsibility

NALA Model Standards and Guidelines for Utilization of Legal Assistants

National Association of Legal Assistants

National Federation of Paralegal Associations (NFPA)

NFPA Model Code of Ethics and Professional Responsibility and Guidelines for Enforcement

Paralegal Advanced Competency Exam (PACE)

Paralegal/legal assistant certification

Paralegal/legal assistant licensure

Respondeat superior

Scope of employment doctrine

Key Terms

associate	injunction	partner
cause of action	malfeasance	respondeat superior

Chapter 3

The Unauthorized Practice of Law

Lawyers use the law as shoemakers use leather: rubbing it, pressing it, and stretching it with their teeth, all to the end of making it fit for their purposes.

—Louis XII, sixteenth-century king of France

Laws are like sausages, it is better not to see them being made.

—Otto von Bismarck, nineteenth-century chancellor of Germany

INTRODUCTION

Although Sarah enjoys her job as a paralegal, she feels perplexed about the fact that many people she knows could not afford the services of her firm or any law firm for that matter. She believes that paralegals should be licensed to independently engage in certain legal services such as basic will drafting, no-fault divorces, and typical landlord/tenant dispute resolutions. Sarah has become a source of information for her neighborhood friends—and their friends—who seek her help on all kinds of legal matters, and is torn between lending a helping hand and violating her professional responsibilities. What can Sarah do to assist her friends without crossing the line and engaging in the unauthorized practice of law?

Few subjects related to the legal profession are as fraught with uncertainty as the unauthorized practice of law (UPL). Lawyers can be disciplined for assisting someone in engaging in the unauthorized practice of law, even if not intending to do so. Paralegals face issues every day that require them to walk a fine line between doing good work and doing too much good. Companies, such as banks and real estate companies, can be sued by state bar associations for intruding into the practice of law. Even private citizens who have no formal connection to the legal profession can find themselves the target of a bar association investigation or charged with civil or criminal violations of unauthorized practice of law statutes. This chapter will focus on what traditionally constitutes the practice of law, what kinds of laws are in place to prohibit UPL, what kinds of activities paralegals are usually prohibited from performing, and what kinds of activities paralegals can safely perform.

The chapter will close with a discussion on the subject of independent contracting paralegals.

WHAT IS THE PRACTICE OF LAW?

It is one thing to say that a person must be licensed in a jurisdiction in order to be called a lawyer. It is another thing to define the practice of law, particularly since those who are not supposed to engage in it need to know the boundaries. While it is intuitive to expect that the practice of law would be defined in a specific rule or statute (statutory law is sometimes referred to as **positive law**), that is not the case in many states. Even though every state has some statute prohibiting the unauthorized practice of law—usually making it a **misdemeanor**, unless fraud is involved—less than a majority of states have statutes that specifically define the practice of law. As described in Chapter 1, legislatures rarely get involved in regulating the practice of law, leaving those tasks to the appropriate appellate court. According to a 1997 study by the ABA State Legislative Clearinghouse, only twelve states and the District of Columbia define the practice of law by statute. For instance, Rhode Island's statute defines the practice of law in this way:

> As used in this chapter, "practice law" means the doing of any act for another person usually done by attorneys at law in the course of their profession, and without limiting this generality, includes:
> (1) The appearance or acting as the attorney, solicitor, or representative of another person before any court, referee, master, auditor, division, department, commission, board, judicial person, or body authorized or constituted by law to determine any question of law or fact or to exercise any judicial power, or the preparation of pleadings or other legal papers incident to any action or other proceeding of any kind before or to be brought before the court or other body;
> (2) The giving or tendering to another person for a consideration, direct or indirect, of any advice or counsel pertaining to a law question or a court action or judicial proceeding brought or to be brought;
> (3) The undertaking or acting as a representative or on behalf of another person to commence, settle, compromise, adjust, or dispose of any civil or criminal case or cause of action;
> (4) The preparation or drafting for another person of a will, codicil, corporation organization, amendment, or qualification papers, or any instrument which requires legal knowledge and capacity and is usually prepared by attorneys at law. R.I. Gen. Laws § 11–27–2.

Washington State's rules of professional conduct provides a general definition, which states, "[T]he practice of law is the application of legal principles and judgment with regard to the circumstances or objectives of another entity or person(s) which require the knowledge and skill of a person trained in the law." The rule then

positive law—A phrase that refers to law made through political, governmental means.

misdemeanor—Generally, a lower classified crime, in comparison to a felony.

goes on to list nonexclusive behaviors that constitute the practice of law, including giving legal advice and representing others in court. Washington Court Rules, General Rule 24(a).

States that do not define the practice of law by positive law choose instead to rely upon the fabric of their common law in order to fashion a working definition. At one time, one could be an attorney without having a formal, legal education. (Thomas Jefferson, lawyer, author of the Declaration of Independence, president, and founder of the University of Virginia, did attend The College of William and Mary for two years, but his legal education was one of personal study under the tutelage of the famous Virginia attorney George Wythe. And, Abraham Lincoln, perhaps the most admired figure in American history, was an outstanding Illinois lawyer who never attended college, much less law school.) State courts determined what one needed to do in order to be eligible to practice law and, as an extension, defined what it meant to be an attorney. Therefore, in many jurisdictions, case law is the starting place for learning about the practice of law.

Interestingly, many of those cases that define the practice of law involve activities that courts found to be the *unauthorized* practice of law. The foundational cases are usually older ones, and a Vermont case serves as a good example. In *In re Flint*, 8 A.2d 655 (Vt. 1937), Flint was found in contempt of court for engaging in the unauthorized practice of law for negotiating a settlement between two prospective litigants. It seems that Flint, who was a sheriff and a law student, arrested a Mr. Pike, and during the trip to the jail, the two started discussing some romantic letters Pike had found that had been written to his wife from a Mr. Whipple. Pike then asked Flint about what could be done (since at that time, a spouse could sue his or her spouse's lover for "alienation of affections"). After putting Pike in a cell, Flint started to advise him about threatening Whipple with a lawsuit and then went to Whipple, advising him about settling a possible lawsuit with Pike. After some jailhouse negotiations, in which Flint would tell each man a different story about what he thought the case was worth, he got the two men to settle any future lawsuit about Pike's wife for $1,000 dollars and he retained $200 dollars for his efforts. After being accused of the unauthorized practice of law, Flint claimed he was not acting as a lawyer because, he said, he only told the men what he would do if he were in their shoes. The court found that unpersuasive, finding that he gave legal advice to the men in that he advised them on the settlement of a legal claim and took a fee for doing so. *Flint* at 657. The court also cited similar cases from other jurisdictions, including one where another court, explaining what it means to practice law, stated, "[W]hen one undertakes to give counsel as to legal status or rights in respect to a pending claim, he is performing a special function reserved for attorneys at law, as much as diagnosis, prognosis, and prescriptions are within the special field of medicine." *Fink v. Peden*, 17 N.E.2d 95, 96 (Ind. 1938). (It does seem odd that a case from 1937 would cite a case from 1938, but it was done.)

An examination of the case law and rules of court leads to a few general principles. First, representing someone in court, including small claims court, is the practice of law. Second, representing someone in an administrative **adjudication** is the practice of law. Third, giving legal advice to someone is the practice of law. Fourth, drafting or completing transactional documents, such as wills, and litigation docu-

adjudication—The process of formally resolving a controversy, based on evidence presented.

ments, such as **pleadings** or **motions**, is the practice of law. Fifth, negotiating on behalf of someone in cases where that person's legal rights (including the right to sue) are involved is the practice of law.

That, however, does not end the inquiry, since the previous list is neither exclusive nor self-explanatory. Furthermore, to state what activities constitute the practice of law also requires one to determine what kinds of people can engage in those activities. Lawyers in good standing can do everything on the list, whereas lawyers who are serving a period of suspension can do nothing on the list. Law students are allowed to practice on a limited basis if meeting the prerequisites stated in their state's Admission and Discipline rules. Those prerequisites usually include completing the second year of law school and a legal ethics course and being certified by their law school's dean as approved for limited licensure. Then, such a law student can only practice under the direct supervision of an attorney who agrees to bear responsibility for the student's work. Law graduates who are awaiting the results of the bar exam can also practice under similar constraints (Exhibit 3-1).

Paralegals can engage in some of those activities in two ways. First, they can engage in certain activities, such as drafting pleadings or assisting clients with discovery requests, under the condition that their work is being conducted under the supervision of an attorney who takes official responsibility for the work, very often as evidenced by his or her signature on the work product. The effective use of supervised paralegals is the essence of the ABA's Model Guidelines for the Utilization of Legal Assistant Services. And, as will be discussed later, federal, state, and local laws have granted to

pleadings—Formal allegations of facts that consist of the plaintiff's claim (the complaint) or the defendant's denial (the answer).

motions—Formal applications to a court (such as a motion for summary judgment), requesting the court to issue an order.

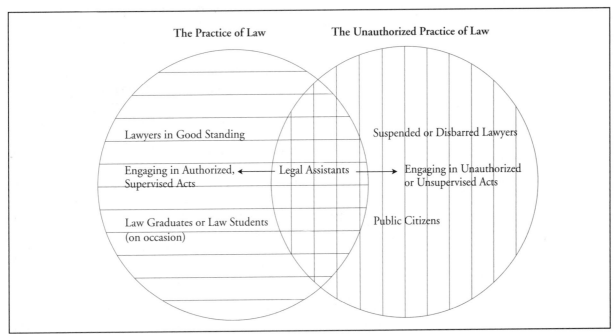

Exhibit 3-1   The Legal Assistant's Place in the Practice of Law

non-lawyers, including those who are not legal assistants, the right to engage in certain legal activities, including some activities listed previously.

Believing that the changing environment of the practice of law called for an examination of whether the ABA should create a uniform definition of the practice of law, the ABA Board of Governors empanelled an entity, The Model Task Force on the Model Definition of the Practice of Law, to work on creating such a definition. Included in the ABA's stated purposes behind the task force's directive was the realization that there is increasing activity of non-lawyers providing services to the public that is difficult to characterize as legal services. The task force released a draft definition in September 2002, seeking comments and suggestions on it by December 2002. The U.S. Justice Department and the Federal Trade Commission responded in writing to the ABA, expressing the opinion that the ABA's definition violates antitrust law by prohibiting the activities of non-lawyer service providers, including real estate brokers and banks, as well as those that sell legal forms or self-help books to the public. In February 2003, a public hearing was held on the model definition at the ABA Midyear meeting.

Notice that the draft definition of the practice of law does cover the work of paralegals and legal assistants in section (d), but it does so without stating that the work of paralegals and legal assistants is the practice of law.

(a) The practice of law shall be performed only by those authorized by the highest court of this jurisdiction.
(b) Definitions:
  (1) The "practice of law" is the application of legal principles and judgment with regard to the circumstances or objectives of a person that require the knowledge and skill of a person trained in the law.
  (2) "Person" includes the plural as well as the singular and denotes an individual or any legal or commercial entity.
  (3) "Adjudicative body" includes a court, a mediator, an arbitrator or a legislative body, administrative agency or other body acting in an adjudicative capacity. A legislative body, administrative agency or other body acts in an adjudicative capacity when a neutral official, after the presentation of evidence or legal argument by a party or parties, will render a binding legal judgment directly affecting a party's interests in a particular matter.
(c) A person is presumed to be practicing law when engaging in any of the following conduct on behalf of another:
  (1) Giving advice or counsel to persons as to their legal rights or responsibilities or to those of others;
  (2) Selecting, drafting, or completing legal documents or agreements that affect the legal rights of a person;
  (3) Representing a person before an adjudicative body, including, but not limited to, preparing or filing documents or conducting discovery; or
  (4) Negotiating legal rights or responsibilities on behalf of a person.
(d) Exceptions and exclusions: Whether or not they constitute the practice of law, the following are permitted:

(1) Practicing law authorized by a limited license to practice;

(2) Pro se representation;

(3) Serving as a mediator, arbitrator, conciliator or facilitator; and

(4) Providing services under the supervision of a lawyer in compliance with the Rules of Professional Conduct.

(e) Any person engaged in the practice of law shall be held to the same standard of care and duty of loyalty to the client independent of whether the person is authorized to practice law in this jurisdiction. With regard to the exceptions and exclusions listed in paragraph (d), if the person providing the services is a nonlawyer, the person shall disclose that fact in writing. In the case of an entity engaged in the practice of law, the liability of the entity is unlimited and the liability of its constituent members is limited to those persons participating in such conduct and those persons who had knowledge of the conduct and failed to take remedial action immediately upon discovery of same.

(f) If a person who is not authorized to practice law is engaged in the practice of law, that person shall be subject to the civil and criminal penalties of this jurisdiction.

At this point, it can be said that the unauthorized practice of law occurs when: (a) a private citizen engages in activities that are only allowed to be done by attorneys; (b) a paralegal exceeds his or her authority as defined by local law and rules of court; and (c) an attorney engages in otherwise lawful behavior during a period of suspension or disbarment.

The following case shows a fourth possibility of the unauthorized practice of law. In the case, an attorney kept his law office open during the period of a short suspension and then unintentionally involved his legal staff in the unauthorized practice of law. While reading the case, pay close attention to the court's expansion of the definition of the practice of law

Case Law

In Re Thonert, 693 N.E.2d 559 (Ind. 1998)

PER CURIAM.

Lawyers who have been suspended from the practice of law may not allow their nonlawyer staff to continue to actively operate their law office and conduct business on behalf of clients during the period of suspension. On July 3, 1997, this Court suspended the respondent, Richard J. Thonert, for a period of thirty days, beginning August 11, 1997, and ending September 10, 1997, for violations of the *Rules of*

Professional Conduct for Attorneys at Law. Matter of Thonert, 682 N.E2d 522 (Ind. 1997). That order specified that the respondent would be automatically reinstated to the practice of law, provided he pay the costs of the underlying proceeding and comply with the requirements of Admis.Disc.R. 23(4)(c). On September 2, 1997, the Commission filed its *Verified Objection to Automatic Reinstatement* stating that during the period of his suspension, the respondent engaged or attempted to engage in the practice of law by acting through non-attorney employees of his office. On September 10, 1997, this Court stayed the respondent's automatic reinstatement pending consideration of the Commission's objections. Thereafter, the parties filed stipulations of fact and a joint petition for ruling. Each fully briefed its position. On October 17, 1997, this Court issued an *Order Imposing Additional Suspension and Lifting Stay of Automatic Reinstatement*, finding that the respondent "violated the order of suspension and that an additional period of suspension, with automatic reinstatement, is warranted." Accordingly, we extended the respondent's suspension from September 10, 1997, until October 17, 1997. This opinion more fully sets forth the facts and circumstances of this case and our analysis underlying our decision to extend his suspension.

I. FACTS

Adopting the parties' stipulations, we now find that the respondent is a solo practitioner with a law office located in Fort Wayne, Indiana. At relevant times, the respondent employed a four-person non-lawyer support staff. The respondent's law practice is one of high volume and relies heavily on the support staff to process paperwork. Much of the practice in routine matters is systematized, relying on support staff to generate the appropriate paperwork upon the occurrence of certain events. On some routine matters, support staff members sign the respondent's name to legal documents. Occasionally, this is done without the respondent's input or review. Prior to his disciplinary suspension on August 11, 1997, the respondent filed motions to continue all matters that were set for hearing or trial during his period of suspension, arranged for another attorney to speak with his clients during that time and to cover any court hearings for which a continuance could not be obtained or which arose during the suspension, and informed his staff that he could not practice law during the suspension. He informed his staff that any questions they had should be directed to specific attorneys the respondent had arranged to be available for consultation.

The respondent was in his office periodically between the effective date of his suspension and August 25, 1997, after which he left the state to visit with relatives. Various questions arose among his staff about what they could and could not do during the period of suspension. For answers, they contacted the office of the respondent's personal attorney. An associate in that office called the respondent and advised him generally as to what actions his support staff could take during the period of suspension. The respondent recorded the conversation and allowed his staff to listen to the tape. He then told his staff members that they were not to provide legal advice to clients, but that they could keep clients informed of court dates or other matters that occurred in their cases, that if they had questions they should contact the attorney with whom the respondent had arranged for them to speak, and that the designation "Attorney at Law" should be removed from the office letterhead. In signed correspondence, the respondent directed them to write "Secretary to Richard J. Thonert." Projects the respondent instructed his staff to undertake during the period of suspension included going through old accounts receivable and sending out new statements, organizing the office, and closing old files. He gave them no specific instructions concerning the preparation and processing of routine forms and correspondence. During the suspension, several clients in fact spoke with the attorney to whom they were referred. That attorney appeared in court on numerous matters, on behalf of the respondent's clients.

While in his office during the period of suspension, the respondent reviewed incoming mail and dictated "informational" letters to clients. The letters, signed by the secretaries, advised of court hearings or other matters relative to specific cases. His staff produced, signed and dispersed form letters advising clients of documents received during the suspension period. The respondent stipulated that not only did he believe that he and his staff were permitted to provide such information to clients, but also that his failure to do so could expose him to further disciplinary action. If a matter on an existing case needed to be continued or some other action was needed, the respondent directed his staff to contact the referral attorney to handle the matter. In some instances, the respondent and/or his staff prepared motions or other documentation and forwarded them to the attorney for signature and filing. If an existing client presented a new matter, or if a potential new client contacted the office, the person either was directed to another attorney or was scheduled to meet with the respondent after the period of suspension expired.

On August 8, 1997, a member of the respondent's support staff prepared and sent a letter to a deputy prosecuting attorney in Allen County requesting his support in a motion for sentence modification. Attached to the letter was a proposed petition for modification of sentence, an agreed entry, and a status report from the client's probation officer. This correspondence was a duplicate of an earlier, pre-suspension request which the respondent had sent to the prosecutor but which the prosecutor apparently had not acknowledged. On August 18, 1997, a member of the respondent's support staff sent a letter to another of the respondent's clients enclosing a charging information and providing instructions relating to discovery material which had been received from the prosecutor in the case. The support staff person indicated that it was the usual practice in the respondent's office to forward to clients discovery materials and other pleadings received by the respondent. The respondent dictated similar letters during his suspension for signature and dispersal by his clerical staff.

On August 20, 1997, a member of the respondent's support staff called the Wells County Prosecutor's Office asking about discovery, charging documents, cause numbers, and hearing dates relative to a criminal action pending against one of the respondent's clients. The call was to follow up on similar inquiries made by the respondent to the prosecutor's office prior to his suspension. On August 21, 1997, a member of the respondent's support staff prepared and sent a letter to an Allen County deputy prosecuting attorney requesting that the prosecutor

agree to modify the conviction of another of the respondent's clients from a Class D felony to a Class A misdemeanor. Attached to the letter was a petition, an agreed entry, and a status report from the probation officer. The correspondence was essentially a duplicate of a prior request made by the respondent to the deputy prosecutor.

On August 25, 1997, a member of the respondent's support staff sent a letter to a Wells County deputy prosecuting attorney concerning one of the respondent's clients. The letter stated, in relevant part:

> Dear [Deputy Prosecuting Attorney]:
> I am writing concerning [client]. His present driving status is HTV [habitual traffic violator]. In order for him to become reinstated, it would be necessary to set aside one or more of the above-referred convictions.
> If vacating one or more of these convictions would be acceptable to your office, I am enclosing the following documents:
> 1. Copy of [client's] Driver's Record
> 2. Agreed Entry/Order
> After you have the opportunity to review your file, please send a letter concerning your position in this matter to our office. I remain,
> Very truly yours, [Secretary]
> Secretary to Richard J. Thonert

The support staff person signing the letter considered the act of producing and dispersing the letter a routine "clerical" task.

On August 26, 1997, a member of the respondent's support staff prepared and sent a letter to an Allen County deputy prosecuting attorney requesting that the prosecutor agree to a petition for post-conviction relief to vacate and set aside a prior traffic offense against another of the respondent's clients. Attached to the letter was a petition for post-conviction relief, an agreed entry, and a proposed order. Again, the correspondence essentially was a duplicate of a request made by the respondent prior to his suspension. The respondent stipulates that numerous other documents similar to those identified above were produced and sent by his staff during his period of suspension. The respondent's bookkeeper received on his behalf no legal fees on new matters during his period of suspension.

On September 7, 1997, after learning that his automatic reinstatement had been stayed upon the Commission's objections, the respondent met with his staff and informed them that the letters mailed to the deputy prosecutors and others went beyond informing clients of the status of their cases, that they should not have been sent, and that they could not continue to be sent during the period of his suspension. The respondent then arranged for the referral attorney to completely supervise the respondent's office pending his reinstatement.

II. COMMISSION'S ALLEGATIONS

In its *Verified Objection,* the Commission concluded that the respondent "attempted to circumvent this Court's order of suspension from the practice of law by continuing to actively operate his law office and conduct business on behalf of clients during the period of suspension." Specifically, the Commission contends that the respondent's law office engaged in the unauthorized practice of law during the respondent's period of suspension. The respondent argues that it was not his intention to violate this Court's order of suspension and that his intention only was to allow his staff to continue to disperse routine correspondence and information to clients and adverse parties as it systematically did before he was suspended.

III. DISCUSSION
This Court has noted that

> The core element of practicing law is the giving of legal advice to a client and the placing of oneself in the very sensitive relationship wherein the confidence of the client, and the management of his affairs is left totally in the hands of the attorney. The undertaking to minister to the legal problems of another creates an attorney-client relationship with regard to whether the services are actually per-

formed by the one so undertaking the responsibility or are delegated or subcontracted to another. It is the opinion of this Court that merely entering into such a relationship constitutes the practice, of law. . . . *The conducting of the business management of a law practice, in conjunction with that practice, constitutes the practice of law* [emphasis added]. *Matter of Perrello,* 270 Ind. 390, 398, 386 N.E.2d 174, 179 (1979)

We have also said that "[to] practice law is to carry on the business of an attorney at law," and "to make it one's business to act for, and by the warrant of, others in legal formalities, negotiations, or proceedings." *Fink v. Peden,* 214 Ind. 584, 17 N.E.2d 95 (1938). A person who gives legal advice to clients and transacts business for them in matters connected with the law is engaged in the practice of law. *State ex rel. Pearson v. Gould* 437 N.E.2d 41 (Ind. 1982). Thus, the practice of law is not defined only as the giving of legal advice or acting in a representative capacity—it also had been extended by this Court to conducting the business management of a law practice.

It is undisputed that the respondent's non-lawyer support staff produced motions, proposed entries, and correspondence seeking legal relief on behalf of clients and sent them to opposing counsel. It is also undisputed that the staff informed clients of upcoming hearing dates, provided instructions to them for answering formal discovery requests and, in a general sense, advised them of the status of their legal proceedings. We find that the communications to public officials undertaken in a representative capacity by the members of the respondent's support staff during his period of suspension, which sought to obtain benefits for individuals represented by the respondent, constituted the practice of law. Likewise, the production and communication of motions, pleadings, and proposed agreed entries, done without the supervision of an attorney licensed to practice in this state, constituted the unauthorized practice of law. Pursuant to court rule, legal assistants may perform services only under the direct supervision of a lawyer authorized to practice in this state. *See* Guideline 9.1: Use of Legal Assistants. A lawyer is responsible for all of the professional actions of a legal assistant performing legal assistant services at the lawyer's direction and should take reasonable measures to ensure that the legal assistant's conduct is consistent with the lawyer's obligations under the *Rules of Professional Conduct. Id.* The respondent himself admits that his staff should not have contacted deputy prosecuting attorneys asking that the state agree to sentence modifications or post-conviction relief and that they should not have sent discovery to clients with instructions as to how to begin preparing factual responses. He states that he should have given clearer and more thorough advice and instruction to his staff about what it could and could not do during his suspension.

The respondent was responsible for ensuring that his staff was adequately informed about what it could and could not do while he was suspended. Guideline 9.l; *see also* Ind. Professional Conduct Rule 5.3. The order imposing his initial suspension was filed July 3, 1997, with the suspension effective August 11. The purpose of the delay between issuance of the order and the effective date of the suspension was to give the respondent time to make arrangements for the care of his clients' legal needs, both substantive and ministerial, to be placed in the expert hands or under the supervision of a licensed attorney. He failed to make adequate arrangements or provide sufficient explanation until his staff had engaged in the unauthorized practice of law. His failure to do so placed his clients at great risk by allowing their cases to be handled by those not trained in the law and licensed to practice.

This case also included less obvious instances of misconduct. The fact that the respondent allowed his support staff to continue "to carry on the business of an attorney at law," i.e., to inform clients of upcoming hearing dates, to apprise them of the status of their legal matters, etc., without the direct supervision of a licensed attorney, constituted the unauthorized practice of law. We caution that to allow non-lawyer staff any contact with clients about the legal status of their cases in the absence of a lawyer's supervision risks harm to the legal rights of the clients. By this decision today, we do not mean to imply that lawyers who have been suspended from the practice of law should simply "walk away" from the practice of law to the detriment of their clients; instead, lawyers should make arrangements for all client needs arising during the period of suspension to be handled by or under the direct supervision of a licensed attorney, or inform all clients who do not choose to use the services of the referral attorney to seek substitute legal counsel of their choice. Admis.Disc.Rule 23(26)(c).

We note, however, that the respondent made a good-faith effort to inform his employees of what they could and could not do during his suspension. When he learned of their communications with clients and prosecutors, he immediately took action to correct the wrongful conduct. He has also expressed sincere remorse for his actions. Because the respondent apparently did not intend to circumvent our July 3, 1997, order of suspension, we find that the brief extension of the suspension already imposed is a sufficient sanction for his misconduct during his period of suspension. The respondent is also admonished of his obligations to comply with the duties of disbarred or suspended attorneys set forth in Admis.Disc.R. 23(26)(b) and discussed in this Court's recent opinions in *Matter of DeLoney,* 689 N.E.2d 431 (Ind. 1997), *Matter of Thonert,* 682 N.E.2d 522, etc.

Case Questions

---

1. Did attorney Thonert's paralegals engage in the unauthorized practice of law, did the attorney do so, or did they all do so?

2. What category of behavior has this court added to the more common definition of the practice of law?
3. If there was another attorney upon whom the suspended attorney's legal staff was relying during the attorney's suspension, then how were the staff's activities unauthorized?
4. Do you think the attorney knowingly contributed to the unauthorized practice of law?
5. Based on the court's reasoning, what would you say a legal assistant could do during the suspension (or even vacation) of his or her supervising attorney?

EXISTING RULES THAT PROHIBIT THE UNAUTHORIZED PRACTICE OF LAW

Although the unauthorized practice of law may be loosely defined, it is certainly specifically forbidden. A variety of statutes, attorney rules of professional responsibility, and paralegal rules of professional responsibility prohibit the unauthorized practice of law, which also includes assisting someone who is engaging in such practice.

Statutes Prohibit UPL

It is against the law for someone who is not an attorney to practice law. But if someone is not attorney, then that person is obviously not a member of the bar. How then does the bar, and its rules of conduct, control that person's behavior? It can be very difficult to do so. But there is a trump card—legislation. All jurisdictions have statutes in place that prohibit the unauthorized practice of law. As an example, Florida's unauthorized practice statute states the following:

> Any person not licensed or otherwise authorized by the Supreme Court of Florida who shall practice law or assume or hold himself or herself out to the public as qualified to practice in this state, or who willfully pretends to be, or willfully takes or uses any name, title, addition, or description implying that he or she is qualified, or recognized by law as qualified, to act as a lawyer in this state, and any person entitled to practice who shall violate any provisions of this chapter, shall be guilty of a misdemeanor of the first degree, punishable as provided in s. 775.082 or 775.083. Fla. Stat. ch. 454.23.

According to § 775.082, the incarceration for a first-degree misdemeanor conviction can be as long as one year; and, according to § 775.083, the fine for a first-degree misdemeanor conviction can be as high as $1,000.

A reading of the Florida statute above shows that it is not just intentionally misleading, lawyer-like activity that is illegal, but also unintentional, unauthorized practice of law. The serious implication of that statute's wording means that one can be guilty of violating the law without trying or even realizing it, and that includes paralegals. In addition, the statute covers attorneys who might violate other related laws, including practicing law while suspended (ch. 454.31) and assisting disbarred or suspended lawyers in the practice of law. The fact that a first-time offender of the unauthorized practice statute is unlikely to be sentenced to a prison term or get a steep fine does not lessen the gravity of that statute—it is a serious thing to practice law without a license. Statutes that make the unauthorized practice of law a crime necessitate the action of a prosecutor to enforce the law. In addition to a local prosecutor's office, a state attorney general's office can bring charges against a violator. Due to the fact that consumer protection is part of the role of an attorney general's office, such enforcement could occur if a state attorney general's office believed that the violator was engaging in fraud in connection with acting as an attorney.

Attorney Rules of Professional Conduct Prohibit UPL

The ABA Model Rules of Professional Conduct and the ABA Model Code of Professional Responsibility prohibit the unauthorized practice of law. However, the focus in those rules is on preventing others who are under the lawyer's authority from the unauthorized practice of law.

As discussed in Chapter 2, Model Rule 5.3 of the ABA Model Rules concerns the supervision of non-lawyer assistants in the law firm, and states:

> With respect to a nonlawyer employed or retained by or associated with a lawyer:
> (a) A partner in a law firm shall make reasonable efforts to ensure that the law firm has in effect measures giving reasonable assurance that the person's conduct is compatible with the professional obligations of the lawyer;
> (b) A lawyer having direct supervisory authority over the nonlawyer shall make reasonable efforts to ensure that the person's conduct is compatible with the professional obligations of the lawyer; and
> (c) A lawyer shall be responsible for conduct of such a person that would be a violation of the Rules of Professional Conduct if engaged in by a lawyer if:
>   (1) the lawyer orders or, with the knowledge of the specific conduct, ratifies the conduct involved; or
>   (2) the lawyer is a partner in the law firm in which the person is employed, or has direct supervisory authority over the person, and knows of the conduct at a time when its consequences can be avoided or mitigated but fails to take reasonable remedial action.

This rule emphasizes three things: design, supervision, and responsibility. Model Rule (MR) 5.3(a) requires the management of the firm to have in place a scheme for ensuring that the professional conduct of non-lawyer employees rises to the ethical standards required of lawyers in the firm. 5.3(b) requires a lawyer in the firm to directly supervise the work of the non-lawyer for the purposes of maintaining standards of professional conduct. And 5.3(c) makes the supervisory lawyer responsible for any misconduct of the non-lawyer if the lawyer causes it to occur, does nothing to prevent its occurrence, or does nothing to minimize the damage of its occurrence. Even though its connection is indirect, this rule concerns the unauthorized practice of law because it makes the firm responsible for all unethical conduct committed by its paralegals.

The ABA Model Code has no provision similar to MR 5.3, but Disciplinary Rule (DR) 4–101 states that a lawyer "shall exercise reasonable care to prevent his employees, associates, and others whose services are utilized by him from disclosing or using confidences or secrets of a client." Also, DR 7–107(J) states that a lawyer "shall exercise reasonable care to prevent his employees and associates from making an extrajudicial statement that he would be prohibited from making."

Model Rule 5.5(b) specifically addresses the unauthorized practice of law by declaring: "A lawyer shall not: (b) assist a person who is not a member of the bar in the performance of activity that constitutes the unauthorized practice of law." The Official Comments to MR 5.5 acknowledge that the practice of law has a definition that is not uniform throughout the country, but it advises lawyers to avoid assisting someone in unauthorized practice, whatever the definition. If a lawyer were to assist a paralegal in the unauthorized practice of law, such assistance would be a violation of both 5.3 (failure to adequately supervise non-lawyer employees) and 5.5 (assisting a non-lawyer in the unauthorized practice of law).

Canon 3 of the ABA Model Code states, "A Lawyer Should Assist in Preventing the Unauthorized Practice of Law." Ethical Consideration 3–5 acknowledges the difficulty of having a uniform definition of the practice of law by providing, "It is neither necessary nor desirable to attempt the formulation of a single, specific definition of what constitutes the practice of law." And EC 3–6 positively addresses paralegals engaging in substantive legal work by stating, "Such delegation is proper if the lawyer maintains a direct relationship with his client, supervises the delegated work, and has complete professional responsibility for the work product. This delegation enables a lawyer to render legal service more economically and efficiently." DR 3–101(A), which is almost identical to MR 5.5(b), states, "A lawyer shall not aid a non-lawyer in the unauthorized practice of law."

Paralegal Codes of Conduct Prohibit UPL

Not surprisingly, all the significant national codes of conduct that have been created by or for paralegals specifically address the significant ethical problem of engaging in the unauthorized practice of law.

The ABA Model Guidelines for the Utilization of Legal Assistant Services

As stated in Chapter 2, the ABA Model Guidelines for the Utilization of Legal Assistant Services is written to and for lawyers and is an adjunct to the Model Rules of Professional Conduct. But the guidelines are not additional rules; hence, the operative word is *guidelines*. And since these guidelines are addressed specifically to the role of the legal assistant, a discussion of them is included in this section on paralegal codes of conduct. The ABA Model Guidelines have four guidelines that deal with the unauthorized practice of law.

Guideline 1 obligates a lawyer to "take reasonable measures to ensure that the legal assistant's conduct is consistent with the lawyer's obligations under the ABA Model Rules of Professional Conduct." How does this relate to the unauthorized practice of law? It does so because one of the Model Rules, 5.3 (previously addressed), requires attorneys to ensure that those who work for them do so in a manner consistent with the lawyer's professional responsibility obligations under the Model Rules. Therefore, if a paralegal engages in the unauthorized practice of law, the paralegal's supervising lawyer will be responsible for such misconduct.

Guideline 2 is an interesting guideline. It provides that a lawyer may allow a paralegal to engage in substantive legal work, the kind traditionally done by lawyers, provided that two conditions are met. The first condition requires the lawyer to be responsible for the legal assistant's work, while the second condition prohibits the lawyer from authorizing the paralegal to do anything that the law (including rules of ethics) says may not be done by non-lawyers. The Comment to Guideline 2 acknowledges what was already been discussed, which is that most jurisdictions do not affirmatively define the practice of law. As such, the Comment emphasizes the need for lawyers to be aware of what is allowed to be delegated to legal assistants in their jurisdiction and to recognize that the activities of legal assistants who are engaging in properly delegated work must be supervised. (The Comment cites a case exemplifying that principle, *Musselman v. Willoughby Corporation*, which is included in Chapter 2.)

Guideline 3 lists three activities for which a paralegal may not be responsible: (1) establishing the attorney-client relationship; (2) establishing the fees to be charged and (3) issuing a legal opinion to a client. Although these activities will be discussed later, it can be noted at this point that the theme associated with them is that of the lawyer needing to maintain a direct relationship with the client. The Comment also states that a lawyer would not be in violation of the guideline if a paralegal "assists" the lawyer in establishing client relationships, fees, or rendering legal opinions.

Guideline 4 concerns appearances of impropriety by putting into the lawyer's hands the duty to inform all relevant parties—clients, courts, and other lawyers—that the lawyer's legal assistant is not a licensed attorney. The Comment avoids requiring a particular method of communicating this fact, but reiterates that it needs to be done so that no one, particularly a client, is confused about the status of a legal assistant. The Comment also gives its approval to paralegal-signed correspondence if the status of the paralegal is clearly given.

The NFPA Model Disciplinary Rules and Ethical Considerations

Rule 1.8 of the NFPA Model Disciplinary Rules and Ethical Considerations (formally titled as such, but inside the NFPA Model Code) specifically addresses the issue by stating, "A paralegal shall not engage in the unauthorized practice of law." Its corresponding Ethical Consideration (EC), 1.8(a), then states, "A paralegal shall comply with the applicable legal authority governing the unauthorized practice of law." However, it does not define what is unauthorized practice. Other rules in the NFPA Model Disciplinary Rules and Ethical Considerations indirectly concern the unauthorized practice of law. Rule 1.3 requires that paralegals "maintain a high standard of professional conduct." EC-1.3(b) states, "A paralegal shall avoid impropriety and the appearance of impropriety." And Rule 1.7 requires that a paralegal's title "be fully disclosed."

NALA Code of Ethics and Professional Responsibility

The NALA Code consists of Canons without commentary or ethical considerations. Canon 1 leaves no doubt concerning the unauthorized practice of law: "A legal assistant must not perform any of the duties that attorneys only may perform nor take any actions that attorneys may not take." Canon 3 prohibits the unauthorized practice activities previously listed in the ABA Guidelines for the Utilization of Legal Assistant Services, but it also includes a prohibition on any activity (even the encouragement of it) "which *could* constitute the unauthorized practice of law" (emphasis added). Such a broad construction shows that the spirit of the Canon, as well as its language, should direct a legal assistant's behavior.

Canon 4 advises a legal assistant against giving any independent legal judgment in place of an attorney. And Canon 5 requires disclosure of non-lawyer status to even the general public and cautions prudence when one is considering how extensively a client may be assisted in the absence of the attorney. Canons 3–5 make reference to the NALA Model Standards and Guidelines for Utilization of Legal Assistants. There, one can find many of the same prohibitions listed in the ABA Guidelines for the Utilization of Legal Assistant Services, the NFPA Model Code of Ethics and Professional Responsibility, and the NALA Code of Ethics. As will be discussed later, the NALA Model Standards and Guidelines lists nine activities that legal assistants may perform under the supervision of an attorney. Included on that list, among other things, are client interviewing, document and correspondence drafting, and discovery device summarizations, including depositions.

WHAT ACTIVITIES ARE PARALEGALS PROHIBITED FROM PERFORMING?

Broad principles need to be supported with specific guidelines in order to be effective. General statements against the unauthorized practice of law, such as those previously discussed, take shape in specific prohibitions. Four categories of prohibitions will be discussed. The first three consist of the holy grail of unauthorized practice and are found in every code of legal ethics: giving legal advice, establishing the attorney-client relationship, and establishing fees. A fourth category includes miscellaneous prohibited activities.

Giving Legal Advice

Avoiding giving legal advice is the cornerstone for any discussion on unauthorized practice, the obvious goal to which all paralegals should aspire. But what does it really mean to give legal advice? It would certainly include, for instance, telling a corporate client being sued for the negligence due to the act of one of its employees that the doctrine of respondeat superior will result in the corporation being liable for any employee negligence. It would also include telling someone that he or she cannot file a lawsuit because the statute of limitations has run out. But does giving legal advice include answering a friend's question about whether his or her pension is protected from his or her spouse in the event of a divorce? Or what about answering a friend's question about getting out of an apartment lease early?

The finer points of the definition of legal advice may vary from jurisdiction to jurisdiction, but there is a consistent theme, which is that giving legal advice involves applying the law, including legal principles, to a specific fact pattern. Clients see attorneys when something has happened or is about to happen to them, whether good or bad. They want to start a business; they want to adopt a baby; they want to sue someone—or, perhaps, they have been sued. These situations require the professional judgment of an attorney, and even if a non-lawyer knows the correct statute or other rule that would apply, he or she should not get involved without the attorney's direction and supervision. Similarly, a nurse might know, based upon his or her education and experience, that a patient has a particular illness yet should not give a diagnosis.

A common problem can arise when paralegals are used effectively. The client, having contact with the paralegal, might seek his or her advice rather than that of the lawyer, particularly when the client realizes that phone calls to the paralegal are cheaper than phone calls to the lawyer. Unless the lawyer has done a sufficient job, in the initial consultation with the client, of explaining the role of the paralegal, the client is likely to be unaware that the paralegal is not authorized to answer his or her legal questions. Even so, the client might not realize that certain questions call for an answer that would qualify as legal advice. For instance, it is natural for someone accused of a crime to be curious to know what the punishment may be. However, even though many prison sentences are standardized and even though a legal assistant might know that a particular first offense would result in a fine only, he or she should refuse to answer the question, "How much time will I get if I'm convicted?"

What about giving legal advice outside the law office? Here, the answer is the same: paralegals may not give legal advice to anyone. Applying the law to a friend's problem is as inappropriate as doing the same for a paying client. Even helping someone who is representing himself is likely to be inappropriate. Although it is a more tempting violation, it would not qualify as pro bono activity. So what can you do? How can you be helpful and responsible? First, answering a general legal question not tied to someone's situation is allowable (although it may be unadvisable, since being wrong is worse than not answering). Second, nothing prohibits anyone who knows how to read the law from showing it to others. Statutes, cases, and regulations are all available for public viewing, and it is absolutely appropriate to help someone find a statute or a case, as long as its meaning is not applied to the friend's problem.

One exception to the prohibition against non-lawyers giving legal advice concerns legal representation behind bars. Jailhouse lawyers, as they are commonly called, are not lawyers at all, but inmates who assist other inmates in the preparation of their appeals or other lawsuits. Such assistance is clearly the unauthorized practice of law, except that is specifically allowed as an exception to the prohibition against UPL by the United States Supreme Court in *Johnson v. Avery*, 393 U.S. 484 (1969).

Establishing the Attorney-Client Relationship

Imagine an attorney attending a Christmas party and, while at the eggnog bowl, being asked about whether he or she has a case for age discrimination after being fired, if a younger person is hired as a replacement. Will that attorney acquire a new client if he or she answers the question? This is not usually the case, although some courts have recently started to focus on what the reasonable belief of the other party was, rather than the attorney's belief, when determining when the attorney-client relationship has attached.

The more common scenario for establishing the attorney-client relationship involves the lawyer, in his or her office, agreeing to take someone's case. One of the substantive tasks for a legal assistant who is being used effectively is client interviewing, including taking part in the initial interview. When interviewing any prospective clients, it is important that paralegals neither express nor imply whether prospective clients have a good case or the kind of case that their firm will take. Since the establishment of the attorney-client relationship can occur in the absence of a written agreement, and since appearances can be reality, the paralegal needs to delicately, but firmly, defer to the attorney any questions concerning whether the firm will take a case.

Establishing Legal Fees

As with the attorney-client relationship, the operative word is *establish*. Establishing fees is closely connected to establishing the attorney-client relationship, since both involve statements that carry with them an implication of professional judgment, the kind that only licensed attorneys are authorized to make. When a fee agreement has been reached, there is a presumption that the client trusts the attorney's expertise in how the client's fees have been determined. However, assuming the firm allows it, paralegals can answer certain fee-related questions, such as what a lawyer's hourly rate is. If the firm has a flat fee for certain services, a legal assistant would be allowed to state it without violating the prohibition on establishing fees. Also, a paralegal could explain to a client how costs and expenses differ from legal fees. Establishment of fees would occur if a paralegal tells a client, or a prospective client, how much a particular legal service will, or is likely to, cost.

Miscellaneous Prohibitions

The three general prohibitions discussed above do not complete the picture on UPL, because there are specific types of conduct that would also constitute UPL if engaged in by paralegals. Knowing and understanding the following miscellaneous prohibitions might even be more valuable than knowing the general prohibitions, due to the fact that the specific prohibitions are situational.

Representation in Court

It almost goes without saying that no one without a license to practice law can represent anyone else in any court proceedings. Such representation would certainly be the unauthorized practice of law, since courtroom advocacy is an integral part of the latter. Courtrooms are the final arbiters of interpersonal conflict, and those peculiar rules of trial procedure and evidence are so important to the process that the decisions made at trial concerning those rules often form the bases for the appeals that are filed. Serving as someone's advocate in a trial or appellate court is so much a part of the lawyer culture that it is what most people think of when they imagine what lawyers do, even though the majority of them are not trial lawyers.

Paralegals are also generally not allowed to represent others in small claims court. *See* Iowa Supreme Court Board of Professional Ethics and Conduct, Op. 88–18 (1989) and 89–30 (1990). California, however, does allow non-lawyers who have been adequately trained to serve as small claims advisors—at no charge—to litigants in small claims court. Cal. Rules of Court 1725. And Michigan prohibits small claims litigants from using attorneys (unless the actual litigant is an attorney), although it does not expressly prohibit the use of non-lawyer representatives in small claims court. Mich. Comp. Laws §§ 600.8401–600.8427.

A person does have the right to represent him- or herself in litigation **pro se**, even if that is a bad idea. In fact, that right to self-representation in federal court is granted by statute and case law. 28 U.S.C. § 1654; *Farretta v. California*, 422 U.S. 806 (1975). A question that often arises in the pro se discussion is whether someone who is not a lawyer can help someone else in a pro se matter. Although an argument could be made that helping someone who is pro se is not the same as serving as someone's lawyer, the right to proceed pro se does not extend to helping someone else who is proceeding pro se, and that includes representing a spouse or other family member. *See Osei-Afriyie by Osei-Afriyie v. Medical College of Pennsylvania*, 937 F.2d 876 (3rd Cir. 1991) (where the court ruled that a father could represent himself, but not his children); *Johnson v. Ivimey*, 488 A.2d 1275 (Conn.App.1985) (where the court allowed a husband to represent himself, but not his wife). However, the general principle against non-lawyers representing others in court can be affected by specific exceptions, such as the South Carolina statute, discussed in the *Robinson* case from Chapter 2, that does allow a non-lawyer to represent others in court if he or she is granted permission by the judge and promises to conduct the representation without any compensation.

Paralegals may attend trials with attorneys from their firms and assist them without fear of engaging in the unauthorized practice of law. Such assistance, including keeping track of documentary evidence, is not unauthorized practice because it is not representation. Instead, it is support of the representation. A Virginia ethics opinion even states that a non-lawyer may appear in court on behalf of someone else for the limited purpose of providing dates for scheduling a trial. Virginia Bar Association Unauthorized Practice Committee, Op. 64 (1984). At the other end of the spectrum, Iowa only allows a paralegal to sit with a bankruptcy client at a bankruptcy hearing if the client's lawyer is also present at the counsel's table. Iowa Supreme Court Board of Professional Ethics and Conduct, Op. 92–24 (1993).

pro se—A Latin phrase that refers to one representing oneself in a legal matter.

Moreover, as an exception to the above prohibition on legal assistants making court appearances on behalf of clients, an Arizona ethics opinion does approve of an attorney delegating to a paralegal who is also a licensed tribal advocate the authority to represent clients before an American Indian tribal court. This opinion states that the jurisdiction of tribal courts is outside the jurisdiction of the Arizona court system and, therefore, the attorney would not be assisting a non-lawyer in the unauthorized practice of law (ER 5.5 of the Arizona Rules of Professional Conduct) when allowing the paralegal to practice in a tribal court. State Bar of Arizona, Ethics Op. 99–13 (1999).

Depositions

Closely related to court representation is the conducting of a deposition, something else a paralegal is not allowed to do. A deposition is similar to a trial in the sense that it is a recorded event and the deponent, like a witness, is put under oath and subject to direct and cross-examination. A deposition requires sufficient legal skill in both asking the questions and listening to the responses. Furthermore, a lawyer representing a deponent has the right to raise objections to certain questions, and the decision to object requires legal judgment. Even if an attorney has a prepared list of questions for a deposition and has instructed his or her legal assistant to ask only what is on the list, the very act of reading the questions to a deponent is the unauthorized practice of law, since the legal assistant is in control of the deposition. However, as is the case with court appearances, paralegals may attend depositions and assist attorneys by helping them manage the order of issues to be covered, for instance.

A variety of jurisdictions have issued ethics opinions disapproving of paralegals, or other nonlawyers, conducting depositions. *See* Colorado Bar Association, Formal Ethics Op. 79 (1989); Iowa Supreme Court Board of Professional Ethics and Conduct, Op. 96–03 (1996); North Carolina Bar Association, Ethics Op. 183 (1994); Oregon Bar Association, Ethics Op. 449 (1980); Pennsylvania Bar Association, Ethics Op. 87–127 (1987) (this ethics opinion states that a paralegal may not even read deposition questions that have been prepared by an attorney, even if the client and opposing counsel approve).

Not even law students are cut any slack when it comes to conducting depositions. Kentucky issued an ethics opinion on the subject of non-lawyers conducting depositions and determined that a lawyer could not delegate the task of taking depositions to non-lawyer employees, including law school graduates who have yet to pass the bar exam. Kentucky State Bar Association, Ethics Op. 341 (1990). Pennsylvania also reached the same conclusion about law students conducting depositions (in this instance, a third-year law student, ranked 5th in the graduating class), and later reaffirmed the position with respect to paralegals. Pennsylvania Bar Association, Ethics Op. 91–137 (1991) and Op. 98–75 (1998).

Alternative Dispute Resolution

Alternative dispute resolution (ADR) has become so prevalent in America that many jurisdictions have some form of rules of court for ADR, distinct

alternative dispute resolution (ADR)—Methods of resolving conflict outside the traditional method of litigation and a trial. Forms of ADR include negotiation, mediation, and arbitration.

from their rules of trial procedure. **Mediation**, one of the major forms of ADR and the process whereby a neutral third party (the mediator) assists the litigants in resolving their dispute through management of a semiformalized bargaining process, is used more and more each year. Although non-lawyers can conduct certain kinds of mediation, lawyers trained in mediation generally conduct mediations connected to legal disputes.

Legal assistants are generally prohibited from conducting legal mediations or representing clients at mediations because, even though a mediation is a conflict resolution form that is wholly distinct in kind from litigation, if it flows from litigation or prospective litigation, it involves the settling of claims and rights that are legal in nature.

A few jurisdictions have specifically discussed the role of non-lawyers in mediations. A Rhode Island ethics opinion states that a lawyer may not form an association with a non-lawyer to provide mediation services. Rhode Island State Bar Association, Op. 87–3 (1988). An Indiana ethics opinion dealt with a question concerning the appropriateness of paralegals conducting pre-suit mediation. While approving of paralegals attending mediations in an attorney-assistance role, the committee decided that a lawyer could not delegate to a paralegal the role of representing a client in pre-suit mediation. Because of the nature of mediation, its decisional flexibility, and the need for legal analysis in settlement evaluations, the committee considered that only lawyers would be appropriate to have such direct client contact. Indiana State Bar Association, Ethics Op. 1 (1997). However, the opinion did state that, with proper supervision and client consent, a lawyer could delegate to a paralegal the authority to engage in pre-suit negotiations on behalf of the client.

As stated, specific exceptions trump general prohibitions, and Florida provides a specific exception. Its Small Claims Court Rules allow a non-lawyer to represent a party to a small claims mediation, provided the court is not opposed and the non-lawyer representative has the party's written authority to appear on his or her behalf. Florida Small Claims Rule 7.090(f). In Maine, a bill was put forward that would have allowed paralegals with degrees from accredited colleges to represent parties in alternative dispute resolutions and small claims matters (Maine H.P. 861 (1987)), but it received an "ought not to pass" recommendation from the legislature's judiciary committee, which turned out to be the case.

Considering that the ABA is very often the precursor to change, in the near future non-lawyers might be granted broader opportunities to engage in mediation. In February 2002, the ABA Section of Dispute Resolution issued its "Resolution on Mediation and the Unauthorized Practice of Law," in which it states that mediation is not the practice of law. Included in the Dispute Resolution Section's statement was the belief that "statutes and regulations should be interpreted and applied in such a manner as to *permit all individuals, regardless of whether they are lawyers, to serve as mediators*" (emphasis added). Regardless of whether jurisdictions follow suit and make it easier for non-lawyers to serve as mediators, that would have no effect on whether non-lawyers are authorized to act as client representatives at mediations involving legal disputes, since representing someone else in a legal dispute is generally allowed for lawyers only.

mediation—A form of ADR in which a third party, known as a neutral, assists the opposing parties in the process of trying to reach a settlement.

Executions of Wills and the Selling of Legal Documents

Paralegals may not execute wills. They may, however, assist lawyers in serving clients with estate planning needs, gathering financial information, collecting records, and even helping with the drafting of wills and other estate-planning documents. A paralegal may also serve as an attesting witness to a will, but the will's execution is a formal transaction that affects the legal rights of others and must conducted by an attorney.

Closely related to executing wills is the practice of selling will kits or other estate-planning devices. Many jurisdictions are opposed to non-lawyers having anything to do with such forms, particularly selling them to the public or assisting member of the public in completing them. *See* Illinois State Bar Association, Advisory Op. 95–7 (1995) (although this opinion specifically stated that accountants could only type and file articles of incorporation for their clients, because anything more would be the unauthorized practice of law, its decision is equally applicable to paralegals); Ohio S. Ct. Board of Board of Commissioners on Grievances and Discipline, Op. 92–15 (1992); Tenn. Op. Atty. Gen. No. 92–02 (1992) (this opinion also disapproves of non-lawyers providing bankruptcy petitions, divorce petitions, and prenuptial agreements).

Nevada dealt with the issue of typing services in *Greenwell v. State Bar of Nevada*, 836 P.2d 70 (Nev. 1992), where the Nevada Bar Association sought a permanent injunction against a typing business that, although it originally sought business typing for lawyers, had started typing legal documents for the public and providing legal advice to its customers. The typing service's defense was that state precedent provided an exception to unauthorized practice for the delivery of simple legal services when lawyers are unavailable. The court was moved by that argument to the point of ordering the bar association to investigate the problem of the unavailability of legal services for the poor, but still determined the activities of the typing business were the unauthorized practice of law, permanently enjoining the business from doing anything other than typing.

California, on the other hand, does have a set of statutes that allows certain individuals, known as "legal document assistants," to sell self-help legal services to members of the public who are representing themselves pro se. Such self-help services includes typing legal forms for others, as well as providing general legal information that has been written by an attorney and making published legal documents available to those who are representing themselves in legal matters. Legal document assistants must register, according to the statutes' prerequisites (which include educational prerequisites), and post a $25,000 dollar **surety bond**. A later statute prohibits legal document assistants from giving legal advice to their customers. *See* Cal. Bus. & Prof. Code §§ 6400-6415. Whatever California's legal document assistants statutes stand for, officially they do not allow one to render independent paralegal services to the public for two reasons. First, legal document assistants are not allowed to offer any services to their customers that involve exercising judgment or giving legal advice. § 6400(g). Second, legal document assistants are *not* paralegals or legal assistants, not only because California has separate statutes concerning paralegals (as mentioned in Chapter 2), but also because the legal document assistant statutes expressly do not

surety bond—A written instrument filed with a court in which one promises to be liable up to the amount stated in the bond in the event of negligence or failure to perform.

apply to paralegals. Section 6401(b). One should contrast California's view on typing services with Nevada's view, as well as Florida's view as expressed in *Florida Bar v. Catarcio*, discussed later in the chapter.

The South Carolina Supreme Court dealt with a paralegal who invoked the court's **original jurisdiction**, in *Doe v. Condon*, 532 S.E.2d 879 (S.C. 2000), asking whether the paralegal, who was employed by an attorney, could conduct estate planning seminars outside the presence of the attorney, and whether the paralegal could meet privately at the attorney's office with the attorney's clients and answer their general questions about wills and other estate-planning devices. Although the court approved of the paralegal interviewing clients and gathering estate planning information from them, it ruled against the paralegal on all of his requests. Specifically, the court found that the paralegal would be engaging in the unauthorized practice of law because what he wanted to do—give estate-planning seminars and answer client questions about estate matters—constituted the giving of legal advice. Although the paralegal claimed that he was only dispensing general information in his seminars, the court considered it more significant that he was conducting the seminars at the behest of the lawyer he worked for and was handing out law firm brochures, which cloaked his seminars in the unauthorized practice of law. *Id.* at 882. As for the client interviews, the court summarily concluded that answering a client's legal questions was the unauthorized practice of law. *Id.* at 883.

Real Estate Closings

Generally, paralegals may not attend and be responsible for any **real estate closing** without attorney supervision, since closings are formal, legal transactions. *See* State Bar of Georgia, Formal Advisory Op. 86–5 (1986), and State Bar of Georgia, Formal Advisory Op. 00–3 (2000) (this opinion specifically says that an attorney may not supervise the paralegal by telephone at the closing; the lawyer must be physically there); Illinois State Bar Association, Real Estate Section Council and Unauthorized Practice of Law Committee, Position Paper (1984) (a reaffirmation of earlier guidelines adopted by the Illinois Bar Association); North Carolina Bar Association, Formal Ethics Op. 13 (2000) (this opinion disapproves of a paralegal attending a real estate closing without the attendance of the supervising lawyer, but it does approve of a paralegal overseeing the execution of the closing documents without the attorney's presence in the room, so long as the attorney is present at the closing conference); Virginia Unauthorized Practice of Law Committee, Op. 183 (1999).

Some jurisdictions, however, do allow a paralegal to attend real estate closings on behalf of a client, provided the supervising lawyer has reviewed the closing documents, the paralegal is properly trained for real estate closings, the client consents, and the paralegal does not give legal advice. *See* Wisconsin State Bar Association, Formal Ethics Op. 95–3 (1995); New York State Bar Association Committee on Professional Ethics, Op. 677 (a paralegal may attend a real estate closing if the supervising attorney is available by telephone). And Guideline 2 of the Connecticut Bar Association's Guidelines for Paralegals specifically allows a paralegal to attend real estate closings even if no lawyer from the paralegal's firm is in attendance.

original jurisdiction—The authority an appellate court has to hear a case directly, before the case proceeds through the trial court and then is appealed.

real estate closing—The formal consummation of a sale of real estate, which usually involves the signing of many documents, payment of the real estate, and delivery of the deed or title.

However, it also states that the paralegal may only act as a messenger and should not give any opinion about the execution of the documents.

A unique exception can be found in the state of Washington, which has a rule of court that allows for the limited practice of real estate closing officers. Found in the Washington Rules on Admission to Practice, Rule 12 permits non-lawyers to apply for board certification as closing officers, authorizing such persons to prepare and complete real estate closing documents. But the rule specifically states that closing officers may not give legal advice. It is important to understand that this type of court rule would not necessarily affect the role of a paralegal because even if a Washington State paralegal applied and received the certification, the right to give legal advice would not be granted, and the paralegal's supervising lawyer would still be responsible for the paralegal's performance as a closing officer.

Representation before Administrative Agencies

While it is clear that paralegals may not represent someone in court, it is not so clear that they may not represent someone before an administrative agency. Administrative agencies, such as a worker's compensation hearing board, are considered quasi-judicial. Their decisions can be binding and are appealable, but the strict rules of evidence generally do not apply and agency hearings are conducted less formally than are trials. When one person represents another before an administrative agency, advocacy is taking place, and advocacy is prohibited for non-lawyers. Later in the chapter, rules that allow non-lawyer representation before administrative agencies will be discussed. At this point, however, it is important to realize that those allowances are jurisdiction specific, and not all administrative agencies allow non-lawyer representation.

Signing Pleadings

Paralegals may draft pleadings but may not be responsible for the pleadings. Pleadings, such as the complaint and the answer, are the initial documents filed in litigation, and lawyers must be legally responsible for all pleadings, as well as motions, filed on behalf of clients. A signature demonstrates such responsibility, and according to Rule 11 of the Federal Rules of Civil Procedure, an attorney representing a party in a lawsuit must sign all pleadings and motions. Likewise, all states have a similar version of Rule 11, and if a paralegal were to sign a pleading or draft and file one that was unsigned by a representing attorney, that would constitute the unauthorized practice of law.

A Florida ethics opinion discussed the propriety of lawyers who are out of their offices having their secretaries or paralegals sign notices of hearings and discovery notices by signing the paralegals' names followed by the lawyers' initials. The Opinion stated that under no circumstances could paralegals sign those documents on behalf of the lawyers who employed them. Florida Bar Association, Ethics Op. 87–11 (1988). Vermont also reached the same conclusion with respect to pleadings. Vermont Bar Association, Advisory Ethics Op. 01–05 (2001).

WHAT ACTIVITIES ARE PARALEGALS PERMITTED TO PERFORM?

Having taken into consideration all the activities that paralegals are not allowed to do, a question occurs: is there anything left for a paralegal to do besides answering the phone? Yes, there is. Remember, though, the key to what a paralegal may do is whether it is generally authorized or, alternatively, whether it has not been specifically prohibited by rules of legal ethics, statutes, or case law.

What Do the Paralegal Ethics Rules Authorize?

The non-lawyer ethics codes affirmatively authorize paralegals to engage in substantive legal work, but the language in the ethics codes ranges from a general affirmation to specific instances of authorized conduct.

The ABA Model Guidelines for the Utilization of Legal Assistant Services

Guideline 2 authorizes an attorney to delegate to a legal assistant any task not otherwise prohibited by law as long as the attorney maintains responsibility for the work product of the legal assistant. The Comment to Guideline 2 quotes from an ABA Ethics Opinion concerning the role of the non-lawyer, noting that an attorney "may employ nonlawyers to do any tasks for him except counsel clients about law matters, engage directly in the practice of law, appear in court . . . so long as it is he who takes the work and vouches for it to the client and becomes responsible for it to the client." ABA Commission on Professional Ethics, Formal Op. 316 (1967). Some of the authorized tasks listed in Comment 2 include legal research, factual investigation, preparation of legal documents, and maintaining any **trust account**.

trust account—A special bank account where the property of the client is held and maintained by the attorney.

The NFPA Model Disciplinary Rules and Ethical Considerations

The NFPA Model Disciplinary Rules and Ethical Considerations is the first part of the NFPA Model Code of Ethics and Professional Responsibility and Guidelines for Enforcement. There is no specific rule in the NFPA Model Disciplinary Rules and Ethical Considerations that addresses what a paralegal is entitled to do. However, some of the Ethical Considerations mention or imply a variety of authorized tasks. The prohibition on communication with parties represented by counsel, found in EC–1.2(b), implies that paralegals would have direct involvement in litigation support, and contact with witnesses. EC–2.3 and 2.4 concern paralegal access to billing records and client assets. EC–1.5 requires paralegals to keep their supervising attorney informed of any confidential information the paralegal may have in connection with the client's case. If the paralegal would have a duty to inform the supervising lawyer of certain facts of which the latter may not be aware, that would imply that a paralegal could do semi-independent legal tasks for the client. Also, EC–1.7 concerns disclosure of the paralegal's title on professional communication, letterhead, and advertisements. That would presume substantive legal work being conducted by paralegals. By contrast, secretaries do not "author" professional communication and are not listed in promotional materials.

The NALA Model Standards and Guidelines for Utilization of Legal Assistants

The Preamble to the NALA Model Standards and Guidelines acknowledges that one of the three most commonly raised questions about legal assistants is what duties a paralegal may perform. Guideline 3 states that legal assistants may perform client representation services as long as the legal assistant does not exercise independent legal judgment; the attorney maintains direct supervision over the legal assistant's work; and the legal assistant's work product merges into the attorney's work product. *Merge*, in this context, means that by the time the client becomes the recipient of the firm's legal services, the substantive work performed by the legal assistant has lost its non-lawyer fingerprints and has taken the identity of the lawyer or firm.

Guideline 5 of the NALA Model Standards and Guidelines is the most succinct source in any rules of legal ethics for the kinds of substantive activities that paralegals can perform. Although nine distinct tasks are listed, not all of them will be discussed here. (Please see Appendix C for Guideline 5 of the NALA Model Standards and Guidelines for Utilization of Legal Assistants.)

- *Paralegals can conduct client interviews.* While not being allowed to establish the attorney-client relationship, it is still significant that paralegals can interview clients, helping to assist in the transformation of their personal problems into legal problems, as well as conveying the empathy that is associated with trained, active listening skills.
- *Paralegals can engage in legal research.* A paralegal who has been through a qualified legal education program should be able to do almost all of the legal research that an attorney would regularly do. Using annotated codes, finding and reading case law, understanding the relationship between digests and headnotes, researching legal encyclopedias, flipping through loose-leaf services, and using Westlaw®, Lexis®, or other electronic legal research services are all activities that a competent paralegal should be capable of doing. In fact, a Virginia ethics opinion acknowledged that paralegals may conduct legal research for lawyers, *or for members of the public* who have provided specific citations that need to be found. Virginia State Bar Association Unauthorized Practice of Law Committee, Op. 127 (1989) [emphasis added].
- *Paralegals can draft legal documents.* This activity is closely related to legal research and is also authorized by Guideline 5. Law clerks write rough drafts for judges; associates in firms write rough drafts for partners. Likewise, a paralegal who shows exemplary writing skills should be used to write the same kinds of rough drafts, including settlement documents, **memorandum of law**, and trial and appellate briefs.
- *Paralegals can draft legal correspondence.* Many kinds of letters are generated in a law office, and all of them can be drafted by paralegals but not all can be signed by paralegals. Some letters, such as a client engagement letter, can be drafted by a paralegal but must become the official letter of the attorney

memorandum of law—An internal memorandum of law is legal analysis of the merits of a client's case. An external memorandum of law is an advocacy document, similar to a brief, presented to a court.

(including being signed by him or her), since such a letter would constitute the practice of law. Other letters, such as perfunctory requests for information or documents, can be drafted and signed by a legal assistant.

- *Paralegals can draft pleadings.* These kinds of litigation documents must be signed by the attorney of record, as required by Rule 11 of the Federal Rules of Civil Procedure; however, nothing prevents paralegals from drafting them. In fact, due to the availability of legal forms books and practice manuals, litigation paralegals might be more adept at drafting pleadings than the average lawyer.
- *Paralegals can assist with discovery.* Paralegals can summarize discovery devices, such as depositions or interrogatories. In fact, briefing cases involves honing the types of skills that can also be valuable in litigation, such as analysis and summarization skills. Depositions and interrogatories can amount to hundreds of pages, and trial preparation can include summarizing those voluminous documents in order to assist in case management.

The NALA Code of Ethics and Professional Responsibility

The nine Canons in the NALA Code of Ethics do not specifically list authorized paralegal activities. Canon 2 states what is found in other codes of ethics: a legal assistant may do only what is authorized, delegated, and properly supervised by an attorney. Likewise, Canon 3 restates the familiar refrain that a legal assistant must not engage in UPL, represent a client in court, establish the attorney-client relationship, establish fees, or give legal advice.

Paralegals and the Representation of Others before Administrative Agencies

An administrative agency, be it federal or state, is often part of the executive branch of government. Government by bureaucracy occurs when the legislature creates an agency and then empowers it to oversee certain aspects of American life that require expertise or constant involvement. For instance, the Internal Revue Code is the source for federal tax laws passed by Congress, while the Internal Revenue Service is the federal agency that oversees the administration of those tax laws. Administrative agencies have two primary sources of power: they make administrative regulations and they adjudicate disputes associated with those regulations. Those adjudications are very much like judicial proceedings. The decisions of a worker's compensation board, for instance, have the effect of law and can be appealed, but usually through all administrative channels before entering the courts. Unlike trial courts, the strict rules of courtroom evidence generally do not apply in administrative hearings, and, on occasion, nonlawyers are allowed to represent others before administrative agencies. Hence, the term *quasi-judicial* is often used in reference to administrative agency adjudications.

Earlier in the chapter, it was stated that representation of others before administrative agencies is generally considered the practice of law because it involves advocating a legal position on behalf of another person. That would lead to an initial presumption that non-lawyers who represent others before administrative agencies are engaging in the unauthorized practice of law. But specific statutes and administrative rules that allow for non-lawyer representation trump that presumption, and *where specifically allowed, such non-lawyer representation is not the unauthorized practice of law.* Nevertheless, even if a federal, state, or local agency approves of non-lawyer representation, appellate courts can still conclude that it is still the unauthorized practice of law. This can get quite confusing.

Representation before Federal Agencies

The federal government does allow non-lawyers to appear on behalf of others in front of its administrative agencies. Section 555(b) of the Administrative Procedures Act states in part:

> A person compelled to appear in person before an agency or representative thereof is entitled to be accompanied, represented, and advised by counsel or, if permitted by the agency, by other qualified representative. A party is entitled to appear in person or by or with counsel or other duly qualified representative in an agency proceeding. 5 U.S.C. § 555(b).

As the statute states, the discretion concerning whether to allow non-lawyer representation is left to each agency, as are the prerequisites that determine the eligibility of those representatives. Some agencies require proven expertise before one may serve as a representative. For instance, the United States Patent Office requires that before patent attorneys or non-lawyer patent agents can practice before the Patent Office, they must be of good moral character and pass the Patent Registration Examination. 37 C.F.R. § 10.7 (2001). The Internal Revenue Service is authorized in 31 U.S.C. § 330 to allow non-lawyer representation, and that is done in 31 C.F.R. § 10.3 (2000) and also in 31 C.F.R. § 10.7(c) (2000), which allows immediate family members to represent each other before the IRS. The Interstate Commerce Commission allows non-lawyers to practice before it as long as they meet the commission's requirements, which include meeting certain educational or experiential prerequisites and passing the practitioner's examination (and paying the examination fee). 49 C.F.R. § 1103.3(a), (b) (2001).

Other federal agencies have a more liberal allowance for non-lawyer representation. The Social Security Administration allows a non-lawyer to act as a representative if that person is competent, which means that a representative knows the significant issues in a claim and has a working knowledge of the key provisions of the Social Security Act, regulations, and rulings. *See* 20 C.F.R. § 404.1705(b), § 404.1740(b)(3)(i), and § 416.1505(b) (2001). The Department of Labor allows non-lawyers to represent parties before the Benefits Review Board, as long as they submit their request in writing to the board and state their education, experience, and relationship to the parties being represented. But the board has the authority to deny a non-lawyer's application because of that person's lack of qualifications. 20 C.F.R. § 802.202 (2001). And the

Immigration and Naturalization Service allows three groups of non-lawyers to represent others: law students (under certain circumstances), accredited representatives (who meet INS accreditation requirements), and "reputable individuals" (who can be anyone appearing at the request of the immigrant, and who are not compensated for their appearance). 8 C.F.R. § 292.1(a) (2001). An interesting case involving the unauthorized representation by a non-lawyer before the Immigration and Naturalization Services (INS) is *In re Disciplinary Action against Tatone*, 456 N.W.2d 717 (Minn.1990), where a lawyer was reprimanded because, for four years, he submitted notices of appearance before the INS, when in reality a non-lawyer, with whom the lawyer shared office space, was representing the clients before the that organization. While reprimanding the lawyer, the court noted that the non-lawyer who represented the clients was not authorized as a non-lawyer, under the INS rules, to represent others. *Id.* And because that person was a non-lawyer (therefore, not subject to professional discipline), the court had nothing to say about his conduct.

Representation before State Agencies

At the state level, the right of a non-lawyer to represent a party in an administrative adjudication is largely determined by state supreme court approval because even if a state statute authorizes non-lawyers to appear in administrative hearings, the state bar association might argue that such activity is the unauthorized practice of law, necessitating court intervention. For instance, after Kentucky amended its worker's compensation statute in 1996 to allow non-lawyer representation of injured workers, the Kentucky Bar Association's Unauthorized Practice of Law Committee issued an opinion that determined that non-lawyers may not represent others before the Kentucky Department of Workers' Claims, and then the Department asked the Kentucky Supreme Court, in *Turner v. Kentucky Bar Association*, 980 S.W.2d 560 (Ky. 1998) to review the statute, in light of the ethics opinion. And, in that case, the court found that the statute violated the separation of powers doctrine (remember *Marbury v. Madison*, from Chapter 1) and was an unconstitutional usurpation of the judiciary's absolute power to make rules relating to the practice of law. It then ruled that non-lawyers may not represent workers before any adjudicative tribunal. *Turner* at 565. However, the court did rule in favor of paralegals at the department advising claimants about their rights in the administrative proceedings and stated the paralegals could even assist claimants at informal arbitrations, provided the paralegals' work was supervised by a department attorney. *Turner* at 564, 565.

Another contentious example of the administrative agency representation controversy occurred in Indiana, where the state attorney general sued to restrain what he considered to be the unauthorized practice of law occurring due to a statute that allowed non-lawyers to appear on behalf of claimants before the state employees' appeals commission. The Indiana Supreme Court ruled that such actions were not the practice of law (and therefore, not UPL), basing its decision, in part, on the fact that the state employees' appeals commission members were not required to possess law degrees, that the potential for public detriment was limited since the commission only heard cases from state employees and not the public at large, and that the decision of the commission was not the final decision that could be made. *State ex rel. Pearson v. Gould,* 437 N.E.2d 41 (Ind. 1981).

The District of Columbia has an exception in its unauthorized practice of law rule that allows a non-lawyer, referred to as a "District of Columbia Practitioner," to practice before District of Columbia agencies, where those agencies specifically allow it and as long as the practitioner discloses in any advertisements that his or her practice is limited to specifically named agencies. D.C. Court of Appeals Rules of Court, Rule 49(c)(5). California, by statute, allows non-lawyers to represent others before the state worker's compensation appeals board (Cal. Bus. & Prof. Code §§ 5501, and 5700), as well as the state unemployment insurance appeals board (Cal. Unemp. Ins. Code § 1957), and a California ethics opinion authorizes law firms to assign their paralegals to represent clients before the Worker's Compensation Appeals Board, provided clients give their consent to the representation and the paralegals' work is adequately supervised. State Bar of California Committee on Professional Responsibility, Formal Op. 1988–103 (1988). Likewise, Michigan has a statute that allows non-lawyers to represent others before the state Unemployment Commission (Mich. Comp. Laws § 421.31), and a Michigan ethics opinion authorizes an employed paralegal to represent others at all administrative hearings where it would not be unlawful for other non-lawyers to do the same, so long as the client consents and the paralegal's supervising attorney is responsible for his or her behavior. Michigan Bar Association, Ethics Op. RI–125 (1992). Illinois's unemployment compensation laws allow any individual who is in an administrative proceeding to be represented by a non-lawyer (80 Ill. Comp. Stat. § 405/806), while its Administrative Code only allows nonlawyers to appear in routine matters, such as agreed continuances (Ill. Admin. Code tit. 50, § 720.40(b) (2001)). And New York's statute on non-lawyer representation is quite broad, stating that "[n]othing herein shall be construed either to grant or to deny to any person who is not a lawyer the right to appear for or represent others before any agency." N.Y. A.P.A. § 501.

Not all bar associations are in favor of even a limited allowance of non-lawyer representation in administrative agencies. For instance, a Delaware ethics opinion states that it would be unethical for a lawyer to delegate to a paralegal the duty to appear before the state industrial accident board to conduct a pretrial conference in a worker's compensation claim. Delaware State Bar Association Committee on Professional Ethics, Op. 1985–3 (1985). Specifically, the committee on professional ethics considered such administrative practice to be adversarial in nature, requiring an understanding of applicable legal principles, as well as the ability to judge the strengths and weaknesses of the client's case.

As the case below shows, one of the key factors to whether a non-lawyer—paralegal or otherwise—can represent someone else before an administrative agency is the level of legal skill considered necessary to adequately represent someone's interest in *that kind of agency.*

Case Law

The Florida Bar re Advisory Opinion on Nonlawyer Representation in Securities Arbitration, 696 So.2d 1178 (Fla. 1997)

PER CURIAM.

Pursuant to rule 10–7.1(1) of the Rules Regulating the Florida Bar, Robert Pearce, a Florida attorney, petitioned the Florida Bar Standing Committee on the Unlicensed Practice of Law (the Committee), for an advisory opinion on the following question: Whether non-attorney companies or individuals who offer advice on securities related matters and represent the public before, during or after any National Association of Securities Dealers (NASD), New York Stock Exchange (N.Y.SE), American Stock Exchange (AMEX), or other stock exchange arbitration proceedings for compensation are engaged in the unauthorized practice of law. . . .

The Committee held a public hearing on the matter in June 1996, where both oral and written testimony was received. Following the hearing, the Committee voted to issue a proposed opinion which finds that non-lawyer representatives in securities arbitration who accept compensation for their services are engaged in the unlicensed and unauthorized practice of law, and that the public is actually being harmed and has the potential for being harmed in the future by this practice. Several nonlawyer securities arbitration representatives filed comments as interested parties in opposition to the proposed opinion. The Standing Committee's proposed opinion is expressly limited to the narrow circumstances in which a securities investor with a claim or claims against a broker is represented before, during or after a securities arbitration to resolve the claim by a non-lawyer retained for compensation. . . .

The Committee is of the opinion that a non-lawyer who is retained to represent an investor in securities arbitration for compensation is engaged in the unauthorized practice at each of the three stages of representation. Specifically, the Committee finds

that the advice given and services rendered before the arbitration affects an investor's legal rights because the representative must determine: (1) whether the investor is compelled to arbitrate under any investor-broker agreement; (2) the effect of eligibility rules and statutes of limitations; (3) the scope of the arbitrator's authority; (4) whether to arbitrate or settle the dispute before filing a claim; (5) the merits of specific claims or defenses; (6) whether attorneys or expert witnesses should be hired to assist in the arbitration; (7) whether the investor should file a petition to stay the arbitration; and (8) the possibility of related or alternative civil actions. The proposed opinion further details that a nonlawyer representative also is engaged in the unlicensed practice of law during the course of the arbitration proceeding because the representation requires, among other things: (1) conducting discovery and any related depositions; (2) presenting evidence, raising objections, examinations of witnesses and voir dire of experts, and opening and closing arguments; and (3) preparing and filing the initial written statements of claims, answers, and counterclaims, as well as written and oral motions and legal memoranda concerning the claims at issue.

As to the third stage of representation, the proposed opinion notes that nonlawyer representatives in securities arbitration are engaged in the unlicensed practice of law even after the arbitration proceeding has concluded because any arbitration award or judgment can be confirmed, vacated, or collected only through an action at law and not through further arbitration or some alternative proceeding. Finally, the Committee notes that the nonlawyer representative in a securities arbitration has overstepped proper bounds because at each of these stages, and throughout the entirety of the representation, the investor places great reliance on the representative to properly prepare and present his or her case.

LACK OF FEDERAL OR STATE REGULATION

The proposed opinion asserts that this Court may—and should—enjoin the activities of non-lawyer securities arbitration representatives because no federal or state rules or regulations specifically authorize these nonlawyer representatives to engage in such activities. The proposed opinion explains that securities arbitration is conducted before self-regulatory organizations (SROs), which are private bodies and not federal offices or agencies. The rules governing the SROs at issue here, namely the National Association of Securities Dealers (NASD), the New York Stock Exchange (N.Y.SE), and the American Stock Exchange (AMEX), are approved by the Securities and Exchange Commission (SEC).

The Committee acknowledges, however, that the rules governing the SROs do not expressly prohibit nonlawyer representation, and that the Arbitrator's Manual published jointly by the SRO's and the Securities Industry Association indicates that parties in securities arbitration "may choose to appear pro se (on their own) or be represented by a person who is not an attorney, such as a business associate, friend, or relative." Nevertheless, the Committee maintains first that neither the rules provision, nor the Manual, constitutes federal legislation preempting this Court's regulatory authority, and, second, that these very general, permissive guidelines do not condone the nonlawyer representation for compensation at issue here. Rather, the Committee maintains in its proposed opinion that these provisions merely recognize, in an informal manner, the right of an investor to appear pro se either by representing himself or with the uncompensated help of a business associate, relative or friend.

Lastly the proposed opinion points to several ways in which the public is harmed by the activities of nonlawyer representatives in securities arbitration. Most importantly, the Committee notes that because the stock brokerage industry arbitration forums have no qualification procedures, and nonlawyer representatives—unlike attorneys—are not supervised or subject to discipline by a state bar or any other regulatory body, instances of misleading advertising, ineffective representation and the unethical conduct of nonlawyer representatives are prevalent but unsanctionable. Specifically, nonlawyers who have been disciplined or suspended by the securities industry or from the practice of law can represent investors in arbitration forums and are not required to meet any ethical standards in their practice. Settlement negotiations and the handling of client's money on deposit goes unregulated.

Testimony before the Committee indicated that nonlawyer representatives are sometimes improperly motivated to settle claims rather than arbitrate because they are unable to go to court to confirm or collect an arbitration award on behalf of their client or defend against a broker's attempt to have the award vacated. Moreover, where claims are not settled and litigation does occur, the investor represented by a nonlawyer is sorely disadvantaged because, at least in the securities setting, the defendant broker or firm is always represented by well-resourced attorneys. And, to make matters worse, investors have no recourse against their compensated representatives for the ineffective representation.

. . . [W]e are persuaded of the need for some regulation of these compensated representatives and approve the UPL Standing Committee's proposed opinion. We conclude that compensated nonlawyer representatives in securities arbitration are engaged in the unauthorized practice of law and pose a sufficient threat of harm to the public to justify our protection. In *State ex rel. Florida Bar v. Sperry*, 140 So.2d 587 (Fla. 1962), this Court set out the framework for determining whether specific activities constitute the practice of law, which bears repeating here. We explained: [I]t is not the nature of the agency or body before which the acts are done, or even whether they are done before a tribunal of any sort or in the private office of an individual, that determines whether that which is done constitutes the practice of law. The best test, it seems to us, is what is done, not where, for the safest measure is the character of the acts themselves. If they constitute the practice of law the fact that they are done in the private office of the one who performs them or before a nonjudicial body in no way changes their character.

It is generally understood that the performance of services in representing another before the courts is the practice of law. But the practice of law also includes the giving of legal advice and counsel to others as to their rights and obligations under the law and the preparation of legal instruments, including contracts, by which legal rights are either obtained, secured or given away, although such matters may not then or ever be the subject of proceedings in a court.

We think that in determining whether the giving of advice and counsel and the performance of services in legal matters for compensation constitute the practice of law it is safe to follow the rule that if the giving of such advice and performance of such services affect important rights of a person under the law, and if the reasonable protection of the rights and property of those advised and served requires that the persons giving such advice possess legal skill and a knowledge of the law greater than that possessed by the average citizen, then the giving of such advice and the performance of such services by one for another as a course of conduct constitute the practice of law. 140 So.2d at 591. . . . For instance, in *Florida Bar v. Brumbaugh*, 355 So.2d 1186 (Fla. 1978), The Florida Bar filed a complaint against Brumbaugh, a self-employed secretary who advertised typing services for "Do-It-Yourself" divorces, wills, resumes, and bankruptcies, alleging that Brumbaugh was practicing law without a license. Id. at 1189. For a fee, Brumbaugh prepared the necessary documents for pleading, filing, and securing a dissolution of marriage, as well as "detailed instructions as to how the suit should be filed, notice served, hearings set, trial conducted, and the final decree secured." Id. at 1100. . . . Additionally, had Brumbaugh typed forms

for her clients, provided she copy only the information given to her in writing by her clients, this too would have been acceptable. However, we ultimately concluded that Brumbaugh's activities constituted the unlicensed practice of law because (1) her customers relied on her to properly prepare the necessary forms for the legal proceeding of a marriage dissolution; (2) she advised clients as to various remedies available to them, or otherwise assisted them in preparing the necessary forms; (3) she inquired into or answered questions of her clients to determine which forms would be necessary, how best to fill out these forms, and how to present the necessary information in court. Id. at 1193–94.

More recently, we addressed the issue of the unlicensed practice of law in the preparation and sales of living trusts in *Florida Bar re Advisory Opinion—Nonlawyer Preparation of Living Trusts*, 613 So.2d 426 (Fla. 1992). In that case, American Family Living Trust petitioned the Florida Bar Standing Committee on the Unlicensed Practice of Law for an advisory opinion concerning: Whether it constitutes the unlicensed practice of law for a corporation or other nonlawyer to draft living trusts and related documents for another where the information to be included in the living trust is gathered by nonlawyer agents of the corporation or by the nonlawyer and the completed documents are reviewed by a member of The Florida Bar prior to execution. Id. at 426. Upon reviewing similar requests from other parties, the Standing Committee held hearings, gathered both oral and written testimony, and subsequently proposed that this Court issue an opinion finding that nonlawyer companies which sell living trusts are engaged in the unlicensed practice of law and the public is or could be harmed by this practice. Id. at 427. . . . Nevertheless, we found that because the "gathering of the necessary information for a living trust" did not constitute the unlicensed practice of law, nonlawyers may properly perform this activity. Id. 680 So.2d at 258-59 (Fla. 1997).

Although we recognize that arbitration was set up to be a nonjudicial alternative for dispute resolution, it is clear that, in light of our caselaw thoroughly discussing the activities that constitute the practice of law, the services provided by nonlawyer representatives in the alternative but still adversarial context of securities arbitration constitutes the practice of law. As the Committee pointedly and accurately notes in its proposed opinion, nonlawyer representatives give specific legal advice and perform the traditional tasks of the lawyer at every stage of the arbitration proceeding in an effort to protect the investor's important legal and financial interests. We cannot ignore such a situation. Because such activities—when performed by nonlawyers—are wholly unregulated and unsanctionable, we further agree with the proposed opinion that these activities must be enjoined. In these circumstances, the public faces a potential for harm from incompetent and unethical representation by compensated nonlawyers that cannot otherwise be remedied. . . .

Finally, we also must reject the position of the interested parties that this Court has been preempted from regulating the unlicensed practice of law in this instance. Specifically, the interested parties maintain that we are precluded from regulating the activities at issue here because the general rules governing the SROs do not prohibit nonlawyer representation and the Arbitrator's Manual, which serves as a handbook for the arbitration process, expressly authorizes lay representation. . . . We agree with the proposed opinion that neither the SRO rules nor the language in the Arbitrator's Manual constitutes federal or state legislative displacement of our authority to protect the public from harm by regulating the unauthorized practice of law.

We do acknowledge that the Securities and Exchange Commission, the federal agency responsible for oversight of securities arbitration, easily could—and may very well choose—to preempt us in enjoining nonlawyer representation by authorizing or regulating the activities of these professionals. Nevertheless, we think that compensated nonlawyer representatives in securities arbitration are engaged in the unauthorized practice of law and the protection of the public requires us to step in where there is no such legislation or regulation. Accordingly, we enjoin nonlawyers from representing investors in securities arbitration proceedings for compensation from the date this opinion becomes final and we approve the Committee's proposed opinion. It is so ordered.

Case Questions

1. How did this lawsuit originate?
2. Why did the court find that non-lawyers could not represent someone in securities arbitration?
3. How does compensation of the non-lawyer representative affect the court's decision?
4. If a non-lawyer cannot do such representation for compensation, then how can it be authorized conduct (if done without compensation)?
5. What examples of authorized non-lawyer conduct were cited by the court?

Local Rules of Court

As discussed in Chapter 1, codes of professional ethics are part of what are called *rules of court*, the kind of rules affecting lawyers and litigation that are adopted by a jurisdiction's highest appellate court. Trial courts are local courts, often organized by counties, and those counties, in conjunction with their own judicial authority structure, are allowed to supplement their state's rules of trial procedure with certain local rules of trial procedure that apply within the county's legal system. Such rules might include special rules on filing documents, making appearances, discovery, and pretrial settlements.

The Seattle–King County Bar Association, for instance, has a Legal Assistant Registration Program in its Bar Association Rules. In order to be eligible to register, legal assistants must meet certain educational and experiential prerequisites. Once registered, legal assistants are entitled, under the bar association's authority, to do certain acts in accordance with the King County local court rules, including checking out files, using the county law library, and presenting agreed orders.

Likewise, some local jurisdictions list specific actions that paralegals are authorized to do, including semi-independent actions. For example, the Allen County Superior Court–Civil Division has local rules of practice, supplementing the Indiana Rules of Trial Procedure, and Rule 21, entitled "Authority of Attorneys' Employees," applies to legal assistants. Section A states, "'legal assistants' . . . shall be limited to the performance of tasks which do not require the exercise of legal discretion or judgment that affects the legal rights of any person." Section D lists four activities that legal assistants are allowed to do: (1) filing and obtaining orders on motions; (2) setting pre-trial conferences and other hearing dates, except trials; (3) examining pleadings and docket sheets; and (4) with the discretion of the court, obtaining approval of orders from the judge's law clerk for notices of hearings, orders to appear and answer interrogatories, stipulations signed and approved by the parties of record, and motions to withdraw appearances. Allen County Superior Court–Civil Division Local Rules of Practice and Procedure, Rule 21 (A), (D).

INDEPENDENT PARALEGAL SERVICES AND THE UNAUTHORIZED PRACTICE OF LAW

As discussed in Chapter 2, lack of paralegal licensure, while perhaps appropriate, has some pitfalls. One of the pitfalls of this unlicensed profession is the lack of clear boundaries on how independent a paralegal may be. To say that a legal assistant must work under the supervision of an attorney presupposes conduct that would clearly be the practice of law if done by the attorney, rather than being supervised by him or her. However, between representing one's self pro se—which all citizens have the right to do—and representing others in litigation and giving legal advice—which only lawyers have the right to do—there lies a gray area of quasi-legal practice. As an example, if someone is allowed to write his or her own will, can someone else provide them the will kit or type it for them? If one can help a friend find a statute at the county courthouse and not be guilty of the unauthorized practice of law, may one also charge a fee for finding that statute? May a bank have its loan officers assist home purchasers in completing the mortgage or other loan documents?

The answers to the above questions vary along state lines and are inconsistent within the case law. The starting point for any answer is to first examine your state's definition of a legal assistant, as found in its state code or rules of professional responsibility. Next, one would need to examine the state's statutes to see if any specific law allows non-lawyers to engage in certain quasi-legal activity, such as a state law that allows non-lawyer service providers to assist parties in obtaining uncontested divorces. Then, legal research would need to be done to analyze the state Supreme Court's view on the matter, as well as any relevant ethics opinions issued by the state disciplinary commission or bar association.

Legal Services Rendered by Non-Lawyers Serving the Public: Treading on Thin Ice

Marilyn Arons, founder of the Parent Information Center, found herself the target of the Delaware State Bar Association because she advised parents of children with special needs about their rights and represented them at school board meetings. In 1997, the Delaware Bar sued Ms. Arons, accusing her of practicing law without a license. She considered herself to be rightfully helping people with public school issues in which lawyers rarely get involved. Ms. Arons is not alone, for in recent years, bar associations have sued a variety of service providers under theories of unauthorized practice of law: banks have been sued in Michigan for charging fees for completing legal documents for loans; a funeral home in Alabama was sued because it charged fees for preparing documents, such as death certificates; Nolo Press, the publisher of legal self-help guides, was sued in Texas for selling its do-it-yourself legal books and computer software.

It is bar associations, and not dissatisfied clients, who have very often brought the increasing number of UPL cases across the country, raising the question of whether such bar association–prompted lawsuits are consumer protection or turf protection. The American Bar Association appointed a commission in 1992, known as the ABA Commission on Nonlawyer Practice, to study and evaluate the implications of non-lawyer practice to society and the legal profession. In 1995, the commission issued its report to the ABA, which included, among other things, recommending increasing the scope of allowable activities for traditional paralegals, considering the possibility of non-lawyer representation in state administrative hearings, examining the ethics rules so as to promote affordable legal services, and promoting non-lawyer assistance as long as it is subject to review. However, the commission's recommendations went nowhere, and were not even presented to the ABA House of Delegates.

On occasion, state legislation has been introduced that would allow paralegals to directly serve the public by engaging in limited legal activities without attorney supervision. States such as California, Illinois, Oregon, Rhode Island, and Washington have contemplated legislation that would allow independent paralegals to draft and execute wills, represent parties at real estate closings, or represent parties in uncontested divorces. (Remember that the Washington statute on real estate closing officers, discussed earlier in the chapter, does not involve independent paralegals.) All those bills, however, died in committee or otherwise failed to pass the legislative process.

That leaves us where we started, treading carefully on the line of demarcation between what is allowed and what is unauthorized. A generality that can be applied to this quagmire is that those who offer typing services or forms preparation directly to the public may do nothing that would involve helping their clientele choose what forms are needed or what information should be used to complete the forms. For example, if one were to purchase a will kit from an individual or entity that sells them, the seller of the kit would be engaging in the unauthorized practice of law if he or she decided, or helped the purchaser decide, what kind of will the purchaser needed, and also if he or she executed the will.

The following case from Florida shows the kinds of specific conduct committed by non-lawyers serving the public that cause courts to be perplexed when they consider whether such conduct is crossing the line into the unauthorized practice of law.

Case Law

Florida Bar v. Catarcio, 709 So.2d 96 (Fla. 1998)

PER CURIAM.

We have for review the referee's report regarding the unlicensed practice of law by respondent, Richard Catarcio. We have jurisdiction. Art. V, §15 Fla. Const. On August 28, 1996, the Florida Bar filed a two-count petition against Catarcio, alleging that he had engaged in the unlicensed practice of law in relation to his preparation of a bankruptcy petition and the manner in which he advertised his legal forms preparation service. Catarcio filed an answer and moved to dismiss the petition, arguing that the Bar's attempt to regulate his conduct was preempted by 11 U.S.C. §110 (1994), which generally regulates the conduct of a "bankruptcy petition preparer," and that the relief sought in the petition would violate the First Amendment of the United States Constitution as it would unlawfully infringe on his commercial speech. We denied Catarcio's motion and a hearing was held before a referee on September 15, 1997. After conducting the hearing, the referee made the findings of fact set forth below.

Catarcio was not and is not a member of the Florida Bar and is therefore not licensed to prac-tice law in Florida. He operates a paralegal service business under the name "American Paralegal Center, Inc.," a Florida corporation, of which he is the sole officer, director, and owner, and his business card shows the Scales of Justice and identifies him as "Richard T. Catarcio, J.D." Catarcio advertises his business in The Flyer, a weekly advertising publication, under the heading "Professional Services" and the subheading "Legal," and the advertisement provides a list of available services, including simple divorce and bankruptcy. The advertisement also contains an offer of "Free Consultation."

In May 1994, Robert Cooper contacted Catarcio for assistance in filing for personal bankruptcy. Cooper met with Catarcio at Catarcio's office, seeking advice as to the appropriateness of filing for bankruptcy, and Catarcio told him that filing for bankruptcy would be proper. Catarcio advised Cooper that he was eligible to file for bankruptcy and that he should file under Chapter 7 of the Bankruptcy Code; Cooper wanted Catarcio to file the bankruptcy petition for him because he thought

Catarcio knew what he was doing. Thereafter, Catarcio advised Cooper and Cooper's ex-wife, Michele Caron, to file for joint bankruptcy, advising Caron that if she did not file for joint bankruptcy, the bankruptcy trustee would "come after" her once Cooper's bankruptcy was completed. Catarcio then orally communicated with Cooper concerning the information to be placed in the bankruptcy petition and what to write in filling out the petition. Catarcio decided where to file the petition and what boxes to check on the bankruptcy forms indicating under which statutes Cooper's property should be exempted, as Cooper did not know what placing check marks in the boxes meant. Catarcio also advised Cooper about what qualified as joint property for the purposes of bankruptcy, selected the legal citations to be placed in the petition to indicate the statutory exemptions claimed, and explained the value of Cooper's personal property which could be claimed as exempt. In addition, Catarcio advised Caron to sign her name as "Cooper" on the joint bankruptcy petition even though she told him that she was divorced and that her legal name at the time was Caron.

Subsequently, when two omissions in the bankruptcy petition were discovered, Cooper again contacted Catarcio. Catarcio advised him to file an amendment to add an omitted creditor, Sears, and to add his vehicle, a van, to the bankruptcy petition. Catarcio informed Cooper that Catarcio would prepare the amendment to the petition and that Cooper "should not worry about it," adding that the effect of the amendment would be that the bankruptcy trustee would be unable to take the van. Catarcio then took the information from Cooper orally to prepare the amendment. Cooper testified that he went to Catarcio to have him properly and competently fill out his bankruptcy forms and that, in preparing the bankruptcy petition and amendment, Catarcio held himself out in such a way that Cooper assumed he was an attorney because of "the way he [Catarcio] talked the law to me [Cooper] about the bankruptcy . . . all these articles and stuff like that."

As a result of filing for joint bankruptcy, neither Cooper nor Caron can obtain credit.

Based on the above findings of fact, the referee concluded that Catarcio had engaged in the unlicensed practice of law by (1) advising Cooper and Caron as to various legal remedies available to them and possible courses of action; (2) taking information from Cooper orally to complete the bankruptcy petition and amendment when the forms being completed were not forms approved by this Court; (3) having direct contact with Cooper and Caron in the nature of consultation, explanation, recommendations, advice and assistance in the provision, selection, and completion of legal forms; (4) inducing Cooper to place reliance upon him in the preparation of his bankruptcy forms; (5) advising Cooper and Caron to file a joint bankruptcy petition when they were not married in contravention of 11 U.S.C. §302(a), which states that joint bankruptcy petitions are filed by a debtor and the debtor's spouse, and by advising Caron to fraudulently sign her name as "Cooper" even though she told him that she was divorced from Cooper and that her legal name at the time was Caron; (6) offering "Free Consultation" in advertising his legal forms preparation service in that it holds him out as able to provide legal services in the nature of consultation and because it goes beyond the limitations placed on nonlawyer advertising by offering more than secretarial and notary services and selling legal forms and general printed materials; and (7) by using the designation "J.D." on his business card in conjunction with his offer of the preparation of legal forms and the depiction of the Scales of Justice.

After arriving at the above conclusions, the referee recommended that this Court find that Catarcio engaged in the unlicensed practice of law based on his conduct in the preparation of Cooper and Caron's joint bankruptcy petition, as well as the manner in which Catarcio advertised his legal forms preparation service. The referee then recommended that Catarcio be enjoined from the unlicensed practice of law and taxed for the costs of these proceedings. Catarcio filed objections to the referee's report, essentially raising the same arguments that he raised in his initial motion to dismiss, and the Bar filed a response. We approve the report of the referee. . . .

We also approve the referee's conclusions and recommendations. This Court has issued numerous decisions proscribing the type of conduct engaged in by Catarcio. See *Florida Bar v. Davide*, 702 So.2d 184 (Fla. 1997) (adopting uncontested referee's report finding nonlawyers engaged in unlicensed practice of law by, among other things, advising persons regarding bankruptcy exemptions); *Florida Bar v. Warren*, 655 So.2d 1131, 1132–32 (Fla. 1995) (enjoining nonlawyer from, among other things, counseling persons as to "the advisability of their filing for protection under the United States bankruptcy laws"); *Florida Bar v. Schramek*, 616 So.2d 979, 984 (Fla.1993) (finding nonlawyer engaged in unlicensed practice of law in many areas, including bankruptcy, by providing services "which require[d] a knowledge of the law greater than that possessed by the average citizen"); *Florida Bar v. King*, 468 So.2d 982. 983 (Fla.1985) (adopting uncontested referee's report finding nonlawyer engaged in unlicensed practice of law by, among other things, having "direct contact in the nature of consultation, explanation, recommendations, advice and assistance in the provision, selection and completion of forms"); *Florida Bar v. Martin*, 432 So.2d 54 (Fla. 1983) (approving referee's report finding nonlawyer's use of designation "J.D." in conjunction with his name constituted unlicensed practice of law); *Brumbaugh*, 355 So.2d at 1194 (enjoining nonlawyer from advising clients as to various available remedies, making inquiries or answering questions as to particular forms which might be necessary, how best to fill out such forms, and where to properly file such forms).

This Court has also adopted rules regulating the unlicensed practice of law which proscribe the type of conduct engaged in by Catarcio. See R. Regulating Fla. Bar 10–2.1(a) (1997) (restricting nonlawyer oral communications solely to those eliciting factual information for the completion of forms

approved by this Court); see also Florida Bar Re Approval of Forms Pursuant to Rule 10–1.1(b) of the Rules Regulating The Florida Bar, 591 So.2d 594, 595 (Fla. 1991) (approving "fill-in-the-blank" forms developed by the Bar for use in "areas amenable to a forms practice").

Federal bankruptcy courts sitting in Florida have found similar conduct constituted the unlicensed practice of law. See *In re Samuels*, 176 B.R. 616, 621–22 (Bankr.M.D.Fla. 1994) (providing exhaustive list of activities constituting the unlicensed practice of law in bankruptcy context in Florida and other jurisdictions, and stating that "[t]he Florida Supreme Court and Florida bankruptcy courts have made it clear that persons wanting to provide services in the bankruptcy area are limited to typing or transcribing written information provided to them by a consumer onto pre-prepared forms"); *In re Calzadilla*, 151 B.R. 622 625–626 (Bankr.S.D.Fla. 1993) (providing what bankruptcy services a nonlawyer may and may not provide); *In re Bachman*, B.R. at 773–775 (applying this Court's *Brumbaugh* decision in bankruptcy context).

We agree with the referee that Catarcio has engaged in the unlicensed practice of law, and we enjoin Richard Catarcio individually, his agents and employees, and any other business entities in which he holds an interest, from engaging in the following activities: (1) advising customers of their rights, duties and responsibilities under Florida or federal law, (2) making inquiries and answering questions as to the particular bankruptcy forms that might be necessary, how best to fill out the forms, the information necessary to complete the forms, and where to properly file such forms, (3) giving advice and making decisions on behalf of others that require legal skill and a knowledge of the law greater than that possessed by the average citizen, (4) advising about or explaining legal remedies and possible courses of action that affect the procedural or substantive legal rights, duties and privileges of persons, (5) counseling customers as to the advisability of filing for protection under United States bankruptcy laws, (6) allowing members of the public to rely on Catarcio to properly prepare legal forms or legal documents affecting individuals' legal rights, (7) using the phrase "Free Consultation" in advertising his legal form preparation service, and from advertising any legal form preparation services beyond the business activities of providing secretarial and notary services, and selling legal forms and general printed information, and (8) using the designation "J.D." following his name in the context of print advertisements, business cards, or other offerings of his legal form preparation services, or in any other manner which could mislead the public into believing Catarcio can assist the public in legal matters. Judgment for costs is entered in favor of The Florida Bar and against Richard Catarcio in the amount of $1,182.44, for which sum let execution issue.

It is so ordered.

Case Questions

1. What conduct did Mr. Catarcio do that qualified as the unauthorized practice of law?
2. Why was he being sued if he had a J.D., as listed on his business card?
3. What conduct did the court state would be permissible for Catarcio to do in his bankruptcy petition preparation service?
4. Has the court's ruling effectively put Catarcio out of business? Why do you think the court prohibited Catarcio from using the phrase "free consultation" in his advertisement?
5. Do you think it is likely that Catarcio was aware that his conduct was unauthorized?
6. Do you think this case is an example of turf protection or consumer protection?

In April 2002, the Florida Supreme Court adopted changes to Rule 4–5.3 of the Florida Rules of Professional Conduct, which is the rule that governs the use of non-lawyer assistants. Surprisingly, the new rule 4–5.3(a) seems to approve of paralegals directly serving the public, because it says, "A person who uses the title of paralegal, legal assistant, or other similar term *when offering or providing services to the public* must work for or under the direction or supervision of a lawyer or an authorized business entity as defined elsewhere in these Rules Regulating The Florida Bar" (emphasis added). And new Comments to the rule state:

> If an activity requires the independent judgment and participation of the lawyer, it cannot be properly delegated to a nonlawyer employee. . . . Additionally, this rule would not permit a lawyer to accept employment by a nonlawyer or group of nonlawyers, the purpose of which is to provide the supervision required under this rule.

The changes adopted to Florida's rule on non-lawyer assistants are quite drastic; however, the rule still requires that lawyers be responsible for the work of paralegals and legal assistants.

The same day Rule 4–5.3 was changed, the Florida Supreme Court also adopted changes to Rule 10–2.1, which governs the unlicensed practice of law. While that rule previously allowed non-lawyers to assist others in filling out legal forms approved by the Florida Supreme Court, a new part of the rule states the following:

It shall constitute the unlicensed practice of law for a person who does not meet the definition of paralegal or legal assistant as set forth elsewhere in these rules to offer or provide legal services directly to the public or for a person who does not meet the definition of paralegal or legal assistant as set forth elsewhere in these rules to use the title paralegal, legal assistant, or other similar term in providing legal services or legal forms preparation services directly to the public. Florida Rules Governing the Investigation and Prosecution of the Unlicensed Practice of Law, 10–2.1(a)(2)

And another new part of the rule 10–2.1(b), which concerns paralegals and legal assistants, states, "A nonlawyer or a group of nonlawyers may not offer legal services directly to the public by employing a lawyer to provide the lawyer supervision required under this rule."

Bankruptcy courts have, consistent with the traditional view, refused to allow independent paralegals to assist members of the public in preparing bankruptcy petitions. Although those courts have allowed non-lawyers to type information that was provided in writing by bankruptcy customers, they stop short when non-lawyers make inquiries of their customers' needs and situations before preparing the bankruptcy petitions. For instance, helping a person fill out schedules of exempt and nonexempt property requires the one doing the assistance to make legal judgments in excess of what is allowed by non-lawyers. *See In re Harris*, 152 B.R. 440 (Bankr. W.D. Pa. 1993). Furthermore, those bankruptcy courts have found that disclaimers signed by customers stating that the assisting independent paralegal has not given legal advice are completely irrelevant to the issue of whether he or she actually crossed the line. In fact, answers given to customers by those paralegals, even when they have sought the advice of lawyers beforehand, constitutes the unauthorized practice of law, and any fees earned must be returned to the bankruptcy customers. *See Matter of Bright*, 171 B.R. 799 (Bankr. E.D. Mich. 1994), where the court provided an extensive analysis on the unauthorized practice of law in bankruptcy settings.

Not every jurisdiction even approves of non-lawyers operating typing services. A Pennsylvania ethics opinion discussed the propriety of a non-lawyer with a paralegal certificate starting a business assisting low-income persons with the completion of bankruptcy and divorce forms. Even though the paralegal claimed that all customers would sign forms stating they had not received any legal advice, the ethics committee found that such a business would violate Pennsylvania's unauthorized practice of law statute. Pennsylvania Unauthorized Practice of Law Committee, Op. 94–102 (1995).

Utah, however, may have just become the first state to authorize much of what has always been thought of as the unauthorized practice of law, when its statehouse passed legislation that will go in effect in May 2004, which defines the practice of law as, "appearing as an advocate in any criminal proceeding or before any court of record in this state in a representative capacity on behalf of another person." Utah H.B. 349. Designed specifically to alleviate the problem of those who make too much to qualify for legal aid but not enough to afford most lawyers, the law allows, by inference, non-lawyers to provide legal services outside the context of court proceedings. The Utah State Bar Association is opposed to the present version of the legislation, but hopes that a compromise can be reached between the legislature and the bar before the law is scheduled to go into effect. Public Letter to Members of the Utah State Bar Association, March 3, 2003 (http://www.utahbar.org/news).

Legal Services Rendered by Non-Lawyers as Independent Contractors to Lawyers

An issue that may be more relevant, at least until the law on independent paralegals changes, is whether a non-lawyer can render legal services to lawyers on an independent contracting basis, as a freelance paralegal. Such an arrangement would provide the kind of outsourcing benefits that have accrued in other industries and professions during the last economic growth cycle (Outsourcing is by no means universally recognized as a win-win situation, but this is not the place for such an analysis). Law firms and corporate legal departments would still be able to use the services of paralegals to do things from manually preparing documents and cases to legal research and writing. However, instead of retaining a legal assistant as an employee, the firm would hire him or her as an **independent contractor**, thereby saving overhead costs on employee taxes, benefits, and employee hiring, training, and firing. Such an arrangement has been used for decades with accountants.

independent contractor—One who is self-employed, but hired to do work for others as needed, such as an attorney, an accountant, or a caterer.

Independent contracting paralegals would then act as entrepreneurs, seeking the immediate legal assistance needs of their clients, who would be lawyers or law firms instead of the general public. Ideally, independent contracting paralegals could work as much—or as little—as they wanted to, retaining their autonomy in much the same way that any self-employed individual would. And with the natural selection that occurs in the marketplace, the better paralegals would become more valuable and earn more money.

Do the present rules of professional responsibility allow for such an arrangement? That depends on the set of rules in place. The ABA Model Rules of Professional Conduct seem to allow independent contracting paralegals. Model Rule 5.3 requires lawyers who have direct supervisory authority over non-lawyer assistants to ensure that those assistants behave compatibly within the Model Rules. The Comment to that rule states in part: "Lawyers generally employ assistants in their practice, including secretaries, investigators, law student interns, and paraprofessionals. Such assistants, *whether employees or independent contractors*, act for the lawyer in rendition of the lawyer's professional services" (emphasis added). The Comment to MR 5.5 (which prohibits lawyers from assisting non-lawyers in the unauthorized practice of law) states that a such rule is not intended to prohibit lawyers from employing the services of paraprofessionals, as long as they properly supervise and retain responsibility for those services. Likewise, the Ethical Considerations following Canon 5 of the ABA Model Code of Professional Responsibility, discussed earlier in the chapter, imply an approval of independent contracting paralegals.

Nothing in the ABA Model Guidelines for the Utilization of Legal Assistant Services prohibits legal assistants from being employed as independent contractors.

The emphasis is on supervision of the delegated tasks. Guidelines 1 and 2 make the lawyer responsible for the professional actions of the legal assistant, and their Comments discuss principles of agency law in the context of lawyers delegating legal tasks to, and supervising the legal work of, legal assistants. The only prohibitions mentioned regarding non-lawyer services are the traditional restrictions of unauthorized conduct: giving legal advice, establishing the attorney-client relationship, establishing fees, and representing clients in court, not the methods in which non-lawyers may be employed.

A statutorily created definition or description of a paralegal or legal assistant can, expressly or impliedly, approve of those who are independent contractors. For instance, California's statutory description of a paralegal includes "a person *who either contracts with or is employed* by an attorney, law firm, corporation, governmental agency, or other entity and who performs substantial legal work under the direction and supervision of an active member of the State Bar of California" (emphasis added). And a later section states, "The terms 'paralegal,' 'legal assistant,' 'attorney assistant,' 'freelance paralegal,' 'independent paralegal,' and 'contract paralegal' are synonymous for purposes of this chapter." Cal. Bus. & Prof. Code §§ 6450(a) and 6454. Similarly, Maine's statutory definition encompasses freelance paralegals by stating, "'Paralegal' and 'legal assistant' mean a person, qualified by education, training or work experience, *who is employed or retained* by an attorney, law office, corporation, governmental agency or other entity and who performs specifically delegated substantive legal work for which an attorney is responsible." Me. Rev. Stat. Ann. tit. 4, § 921 (emphasis added).

Also, the definition of a paralegal adopted by a jurisdiction's rules of court or bar associations can impliedly approve of those who are independent contractors. The American Bar Association's definition of a legal assistant was revised in 1997 and states in part, "A legal assistant or paralegal is a person qualified by education, training or work experience *who is employed or retained* by a lawyer" (emphasis added). As was discussed in Chapter 2 concerning legal assistants joining state bar associations, Article I, Section 6 of the Michigan Bar Association Bylaws describes a legal assistant as "[a]ny person *currently employed or retained* by a lawyer" (emphasis added). And New Hampshire states, in its guidelines on the use of legal assistants, that its definition of a legal assistant "is intended to cover *all lay persons who are employed by or associated with* a member of the Bar but who are not admitted to practice law in the State of New Hampshire." N.H. R. S. Ct., Rule 35 (emphasis added). New Mexico's definition of a legal assistant also incorporates the revised ABA definition of a qualified person who is "*employed or retained* by a lawyer." N.M. Rules Governing Legal Assistant Services, Rule 20-102(A) (emphasis added).

Some states have addressed the issue of independent contractors in ethics opinions. For example, South Carolina approved of the use of lawyers employing independent contract paralegals in a 1996 ethics opinion. Specifically, the question asked was whether a lawyer could use a contract-paralegal service to assist the lawyer in a probate practice, paying the paralegal service and then billing the client for the paralegal's work. The opinion stated that such an arrangement was allowed, provided the client is aware of the billing arrangement and the lawyer properly supervises, and remains responsible for, the paralegal's work. South Carolina Bar Association, Ethics Advisory Op. 93-13 (1996). Utah recently issued an ethics opinion (in September 2002) that also approves of independent contracting paralegals, concluding that, "Utah lawyers may hire outside paralegals on an independent-contractor basis, provided the paralegal does not control the lawyer's professional judgment." Utah State Bar Association, Ethics Advisory Committee Op. 02–07 (2002).

New Jersey reversed itself in 1992, when its Supreme Court acknowledged that lawyers were responsible to supervise legal assistants, "whether they are employees of the firm or independent contractors." *In Re Ethics Opinion No. 24 of the Committee on the Unauthorized Practice of Law*, 607 A.2d. 962 (N.J. 1992). Previously, the New Jersey Committee on the Unauthorized Practice of Law had concluded, in an ethics opinion, that freelance paralegals were engaging in the unauthorized practice of law, due to the intrinsic lack of supervision occurring in such relationships. New Jersey Supreme Court Committee on the Unauthorized Practice, Advisory Op. 24 (1990).

Key parts of the New Jersey Supreme Court's decision approving of independent contracting paralegals are reproduced below.

Case Law

In Re Ethics Opinion No. 24 of the Committee on the Unauthorized Practice of Law, 607 A.2d. 962 (N.J. 1992)

GARIBALDI, J.

The New Jersey Supreme Court Committee on the Unauthorized Practice of Law (the "Committee") concluded in Advisory Opinion No.24, 126 *N.J.L.J.* 1306, 1338 (1990), that "paralegals functioning outside of the supervision of an attorney-employer are engaged in the unauthorized practice of law." Petitioners are several independent paralegals whom attorneys do not employ but retain on a temporary basis. They ask the Court to disapprove the Advisory Opinion. Like paralegals employed by attorneys, independent paralegals retained by attorneys do not offer their services directly to the public. Nonetheless, the Committee determined that independent paralegals are engaged in the unauthorized practice of law because they are performing legal services without adequate attorney supervision. We agree with the Committee that the resolution of the issue turns on whether independent paralegals are adequately super-

vised by attorneys. We disagree with the Committee, however, that the evidence supports a categorical ban on all independent paralegals in New Jersey.

I.

The Committee received inquiries from various sources regarding whether independent paralegals were engaged in the unauthorized practice of law. Pursuant to its advisory-opinion powers under *Rule* 1:22–2, the Committee solicited written comments and information from interested persons and organizations. In response, the Committee received thirty-seven letters from a wide variety of sources. Additionally, the State Bar Association's Subcommittee on Legal Assistants ("Legal Assistant Subcommittee"), the National Association of Legal Assistants ("NALA"), and the National Federation of Paralegal Associates ("NFPA") provided the Committee with information on regulation, education, certification, and the ethical responsibilities of paralegals. The Committee characterized the information that it received in two ways: first, the material expressed positive views on the value of the work performed by paralegals; second, all of the materials expressly or implicitly recognized that the work of paralegals must be performed under attorney supervision. None distinguished between paralegals employed by law firms and those functioning as independent contractors offering services to attorneys.

. . . Two attorneys appeared before the Committee. One testified that as long as attorneys supervise independent paralegals, that those paralegals do not work full-time for one attorney or firm does not matter. The second attorney, a sole practitioner, testified that independent paralegals provide many benefits to both small firms and the general public alike. The Committee, he suggested, should focus on others, known as "legal technicians" or "forms practitioners," who offer their services directly to the public, rather than on independent paralegals who do not offer their services directly to the public but who are retained by attorneys.

II.

. . . The Committee summarized its findings as follows:

When the paralegal is employed by the attorney, the nature of the employment relationship makes it possible for the attorney to make the decisions as to which matters are appropriate for handling by the paralegal and which matters require direct hands-on work by the attorney. When the attorney and the paralegal are separated both by distance and the independent nature of the paralegal's relationship with the attorney, the opportunity for the exercise of that most important judgment by the attorney becomes increasingly difficult. This is not to say that there are not matters that could be handled by an independent paralegal with appropriate supervision by the attorney contracting with the paralegal. The problem is that the decisions as to what work may be done by the parale-

gal should be the attorney's to make but the distance between attorney and paralegal mandated by the independent relationship may result in the making of those decisions by the paralegal or by default. It is the view of the Committee, moreover, that the paralegal practicing in an independent paralegal organization, removed from the attorney both by distance and relationship, presents far too little opportunity for the direct supervision necessary to justify handling those legal issues that might be delegated. Without supervision, the work of the paralegal clearly constitutes the unauthorized practice of law. We found, from the testimony and materials presented to our Committee, that the opportunity for supervision of the independent paralegal diminishes to the point where much of the work of the independent paralegal, is, in fact, unsupervised. That being the case, the independent practice by the paralegal must involve the unauthorized practice of law. The fact that some of the work might actually be directly supervised cannot justify the allowance of a system which permits the independent paralegal to work free of attorney supervision and control for such a large part of the time and for such a large part of the work. [Ibid.]

Based on those findings, the Committee concluded that attorneys are currently unable to supervise adequately the performance of independent paralegals, and that by performing legal services without such adequate supervision those paralegals are engaging in the unauthorized practice of law. Ibid. We granted petitioners' request for review,—N.J.—(1991), and the Chairperson of the Committee granted their motion to stay the enforcement of Opinion No. 24.

III.

. . . The practice of law is not subject to precise definition. It is not confined to litigation but often encompasses "legal activities in many non-litigious fields which entail specialized knowledge and ability." Therefore, the line between permissible business and professional activities and the unauthorized practice of law is often blurred. [Id. at 236, 507A.2d 711 (citations omitted).]

. . . There is no question that paralegals' work constitutes the practice of law. *N.J.SA. 2A:170–78* and *79* deem unauthorized the practice of law by a nonlawyer and make such practice a disorderly persons offense. However, *N.J.SA. 2A:170–81(f)* excepts paralegals from being penalized for engaging in tasks that constitute legal practice if their supervising attorney assumes direct responsibility for the work that the paralegals perform. *N.J.SA.2A:170–81(f)* states:

> Any person or corporation furnishing to any person lawfully engaged in the practice of law such information or such clerical assistance in and about his professional work as, except for the provisions of this article, may be lawful, but the lawyer receiving such information or service shall at all times maintain full professional and direct responsibility to his client for the information and service so rendered.

Consequently, paralegals who are supervised by attorneys do not engage in the unauthorized practice of law.

IV.

. . . New Jersey's Advisory Committee on Professional Ethics also has recognized the value of paralegals to the legal profession:

> It cannot be gainsaid that the utilization of paralegals has become, over the last 10 years, accepted, acceptable, important and indeed, necessary to the efficient practice of law. Lawyers, law firms and, more importantly, clients benefit greatly by their work. Those people who perform paraprofessionally are educated to do so. They are trained and truly professional. They are diligent and carry on their functions in a dignified, proper, professional manner. ACPE Op. 647, 126 *N.J.L.J.* 1525, 1526 (1990).

V.

No judicial, legislative, or other rule-making body excludes independent paralegals from its definition of a paralegal. For example, the ABA defines a paralegal as follows:

> A person qualified through education, training or work experience; is employed or *retained* by a lawyer,

law office, government agency, or other entity; works under the *ultimate* direction and supervision of an attorney; performs specifically delegated legal work, which, for the most part, requires a sufficient knowledge of legal concepts; and performs such duties that, absent such an assistant, the attorney would perform such tasks. (emphasis added)

The ABA definition expands the role of a legal assistant to include independent paralegals, recognizing that attorneys can and do retain the services of legal assistants who work outside the law office.

VI.

Under both federal law and New Jersey law, and under both the ABA and New Jersey ethics Rules, attorneys may delegate legal tasks to paralegals if they maintain direct relationships with their clients, supervise the paralegal's work and remain responsible for the work product. Neither case law nor statutes distinguish paralegals employed by an attorney or law firm from independent paralegals retained by an attorney or a law firm. Nor do we. Rather, the important inquiry is whether the paralegal, whether employed or retained, is working directly for the attorney, under that attorney's supervision. Safeguards against the unauthorized practice of law exist through that supervision. Realistically, a paralegal can engage in the unauthorized practice of law whether he or she is an independent paralegal or employed in a law firm. Likewise, regardless of the paralegal's status, an attorney who does not properly supervise a paralegal is in violation of the ethical Rules. Although fulfilling the ethical requirements of *RPC* 5.3 is primarily the attorney's obligation and responsibility, a paralegal is not relieved from an independent obligation to refrain from illegal conduct and to work directly under the supervision of the attorney. A paralegal who recognizes that the attorney is not directly supervising his or her work or that such supervision is illusory because the attorney knows nothing about the field in which the paralegal is working must understand that he or she is engaged in the unauthorized practice of law. In such a situation an independent paralegal must withdraw from representation of the client. The key is supervision, and that supervision must occur regardless of whether the paralegal is employed by the attorney or retained by the attorney.

We were impressed by the professionalism of the paralegals who testified before the Committee. They all understood the need for direct attorney supervision and were sensitive to potential conflict-of-interest problems. Additionally, they all recognized that as the paralegal profession continues to grow, the need to define clearly the limits of the profession's responsibilities increases.

. . . We recognize that distance between the independent paralegal and the attorney may create less opportunity for efficient, significant, rigorous supervision. Nonetheless, the site at which the paralegal performs services should not be the determinative factor. In large law firms that have satellite offices, an employed paralegal frequently has less face-to-face contact with the supervising attorney than would a retained paralegal. Moreover, in this age of rapidly-expanding instant communications (including fax tele-transmissions, word processing, computer networks, cellular telephone service and other computer-modem communications), out-of-office paralegals can communicate frequently with their supervising attorneys. Indeed, as technology progresses, there will be more communication between employers and employees located at different sites, even different states. That arrangement will be helpful to both the paralegal and the attorney. Parents and disabled people, particularly, may prefer to work from their homes. Sole practitioners and small law firms will be able to obtain the services of paralegals otherwise available only to large firms.

Moreover, nothing in the record before the Committee suggested that attorneys have found it difficult to supervise independent paralegals. Indeed, the paralegals testified that the use of word processing made an attorney's quick review of their work possible. Most of the independent contractors who testified worked under the supervision of attorneys with whom they had regular communication.

Although a paralegal's unsupervised work does constitute the unauthorized practice of law, that issue is not unique to independent paralegals. Rather, we emphasize again, it is the lack of educational and regulatory standards to govern their practice that is at the heart of the problem.

VII.

Regulation and guidelines represent the proper course of action to address the problems that the work practices of all paralegals may create. Although the paralegal is directly accountable for engaging in the unauthorized practice of law and also has an obligation to avoid conduct that otherwise violates the Rules of Professional Conduct, the attorney is ultimately accountable. Therefore, with great care, the attorney should ensure that the legal assistant is informed of and abides by the provisions of the Rules of Professional Conduct.

Although an attorney must directly supervise a paralegal, no rational basis exists for the disparate way in which the Committee's opinion treats employed and independent paralegals. The testimony overwhelmingly indicates that the independent paralegals were subject to direct supervision by attorneys and were sensitive to potential conflicts of interest. We conclude that given the appropriate instructions and supervision, paralegals, whether as employees or independent contractors, are valuable and necessary members of an attorney's team in the effective and efficient practice of law.

Subsequent to the issuance of the Committee's decision, the State Bar Association forwarded a resolution to this Court requesting the establishment of a standing committee on paralegal education and regulation. We agree that such a committee is necessary, and will shortly establish it to study the practice of paralegals and make recommendations. The committee may consider guidelines from other states, bar associations, and paralegal associations in formulating regulations for New Jersey paralegals. Any such regulations or guidelines should encourage the use of paralegals while providing both attorneys and paralegals with a set of principles that together with the Rules of Professional Conduct can guide their practices. The guidelines drafted will not be static but

subject to modification as new issues arise.

We modify Opinion No. 24 in accordance with this opinion.

Case Questions

1. Why did the Unauthorized Practice Committee decide in 1990 that independent paralegals were engaging in the unauthorized practice of law?
2. Did the court define the practice of law? Why or why not?
3. What reasons did the court give in support of its decision that paralegals in New Jersey could act as independent contractors?
4. Did the court put any limits on the role of independent contracting paralegals? Whom can independent paralegals serve?

Indiana dealt with a similar quandary. Guideline 9.1 of the Indiana Rules of Professional Conduct specifically states, "Independent legal assistants, to-wit, those not employed by a specific firm or by specific lawyers are prohibited." However, Rule 5.3 of the Indiana Rules of Professional Conduct mirrors the ABA version, and mentions in its Comment the use of "independent contractors." Dealing with the textual inconsistency, the Legal Ethics Committee of the Indiana State Bar Association concluded in 2000 that an attorney could appropriately use the services of an independent contracting paralegal as long as he or she supervised the work and otherwise complied with the Guidelines in the Indiana Rules that concern the use of paralegals. Indiana State Bar Association, Ethics Op. 3 (2000). However, as is the case with this Indiana ethics opinions, all ethics opinions are only advisory and do not have the force of law. Therefore, it could be said that independent contracting paralegals could only safely operate in those jurisdictions where statutes or case law authorize such endeavors.

ETHICS 2000 AND THE UNAUTHORIZED PRACTICE OF LAW

Proposal by the Ethics 2000 Commission

The Ethics 2000 Commission substantially revised Model Rule 5.5. MR 5.5(b), which concerns assisting a non-lawyer in the unauthorized practice of law, has been changed to 5.5(c), and has been revised to say that a lawyer shall not assist "another person" rather than "a person who is not a member of the bar." This change was made to simplify the unauthorized practice rule and to make it apply to assisting lawyers admitted to practice in another jurisdiction, as well as non-lawyers. There are many new Comments to MR 5.5, including a new sentence in one Comment that implicates the use of independent contracting paralegals as well as the allowance of limited, legal services providers: "Lawyers may assist independent nonlawyers authorized by the law of a jurisdiction to provide particular legal services, for example, paraprofessionals authorized to provide some kinds of legal services."

The other revisions to MR 5.5 and its Comments concern adding new sections that specifically address lawyers practicing law in jurisdictions other than where they are licensed.

Action Taken by the ABA House of Delegates

The House of Delegates took no action on adopting or rejecting the revised 5.5 because the ABA Commission on Multijurisdictional Practice is examining that rule as part of its own work.

Summary

The practice of law is allowed only for licensed attorneys not under suspension. What constitutes practicing law is usually defined by case law, although some jurisdictions have statutes or rules of court that define it and all jurisdictions have statutes that prohibit the unauthorized practice of law, making it a crime. Certain actions are commonly considered the practice of law: representing someone in court; representing someone before an administrative agency in an adjudication; giving legal advice; drafting or completing legal documents; negotiating on behalf of someone where that person's legal rights are involved; and carrying on the business aspects of a law practice.

The unauthorized practice of law is committed when a non-lawyer engages in activities that can only be done by licensed attorneys, when a legal assistant exceeds his or her authority as defined by the rules of professional conduct, and also when a paralegal engages in otherwise appropriate activities that are unsupervised by the delegating attorney. The rules of ethics list three activities that paralegals are specifically prohibited from performing: giving legal advice, establishing the attorney-client relationship, and establishing fees. The giving of legal advice occurs when one applies legal principles to a specific set of facts. Although paralegals may engage in initial client interviews, they may not say or do anything that gives the impression that a lawyer-client relationship has been established. Paralegals should be careful when answering client questions about fees that no statements are made that appear to create a fee arrangement.

Other additional activities that legal assistants are not allowed to perform include representing others in court, conducting depositions, representing others in legal mediations, executing wills, conducting real estate closings, representing others in administrative proceedings, and signing pleadings and other litigation documents. However, some jurisdictions make limited exceptions to the above-named prohibitions.

All of the national rules of ethics dedicated for the use of legal assistants authorize them to perform a variety of substantive legal functions, as long as those functions are properly delegated and supervised by attorneys who maintain responsibility for the work product. Such activities include client interviewing, trial preparation, case management, and legal research and writing.

Federal law provides that federal agencies may allow non-lawyers, including paralegals, to represent clients in administrative adjudications. At the state level, some administrative practice by non-lawyers is also allowed. Where federal and state laws allow a non-lawyer to represent others before administrative agencies, such representation is conditioned on the non-lawyer representatives meeting certain educational or experiential prerequisites. Local rules of court and local bar association guidelines might also allow paralegals to engage in other court-approved activities.

Independent paralegals may only directly serve the public in ways that are specifically authorized by law or in ministerial functions such as typing services or document preparation. Some statutes even allow non-lawyers to render certain law-related services to the public. However, such services generally prohibit these legal services providers from helping their customers decide what best suits their legal needs. Some jurisdictions, however, allow legal assistants to be employed as independent contractors to law firms as long as there is appropriate lawyer supervision of the contracted work, as well as lawyer responsibility for the work product. And the Ethics 2000 version of Model Rule 5.5 now includes a new Comment that implies an approval of lawyers using the services of independent contracting paralegals, although the ABA House of Delegates made no decision on it.

Points to Ponder

1. After rereading the chapter's opening vignette, what advice would you give Sarah concerning how she could help her friends yet remain ethical?
2. After examining your jurisdiction's Admission and Discipline Rules, determine if any allowances are made for law students to practice law on a limited basis.
3. What activities are most associated with the practice of law and therefore only allowed to be performed by lawyers?
4. What does it mean to give legal advice?
5. What rules in the ABA Model Rules of Professional Conduct affect the unauthorized practice of law?
6. What attorney rules of ethics in your jurisdiction affect the unauthorized practice of law? Are they different from either the ABA Model Rules or ABA Model Code?
7. Does your jurisdiction incorporate into its set of rules the ABA Model Guidelines for the Utilization of Legal Assistant Services?
8. In what two ways could a paralegal's conduct, even if technically accurate, be considered the unauthorized practice of law?
9. Does your state define the practice of law by statute?
10. Why do you think the ABA did not act on the recommendations of the 1995 committee appointed to examine the changing role of non-lawyer practice?
11. What does it mean to establish the attorney-client relationship or to establish fees?
12. What kinds of activities could a paralegal in a sole practitioner's office do while the attorney is on vacation?
13. Do you think the law should prohibit non-lawyers from assisting others who are representing themselves in court?
14. Why is a paralegal not allowed to take a deposition?
15. Does your jurisdiction allow non-lawyers to conduct real estate closings?
16. Why is it said that what occurs in an administrative agency adjudication is quasi-judicial?
17. What determines whether a non-lawyer is allowed to represent someone before an administrative agency?
18. Does your jurisdiction allow non-lawyers to represent others before any administrative agencies?

19. Does your jurisdiction have any local court rules that authorized paralegals to engage in any legal acts?
20. What kinds of problems can occur when non-lawyers are allowed to provide limited legal services to the public?
21. What advantages occur when legal assistants are allowed to act as independent contractors to lawyers?
22. Does your jurisdiction allow the use of independent contracting paralegals?

Key Concepts

Administrative agency adjudication

Alternative Dispute Resolution

Arbitration

Establishing fees

Establishing the attorney-client relationship

Giving legal advice

Independent contracting paralegal/legal assistant

Mediation

Practice of law

Pro se representation

Real estate closing

Unauthorized practice of law (UPL)

Will execution

Key Terms

adjudication	memorandum of law	positive law
alternative dispute resolution (ADR)	misdemeanor	pro se
	motions	real estate closing
independent contractor	original jurisdiction	surety bond
mediation	pleadings	trust account

Chapter 4

Confidentiality

[F]ew love a spokesman for the despised and the damned.

—Clarence Darrow, one of America's
greatest criminal defense lawyers

*Of course people are getting smarter nowadays; they are letting
lawyers, instead of their conscience, be their guides.*

—Will Rogers, humorist

INTRODUCTION

While working on a criminal case, Rachel came across some information that she regretted having found. The firm's client, William, has been accused of sexual assault; the trial is to begin in a few weeks. William is accused of sexually assaulting a woman he met in a hotel bar, while at an out-of-town convention. William claims that they engaged in consensual sex, which makes his testimony critical. While going through William's files, Rachel sees a reference to another file and its file number. Rachel tracks down that file and opens it to discover that William has, on two prior occasions within the last eight years, paid large sums of money to women who accused him of "acquaintance rape." Both cases involved William meeting women in a club or a bar while on trips out of the state. Although William was never brought to trial, he was sued each time and reached settlements with both women. Copies of the settlements in the file, which were drafted by Rachel's boss, require each woman not to ever discuss the facts of the dispute or the amount of money she received. Rachel now cannot stand to look at William, believing that he is a serial rapist. She knows the prosecuting attorney will never learn about these two incidents, but she believes if that information came to light, it might help establish a modus operandi (habitual method of procedure). Rachel is considering making an anonymous tip to the prosecuting attorney's office about these other incidents because she fears that William will get away with another assault. Should she do this? If not, is there anything else she can or should do?

One of the hallmarks of the legal profession is its formalized respect for the sanctity of communications between clients and their attorneys. As with doctor-patient and priest-penitent relationships, it is common knowledge that an attorney will not, and indeed may not, disclose to the client's disadvantage what the client tells the attorney. This chapter will explore the concept of lawyer-client confidentiality, which is found in two related bodies of law. First, there will be a discussion of the professional responsibility rules that concern the duty of confidentiality, including when that duty arises, its extension to the legal assistant and what exceptions would allow an attorney to disclose confidential information.

Connected to the duty of confidentiality is the attorney-client privilege, which is generally found in statutes on witness competency and prohibits attorneys from testifying against their clients. The attorney client privilege also takes shape in what is known as the work product rule, which is found in the rules of civil procedure and concerns the nondisclosure of certain kinds of **discovery** material. This chapter will explain the nature of the attorney-client privilege and the work product rule, and why paralegals need to be aware of its ramifications when working on discovery matters. Finally, this chapter will discuss inadvertent disclosure—what happens when protected attorney-client materials are accidentally turned over to the other party.

discovery—A pre-trial procedure used in litigation where parties gain information from each other. Discovery is designed to promote open disclosure of relevant evidence and is supposed to operate without court involvement.

THE DUTY OF CONFIDENTIALITY

The protection provided by the duty of confidentiality has many facets. First, there is the comfort that comes from knowing that what one says to his or her lawyer is private. That knowledge helps clients overcome some of the fear associated with talking about their problems, embarrassments, or mistakes. Beyond the fear factor, there are practical benefits that accrue when clients fully disclose information to their attorneys. As specialists, lawyers need all the facts before them to best assess whether a client's situation is actually a legal problem or, if so, how extensive the legal problem is. If clients only told their attorneys those things the clients thought were relevant or important, then their hired experts would be hindered from working effectively on their behalf. Whether a lawyer's activities fall into the categories of problem avoidance (estate planning or contract drafting) or of problem solving (litigation), both activities require uninhabited fact gathering before proceeding and neither activity can be carried out as anticipated by the client without full disclosure with the attorney.

Distinctions between the Confidentiality Rules of the Model Rules and Those of the Model Code

The starting point for the duty of confidentiality is ABA Model Rule 1.6, wherein, in section (a), it states, "A lawyer shall not reveal information relating to representation of a client unless the client consents after consultation, except for disclosures that are impliedly authorized in order to carry out the representation, and except as stated in paragraph (b)." The Model Rule differs from the Model Code's confidentiality rule in

Model Rule 1.6	DR 4–101
• covers all client information, regardless of the source and when the lawyer acquires it	• covers the client's confidences and secrets gained in the lawyer-client relationship
• generally covers client statements made in the presence of third parties	• generally does not cover client statements made in the presence of third parties
• has an implied attorney-representation exception	• has no implied attorney-representation exception
• has no exception that specifically concerns collecting fees	• has an exception that specifically concerns collecting fees
• allows disclosure to prevent client criminality only if criminality is likely to result in imminent death or substantial bodily harm	• allows disclosure to prevent client criminality for any crime

Exhibit 4-1   The Model Rules vs. the Model Code: Confidentiality

that DR 4–101 prohibits the disclosure of only such information as is "gained in" the lawyer-client relationship that the client either has asked be kept confidential or "the disclosure of which would be embarrassing or would be likely to be detrimental to the client." This distinction is important because, under MR 1.6, all information relating to the representation starts out as being confidential, from whatever the source, and this includes information the lawyer may have acquired from any source, even before having entered into a professional relationship with the client (Exhibit 4–1).

The following case is an example of the broader protection provided to clients in jurisdictions that have adopted ABA MR 1.6.

Case Law

In Re Anonymous, 654 N.E.2d 1128 (Ind. 1995)

PER CURIAM.

The respondent has been charged by the Disciplinary Commission in a verified complaint for disciplinary action with violating Rules 1.6 (a), 1.8 (b), and 1.16 (a)(1) of the *Rules of Professional Conduct for Attorneys at Law.* The Commission and the respondent now tender for this Court's approval a statement of circumstances and conditional agreement for discipline, pursuant to Ind.Admission and Discipline Rule 23, Section 11 (g). In their agreement, the parties agree that the proper sanction for the respondent's misconduct is a private reprimand and that the facts and circumstances of this case

should be set forth in an anonymous opinion to educate the Bar. We approve the parties' agreement, and herein more fully set forth the facts and circumstances of this case.

As stipulated by the parties, the respondent was contacted by an individual (the "mother") in April or May of 1994 about representing her in seeking a child support arrearage due to her from the father ("father") of her minor child. She supplied the respondent with records concerning her support action and her income. Also included in these documents was information regarding the father, including the fact that he was going to receive a substantial inheritance, his salary, his place of employment, and his address. In the course of reviewing the documents supplied by the mother, the respondent discovered that on July 17, 1992, a judgment had been entered against the mother and father, making them jointly liable for almost $4,500 of medical and hospital debt resulting from the birth of their child. The judgment was in favor of the local county welfare department. The respondent was, at all times relevant to this proceeding, the attorney under contract to represent the local county welfare department.

The respondent contacted the mother to determine if the medical debt owed to the welfare department had been paid by either her or the father. It had not. The respondent then informed the mother that he would be unable to represent her in the case because of a conflict of interest, then forwarded her documents, at her request, to another attorney. Thereafter, the respondent received approval from the local county welfare department to file a collection suit against the father, which he did on April 26, 1994. Later, the father's counsel joined the mother as a party defendant in the collection suit. The respondent ultimately obtained a summary judgment against the mother and the father. The respondent did not withdraw from the case after the mother was joined as a party defendant.

We find that, by revealing information relating to the representation of the mother without her consent, the respondent violated Ind.Professional Conduct Rule 1.6(a). By using that information to her disadvantage without her consent, he violated Prof.Cond.R. 1.8(b). By failing to withdraw as counsel for the local welfare department during the collection suit against the mother when such representation violated the *Rules of Professional Conduct,* the respondent violated Prof. Cond.R. 1.16(a)(1).

The respondent and the Commission agree that several factors mitigate the severity of his misconduct. They agree that the information gained by the respondent about the mother's case was readily available from public sources and not confidential in nature. The respondent declined to represent the mother after he learned of her outstanding debt owed to the county welfare department, and advised her to seek other counsel. He did not at any time request that she sign an employment agreement, seek a retainer fee, or otherwise charge her. We see no evidence of selfish motive on the respondent's part.

The respondent's use of information gained during consultations with the mother represents misuse of information entrusted to him in his capacity as a lawyer. Such conduct not only threatens harm to the individuals involved, but also erodes the integrity of the profession. At the same time, we note that the respondent appears to have had no sinister motives. For these reasons, we accept the agreed sanction of a private reprimand.

Case Questions

1. What information did the lawyer learn about the mother that the court considered confidential?
2. Why would it have been confidential if it did not relate to the mother's claim against the father for back child support?
3. Notice that this case also involves a conflict of interest, which is the subject of Chapter 5. With that in mind, why do you think the lawyer's conduct implicated a conflict of interest if he ceased representing the mother, never even charging her a fee, before representing the county welfare department against the father?

MR 1.6 leaves no room for the attorney to speculate as to whether divulging client information would be detrimental or embarrassing to the client. In a Wisconsin case, an attorney working on a corporate acquisition for a client purchased shares in the company his client was going to acquire, and then later sold those shares at a profit. Such an act violated not only laws against insider trading, but also the duty of confidentiality, even though no allegation was made that the corporate client was harmed by the attorney's purchase of the acquiring company's stock. *In re Marick,* 554 N.W.2d 204 (Wis. 1996).

MR 1.6 is also broader than DR 4–101 in that the former gives the attorney implied authority to divulge information that is necessary to the representation, whereas the latter requires that information be divulged only after the client consents. For instance, in a settlement negotiation with an insurance company, a plaintiff's lawyer practicing in a Model Rules–based jurisdiction would not need the client's permission to detail the extent of his or her injuries or complications from those injuries in order to improve the likelihood of settlement or increase his or her recovery. Another kind of authorized disclosure occurs when an attorney discusses client matters with another member of the firm unless the client specifically has requested that certain information not be discussed with other members of the firm.

One aspect of client confidentiality that tends to bother the general public is when a lawyer knows facts about a past crime that might bring resolution to the community or the victim's family but fails to disclose that information. Although unjust in the eyes of the public, it is fundamental to the doctrine of confidentiality that attorneys, and their employees, refuse to reveal information relating to their clients' past criminal conduct.

When Does the Duty of Confidentiality Arise?

Clearly, the duty of confidentiality attaches to the attorney-client relationship, once it is established, but it also applies before a client has signed a fee agreement or paid a **retainer**. It would certainly be destructive to the policy behind confidentiality to leave unprotected those statements made by prospective clients in the course of seeking representation, but before a lawyer has agreed to take the case.

But what if the lawyer does not take the client's case or the client chooses another lawyer? When a prospective client consults an attorney in good faith for the purposes of seeking assistance or representation, the duty of confidentiality may arise even if the attorney declines representation or does nothing on behalf of the would-be client. *See* ABA Commission on Ethics and Professional Responsibility, Formal Op. 90–358 (1990); *Gilmore v. Goedecke,* 954 F. Supp. 187 (E.D. Mo. 1996) (in that case, a firm was disqualified from defending its long-standing client in an age discrimination suit because the plaintiff had called a lawyer in the firm and discussed the matter by phone). If, however, a prospective client consults an attorney simply for the purpose of disqualifying that attorney (or firm), such shrewdness will not necessarily result in a finding that such a consultation was protected. Imagine if, after the presidential election of 2000, former vice president Al Gore visited Theodore Olson (who would later represent then-governor George W. Bush before the United States Supreme Court) to discuss retaining Mr. Olson in any future election litigation. If such a visit were made in order to disqualify Mr. Olson when Governor Bush retained him, it would be unlikely that a court would

retainer—A payment, similar to an advance, made to an attorney, which is made to secure the lawyer's availability. When a retainer is called a general retainer, it is usually nonrefundable because the lawyer has earned the retainer upon payment. When a retainer is called a special retainer, it is usually a refundable payment, much like an advance. See Chapter 7.

find the initial Gore-Olson consultation to be worthy of invoking the confidentiality doctrine. That kind of conflict will be discussed in Chapter 5.

For How Long Does the Duty of Confidentiality Apply?

Near the end of the movie *The Firm*, Tom Cruise's character, Mitch McDeere, uses a brilliant simile to explain to the mafia boss, whom Mitch unwittingly represents, how the ethics rule of confidentiality will protect the Mafioso from the Justice Department's prosecution of Mitch's firm, and thereby protect Mitch from the Mafioso's inclination to kill him. Mitch compares himself—as long as he is alive—to a ship carrying a cargo that will never reach port.

The attorney's duty of confidentiality is a **fiduciary** duty based on loyalty. It is not simply an obligation based on contract law, in which the obligations contracting parties have toward one another usually end when both parties have performed their part of the bargain. Unless an exception applies, the lawyer's duty of confidentiality survives the representation of the client. The **Restatement** (Second) of Agency § 396 (1957) put it this way: "The confidences communicated by a client to his attorney must remain inviolate for all time if the public is to have reverence for the law and confidence in its guarantees." This duty generally continues beyond the death of the client, or former client, unless limited exceptions can be found, such as if the information needed is sought in connection with a criminal matter and the party seeking disclosure of the privileged information has met its high burden of showing need for the information. *In re Sealed Case*, 107 F.3d 46 (D.C. Cir. 1997).

fiduciary—One who has a legal duty to act in the best interests of another. Lawyers are fiduciaries to their clients, as parents are to their minor children.

Restatement—Unified, systematic statements on the common law, created by the American Law Institute. There are many restatements, including the Restatement of Contracts, the Restatement of Agency, and the Restatement of Torts.

Do the Principles of Confidentiality Apply to the Lawyer's Employees?

The short answer is yes, the principles of confidentiality do apply. As a general principle, all the rules of professional responsibility apply to all non-lawyer assistants of the lawyer. Model Rule 5.3(a) requires partners in a law firm to ensure that their non-lawyer employees conduct themselves in conformity with all the obligations of lawyers, and MR 5.3(b) makes those lawyers who supervise non-lawyer employees specifically responsible to ensure that the conduct of all their employees is compatible with the same obligations as those of lawyers. The Comments to MR 5.3 specifically mention that lawyers should warn their nonlawyer employees about their obligation not to breech the duty of confidentiality. The ABA Model Code originally expressed the same idea concerning non-lawyer employees and their duty to keep client confidences, in DR 4–101(D). In a Pennsylvania case, a defendant was convicted of first-degree murder, in part because the district attorney subpoenaed the defense attorney's secretary who received the phone call from the defendant in which the defendant said to the secretary, "I just committed a homicide. I have to talk to Sam [the attorney]." On appeal, the court ruled that the statement to the secretary was privileged communication because it was made for the purposes of seeking legal advice. *Pennsylvania v. Mrozek*, 657 A.2d 997 (Pa. 1995). (There is much more on the attorney-client privilege and how it applies to statements made to paralegals in a later section, "The Attorney-Client Privilege: Related to the Duty of Confidentiality.")

Specifically, the obligation of confidentiality applies to legal assistants. Guideline 6 of the ABA Model Guidelines for the Utilization of Legal Assistant Services makes lawyers responsible to ensure that legal assistants keep client confidences. The NALA Code of Ethics, Canon 7, requires legal assistants to "protect the confidences of a client," and Rule 1.5 of the NFPA Model Disciplinary Rules and Ethical Considerations states: "A paralegal shall preserve all confidential information provided by the client or acquired from other sources before, during, and after the course of the professional relationship." This standard would require a member of the NFPA to treat as confidential any information relating to a former client that has come to that paralegal's attention after the client has ceased using the services of the paralegal's firm (which will usually mean the information has come from a third party). An interesting example of the tension between lawyer rules of ethics and paralegal association rules of ethics can be found in EC 1.5(d), which establishes the circumstances under which a paralegal may disclose confidential information. Although it closely mirrors the exceptions of the ABA Model Rules, its client-consent exception covers consent made in writing, a standard not used in the Model Rules or the Model Code.

How Is Confidentiality Affected When the Client Is an Organization?

When the client is a person, confidentiality issues are relatively straightforward. However, when the client is an organization, such as a corporation, a discussion about client confidentiality is a bit more layered, and is also affected by conflicts of interest issues, which are the subject of Chapter 5. First, it is important to understand the role of the **constituent**: organizations have constituents, including directors, officers, employees, and shareholders. When a lawyer represents an organization, it is generally the case that the organization is the beneficiary of client confidentiality because the organization itself is the client, rather than the various constituents. Second, since corporations are inanimate creations, they can only act through their authorized agents, usually the board of directors or high-ranking executive officers.

For instance, if a high-ranking employee told the company's attorney about illegal corporate activities in which the employee had engaged, the attorney would not violate the duty of confidentiality by telling such a secret to the corporation's president or board of directors. *See* D.C. Bar Legal Ethics Comm. Op. 269 (1997). However, if a third party, such as the government, wanted that the attorney to divulge what the employee told the attorney, the attorney-client privilege (which is explained later in this chapter) would generally protect against such disclosure. The

constituent—A part of something else that is a distinct entity.

leading case in the area of attorney-client privilege in the corporate environment is *Upjohn v. United States*, 449 U.S. 383 (1981), in which the United States Supreme Court held that what a corporation's employee told the corporation's lawyer in connection with a corporation-directed investigation was protected by the attorney-client privilege. Anyone working as a legal assistant at an in-house, corporate legal department needs to bear in mind that information derived from various constituents is confidential with respect to the organization, but not necessarily confidential with respect to other constituents of the organization, such as corporate officers.

Are Certain Kinds of Client Information Considered Not Confidential?

Under ABA Model Code DR 4–101, information was considered confidential if (a) it was made in the course of the lawyer-client relationship and (b) the client requested that the information be kept confidential or the information if released would be embarrassing or detrimental to the client. That standard places a stronger burden on the client and provides more protection to lawyers and their legal assistants accused of violating the rule of confidentiality. Model Rule 1.6 is more expansive, not treating either the nature of the client information, its source, or the date when the lawyer becomes aware of it, as being controlling in determining whether such information must be kept confidential.

Statements Made in the Presence of Third Parties

One of the more puzzling aspects of confidentiality concerns a case where a client, or prospective client, says something that generally would be thought of as confidential but says it in the presence of someone else—someone not governed by this duty. For instance, if a prospective client brings a friend to the lawyer's office as an emotional support, it is possible that what the prospective client tells the lawyer will not be covered by the attorney-client privilege. This is because a court could consider that the statements were never originally confidential since the speaker made them in the presence of the third party. Although the lawyer would still be subject to discipline for voluntarily repeating the statements, he or she could be subpoenaed to testify about what was said. For example, in a Minnesota case, a divorce lawyer met with a husband and wife to discuss the financial ramifications of their divorce. Later, when the husband was tried for his wife's murder, the lawyer was called as a witness to testify about what was said in that discussion. On appeal, the husband argued that his lawyer's testimony was a violation of the attorney-client privilege. However, the court disagreed, finding that, since only the husband was the lawyer's client, what was said in the office that day was not protected by attorney-client privilege because of the presence of the wife. *State v. Rhodes*, 627 N.W.2d 24 (Minn. 2001). Moreover, a third party, who would obviously not be affected by the duty of confidentiality or the attorney-client privilege, could certainly testify about what was discussed between a lawyer and a client.

The following concerns a famous celebrity murder case. Jean Harris was accused of murdering her boyfriend, Dr. Herman Tarnower, the author of the national bestseller *The Scarsdale Diet*. The case created many national headlines, and the appeal concerned, in part, the problem with talking to one's lawyer but doing so in a public way.

Case Law

People v. Harris, 442 N.E.2d 1205 (N.Y. 1982)

GABRIELLI, J.

Defendant, Jean Harris, was convicted, following a jury trial, of murder in the second degree and criminal possession of a weapon in the second and third degrees. This appeal presents for our consideration several purported errors occurring during the course of that trial, which defendant urges mandate reversal of the judgment of conviction. Inasmuch as our resolution of these issues leads us to the conclusion that reversible error was not committed, there should be an affirmance.

Defendant's trial for murder arose out of the shooting death of Dr. Herman Tarnower in his home on March 10, 1980. The People's case proceeded on the theory that Mrs. Harris, who had been Dr. Tarnower's paramour and companion for nearly 14 years, went to his home on the evening of the shooting and, acting out of jealous rage over the doctor's relationship with a younger woman, deliberately shot and killed him. One of the prosecution's witnesses, Dr. Tarnower's house manager, testified to the difficulties that had resulted from the doctor's relationships with the two women. Mrs. Harris's oral statements, testified to by the police officers who were investigating the shooting, were also relied upon as evidence of her motivation in going to the Tarnower estate on the evening of the shooting. The prosecution also utilized the so-called "Scarsdale letter," written by Mrs. Harris to the doctor over the weekend prior to his death, as strong evidence of Mrs. Harris's state of mind. In

this letter, which contained several unflattering references to the younger woman in Dr. Tarnower's life, Mrs. Harris described her feelings of anguish and rejection over the doctor's apparent preference for this younger woman.

The defense theory was that Mrs. Harris, physically agitated by the lack of medication she had been taking for some time and suffering from recent failures and disappointments in her professional life, had determined that she wanted to end her life. Intending to see Dr. Tarnower once more before she died, Mrs. Harris drove to his home on March 10, hoping only to speak with him for a few moments. She entered the doctor's home and went into his bedroom, where she found him sleeping. Mrs. Harris was unable to rouse the doctor in order to have a conversation with him. Apparently upset by his lack of responsiveness and the presence of the belongings of the other woman in the bathroom, Mrs. Harris decided to kill herself there in the doctor's bedroom. According to Mrs. Harris, as she attempted to carry out her desire, the doctor, who had by now awakened, tried to prevent her from shooting herself. Several struggles ensued, during which Mrs. Harris's gun discharged, shooting Dr. Tarnower and inflicting four gunshot wounds from which he died. Evidence concerning Mrs. Harris's version of these events and her state of mind on the night of the shooting and previously thereto was presented largely through the testimony of Mrs. Harris herself. The defense also relied upon a will and certain letters, written by Mrs. Harris just prior to her departure for the Tarnower estate on March 10, to demonstrate her belief that she would never return to her home, because she intended to end her life. In addition, the defense offered a number of witnesses who testified that Mrs. Harris had indeed been distraught over recent events occurring in connection with her position as headmistress of the Madeira School. . . .

I

On the night of her arrest at the Tarnower residence, defendant made a statement over the telephone to her attorney. She contends that the introduction into evidence of that statement, testified to by a police officer who overheard it, violated her right to counsel under the Constitution of this State. It appears that Mrs. Harris, having been read her *Miranda* rights several times, having waived those rights and made statements to the police officers who were investigating the shooting, was thereafter asked if she would like to make a telephone call. Mrs. Harris responded that she would like to call a lawyer friend. After an attempt to make this call at a nearby telephone was unsuccessful, one of the officers, Lieutenant Flick, went into the house manager's bedroom to place the call for Mrs. Harris. When the lieutenant reached Mrs. Harris's party, he left the bedroom to so inform her. Officer Tamilio, at Lieutenant Flick's request, assisted Mrs. Harris to the bedroom. When they entered the room, the house manager's husband was already there, standing a few feet from the telephone. Immediately upon picking up the telephone, Mrs. Harris made the statement: "Oh, my God, I think I've killed Hy." Its admission into evidence is now challenged.

It is clear that, at the time Mrs. Harris made this statement, her right to counsel had attached by virtue of her request to speak with an attorney (*People v. Cunningham,* 49 N.Y.2d 203). Once the right to counsel had been invoked, no further questioning of Mrs. Harris would have been per-

missible, unless she had affirmatively waived her rights in the presence of her attorney (*People v. Rogers,* 48 N.Y.2d 167; *People v. Hobson,* 39 N.Y.2d 479). Notwithstanding this rule, statements made by a defendant who has invoked the right to counsel may nevertheless be admissible at trial if they were made spontaneously. In order for such statements to be characterized as spontaneous, it must "be shown that they were in no way the product of an 'interrogation environment,' the result of 'express questioning or its functional equivalent'" (*People v. Stoesser,* 53 N.Y.2d 648, 650). . . .

Although we hold today that a statement properly characterized as spontaneous is no less so simply because it was made to an attorney, a further aspect of the admissibility of such statements should be considered. Given that the communication received in evidence was made to an attorney, the attorney-client privilege is implicated, in addition to the right to counsel. This privilege protects those communications made by a defendant to an attorney that are intended to be confidential (*People v. Buchanan,* 145 N.Y. 1; *Baumann v. Steingester,* 213 N.Y. 328). It cannot be said, on the facts of this case, that Mrs. Harris, in speaking over the telephone to a lawyer in the known presence of both a police officer and the house manager's husband, intended this communication to be confidential. Generally, communications made in the presence of third parties, whose presence is known to the defendant, are not privileged from disclosure (see Richardson, Evidence [10th ed], § 413; 8 Wigmore, Evidence [McNaughton rev], § 2311). We see no reason to depart from this general rule simply because one of those parties present was a police officer, who, as has been noted, did nothing to purposely overhear the conversation or conceal his presence from defendant. Thus, we conclude that defendant's attorney-client privilege was not violated by the officer testimony regarding this communication and that the testimony was properly admitted by the trial court. . . .

Case Questions

1. What reason was given why the statement Ms. Harris clearly made to her lawyer was not covered by the attorney-client privilege?
2. Do you think Ms. Harris was aware that she was waiving the attorney-client privilege by talking on the phone to her lawyer in the presence of others?
3. Is it unfair to say that there was no cloak of confidentiality surrounding her statement since she was in police custody and had invoked her right to counsel, and since she knew she was talking to her lawyer?

In the following case, on the other hand, the court takes the view that there are occasions where statements made by third parties to lawyers can be considered as confidential statements, and thus protected by the attorney-client privilege.

Case Law

Palomba v. Sullivan, 1998 WL 928392 (Conn. Super. Ct. 1998)

PELLEGRINO, J.

The Plaintiff's decedent, Carla Palomba (hereinafter Plaintiff), a passenger in an automobile, died as result of injuries sustained in an accident when the automobile she was riding in collided with another automobile. The instant action was instituted against both the drivers and the owners of the vehicles involved in the accident. This motion for protective order follows a deposition of Candice Palomba, a non-party who is the sister of the Plaintiff.

At the deposition, Candice Palomba was asked by counsel for one of the Defendants about conversations at a meeting attended by herself, attorney Bruce Diamond, her mother Judith Palomba and her sister Crystal Palomba. The meeting was held prior to the commencement of this action. Mr. Diamond represents that he acted as legal counsel for the entire Palomba family, including Candice Palomba, during the meeting. Candice Palomba has invoked the attorney-client privilege in refusing to answer questions, at the deposition, as to whether attorney Diamond

had given her any information about the accident during the meeting.

"The attorney-client privilege protects communications between client and attorney when made in confidence for the purpose of seeking or giving legal advice." *Ullmann v. State*, 230 Conn. 698, 711, 647 A.2d 324 (1994). "Whether a communication is privileged is a question of law for the trial court." *Miller v. Anderson*, 30 Conn. Sup. 501, 505, 294 A.2d 344 (App. Div. 1972). "[An] . . . initial consultation between the defendant and his trial counsel . . . [may fall] within the scope of the privileged communication. *The client may not be required to divulge the advice which his attorney gave him*" (Emphasis added.) (*Id.*, 505.)

"When two or more people consult an attorney together on a matter of joint interest, these competing considerations are normally resolved by allowing their communications to be privileged as to the outside world, though not as to each other in a later controversy between themselves." *State v. Cascone*, 195 Conn. 183, 186–87, 487 A.2d 186 (1985).

"... [A] direct communication from a client to his attorney either made in or sent to the attorney's office; in such a case, relatively little factual foundation would ordinarily be required to establish the privilege and, so, the inadmissibility of any question concerning the subject matter of the communication." *State v. Hanna*, 150 Conn. 457, 467, 191 A.2d 124 (1963). "[E]ven if [an attorney] never communicated specific legal opinions . . . that fact would not change the nature of the attorney-client relationship. . . . It is not the rendering of legal advice that establishes the attorney-client relationship. If that were the case, the initial communications between the client and attorney, those that are often the most sensitive and most in need of confidentiality, would be unprotected. Rather it is the client's seeking of legal advice . . . that establishes the relationship. . . ." *Shew v. Freedom of Information Comm.*, Superior Court, judicial district of Hartford/New Britain at Hartford, Docket No. 539639, 15 CONN. L. RPTR. 309 (September 19, 1995) (Maloney, J.), affirmed on other grounds, 245 Conn. 149, (1998).

Connecticut's courts have addressed similar factual circumstances as the one presented in the instant case in terms of the presence of a third party during an attorney-client conversation. In *Grodovich v. Immediate Medical Care, CTR*, Superior Court, judicial district of Hartford/New Britain at Hartford, Docket No. 515617, 12 CONN. L. RPTR. 234 (August 4, 1994) (Wagner, J.), the court addressed an issue wherein "the plaintiff now moves to compel [the defendant] to disclose matters he discussed with his insurance representative in the presence of his attorney, the defendants objecting to that motion on the basis of attorney-client privileges." (*Id.*) The court held that

> [i]n the present case, the expectation of privacy continues. . . . The legal and economic interests of the defendants and the insurance company are so thoroughly intertwined, that the mere presence of the insurance agent does not cause the privilege to be waived, but the privilege continues to protect the confidentiality of the communications.

In this case, the members of the Palomba family sought legal advice from Attorney Diamond concerning the death of their sister, the Plaintiff in this action. Those communications are privileged and therefore the court will grant the Plaintiff's motion for protective order.

Case Questions

1. On what legal theory does the court find that the statements the sister of the decedent made to the attorney were confidential and, therefore, covered by the attorney-client privilege?
2. Who is the client here?
3. Based on the court's reasoning, and assuming the sister had a boyfriend, would the result be the same if the sister had brought her boyfriend to the initial meeting? If the sister had told her boyfriend about what happened that day in the lawyer's office, could the boyfriend be deposed about what the sister told him?

The Client's Identity

The client's identity can be considered information that is not confidential, but not without exception. Generally, the client's identity is a fact that, in and of itself, does not qualify as protected information. See *In re Subpoena to Testify before Grand Jury*, 39 F.3d 973 (9th Cir. 1994), a case where a lawyer was required to divulge the identity of a client who happened to give the attorney a counterfeit

$100 dollar bill. In circumstances where revealing the client's identity can convey information that is privileged, such as acknowledging guilt that would have led the client to seek legal advice, this can serve as the basis for rightfully withholding the client's identity. *In re Grand Jury Subpoena*, 976 F.2d 1314, 1317 (9th Cir. 1992). In a Delaware case, a client accusing her lawyer of wrongful sexual advances was denied, on the grounds of confidentiality, the right to access the lawyer's client list. *Brett v. Barques*, 706 A.2d 509 (Del. 1998).

The Client's Location

prima facie—On its face, or on the surface.

Where a client is located can also be desired information, particularly if he or she is a parent in a custody dispute and has gone into hiding with the children who are the subject of the dispute. A client's location is information that is received in the course of representation, so it is, **prima facie**, protected information. However, lawyers must abide by the final orders of a court, and if, for instance, a court orders a lawyer to divulge the location of the client—and the lawyer has exhausted all available appeals—the lawyer is then required to disclose the otherwise confidential information, but on as limited a basis as possible. *See* ABA Comm. On Ethics and Professional Responsibility, Formal Op. 94–385 (1994).

Fee Arrangements

Fee arrangements made between clients and their lawyers are usually not considered to be confidential information. One exception to that is the doctrine of "last link," which also applies to client identity controversies. This doctrine stems from a famous case, *Baird v. Koerner*, 279 F.2d 623 (9th Cir. 1960), and holds that if otherwise unprotected information would, if disclosed, serve as the last link to implicate the client in criminal activity, then that information is protected. When insurance companies are third-party payers of the client's legal bill, they often want the legal fees audited. Many state ethics committees are opposed to such transfer of billing information without client consent, on the grounds that such disclosure would compromise attorney-client confidentiality and could disclose legal strategies. Alaska Bar Ethics Commission, Op. 99–1 (1999); D.C. Bar Legal Ethics Comm., Op. 290 (1999); Md. State Bar Ass'n Comm. On Ethics, Op. 99–7 (1998).

Disclosures after the Client Waives the Privilege

The attorney-client privilege, which is closely connected to the doctrine of confidentiality and will be discussed later in the chapter, is the client's privilege, and the attorney exercises the privilege on behalf of the client. Unless authorized, the attorney usually may not waive the privilege because only the client has the right to waive it. However, if the client waives the privilege, the attorney's duty with respect to what has been waived ends. For example, as Timothy McVeigh's execution was drawing near, he granted interviews and wrote many letters to two journalists, who then published a book based on the correspondence, titled *American Terrorist: Timothy McVeigh and the Oklahoma City Bombing* (Regan Books, 2001). Renowned defense attorney Stephen Jones, who represented McVeigh at the trial, granted interviews contemporaneous with the scheduled execution date and challenged some of the statements made by McVeigh, particularly his assertion that he acted alone. Jones's statements to the press would not qualify as violating the doctrine of client confidentiality since McVeigh went public first with his assertions, some of which were highly critical of Jones's representation.

Paralegals should be extremely cautious with regard to the above kinds of information that might not be considered confidential. Even if a paralegal could, after conducting legal research in his or her jurisdiction, feel confident that a client's identity would not be confidential information, it is best to treat it as confidential and not disclose it unless specifically authorized by a supervising attorney. Ultimately, whether information is or is not confidential can be up to a court to decide, and any error of disclosure could place the paralegal's attorney at risk of being accused of failing to properly supervise non-lawyer employees. Also, one could argue that determining whether a client's identity is or is not confidential information constitutes making a legal judgment, which would make it something only lawyers are authorized to do.

EXCEPTIONS TO THE DUTY OF CONFIDENTIALITY

Although the duty of confidentiality is one of the sacred principles associated with the practice of law, it is not without its own exceptions. All jurisdictions, whether operating under the Model Code of Professional Responsibility or the Model Rules of Professional Conduct, provide exceptions that allow lawyers to disclose information that would otherwise be considered private. As the following primary exceptions are considered, be aware that the exceptions are discretionary; almost nothing in the ethics rules requires a lawyer to use a confidentiality exception. However, when lawyers make decisions to disclose client information, based upon their jurisdiction's exceptions, they are required to limit their disclosure to only that which is necessary for the purposes of the exception.

Implied Authorizations

As stated earlier in the chapter, lawyers are allowed to divulge such client information as would be required to carry out the representation. Without such an implied authority, a lawyer or a legal assistant could not adequately draft a complaint, since a complaint must allege facts (such as the nature of the client's injuries) that establish a cause of action. Moreover, the Comments to Model Rule 1.6 state that a lawyer has implied authority during litigation to admit to facts that cannot properly be denied. However, this kind of disclosure can sometimes be found to be inappropriate if given without the client's consent. ABA Comm. On Ethics and Professional Responsibility, Formal Op. 93–370 (1993). (An attorney should not reveal to a judge the client's instructions on settlement authority limits or the attorney's opinions on settlement.) In a West Virginia case, a state attorney general was reprimanded for revealing client information without the client's consent. Even though the information was not considered a "client secret," it was still client information. And even though it was information that could have been found in a public document, the Court determined that its disclosure was not impliedly authorized. *Lawyer Disciplinary Bd. v. McGraw*, 461 S.E.2d 850 (W. Va. 1995). The Model Code is stricter with respect to implied authority by requiring that the attorney obtain the client's consent before revealing confidences. DR 4–101(B) and (C).

The sharing of client information among lawyers in a firm (and their employees) is normally considered an acceptable disclosure when other members of the firm are needed to help with the client's case. However, if the client requests that certain information not be disclosed to other members of the firm, then there is no implied authorization exception. Likewise, if a lawyer shares client information or files with lawyers of other firms in order to get their assistance but does not obtain the client's consent, that disclosure would be unauthorized. *See In re Mandelman*, 514 N.W.2d 11 (Wis. 1994); ABA Comm. On Ethics and Professional Responsibility, Formal Op. 98–411 (1998).

The Prevention of Client Criminal Conduct or Fraud

If a client tells his or her attorney (or the attorney's legal assistant) about crimes that he or she has committed, that information is absolutely protected. Even if its disclosure would help convict an evil person or provide closure to the victim or his or her family, or is done for another good reason, a lawyer would be subject to discipline for doing so.

However, attorneys are allowed to disclose client information in order to prevent a client from committing a future criminal act. Under the Model Code, the attorney is allowed to disclose information necessary to prevent the client from committing *any crime*, regardless of its severity. DR 4–101(C)(3). Under the Model Rules, the lawyer is only allowed to disclose information that is necessary to prevent the client from committing a crime "that the lawyer believes is likely to result in imminent death or substantial bodily harm." MR 1.6(b). Such a standard means that a lawyer in a Model Rules jurisdiction would not be allowed to report a client to the Internal Revenue Service, even if he or she knew the client was about to commit tax fraud, since such a crime would not likely result in imminent death or substantial bodily harm.

Concerning the kinds of crimes that implicate MR 1.6(b), it is the lawyer's reasonable belief about the likelihood of death or harm that triggers the disclosure. In a Massachusetts case, an apartment building maintenance man who had been fired went to see an attorney at a legal services office. After the discussion, the attorney, contacted the police to report that he believed the maintenance man was planning on setting fire to the building. In rendering an opinion concerning the attorney-client privilege as it related to the government's attempt to force the attorney to testify about the conversation, the court found nothing inappropriate about the attorney's initial disclosure to the police. *Purcell v. District Attorney for Suffolk County*, 676 N.E.2d 436 (Mass. 1997). Illinois's confidentiality rule, for instance, is stricter than its ABA counterpart with respect to serious crimes. It requires, rather than allows, a lawyer to disclose client information, "*to the extent it appears necessary* to prevent the client from committing an act that would result in death or serious bodily harm" (emphasis added). Illinois Rules of Professional Conduct 1.6(b).

Fraud is a word that has different definitions in different legal contexts, but generally it can be thought of as an intentional deception that results in some injury or disadvantage to another person. If a client uses his or her attorney's services to perpetrate or complete a fraud, the attorney, upon recognizing the impending or continuing fraud, has limited rights to rectify the situation, including withdrawing from the representation. *See* ABA Model Rule 1.16(b). Furthermore, some courts have held that lawyers may disclose client information in order to extinguish the fraud. For example, in a New Jersey case, a lawyer had prepared mutual wills for a husband and wife (meaning that each spouse's heirs could inherit the estate of the deceased spouse). The firm then discovered that the husband had recently fathered an illegitimate child and had kept that fact from his wife. That could have resulted in the wife's estate passing to this out-of-wedlock child. The law firm sought the court's approval to disclose the confidential information of one co-client to another co-client, and was granted permission under the fraud exception, particularly since New Jersey's version of MR 1.6 was broader than the ABA version, providing more leeway to disclose confidences when fraud is contemplated by the client's use of the lawyer's services. *A. v. B.*, 726 A.2d 924 (N.J. 1999).

However, California is a jurisdiction where the confidentiality exceptions do not apply as liberally. California's confidentiality rule, without exception, requires attorneys to "maintain inviolate the confidence, and at every peril to himself or herself to preserve the secrets, of his or her client." Cal. Bus. & Prof. Code § 6068(e). This does not mean that a California attorney must refrain from allowing the client to use his or her services to continue ongoing criminal or fraudulent activity, but California's confidentiality requirement is considered to be the strictest in the country since it has no express exceptions. In fact, a local bar association ethics opinion decided that an attorney may not warn a co-defendant or the police even after an attorney's client left the law office waving a gun and threatening to kill the co-defendant. San Diego County Bar Ass'n Legal Ethics and Unlawful Practices Comm., Op. 1990–1 (1990).

A related question involves whether a lawyer may warn third parties who might be at risk that the client has a serious disease. A few state ethics opinions have decided that attorneys who are aware of their clients' conditions may not automatically reveal such information to the clients' sexual partners or certain members of the public, such as customers in the restaurant where the client works. Pa. Bar Ass'n Comm. On Legal Ethics and Professional Responsibility, Op. 93–115 (1993); N.C. State Bar Ethics Comm., Op. 117 (1992); Del. Bar Ass'n Professional Ethics Comm., Op. 1988–2.

fraud—An intentional deception that results in a legal injury to another. Fraud usually involves a material misrepresentation (which can include silence) made to deceive the other party, reliance by the other party on the misrepresentation, and resulting harm.

The Defense of a Claim against the Lawyer

Self-preservation is an innate response to danger, and when lawyers are the targets of allegations, they are allowed to reveal client information, including confidential information, in order to defend themselves against such allegations. The Model Rules allow a lawyer to reveal information the lawyer believes necessary

> to establish a claim or defense on behalf of the lawyer in a controversy between the lawyer and the client, to establish a defense to a criminal charge or civil claim against the lawyer based upon conduct in which the client was involved, or to respond to allegations in any proceeding concerning the lawyer's representation of the client. MR 1.6(b)(2).

The Model Code similarly states that confidences or secrets can be disclosed as is necessary for a lawyer "to defend himself or his employers or associates against an accusation of wrongful conduct." DR 4–101(C)(4).

Three kinds of situations are applicable to this type of exception. First, there are occasions where clients sue their own attorneys. In a lawsuit alleging legal malpractice, for instance, the attorney would be authorized to disclose client information as necessary to defend the lawsuit. Second, it is possible that an attorney might be charged with a crime with respect to representing a client. In that event, the attorney would be entitled to disclose client information as would be necessary to present a defense. A Pennsylvania ethics opinion addressing that issue decided that when a client who is under investigation for securities violation defends him- or herself on the grounds that it was the lawyer's fault, the lawyer is allowed to contact the Securities and Exchange Commission and disclose client information sufficient to clear him- or herself of wrongdoing. Pa. Bar Ass'n Comm. On Legal Ethics and Professional Responsibility, Op. 96–48. Third, when charged by a disciplinary commission with professional responsibility violations connected to client representation, an attorney would, by necessity, be allowed to disclose client information in order to rebut and defend against the charges. For instance, if a disciplinary commission charges an attorney with failure to use diligence with respect to a client's case, he or she would be allowed to disclose to the disciplinary commission information and materials that would help establish that he or she acted with due diligence when handling the client's matter.

The Collection of Fees

Both the Model Code (by expressly stating it) and the Model Rules (by implication) allow a lawyer to disclose client information necessary to collect the agreed fee from him or her. Although it may seem self-serving for the legal profession to grant itself a confidentiality exception in order to get paid, without such an exception law firms would be in an unenviable position of trying to prove their right to be paid the agreed fee in cases where the client's refusal to acknowledge the work would be the last word. Even though attorneys are fiduciaries to their clients, clients are not allowed to use such a relationship to their inequitable advantage.

As provided with earlier exceptions, the disclosure can only be what is necessary to collect the fee. There are occasions when law firms hire collection agencies to obtain unpaid client fees. In order for the collection agency to do its job, it needs certain client information, which begs the question of whether such a disclosure by the firm would be authorized. On the one hand, a collection agency hired by the firm would be an agent of the firm, which would seem to mean that such a disclosure would be authorized in the similar way that disclosures to paralegals working on the client's case are authorized. A few state ethics opinions have authorized attorneys giving client information to collection agencies, but not those collection agencies that keep records for credit reports purposes. N.Y. State Bar Ass'n Comm. on Professional Ethics, Op. 684 (1996); S.C. Bar Ethics Advisory Comm., Op. 94–11 (1994); Ohio Sup. Ct. Bd. of Comm'rs on Grievances and Discipline, Op. 91–16 (1991). On the other hand, the use of collection agencies to collect legal fees can be seen as heavy-handed, and not all states allow such disclosure. Texas, for instance, disapproves of lawyers sharing client information with collection agencies without obtaining client consent. State Bar of Texas Professional Ethics Comm., Op. 495 (1994). And Florida allows lawyers to use collection agencies against former clients, but not present clients. Fla. Bar Professional Ethics Comm., Op. 90–2 (1991).

TECHNOLOGY AND CLIENT CONFIDENTIALITY

One of the ironies about the technological age in which we presently live is that all the time-saving devices invented in the last few decades—including microwave ovens, desktop and laptop computers, fax machines, and electronic organizers—give us more time to work. If it now takes fifteen minutes to prepare a client's bill (thanks to computerized record-keeping and billing software) where once it took an hour, the remaining forty-five minutes are considered anything other than free time. Another technology irony is that the more electronic devices benefit our lives, the less our lives have privacy. Increasingly, people are becoming victims of identity theft as more and more professional and personal information is stored and accessed on electronic files, which can be accessed by hackers or destroyed by electronic viruses. As it concerns the law office, three common methods of communication—e-mail, faxes, and mobile phones—have become recent client confidentiality issues needing to be addressed.

E-mail Messages and Client Confidentiality

E-mail messages, especially those that are unencrypted, are anything but private. Even if deleted, e-mail is still susceptible to being recovered from the e-mail servers that were used in the transmission, as well as from the hard drive on which it was created. Perhaps no better example of the public nature of e-mail can be found than in *United States v. Microsoft*, one of the most significant and expensive legal cases in history, which pitted the United States government against the world's largest computer software company and its co-founder and chief executive officer, Bill Gates, the world's richest man. The case, in which the government successfully accused Microsoft of being a monopoly and violating antitrust laws, took many years to complete and resulted in a verdict against Microsoft in April 2000 (although Microsoft won at the appellate level and the case was eventually settled). Fascinatingly enough, much of the government's ammunition against this computer software giant included hundreds of damaging e-mails sent by Microsoft executives, including Gates himself, which tended to support the government's theory that Microsoft had engaged in unfair, pillaging business practices with respect to its Internet Explorer web browser. A thorough and fascinating account of the case and its major players is found in Ken Auletta's book, *World War 3.0: Microsoft and Its Enemies* (Random House, 2001). As reported in the book, David Boies, the lawyer who represented the U.S. government and won the case at the trial level (and later represented Al Gore in the 2000 election litigation), a lawyer considered by some to be the best trial lawyer in America, is someone who would not even use e-mail (Auletta, 11).

Is the use of e-mail to communicate with clients, or about client matters, a violation of the professional duty of confidentiality? Is confidentiality lost when a lawyer gives legal advice by way of an e-mail document? The American Bar Association's Ethics Committee considered this controversy when it issued an ethics opinion on the subject in 1999. The ABA's conclusion was that the use of unencrypted e-mail does not violate the doctrine of confidentiality, as expressed in MR 1.6(a), because there is a reasonable expectation of privacy in e-mail. The committee reasoned that just because e-mail is susceptible to interception does not mean it should not automatically be used. The committee considered e-mail no more of a risk to interception than other methods of communication—postal mail, telephone conversations—that can also be intercepted. Furthermore, the reasonable expectation of privacy is bolstered by federal law, which prohibits the interception of electronic communication (wiretapping). 18 U.S.C.A. § 2511. However, the opinion did state that if the nature of an e-mail message to be sent to the client was highly sensitive, then a lawyer should seek the client's wishes on sending the communication through another means. ABA Standing Committee on Ethics and Professional Responsibility, Formal Op. 99–413 (1999).

Some states have also issued ethics opinions regarding e-mail, most of them deciding that confidentiality requirements are not breached by its use. South Carolina originally held that the use of e-mail for client communications was inappropriate unless the client expressly waived the confidentiality protection. S.C. Bar Ethics Advisory Comm. Op. No. 94–27 (1994). Three years later, however, South Carolina reversed itself. S.C. Bar Ethics Advisory Comm. Op. No. 97–08 (1997). Other jurisdictions endorse the use of e-mail: Alaska Bar Ass'n Op. 98–2 (1998); D.C. Bar Op. 281 (1998); Delaware State Bar Ass'n Comm. on Prof. Ethics Op. 2001–2 (2002); Illinois State Bar Ass'n Advisory Op. on Professional Conduct No. 96–10 (1997); Ky. Bar Ass'n Ethics Comm. Advisory Op. E–403 (1998); New York State Bar Ass'n Comm. on Professional Ethics Op. 709 (1998); North Dakota State Bar Ass'n Ethics Comm. Op. 97–09 (1997); Utah State Bar Ethics Advisory Op. 00–01 (2000); Vermont Advisory Ethics Op. 97–5 (1997).

A few ethics opinions have taken a more cautious approach to the use of e-mail. Pennsylvania advises that lawyers get client consent before using e-mail to communicate with them. Pennsylvania Bar Ass'n Comm. on Legal Ethics Op. 97–130 (1997). Arizona advises that lawyers use encrypted e-mail or warn clients about e-mail risks. State Bar of Arizona Advisory Op. 97–04 (1996). And two states have issued ethics opinions advising against the use of e-mail: Iowa Bar Ass'n Op. 1997–1 (1997) and North Carolina State Bar Opinion 215 (1995).

Fax Machines and Client Confidentiality

Facsimile (fax) machines are usually kept in a central location in an office facility, which makes their use to transmit client information slightly more risky than e-mail, since anyone in an office can intercept a fax as it comes from the fax machine. Fax numbers can also be dialed incorrectly, resulting in the wrong fax machine receiving what should have been faxed elsewhere. But the same ABA ethics opinion that discussed the appropriateness of e-mail also made reference to faxes and, while failing to expressly declare fax use ethical, found that the use of faxes has become so commonplace that courts take for granted that it is an appropriate method of communicating that does not violate the duty of confidentiality. ABA Standing Comm. on Ethics and Professional Responsibility, Formal Op. 99–413 (1999). And an earlier opinion considered the attorney-client privilege would not be ruined in the event a fax was accidentally sent to the wrong place. ABA Standing Comm. on Ethics and Professional Responsibility, Formal Op. 94–382 (1994).

Mobile Phones and Client Confidentiality

Like e-mail, mobile phone usage is susceptible to eavesdropping, unintentional or otherwise. During his meteoric rise and fall as Speaker of the United States House of Representatives, Newt Gingrich found himself the subject of yet another controversy when a phone conversation he was having in 1996 with another Republican congressman (discussing how to handle ethics charges made against Gingrich) who was on a mobile phone was secretly tape-recorded by an elderly couple who claimed that they just happened to pick up the conversation on a scanner in their car while Christmas shopping for their grandchild. They then gave the recording to Democratic congressman Jim McDermott, who was a member of the House Ethics Committee. Eventually, the tape recording ended up in the hands of the national press, who released its contents. Because it is illegal to intentionally intercept someone's phone conversation, the couple was prosecuted, pleaded guilty to violating 18 U.S.C. § 2511, and were fined $500 dollars. The congressman whose mobile phone conversation was illegally tape-recorded then sued congressman McDermott, claiming he illegally gave the tape to the news media. And in May 2002, McDermott acknowledged in court filings that he did leak the tape recording to the press, but claimed that it was within his free speech rights.

More than a few bar associations have weighed in on the use of cordless or mobile phones, expressing cautious approval. New Hampshire and Massachusetts have issued ethics opinions cautioning lawyers against using cordless or mobile phones, stating that before talking about sensitive matters with their clients on mobile phones, lawyers should explain to their clients the risks of talking on unprotected lines and the implications that such a phone conversation might be seen as a waiver of attorney-client privilege and then get their clients' consent before continuing. N.H Bar Ass'n Ethics Comm. Opinion 1991–92/6; Mass. Bar Ass'n, Ethics Comm. Opinion No. 1994–5 (1994). Iowa, North Carolina, and Washington have issued similar opinions that obligate attorneys, when talking on mobile or cordless or portable phones (or when they believe their clients are using such phones) to inform their clients about the likelihood of loss of confidentiality. Iowa State Bar Ass'n Opinion 90–44 (1990); N.C. State Bar Ass'n, Ethics Comm. Opinion 251 (1995); Washington State Bar Ass'n Informal Ethics Op. 91–1 (1991). Arizona advises its attorneys to use caution when talking about client matters on mobile phones, but refrains from stating that all client discussions on mobile phones are automatically unethical. State Bar of Ariz. Comm. on Rules of Professional Conduct Opinion 95–11 (1995). And the Delaware ethics opinion (cited earlier), that approved of the use of e-mail also discussed the use of mobile phones, concluding that such use is not a violation of Delaware's confidentiality rule. This decision was reached in part because of the federal statutes that prohibit mobile phone interception and disclosure. Delaware State Bar Ass'n Comm. on Prof. Ethics Op. 2001–2 (2002).

ETHICS 2000 AND THE DUTY OF CONFIDENTIALITY

Proposal by the Ethics 2000 Commission

informed consent—Giving one's agreement to take a certain action, including doing nothing, after having had the possible ramifications and consequences of taking that action fully explained.

The ABA's Ethics 2000 Commission made such significant recommendations regarding MR 1.6 that it has been reorganized. A few changes are worthy of mention. First, whereas MR 1.6 allows for disclosure after client consultation and consent, the new version requires that clients give **informed consent**. The new version gives attorneys broader discretion to disclose confidential information as well. Confidences can be disclosed to prevent "reasonably certain death or substantial bodily harm," and with no prerequisite that the client be involved in criminality. Confidences can also be disclosed to prevent a fraud or economic harm in which the client has used, or is using, the lawyer's services. Moreoever, confidences can be disclosed to prevent, minimize, or remedy substantial economic loss that is a result of the client using the lawyer's services. In addition, the new version expressly allows lawyers to disclose confidences in order to seek legal advice regarding application of the ethics rules, as well as to comply with law or a court order.

Action Taken by the ABA House of Delegates

The House of Delegates approved the change allowing disclosing of client confidences to prevent reasonably certain death or substantial bodily harm, as well as to seek legal advice. However, it rejected the proposal allowing for disclosures necessary to prevent a crime or fraud caused by the client's use of the lawyer's services. Moreover, the Ethics 2000 Commission withdrew the proposed change allowing for disclosure of client information necessary to prevent or rectify economic harm caused by the client's criminal or fraudulent use of the lawyer's services.

THE ATTORNEY-CLIENT PRIVILEGE: RELATED TO THE DUTY OF CONFIDENTIALITY

There is a slight misunderstanding concerning the duty of confidentiality and the attorney-client privilege in that the two ideas are sometimes discussed as if they were identical. They actually are two branches of the same tree. Although *attorney-client privilege* is a phrase that might be used in cases dealing with confidentiality, the duty of confidentiality is a professional responsibility doctrine that obligates attorneys and their agents to keep client information and communication confidential.

The attorney-client privilege, on the other hand, is not an ethics doctrine but rather a discovery or evidentiary doctrine. The attorney-client privilege prevents lawyers from being forced to testify against their clients, and is usually formalized in legislation that concerns the competency of witnesses, rather than in the rules of court that govern trial procedure or the professional responsibilities of attorneys. For instance, Indiana's attorney-client privilege is found in the statute that also includes the doctor-patient privilege, the clergy-parishioner privilege, and the husband-wife privilege. It simply states, "Except as otherwise provided by statute, the following persons shall not be required to testify regarding the following communications: (1) Attorneys, as to confidential communications made to them in the course of their professional business, and as to advice given in such cases." Ind. Code § 34–46–3–1(1). Oklahoma's attorney-client privilege is a separate statute that includes definitions for key words in the statute, as well as conditions for the application of, and exemption from, the privilege. Oklahoma's attorney-client privilege statute also encompasses paralegals because it covers confidential communication between the client and "his attorney's representative." Okla. Stat. tit. 12, § 2502(B)(1). An attorney's representative is defined as "one employed by the attorney to assist the attorney in the rendition of professional legal services." § 2502(A)(3).

Connected to the attorney-client privilege is the work product rule, which will be discussed in detail later in the chapter. However, at this point, one should recognize that there are three related concepts in this area, each with their own primary authority source: the duty of confidentiality (found in the professional responsibility rules); the attorney-client privilege (usually found in the statutes on witness

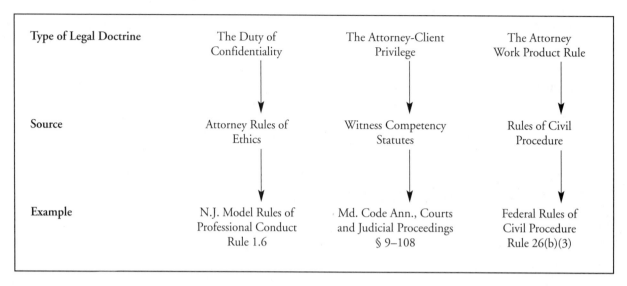

Exhibit 4–2 The Relationship among the Confidentiality Doctrines

Type of Legal Doctrine	The Duty of Confidentiality	The Attorney-Client Privilege	The Attorney Work Product Rule
Source	Attorney Rules of Ethics	Witness Competency Statutes	Rules of Civil Procedure
Example	N.J. Model Rules of Professional Conduct Rule 1.6	Md. Code Ann., Courts and Judicial Proceedings § 9–108	Federal Rules of Civil Procedure Rule 26(b)(3)

competency, although there are exceptions: for instance, Delaware's attorney-client privilege is found in Rule 502 of the Delaware Rules of Evidence); and the work product rule (found in the rules of civil procedure). In most instances, attorneys cannot be forced to give testimony that concerns their clients because the attorney-client privilege protects that kind of confidential information. The attorney-client privilege can also shield the attorney from being forced to testify about conversations the attorney had with the client before the lawyer-client relationship began (Exhibit 4–2).

As the following tragic case shows, conversations prospective clients have with paralegals can be covered by the attorney-client privilege as well.

Case Law

Mayberry v. State, 670 N.E.2d 1262 (Ind. 1996)

Sullivan, Justice.

We affirm defendant Elizabeth Mayberry's conviction for the murder of minister Roland Phillips, committed as he concluded his Sunday sermon at the North Salem United Methodist Church.

In May, 1992, defendant met Phillips, a student pastor at the North Salem United Methodist Church, at a singles retreat sponsored by the United Methodist Church. Defendant and Phillips dated for several months after the retreat. During the course of their relationship, defendant, then 35 years old, claims that Phillips encouraged her to allow him to kiss her using his tongue, engage in consensual, mutual, oral sex with him, fondle and kiss her breasts, and digitally penetrate her vagina. Defendant had never before had intimate physical contact with a man. Phillips would later deny to church officials that he had ever engaged in oral sex with defendant. Defendant's relationship with Phillips took a turn for the worse in August of 1992. In an attempt to salvage the relationship, defendant wrote Phillips letters inquiring into the status of their relationship. In one of these letters, she asked Phillips to attend counseling with her. In November, 1992, defendant received a letter from Phillips in which he stated that their relationship was over. This letter deeply hurt defendant and made her angry.

In December, 1992, defendant filed a complaint with the United Methodist Church (UMC) in which she alleged that Phillips had engaged in sexual misconduct. When speaking about her relationship with Phillips to Reverend Harry Coleman, defendant stated: "My concern is for the next woman with whom he chooses to have a relationship. What kind of damage will he do to her life? He says his behavior is a pattern. I believe it is one which must be broken." After several hearings on defendant's complaint, the UMC Committee on Ordained Ministry determined, in May, 1993, that Phillips was to retain his position as a student pastor. Upon learning the result of her complaint, the defendant became extremely distraught.

Despite the fact that defendant sought counseling, in June, 1993, she started having thoughts about killing herself. . . . On August 2, 1993, defendant purchased a handgun and box of ammunition in Bloomington. On August 19, 1993, a firearms expert and trainer spent two hours with defendant at her house showing her how to use and care for the gun. On September 18, 1993, defendant loaded the gun with five cartridges. On Sunday morning September 19, defendant, with the gun concealed in her purse, drove to North Salem United Methodist Church. Defendant arrived in front of the church at about 11:00 A.M. and parked her car across the street. Upon entering the sanctuary, defendant never took her eyes off of Phillips, who was delivering a sermon from the pulpit. Defendant walked down the center aisle toward the pulpit. As she approached the pulpit,

Phillips turned and looked at her and told her that he would speak with her after the service concluded. Defendant stood silently at the left side of the pulpit and watched Phillips finish his sermon. Phillips finished his sermon, asked the congregation to stand, and announced the last hymn. Defendant pulled the gun out of her purse, aimed it directly at Phillips and fired twice. Phillips's knees buckled and he fell to the floor. Defendant exclaimed: "You raped me! You raped me!" Phillips responded: "No I didn't. No I didn't." Defendant walked closer to Phillips and fired the gun two more times. . . . The paramedics arrived shortly thereafter and took Phillips to the hospital where he died due to loss of blood from gunshot wounds to the neck, chest, wrist, and leg.

On September 20, 1993, the State filed an information charging defendant with Murder. On October 11, 1993, defendant filed a notice of insanity pursuant to Indiana Code § 35–36–2–1 (1993). Defendant's jury trial commenced on June 13, 1994. The jury found defendant guilty but mentally ill of Murder on June 22, 1994. The trial court sentenced defendant to a term of sixty years on July 20, 1994.

In a hearing outside the presence of the jury, defense witness Jennie Maretto, a friend of Phillips and a paralegal for a law firm in Fishers, Indiana, testified that Phillips contacted her at work to obtain legal advice regarding a letter he wrote to the UMC in response to the complaint that defendant had filed. Maretto testified that she felt that she was not legally able to give Phillips legal advice but would have to consult with an attorney. Maretto stated that Phillips asked her to consult an attorney. Maretto also testified that she gave a statement regarding her conversations with Phillips to Officer Danny Williams. When defense counsel inquired about the letter Phillips asked Maretto to look over, the State asserted the attorney-client privilege on Maretto's behalf as to any communication between Maretto and the victim. The trial court sustained the State's objection to the admission of Maretto's testimony.

In an offer to prove, the defense introduced into evidence a police report prepared by Officer

Williams. In the report, Officer Williams states that when he spoke with Maretto she informed him that Phillips had contacted her to obtain legal advice. The report also states that Maretto advised the officer that Phillips stated that Phillips and defendant had engaged in consensual, mutual oral sex.

Defendant contends that the trial court erroneously determined that the attorney-client privilege attached to comments Phillips made to Maretto because Maretto did not adequately establish that Phillips contacted her in an effort to employ an attorney for professional advice or aid. In *Colman v. Heidenreich*, 269 Ind. 419, 381 N.E.2d 866 (1978), this court made the following observations:

> The attorney-client privilege is a very important provision in our law for the protection of persons in need of professional legal help. It makes provision for a person to give complete and confidential information of an attorney, so that the attorney may be fully advised in his services to the client. At the same time, it assures the client that these confidences will not be violated. *Colman*, 269 Ind. at 421, 381 N.E.2d at 868.

Indiana Code §34–1–14–5 (1993) provides that attorneys shall not be competent witnesses "as to confidential communications made to them in the course of their professional business, and as to advice given in such cases." This "attorney-client privilege not only plays a role in our law of evidence but is also fundamental to our rules of professional conduct which forbid attorneys from revealing 'information relating to representation of a client unless the client consents after consultation.' See Ind.Professional Conduct Rule 1.6." *Corll v. Edward D. Jones & Co.*, 646 N.E.2d 721, 724 (Ind. Ct. App. 1995). As long as an attorney is consulted on business within the scope of the attorney's profession, "it is of no moment to the privilege's application that there is no pendency or expectation of litigation. Neither is it of any moment that no fee has been paid." *Colman*, 269 Ind. at 423, 381 N.E.2d at 869 (citations omitted). Rather, the essential prerequisites to invocation of the privilege are to establish by a preponderance of

the evidence (i) the existence of an attorney-client relationship and (ii) that a confidential communication was involved. *See Colman*, 269 Ind. at 423, 381 N.E.2d at 869. To meet the burden of showing that an attorney client relationship existed, the State had to, at the very least, establish that the communication at issue occurred in the course of an effort to obtain legal advice or aid, on the subject of the client's rights or liabilities, from a professional legal advisor acting in his or her capacity as such. *Id.; United States v. Demauro*, 581 F.2d 50, 55 (2nd Cir. 1978).

Defendant suggests that Phillips's communications with his friend Maretto are privileged "only if his asking her to have an attorney look over his papers can be construed to be an attempt by Phillips to employ legal counsel." Defendant also states that the State failed to meet its burden of establishing that Maretto's communications with Phillips were privileged because she did not testify that Phillips intended to or sought to employ her firm to represent him concerning his difficulties with the complaint defendant filed with the church. Defendant misstates the State's burden. Although Maretto and Phillips were social friends, the record reveals that Phillips approached Maretto at the law firm where she worked as a paralegal/office manager and asked her to consult an attorney regarding his legal concerns. We believe these facts can be read to establish that the communications at issue occurred in the course of an effort to obtain legal advice or aid from a professional legal advisor in his capacity as such. *Colman*, 269 Ind. at 423, 381 N.E.2d at 869; *Demauro*, 581 F.2d at 55. Therefore, we cannot say that the trial court erred in determining that the State met its burden of showing the existence of an attorney-client relationship. And if the communications at issue occurred during an attempt to procure professional legal aid, confidential communications were involved here. *See Colman*, 269 Ind. at 423, 381 N.E.2d at 869. Therefore, the trial court did not abuse its discretion in determining that the communications between Maretto and Phillips were subject to the attorney-client privilege.

Case Questions

1. What was the argument made by the defendant when she asserted that the statements the victim made to his paralegal friend were not covered by the attorney-client privilege?
2. What was the argument made by the State when it asserted that the statements were covered by the attorney-client privilege?
3. What evidence was there that the victim talked to the paralegal's attorney about the matter?
4. Why did the State want the attorney-client privilege to cover the statements the victim made to his paralegal friend?
5. Do you think the victim contacted his paralegal friend because she was his friend or because she was a paralegal? Does it matter?

The Basics of Discovery

Although television shows about lawyers often save the key witness or piece of evidence as a surprise for the thrilling ending, the reality of litigation is that the rules of discovery are designed to avoid surprises at trial by allowing each side to have access to the other side's case. This information gathering is done through **interrogatories** of the parties, depositions of parties and witnesses, examination of the parties' documents or other things, entry on the parties' land or other property for the purposes of inspection, physical and mental examinations, and requests for admissions. Federal Rules of Civil Procedure, Rule 26(A) (2000). The attorney-client privilege is implicated when lawyers, upon being asked for certain discovery items, claim that such information is protected against disclosure by the attorney-client privilege. Though this is not a civil procedure or evidence book, a limited discussion of the basic operation of discovery will help put the attorney-client privilege in context.

interrogatories—An interrogatory is a discovery device that involves one party sending to the other party a set, or sets, of questions that are to be answered under oath and in writing.

What can be discovered is governed by Civil Procedure Rule 26(B), which states in part:

> (B) Scope of discovery. Unless otherwise limited by order of the court in accordance with these rules, the scope of discovery is as follows:
>
>   (1) Parties may obtain discovery regarding any matter, not privileged which is relevant to the subject-matter involved in the pending action, whether it relates to the claim or defense of the party seeking discovery or the claim or defense of any other party. . . . It is not ground for objection that the information sought will be inadmissible at trial if the information sought appears reasonably calculated to lead to the discovery of admissible evidence. Federal Rules of Civil Procedure, Rule 26(B).

What can be obtained in discovery is much broader than what can be presented as evidence in the event of a trial, because the above rule allows a party to seek discovery of any information if that information could reasonably lead to the discovery of other information that would be admissible at trial. For example, a party's offer to settle a lawsuit is generally inadmissible at trial, but interrogatories and depositions can be used to find out if a party made an offer to settle the case.

The Basics of the Work Product Rule

Since client information is to be protected by the duty of confidentiality and the attorney-client privilege, discovery requests could seemingly always be thwarted by the other side simply by claiming that the information being sought is confidential, end of story. That is where Rule 26(B)(3) comes to the rescue, by distinguishing between kinds of attorney-client information and then determining if and when the attorney-client privilege protects against the disclosure of that information to the other side. Rule 26(B)(3) states, in part:

> (3) *Trial preparations: Materials.* Subject to the provisions of subdivision (B)(4) or this rule, a party may obtain discovery of documents and tangible things otherwise discoverable under subdivision (B)(1) of this rule and prepared in anticipation of litigation or for trial by or for another party or by or for that other party's representative (including his attorney, consultant, surety, indemnitor, insurer, or agent) only upon a showing that the party seeking discovery has substantial need of the materials in the preparation of his case and that he is unable without undue hardship to obtain the substantial equivalent of the materials by other means. In ordering discovery of such materials when the required showing has been made, the court shall protect against disclosure of the mental impressions, conclusions, opinions, or legal theories of an attorney or other representative of a party concerning the litigation.

The above section is commonly referred to as the *work product rule*. The first part of the rule allows one side in litigation to compel the other side to disclose tangible information that was prepared in anticipation or connection with litigation by the other side, provided (a) the side desiring the tangible information demonstrates a substantial need of it; and (b) the side desiring the tangible information demonstrates that they would be unable to obtain the same information on their own without incurring extreme hardship. For example, imagine a plaintiff sues a defendant over a car accident and, before the defendant has an opportunity to examine and photograph the plaintiff's car, it is mistakenly crushed at the junkyard. Under the work product rule, the defendant would be able to have access to the photographs taken by the plaintiff's lawyer (or the lawyer's agents, such as investigators) since they were taken by the plaintiff in connection with the litigation and since there would be no way for the defendant to make his or her own examination of the car.

The second part of the rule is sometimes referred to as the *attorney-opinion work product rule;* it serves as an exception to the exception that certain kinds of client information must be disclosed to the other side. This part of the rule absolutely protects from disclosure any otherwise discoverable client information if what is sought would reveal the attorney's legal strategies, theories, or opinions about the case. To continue the above example, the attorney-opinion aspect of the work product rule would protect the plaintiff from being compelled to turn over to the defendant any and all notes written by the plaintiff's lawyer that would show the plaintiff's game plan at trial (perhaps demonstrating that the defendant was negligently driving the car). The attorney-client privilege would also prevent the plaintiff, in an attempt to find out if the defendant stated or implied he or she might be at fault, from compelling his or her attorney to turn over notes of interviews with him or her. The defendant's attorney would be prohibited from disclosing that information because of the ethical duty of confidentiality (the first branch of the confidentiality tree), and in this instance, such discussions would be protected from discovery by the attorney-client privilege (the second branch).

Attorney-Client Privilege, the White House, and the First Lady

A controversial example of the relationship of the attorney-client privilege and attorney notes involved the Whitewater Investigation and then–first lady, Hillary Clinton. Long before the country ever heard of an intern named Monica Lewinsky and a former **solicitor general** named Kenneth Starr, the **Office of Independent Counsel (OIC)**, originally headed by Robert B. Fiske, Jr., was appointed to investigate the possible crimes committed back in Arkansas by the Clintons and their Whitewater land investment partners, James and Susan McDougal. As part of that investigation, the OIC issued a grand jury subpoena to the White House, directing it to turn over to the grand jury any and all notes taken by two White House lawyers during meetings held in the White House that included the presence of Mrs. Clinton and her personal lawyer. The White House Counsel's Office and Mrs. Clinton argued in response that the notes were protected by the attorney-client privilege. However, the Eighth Circuit Court of Appeals disagreed, in *In re Grand Jury Subpoena Duces Tecum*, 112 F.3d 910 (8th Cir. 1997). The Court ruled that the White House Counsel represents the public's interests, not the interests of the first lady. Therefore, since the White House Counsel's client is the United States and the OIC is a part of the U.S. government, White House lawyers cannot assert the attorney-client privilege against their own client, particularly when the OIC's investigation concerned the affairs of the Clintons before Mr. Clinton was elected president.

The Eighth Circuit Court of Appeals also found unpersuasive the argument that the attorney-client privilege applied to the conversations and the notes the White House lawyers took of those conversations because Mrs. Clinton believed the attorney-client privilege applied, since she and her personal lawyer also attended those meeting in the White House. Instead, the court found that argument irrelevant since Mrs. Clinton correctly did not assert that she believed that the White House lawyers were representing her personally. Also, the White House claimed the notes were protected by the work product doctrine, since the notes were prepared in anticipation of the OIC's investigation of Mrs. Clinton, which was something

solicitor general—The third ranking member of the U.S. Justice Department. The solicitor general represents the federal government before the U.S. Supreme Court.

Office of Independent Counsel (OIC)—A statutorily created special legal office, empowered to investigate and prosecute misconduct by members of the executive branch of government and other high-ranking government officials.

akin to litigation. To that argument, the court reiterated that since the OIC was not investigating the White House, but rather was investigating its occupants for activities occurring in Arkansas, the work product doctrine did not apply. Since the Supreme Court refused to review the decision, it became the final word on the matter. Some critics argue the decision will cause a chill in the communication lines between public officials and government lawyers and that it chips away at the attorney-client privilege. Others, however, contend the decision may be politically controversial but is not legally controversial since it restates a common notion, which is that government lawyers take as their client the government, that is, the public.

Inadvertent Disclosure: What to Do When Mistakes Occur

As has been discussed, even though the rules of discovery are meant to facilitate the sharing of information between parties, there are certain kinds of information that do not have to be disclosed to the other side. But mistakes happen. Imagine, in anticipation of the Super Bowl, the quarterback from one team accidentally gives his script for his team's first fifteen offensive plays to a player from the opposing team. Would the opposing team be required to inform the quarterback and his coach of the mistake, or be expected not to prepare for those plays? Or, suppose at a poker game, a player holds his or her cards so sloppily that the nearest player can see them. Would anyone expect the beneficiary of such sloppiness to pretend that nothing was seen, and not take advantage of such good luck? Of course not. Opponents in all endeavors look for each other's mental errors precisely to take full advantage, and almost no one would expect anything different.

Litigation can be different, however. During the paper-burying process of discovery, a law firm might, on occasion, unintentionally send to the other firm documents or other tangible items that should not have been sent because they were protected work product material. When either firm horrifyingly or pleasantly discovers the error, what happens next can depend on the jurisdiction.

Material Inadvertently Disclosed Retains Its Privileged Status
The ABA Ethics Commission issued an opinion concerning inadvertent disclosure in 1992. Specifically, the question addressed concerned a lawyer who received privileged information by a fax that was erroneously sent. The ABA reached the conclusion that if a lawyer receives information from the opposing party that the lawyer believes to be confidential or protected, the lawyer should: (a) refrain from further examining the materials; (b) inform the lawyer who sent the materials; and (c) abide by the wishes of the sending lawyer. ABA Comm. on Ethics and Professional Responsibility, Formal Op. 92–368 (1992). Some state ethics opinions adhere to that advice and require attorneys who are erroneously sent confidential or protected materials to return those materials to opposing counsel without further examining them. Oregon State Bar Legal Ethics Comm., Op. 1998–150 (1998); Standing Comm. on Legal Ethics of Virginia State Bar, Op. 1702 (1997).

The following case, involving a divorce client suing her law firm for malpractice, illustrates the view that inadvertent disclosure does not result in an effective waiver of the attorney-client privilege. The parts of the court's decision addressing the law of attorney malpractice are redacted from the version below. While reading the case, notice how the Court adopts the ABA's position on inadvertent disclosure.

Case Law

Corey v. Norman, Hanson & DeTroy, 742 A.2d 933 (Maine 1999)

CLIFFORD, J.

Susan W. Corey appeals from a summary judgment (Cumberland County, Cole J.) entered in favor of the defendants. The court concluded that Susan failed to establish the necessary elements to establish malpractice in her action brought against the law firm of Norman, Hanson & DeTroy and the accounting firm of Dawson, Smith, Purvis & Bassett, P.A. (referred to collectively as NH&D). Susan contends that the trial court erred in basing its decision to grant a summary judgment on what it concluded was an insufficient statement of material facts filed by Susan pursuant to M.R. Civ. P. 7(d)(2). Susan also appeals from an order (Saufley, J.) requiring her attorney to return to the attorney for NH&D a document that the trial court found to be privileged. She contends that the court erred in finding that an inadvertent disclosure of a privileged document does not constitute a waiver of the attorney-client privilege. We affirm both the summary judgment and the court's order regarding the privileged document.

In the spring of 1995, Susan retained attorney Peter DeTroy of NH&D to represent her in divorce proceedings against her then husband John B. Corey, a dentist specializing in periodontics. DeTroy hired Dawson, Smith, Purvis & Bassett, P.A., certified public accountants, to value assets of the marital estate and to assist in distinguishing between marital and nonmarital property for purposes of the divorce. The parties agreed that John Corey's

dental practice was marital property. DeTroy stipulated to the $37,700 valuation of the dental practice proposed by John's attorney. No formal appraisal of the dental practice was conducted by DeTroy or the accountants he hired. The divorce was finalized in March of 1996. In the divorce judgment, the stipulated value of the dental practice was accepted by the court and the practice was set aside to John. More than $1.6 million in marital property was awarded to Susan. In addition, John was ordered to pay his former wife alimony in excess of $300,000 over ten years.

In January of 1997, Susan filed a complaint in the Superior Court charging NH&D with professional negligence. Susan alleged that . . . NH&D breached that duty by failing to obtain an independent valuation and by stipulating to the $37,700 valuation of the dental practice. This breach, Susan alleges, "caused the dental practice, a valuable marital asset, to be seriously undervalued," thereby resulting in a property distribution to Susan "of substantially less value than that to which she was entitled." The $37,700 figure to which NH&D stipulated was the value of the dental and business equipment less debt, and did not account for the good will of the dental practice, which, Susan contends, has a substantial value. . . .

The Superior Court entered a summary judgment in favor of NH&D based on Susan's failure to present sufficient evidence of any loss that was proximately caused by negligence on the part of NH&D.

Therefore, the court concluded, her claim for damages was overly speculative. Susan has appealed from that judgment. . . .

II. ATTORNEY-CLIENT PRIVILEGE

On February 4, 1997, Michael Waxman, Susan's attorney, went to the office of Harrison L. Richardson, the attorney for NH&D, to view NH&D's file regarding the Corey divorce. Richardson was not in his office, but he had told his secretary to photocopy any documents Waxman wished to have. Inadvertently placed in the boxes of documents available for Waxman's review was a memorandum with the phrase "CONFIDENTIAL AND LEGALLY PRIVILEGED" written at the top of the page. The memorandum is a summary of a telephone conference between Richardson and DeTroy, the attorney who represented Susan in her divorce. Waxman requested and received a copy of the document from a firm secretary without the knowledge of Richardson. The secretary contacted Waxman later that day to request the return of the copy of the document. Waxman refused that request, believing that he did not have an obligation to return the document because the attorney-client privilege was waived by the inadvertent disclosure of the document. He then informed Richardson, in writing, of his receipt of the document.

The Superior Court granted NH&D's motion for a protective order and required Waxman to return his copy of the memorandum to Richardson and to make no further use of it. An appeal of that ruling is now before us. . . .

The purpose of the attorney-client privilege "is to encourage clients to make full disclosure to their attorneys," *see Fisher v. United States*, 425 U.S. 391, 403 (1976), and "to protect not only the giving of professional advice to those who can act on it but also the giving of information to the lawyer to enable him to give sound and informed advice," *see Upjohn Co. v. United States*, 449 U.S. 383, 390 (1981). Any rule regarding inadvertent disclosures must uphold this underlying purpose.

In ordering the return of the inadvertently disclosed privileged document, the trial court, adopting the rule first established in *Mendenhall v. Barber-Greene Co.*, 531 F. Supp. 951 (N.D. Ill. 1982), concluded: A truly inadvertent disclosure cannot and does not constitute a waiver of the attorney-client privilege. The issue for counsel and the court upon a claim of inadvertent disclosure must be whether the disclosure was actually inadvertent, that is, whether there was intent and authority for the disclosure. . . . If receiving counsel understands the disclosure to have been inadvertent, no waiver will have occurred. Unless receiving counsel has a reasonable belief that the disclosure was authorized by the client and intended by the attorney, the receiving attorney should return the document and make no further use of it. See id. at 954-55. We agree with the Superior Court and its adoption of the common sense rule set out in *Mendenhall*. . . . Underlying this rule is the notion that the client holds the privilege, and that only the client, or the client's attorney acting with the client's express authority, can waive the privilege. . . .

The rule adopted by the Superior Court, which we now adopt, is consistent with the rule adopted by the American Bar Association's committee on Ethics and Professional Responsibility: A lawyer who receives materials that on their face appear to be subject to the attorney-client privilege or otherwise confidential, under circumstances where it is clear they were not intended for the receiving lawyer, should refrain from examining the materials, notify the sending lawyer and abide the instructions of the lawyer who sent them. ABA Comm. on Ethics and Professional Responsibility, Formal Op. 92–368 (1992); see also ABA Comm. on Ethics and Professional Responsibility, Formal Op. 94–382 (1994).

We agree with the Superior Court's rejection of the alternate approaches followed by other courts. In one line of cases, an inadvertent disclosure of a privileged document can amount to a waiver of the privilege if the client and the client's attorney did not take adequate steps to prevent the disclosure. *See Gray v.*

Bicknell, 86 F.3d 1472, 1483-84 (8th Cir. 1996); *see also Hartford Fire Ins. Co. v. Garrey*, 109 F.R.D. 323, 331-32 (N.D. Cal. 1985). The Gray approach has been criticized as creating an uncertain, unpredictable privilege, dependent on the proof of too many factors concerning the adequacy of the steps taken to prevent disclosure. *See Berg Elecs., Inc. v. Molex, Inc.*, 875 F. Supp. 261, 262-63 (D. Del. 1995). Another line of cases concludes that all inadvertent disclosures of documents constitute a waiver of the privilege because the information is no longer confidential. *See International Digital Sys. Corp. v. Digital Equip. Corp.*, 120 F.R.D. 445, 449-50 (D. Mass. 1988); John Henry Wigmore, Evidence in Trials at Common Law § 2325(3) (John T. McNaughton ed., 1961). Although this approach has been adopted by the United States District Court for the District of Maine, *see Federal Deposit Ins. Corp. v. Singh*, 140 F.R.D. 252, 253 (D. Me. 1992), it takes away from the client the ability to control when the privilege is waived and discourages communication between attorneys and clients.

The Superior Court was correct in concluding that there was no waiver of the privilege, and in ordering the return of the document and prohibiting the disclosure of its contents.

The entry is: Order regarding the privileged document is affirmed; judgment affirmed.

Case Questions

1. Do you think the receiving attorney did anything wrong by examining the letter he was given by the secretary for the opposing lawyer?
2. Why did the court state that the attorney-client privilege had not been waived despite a clear occurrence of inadvertent disclosure?
3. Based on this decision, under what circumstances would the attorney-client privilege be waived?

In 1994 the ABA dealt with a slightly different question, which concerned what to do when a lawyer receives privileged materials from a third party (such as a disgruntled former employee of the opposing party or law firm), instead of erroneously from the opposing lawyer. Similar to the 1992 opinion, the ABA decided that the lawyer, once discovering the privileged materials, should contact the opposing party to inform them of the situation and then follow their instructions. ABA Comm. on Ethics and Professional Responsibility, Formal Op. 94–382. Some states have expressed similar sentiment to the effect that lawyers should not take advantage of the situation when a third party sends them privileged information. North Carolina State Bar Ethics Comm., 252 (1997); Standing Comm. on Legal Ethics of Virginia State Bar, Op. 1702 (1997). Other states, however, consider such a fortuitous finding to incur no duty by the receiving lawyer to rectify the situation. Maryland State Bar Ass'n Comm. on Ethics Op. 96–38 (1996); Ohio Sup. Ct. Bd. of Comm'rs on Grievances and Discipline Op. 93–11 (1993).

The following case involves a curious form of inadvertent disclosure by a third party: the third party is the plaintiff, who also happens to be her attorney's paralegal.

Case Law

Lipin v. Bender, 193 A.D.2d 424 (N.Y. App. Div. 1, 1993)

Appeal from the Supreme Court, New York County (Karla Moskowitz, J.).

This is seemingly a matter of first impression, the issue being whether, under the unique circumstances presented, dismissal of the complaint is an appropriate sanction for plaintiff's surreptitious removal and use of confidential documents constituting privileged material and defense counsel's attorney's work product. The underlying facts are not in dispute. Plaintiff, a former high ranking employee of defendant American Red Cross in Greater New York (NYRC), brought this action for sexual harassment and discrimination pursuant to New York's Human Rights Law and 42 U.S.C. § 1983 and 1985.

On June 28, 1991, the parties appeared before Special Referee Birnbaum in a hearing room on the second floor of the New York County Courthouse at 60 Centre Street to argue certain discovery matters. Plaintiff, who since her termination by NYRC had been working as a paralegal for her attorney in this matter, found immediately in front of her at her "customary" location at the counsel table, a stack of documents of some 200 pages. It is unclear why and by whom the documents were placed in that precise location and not otherwise safeguarded, but counsel for defendants were sitting directly across the 12 by 6 foot counsel table.

Typed on the top page of the stack of documents was the heading:

"Weil, Gotshal & Manges MEMORANDUM
Two Files From Lawrence J. Baer
Re: *Joan Lipin* v *American Red Cross*"

The documents contained a series of internal memoranda prepared by counsel containing notes of various interviews with defendant Bender and other individuals employed or associated with NYRC concerning this action. The documents also included digests of depositions which had previously been taken in this action.

As counsel were engaged in argument concerning certain discovery matters, plaintiff slipped these documents off the table, placed them on her lap, and began to read them. As plaintiff read through the documents, she recognized that they were interviews with various witnesses relevant to this action. According to the hearing testimony, "I decided that I was going to obtain possession of these papers for my own protection." When argument before the Special Referee had ended, plaintiff informed her attorney that she had just read various inflammatory statements taken in interviews concerning her, and that she was "horrified." Counsel stated that he would not read the documents until he had obtained a "second opinion." During the luncheon recess, plaintiff went to counsel's office and copied the documents.

Counsel examined the documents on Sunday, June 30, 1991. According to him, the documents contained inflammatory references to plaintiff, as well as evidence of a "conspiracy to ruin her career." After conferring with the attorney who had originally referred the matter to him, both attorneys formed the opinion that they were entitled to retain the documents under a claim of right, and that any claim of confidentiality had been waived in view of the circumstances of the discovery of the documents—that they had been left unsecured, directly in front of the plaintiff, in a public area, such that plaintiff had been "invited" to read the documents.

Thereupon, plaintiff's counsel requested that opposing counsel attend a "settlement" conference at his offices at 2:00 P.M. on Tuesday, July 2, 1991. At that time, plaintiff's counsel made various demands, including (1) that Weil, Gotshal & Manges withdraw as counsel based upon a conflict of interest in representing both defendants Bender and NYRC, (2) a monetary settlement, and (3) "suitable action" to withdraw, with an apology for false information allegedly disseminated concerning plaintiff. In response to these demands, defense counsel demanded return of the documents and an explanation as to the manner in which plaintiff had obtained them. Plaintiff's counsel refused to reveal how the documents had been obtained, and also refused to return the copies which had been made, asserting that in any event he had no control over his client, who could conceivably give the documents to the mass media.

Defendants immediately sought, by order to show cause, an order pursuant to CPLR 3103 N.Y.C.P.L.R. suppressing the privileged documents, disqualifying plaintiff's attorney, and imposing sanctions. Pending a hearing, the IAS Court directed that no use be made of the documents and that any and all copies made of the documents be secured.

An evidentiary hearing was held, at which plaintiff revealed the manner in which she had removed the documents. Plaintiff admitted that in her employment as a paralegal, she was aware of the nature of the attorney-client privilege. Plaintiff further revealed that counsel had advised her, on the day the documents were obtained, that "you can't lie so you have to say yes, you by mistake picked up his documents." The plaintiff insisted, however, that the documents were not taken by mistake, but rather, "it was my own recognizance and my own protection." Following the hearing, defendants moved to amend their motion to seek dismissal of the complaint, based upon the hearing testimony given by plaintiff.

In a decision read into the record, the court found that the documents were on their face clearly attorney's work product, and that plaintiff, as an employee of her counsel, had an obligation to return those documents to opposing counsel. Instead, copies of the documents were made, for which there was "no justification." The court stated, "I have to

conclude that the actions of the plaintiff and her attorney were so egregious in taking this material * * * so heinous that the only remedy, as much as I dislike to do this, is to dismiss the lawsuit."

In *Matter of Beiny* (129 A.D.2d 126), counsel for petitioner in a trust accounting proceeding clandestinely obtained, by means of an improperly issued subpoena, discovery of confidential and privileged material from the adverse party's former law firm without notifying that party. This Court, in modifying the order of the Surrogate so as to disqualify petitioner's counsel in addition to the previously ordered suppression of the 107 improperly obtained documents, found that the sanction of disqualification, while regrettable, in that it deprived petitioner of his chosen counsel, was necessary

> "not only to sanitize the proceeding but to prevent the offending lawyer or firm from deriving any further benefit from information obtained and used in violation of basic ethical precepts and statutory obligations * * * [T]o impose a sanction short of disqualification would be to treat the conduct at issue with a degree of lenity practically inviting its recurrence. Our principal concern under the circumstances must be to preserve the integrity of the process by which rights are vindicated. (*Supra,* at 143–144.)

Under the circumstances of this case, although there is not the premeditation found in *Beiny (supra,* at 133), plaintiff's initial conduct is equally or even more egregious in terms of an appropriate sanction inasmuch as it was plaintiff herself who seized the opportunity presented to obtain an unfair advantage over her adversaries in this litigation. Her improper conduct was then compounded by counsel, who could have readily returned the documents or sought further direction from the court, rather than permitting his client to return this office and make copies of the disputed documents and then sought to take advantage of such improper conduct by scheduling a "settlement conference."

Although plaintiff's contention that CPLR 3103 N.Y.C.P.L.R. does not authorize a court to dismiss a complaint for discovery abuses has some facial appeal, as noted by Professor Siegel in his Practice Commentaries to the section, the factual variations that arise from case to case are limitless and a detailed listing of all possible abuses and remedies would be impractical and unwise. "If, for any reason sufficient to invoke that undefinable commodity known as judicial 'discretion,' an adjustment in the use of disclosure is called for by the facts of any case, CPLR 3103 N.Y.C.P.L.R. is at hand to confer the discretion." (Siegel, Practice Commentaries, McKinney's Cons Laws of NY, Book 7B, CPLR C3103:1, at 356.)

Thus, although the statute does not list dismissal as a remedy for a discovery abuse, it does not purport to set forth an exhaustive list of remedies, leaving the court the wide discretion to make "an appropriate order" to prevent the abuse of disclosure devices, including but not limited to suppression of information improperly obtained. Under the unique circumstances presented, particularly the sort of willful misbehavior engaged in by plaintiff and her attorney, we conclude that the IAS Court did not improvidently exercise its discretion in invoking the drastic sanction of dismissal of the complaint.

We have considered plaintiff's other points and find them without merit. Her attempt to portray the defendants as having engaged in dilatory and sharp practices appears to have but one purpose—to obscure the issue of her own misconduct. Moreover, there is no support for her claim that defendants waived any attorney-client privilege and, regardless of whether the documents were privileged, the highly improper manner in which they were obtained, combined with their subsequent use by plaintiff's counsel to defendants' detriment, constitutes a sufficient basis for the court's action *(see, Matter of Beiny, supra,* at 136). "[I]t is not unduly harsh to expect and indeed to require that civil litigants gather the information needed to prosecute or defend their actions in conformity with the applicable CPLR provisions." *(Supra,* at 137.)

Concur—Sullivan, J.P., Rosenberger, Kupferman and Asch, JJ.

Case Questions

1. How did the controversial materials end up in the plaintiff's hands?
2. Did the plaintiff know that the materials were covered by the attorney-client privilege?
3. Why did the plaintiff's attorney allow the materials to be copied?
4. Why did the defendant amend its motion, requesting the complaint be dismissed?
5. Is it fair that the plaintiff's serious claims be dismissed as a sanction for the misbehavior of her and her attorney?

Inadvertent Disclosure Results in Waiver

waived—To waive a right or prerogative is to give it up. A waiver can be implied.

Another response to the inadvertent disclosure of privileged materials is to declare that the privilege has been **waived**, and the other side has the right to use the materials. Even though the attorney-client privilege belongs to the client, and the attorney may have committed the error, the privilege can be waived without the client's express consent since the client acts through his or her appointed agent, the attorney. Some state ethics opinions expressly disagree with the 1992 ABA ethics opinion mentioned above (which requires the receiving lawyer to take no advantage of the mistakenly sent privileged materials), arguing that the ABA's position is too idealistic. Comm. on Professional Ethics of Illinois State Bar Ass'n Op. 98–4 (1999); D.C. Bar Legal Ethics

Commission Op. 256 (1995). These jurisdictions distinguish between two situations. In the first situation, the receiving lawyer is aware of the other lawyer's mistake, and then proceeds to examine the materials. That would be considered unethical. In the second situation, the receiving lawyer is unaware of the mistaken disclosure before examining the protected materials. Here, these opinions state that there is no ethics violation if the receiving lawyer uses those materials because a lawyer's ethical duty to zealously represent the client (Model Rule 1.3 and Model Code Canon 7) should take priority over helping the other, careless lawyer correct his or her mistake.

The view that inadvertent disclosure results in waiver is followed in certain federal jurisdictions. One of the more famous cases, *In re Grand Jury Investigation of Ocean Transportation*, 604 F.2d 672 (D.C. Cir. 1979), involved a subpoena that the Anti-Trust Division of the U. S. Government issued to a company. Although the company instructed its lawyer not to disclose any materials covered by the attorney-client privilege, the lawyer turned over two sets of documents that the company, after firing its first lawyer and retaining a different lawyer, later claimed were protected. The Court of Appeals ruled that the company absolutely waived the privilege with respect to the first set of documents because the original lawyer did not even mark those documents as protected or privileged. Therefore, it could not later be claimed by the second lawyer that the materials were privileged when sent to the Government. The second set of documents, however, was marked with a "P." Regarding those documents, the court found that the privilege was also waived because the government, upon discovering the materials, contacted the original counsel inquiring whether the materials were, in fact, protected. The original counsel inexplicably stated they were not, and it was not until over a year had passed that the original counsel claimed those materials were privileged (the second lawyer being the one who issued the formal demand that the materials be returned). Since the government acted appropriately upon its discovery of the materials, and because so much time had passed during the interim—which included the Government's use of the materials—it was too late to try to close the Pandora's box.

Other federal courts hold a similar view that inadvertent disclosure results in a waiver of the privilege. *See Weil v. Investment/Indicators, Research & Management, Inc.*, 647 F.2d 18 (9th Cir 1981); *Liggett Group v. Brown & Williamson Tobacco Corp.*, 116 FRD 205, (M.D. N.C. 1986); *International Digital Systems Corp. v. Digital Equipment Corp.*, 120 FRD 445 (D. Mass. 1988).

Some state courts also hold that inadvertent disclosure can result in waiver of the attorney-client privilege, as the following case from Oregon shows.

Case Law

Goldsborough v. Eagle Crest Partners, Ltd., 848 P.2d 1049 (Oregon 1992)

VAN HOOMISSEN, J.

The sole question in this case is whether defen-

dant waived its lawyer-client privilege as to a letter that defendant wrote to its lawyer and that defendant's lawyer voluntarily gave plaintiff in response to plaintiff's pretrial request for production of documents. The trial court ruled that defendant waived its privilege, and the Court of Appeals affirmed. *Goldsborough v. Eagle Crest Partners, Ltd.,* 105 Or. App. 499, 805 P.2d 723 (1991). We also affirm. Plaintiff sued her employer for statutory remedies pursuant to ORS 659.121 (1) and for common law wrongful discharge, alleging that defendant had fired her in violation of ORS 659.030 as retaliation for her filing an administrative claim of sex discrimination. Before trial, plaintiff served on defendant a request for production of documents, ORCP 43, seeking: "3. Any and all correspondence between defendants and any other entity *other than defense counsel* regarding plaintiff." (Emphasis added.) In response, defendant's lawyer voluntarily gave plaintiff a letter written by defendant's personnel director to defendant's lawyer concerning plaintiff's employment. [The letter stated in part: "In reviewing my notes on Vicki's interview of October 27th, she made the following statement, 'Yes, a lot of guys come on to me, I try and support four kids.' There has to be a reason guy's *[sic]* 'come on' to her. . . . At present, Vicki's performance has been 'Excellent,' so I'll just have to wait."]

At trial, plaintiff offered the letter in evidence. Defendant's lawyer objected, arguing for the first time that the letter was privileged and that defendant did not intend to waive its lawyer-client privilege when the letter was given to plaintiff. Defendant offered no evidence, and did not argue, that the disclosure was inadvertent, mistaken, or not authorized by the client. In response, plaintiff conceded that the letter was a confidential communication, but argued that, because of the voluntary disclosure during discovery, defendant had waived its privilege. Defendant's lawyer acknowledged that he had voluntarily disclosed the letter, but argued that, notwithstanding, defendant did not intend to waive its privilege and, further, that the burden was on plaintiff to show that the client specifically consented to a waiver. The trial court ruled that the privilege had been waived and admitted the letter in evidence. The jury

later found for plaintiff and awarded her damages.

On appeal, defendant contended that the trial court erred in admitting the letter into evidence and requested a new trial. ORCP 64B(6). Finding no Oregon cases directly on point, and relying primarily on federal cases, the Court of Appeals affirmed, stating: "Defendant has the burden to show that the letter was privileged and that it did not waive the privilege. Defendant concedes that it voluntarily disclosed the document. . . ." The Court of Appeals rejected defendant's argument that there must be "specific evidence of authorization" by the client in order to find that a lawyer's disclosure of a privileged document is a waiver. . . .

On review, defendant argues, as it did in the Court of Appeals, that its lawyer's voluntary disclosure of the letter during discovery did not waive its privilege and that it had no such intent here. Defendant reasons that, because the lawyer-client privilege belongs to the client (and not to the lawyer) and because a waiver is an intentional relinquishment of a known right, its lawyer's voluntary disclosure was not an intentional relinquishment of a known right by the client. Defendant argues further that there can be no waiver found without specific evidence of the client's consent, and that the burden is on plaintiff to show that the client specifically consented to a waiver.

OEC 503(2)(a) provides in part: "A client has a privilege to refuse to disclose and to prevent any other person from disclosing confidential communications made for the purpose of facilitating the rendition of professional legal services to the client."

OEC 511 provides in part: "A person upon whom [OEC 503 to 514] confer a privilege against disclosure of the confidential matter or communication waives the privilege if the person * * * voluntarily discloses or consents to disclosure of any significant part of the matter or communication. This [rule] does not apply if the disclosure is itself a privileged communication." . . .

By traditional doctrine, waiver is the intentional relinquishment of a known right. *Johnson v. Zerbst,* 304 U.S. 458, 464, 58 S Ct 1019, 82 L Ed 1461

(1938). However, in the confidential privilege situations, once confidentiality is destroyed through voluntary disclosure, no subsequent claim of privilege can restore it, and knowledge or lack of knowledge of the existence of the privilege appears to be irrelevant. California Evidence Code § 912; 8 Wigmore § 2327. Kirkpatrick, Oregon Evidence 282-83 (2d ed 1989).

See Smith v. Aleyska Pipeline Service Co., 538 F. Supp. 977, 980-82 (D Del 1982), *aff'd* 758 F.2d 668 (1st Cir 1984), *cert den* 471 U.S. 1066 (1985) (lawyer-client privilege waived when the lawyer, acting on behalf of the client, voluntarily sent to the opposing party a copy of an opinion letter addressed to the client concerning the litigation).

Defendant relies primarily on *Bryant v. Dukehart,* 106 Or. 359, 210 P. 454 (1923), a pre-Oregon Evidence Code case. In *Bryant,* there was no showing that the party claiming the privilege had turned over the privileged material. Indeed, it was not known how the privileged material reached the opposing party. Here, defendant admits that its lawyer voluntarily gave the letter to plaintiff during pretrial discovery. . . .

It is common practice for clients to authorize their lawyers to respond to discovery requests. In the absence of evidence to the contrary, an inference may be drawn that a lawyer who voluntarily turns over privileged material during discovery acts within the scope of the lawyer's authority from the client and with the client's consent. The lawyer's action in voluntarily giving privileged material in response to a demand for discovery is at least an implicit representation by the lawyer that the lawyer has the client's consent to do so, *i.e.,* that the client has waived the privilege. A voluntary disclosure by a client's lawyer

under facts such as those present here is, accordingly, sufficient to permit a trial court to find a waiver.

A court need not necessarily conclude that the lawyer-client privilege has been waived when a document has been produced during discovery. Factors to be considered by the court may be whether the disclosure was inadvertent, whether any attempt was made to remedy any error promptly, and whether preservation of the privilege will occasion unfairness to the opponent.

McCormick, Evidence 342-43, § 93 (4th ed 1992). As noted above, defendant conceded that its lawyer voluntarily gave the letter to plaintiff in response to plaintiff's discovery request. Plaintiff had not requested the letter. Defendant offered no evidence, and did not argue, that the disclosure was mistaken, inadvertent, or unauthorized by the client. Defendant argued only that it did not intend to waive its privilege when its lawyer voluntarily gave plaintiff the letter and that proof of the client's specific consent is necessary to find a waiver. There was no evidence or argument that the disclosure was mistaken or inadvertent or that defendant's lawyer was acting outside the scope of his authority. There is no general legal requirement that a client have specifically consented to the release of a particular document in order for a waiver to be established.

We conclude that there was sufficient evidence to support the trial court's ruling under OEC 104(1) that defendant waived its privilege. We therefore hold that the trial court did not err in admitting the letter in evidence.

The decision of the Court of Appeals and the judgment of the circuit court are affirmed.

Case Questions

1. Why does this court disagree with the premise that the attorney-client privilege is not waived unless the client affirmatively waives it?
2. What factors in the court's reasoning helped it reach the conclusion that the privilege had been lost?
3. Do you agree with this court's view on inadvertent disclosure, or do you agree with the ABA's position on inadvertent disclosure?

THE LEGAL ASSISTANT AND CONFIDENTIALITY

It is critical that the non-lawyer employee understand the ramifications of violating the duty of confidentiality. The first step for the legal assistant is to determine what kind of confidentiality rule is in place in his or her jurisdiction. If the legal assistant is working in a state that follows the ABA Model Rules, then more than just client "secrets" are confidential; all client information, from whatever the source, is considered confidential and must be held sacred. Examining one's jurisdiction's confidentiality rule will allow the legal assistant to see if the rule has broader exceptions than the Model Code or Model Rules (as does New Jersey's), more stringent exceptions (as does Illinois's), or no exceptions (as does California's).

How Does the Attorney-Client Privilege Cover the Legal Assistant?

As stated earlier in the chapter, if a client or prospective client contacts a legal assistant for the purposes of seeking legal advice from the lawyer, the statement made to the legal assistant can be considered protected by the attorney-client privilege. The fact that the statement was made to a non-lawyer does not ruin the attorney-client privilege because the more important fact concerns the type of statement and the manner in which it was made: the statement was the kind the attorney-client privilege covers (seeking legal advice), and was made to an authorized agent of the lawyer who received the statement within the scope of employment (the legal assistant).

A more difficult question involves whether the attorney-client privilege applies to the paralegal's work, performed at the direction of the supervising attorney on behalf of a client matter. If, for example, the information gathered during litigation by an attorney's paralegal were outside the scope of the attorney-client privilege, the paralegal's role would then be relegated to that of a secretary and would include no substantive work assignments.

Fortunately, that is not how courts apply the attorney-client privilege. One of the more famous cases in this area is *Samaritan Foundation v. Superior Court*, 844 P. 2d 593 (Ariz. App. Div. 1 1992), which was later vacated in part on other grounds by *Samaritan Foundation v. Goodfarb*, 862 P.2d 870 (Ariz. 1993). In that case, parents of a baby who had a cardiac arrest during surgery sued the hospital and two doctors. Following the surgery, the hospital's legal department assigned a nurse-paralegal to interview three nurses and a scrub technician who witnessed the surgery. During the litigation, the plaintiffs deposed those four witnesses, who then claimed they could not remember what had happened in the operating room. When the plaintiffs learned that the witnesses had been interviewed soon after the surgery, they petitioned the trial court to order disclosure of the summaries of the interviews taken by the paralegal, arguing that since she was not an attorney, her notes were not covered by the attorney-client privilege statute, which did not include paralegals (although the statute did include an attorney's secretary, stenographer, or clerk). However, the court concluded that, because the law has recognized that lawyers may appropriately and efficiently act through their paralegals, they should not have to stop assigning litigation tasks to paralegals just to maintain the privilege. Therefore, it held that, "a lawyer does not forfeit the attorney-client privilege by receiving otherwise privileged client communications through the conduit of a properly supervised paralegal employee." *Id* at 599–600.

Other courts have also held that the attorney-client privilege and the work-product rule can apply to the work of the paralegal, or some other agent of the attorney. *See State v. Post*, 513 N.E.2d 754 (Ohio 1987). However, it is not true that everything a paralegal does during litigation is protected by the attorney-client privilege or covered by the work product rule. Courts usually hold that in order for a nonlawyer's work to be covered by the attorney-client privilege, the work must be of such a nature that the performance of it required professional skill. If the non-lawyer's work required no particular expertise and could have been done by a layperson, the argument could be made that the work should not be protected by the privilege. In fact, in *Samaritan Foundation v. Superior Court*, discussed earlier, the court made sure to emphasize that it was not creating a paralegal-client privilege. It was only applying the attorney-client privilege where the paralegal's work was of such a substantive nature that it warranted being covered by the attorney-client privilege. *Samaritan Foundation v. Superior Court* at 600.

Determining exactly what types of litigation-related work require professional skill is not as easy as it seems. The fact that documents might take more than a few hours to prepare does not necessarily mean that professional skill was required to prepare them. In a New York case, plaintiffs sued a car company for injuries sustained in a car accident. During discovery, the plaintiff's attorney traveled to the defendant's offices in Dearborn, Michigan, in order to examine boxes of documents concerning the design and development of the automobile plaintiff was driving at the time of the accident. About thirty of the seventy-six boxes were not available because, according to the defendant's attorneys, they were protected and confidential materials. Upon learning that one of the defendant's attorneys and two paralegals had reviewed all the boxes and prepared indexes describing the contents of the boxes, the plaintiff sought the indexes, and the defendant claimed the indexes were also privileged. The court found that indexes were not protected by the work product rule because the defendant presented no evidence that the indexes were created by using "any particular legal skills." *Bloss v. Ford Motor Co.*, 126 A.D.2d 804, 805 (N.Y. App. Div. 1987).

Tips to Protect Confidentiality and the Attorney-Client Privilege

Certain practices can be deployed to minimize unintended breaches of confidentiality. First, lawyers and paralegals need to be vigilant about discussing client matters outside the office, especially in public places like the hallways of the courthouse or in restaurants. The word *overheard* is in the dictionary for a reason. Client matters should also not be discussed at home with family members or with personal acquaintances for this simple reason: what is the guarantee that the person to whom you tell client matters will not violate a promise to you to keep things confidential when he or she knows that you are already in violation?

At the office, a few extra steps to ensure protection of client information can be taken. Although e-mail can be sent unencrypted without violating the duty of confidentiality, it should be sent encrypted since encryption of e-mail is relatively easy to accomplish. Having on file the client's permission to communicate by e-mail can protect against later malpractice charges. Paralegals should also change their computer passwords regularly in order to make it more difficult for others to access that account. Files should never be left in the open, or even given to unauthorized personnel in the firm, since there is no such thing as an absolute, implied authorization that covers all employees of a law firm. Phone conversations with clients or about client matters should not occur within earshot of others. Mobile phones should not be used to discuss client matters. And those legal assistants who work for lawyers who share common office space (such as waiting or conference rooms) with other lawyers who are not in a partnership need to be especially careful. Since what a client says in public areas can be considered unprotected by the attorney-client privilege, then receptionists, secretaries, and legal assistants should do their best to prevent clients—and prospective clients—from discussing their situation in common areas. And if an occasion occurs where the client tells the paralegal something, but requests that the paralegal not pass that information on to the lawyer, the paralegal needs to tactfully explain to the client that the duty of confidentiality starts with the attorney. Paralegals may withhold no client information from their supervising attorneys, regardless of any client requests to the contrary.

Since paralegals do considerable amounts of discovery work, it is critical that they never send discovery materials to the opposing party's counsel without making sure the materials can be sent. Although many jurisdictions refuse to consider the attorney-client privilege has been waived by inadvertent disclosure, there is no guarantee that harm will not come to the client (or paralegal) due to the error. Asking a supervising lawyer whether certain documents should be sent, even if the original instructions by the attorney were that the documents should be sent, can prevent the paralegal from being wrongfully blamed for sending protected materials. Because lawyers balance many cases at the same time, good legal assistants should take it upon themselves to be a bit paranoid and, if in doubt, ask their supervising lawyers for confirmation that what was instructed to be sent should in fact be sent.

When marking discovery materials as protected, legal assistants should mark them in a permanent way, because post-it notes and other labels can fall off privileged materials. If inadequately labeled privileged materials are mistakenly sent to the opposing party's counsel and the receiving counsel is initially unaware of the mistake, the attorney-client privilege can be considered waived in certain jurisdictions. Even if a court were to find that the privilege has not been lost by inadvertent disclosure of protected materials, that in no way protects the firm if and when the disgruntled client files a grievance with the disciplinary commission or a malpractice action against the firm.

Summary

The doctrine of confidentiality is one of the foremost ethical considerations in the law, and it takes shape in two interrelated concepts: the duty of confidentiality and the attorney-client privilege. The duty of confidentiality is found in the rules of professional responsibility, while the attorney-client privilege is located in the litigation-related rules of discovery and evidence.

Jurisdictions that apply the Model Rules consider client information, from whatever the source, protected as confidential. However, jurisdictions that apply the Model Code consider client confidences and secrets protected. Client confidentiality attaches before the client has retained the lawyer's services and survives the lawyer-client relationship. If the client is an organization, the organization, and not its constituents, is the recipient of the duty of confidentiality. If the client makes statements to his or her lawyer in a context that can reasonably be construed as not made in confidence, those statements can be obtained if a court considers that the context effected a waiver of the attorney-client privilege. Certain kinds of information, such as fees or the client's identity, can be considered not covered by the duty of confidentiality. Agents of the lawyer, such as the lawyer's paralegal, are also covered by the duty of confidentiality and are expected to treat client information in the same manner as is expected of the lawyer. Lawyers have implied authorization to disclose client information that is necessary to proceed with the representation, such as in settlement negotiations.

Both the Model Rules and the Model Code allow a lawyer to disclose client information, even sensitive information, under certain, exceptional circumstances. The duty of confidentiality can be breeched in order to prevent the client from committing serious crimes or fraud or to defend against criminal charges or charges made by the client or collect fees. When the law allows an attorney to disclose client information, the attorney may only disclose that which is essential for the purpose of the exception.

Although there are risks involved in using certain technology to conduct client business or to communicate with clients, many jurisdictions do not prohibit attorneys from using e-mail, fax machines, or mobile phones. Some jurisdictions advise obtaining client consent before using e-mail or mobile phones, and a few jurisdictions caution against using either technology.

The American Bar Association's Ethics 2000 proposal for Model Rule 1.6 was significantly different from its prior version. However, the House of Delegates did not accept all of the proposed changes. The House of Delegates approved the change allowing disclosing of client confidences to prevent reasonably certain death or substantial bodily harm, as well as to seek legal advice, but it rejected the proposal allowing for disclosures necessary to prevent a crime or fraud caused by the client's use of the lawyer's services.

The attorney-client privilege is a concept derived from the rules of discovery and evidence. It generally protects against lawyers being compelled to testify against their clients or disclosing client information in litigation and is usually found in statutes on witness competency rather than in the rules of ethics. The work product rule, as found in Civil Procedure Rule 26, does allow a limited exception for client information that was prepared in anticipation of litigation to be turned over to the other party under extreme circumstances. However, even within that exception, parties are not allowed access to materials that express the legal strategies or theories of the other parties' attorneys. The attorney-client privilege covers employees of the attorney, including legal assistants who are the recipients of information made by clients or prospective clients. If, during the course of discovery, lawyers inadvertently disclose privileged materials to the other party, that mistake can result in a waiver of the attorney-client privilege, although many jurisdictions consider inadvertently disclosed materials to remain covered by the privilege.

Legal Assistants are expressly authorized to deal in client matters and can have access to client information. While working on client matters, legal assistants should take precautions to prevent unauthorized persons from having access to client information, and should refrain from discussing client matters with those not covered by attorney-client confidentiality. Moreover, while working on discovery matters, legal assistants should exercise great caution when marking materials as protected materials and also when turning discovery materials over to the other parties' attorneys, since it is possible that inadvertent disclosure can result in a waiver of the attorney-client privilege, if not a malpractice claim. For a paralegal's work to be covered by the attorney-client privilege or the work product rule, it needs to be the kind of work that requires some level of professional skill.

Points to Ponder

1. What are the reasons why the duty of confidentiality is such a hallowed concept?
2. How does the Model Rules version on confidentiality differ from the Model Code version?
3. What is the difference between client information and client confidences?
4. How does the Ethics 2000 version of MR 1.6 differ from its prior version?
5. Using your jurisdiction's rules, determine whether your jurisdiction's confidentiality rule is based on the Model Code or the Model Rules and whether your jurisdiction's rule is different from its ABA counterpart.
6. When would an attorney have an implied authorization to disclose client information?
7. What kinds of information can generally be considered as not confidential?
8. When, as an exception, could the information identified in (7) be considered confidential?
9. How do the confidentiality rules affect legal assistants?
10. What makes the doctrine of confidentiality more difficult to grasp in cases where the client is an organization, such as a corporation?
11. Going back to the scenario at the beginning of the chapter, what advice would you give Rachel about her dilemma concerning whether to do anything about the information that the client, William, has settled with other women who accused him of sexual assault?
12. What are the basic exceptions to the requirement that client information be kept confidential?
13. What policy concern is consistent behind all of the exceptions identified in (12)?
14. Do you think a lawyer should be allowed to tell a grieving family where their child is buried if he or she knows where the client buried the body and the client has already been found not guilty? What if the client has been found guilty? If the lawyer discloses the information, should he or she be disbarred for breeching one of the duties of professional responsibility?
15. What limitations apply when a lawyer is considering disclosing client information to prevent a crime or fraud?
16. Do you think a lawyer should be obligated to disclose to a client's sexual partner that the client has an infectious disease?
17. What is the attorney-client privilege?
18. What is the work product rule?
19. When would a paralegal be covered by the attorney-client privilege?

20. What distinguishes the two kinds of work product?
21. Why do jurisdictions consider that the attorney-client privilege has not been waived in cases where privileged materials have been inadvertently disclosed to the other party?
22. What is the criticism of the ABA ethics opinion stating that when lawyers are in receipt of protected materials mistakenly sent to them that they should not examine them and instead should follow the other lawyer's wishes about returning the materials?
23. Do you think a lawyer should be allowed to take advantage of the opposing party's otherwise protected materials when it is erroneously sent to him or her?
24. In addition to techniques mentioned in the chapter, are there other techniques paralegals can use to help ensure client confidentiality?
25. In addition to techniques mentioned in the chapter, are there other techniques legal assistants can use to help ensure that they are not involved in inadvertent disclosure?

Key Concepts

Attorney-client privilege	Implied authorizations
Attorney-opinion work product rule	Inadvertent disclosure
Confidentiality exceptions	Informed consent
Corporate constituents	Last link doctrine
Discovery	Privileged materials
Duty of confidentiality	Witness competency statutes
Encrypted e-mail	Work product rule
Fiduciary	

Key Terms

constituent	interrogatories	restatement
discovery	Office of Independent Counsel (OIC)	retainer
fiduciary		solicitor general
fraud	prima facie	waived
informed consent		

Chapter 5

Conflicts of Interest

*No man is above the law and no man is below it; nor do we ask
any man's permission when we ask him to obey it.*

—President Teddy Roosevelt

When the President does it, that means it is not illegal.

—President Richard Nixon

INTRODUCTION

If a hall of fame for great American lawyers were to be built, the first inductee
might be John Adams. Although one of the most significant founding fathers and
early presidents (see Chapter 1), Adams had a genteel personality less memorable
than those of Benjamin Franklin and Patrick Henry and a presidency sandwiched
between two historical giants, George Washington and Thomas Jefferson. Like
Jefferson, Adams was a lawyer. In fact, as a Boston-area resident, Adams was
involved in one of the most wrenching legal cases of the colonial period. On March
5, 1770, British soldiers in Boston fired on an angry crowd that had begun throwing rock-filled snowballs and sticks at a British sentry. Five people were killed in
what became known as the Boston Massacre, including Crispus Attucks, a free
black man, who has been called America's first casualty of the fight for independence. The British soldiers were charged with murder and in desperate need of a
capable lawyer, since most in Boston thought the trial would be a formality to the
soldiers' execution. Although he was an area resident with ties to the local protest
movement, John Adams agreed to serve as the soldiers' lead defense counsel, all
other local lawyers having turned down the defendants' requests. His was the task
of convincing the jury that in response to the activities of the mob in the street that
day, the soldiers had fired in self-defense. So successful was Adams in the six-day
trial (the first trial in Massachusetts to last longer than a day) that all but two of the
defendants were acquitted. Moreover, the two convictions were for manslaughter,
rather than murder, and the punishment was thumb branding rather than death.

How was John Adams treated during this ordeal? He was reviled by his fellow
townspeople and patriots for his lack of loyalty to their cause. Those fellow towns-

people included John Adams's cousin, Samuel Adams, believed by some to have been the instigator behind the mob gathering that day. (Samuel Adams would later achieve immortality for instigating the Boston Tea Party.) John Adams's wife and children were also treated maliciously. Adams, however, believed that every accused person had a right to a fair trial. So great was the tension over the conflict between Adams's political and personal beliefs as a New England colonial and his professional obligations as a lawyer that he wrote in his diary that during that time period, he was "never in more misery my whole life." However, John Adams's duty to the law was so strong that he later wrote of his defense of the Boston Massacre defendants, "It was, however, one of the most gallant, generous, manly and disinterested Actions of my whole Life, and one of the best Pieces of Service I ever rendered my Country." *The Diary and Autobiography of John Adams.* (L. H. Butterfield, Editor. Harvard University Press, 1961). Such a wonderful testament to professionalism in the face of a conflict of interest is even more impressive in light of the fact that Adams reported that he was never even thanked by the highest-ranking British officer for whom Adams had obtained an acquittal.

When a lawyer undertakes to represent a client, he or she not only pledges confidentiality to the client but also pledges, in a more general sense, loyalty to the client. Loyalty is the starting point for conflicts of interest rules. Because lawyers are fiduciaries, they are bound to put their clients' interests ahead of their own. Although it may have been advantageous for the cause of the New England protestors—a group to whom John Adams belonged—that the British soldiers be found guilty of the Boston Massacre, upon agreeing to take the case, John Adams's loyalties to his friends and fellow citizens took a backseat to the loyalty to his clients. If the same situation were to occur today, it would be very interesting to see if the conflicts of interest rules would even allow a lawyer like John Adams to undertake such a representation.

The duty of loyalty takes effect most directly in the rules of professional responsibility that concern conflicts of interest: ABA Model Rules 1.7 through 1.11, and 1.13; and DR 5-101 through 107, DR 7–106, and DR 9–101 of the ABA Model Code. Because legal assistants are obligated to comport themselves in the same professional manner as lawyers, legal assistants also need to be concerned with the various conflicts that can occur in the lawyer-client relationship. However, because legal assistants do not directly advocate on the client's behalf, the conflicts rules may not always be directly applicable to them. This chapter's discussion will include an examination of conflicts of interest that arise in the following situations: when two present clients of the lawyer are in conflict with one another; when a present client is in conflict with a former client; when two present clients are seeking joint representation; and when a client's interest may be in conflict with the lawyer's interests. We will also analyze certain kinds of transactions between lawyers and clients that are either prohibited or severely limited. Finally, we will examine the difficulties that occur when lawyers and legal assistants move from one firm to another and then represent clients whose interests are in opposition to a party represented by the firm where the lawyers or legal assistants used to work. This is known as imputed disqualification, and here, the law generally provides more leeway to paralegals than it does to lawyers. Bear in mind as the conflicts rules are examined that the lawyer and the paralegal's right to earn a living and the general public's freedom to have the lawyer of their choice will occasionally allow for exceptions to the conflicts rules.

The Model Rules' Starting Point for Conflicts of Interest

The source for many jurisdictions' general rule on conflicts of interest states the following:

(a) A lawyer shall not represent a client if the representation of that client will be directly adverse to another client, unless:
   (1) the lawyer reasonably believes the representation will not adversely affect the relationship with the other client; and
   (2) each client consents after consultation.
(b) A lawyer shall not represent a client if the representation of that client may be materially limited by the lawyer's responsibilities to another client or to a third person, or by the lawyer's own interests, unless:
   (1) the lawyer reasonably believes the representation will not be adversely affected; and
   (2) the client consents after consultation. When representation of multiple clients in a single matter is undertaken, the consultation shall include explanation of the implications of the common representation and the advantages and risks involved. ABA Model Rule 1.7.

Section (a) of the rule concerns actual conflicts of interest between different clients, while section (b) concerns possible conflicts between different clients, between the client and a third party, and between the client and the lawyer's own interests. This rule, as with many rules, has exceptions, but in this case do the exceptions overshadow the rule? If a client can consent to the representation notwithstanding the conflict, as is the case in both sections of MR 1.7, then is anything prohibited by the rule? Yes, there are some absolutes. The Comment to MR 1.7 states that clients may not be given the opportunity to give consent to continued representation involving directly adverse conflicts when "a disinterested lawyer would conclude that a client should not agree to the representation." While what is direct or material may not always be clear, it is clear that in such situations, the client cannot consent to the lawyer's continuing representation.

The Model Code and General Conflicts of Interest

The Model Code of Professional Responsibility has a rule that is similar to MR 1.7. DR 5–101(A) states, "Except with the consent of his client after full disclosure, a lawyer shall not accept employment if the exercise of his professional judgment on behalf of the client will be or reasonably may be affected by his own financial, business, property, or personal interests." DR 5-105(A) states that a lawyer

> shall decline proffered employment if the exercise of his independent professional judgment in behalf of a client will be or is likely to be adversely affected by the acceptance of the proffered employment, or if it would be likely to involve him in representing differing interests, except to the extent permitted under DR 5-105(C).

Section (C) states:

> a lawyer may represent multiple clients if it is obvious that he can adequately represent the interest of each and if each consents to the representation after full disclosure of the possible effect of such representation on the exercise of his independent professional judgment of behalf of each.

COMMON CONFLICTS OF INTEREST

Because there is more than one conflicts of interest rule, the possibilities of conflicts that face attorneys and their nonlawyer employees are many (Exhibit 5–1). An analysis of all the conflicts of interests envisioned by the rules is beyond the scope of this text. But there are some conflicts of interest that are more likely than others to occur, six of which will be explained below.

Double Representation: One Lawyer Representing the Plaintiff and the Defendant

A lawyer cannot represent the plaintiff and the defendant in the same lawsuit because there is no more direct conflict that can occur between parties than when they are on opposite sides of litigation. Suppose someone who is sued for negligence stemming from an automobile accident would try to retain a lawyer to represent them against the plaintiff, only to find out the lawyer is already representing the plaintiff. The lawyer can have no loyalty to either client if representing both of them at the same time, against one another. *See Alex Munoz Gen. Contractor, Inc. v. MC3D, Inc.,* 1998 WL 831806 (N.D. Ill. Nov. 25, 1998) (a law firm that represents a corporation cannot also represent the shareholders of the corporation in a lawsuit against the corporation). Some states, such as Texas, expressly prohibit lawyers from representing opposing parties in the same litigation. Texas Disciplinary Rules of Professional Conduct, Rule 1.06(a) (1999).

Perhaps you have heard about married couples going through a divorce and using the same lawyer, due to the fact that the divorce was amicable and both spouses agreed to all terms related to it. While it is possible that such a non-confrontational divorce could be obtained (with both spouses satisfied with the cost

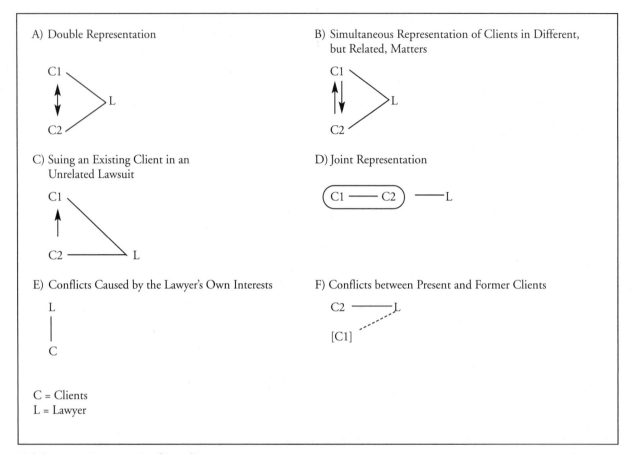

Exhibit 5-1   Common Conflicts of Interest

savings that come from sharing one lawyer), it is important to remember that spouses getting divorced are officially antagonists to each other, so sharing the same lawyer is like playing with matches. Some jurisdictions expressly prohibit a lawyer from representing both spouses in a divorce, regardless of the circumstances. For instance, Utah has an ethics opinion that prohibits it. Utah Bar Ethics Op. 116 (1992). And two West Virginia cases show the evolution of such a prohibition. In the first one, the West Virginia Supreme Court held that an attorney may not represent both spouses in any stage of a separation or divorce. *Walden v. Hoke*, 429 S.E.2d 504 (W.Va.1993). And in the second case, an attorney was sanctioned because, while representing the husband in an amicable divorce, he also prepared the response to the divorce complaint for the wife, who was representing herself, pro se. Although the lawyer prepared the wife's answer at the request of the husband, that fact did not alter the court's view that the lawyer violated his duty of loyalty to the husband. *Lawyer Disciplinary Bd. v. Frame*, 479 S.E.2d 676 (W.Va. 1996). In a Georgia case, the court upheld the jury's finding of punitive damages against a lawyer who represented a wife in a divorce, wherein the lawyer and her paralegal forged the husband's signature, this following the lawyer's initial representation of the husband in the divorce. *Peters v. Hyatt Legal Services*, 469 S.E.2d 481 (Ga. Ct. App. 1996).

There are, however, some jurisdictions that have given limited approval to divorcing spouses sharing their lawyer. An Oregon ethics opinion initially states that such a representation is inappropriate, but it then lists ten divorce-related factors and states that if all ten are present, then dual representation may be appropriate. Oregon Formal Op. 1991–86 (1991). Some of those factors include there being no minor children, the wife not being pregnant at the time of the divorce, and the couple having no substantial assets or liabilities. And in an Indiana case where a lawyer was charged with violating Ind. Rule 1.7 for representing both spouses in a divorce, the court concluded that the evidence was inconclusive about whom the lawyer represented in the divorce. Nonetheless, it stated that, "[r]egardless, the evidence does establish that the [lawyer's] actions were taken with the full knowledge and consent of the husband and the wife." *Matter of Lively*, 658 N.E.2d 903, 905 (Ind. 1995).

Which Client Gets the Lawyer?

Whom should the lawyer represent if the plaintiff and the defendant are current clients? The Comments to MR 1.7 state that when such conflicts of interest arise, whether at the beginning, or during the course, of representation, the lawyer is obligated to withdraw from the representation. MR 1.16(a)(1) also requires that a lawyer withdraw from representing a client if "the representation will result in violation of the rules of professional conduct." Therefore, if an attorney is requested by two current clients to represent them in litigation against each other, he or she must decline both requests. And if, during the course of representing a client, the attorney becomes aware that the representation will cause a direct conflict with another client, he or she must withdraw. Direct conflicts can also occur when another client is not an opposing party but might be involved as a witness on the opposing side. A 1992 ABA ethics opinion even stated that a lawyer may not represent a client in litigation if he or she would be required, in the course of the litigation, to cross-examine another of his or her own clients. ABA Comm. on Ethics and Professional Responsibility, Formal Op. 92–367 (1992).

A slightly different problem occurs when a lawyer represents two current clients in a matter that has not yet reached the situation where one client is suing the other. Imagine, for instance, an attorney acting as an advisory intermediary between two clients discussing the terms for the sale of a piece of real estate. If the performance of the contract terms is thought to be insufficient by one of the parties, such conflict could lead to litigation. Although the exception to the above-cited rule requires client consent, a client can only be given the option to consent after the lawyer determines that the conflict is not a direct conflict. See *Florida Bar v. Sofo*, 673 So. 2d 1 (Fla. 1996), in which a lawyer was disciplined for representing different corporations in the same matter, which eventually became contentious.

Simultaneous Representation of Clients in Different, but Related, Matters

A lawyer cannot properly represent both the plaintiff and the defendant in the same lawsuit, that much is clear. But a similar conflict can arise when a lawyer represents two clients who are in different lawsuits that involve a related issue or antagonist positions. For example, imagine an attorney representing a defendant in a tort action that results in settlement following mediation. Following the mediation, however, the defendant refuses to honor the settlement agreement and the plaintiff seeks the representation of the defendant's lawyer who helped negotiate the settlement. Even though attempting to enforce a settlement agreement is distinct from the original cause of action, the defendant's lawyer cannot represent the plaintiff because the connection between the two matters is too close. For example, in a Florida case, a lawyer was reprimanded for the following reasons: she represented an employee in a successful unemployment compensation case; the employer then brought a suit against the employee, which was dismissed; then, when the employee brought a malicious prosecution suit against the employer, the lawyer represented the employer. *Florida Bar v. Milin*, 502 So.2d 900 (Fla. 1986).

This kind of conflict of interest can also occur in settings other than litigation. For example, in an Indiana case, a lawyer who was representing a client in a bankruptcy proceeded to sell a car to that client that the lawyer was leasing from another client (but was authorized to sell). The lawyer never informed the client who purchased the car that he was selling it on behalf of another client. In reprimanding the lawyer, the court mentioned that both clients' interests were clearly antagonistic since a buyer and seller have opposite aims, with the seller wanting the highest price possible and the buyer wanting the lowest price possible. Therefore, the lawyer should have informed the purchasing client about the conflict of interest and given that client an opportunity to seek independent representation for the purchase of the car, or to consent to the lawyer's continued representation. *In re Horine*, 661 N.E.2d 1206 (Ind. 1996).

Suing an Existing Client in an Unrelated Suit

In *The Godfather*, Vito Corleone is the only client of his lawyer, who also happens to be one of Corleone's sons. Such is not the case for most real-life lawyers, who have many clients and, as law firms get bigger and establish offices in different cities or even countries, it is possible that lawyers from one office of the same firm might be asked to be involved in litigation against another party who is a client from another office of the same firm. Although the firm could not represent both sides to the same litigation, it is possible that it could be involved in the unrelated suit against another client, if both clients gives their consent. This would require one of the clients using a different firm for their representation, or else the matter would no longer be "unrelated." The Comments to MR 1.7 acknowledge such a representation by saying that a corporate or government lawyer may serve as an advocate against the corporate enterprise or government in unrelated matters if doing so would not adversely affect the lawyer's relationship with the main client and if both parties consent after consultation. Not only is a conflict of loyalties a pitfall in such a representation, but there is also a danger of a breach of the duty of confidentiality, possibilities that need to be discussed with both clients as part of the consent consultation.

Conflicts issues of this type can be difficult to grasp because, outside the clearly prohibited representations, whether consent can be given or whether the representation is appropriate is extremely fact sensitive. In an older case, a lawyer was sanctioned for representing a husband in a worker's compensation claim while at the same time representing the man's wife in the couple's divorce. The court called the unrelated representations "decidedly antagonistic." *Memphis & Shelby County Bar Ass'n v. Sanderson*, 52 Tenn. App. 684, at 707 (Tenn. App. 1963). In another case, a law firm represented a bank in a matter and then was disqualified from representing a defendant that was being sued by the bank in an unrelated matter involving a **trust**. *Harrison v. Fisons Corp.*, 819 F. Supp. 1039 (M.D. Fla. 1993).

The American Bar Association, as well as state and local bar associations, have issued ethics opinions in this area of conflicts of interest. The ABA issued an opinion in1995 that held that a lawyer who represents a corporate entity is not *per se* disqualified from representing a client in an unrelated matter that is adverse to an affiliate of the corporate entity, but the corporate entity must give its consent to the representation. ABA Comm. on Ethics and Professional Responsibility, Formal Op. 95–390 (1995). And in 1991, the ABA cautioned against lawyers simultaneously representing individual partners of a partnership and the partnership on unrelated matters because of the chance that the lawyer will come into confidential information that he or she would not be allowed to convey to the other client and that might require him or her to withdraw from representing both clients. ABA Comm. on Ethics and Professional Responsibility, Formal Op. 91–361 (1991). The Illinois ethics committee found that it is not automatically inappropriate for a lawyer to represent a city government that is a defendant in a personal injury suit and also represent a party suing the same city in a zoning case, as long as both clients consent following consultation. Ill. State Bar Ass'n Comm. on Professional Ethics, Op. 94–21 (1995). And a Philadelphia ethics opinion said that a law firm may represent unrelated clients in unrelated matters and advocate antagonistic positions, but if both cases result in appeals to the same appellate court, then the firm must obtain both clients' consent to continue the representation. Philadelphia Bar Ass'n Professional Guidance Comm., Op. 89–27 (1990).

trust—A legal mechanism where property is held by one party for the benefit of another. A trust is created when the Donor transfers the property into the trust, where the Trustee holds the legal title to the property, while the Beneficiary of the trust has the equitable title in the property, which means the benefits (income) of the trust are provided to the beneficiary.

Issue Conflicts

Issue conflicts, rather than actual, positional conflicts, can arise in this area as well. An issue conflict occurs when a lawyer makes a legal argument on behalf of one client that, if successful, could be detrimental to the situation of another of the lawyer's clients. Suppose that in 1995, the Los Angeles Police Department tried to hire Johnny Cochran to defend it against charges stemming from the formal investigation, following the Rodney King riots, of allegations that it had historically conspired against minorities and occasionally planted evidence against suspects. Even though Johnny Cochran is a more than capable defense attorney, he was, at that time, advocating an argument on behalf of his client, O. J. Simpson, which included specifically arguing that the Los Angeles Police Department did conspire against a minority and planted evidence. Even though the two, separate lawsuits do not involve the same parties (the state of California, not the police department, was prosecuting O. J. Simpson), there is a clear issue conflict here. It would be unlikely, therefore, that O. J. Simpson could consent (assuming he wished to) to such a dual representation involving antagonistic issues. A 1993 ABA ethics opinion, speaking to the problem of issue conflicts, makes it more likely that issue conflicts can be overcome with client consent if the two matters are pending in different jurisdictions. ABA Comm. on Ethics and Professional Responsibility, Formal Op. 93–377 (1993).

Joint Representation: Two Clients with the Same Lawyer

When two clients seek joint representation by the same lawyer, they appear to have interests that are aligned. Unlike two parties on opposite sides of the lawyer's conference table, being on the same side does not present a problem under Model Rule 1.7(a). But what starts out on friendly terms can eventually take a turn for the worse, and Model Rule 1.7(b) governs those types of potential conflicts. Three areas of joint representation will be discussed: joint representation in criminal cases, joint representation in civil cases, and joint representation in non-litigation settings.

Joint Representation in Criminal Cases

Should an attorney represent co-defendants in a criminal case? According to the Comments to MR 1.7, "The potential for conflict of interest in representing multiple defendants in a criminal case is so grave that ordinarily a lawyer should decline to represent more than one codefendant." For example, when Lyle and Erik Menendez were charged with murdering their parents, each brother had his own defense lawyer, even though one brother's defense was aligned with the other (both involved parental abuse and self-defense). Because a criminal defendant's liberty is at stake, the possibility that one co-defendant's defense could be at odds with that of another is so grave that many legal scholars believe joint representation should not be undertaken.

On the other hand, criminal defendants do have a constitutional right to defense counsel, a choice that could include a co-defendant's counsel. But a defendant's desire to have the same lawyer as a co-defendant's can be trumped by the conflict of interest dangers. The United States Supreme Court has issued several cases on joint representation of co-defendants in criminal cases. In *Wheat v. United States*, 486 U.S. 153 (1986), the Court upheld a district court's refusal to allow a defendant in a drug conspiracy case to use the lawyer of two fellow defendants (both of whom had consented to the joint representation and one of whom had pled guilty to a lesser charge). Even though the Court acknowledged a defendant's generalized right to choose his or her own lawyer, it stated that a defendant's Sixth Amendment rights are not violated when a trial court sees an actual conflict of interest and refuses to allow the joint representation. *Id.* at 162. Two other Supreme Court cases, *Holloway v. Arkansas*, 435 U.S. 475 (1978), and *Glasser v. United States*, 315 U.S. 60 (1942), show the Court's unfavorable position on joint representation in criminal cases. One state even took the position that convictions will be reversed when there is joint representation of co-defendants unless the trial record shows that the defendants made a written request for joint representation and then clearly waived the possibility of conflicts of interest. *Shongutsie v. State*, 701 P.2d 361 (Wyo. 1992).

Joint Representation in Civil Cases

Clients who seek joint representation in civil litigation must still be consulted as to the ramifications that their joint interests might diverge. The likelihood that the representation of one client will adversely affect the lawyer's relationship with the other client is increased in a corporate setting if the lawyer represents both a corporation and members of its board of directors. If, for instance, the corporation and the board members are sued for misconduct in a **shareholder's derivative lawsuit**, the lawyer who represents the corporation and the board will be in a bind and may have to **recuse** him- or herself from either representation, as will be discussed later in the chapter.

When co-plaintiffs are considering settling, conflicts can arise if some plaintiffs want to settle but others do not. The ABA has stated that when there is disagreement about settlement among co-plaintiffs in a mass tort case, the lawyer must first obtain a waiver of conflicts from the co-plaintiffs who do not want to settle or else obtain independent counsel for them before proceeding further on behalf of the plaintiffs who want to settle. ABA Comm. on Ethics and Professional Responsibility, Formal Op. 371 (1993). In an Arizona case, an attorney represented co-defendants being sued for breach of contract and fraud. In the course of the litigation, it became clear that the co-defendants had inconsistent positions, but rather than informing them about the conflict, the attorney continued to represent both clients. He then showed his divided loyalty in a letter to one client when, in reference to the defense of the other client, he wrote, "it is to *our obvious advantage* to assure that [the other client] is as friendly as possible to us." *In re Shannon*, 876 P.2d 548, 557 (Ariz. 1994). Needless to say, the attorney was severely disciplined. *Id.* at 577.

As litigation progresses, specific theories of liability can evolve as investigation and discovery take place. Although joint defendants and joint plaintiffs might seem to have identical claims or objectives, the attorney representing the simultaneous parties may come to realize that the parties have conflicting interests, despite the similar objectives.

The following case from Florida shows, almost comically, how extreme conflicts can arise when an attorney represents two plaintiffs in the same litigation.

shareholder's derivative lawsuit—A lawsuit in which a shareholder of a corporation, on behalf of the corporation, sues the corporation's board of directors, alleging that their actions have harmed the corporation. Any benefits from the derivative lawsuit flow to the corporation, not personally to the shareholder.

recuse—When someone, such as a judge or other person of influence, removes him or herself from participation in a matter, because of a conflict of interest.

Case Law

Florida Bar v. Mastrilli, 614 So.2d 1081 (Fla. 1993)

PER CURIAM.

This cause is before the Court on complaint of The Florida Bar for review of the referee's recommendation that Kenneth W. Mastrilli, an attorney, be disciplined for ethical violations. We have jurisdiction. Art. V, § 15, Fla. Const.

The referee's findings of fact are supported by substantial competent evidence and thus are accepted by this Court. In 1989, Mastrilli undertook representation of two women allegedly injured in an accident while one was the driver and one was the passenger in the same vehicle. Mastrilli issued demand letters on behalf of the passenger against the insurance carrier of the driver on grounds the latter had been negligent, resulting in alleged injuries to the passenger totalling $100,000.00. The driver's insurance policy would cover only $50,000.00 of any loss.

When the insurance company denied payment, Mastrilli then filed suit in 1990 against the driver on behalf of the passenger. In effect, he filed suit against his own client in the same matter for which he had been retained. The driver terminated Mastrilli's employment when she received the complaint and learned she had been sued by her own attorney. The passenger's lawsuit eventually was settled for $20,000.00, within the limits of liability.

The referee concluded that Mastrilli had violated Rules of Professional Conduct 4–1.7(a) and 4–1.7(b) and noted that Mastrilli has shown no remorse for his actions. The referee then recommended discipline of six months' suspension.

Mastrilli now argues that he was merely negligent in failing to discover a conflict of interest and that, in any event, no harm has come to either client. We do not agree with Mastrilli's representation that he was merely negligent. Mastrilli undertook representation of both the passenger and driver, and he either knew or should have known that their interests were adverse when he sued one on behalf of the other. The Florida Standard for Imposing Lawyer Sanctions 4.32 states:

> Suspension is appropriate when a lawyer knows of a conflict of interest and does not fully disclose to a client the possible effect of that conflict, and causes injury or potential injury to a client.

Here, Mastrilli either knew or should have known of the conflict; and there was a potential that his actions would expose his client, the driver, to a personal liability of up to $50,000.00. Accordingly, suspension is warranted. Accordingly, we adopt the referee's findings of fact and findings that Mastrilli violated the rules of conduct noted above. We suspend Mastrilli from the practice of law for a period of six months. The suspension will be effective thirty days from the filing of this opinion so that Mastrilli can close out his practice and protect the interests of existing clients. If Mastrilli notifies this Court in writing that he is no longer practicing and does not need the thirty days to protect existing clients, this Court will enter an order making the suspension effective immediately. Mastrilli shall accept no new business from the date this opinion is filed. Costs in the amount of $2,451.12 are hereby assessed against Mastrilli, for which sum let execution issue.

Case Questions

1. Reread your state's version of MR 1.7 and then decide whether Mr. Mastrilli was capable of joint representation of both plaintiffs in the first place.
2. Do you think that the plaintiff/driver was likely to be aware of the theory her lawyer had in mind for her fellow plaintiff/passenger?
3. Why could it be said, despite Mastrilli's defense argument, that it is worse to be negligent in failing to see the conflict of interest in this joint representation than to proceed despite the observable conflict?

Joint Representation in Nonlitigation Settings

Two spouses getting divorced clearly should have independent representation. But should two spouses seek independent representation when having a will drafted? Probably they should not: most marital wills will rarely involve the kinds of conflicts of interest envisioned by the conflicts rules since most spouses likely share the same wishes about passing on their assets. However, when an engaged couple enters into a **prenuptial agreement**, should each party have independent representation? Although a prenuptial agreement is a transactional document made between two people whose personal interests are so aligned that they want to get married, the possibility of a conflict still exists since a prenuptial agreement is like a **liquidated damages clause** in a contract: it concerns breach of the relationship. Courts have voided prenuptial agreements due to conflicts problems in cases where one lawyer seemed to represent both parties but was really representing one to the disadvantage of the other. *See Rowland v. Rowland*, 599 N.E.2d 315 (Ohio Ct. App. 1991). Conflicts can also arise when divorcing couples have other legal matters pending in which they are joint parties. For instance, suppose a husband and wife are divorcing. The husband has a divorce attorney, while the wife does not. At the same time, the couple is in bankruptcy proceedings and the husband's divorce attorney represents both spouses in that matter. Is this an impermissible conflict? An ethics opinion says yes, because the lawyer's interest in advocating for his client in the divorce is sufficiently threatened by representing the wife and the husband in the bankruptcy. Ill. State Bar Ass'n Comm. on Professional Ethics, Op. 98–06 (1998).

Similar conflicts can arise when buyers and sellers of real estate share the same lawyer. Since the buyer wants to pay as little as possible and the seller want to sell for as much as possible, the lawyer representing them both faces the risk that buyer's remorse, seller's remorse, or other problems are likely to be directed at the lawyer who, one party may feel, did not adequately look out for him or her. Some states, such as New Jersey, prohibit buyers and sellers in complex real estate transactions from sharing the same lawyer. *Baldasarre v. Butler*, 625 A.2d 458 (N.J. 1993). However, other states, such as New York, Florida, and Massachusetts, allow lawyers to represent sellers and buyers (or lenders and buyers) if the parties consent and the lawyer clearly explains the terms to all parties. *In re Pohlman*, 604 N.Y.S.2d 636

prenuptial agreement—A contract entered into by two people intending to marry each other, in which the people agree in writing to their respective property rights in the event of divorce or death.

liquidated damages clause—A part of a contract that predetermines the monetary damages one party would owe the other in the event of breach of contract. Liquidated damages need to be a reasonable estimate of the damages suffered in order to be valid.

(App. Div. 1993); *Florida Bar v. Belleville*, 591 So. 2d 170 (Fla. 1991); Mass. Bar Ass'n Ethics Comm., Op. 90–3 (1990).

The following case from Florida shows what can happen when one lawyer represents both parties to a real estate transaction and one of the parties is underrepresented.

Case Law

Florida Bar v. Clark, 513 So.2d 1052 (Fla.1987)

PER CURIAM

This disciplinary proceeding is before the Court for consideration of the referee's report. The referee found the respondent attorney, Frank Clark, III, guilty of professional misconduct and recommended disbarment. The respondent has not filed a petition for review. As provided by Rule 3–7.6 of the Rules Regulating The Florida Bar, this Court must review the referee's report and render an appropriate judgment.

The referee found that Lois Resch agreed to purchase a condominium from Ronald A. and Angela Kenney. Ms. Resch agreed to assume the obligations of first and second mortgages on the property. The parties to the sale met at respondent's office for the closing. Ms. Resch had the impression that respondent as attorney was advising both the Kenneys and herself. Respondent, the referee found, did nothing to discourage this impression. The closing statement reflected that the two parties to the sale were each charged half of the attorney's fee exacted for the transaction. Ms. Resch executed documents assuming responsibility for the two existing mortgages. She was provided payment coupon books and was instructed to make payments without contacting the mortgagees.

Later Ms. Resch discovered that the mortgagees were under no obligation to allow her to assume the mortgages and that neither the sellers nor respondent had sought consent for the assumption of the mort-

gages. As a result the mortgagees declared the loans due and Ms. Resch was forced to refinance the indebtedness in order to retire the preexisting mortgages. She obtained a less favorable interest rate and had to pay arrearages that had accrued before her purchase.

Although not recited by the referee, record testimony also showed that in addition to assuming the two mortgages, Ms. Resch also signed a promissory note in favor of the sellers, Mr. and Mrs. Kenney. They sold the note to a third party. When Ms. Resch discovered the nonassumable nature of the mortgages, she suspended payment on the note. The purchaser of the note filed a legal action to collect the amount due. The purchaser was represented in that legal action by the respondent.

The referee found that respondent had violated the following Disciplinary Rules of the former Florida Bar Code of Professional Responsibility: D.R. 5–105(A), for accepting employment when it was likely to affect the representation given to another client; D.R. 5–105(B), for continuing multiple employment when his independent professional judgment was likely to be adversely affected; D.R. 6–101(A)(2), for handling a matter without adequate preparation; and D.R. 6-101(A)(3), for neglecting a legal matter entrusted to him. . . .

We approve the referee's report. Frank Clark, III, is hereby disbarred. As it appears that he is presently under suspension for nonpayment of bar dues, this disbarment shall take effect immediately.

Case Questions

1. Was Clark the attorney for Ms. Resch? Why or why not?
2. What legal misunderstandings caused Ms. Resch so many problems?
3. In addition to his underrepresentation of Ms. Resch, what else did Clark do that may have contributed to his disbarment?

Conflicts of interest are at stake when the same lawyer in a private adoption represents the adoptive and biological parents. For instance, if the biological mother would like some periodic visitation rights or information about the child's well-being, but the adoptive parents are opposed, each side will need independent representation. Two New York cases involving joint representation of biological and adoptive parents have shown the courts' disapproval. *In re Michelman*, 616 N.Y.S.2d 409 (App. Div. 1994); *In re Adoption of Vincent*, 602 N.Y.S.2d 303 (Fam. Ct. 1993). Furthermore, the ABA has opposed joint representation of biological and adoptive parents in private adoptions. ABA Comm. on Ethics and Professional Responsibility, Informal Op. 87–1523 (1987).

Conflicts Caused by the Lawyer's Own Interests

Could John Adams adequately represent the Boston Massacre defendants under today's rules on conflicts of interest? Clearly, a lawyer in favor of independence, with friends and family members involved in the same cause, has to have a considerable internal conflict when faced with the prospect of representing British soldiers accused of murdering that lawyer's fellow colonials. While Model Rule 1.7(a) concerns representations that involve conflicts between clients of the lawyer, MR 1.7(b) concerns how the lawyer's ability to represent the client is affected by the lawyer's responsibilities to a third person, as well as the lawyer's own interests. It prohibits a lawyer from taking a case if the representation of the client, "may be materially limited by the lawyer's responsibilities to another client or to a third person, or by the lawyer's own interests." But if the lawyer believes that this type of conflict of interest will not adversely affect his or her representation of the client, then he or she can continue the representation after seeking the client's consent. Had this type of rule existed in 1770, John Adams could have ethically represented the British soldiers, because they obviously would have consented to Adams's representation, considering no other lawyers would take their case. The kinds of personal interests that may materially limit the lawyer's representation of the client include financial, business, or personal interests. Certain, specific kinds of interests are covered later in this chapter, in the section titled "Special Circumstances: Prohibited Transactions."

Financial Interests

Although a lawyer may refuse a case because of financial concerns, it is unethical to base representation decisions on his or her own financial interests. The United States Supreme Court, when dealing with a case involving the propriety of a civil rights case settlement being conditioned on the plaintiffs waiving their right to have the defendant pay the plaintiffs' legal fees, not only stated that such fees waivers can be accomplished, but also found that there is really no ethical dilemma for the plaintiffs' attorney because the attorney's duty to advise the plaintiffs about the decision to settle should be made only with respect to the clients' interests, without any consideration of the lawyer's financial interests. *Evans v. Jeff D.*, 476 U.S. 717, at 728 (1986).

Business Interests

If a lawyer has a business interest connected to representation of the client, it may cloud his or her advice. Such a business interest is not an automatic impediment, but the lawyer needs to make the client aware of the possible conflict and seek his or her consent in order to continue the representation. For example, in a Wisconsin case, an attorney represented a restaurant corporation in which he was also a shareholder and director. When another client later asked the attorney to represent him in some business dealings with the restaurant corporation, this client was aware that the attorney represented the restaurant corporation but unaware that the attorney had a personal, business interest in the restaurant corporation. The attorney never advised the client about his own business interest in the corporation nor how it might be affected by the actions desired by the client. The lawyer was disbarred for this and other conflicts of interest violations. *In re Charlton*, 498 N.W.2d 380 (Wis. 1993).

Sexual Relationships with Clients

Strangely enough, the dating and intimate relationships between lawyers and their clients depicted in television and film might be the most accurate portrayal of all that passes for the practice of law, because there is plenty of case law concerning such relationships. However, usually left out of the fictionalized stories are the charges the clients will eventually bring against their paramours. Nevertheless, neither the Model Rules nor the Model Code have an express prohibition on such relationships (but see the summary of Ethics 2000 and Model Rule 1.8 at the end of this chapter).

The dangers associated with lawyers engaged in intimate relationships with their clients are primarily two-fold. First, there is the problem of coercion or duress. The lawyer-client relationship is not an equal relationship (remember that lawyers are fiduciaries to their clients) and, on many occasions, clients are in varying states of vulnerability. That combination can lead to clients succumbing to pressure for sex because they feel they must comply with their lawyers' wishes. Courts are quick to find violations of MR 1.7(b), as well as MR 1.8, and other rules, when lawyers engage in such coercion. An Illinois case illustrates the coercion problem. A lawyer was suspended from the practice of law for three years because he had engaged in sexual relations with four clients, all encounters occurring at least seven years before the charges were brought. The clients were female divorce clients who claimed a similar pattern of sexual contact: the lawyer approached them in a sexual way in his office upon the first or second meeting and then had sex with them on later occasions; he also took nude pictures of some of them. All the clients claimed they felt they had to have sex with the lawyer because they feared that if they did not, their cases would be harmed or they would lose the retainer money they had paid him. Despite the lawyer's denial that any sexual relations occurred with these clients while he or his firm were representing them, he also argued that he could not be sanctioned because there was no express rule in Illinois forbidding lawyer-client sexual contact. The court found the argument unpersuasive, stating that the ethics rules are not manuals intended to govern a lawyer's conduct only when specifically covering every conceivable situation. *In re Rinnella*, 677 N.E.2d 909, 914 (Ill. 1997). And in a Kansas case, a lawyer was disbarred for having sexual relations with what the court termed "vulnerable divorce clients," even though there was no specific rule forbidding it. *In re Berg*, 955 P.2d 1240 (Kans. 1998).

The other danger involves the loss of objectivity that can accompany even those lawyer-client sexual relationships that are not a result of coercion or intimidation. Even if such intimacies would reasonably be considered mutual, such mixing of personal and professional relationships can cause the lawyer to represent the client in a way that is advantageous to the former's personal interest. The ABA issued a formal opinion on this topic in 1992 and, while not expressly opposing all lawyer-client sexual involvement, it did advise lawyers against such behavior and stated that if such sexual relationships lead to impaired representation, "the lawyer will have violated the ethical obligations to the client." ABA Comm. on Ethics and Professional Responsibility, Formal Op. 92–364 (1992).

Some states have issued stronger statements than the ABA opinion, including Alaska (Alaska State Bar Gen. Counsel. Op. 92–6), Pennsylvania (Pa. Bar Ass'n Comm. on Legal Ethics and Professional Responsibility, Op. 97–100), and Maryland (which changed its Comment to MR 1.7 to discuss the matter). Some jurisdictions, such as Washington State, have modified their conflicts of interest rules by expressly prohibiting lawyers from having sexual relationships with their *current* clients. Wash. R.P.C., Rule 1.8(k). And some jurisdictions, such as California, have modified their conflicts of interest rules to include sexual relationships with clients but have framed the rules in terms of whether the representation is conditioned on sexual relations, whether the client is coerced into sexual relations, or whether the representation will be adversely affected by such relations. Cal. Bus. & Prof. Code § 6106.9; Cal. R.P.C. 3-120.

How does this controversial subject apply to the paralegal? On the one hand, the stakes are different when paralegals and clients are sexually involved because the dangers of coercion seem to be nonexistent. This is because the paralegal does not represent the client and is in no position to threaten him or her with limited or no representation. Also, because legal assistants do not actively represent the client and are prohibited from giving legal advice, the dangers of impaired representation due to such personal relationships seem not to apply. For example, Washington State's prohibition on lawyers having sexual relationships with their clients defines, for the purpose of the prohibition, a lawyer as "any lawyer who assists in the representation of the client, but does not include other firm members who provide no such assistance." Wash. R.P.C. 1.8(k)(3).

There is, however, another facet to consider. Relationships can dissolve, and when they do, both sides can have hurt feelings. That can lead a client, even long after the breakup, to bring charges against the lawyer or sue him or her for malpractice. Even if such charges would not lead to a judgment against the lawyer, the legal costs alone, as well as the embarrassment, should be enough to cause legal assistants to avoid romantic relationships with their firms' clients.

companion cases—Two or more appellate cases that are connected because they involve the same parties in similar legal situations, or different parties with the same legal issue.

Although the following **companion cases** do not involve a paralegal, notice that these are the kinds of cases that could involve a paralegal. The first case involves a disciplinary process against an attorney for having a sexual relationship with his client. The second case concerns the malpractice case against the same attorney. As you read excerpts from the first case, notice the court's analysis of the nature of the relationship between the lawyer and his client. Then, while reading excerpts from the second case, notice the different version of the personal history as it was presented at trial by the client against her former lawyer and also try to determine why the client sued her lawyer.

Case Law

In re DiSandro, 680 A.2d 73 (R.I. 1996)

PER CURIAM

This matter is before the court pursuant to a decision and recommendation of the Supreme Court Disciplinary Board (board) that the respondent, Edmond A. DiSandro, be publicly censured. The facts giving rise to these proceedings are as follows. In 1977 Maria del Rosario Vallinoto (Vallinoto) married Dennis Ledo. In 1987 the husband filed an action for divorce against Vallinoto in the Family Court. Among the issues involved in the divorce case were custody of a minor child of the marriage and distribution of the marital assets. Vallinoto retained the services of an attorney to represent her in the divorce filed by her husband. She quickly became dissatisfied with the quality of that attorney's representation and discharged him approximately one month later. She retained a second attorney but dis-

charged that attorney after approximately two months. In May of 1987 she retained the services of respondent, who represented her to the conclusion of the divorce proceedings. The record discloses that Vallinoto received custody of the minor child of the marriage and was awarded approximately 60 percent of the marital assets.

In January of 1991 Vallinoto filed a multicount civil action in the Superior Court against respondent and his firm, alleging, inter alia, legal malpractice, battery, deceit, negligence, and the intentional infliction of emotional distress. A disciplinary complaint was also filed on her behalf with the Supreme Court Disciplinary Counsel. The civil action resulted in a jury verdict in favor of Vallinoto in the amount of $225,000. *Vallinoto v. DiSandro*, C.A. 91–390. These disciplinary proceedings commenced upon the conclusion of the civil action before the Superior Court. The board concluded that the sexual relations between respondent and Vallinoto were consensual. In reaching this conclusion, the board heard the testimony of Vallinoto and of respondent and had the opportunity to observe their demeanor and to assess their credibility. Vallinoto testified that she and respondent acted as boyfriend and girlfriend in front of others and that she was cordial to respondent's office staff. A friend of Vallinoto's testified at the disciplinary hearing that Vallinoto had told her that she was dating respondent. Vallinoto presented respondent with gifts, including a Christmas gift and a tape of love songs. The documentary exhibits before the board included a birthday card from Vallinoto to respondent with the written notation, "Love, Rosario," and another card with the printed notation, "You've got me right where I want me."

Rule 1.7 (b) of the Rules of Professional Conduct is substantially similar to Disciplinary Rule 5–101 (A). Rule 1.7 (b) provides, in pertinent part:

> A lawyer shall not represent a client if the representation of that client may be materially limited . . . by the lawyer's own interests, unless:
> (1) the lawyer reasonably believes the representation will not be adversely affected; and
> (2) the client consents after consultation.

As we noted in *In the Matter of Robert F. Dipippo*, No. 96–235–M.P. (R.I., filed July 10, 1996), there is no specific prohibition contained within the Rules of Professional Conduct (or the Code of Professional Responsibility) regarding sexual activity between attorneys and their clients. However, any attorney who practices in the area of domestic relations must be aware that the conduct of the divorcing parties, even in a divorce based on irreconcilable differences (a so-called no-fault divorce) may have a significant impact on that client's ability to secure child custody and/or may materially affect the client's rights regarding distribution of marital assets. An attorney who engages in sexual relations with his or her divorce client places that client's rights in jeopardy. The lawyer's own interest in maintaining the sexual relationship creates an inherent conflict with the obligation to represent the client properly. When an attorney represents a divorce client in a case in which child custody, support, and distribution of marital assets are at issue, the attorney must refrain from engaging in sexual relations with the client or must withdraw from the case.

We note that although the respondent's conduct may have placed his client's case in jeopardy, no actual adverse effect on the outcome of the client's case resulted. Accordingly we accept the recommendation of the board and impose the sanction of public censure upon the respondent. Had the client's case actually been prejudiced by the respondent's conduct, a more serious sanction may have been appropriate.

Vallinoto v. DiSandro, 688 A.2d 830 (R.I. 1997)

Bourcier, Justice

This case comes before us on appeal from a final judgment entered in the Superior Court following a jury's verdict in favor of the plaintiff, Maria Del Rosario Vallinoto (Vallinoto), and against the defendant, Edmond A. DiSandro (DiSandro). . . .

In May 1987, Vallinoto retained DiSandro to represent her in a divorce action brought against her by her former husband, Dennis Ledo (Ledo).

Vallinoto, a citizen of Spain, married Ledo while living in Spain in 1977. They thereafter moved to this country. Ledo was an American citizen, but Vallinoto was not and was here on a so-called "green card." The marriage produced one child, Christina, who was also an American citizen. Vallinoto's marriage was by no means a tranquil or a happy one. She testified that during the course of her marriage to Ledo she had been restricted to the marital home, verbally abused, badgered, and belittled. She claims to have suffered severe mental depression and stress, to have entertained suicidal thoughts, and to have been "isolated" and "victimized" by Ledo throughout the course of their ten-year marriage. It was Ledo, however, who commenced the fateful divorce proceedings, with Vallinoto later counterclaiming for divorce.

After having retained and then dismissing two other attorneys with whom she had become dissatisfied in the course of the divorce proceedings, Vallinoto retained DiSandro in May of 1987. DiSandro's legal efforts on her behalf appear to have been both well performed and successful. DiSandro was able to obtain for her an increase in the weekly child support payments previously ordered for her daughter, Christina, from $15 to $30 per week to $150 to $200 per week. Moreover, at the time that her divorce became final on April 25, 1989, Vallinoto was awarded custody of Christina, 60 percent of the marital assets, several priceless paintings and heirlooms, and attorney's fees. Vallinoto, by her own account, acknowledged receiving excellent legal representation from DiSandro in her divorce proceedings as well as successful final results, all clearly evidenced in her final judgment of divorce. Unfortunately, however, DiSandro's relationship with Vallinoto extended far beyond his legal representation of her.

In August of 1987, some three months after having been retained to represent Vallinoto in her divorce action, DiSandro and Vallinoto became involved in an intimate physical relationship. That relationship continued until Vallinoto's last hearing on her divorce petition in December of 1988. DiSandro viewed the relationship as consensual. Vallinoto, on the other hand, alleged that she was compelled to perform sexual acts with DiSandro in part because of an alleged threat that DiSandro had once made to her, stating that if he discontinued his representation of her, she would be deported and lose custody of her child. She also alleged, in like vein, that DiSandro told her that he had undertaken to

represent her only because she had been referred to him by a mutual friend and that good lawyers like himself usually did not take cases that other lawyers had started, which she interpreted to mean that if he withdrew as her counsel in her case, other good attorneys would not undertake to represent her. Vallinoto asserted that as a result of those implied threats, she felt compelled to comply with DiSandro's sexual demands, fearing that he would terminate his representation of her and that she would not thereafter be able to engage another competent attorney. Over the course of their approximately eighteen-month relationship, Vallinoto estimated that she and DiSandro were actively intimate almost 200 times, all without her consent. She later testified at disciplinary board hearings that the 200 number was really a guess on her part. In any event, the occurrence rather than the number is the significant factor.

During the jury trial below, DiSandro's law partner, Z. Hershel Smith (Smith), was called as a witness by Vallinoto to testify with regard to the nature of the relationship that existed between Vallinoto and DiSandro. Smith testified that contrary to Vallinoto's view of her relationship with DiSandro, he considered Vallinoto to be DiSandro's girlfriend. He recalled that at Christmas time, Vallinoto cheerfully came to DiSandro's law office and gave gifts to the office personnel, including DiSandro. Vallinoto herself testified that in the course of the relationship she frequently sent different greeting cards to DiSandro, many of which ended with an expression of "love" obviously intending to convey that emotion to DiSandro. Among the many trial exhibits was a greeting card containing the phrase "you got me right where I want me." By the time Vallinoto's divorce became final in early 1989, the affairs, both legal and nonlegal, between her and DiSandro had ended. She returned, however, to DiSandro some eight months later, seeking legal assistance on another matter in which she was being sued by her former husband, Ledo. She and DiSandro did not renew their sexual intimacy during that particular attorney-client relationship, and Vallinoto has never complained of DiSandro's handling of that matter for her.

The record also reveals that Vallinoto's extramarital interests, however, were not restricted to her attorney's participation. She admitted that during her ongoing sexual relationship with DiSandro and prior to the time of concluding her divorce petition hearings and continuing on thereafter into late 1989, she was dating someone other than DiSandro. In the summer of 1989 she traveled to Hawaii with that other person and shared the same hotel room with him for some two weeks. Later, in early 1990, she then began dating a new and different man. It was while planning with this latest man to purchase a larger house in which to live together that she decided to tell him of her previous sexual relationship with DiSandro. She eventually married that man in December 1990. It was some three weeks later, in January 1991, that she decided, with the encouragement of her new husband, to commence her litigation seeking monetary damages from DiSandro.

In her civil action . . . [s]he sought compensatory as well as punitive damages . . . and the jury returned a general verdict for Vallinoto, covering all claims, for $25,000 in compensatory damages and $200,000 in punitive damages. DiSandro appealed. . . .

The case before us involves . . . a negligence-based legal malpractice claim as opposed to a legal malpractice claim based on a breach of fiduciary duty. However, under either theory, plaintiff's claim for legal malpractice would fail. There is no relevant probative evidence in the trial record that suggests to us that the legal services rendered by DiSandro were made contingent on sexual involvement with Vallinoto. She clearly had the ability and the knowledge to discharge and leave DiSandro at any time if she was ever dissatisfied with his legal representation in her divorce case. She had earlier, prior to retaining DiSandro, discharged two previous attorneys with whom she had been dissatisfied. Moreover, according to her testimony, there were more than 200 incidents of sexual encounters between her and DiSandro,

some taking place after romantic dinners at intimate restaurants and others during sleepovers at DiSandro's house. The numerous greeting cards she sent to DiSandro over the many months of the relationship, all expressing her love and affection for him, seem to indicate that it was a two-way affair. Additionally, she returned to DiSandro for legal representation long after the incidents of the alleged forced sexual relations concerned in her civil action had terminated and at a time when she was dating at least two other men, one of whom she married just before filing her action against DiSandro.

All those facts suggest to us that DiSandro's legal representation was kept separate and apart from the personal relationship that he embarked upon with Vallinoto. Accordingly, even though we certainly cannot and do not condone or excuse DiSandro's actions involving his extralegal relationship with his client, there is an absence of evidence in the record before us that would support Vallinoto's contention that DiSandro's legal services departed from the standard of due care required of DiSandro in his handling of her divorce case litigation by the attorney-client relationship.

We note additionally that even if a factfinder were to find that the legal services by DiSandro were a quid pro quo for sexual favors, Vallinoto's claim would still fail because of the complete absence of any competent and relevant probative evidence of damages that resulted to her legal position, or to her legal detriment personally, as a result of DiSandro's inappropriate sexual activities. She testified that DiSandro did an "excellent" job in representing her in her divorce action. She in fact received more than she had ever anticipated at the conclusion of her divorce proceeding. She was awarded custody of her child, an increase in support payments, 60 percent of the marital assets and several priceless paintings and heirlooms, as well as her attorney's fees. Her divorce action by all accounts, including hers, was certainly settled satisfactorily, and that result reflects the competency of DiSandro's legal representation. The complete absence of any evidence of damages resulting to her from his legal efforts on her behalf prevents any recovery on a negligence-based legal malpractice claim such as the one Vallinoto asserts in her complaint.

Accordingly, we conclude . . . the trial justice erred in not granting DiSandro's motion for a directed verdict on the malpractice count. . . .

Flanders, Justice, dissenting

I respectfully dissent because I believe that the defendant Edmond A. DiSandro's sexual depredation of the plaintiff while serving as her divorce attorney constituted a flagrant breach of the fiduciary duties he owed to his client and that this breach constituted legal malpractice. When, as here, a lawyer handling a divorce for a client enters into a sexual relationship with that client, I believe that lawyer has committed legal malpractice, regardless of the legal results obtained and how well the lawyer has performed the necessary legal services. Such misconduct is "a wrong that is distinct and independent from professional negligence _but still is legal malpractice._" (Emphasis added.) 2 Ronald E. Mallen & Jeffrey M. Smith, _Legal Malpractice_ § 14.1 at 229 (4th ed. 1996). . . .

[The majority and dissenting opinions were quite long, dealing with five separate issues. Ultimately, the majority reversed the jury's verdict, and remanded the case for a new trial, while the dissent wrote that the jury's verdict was sustainable.]

Case Questions

---

1. Bearing in mind that the same court issued both of the above opinions—although the first opinion dealt with the disciplinary charges, while the second opinion concerned the civil lawsuit—what differences are noticeable in the presentation of the facts against the attorney?
2. What did the client accuse her lawyer of doing to her? Why did the court refuse to agree with the jury's finding that her charges were valid?
3. Why did the court only reprimand the lawyer in the disciplinary case?
4. Why do you think the client filed a lawsuit against the attorney years after the representation ceased?
5. Based on both of the court's opinions, do you think a lawyer who does not have divorce clients (or who has divorce clients without any children or property disputes) may have sexual relationships with clients?
6. Do you think the court unfairly painted the amorous character of the client with too broad a brush in order to justify its decision, or do you think she got what she deserved for concocting a convoluted tale of woe? (One of the footnotes from the disciplinary case _In re DiSandro_, read in part: "The evidence presented to the Superior Court, tried before a jury, and that presented to the disciplinary board was significantly different. At the civil trial Vallinoto testified that she had been 'raped' 200 times by respondent. In the disciplinary proceeding, however, she acknowledged that there were far fewer incidences of sexual contact between her and respondent.")

Conflicts between Present and Former Clients

As discussed in Chapter 4, lawyers continue to owe certain fiduciary duties to former clients, even those clients who fired their lawyers. Model Rule 1.9 concerns the duty of loyalty to former clients by establishing grounds whereby a lawyer would be prohibited from representing a present client because of the lawyer's prior-established duty to a former client. MR 1.9(a) states the following:

A lawyer who has formerly represented a client in a matter shall not thereafter represent another person in the same or a substantially related matter
in which that person's interests are materially adverse to the interests of the
former client unless the former client consents after consultation.

The Model Code of Professional Responsibility had no disciplinary rule counterpart to MR 1.9, but Canon 9, which said, "A lawyer should avoid even the
appearance of impropriety," was thought to cover former client conflicts, including
those conflicts occurring when lawyers move to different firms. Since impropriety
was undefined in the Model Code, little guidance was given by such a Canon.

MR 1.9(a) provides more leeway to the lawyer than does MR 1.7(a). Notice
that under MR 1.7(a), the lawyer could seek both clients' consent to continue representing them when a conflict was discovered *only if* the lawyer concluded that the
continued representation of one client would *not be directly adverse* to the other
client. But MR 1.9(a) allows the lawyer to seek the consent of the former client *even
if the representation of the present client involves the same or a substantially related matter that is materially adverse to the former client.* Therefore, if the lawyer concludes
that a present client's case is not the same or substantially related to a former client's
case, the lawyer need not seek the former client's consent to continue representing
the present client. If the former client believes that his or her lawyer should not be
representing parties who have adverse interests to the former client and sues the
lawyer for malpractice or seeks to enjoin the lawyer's continued representation, the
correct presumption (usually unstated in the case law) is that the lawyer did not
seek the former client's consent before embarking upon the present client's representation. *See Hyman Cos., v. Brozost*, 964 F. Supp. 168 (E.D. Pa. 1997); *see also
Damron v. Herzog*, 67 F.3d 211 (9th Cir. 1995).

Two important determinations need to be made for this kind of conflict of
interest analysis: when is a client a former client and when is the lawyer-client relationship created for the new client?

When Is a Client a Former Client?

If a client fires his or her lawyer, then clearly the client is a former client. When
a client hires a lawyer to draft a will, then it is logical to presume that once the will's
execution is complete and the client pays the fee, the lawyer-client relationship is
complete. But identifying the end of every lawyer-client relationship is not always
easy. Because there is no concrete standard on when a present client becomes a former client, sometimes it is to the law firm's advantage to consider the client as being
a former client, since the conflicts rule of MR 1.9 is less strict than that of MR 1.7.
This can lead to the problem of the "hot potato" client, who is dropped (and then
becomes the former client) in favor of a new client with interests conflicting. In a
federal case involving the former client conflict, the court stated that law firms may
not drop clients like hot-potatoes in favor of newer, more profitable clients. *Munoz
Gen. Contractor, Inc., v. MC3d, Inc.*, 1998 WL 831806 (N.D. Ill, Nov. 25, 1998).
And at least one state ethics committee has stated that lawyers may not drop a
client so as to reap the benefits of the more lenient standard associated with former

client conflicts. State Bar of Mich. Comm. on Professional and Judicial Ethics, Op. RI–139 (1992).

When Is the Lawyer-Client Relationship Created?

The second component also has its fuzzy aspects. On the clear side, the lawyer-client relationship is obviously created when a lawyer accepts the client's case and sends the client an **engagement letter** or when the client pays a retainer to the lawyer. But the fuzzy part is trying to determine if the lawyer-client relationship is created even if the lawyer engages in no representation of the prospective client. The answer to that question usually revolves around whether the lawyer became aware of confidential information in the initial consultation with the prospective client or whether he or she rendered any advice to the prospective client. In a Nebraska case, the disgruntled buyer of a house costing over $200,000 called an attorney at the latter's home to discuss her situation. Almost two years later, the buyer (represented by a different firm) sued the seller of the house to rescind the real estate contract and the seller retained a different lawyer at the same firm of the attorney who had the phone conversation with the buyer many months earlier. Despite the fact that the buyer of the house was never billed by the attorney for the at-home phone call (in fact, the attorney claimed to not remember talking with the buyer on the phone), she was able to disqualify the firm representing the seller due to the theory that she was a former client of the firm and the firm was wrongfully representing the seller in the same matter. *Richardson v. Griffiths*, 560 N.W.2d 430 (Neb. 1997). See "Imputed Disqualification: Effects on the Firm of One Lawyer's Conflict" later in this chapter.

Intentionally Creating a Lawyer-Client Conflict

Connected to the problem of prospective clients being considered former clients for the purposes of conflicts in substantially related legal matters is the situation where clients might intentionally try to create a conflict of interest. As was mentioned in Chapter 4, a client could try to retain a particular lawyer solely for the purpose of preventing that lawyer (and his or her firm) from being used in future litigation by an opposing party to the client. Such a practice is the inverse of the hot-potato trick that lawyers have been known to play. The idea of retaining a lawyer just to make him or her a victim of the conflicts rules is frowned upon by some authorities. An Indiana ethics opinion, dealing with lawyers sending their divorce clients to other lawyers for the purpose of preventing them from representing the divorce clients' spouses, found that, although the rules do not expressly prohibit such activities, such behavior violates the spirit of the ethics rules. Indiana State Bar Association Ethics Opinion no. 2 (2000). A Maryland case illustrates such a maneuver almost perfectly. *Davis v. York International Corp.* 1993 WL 180224 (D.C. Md. 1993) concerned a lawyer who was teaching a continuing legal education seminar. During the course of the seminar, an attorney in attendance asked the teacher for advice about one of her current cases. Later, the teacher represented an opponent of this former student's client, whereupon the former student sought to disqualify the teacher on the theory that he had become her lawyer by

engagement letter—A letter from a lawyer to a client that formally acknowledges that the firm has accepted the client's case and sets forth the terms of the representation.

answering her legal question at the seminar. The court disagreed, finding that no lawyer-client relationship was created simply because the lawyer teaching the seminar answered the student's question.

Model Rule 1.9(b) concerns conflicts that can occur when lawyers move to different firms, as does MR 1.10; that kind of conflict and its resolution will be discussed in the section on imputed disqualification. MR 1.9(c) is similar to MR 1.6 in that it prohibits lawyers from using the confidential information of their former clients in any way that is detrimental to them except for disclosures that are authorized (see Chapter 4).

SPECIAL CIRCUMSTANCES: PROHIBITED TRANSACTIONS

The conflicts rules examined so far can be difficult to grasp because they are general rules whose application is broad. Determining whether a client's case will be adversely affected because of a conflict is not subject to a mathematical analysis. But there are some specific behaviors of lawyers that are forbidden or carefully limited. Those prohibited transactions are covered in ABA Model Rule 1.8, which compliments Model Rule 1.7. Not only does MR 1.8 cover certain transactions whose conflict relates generally to MR 1.7, it also covers certain transactions that are not implicated by MR 1.7 but are prohibited due to the risk of attorneys taking unfair advantage in certain situations.

Business Transactions with Clients

Model Rule 1.8(a) prohibits lawyers from entering into a business transaction with a client unless: (1) the terms are fair and presented to the client in straightforward, written language; (2) the client is given a fair chance to seek another lawyer's advice concerning the pending business transaction; and (3) the client consents to the transaction in writing. (See ABA Comm. on Ethics and Professional Responsibility, Formal Op. 00–416 (2000), and Formal Op. 00–418 (2000) for more on business transactions with clients.) This rule does not apply to former or prospective clients, only present clients. And unlike almost every other contract, whose agreement is a result of the dog-eat-dog world of negotiations, this rule requires that the terms are fair to the client.

This rule also applies to the lawyer obtaining a possessory interest or **security interest** that is adverse to the client, such as if the lawyer were purchasing an apartment complex where a client was a tenant, if planning on purchasing a client's real estate at a foreclosure sale, or if the client were to execute a promissory note to him or her as part of a fee arrangement. And, certainly, the rule would apply to lawyers borrowing money from, or lending money to, their clients. The Comments to this rule make clear that it does not apply to common commercial transactions between a lawyer and client for products (for example, the client is the Dell Computer Co. and the lawyer buys Dell

security interest—Where a creditor secures the repayment of a loan by taking legal title to certain property of the debtor, known as collateral. In the event of default, the creditor has rights to the collateral. A mortgage is an example of a security interest.

computers for the firm) or services (the client is The Charles Schwab Co. and the lawyer has a Schwab brokerage account) that the client sells to others.

Even if the business arrangement has terms that are fair to the client, a violation will still be found if the terms are not adequately disclosed to the client or if the client is not given the requisite triggers for consent. This restriction has also been found to apply even when the client is extremely sophisticated in business matters. *See In re Ober*, 714 A.2d 856 (Md. 1998). But some transactions are considered improper, regardless of client consent. For instance, Rhode Island prohibits attorneys from selling insurance products to their estate planning clients and prohibits attorneys who sell insurance from selling estate planning legal services to their insurance clients. R.I. Sup. Ct. Ethics Advisory Panel, Op. 96–26 (1996).

One of the problematic transactions in this type of conflict occurs when lawyers sell property to or buy it from their clients. Lawyers not only occupy a superior bargaining position because of the trust their clients place in them, but they also tend to be quite a shrewd group of people. These advantages can lead to **undue influence**. In an illustrative New Jersey case, a divorce client moving out of state asked her lawyer to find a buyer for her house, hoping to get $95,000. Another of the lawyer's clients was interested in buying the house for that price, but after the lawyer received the signed contract from the seller, he never contacted the other client to tell him to sign the contract. Both clients never knew that the other was willing to complete the sale. Then, a few months later, the lawyer bought the house from the seller for $85,000, and within ten days he then resold the house to another buyer for $150,000. The court suspended the lawyer for one year, noting, in part, that the lawyer never properly informed the seller of the true value of her home nor kept either client informed of their respective rights to seek independent representation in their dealings with him. *In re Dalto*, 614 A.2d 1344 (N.J. 1992).

undue influence—Where one party, in a position of strength over another party who is in a position of weakness, causes that party to enter into a contractual relationship with the superior party, or causes that party to give a gift to the superior party. Undue influence takes away the free will of the weaker party because of the unfair influence of the superior party.

Using Client Information to the Client's Detriment

Model Rule 1.8(b) prohibits lawyers from using information—not just confidential information—gained in the lawyer-client relationship to the disadvantage of the client, with limited exception (including client consent). This prohibition is connected to other conflicts already covered by other rules. First, this rule has been applied to situations where lawyers have engaged in business transactions disadvantageous to the client, based upon information learned during the representation. Second, this rule has also been applied to situations where lawyers have begun sexual relationships with their clients after learning, during the course of the representation, of their emotional or sexual vulnerability.

Gifts from Clients

Model Rule 1.8(c) expressly prohibits a lawyer from drafting any instrument (such as a will or trust) that gives any substantial gift to the lawyer unless he or she is related to the party making the gift. Self-dealing and undue influence are the obvious concerns here; notice that there is no client consent exception. There is an exception, however, for lawyers' relatives, such that a lawyer could draft a will for his or her parents that included bequests to the lawyer him- or herself. Just what makes a gift a "substantial gift" is not monetarily defined, but the Comments say that an appropriate gift "meets a general standard of fairness."

States that operate under the Model Code of Professional Responsibility might allow for gifts to lawyers in wills drafted by those lawyers, because there is no Model Code counterpart to MR 1.8(c). In an interesting Washington State case, a lawyer was found not to have violated the ethics rules by drafting a will for a client in which the lawyer himself was named as a 10 percent beneficiary under the will because, when the will was drafted, the Model Code's disciplinary rules were in effect. However, the lawyer was disciplined for not deleting himself from the will when he revised it a few years later (he actually increased his share to 20 percent), which was after the Model Rules had been adopted. *In re Gillinghamn*, 896 P.2d 656 (Wash. 1995). Inexplicably, the lawyer defended himself by blaming his paralegal for the second will, claiming the paralegal drafted it. The court considered that argument groundless—regardless of its truthfulness—since lawyers are obviously responsible for the acts of their paralegals.

Other than gifts presented in an instrument, nothing in MR 1.8(c) prevents lawyers from accepting gifts from clients. But courts and commentators have considered the substantial gift language as it relates to instruments as applicable to gifts to lawyers in general. The Comments to MR 1.8 mention as appropriate gifts of appreciation, token gifts, and holiday gifts made by clients to their lawyers.

Gifts to Legal Assistants

A legal assistant can also be the object of a client's affection and generosity. Although nothing in the language of the rule makes it applicable to client gifts to the lawyer's employees, such gifts are not without similar appearances of undue influence or impropriety. If the firm has no policy that prohibits employees from accepting client gifts, then the legal assistant is wise to seek the permission of the firm before accepting anything other than minor tokens of appreciation. And if it is too late to seek permission, seek ratification instead.

Even though the legal assistant is not the client's advocate, that does not prevent a disgruntled party from suing him or her in the belief that he or she overreached in a personal relationship with a client. An Illinois case that displays an ever-increasing friendship between a lawyer's paralegal and the lawyer's client should serve as a caution to all legal assistants. In that case, a paralegal became friends with an elderly client following the death of the client's wife. The paralegal would visit the widower at his apartment, helping him with household duties and getting his groceries. Eventually, the paralegal suggested that the widower move to a safer apartment, which just happened to be in a building owned by the lawyer. The widower also gave his checkbook to the paralegal so she could pay his bills. Although she was not paid for her assistance, the widower gave her gifts in return. Finally, the widower called the lawyer to the apartment with a request to transfer ownership of his bank accounts to his "sweetheart" (the paralegal) and also to draft a will giving the lawyer and the paralegal $3,000 each. Following the widower's death, the paralegal withdrew all the money out of the bank accounts, and the widower's relatives sued after they discovered that the bank accounts held over $165,000! Their lawsuit was based on a legal theory that attempted to hold the paralegal liable as a fiduciary to the widower because she was an employee of the lawyer, who was a fiduciary to the widower/client. The relatives, however, never sued the attorney. Although the court refused to hold that paralegals are liable as fiduciaries to their lawyers' clients and never found that the paralegal acted improperly, the mess could have been avoided if the paralegal had initially told her lawyer about the relationship and also if the lawyer had formulated a policy on gifts from clients to his staff, as well as himself. *In re Estate of Divine*, 635 N.E.2d 581 (Ill. App. 1 Dist. 1994)

Media Rights In the Client's Story

Model Rule 1.8(d) prohibits a lawyer from acquiring the media rights related to a client's case while he or she still represents the client. Even if the client's limited payment options would make exchanging the literary or media rights of his or her case for representation a financially feasible option, it may not be done before or during the course of the representation. This rule is designed to prevent lawyers, especially in celebrity or controversial cases, from altering their representation of their clients in order to make the "story" more interesting or scandalous instead of doing what would be in their clients' best interest.

One of the most famous celebrity cases in U.S. history involved the 1974 kidnapping of Patty Hearst, granddaughter of William Randolph Hearst, the publishing tycoon and loosely drawn subject of the Orson Welles movie *Citizen Kane*. While with the terrorists who kidnapped her, Patty Hearst was caught on tape robbing a bank and was later prosecuted for the robbery. F. Lee Bailey, perhaps the most famous criminal defense lawyer of the last fifty years, represented her, arguing that she was brainwashed by the terrorists and not responsible for her actions. Hearst was convicted and, after firing Bailey, argued on appeal that Bailey's representation of her was detrimentally affected because he wrongfully acquired the publication rights to her story while he was still her lawyer. Their agreement required Hearst to fully cooperate with Bailey's account of her story and to not publish her own version of her story within 18 months of the publication of Bailey's version. Despite Bailey's argument that the agreement was made after the trial and was necessary to pay for his fees, the court found it to be an impermissible conflict of interest and a violation of the ABA Model Code of Professional Responsibility. *United States v. Hearst*, 638 F.2d 1190 (9th Cir. 1980). (See Chapter 7 for more on F. Lee Bailey's legal ethics scrapes.)

pro bono—Legal services provided to a client free of charge, or at a reduced rate. The original Latin form was pro bono publico, which means for the public good or welfare.

Helping the Client Financially

Although bar associations encourage **pro bono** activities, lawyers are generally prohibited by Model Rule 1.8(e) from giving financial assistance to their clients. Two exceptions are granted in that rule. First, lawyers may pay a client's litigation costs and expenses in advance. Such an exception would allow the lawyer to make the client's obligation to repay those costs dependent upon a favorable outcome (the contingency fee, for example). And second, the rule also allows lawyers to pay, without the need for reimbursement, the litigation costs of their **indigent** clients.

indigent—Poor, determined to be incapable of paying for a lawyer's services.

Outside the above exceptions, lawyers may not provide a direct financial benefit to their clients. Paying a client's living expenses is not allowed, nor is lending the money, instead; only the advancing of litigation expenses is allowed. Although such a rule might seem cold-hearted, it is predicated on a prior stated concern that lawyers would acquire a financial stake in the litigation and base their legal advice on factors other than professional objectivity. Such a rule can, however, lead to ironic outcomes. For example, in a Mississippi case, a personal injury lawyer helped pay the living expenses of a client whose leg was amputated in a motorcycle accident, including giving the client's girlfriend money to purchase Christmas gifts for her children, paying the client's child support to his ex-wife, and loaning the client money to pay for his prosthetic leg. However, the client brought charges against the lawyer for these actions two years later, and the court disciplined him for his generosity with a private reprimand. *Mississippi Bar v. Attorney HH*, 671 So.2d 1293 (Miss. 1996). As odd an outcome as this might seem, it is supported by a 1954 ABA opinion that prohibits lawyers from advancing living expenses to their clients (ABA Comm. on Ethics and Professional Responsibility, Formal Op. 288—1954), as well as state ethics opinions (State Bar of Ariz. Comm. on Rules of Professional Conduct, Op. 95–01).

Someone Other Than the Client Paying the Legal Expenses

If someone is sued for automobile negligence, the benefits of car insurance become immediately cognizable because many policies provide legal coverage. As a result, the client does not have to pay legal fees—at least up to the amounts of the legal expenses coverage. Model Rule 1.8(f) is designed to protect the client in the situation where a third party is paying the legal costs by requiring that: (1) the client must consent to such an arrangement; (2) the lawyer's judgment must in no way be affected by the payment arrangement; and (3) the lawyer must maintain client confidentiality. The pitfall that can occur when someone other than the client pays his or her legal fees is that the person paying the bill could possibly have interests that are adverse to the client's interests, which could affect the lawyer's loyalty to the client. The rules make clear that, regardless of who pays the bill, the client's interests must prevail.

Although third-party payers can come in a variety of forms, the insurance company is of principal concern here. Clearly, there are occasions where the insurance company's interests can be adverse to the interests of the insured (client), such as if the insurance company wants the case settled but the client does not want to settle. Many ethics opinions have been issued that state that the lawyer must act in conformity with the client's wishes. ABA Comm. on Ethics and Professional

Responsibility, Formal Op. 01–412 (2001) (the lawyer may not reveal to the insurance company confidential information that is materially adverse to the client's interest unless the client consents); Florida Bar Professional Ethics Comm., Op. 98–2 (1998) (the lawyer may not allow his or her independent judgment to be affected when accepting set fees for representing the insurance company's customers); Pennsylvania Bar Ass'n Comm. on Legal Ethics and Professional Responsibility, Op. 97–119 (1997) (a law firm may not release confidential information or "work product" to the insurance company's auditing agency in order to support the legal fees being billed to the insurance company).

Settlement of Combined Claims

When a lawyer represents joint clients, including class action plaintiffs, and a settlement of claims is being considered, Model Rule 1.8(g) requires that *all* clients give their consent to the settlement before the lawyer accepts any settlement on their behalf. The rule predicates the clients' consent on a consultation that would explain the meaning of the settlement to the respective joint clients. When a lawyer makes an **aggregate settlement** on behalf of all the lawyer's clients but without all the clients having been consulted, much less given the opportunity to refuse consent, the lawyer can end up paying for that error figuratively (being professionally disciplined) and literally (having to reimburse the clients who were not consulted). *See State ex rel. Oklahoma Bar Ass'n v. Watson*, 897 P.2d 246 (Okla. 1994).

aggregate settlement—A settlement made by all parties on the same side of a case. Sometimes called a joint settlement.

Agreements Limiting the Lawyer's Liability

Model Rule 1.8(h) is really two rules rolled into one, both of which concern the propriety of lawyers limiting their liability with clients. The first part of the rule puts limits on a lawyer's ability to prospectively limit his or her liability with the client at the outset of the representation by allowing it only if (a) it is permitted in the lawyer's jurisdiction and (b) the client is independently represented. Some states, such as Ohio, believe it is unsettling to the public to have lawyers tell their new clients that they should go see another lawyer to get advice about agreeing to limit the first lawyer's liability for future negligence, and so are in opposition to these type of agreements. S.Ct. Ohio Board of Commissioners on Grievances and Discipline Op. No. 96–9 (1996). Sometimes, lawyers insert **arbitration** clauses in their retainer agreements, and ethics commissions and courts generally do not oppose such clauses because arbitration agreements do not limit the lawyer's liability but, instead, choose a method for resolving liability claims. Virginia Ethics Op. 1707 (1998); State Bar of California Committee on Professional Responsibility and Conduct, Formal Op. 1989–116 (1989).

arbitration—An alternative dispute resolution mechanism where parties agree to submit their dispute to a neutral third party, called an arbitrator, who renders a decision, which is usually binding. Arbitration, usually a creature of contract, is quicker and, therefore, less expensive than traditional litigation.

The other part of MR 1.8(h) involves a lawyer settling an existing malpractice claim with a present or former client. In order for a lawyer to settle such a dispute with a client or former client, he or she must first advise the client in writing of the client's right to seek another lawyer's advice concerning any settlement. Although adults are generally free to make any contract they desire, the rules presume that disgruntled clients are in a disadvantageous bargaining position with their (former) lawyers when negotiating such financial settlements. For example, in a Florida case, a lawyer hired a second lawyer to file an appearance on behalf of the first lawyer's client. The second lawyer negligently failed to timely file the appearance, so the client's case was dismissed. Even though the client was already represented by the original lawyer, the second lawyer was disciplined for settling the malpractice claim with the client without first advising the client of the need to seek independent representation. *Florida Bar v. Jordan*, 705 So.2d 1387 (Fla. 1998).

Related Lawyers Opposing Each Other

Model Rule 1.8(i) is designed to protect clients where the family relationships of the lawyers might affect their representation. The rule states that lawyers who are related as either parents, children, siblings, or spouses may not oppose each other in litigation unless each client consents, after being made aware of the family relationships involved. This rule only requires client consent if the related lawyers are directly opposing each other.

The Lawyer's Ownership of the Client's Case

Model Rule 1.8(j) is a hybrid of two common law crimes: **barratry** and **champerty**. Barratry involved someone stirring up groundless litigation (today sometimes called ambulance chasing), and champerty involved a lawyer making an agreement to pay the client's litigation expenses in exchange for owning part of the client's eventual damages award. This rule makes it unlawful for a lawyer to have an ownership interest in the client's cause of action, with two exceptions. First, the lawyer can, in an attempt to get paid, obtain a lien against the client, which ultimately allows the lawyer to have the client's assets seized in order to pay the legal fees. Second, the lawyer can make a contingency fee arrangement with the client that is "reasonable" and in civil cases only (see the discussion on contingency fees in Chapter 7).

    The difference between a contingency fee, which is allowed, and an ownership fee, which is not allowed, can be difficult to distinguish. Summarily, contingency fees are payable to the lawyer from a recovery the plaintiff gets following the conclusion of a claim made against the defendant. For example, in a Hawaii case, a lawyer represented the male half of an unmarried couple fighting over a jointly owned house. The couple was close to agreeing that the man would sell his interest in the house to the woman for $25,000, a sum the man's lawyer called ridiculous. But later, the lawyer purchased the man's interest in the house for the same amount (this purchase ended the client's financial obligation to the lawyer) and executed a contract that stated that the male client understood he was waiving the lawyer's

barratry—Historically, barratry was the crime of stirring up frivolous, or groundless, litigation.

champerty—An agreement between the lawyer and client where the lawyer agrees to pay the costs of the litigation in exchange for the client transferring to the lawyer the client's ownership in any future judgment. The historical prohibition of champerty has been relaxed by the allowances of contingency fees.

conflict of interest (something the lawyer never explained to the client). The court considered the lawyer's purchase to be an impermissible ownership interest in the subject matter of the cause of action. *Lee v. Aiu*, 936 P.2d 655. (Haw. 1997).

The Model Code and Prohibited Transactions

Many of the listed prohibitions in MR 1.8 are found in the Model Code of Professional Responsibility's Disciplinary Rules (DR 5–104, DR 4–101, DR 5–103, DR 5–105, DR 5–106, and DR 6–102) and Ethical Considerations (EC 5–3 and EC 5–5). But the Model Code has no rules that allow lawyers to pay the litigation costs of their indigent clients, concern settling malpractice claims with former clients, or prohibit related lawyers from opposing each other.

CONFLICTS WHEN THE CLIENT IS A CORPORATION OR OTHER ORGANIZATION

ABA Model Rule 1.13 addresses conflicts that can arise when the client is an entity, such as a corporation or a partnership. Although the text of the rule is voluminous, covering many issues, two of those issues will be discussed: determining who the client is in a corporate setting and learning how conflicts of interest are affected by corporate criminal activity.

Who Is the Client?

MR 1.13(a) makes it clear that the organization is the client, and not the persons who control, work at, or own the organization, all of whom are known as the organization's constituents. What is not clear is how this works in reality. Imagine that a lawyer represents Martha Stewart Living Omnimedia, Inc., the publicly traded company founded by Martha Stewart to run her television and radio show, produce her publications, and sell her products. Clearly, Martha Stewart is the boss at the company; she is its chief executive officer as well as the chair of the board of directors. But the company, not Martha, is the client. This means that the lawyer's duty of loyalty is owed to the company. But Martha, as the boss, is the company's head and, therefore, has the right to direct the lawyer's activities on behalf of the company. (See the Comments to MR 1.13 for more explanation on the corporate client and those who control it.)

Employees and shareholders are also constituents. And as the rule and its Comments make clear, when the interests of the constituents and the organization are in conflict, the lawyer must protect the interests of the organization. In fact, MR 1.13(d) says that in such situations, the lawyer needs to explain to the constituents that the organization is the client, and not they. But such conflicting interests can occur after the fact. In a federal case, a school principal who lost her job filed a wrongful termination suit against her school district. Part of her legal strategy included attempting to disqualify the school district's lawyer on the theory that the lawyer advised her on matters relating to her decision to fire several employees during her tenure as principal. Therefore, she argued, she was the lawyer's client. However, the court disagreed, finding that the lawyer-client relationship never attached because she sought the lawyer's advice on official matters, not personal matters. He was the lawyer for the school (the entity), not for the principal (the constituent). *Cole v. Ruidoso Mun. Schools*, 43 F.3d 1373 (10th Cir. 1994) (Exhibit 5–2).

What If the Organization Is Engaging in Illegal Activity?

How does an organization engage in illegal activity? Since it is inanimate, it acts through its authorized representatives. For example, when the Ford Motor Co. was tried for criminal homicide in 1980 in connection with the deaths of three women caused by the Ford Pinto and when the accounting firm of Arthur Anderson was convicted in 2002 of obstruction of justice in connection with the shredding of Enron financial documents, both sets of charges were made under the legal doctrine that the companies were liable for acts committed or ratified by their high-ranking employees.

   If a corporate lawyer believes that representatives of the organization are acting illegally, it is his or her responsibility to inform the highest executive of the organization about the misdeeds. *See* ABA Comm. on Professional Ethics, Formal Op. 93–375 (1993). The lawyer cannot be a whistle-blower and inform outsiders about the ille-

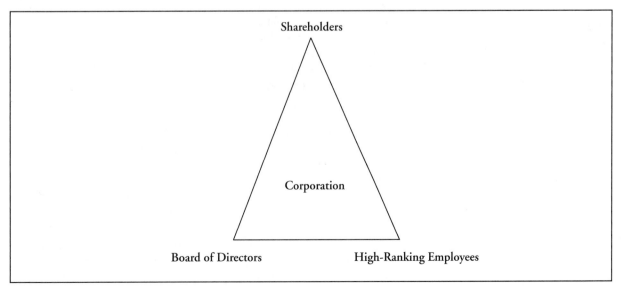

Exhibit 5-2   Corporations and Their Constituents

gal activities because such disclosure would violate the duty of confidentiality and also because it could harm the corporation/client. If the chief executive officer refuses to rectify the illegal activities, the lawyer could resign from the representation, assuming no confidences would be revealed by the method in which this is done.

Some courts consider the duty of confidentiality so important that they do not allow in-house corporate lawyers to sue their former employers for retaliatory discharge after having been fired for blowing the whistle on them. For example, in an Illinois case, a corporation's attorney was fired for threatening to report the fact that the corporation was planning on selling defective dialyzer machines. In the ensuing lawsuit, the court found that the lawyer's duty not to disclose client information outweighed his desire to protect the public. *Balla v. Gambro, Inc.*, 584 N.E.2d 104 (Ill. 1991). Other jurisdictions give fired corporate counsel a limited right to sue their former employer, assuming the allegations can be proved without disclosing confidential information. *See also General Dynamics Corporation v. Superior Court*, 32 Cal. Rptr. 2d 1 (Cal. 1994); *Fox Searchlight Pictures v. Paladino, Inc.*, 106 Cal. Rptr. 2d 906 (Cal. Ct. App. 2001).

Change in this area might be around the corner, however. The Montana Supreme Court decided in 2000 that Montana's Rules of Professional Conduct do not prevent in-house counsel from suing his or her employer for wrongful termination and using confidential information in order to establish the claim. *Burkhart v. Semitool, Inc.*, 5 P.3d 1031 (Mont. 2000). And the ABA issued a trail-blazing ethics opinion in September 2001 declaring that the ABA Model Rules do not prohibit a lawyer from suing his or her former client and employer for wrongful termination, even if the suit involved disclosing confidential information. ABA Commission on Professional Ethics, Formal Op.01–424 (2001). The ABA did state, however, that only the amount of confidential information necessary to establish the lawyer's claim for wrongful discharge could be disclosed. Then, the Tennessee Supreme Court decided in May 2002 that in-house counsel has the right to sue his or her corporate employer for wrongful termination and may also use confidential information in order to establish the claim. *Crews v. Buckman Laboratories Intern., Inc.*, 2002 WL 1050247 (Tenn. May 24, 2002). But the Court limited a lawyer's right to disclose client confidences and secrets to only that which is necessary and those who need to know.

The Legal Assistant as a Corporate Employee

The legal assistant working in a corporate law department might become aware of information that implicates the company in inappropriate or illegal activities. This puts him or her in a difficult position since the employer is his or her client. Generally, employees have no inherent duty to protect their employer's discriminatory or illegal activities. On many occasions, corporate criminal activity is only established with the help of the whistle-blower. For instance, the IRS has the authority to reward those who report on the tax fraud of others—including their employers—by giving the whistle-blower a percentage of whatever the IRS recovers from the tax cheat. *See* IRS Publication no. 733. A sense of justice or moral outrage might compel the legal assistant to report the misdeeds of their corporate employer. That may be done, but only to authorities within the company. Any whistle-blowing done outside the company (to the government or the press) would be wrong, because legal assistants, being bound by the same rules of confidentiality as lawyers, must protect their clients' confidences, even harmful confidences. Even in Montana and Tennessee, corporate paralegals should not believe themselves free to do what those courts have recently allowed lawyers to do, since those cases involve lawyers, not non-lawyer employees of corporate law departments.

The Model Code and the Corporate Entity

The Disciplinary Rules of the Model Code of Professional Responsibility had no singular rule that was equivalent to MR 1.13. However, DR 5–107(B) required a lawyer who was employed by someone to render legal services for another to refuse to allow the employing person to affect his or her judgment. And EC 5–18 provided that a "lawyer employed or retained by a corporation or similar entity owes his allegiance to the entity and not to a stockholder, director, officer, employee, representative, or other person connected with the entity."

IMPUTED DISQUALIFICATION: ONE LAWYER'S CONFLICT AFFECTING THE FIRM

So far, the kinds of conflicts of interests that have been discussed required a determination of whether the lawyer may continue to represent his or her client despite a conflict of interest the lawyer does, or might, have. If the lawyer cannot obtain the client's consent for those conflicts that allow for client consent, the lawyer must withdraw. Likewise, the lawyer must withdraw for those direct, or materially adverse, conflicts, for which the rules do not allow client consent. This seems simple enough. But can another lawyer in the same firm take a case that the conflicted lawyer either may not take or may not continue? Or is the whole firm disqualified if one of its lawyers is disqualified?

The General Policy: Disqualification

ABA Model Rule 1.10(a) covers the kinds of situations where the disqualification of one lawyer in the firm will be imputed to the entire firm. The gist of MR 1.10(a) is that *all lawyers in a firm* are disqualified from representing a client *if any lawyer in the firm* would be disqualified due to the application of four situations: (1) the general conflicts found in MR 1.7; (2) the client gift prohibition of MR 1.8(c); (3) the former client conflicts found in MR 1.9; and (4) cases where the lawyer acts as an intermediary between clients, found in MR 2.2. Except for the gift prohibition, the imputed disqualification situations are quite broad since, as an example, the general lawyer conflicts encompassed by MR 1.7 are broad.

This is a strict rule that makes an entire law firm bear the responsibility for the conflict of one of their lawyers because of the overriding concern for loyalty to the client. This imputed disqualification rule also presumes that all lawyers in the firm have access to, and share in, all of the firm's clients' confidential information. For example, in a New Jersey case, a local police officer who was also licensed to practice law wrote the state ethics committee for advice about any limitations that might apply to a law firm he was considering joining on a part-time basis. The committee decided—and the New Jersey Supreme Court affirmed—that the law firm would be able to represent no private defendants in criminal matters arising in the municipality where the police officer was employed if he joined the law firm. Such imputed disqualification was based, in part, on the **appearance of impropriety** standard being applied to MR 1.10(a), since clearly the lawyer/police officer could not represent any clients accused of crimes in the township where he was employed as a police officer. *In re Advisory Committee*, 616 A.2d 1290 (N.J. 1992). The Model Code applied a tougher standard than does the Model Rules in that DR 5–105(D) required that if a lawyer was disqualified from representing the client for any reason under the Model Code, then no lawyer associated with the first lawyer was able to take the case.

appearance of impropriety—A standard of ethical conduct, found in the Model Code of Professional Responsibility, in which lawyers are advised to avoid certain activities because those activities look bad, rather than actually being bad.

Imputed Disqualification: Formerly Associated Lawyers

The Comments to MR 1.10 make clear that section (a) concerns lawyers who are currently associated with each other. MR 1.10(b), however, applies to situations where conflicts are imputed to a law firm because of a conflict-affected lawyer who used to work at the firm. This section does allow a law firm to represent a client whose interests are adverse—even materially adverse—to another client who was represented by a lawyer when that lawyer used to work at that firm, provided two conditions exist. First, the matter cannot be the same or substantially related to the matter with which the formerly associated lawyer was connected. And second, if the matter is the same or substantially related, there can be no remaining lawyer in the firm who has any confidential information about the matter in question. As an example, suppose that attorney A at law firm 1 represented a plaintiff in a sexual harassment case against the plaintiff's former employer. Then, attorney A leaves that law firm and moves to law firm 2, taking that plaintiff with her. Later, the employer from the sexual harassment case comes to law firm 1, seeking representation on a zoning matter. Can law firm 1 represent the employer? Yes, because the matter is not the same, which means there is no need to consider whether any lawyer possesses confidential information about the sexual harassment plaintiff.

Now, suppose that attorney A at law firm 1 represented the employer against a charge of sexual harassment by one of its employees. Then, attorney A leaves that law firm and moves to law firm 2, taking the employer/client with her. Later, another employee of that company comes to law firm 1, seeking representation in a claim of sexual harassment against that employer/former client. Can law firm 1 represent that employee? Probably not, because the matter (a sexual harassment allegation) is substantially related to the kind of case lawyer A worked on for the employer/client when she worked at law firm 1, and there is a strong presumption that other lawyers in law firm 1 had access to confidential information of the employer/client when lawyer A was associated with that firm.

The Presumption of Shared Confidences

However, the presumption that other remaining lawyers in the firm had access to confidential information can be rebutted if the courts are willing to consider such an argument. In a Missouri case, a husband and wife were divorcing and the husband tried to disqualify the law firm that represented the wife because that firm recently hired a lawyer who, at one time, was employed by the law firm representing the husband. The court, in denying the disqualification motion, found that disqualification was inappropriate in light of these facts: the lawyer in question never represented the husband at the former law firm, nor was she representing the wife at the present law firm, and the husband never alleged that the lawyer in question ever learned any of his case's information, confidential or otherwise, while working at the law firm that had represented him. *In re Marriage of Carter*, 862 S.W.2d 461 (Mo. Ct. App. 1993). Even if a lawyer at the former firm performed legal research for the client before moving to the firm representing the client's opponent, that might not necessarily require the new firm to be disqualified from representing the client's opponent if there is no evidence that the lawyer acquired confidential information while working at the first firm. *See Pacific Employers Ins. Co. v. P.B. Hoidale Co.*, 804 F. Supp. 137 (D. Kan. 1992).

Some jurisdictions do not accept the position that the presumption of shared confidential information is a rebuttable presumption. Instead, these courts draw a strict line that requires disqualification of a law firm that employs a lawyer who used to work at the firm whose client is involved in the same, or substantially the same, matter as a client of the new firm. *See State ex rel. FirsTIER Bank v. Buckley*, 503 N.W.2d 838 (Neb. 1993); *Elan Transdermal Ltd. v. Cygnus Therapeutic Sys.*, 809 F. Supp. 1383 (N.D. Cal. 1992).

Imputed Disqualification and Client Consent

MR 1.10(c) does allow imputed disqualification obstacles to be overcome by client consent, but only the kind of client consent allowed under MR 1.7, the general conflict of interest rule. That rule allows clients to give their consent to their lawyers' continued representation, despite the presence of a conflict of interest, but not in all situations. (Remember, client consent would not cure the conflict of two clients suing each other and wanting to share the same lawyer.)

Consent can sometimes be found to have occurred passively if the affected client waits too long to oppose the disputed representation. Occasionally, courts have found that, by delaying for too long, clients have waived the right to oppose their former lawyer's representation of a client affected by MR 1.10. For instance, in a federal case in California, a former client was found to have waived the right to object to his former lawyer's representation of an adverse party because he did not formally object to the representation until over a year after becoming aware of the adverse representation. *Employers Ins. of Wausau v. Albert D. Seeno Const. Co.,* 692 F. Supp. 1150 (N.D. Cal. 1988).

IMPUTED DISQUALIFICATION: THE USE OF SCREENS FOR THE TAINTED EMPLOYEE

So far, we have learned that, generally, in cases where a lawyer would be disqualified from representing a client, the entire firm would be disqualified (unless the client consents), due to the presumption that all lawyers in the firm have access in, and share, the confidential knowledge of all the firm's clients. But that presumption can be overcome by evidence that the affected lawyer had no confidential information because the lawyer only worked at the former law firm but did no work on behalf of the client at the former firm who is attempting to disqualify the lawyer's present firm. But what if the lawyer did work on a matter for the client (client A) before moving to a new firm, which is representing a client (client B) with a position adverse to client A? This would require disqualification of the new firm, since the affected lawyer actually possesses confidential information of client A, unless the "tainted" lawyer can be effectively "screened" from the other lawyers in the firm.

The Use of Screens for Tainted Lawyers

Nothing in MR 1.10's rule or Comments mentions screening as a technique to avoid disqualification, but it is specifically mentioned in Model Rule 1.11(a)(1) as allowable for former government lawyers working in private practice. This allows, for instance, a lawyer working for the federal government in the Securities and Exchange Commission (SEC) and involved in investigating and prosecuting **insider trading** to move to a private firm where lawyers in the firm represent those targeted by the SEC. The policy behind allowing former government lawyers to be screened is that, by allowing screening, the government can attract highly competent attorneys (who will earn much less than if they were in private practice), since those lawyers need not fear that their future employability will be at risk when they leave government service to practice the same type of law, except on the other side.

Some courts have expanded the concept of screening for former government lawyers to lawyers not involved in former government work. The first significant case in which screening for private practice lawyers switching firms was approved was *Schiessle v. Stephens,* 717 F.2d 417 (Seventh Cir. 1983). A screen is sometimes also referred to as a "Chinese wall" (a bad analogy since the Great Wall of China was breached without great difficulty by the Mongol conqueror Genghis Khan), or an "ethical wall," or a "cone of silence." The following internal mechanisms, put in place by the firm with the tainted lawyer, can help to show that he or she has been

insider trading—The buying or selling of a company's stock, by the company's insiders, based on information the insiders know, and before that information is released to the public. Insiders are usually defined as executive officers, directors, or shareholders of a corporation owning at least 10 percent of the corporation's stock.

effectively screened: (1) the lawyer is prevented from having any involvement in the controversial case; (2) the lawyer is prevented from having any access to the files of the case; (3) the lawyer declares under oath that he or she did not, nor will not, disclose any information of the former client to any other lawyer in the firm; and (4) the lawyer is prevented from sharing in the fees from the case. *See* D.C. Bar Comm. on Legal Ethics, Op. 279 (1998). (This opinion discusses the appropriate measures taken to screen an infected government lawyer, as well as nonlawyer employees, including paralegals, and cites many cases where screens have been approved.)

A few jurisdictions expressly allow screening for private practice lawyers in their rules of court, thereby avoiding the problem of waiting for the courts to get involved. For instance, Michigan, Pennsylvania, and Oregon have amended their imputed disqualification rules and now allow such lawyers to be screened. *See* Mich. Rules of Professional Conduct, Rule 1.10(b); Pa. Rules of Prof. Conduct, Rule 1.10(b); Or. Code of Prof. Responsibility, DR 5–1–5(I).

More than a few jurisdictions, however, do not approve of screens for lawyers in private practice, finding that the interest of protecting the former client's confidential information is paramount to the lawyer's economic interest in seeking new employment at a firm that might put that former client's interest at risk. Arizona, Georgia, New Jersey, and Kansas are some of the states that prohibit the screening of private practice lawyers moving to other firms. A California case discussing the Chinese wall doctrine specifically limited it to former government lawyers and stated that California law was clear that screens could not be used to overcome imputed disqualification caused by lawyers switching firms. *Henriksen v. Great American Savings & Loan*, 14 Cal. Rptr. 2d 184 (Ct. App. 1992).

Screens for Non-Lawyer Employees: The News Is Pretty Good

There are two ways of viewing a lawyer as tainted: either the lawyer simply worked at another firm (firm 1) where there was a client (client A) with a matter adverse to a client (client B) at the lawyer's present firm (firm 2), or the lawyer actually worked on the former client's (client A) case and then moved to the present firm (firm 2), which represents a client (client B) with a matter adverse to client 1. Both situations could require firm 2 to be disqualified from representing client B (assuming client A moves to have the firm disqualified). Likewise, both types of imputed disqualification could be avoided by screening the tainted lawyer, assuming the jurisdiction allows for such screens.

Both these situations are just as likely to occur where legal assistants are involved and, logically, the use of screens for lawyers has been extended to non-lawyer employees. In fact, the use of screens for non-lawyer employees is better received across the country than the use of screens for lawyers. The American Bar Association issued an ethics opinion in 1988 that approved the use of screens for non-lawyer employees (such as paralegals and investigators) moving between firms who are representing opposing clients, as long as the non-lawyer employees did not work on both sides of the same matter. The concern expressed by the ABA opinion was two-fold: to protect client confidences and to protect the employability of highly skilled non-lawyer employees, who would otherwise lose their chance of being hired at other firms if they were held to the same imputed disqualification standards as lawyers. ABA Comm. on Ethics and Professional Responsibility, Informal Op. 88–1526 (1988). Other jurisdictions have issued their own ethics opinions approving of screens for paralegals or legal assistants, as well as secretaries: Ala. Office of General Counsel, Op. 91–02 (1991); State Bar of Mich. Comm. on Professional and Judicial Ethics, Op. RI–285 (1996); State Bar of Mich. Comm. on Professional and Judicial Ethics, Op. R–115 (1992); Mo. Office of the Chief Disc. Counsel, Op. 980149 (1998); Neb. St. Bar Assoc. Advisory Comm. Op. 94–4 (1994); N.J. Sup. Ct. Advisory Comm. on Professional Ethics, Op. 665 (1992); N.C. State Bar Ethics Comm. Op. 176 (1994); Ethics Comm. of State Bar Ass'n of N.D., Op. 98–1 (1998); Pa. Bar Assoc. Formal Op. 98–75 (1998); Vt. Bar Assoc. Advisory Ethics Op. 97–9 (1997).

Many Courts Approve of Screens for Legal Assistants

There is a lot of case law that shows approval of screens for legal assistants as a way of avoiding the disqualification of the legal assistant's new firm. Some of the factors that tend to be significant for law firms trying to avoid vicarious disqualification include the following: (a) the size of the firm (the larger the firm, the better the chances that the screen will prevent the tainted lawyer or non-lawyer employee from having contact with the members of the firm working on the matter that is the subject of the disqualification motion, especially if the tainted employee works at a different office of the firm than where the matter is being represented); (b) the level of departmentalization at the firm (the clearer the lines of distinction between different departments of the firm, the more believable it is that the screen being employed will prevent the tainted employee from having contact with the members of the department working on the matter); and (c) the methods employed in creating the screen (such as a memo to the firm employees informing them of the screening measure in place for the affected employee, a letter to the former client of the affected employee that informs them of the screening measures that were taken, and an affidavit of the affected employee in which the affected employee affirms an oath to work within the screen and keep confidential all information of the former client) (Exhibit 5–3).

As recently as April 2002, another court approved, for the first time, the use of screens for non-lawyer employees. In *Hayes v. Central States Orthopedic Specialists, Inc.*, 5 P.3d 562 (Okla. 2002), the Oklahoma Supreme Court dealt with an appeal involving a plaintiff who disqualified the defendant's law firm because a secretary who worked at the plaintiff's law firm left her employment there and went to work for the defendant's law firm. Reversing the decision of the trial court, the supreme court concluded two things: (1) the plaintiff waived the right to disqualify the defendant's firm because of waiting over eight months before objecting to the secretary's employment change; and (2) the use of a "Chinese wall" screening device can be an effective device to prevent a law firm from being disqualified after it has hired a non-lawyer employee who used to

1. The screen is put in place at the time the tainted legal assistant moves to the new firm.
2. The legal assistant signs an affidavit declaring that he or she will have no involvement in the case that is the subject of the conflict controversy and that no information from the former firm's client has been, or will be, disclosed to anyone at the new firm.
3. The new firm physically separates the legal assistant from the lawyer or lawyers working on the affected case.
4. The new firm instructs all members, particularly those working on the case, not to discuss the affected case with the legal assistant.
5. A memo is sent to all members of the firm confirming the screening instructions.
6. A letter is sent to the legal assistant's former firm, informing it of the screening measures that are in place to protect against any breech of confidentiality.

Exhibit 5-3   Elements of an Effective Legal Assistant Screen

work at the opposing party's law firm. Specifically, the court applied the logic of screens for government lawyers in allowing screens for non-lawyer assistants at private law firms, finding that—like government lawyers—non-lawyer assistants do not have a financial stake in the outcome of the cases on which they work, and they cannot choose their clients. To its credit, the Oklahoma Supreme Court acknowledged that, in reaching its decision, it considered the **amicus curiae** brief filed by the National Association of Legal Assistants, arguing in support of screens for non-lawyer assistants. *Id.*, at 564.

The fact that jurisdictions are on record as approving of a screen as a way to avoid imputed disqualification does not mean that courts will not disqualify a firm that claims to have had a screen in place. The following case is famous in the area of non-lawyer screening, with a deceitful paralegal at the center of the controversy.

amicus curiae—A Latin phrase that means "friend of the court." An amicus curiae brief is a brief filed by one who is not a party to the lawsuit, but who believes the court needs to read the legal perspective presented in the amicus brief in order to make a correct decision.

Case Law

In Re Complex Asbestos Litigation, 283 Cal. Rptr. 732 (Cal. App. 1991)

Chin, J.

Attorney Jeffrey B. Harrison, his law firm, and their affected clients appeal from an order disqualifying the Harrison firm in nine asbestos-related personal injury actions. The appeal presents the difficult issue of whether a law firm should be disqualified because an employee of the firm possessed attorney-client confidences from previous employment by opposing counsel in pending litigation. We hold that disqualification is appropriate unless there is written consent or the law firm has effectively screened the employee from involvement with the litigation to which the information relates.

FACTS

Michael Vogel worked as a paralegal for the law firm of Brobeck, Phleger & Harrison (Brobeck) from October 28, 1985, to November 30, 1988. Vogel came to Brobeck with experience working for a law firm that represented defendants in asbestos litigation. Brobeck also represented asbestos litigation defendants, including respondents. At Brobeck, Vogel worked exclusively on asbestos litigation. During most of the period Brobeck employed Vogel, he worked on settlement evaluations. He extracted information from medical reports, discovery responses, and plaintiffs' depositions for entry on "Settlement Evaluation and Authority Request" (SEAR) forms. The SEAR forms were brief summaries of the information and issues used by the defense attorneys and their clients to evaluate each plaintiff's case. The SEAR forms were sent to the clients.

Vogel attended many defense attorney meetings where the attorneys discussed the strengths and weaknesses of cases to reach consensus settlement recommendations for each case. The SEAR forms were the primary informational materials the attorneys used at the meetings. Vogel's responsibility at these meetings was to record the amounts agreed on for settlement recommendations to the clients. Vogel sent the settlement authority requests and SEAR forms to the clients. He also attended meetings and telephone conferences where attorneys discussed the recommendations with clients and settlement authority was granted. Vogel recorded on the SEAR forms the amount of settlement authority granted and distributed the information to the defense attorneys. The SEAR form information was included in Brobeck's computer record on each asbestos case. The SEAR forms contained the plaintiff's name and family information, capsule summaries of medical reports, the plaintiff's work history, asbestos products identified at the plaintiff's work sites, and any special considerations that might affect the jury's response to the plaintiff's case. . . .

In 1988, Vogel's duties changed when he was assigned to work for a trial team. With that change, Vogel no longer was involved with the settlement evaluation meetings and reports. Instead, he helped prepare specific cases assigned to the team. Vogel did

not work on any cases in which the Harrison firm represented the plaintiffs. . . . [In October 1988] Brobeck gave Vogel two weeks' notice of his termination, though his termination date was later extended to the end of November. Vogel contacted a number of firms about employment, and learned that the Harrison firm was looking for paralegals. The Harrison firm recently had opened a Northern California office and filed a number of asbestos cases against respondents. Sometime in the second half of November 1988, Vogel called Harrison to ask him for a job with his firm. In that first telephone conversation, Harrison learned that Vogel had worked for Brobeck on asbestos litigation settlements. Harrison testified that he did not then offer Vogel a job for two reasons. First, Harrison did not think he would need a new paralegal until February or March of 1989. Second, Harrison was concerned about the appearance of a conflict of interest in his firm's hiring a paralegal from Brobeck. Harrison discussed the conflict problem with other attorneys, and told Vogel that he could be hired only if Vogel got a waiver from the senior asbestos litigation partner at Brobeck. Vogel testified that he spoke with Stephen Snyder, the Brobeck partner in charge of managing the Northern California asbestos litigation. Vogel claimed he told Snyder of the possible job with the Harrison firm, and that Snyder later told him the clients had approved and that Snyder would provide a written waiver if Vogel wanted. In his testimony, Snyder firmly denied having any such conversations or giving Vogel any conflicts waiver to work for Harrison. The trial court resolved this credibility dispute in favor of Snyder. . . . Harrison did not contact Brobeck to confirm Vogel's claim that he made a full disclosure and obtained Brobeck's consent. Nor did Harrison tell Vogel that he needed a waiver from Bjork [another firm doing asbestos-related work, where Vogel was employed immediately before his employment with Harrison].

[A]t the end of February 1989, Vogel was asked to finish another paralegal's job of contacting asbestos plaintiffs to complete client questionnaires.

The questionnaire answers provided information for discovery requests by the defendants. Vogel contacted Bjork and others to request copies of discovery materials for the Harrison firm. Vogel also assisted when the Harrison firm's asbestos trial teams needed extra help. In March 1989, Snyder learned from a Brobeck trial attorney that Vogel was involved in asbestos litigation. In a March 31 letter, Snyder asked Harrison if Vogel's duties included asbestos litigation. Harrison responded to Snyder by letter on April 6. In the letter, Harrison stated Vogel told Snyder his work for the Harrison firm would include periodic work on asbestos cases, and that Harrison assumed there was no conflict of interest. Harrison also asked Snyder to provide details of the basis for any claimed conflict. There were no other communications between Brobeck and the Harrison firm concerning Vogel before the disqualification motion was filed.

In June, a Harrison firm attorney asked Vogel to call respondent Fibreboard Corporation to see if it would accept service of a subpoena for its corporate minutes. Vogel called the company and spoke to a person he knew from working for Brobeck. Vogel asked who should be served with the subpoena in place of the company's retired general counsel. Vogel's call prompted renewed concern among respondents' counsel over Vogel's involvement with asbestos litigation for a plaintiff's firm. On July 31, counsel for three respondents demanded that the Harrison firm disqualify itself from cases against those respondents. Three days later, the motion to disqualify the Harrison firm was filed; it was subsequently joined by all respondents.

The trial court held a total of 21 hearing sessions on the motion, including 16 sessions of testimony. During the hearing, several witnesses testified that Vogel liked to talk, and the record indicates that he would volunteer information in an effort to be helpful. A critical incident involving Vogel's activities at Brobeck first came to light during the hearing. Brobeck's computer system access log showed that on November 17, 1988, Vogel accessed the computer

records for 20 cases filed by the Harrison firm. On the witness stand, Vogel at first flatly denied having looked at these case records, but when confronted with the access log, he admitted reviewing the records "to see what kind of cases [the Harrison firm] had filed." At the time, Vogel had no responsibilities for any Harrison firm cases at Brobeck. The date Vogel reviewed those computer records was very close to the time Vogel and Harrison first spoke. The access log documented that Vogel opened each record long enough to view and print copies of all the information on the case in the computer system. . . . Vogel denied recalling what information for the Harrison firm's cases he saw on the computer, and Brobeck's witness could not tell what specific information was on the computer that day.

Vogel, Harrison, and the other two witnesses from the Harrison firm denied that Vogel ever disclosed any client confidences obtained while he worked for Brobeck. However, Harrison never instructed Vogel not to discuss any confidential information obtained at Brobeck. Vogel did discuss with Harrison firm attorneys his impressions of several Brobeck attorneys. After the disqualification motion was filed, Harrison and his office manager debriefed Vogel, not to obtain any confidences but to discuss his duties at Brobeck in detail and to assess respondents' factual allegations. During the course of the hearing, the Harrison firm terminated Vogel on August 25, 1989.

The trial court found that Vogel's work for Brobeck and the Harrison firm was substantially related, and that there was no express or implied waiver by Brobeck or its clients. The court believed there was a substantial likelihood that the Harrison firm's hiring of Vogel, without first building "an ethical wall" or having a waiver, would affect the outcome in asbestos cases. The court also found that Vogel obtained confidential information when he accessed Brobeck's computer records on the Harrison firm's cases, and that there was a reasonable probability Vogel used that information or disclosed it to other members of the Harrison firm's staff. The court refused to extend the disqualification beyond those cases where there was tangible evidence of interference by Vogel, stating that on the rest of the cases it would require the court to speculate. The trial court initially disqualified the Harrison firm in all 20 cases Vogel accessed on November 17, 1988, which included 11 cases pending in Contra Costa County. However, on further consideration, the trial court restricted its disqualification order to the nine cases pending in San Francisco. The Harrison firm timely noticed an appeal from the disqualification order, and respondents cross-appealed from the denial of disqualification in the Contra Costa County cases and all asbestos litigation.

DISCUSSION

The courts have discussed extensively the remedies for the ethical problems created by attorneys changing their employment from a law firm representing one party in litigation to a firm representing an adverse party. Considerably less attention has been given to the problems posed by nonlawyer employees of law firms who do the same. The issue this appeal presents is one of first impression for California courts. While several Courts of Appeal have considered factual situations raising many of the same concerns, as will be discussed below, the decisions in those cases hinged on factors not present here. In short, this case is yet another square peg that does not fit the round holes of attorney disqualification rules. . . .

The Harrison firm argues that conflict of interest disqualification rules governing attorneys should not apply to the acts of nonlawyers, citing *Maruman Integrated Circuits, Inc. v. Consortium Co.* (1985) 166 Cal.App.3d 443, [212 Cal.Rptr. 497] and *Cooke v. Superior Court* (1978) 83 Cal.App.3d 582 [147 Cal.Rptr. 915]. The courts in both cases refused to disqualify attorneys who possessed an adverse party's confidences when no attorney-client relationship ever existed between the party and the attorney sought to be disqualified. . . .

A law firm that hires a nonlawyer who possesses an adversary's confidences creates a situation, similar

to hiring an adversary's attorney, which suggests that confidential information is at risk. We adapt our approach, then, from cases that discuss whether an entire firm is subject to vicarious disqualification because one attorney changed sides. (See, e.g., *Klein v. Superior Court, supra,* 198 Cal.App.3d at pp. 908-914; *Chambers v. Superior Court* (1981) 121 Cal.App.3d 893 [175 Cal.Rptr. 575].) The courts disagree on whether vicarious disqualification should be automatic in attorney conflict of interest cases, or whether a presumption of shared confidences should be rebuttable. (See *Klein, supra,* at pp. 910–913.) An inflexible presumption of shared confidences would not be appropriate for nonlawyers, though, whatever its merits when applied to attorneys. There are obvious differences between lawyers and their nonlawyer employees in training, responsibilities, and acquisition and use of confidential information. These differences satisfy us that a rebuttable presumption of shared confidences provides a just balance between protecting confidentiality and the right to chosen counsel.

The most likely means of rebutting the presumption is to implement a procedure, before the employee is hired, which effectively screens the employee from any involvement with the litigation, a procedure one court aptly described as a "'cone of silence.'" (See *Nemours Foundation* v. *Gilbane, Aetna, Federal Ins.* (D.Del. 1986) 632 F. Supp. 418, 428.) Whether a potential employee will require a cone of silence should be determined as a matter of routine during the hiring process. It is reasonable to ask potential employees about the nature of their prior legal work; prudence alone would dictate such inquiries. Here, Harrison's first conversation with Vogel revealed a potential problem—Vogel's work for Brobeck on asbestos litigation settlements.

The leading treatise on legal malpractice also discusses screening procedures and case law. (1 Mallen & Smith, Legal Malpractice (3d ed. 1989) §§ 13.18–13.19, pp. 792–797.) We find several points to be persuasive when adapted to the context of employee conflicts. "Screening is a prophylactic, affirmative measure to avoid both the reality and appearance of impropriety. It is *a* means, but not *the* means, of rebutting the presumption of shared confidences." (*Id.,* § 13.19, at p. 794, original italics, fn. omitted.) Two objectives must be achieved. First, screening should be implemented before undertaking the challenged representation or hiring the tainted individual. Screening must take place at the outset to prevent any confidences from being disclosed. Second, the tainted individual should be precluded from any involvement in or communication about the challenged representation. To avoid inadvertent disclosures and to establish an evidentiary record, a memorandum should be circulated warning the legal staff to isolate the individual from communications on the matter and to prevent access to the relevant files. (*Id.,* at pp. 795–796.) . . .

Respondents' alternative formulation, that a substantial relationship between the type of work done for the former and present employers requires disqualification, presents unnecessary barriers to employment mobility. Such a rule sweeps more widely than needed to protect client confidences. We share the concerns expressed by the American Bar Association's Standing Committee on Ethics and Professional Responsibility:

> It is important that nonlawyer employees have as much mobility in employment opportunity as possible consistent with the protection of clients' interests. To so limit employment opportunities that some nonlawyers trained to work with law firms might be required to leave the careers for which they are trained would disserve clients as well as the legal profession. Accordingly, any restrictions on the nonlawyer's employment should be held to the minimum necessary to protect confidentiality of client information. (Imputed Disqualification Arising from Change in Employment by Nonlawyer Employee, ABA Standing Com. on Ethics & Prof. Responsibility, Informal Opn. No. 88–1526 (1988) p. 3.)

Respondents' suggested rule could easily result in nonlawyer employees becoming "Typhoid Marys," unemployable by firms practicing in specialized areas

of the law where the employees are most skilled and experienced. . . .

Absent written consent, the proper rule and its application for disqualification based on nonlawyer employee conflicts of interest should be as follows. The party seeking disqualification must show that its present or past attorney's former employee possesses confidential attorney-client information materially related to the proceedings before the court. The party should not be required to disclose the actual information contended to be confidential. However, the court should be provided with the nature of the information and its material relationship to the proceeding. (See *Elliott* v. *McFarland Unified School Dist., supra,* 165 Cal.App.3d at p. 572.) Once this showing has been made, a rebuttable presumption arises that the information has been used or disclosed in the current employment. . . . To rebut the presumption, the challenged attorney has the burden of showing that the practical effect of formal screening has been achieved. The showing must satisfy the trial court that the employee has not had and will not have any involvement with the litigation, or any communication with attorneys or coemployees concerning the litigation that would support a reasonable inference that the information has been used or disclosed. If the challenged attorney fails to make this showing, then the court may disqualify the attorney and law firm. . . .

There can be no question that Vogel obtained confidential attorney-client information when he accessed the Harrison firm's case files on Brobeck's computer. Respondents need not show the specific confidences Vogel obtained; such a showing would serve only to exacerbate the damage to the confidentiality of the attorney-client relationship. As discussed above, respondents had to show only the nature of the information and its material relationship to the present proceedings. They have done so. To blunt the impact of Vogel's misconduct, the Harrison firm argues that the cases on the computer were newly filed and that no evidence showed the computer information to be more than appeared on the face of the complaints, which are public records. The argument is wrong on both points. While many of the cases were entered on the computer little more than a week earlier, others were entered weeks or months before Vogel looked at them. Moreover, the fact that some of the same information may appear in the public domain does not affect the privileged status of the information when it is distilled for an attorney-client communication. . . .

CONCLUSION

We realize the serious consequences of disqualifying attorneys and depriving clients of representation by their chosen counsel. However, we must balance the important right to counsel of one's choice against the competing fundamental interest in pre-serving confidences of the attorney-client relationship. . . . Attorneys must respect the confidentiality of attorney-client information and recognize that protecting confidentiality is an imperative to be obeyed in both form and substance. A requisite corollary to these principles is that attorneys must prohibit their employees from violating confidences of former employers as well as confidences of present clients. Until the Legislature or the State Bar chooses to disseminate a different standard, attorneys must be held accountable for their employees' conduct, particularly when that conduct poses a clear threat to attorney-client confidentiality and the integrity of our judicial process.

The order of the trial court is affirmed. Each party shall bear its own costs.

Case Questions

1. What specific facts indicate the deceitfulness of Vogel, the paralegal?
2. What standard for imputed disqualification did the Brobeck firm want the court to apply? Why did the court apply a more lenient standard?
3. What screening mechanism did the court adopt?
4. Why did the court believe that the Harrison firm was in possession of Brobeck's confidential client information?
5. How did Harrison's own conduct contribute to the court's decision to affirm his firm's disqualification?

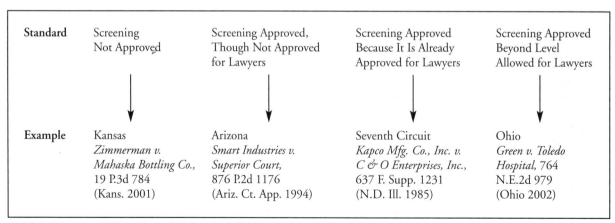

Standard	Screening Not Approved	Screening Approved, Though Not Approved for Lawyers	Screening Approved Because It Is Already Approved for Lawyers	Screening Approved Beyond Level Allowed for Lawyers
Example	Kansas *Zimmerman v. Mahaska Bottling Co.,* 19 P.3d 784 (Kans. 2001)	Arizona *Smart Industries v. Superior Court,* 876 P.2d 1176 (Ariz. Ct. App. 1994)	Seventh Circuit *Kapco Mfg. Co., Inc. v. C & O Enterprises, Inc.,* 637 F. Supp. 1231 (N.D. Ill. 1985)	Ohio *Green v. Toledo Hospital,* 764 N.E.2d 979 (Ohio 2002)

Exhibit 5-4 The Shifting Screening Standards for Paralegals Switching Firms

Not All Courts Approve of Screens for Legal Assistants

When courts approve of legal assistant screening, they usually do so in one of three possible stances (Exhibit 5-4): (a) the screening is approved, despite the fact that lawyer screening is not approved; (b) the screening is approved because lawyer screening is already approved; or (c) the screening is approved at a level beyond that allowed for lawyer screening (such is the standard in *In re Complex Asbestos Litigation*, above). And, as the above case shows, the fact that a jurisdiction approves of non-lawyer screening does not mean it will refuse to disqualify a law firm that has hired a legal assistant from the opposing party's firm. The screen must be real—and not simply claimed—and in effect at the time the legal assistant is hired; moreover, its effects must be demonstrable to the opposing firm, as well as the trial court at the disqualification hearing.

However, not all jurisdictions approve of non-lawyer screening measures as a way of a firm avoiding disqualification when the firm has hired a non-lawyer employee who was formerly employed at the opposing party's firm. Some ethics opinions expressly reject the screening of tainted non-lawyer employees. Kansas Bar Association Professional Ethics Advisory Comm. Op. 90–05 (1990). And, by judicial decision, certain jurisdictions disapprove of non-lawyer screening. *See Zimmerman v. Mahaska Bottling Co.*, 19 P.3d 784 (Kans. 2001); *Glover Bottled Gas Corp. v. Circle M. Beverage Barn, Inc.*, 514 N.Y.S.2d 440 (N.Y. Sup. Ct.1987); *Williams v. Trans World Airlines*, 588 F.Supp. 1037 (W.D. Mo. 1984). These jurisdictions apply an ironic logic, which is: (a) if legal assistants work on behalf of lawyers, and (b) if the professional responsibility rules make the lawyer responsible for ensuring that the conduct of non-lawyer employees is compatible with the professional obligations of the lawyer (MR 5.3 and also, in a way, DR 4–101[D]), then (c) if the jurisdiction does not approve of screens for lawyers, it could not approve of screens for non-lawyers even under some general theory of leniency or employability. The irony is that equating legal assistants to lawyers in an area such as imputed disqualification, while professionally laudable, places equal employability limitations on legal assistants, law firm employees who are paid considerably less than their lawyer counterparts.

The following case is a benchmark for the alternate view that non-lawyer screening should not be allowed.

Case Law

Ciaffone v. District Court, 945 P.2d 950 (Nev. 1997)

PER CURIAM

On May 27, 1993, petitioners Linda Ciaffone, Joseph Ciaffone, and Carla Ciaffone, individually, and Kathleen Hornbrook as Special Administratrix, on behalf of the estate of Joseph Ronald Ciaffone, the deceased, ("Ciaffones") filed a wrongful death action against Skyline Restaurant & Casino ("Skyline") for the shooting of Joseph Ciaffone. The law firm of Gillock, Koning, Markley & Killebrew, P.C. ("Gillock firm") represented the Ciaffones while Skyline retained the law firm of Thorndal, Backus, Armstrong & Balkenbush ("Thorndal firm"). The case was scheduled for trial in April 1996, but was continued until December 30, 1996.

On February 11, 1995, Ingrid Decker ("Decker") was employed by the Thorndal firm through a "temp" agency and worked in the word processing unit. On March 25, 1995, Decker was hired directly by the Thorndal firm to serve as a legal secretary to attorney David Clark ("Clark"). Although Clark was not assigned to the Ciaffone v. Skyline Restaurant & Casino ("Ciaffone v. Skyline") litigation, Decker admits that she performed some work on Ciaffone v. Skyline in a limited "overflow" secretarial capacity.

After Clark left the Thorndal firm, Decker remained for several months. Decker sat from March 18, 1996, to March 25, 1996, as a floating secretary to attorney of record in Ciaffone v. Skyline, Janiece Marshall ("Marshall"). Although Decker claims she did not do any work on Ciaffone v. Skyline while working for Marshall, she does admit that she may have done some work in Ciaffone v. Skyline in her brief duties as a word processor at the Thorndal firm.

On September 9, 1996, Decker began her employment at the Gillock firm as a secretary to Julie A. Mersch ("Mersch"), attorney of record in Ciaffone v. Skyline. The Gillock firm made efforts to screen Decker from any involvement in the Ciaffone v. Skyline case; the trial court found these efforts sufficient, despite some minor involvement by Decker with the case.

On November 25, 1996, the Thorndal firm moved to disqualify the Gillock firm based on Decker's involvement in Ciaffone v. Skyline and the absence of any authority in Nevada recognizing nonlawyer screening. Judge Sobel, based on

written motions, affidavits, and an informal hearing, ruled as follows:

> The Motion to Disqualify poses at least two significant issues.
>
> First, should "screening" be allowed where a nonlawyer is involved? I think it should be permitted, but there is a complete absence, as far as I can tell, of applicable Nevada law permitting it. . . .
>
> Second, was the screening effective with respect to Ingrid Decker? I believe that the screening was effective in this case, and that Decker did not, after taking her new employment, have the significant participation in the case that the nonlawyer had in [Smart Industries Corp. v. Superior Court, 876 P.2d 1176 (Ariz. Ct. App. 1994)].
>
> However, I feel constrained as a trial judge to find that neither by rule or case has our state yet recognized screening. . . .
>
> I believe if screening is to take place with respect to nonlawyers in Nevada, in the face of rules that apparently do not permit it, it should be the Supreme Court, the maker of Supreme Court rules, and not me, who gives permission for screening.
>
> The Motion to Disqualify is therefore granted reluctantly.

Ciaffones then petitioned this court for a writ of mandamus ordering the district court to reinstate the Gillock firm as attorneys of record. . . .

Skyline argues that regardless of the efforts taken by the Gillock firm to screen Decker from participation in Ciaffone v. Skyline, no statute or case law exists in Nevada permitting nonlawyer screening. Skyline further contends that because Nevada law does not authorize screening when lawyers move from one private firm to another, nonlawyers should be held to the same standard. We conclude that Skyline's argument correctly states Nevada law.

Although Nevada has not addressed the problem of nonlawyer screening, this court has taken the position in SCR 160(2) that *lawyer screening* is prohibited. In part, SCR 160(2) provides:

When a lawyer becomes associated with a firm, the firm may not knowingly represent a person in the same or a substantially related matter in which that lawyer, or a firm with which the lawyer was associated, had previously represented a client whose interests are materially adverse to that person and about whom the lawyer had acquired information protected by Rules 156 and 159(2) that is material to the matter.

SCR 156 and 159(2) address the disclosure of confidential and privileged information between the attorney and client. Additionally, SCR 187 requires lawyers to hold nonlawyer employees to the same professional standards. In relevant part, SCR 187 states:

> With respect to a nonlawyer employed or retained by or associated with a lawyer:
>
> 1. A partner in a law firm shall make reasonable efforts to ensure that the firm has in effect measures giving reasonable assurance that the person's conduct is compatible with the professional obligations of the lawyer;
> 2. A lawyer having direct supervisory authority over the nonlawyer shall make reasonable efforts to ensure that the person's conduct is compatible with the professional obligations of the lawyer. . . .

When SCR 187 is read in conjunction with SCR 160(2), nonlawyer employees become subject to the same rules governing imputed disqualification. To hold otherwise would grant less protection to the confidential and privileged information obtained by a nonlawyer than that obtained by a lawyer. No rationale is offered by Ciaffones which justifies a lesser degree of protection for confidential information simply because it was obtained by a nonlawyer as opposed to a lawyer. Therefore, we conclude that the policy of protecting the attorney-client privilege must be preserved through imputed disqualification when a nonlawyer employee, in possession of privileged information, accepts employment with a firm who represents a client with materially adverse interests. . . . Therefore, we

decline to carve out an exception allowing screening of nonlawyers in situations where lawyers would be similarly disqualified.

In contrast, Ciaffones cite Smart Industries Corp. v. Superior Court, 876 P.2d 1176 (Ariz. Ct. App. 1994), for the proposition that jurisdictions may expressly prohibit lawyer screening while allowing nonlawyer screening. In justifying this seemingly contradictory position, the *Smart Industries* court adopted the rationale of ABA Informal Opinion 88–1526 (June 22, 1988): *Imputed Disqualification Arising From Change in Employment by Nonlawyers Employees.*

> It is important that nonlawyer employees have as much mobility in employment opportunity as possible consistent with the protection of clients' interest. To so limit employment opportunities that some nonlawyers trained to work with law firms might be required to leave the careers for which they are trained would disserve clients as well as the legal profession. *Smart Industries,* 876 P.2d at 1183.

The reasoning of *Smart Industries* implicitly recognizes that a nonlawyer's employment opportunities or mobility must be weighed against client confidentiality before disqualification occurs. While this approach may appear fairer to the paralegal/secretary, it has been roundly criticized for ignoring the realities of effective screening and litigating that issue should it ever arise. For example, one commentator explained that *a majority of courts have rejected screening* because of the uncertainty regarding the effectiveness of the screen, the monetary incentive involved in breaching the screen, the fear of disclosing privileged information in the course of proving an effective screen, and the possibility of accidental disclosures. M. Peter Moser, *Chinese Walls: A Means of Avoiding Law Firm Disqualification When a Personally Disqualified Lawyer Joins the Firm,* 3 Geo. J. Legal Ethics 399, 403, 407 (1990). Accordingly, we conclude that adherence to the existing SCR scheme is the better rule. We, therefore, refrain from creating an exception to the imputed disqualification rule embodied in SCR 160. Thus, we conclude a writ of mandamus is not warranted.

Case Questions

1. Is Ms. Decker's previous employment at the Thorndal firm what caused the disqualification of the Gillock firm?
2. What evidence is there that Ms. Decker was in possession of confidential information?
3. Why does the court criticize the ABA opinion approving of non-lawyer screens and the line of cases that follow such a theory?
4. What is the policy behind the strict rule laid down by the court?
5. What could legal assistants, like Ms. Decker, do to avoid a future disqualification?

Final Thoughts on Imputed Disqualification and Legal Assistant Screening

Even in jurisdictions where legal assistant screening is not allowed, there are two ways to avoid lawyer or law firm disqualification when a legal assistant switches sides. First, if the legal assistant acquired no confidential information at his or her former law firm, then whether the jurisdiction approves of screens is usually moot, since screens are necessary if the legal assistant has acquired confidential information. The presumption of shared confidences—which applies to lawyers switching firms—does not necessarily apply to non-lawyer employees simply because they worked at a firm that had a client in opposition to a client at the non-lawyer employee's new firm. Notice that even in the *Ciaffone* case, which takes a strict position on paralegal screening, although the court refused to allow for Ms. Decker to be screened, thereby disqualifying her present employer/law firm, it mentioned that disqualification was necessary because she was "in possession of privileged information."

Second, even if the legal assistant acquired confidential information, the legal assistant's new firm does not have to be disqualified if the former client consents to waive the disqualification. Just because a jurisdiction does not allow for the unilaterally imposed screening of a legal assistant does not prevent a screen from being employed in cases where both sides agree to it. Such consent would obviously be contingent on demonstrable measures that show the effective screening of the legal assistant.

Finally, those legal assistants and other non-lawyer employees who work for government agencies need not worry whether their jurisdiction approves of lawyer screening and, by extension, non-lawyer screening. The lawyer screening controversy involves lawyers moving between private firms. But screening is explicitly accepted in the ethics rules as a fail-safe device for lawyers—and, by extension, non-lawyers—moving from government work to private employment.

THE LEGAL ASSISTANT AND CONFLICTS OF INTEREST RULES

All three of the major sets of ethics rules designed to apply specifically to non-lawyer employees have rules concerning conflicts of interest. Guideline 7 of the ABA Model Guidelines for the Utilization of Legal Assistant Services states that a lawyer should have measures in place that prevent the legal assistant from having the kinds of conflicts of interest that apply to the lawyer.

The NALA Code of Ethics and Professional Responsibility has no Canon that specifically discusses conflicts of interest, but Canon 7 requires a legal assistant to protect the confidences of a client. Guideline 1, Section 3, of the NALA Model Standards and Guidelines for Utilization of Legal Assistants warns legal assistants to "avoid any action which would involve the attorney in a violation of the Rules [of Professional Responsibility], or give the appearance of professional impropriety." The Comment to Guideline 1 discusses conflicts of interest.

Rule 1.6 of the NFPA Model Disciplinary Rules and Ethical Considerations states, "A paralegal shall avoid conflicts of interest and shall disclose any possible conflict to the employer or client, as well as to the prospective employers or clients." There are seven Ethical Considerations that follow the rule, many of which concern the conflicts that can arise when a paralegal changes employment. In fact, EC–1.6(d) requires a paralegal to maintain a "record keeping system that identifies clients, matters, and parties with which the paralegal has worked, to be able to determine whether an actual or potential conflict of interest exists."

TIPS ON AVOIDING CONFLICTS OF INTEREST

What follows are a few strategies for minimizing the traditional conflicts of interest problems between clients, and also between employers.

Protecting the Interests of Present and Former Clients

While working at the law firm, the paralegal can do a few things to help limit conflicts of interest problems. The client intake form needs to include questions concerning other lawsuits in which the prospective client may have been involved. Then, conflicts checking systems should be in place to allow the paralegal to find categories of the firm's former and present clients, including protected persons connected to the clients, such as spouses, or business partners, to see if any adverse representation conflicts are involved. The conflict checking system should also include information about the lawyers and paralegals in the firm, since they may have formerly worked at firms that represented parties in matters adverse to the prospective client, which would necessitate the implementation of a screening device.

Legal Ethics

Protecting Oneself When Seeking Different Employment

When seeking other legal employment, the paralegal needs to walk a fine line between protecting the client confidences of former clients and alerting prospective employers to potential conflicts of interest. Because screening is acceptable in all jurisdictions for legal employees moving from government employment to private employment, the former government paralegal need not fear losing a job opportunity because of a dilemma involving a potential conflict with a former client. And because paralegal screening is approved in many jurisdictions for paralegals moving between private firms, the job-changing paralegal can alert the interviewer to possible conflicts without risk that such a contingency would thwart a job offer. Remember, for screening to be effective, it must be put in place at the time the firm becomes aware of an imputed disqualification problem. If a law firm is unaware of potential conflicts when it hires a paralegal and an opposing firm seeks to disqualify the paralegal's new firm, the fact that the jurisdiction may provide greater screening leeway to non-lawyer employees than it does to lawyers will be of little benefit to the firm or its soon-to-be unemployed paralegal. However, the paralegal must be extremely careful not to disclose former client confidences when alerting a prospective employer about potential former client conflicts.

ETHICS 2000 AND CONFLICTS OF INTEREST

There have been more than a few changes made to the conflicts of interest rules by the Ethics 2000 Commission, some of which will be summarized here.

MR 1.7 and Current Client Conflicts

Proposal by the Ethics 2000 Commission

The newer version of MR 1.7 is structurally different; the rule is entirely rewritten. The emphasis now is on what is referred to as a "concurrent conflict of interests." There is a single paragraph that defines concurrent conflict of interest to mean either directly adverse conflicts between current clients or conflicts occurring when there is a "significant risk that the representation of one or more clients will be materially limited by the lawyer's responsibility to another client, a former client, or a third person or by a personal interest of the lawyer." The new version also makes it explicitly clear that the lawyer may not seek client waiver in certain kinds of conflicts, such as when two clients of the same lawyer are suing each other. The proposal requires informed consent (as opposed to the words "consent after consultation," as used in the present version) and also requires that in order for the lawyer to establish that the client has given informed consent, the consent must be given in writing. Informed consent is a fuller concept than consent; it is defined in Ethics 2000 Rule 1.0(e) to include the lawyer "communnicat[ing] adequate information and explanation about the material risks of and reasonably available alternatives to the proposed course of conduct."

Action Taken by the ABA House of Delegates
Approved.

MR 1.8 and Specific Prohibitions

Proposal by the Ethics 2000 Commission
The Ethics 2000 Commission made certain stylistic and substantive changes to MR 1.8, including re-titling it in order to make it more compatible with the new MR 1.7. Included in these parallel changes is continuing the requirement of informed consent being given by the client in writing in places where the present MR 1.8 simply requires consent after consultation. The rule prohibiting lawyers from drafting instruments for clients who give the lawyer a gift except where the donee is related to the lawyer has now been modified to include a prohibition on lawyers soliciting substantial gifts from their clients. The exception for when the lawyer drafts a gift instrument for a related person who gives a gift to the lawyer now defines related persons and includes in that definition, an "individual with whom the lawyer or client maintains a close, familial relationship."

MR 1.8 now places no prohibition on lawyers making agreements with their clients that limit the lawyer's malpractice liability with the client, but still requires that the client have independent representation when considering whether to limit the lawyer's liability. The part of the rule that allows clients and former clients to settle claims with their lawyer now includes "potential claims," such as if the client signs a release of liability as part of the resolution over contested legal fees.

The rule that prohibits related lawyers opposing each other in litigation without client consent has been deleted. The commission believed the rule was both under- and overinclusive, so instead it added a Comment to MR 1.7 that concerns conflicts of interest growing out of a lawyer's family relationships.

There is a new rule in MR 1.8 that expressly prohibits sexual relationships between lawyers and their clients, with the only exception being if there was a consensual sexual relationship existing between the parties at the time the lawyer-client relationship began. Some jurisdictions have prohibited such controversial sexual relationships when they involved coercion (such as a means to reduce or forgive one's legal fees), but the commission believed a total ban alerts both lawyers and clients to the severity of the conflict due to the view that since the relationship between a lawyer and their client is "almost always unequal," it can involve unfair exploitation. Furthermore, the commission took the position that the lawyer's objectivity is sacrificed when there is such a sexual relationship. (As a side note, interested lawyers other than the post-suspended Bill Clinton might want to know if the ABA has a definition of "sexual relationship." California does, in its sexual relations prohibition.)

MR 1.8 now adds an imputation rule—specifically covering what MR 1.10 generally covers—that makes all lawyers associated in a firm prohibited from engaging in any of the proscriptions of MR 1.8 if any lawyer is so prohibited, except for the sexual relationship prohibition.

Action Taken by the ABA House of Delegates
Approved.

MR 1.9 and Former Client Conflicts

Proposal by the Ethics 2000 Commission
This rule has been slightly re-titled, and also includes the change that for waiver of a conflict to be given by the former client, the former client needs to give "informed consent, confirmed in writing."

Action Taken by the ABA House of Delegates
Approved.

MR 1.10 and Imputed Disqualification

Proposal by the Ethics 2000 Commission
MR 1.10 has a new title and some changes. Included in the changes is one that makes an imputed disqualification exception that would not prohibit a firm from representing a client when a lawyer in the firm would be prohibited due to a "personal interest" conflict, as long as there is no significant risk that the representation will be materially limited by the continued representation. This exception would allow, for instance, one lawyer in a firm to represent a born-again Christian seeking to have a Bible-study class allowed at the public college he or she attends, even though another lawyer in the firm is an atheist and would refuse such a case due to a personal conflict of interest with the client's objective.

Another significant change proposed for MR 1.10 is a new section that would allow for a lawyer who has moved to another law firm and has a former-client conflict with a client of the lawyer's new firm to be screened, thereby preventing the imputed disqualification rule from applying to the entire firm. The commission believed that the experiences of jurisdictions that already allow screening to take place has been favorable enough to promote the practice expressly. However, a lawyer who played a significant part in the matter that is the cause of the former client/former firm versus present client/present firm dispute may still not be screened, and the entire firm would still be disqualified. And a new comment for this rule now includes a discussion on paralegals and expresses the view that the paralegal's new firm would not be disqualified by his or her conflict if he or she is screened.

Action Taken by the ABA House of Delegates
The House of Delegates accepted the proposal on personal interest conflicts, but it rejected the proposal allowing lawyers to be screened. The House did accept, however, the proposed Comment that approved of paralegal screening.

MR 1.11 and Conflicts of Former and Current Government Employees

Proposal by the Ethics 2000 Commission

There are many changes made to this rule, including a re-titling, designed to include not only former government lawyers, but also lawyers who move between government agencies. One of the changes is an addition to the rule that makes government lawyers subject to rule MR 1.9, as are other lawyers. Some terms, such as "consent after consultation," are changed (to "informed consent"), and others, such as "confidential government information," are defined. There are also new Comments that explain the relationship between MR 1.9 and MR 1.11.

Action Taken by the ABA House of Delegates

Approved.

MR 1.13 and Corporate Attorneys

There are minor grammatical changes made to this rule, which were adopted by the House of Delegates, but no changes in the rule's substance were proposed.

Summary

Lawyers and their non-lawyer employees are advised to avoid conflicts of interest with their clients. As with the rules that concern confidentiality, rules concerning conflicts of interest are grounded in the fiduciary obligation of loyalty. There are more than a few conflicts of interest rules in the ABA Model Rules of Professional Conduct, but MR 1.7 is the general conflicts of interest rule. It prohibits lawyers from representing a client if that representation will be directly adverse to another of the lawyer's clients. Exceptions are provided for client consent, but only if the lawyer first believes that the representation will not adversely affect the other client.

MR 1.7 also prohibits a lawyer from representing a client if that representation might be materially limited by the lawyer's duty to another client or other person or by the lawyer's own interests. Again, exceptions are provided that allow for client consent, but only after the lawyer reaches the conclusion that the representation will not be adversely affected. An example of the kind of conflict of interest that would not allow the lawyer to seek client consent is where the plaintiff and defendant are seeking the representation of the same lawyer. The kinds of common conflicts that can occur include clients suing each other in unrelated matters, joint representation, and client conflicts caused by the lawyer's own personal interests, such as a business interest.

Specific transactions between lawyers and their clients are either expressly prohibited or severely limited. Such transactions include lawyers entering into business transactions with their clients, lawyers receiving gifts from their clients, lawyers negotiating for the media rights to a client's story, lawyers giving financial assistance to their clients, lawyers accepting payments for a client's bill from a third party, and lawyers making malpractice limitation agreements with their clients. Where such transactions are allowed, the acceptable procedure includes the lawyer consulting with the client about the ramifications of a proposed transaction and advising the client of the opportunity to seek the advice of another lawyer. Occasionally, the client's consent to such transactions must be made in writing.

Lawyers and legal assistants working for corporate legal departments (or other kinds of entities) need to be aware that the client is the entity, and not its constituents. Conflicts of interest can occur when those individuals who employ the legal department are acting in a way that is detrimental to the entity. If the corporation or certain employees within it are violating the law, the corporate legal team owes its allegiance to the entity, which means that the legal department may not violate the duty of confidentiality and report such illegal activity.

When certain kinds of conflicts of interest prevent a lawyer from representing a client, then, as a general rule, every other lawyer in the firm is also prevented from representing the client. Such a policy, known as imputed disqualification, is predicated on the assumption that all members of the firm have access to, and share in, the confidential information of all the clients in the firm. Imputed disqualification can also occur when lawyers move from government service to private employment and when lawyers move between law firms. Following such job switches, imputed disqualification is required if the lawyer's new firm represents a client in a matter that is adverse and substantially related to the former client. Imputed disqualification can be avoided if the former client consents by waiving the imputed disqualification.

Former government lawyers are expressly allowed to be screened and thereby avoid the harshness of imputed disqualification. Although the ethics rules do not provide for screening for lawyers moving between firms, some jurisdictions allow for it in their case law. To be effective, a screen must be put in place at the time the firm becomes aware of the imputed disqualification conflict. The mechanisms of an effective screen include separating the tainted lawyer from the case and its files, informing the other lawyers and support staff to refrain from discussing the case with the tainted lawyer, and preventing the tainted lawyer from sharing in the fees from the case.

When legal assistants move to another firm, they are faced with same realities of imputed disqualification. However, the American Bar Association expressly approves of legal assistant screening, and many jurisdictions allow legal assistants to be screened. Some jurisdictions even allow paralegals to be screened in situations where lawyers cannot. However, some jurisdictions do not allow paralegals to be screened, finding that the interests of client confidentiality outweigh the employability options of paralegals and holding paralegals to the same imputed disqualification standards as lawyers. All the major ethics codes drafted by or for legal assistants have rules or ethical considerations that advise legal assistants to avoid conflicts of interest, including conflicts of a personal nature.

Conflicts checking systems can be used with new or prospective clients as a means to detect possible conflicts with the firm's present or former clients. Such systems can be computerized, or they can be maintained by file cards. When legal assistants take positions with other firms, they need to be careful to disclose any possible former client conflicts without violating any confidences of the former clients.

The Ethics 2000 Commission has proposed significant changes to the ABA Model Rules that concern conflicts of interest. Some of these changes to MR 1.7 include making it clear where client consent may not be sought, and replacing the phrase "consents after consultation" with "informed consent." MR 1.8 has been changed to require clients to give their written consent where consent is needed for certain lawyer-client transactions; it prohibits lawyers from soliciting substantial gifts from their clients; and it prohibits lawyers from having sexual relationships with their clients. The proposal to change MR 1.10 on imputed disqualification to allow for an exception that concerns conflicts caused by the lawyer's personal interests was accepted by the ABA House of Delegates, but the proposal to expressly provide for screening where lawyers move between private firms was rejected by the House of Delegates. Fortunately, the Comment approving of paralegal screening was accepted.

Points to Ponder

1. Could John Adams represent the Boston Massacre defendants if the Model Rules of Professional Conduct or the Model Code of Professional Responsibility were in effect then?
2. Why do the rules of ethics take conflicts of interest so seriously?
3. How does the general conflicts of interest rule work? What determines if the lawyer cannot seek the client's consent to continue the representation when a conflict is discovered?
4. How is Model Rule 1.7(a) different than MR 1.7(b)?
5. When, if at all, could a firm represent one client who has sued another client?
6. What risks are involved when a lawyer simultaneously represents two or more clients on the same side of litigation?
7. What risks are involved when a lawyer simultaneously represents two clients in a non-litigation matter, such as when one client sells property to another client?
8. What kinds of client conflicts can be caused by the lawyer's own interests?
9. Does your jurisdiction expressly prohibit lawyers being sexually involved with their clients? Do you think legal assistants should be held to the same standard as lawyers with respect to romantic relationships with clients?
10. How does the rule related to a lawyer's obligation to former clients differ from the general conflicts of interest rule?
11. What is the hot potato client?
12. For the purposes of the former-client conflict of interest, when has someone become a client (and, therefore, deserving of the former-client protection)?
13. Under what conditions can a lawyer enter into a business relationship with a client?
14. Why does the law presume that lawyers and clients cannot negotiate from a position of equal strength, as is the case with most other business negotiations?
15. Under what conditions can a lawyer accept a gift from a client?
16. Do you think it should be permissible for a legal assistant to be included in a client's will?
17. What is the policy behind prohibiting lawyers from rendering financial aid to their clients in almost all situations?
18. Can a third party pay a client's legal expenses? If not, why not? If so, what possible conflicts can occur?
19. Does your jurisdiction allow lawyers to limit their malpractice liability with their clients?
20. Situations such as lawyers engaging in business transactions with their lawyers or limiting their liability with their clients call for the lawyer to advise the client about the propriety of seeking independent representation before moving forward. Why is it, however, that such advice could be of little value?
21. How are the conflicts of interest dynamics different when the client is a corporation or other entity?
22. When working in the legal department of a corporation, what steps should the paralegal take, upon discovering illegal behavior, to protect the client as well as the paralegal's employment?
23. What is imputed disqualification? What policy is promoted by imputed disqualification?
24. For what kinds of job switches do the rules specifically allow lawyers to be screened?
25. Where jurisdictions allow tainted lawyers to be screened and thereby avoiding imputed disqualification for the firm, what kinds of evidence show that the screen is effective?
26. Why does the ABA take a more lenient position on legal assistant screening than it does on lawyer screening?
27. On what basis do certain jurisdictions forbid legal assistant screening?

28. Does your jurisdiction allow for legal assistant screening?
29. How can the paralegal help assess possible conflicts of interest with prospective or new clients?
30. When a paralegal is seeking different legal employment, what can be done to avoid future conflicts problems at the prospective employer?
31. Do you think there are any significant differences between the conflicts of interest rules of the ABA Model Rules and the ABA Model Code?
32. Do you think there are any significant changes in the Ethics 2000 conflicts of interest rules, as compared to the ABA Model Rules?

Key Concepts

Appearance of impropriety

Barratry

Champerty

Conflict of interest

Former client conflict

Hot potato client

Imputed disqualification

Issue conflict

Joint representation

Presumption of shared confidences

Screen (or ethical wall or cone of silence)

Simultaneous representation

Tainted employee

Undue influence

Key Terms

aggregate settlement	companion cases	pro bono
amicus curiae	engagement letter	recuse
appearance of impropriety	indigent	security interest
arbitration	insider trading	shareholder's derivative lawsuit
barratry	liquidated damages clause	trust
champerty	prenuptial agreement	undue influence

Advertising and Solicitation

What kills a skunk is the publicity it gives itself.

—Abraham Lincoln

I'm not an ambulance chaser. I'm usually there before the ambulance.

—Melvin Belli, the lawyer known as the King of Torts

Chapter 6

INTRODUCTION

The subjects of advertising and solicitation sit at the intersection of commerce and profession. While the marketing of sneakers, sandwiches, and sink cleansers is commonplace and acceptable, the marketing of legal services is commonplace but not fully acceptable. Many lawyers and consumers bemoan the television commercials that tell daytime viewers that if they have been injured, for instance, they should call the 800 number on the screen to talk to lawyers who "have graduated with honors," "have years of experience fighting big insurance companies," or "grew up in the same community where they work." Beyond the general marketing of legal services is the solicitation of legal services, which involves personally seeking legal business through the direct contact of prospective clients. This chapter will examine the controversial subject of lawyer advertising and solicitation, including an analysis of the rules and significant cases that control the marketing of legal services and its solicitation. Technological changes have expanded the lawyer's ability to advertise and solicit, and this chapter will also examine what newer rules or guidance concern the marketing of legal services on the Internet.

A SHORT HISTORY OF LAWYER ADVERTISING

Today we accept as commonplace the practice of lawyer advertising. From television to radio commercials and from the yellow pages to the foldout advertisements in the front of the phone book, the fact that lawyer advertising is prevalent would lead one to safely conclude that is a lawful practice. But a quick history lesson will show that lawyer advertising was once considered unlawful, and before that it was just considered in poor taste. Eventually, the U.S. Supreme Court changed its own view on the subject, to the disappointment of many bar associations.

From the Nineteenth Century to the 1950s

As was mentioned in Chapter 1, the American Bar Association's first rules of ethics, the 1908 Canons of Professional Ethics, were based on the Alabama Code of Ethics of 1887, which was the first formal set of lawyer ethics rules in the United States. Prior to the creation of those rules of conduct, lawyers regulated themselves similarly to the way English lawyers did, simply through tradition and the following of professional etiquette. Nothing prohibited lawyers from advertising, and lawyers, from future President Abraham Lincoln to future Supreme Court Justice Howell Jackson, advertised their services. The Alabama Code of Ethics also did not prohibit lawyer advertising; Canon 16 of the Alabama Code allowed for lawyer advertising in newspapers (calling for restraint in the method of presentation), but prohibited solicitation. Other states, however, began to find advertising to be inappropriate. For instance, in 1893, the Colorado Supreme Court suspended an attorney who placed an advertisement in a newspaper for his divorce practice, stating, "The ethics of the legal profession forbid that an attorney should advertise his talent or skill, as a shopkeeper advertises his wares." *People ex rel. Attorney General v. MacCabe*, 32 P. 280 (Col. 1893) (Exhibit 6–1).

circulars—Notices or advertisements sent to certain groups of
people.

That first ABA Canons of Professional Ethics altered the Alabama Code's view on advertising by stating in Canon 27 that that "solicitation of business by **circulars** or advertisement, or by personal communications, or interviews, not warranted by personal relations, is unprofessional." An early ABA ethics opinion that concerned Canon 27 found that "[a]ny conduct that tends to commercialize or bring 'bargain counter' methods into the practice of law, lowers the profession in public confidence and lessens its ability to render efficiently that high character of service to which the members of the profession are called." ABA Comm. on Professional Ethics and Grievances, Formal Op. 1 (1924). By 1951, the ABA had modified Canon 27 to allow lawyers to list themselves in telephone books and legal directories, a modification many lawyers opposed.

J. T. STUART AND A. LINCOLN,
ATTORNEYS and Counsellors at Law, will practice, conjointly, in the Courts of this Judicial Circuit.— Office No. 4 Hoffman's Row, up stairs.
Springfield, april 12, 1837.   4

THE partnership heretofore existing between the un-

Exhibit 6-1   1837 Advertisement of Abraham Lincoln and His Law Partner

The Supreme Court's View Shifts from the 1940s through the 1970s

Regardless of whether one finds lawyer advertising to be distasteful, it would seem that lawyers would have a freedom of speech right to advertise their services, or even solicit clients. But the First Amendment's protections are greatest in the areas of religious speech and political speech; **commercial speech**—communication connected to business or capitalism—is not on that level, and can easily be restricted. Therefore, when states began to prohibit certain kinds of commercial advertising beyond telephone book listings, courts, including the Supreme Court, upheld the states' prerogative to restrict such forms of commercial speech. *See Valentine v. Chrestensen*, 316 U.S. 52 (1942). The law on lawyer advertising was clear: it was prohibited. But, by 1976, the U.S. Supreme Court, in *Virginia State Board of Pharmacy v. Virginia Citizens Consumer Council*, 425 U.S. 748 (1976), overturned a statute that prohibited drug price advertisements by pharmacies, finding that the benefits of such price advertising outweighed the state's interests in regulating such business practices. However, the decision's effect was limited to pharmacies.

commercial speech— Communications made for business purposes. Speech made in the pursuit of capitalism is commercial speech, and it is less protected under free speech doctrines than religious or political speech.

The seminal case for attorney advertising occurred one year later, in *Bates v. State Bar of Arizona*, 433 U.S. 350 (1977). In *Bates*, two lawyers who advertised their legal clinic's services were found to be in violation of the Arizona disciplinary rules against advertising. The U.S. Supreme Court took the appeal and forever changed the restrictions on lawyer advertising.

Before reading *Bates*, look at the advertisement at the beginning of the opinion, which was the subject of the controversy (Exhibit 6–2, on the next page). Then, while reading the case, pay attention to the arguments the state of Arizona put forward in support of its prohibition of lawyer advertising, as well as the Court's response to those arguments.

Case Law

Bates v. State Bar of Arizona, 433 U.S. 350 (1977)

Mr. Justice BLACKMUN delivered the opinion of the Court.

As part of its regulation of the Arizona Bar, the Supreme Court of that State has imposed and enforces a disciplinary rule that restricts advertising by attorneys. This case presents two issues: whether §§1 and 2 of the Sherman Act, 15 U.S.C. §§1 and 2, forbid such state regulation, and whether the operation of the rule violates the First Amendment, made applicable to the State through the Fourteenth. [The part of the opinion dealing with the Sherman Act has not been included.]

Appellants John R. Bates and Van O'Steen are attorneys licensed to practice law in the State of Arizona. As such, they are members of the appellee, the State Bar of Arizona. After admission to the bar in 1972, appellants worked as attorneys with the Maricopa County Legal Aid Society. In March 1974,

Exhibit 6-2   Appendix to Opinion of the Court

appellants left the Society and opened a law office, which they call a "legal clinic," in Phoenix. Their aim was to provide legal services at modest fees to persons of moderate income who did not qualify for governmental legal aid. In order to achieve this end, they would accept only routine matters, such as uncontested divorces, uncontested adoptions, simple personal bankruptcies, and changes of name, for which costs could be kept down by extensive use of paralegals, automatic typewriting equipment, and standardized forms and office procedures. More complicated cases, such as contested divorces, would not be accepted. Because appellants set their prices so as to have a relatively low return on each case they handled, they depended on substantial volume. After conducting their practice in this manner for two years, appellants concluded that their practice and clinical concept could not survive unless the availability of legal services at low cost was advertised and in particular, fees were advertised. Consequently, in order to generate the necessary flow of business, that is, "to attract clients," appellants on February 22, 1976, placed an advertisement in the Arizona Republic, a daily newspaper of general circulation in the Phoenix metropolitan area. As may be seen, the advertisement stated that appellants were offering "legal services at very reasonable fees," and listed their fees for certain services.

Appellants concede that the advertisement constituted a clear violation of Disciplinary Rule 2–101(B), incorporated in Rule 29(a) of the Supreme Court of Arizona, 17A Ariz.Rev.Stat., p. 26 (Supp. 1976). . . . In the instant case we are confronted with the arguments directed explicitly toward the regulation of advertising by licensed attorneys.

The issue presently before us is a narrow one. First, we need not address the peculiar problems associated with advertising claims relating to the quality of legal services. Such claims probably are not susceptible of precise measurement or verification and, under some circumstances, might well be deceptive or misleading to the public, or even false.

Appellee does not suggest, nor do we perceive, that appellants' advertisement contained claims, extravagant or otherwise, as to the quality of services. Accordingly, we leave that issue for another day. Second, we also need not resolve the problems associated with in-person solicitation of clients at the hospital room or the accident site, or in any other situation that breeds undue influence by attorneys or their agents or "runners." . . .

The heart of the dispute before us today is whether lawyers also may constitutionally advertise the prices at which certain routine services will be performed. Numerous justifications are proffered for the restriction of such price advertising. We consider each in turn:

1. *The Adverse Effect on Professionalism.* Appellee places particular emphasis on the adverse effects that it feels price advertising will have on the legal profession. The key to professionalism, it is argued, is the sense of pride that involvement in the discipline generates. It is claimed that price advertising will bring about commercialization, which will undermine the attorney's sense of dignity and self-worth. The hustle of the marketplace will adversely affect the profession's service orientation, and irreparably damage the delicate balance between the lawyer's need to earn and his obligation selflessly to serve. Advertising is also said to erode the client's trust in his attorney: Once the client perceives that the lawyer is motivated by profit, his confidence that the attorney is acting out of a commitment to the client's welfare is jeopardized. And advertising is said to tarnish the dignified public image of the profession.

We recognize, of course, and commend the spirit of public service with which the profession of law is practiced and to which it is dedicated. The present Members of this Court, licensed attorneys all, could not feel otherwise. And we would have reason to pause if we felt that our decision today would undercut that spirit. But we find the postulated connection between advertising and the erosion of true professionalism to be severely strained. At its core, the argument presumes that attorneys must conceal from themselves and from their clients the real-life fact that lawyers earn their livelihood at the bar. We suspect that few attorneys engage in such self-deception. And rare is the client, moreover, even one of the modest means, who enlists the aid of an attorney with the expectation that his services will be rendered free of charge. . . . In fact, the American Bar Association advises that an attorney should reach "a clear agreement with his client as to the basis of the fee charges to be made," and that this is to be done "[a]s soon as feasible after a lawyer has been employed." . . . If the commercial basis of the relationship is to be promptly disclosed on ethical grounds, once the client is in the office, it seems inconsistent to condemn the candid revelation of the same information before he arrives at that office.

Moreover, the assertion that advertising will diminish the attorney's reputation in the community is open to question. Bankers and engineers advertise, and yet these professions are not regarded as undignified. In fact, it has been suggested that the failure of lawyers to advertise creates public disillusionment with the profession. The absence of advertising may be seen to reflect the profession's failure to reach out and serve the community: Studies reveal that many persons do not obtain counsel even when they perceive a need because of the feared price of services or because of an inability to locate a competent attorney. Indeed, cynicism with regard to the profession may be created by the fact that it long has publicly eschewed advertising, while condoning the actions of the attorney who structures his social or civic associations so as to provide contacts with potential clients.

It appears that the ban on advertising originated as a rule of etiquette and not as a rule of ethics. Early lawyers in Great Britain viewed the law as a form of public service, rather than as a means of earning a living, and they looked down on "trade" as unseemly. . . . Eventually, the attitude toward advertising fostered by this view evolved into an aspect of the ethics of the profession. But habit and tradition are not in themselves an adequate answer to a constitutional challenge. In this day, we do not belittle the person who earns his living by the strength of his arm or the force of his mind. Since the belief that lawyers are somehow "above" trade has become an anachronism, the historical foundation for the advertising restraint has crumbled.

2. _The Inherently Misleading Nature of Attorney Advertising._ It is argued that advertising of legal services inevitably will be misleading (a) because such services are so individualized with regard to content and quality as to prevent informed comparison on the basis of an advertisement, (b) because the consumer of legal services is unable to determine in advance just what services he needs, and (c) because advertising by attorneys will highlight irrelevant factors and fail to show the relevant factor of skill.

We are not persuaded that restrained professional advertising by lawyers inevitably will be misleading. Although many services performed by attorneys are indeed unique, it is doubtful that any attorney would or could advertise fixed prices for services of that type. The only services that lend themselves to advertising are the routine ones: the uncontested divorce, the simple adoption, the uncontested personal bankruptcy, the change of name, and the like: the very services advertised by appellants. Although the precise service demanded in each task may vary slightly, and although legal services are not fungible, these facts do not make advertising misleading so long as the attorney does the necessary work at the advertised price. The argument that legal services are so unique that fixed rates cannot meaningfully be established is refuted by the record in this case: The appellee, State Bar itself sponsors a Legal Services Program in which the participating attorneys agree to perform services like those advertised by the appellants at standardized rates.

The second component of the argument—that advertising ignores the diagnostic role—fares little better. It is unlikely that many people go to an attorney merely to ascertain if they have a clean bill of legal health. Rather, attorneys are likely to be employed to perform specific tasks. Although the client may not know the detail involved in performing the task, he no doubt is able to identify the service he desires at the level of generality to which advertising lends itself.

The third component is not without merit: Advertising does not provide a complete foundation on which to select an attorney. But it seems peculiar to deny the consumer, on the ground that the information is incomplete, at least some of the relevant information needed to reach an informed decision. The alternative—the prohibition of advertising—serves only to restrict the information that flows to consumers. Moreover, the argument assumes that the public is not sophisticated enough to realize the limitations of advertising, and that the public is better kept in ignorance than trusted with correct but incomplete information. We suspect the argument rests on an underestimation of the public. In any event, we view as dubious any justification that is based on the benefits of public ignorance. . . .

3. *The Adverse Effect on the Administration of Justice.* Advertising is said to have the undesirable effect of stirring up litigation. The judicial machinery is designed to serve those who feel sufficiently aggrieved to bring forward their claims. Advertising, it is argued, serves to encourage the assertion of legal rights in the courts, thereby undesirably unsettling societal repose. There is even a suggestion of barratry.

But advertising by attorneys is not an unmitigated source of harm to the administration of justice. It may offer great benefits. Although advertising might increase the use of the judicial machinery, we cannot accept the notion that it is always better for a person to suffer a wrong silently than to redress it by legal action. As the bar acknowledges, "the middle 70% of our population is not being reached or served adequately by the legal profession." ABA, Revised Handbook on Prepaid Legal Services 2 (1972). Among the reasons for this underutilization is fear of the cost, and an inability to locate a suitable lawyer. Advertising can help to solve this acknowledged problem: Advertising is the traditional mechanism in a free-market economy for a supplier to inform a potential purchaser of the availability and terms of

exchange. The disciplinary rule at issue likely has served to burden access to legal services, particularly for the not-quite-poor and the unknowledgeable. A rule allowing restrained advertising would be in accord with the bar's obligation to "facilitate the process of intelligent selection of lawyers, and to assist in making legal services fully available." ABA Code of Professional Responsibility EC 2–1 (1976).

4. *The Undesirable Economic Effects of Advertising.* It is claimed that advertising will increase the overhead costs of the profession, and that these costs then will be passed along to consumers in the form of increased fees. Moreover, it is claimed that the additional cost of practice will create a substantial entry barrier, deterring or preventing young attorneys from penetrating the market and entrenching the position of the bar's established members.

These two arguments seem dubious at best. Neither distinguishes lawyers from others . . . and neither appears relevant to the First Amendment. The ban on advertising serves to increase the difficulty of discovering the lowest cost seller of acceptable ability. As a result, to this extent attorneys are isolated from competition, and the incentive to price competitively is reduced. Although it is true that the effect of advertising on the price of services has not been demonstrated, there is revealing evidence with regard to products; where consumers have the benefit of price advertising, retail prices often are dramatically lower than they would be without advertising. It is entirely possible that advertising will serve to reduce, not advance, the cost of legal services to the consumer.

The entry-barrier argument is equally unpersuasive. In the absence of advertising, an attorney must rely on his contacts with the community to generate a flow of business. In view of the time necessary to develop such contacts, the ban in fact serves to perpetuate the market position of established attorneys. Consideration of entry-barrier problems would urge that advertising be allowed so as to aid the new competitor in penetrating the market.

5. *The Adverse Effect of Advertising on the Quality of Service.* It is argued that the attorney may advertise

a given "package" of service at a set price, and will be inclined to provide, by indiscriminate use, the standard package regardless of whether it fits the client's needs. Restraints on advertising, however, are an ineffective way of deterring shoddy work. An attorney who is inclined to cut quality will do so regardless of the rule on advertising. And the advertisement of a standardized fee does not necessarily mean that the services offered are undesirably standardized. Indeed, the assertion that an attorney who advertises a standard fee will cut quality is substantially undermined by the fixed-fee schedule of appellee's own prepaid Legal Services Program. Even if advertising leads to the creation of "legal clinics" like that of appellants' clinics that emphasize standardized procedures for routine problems it is possible that such clinics will improve service by reducing the likelihood of error.

6. *The Difficulties of Enforcement.* Finally, it is argued that the wholesale restriction is justified by the problems of enforcement if any other course is taken. Because the public lacks sophistication in legal matters, it may be particularly susceptible to misleading or deceptive advertising by lawyers. After-the-fact action by the consumer lured by such advertising may not provide a realistic restraint because of the inability of the layman to assess whether the service he has received meets professional standards. Thus, the vigilance of a regulatory agency will be required. But because of the numerous purveyors of services, the overseeing of advertising will be burdensome.

It is at least somewhat incongruous for the opponents of advertising to extol the virtues and altruism of the legal profession at one point, and, at another, to assert that its members will seize the opportunity to mislead and distort. We suspect that, with advertising, most lawyers will behave as they always have: They will abide by their solemn oaths to uphold the integrity and honor of their profession and of the legal system. For every attorney who overreaches through advertising, there will be thousands of others who will be candid and honest and straightforward. And, of course, it will be in the latter's interest, as in other cases of misconduct at the bar, to assist in weeding out those few who abuse their trust.

In sum, we are not persuaded that any of the proffered justifications rise to the level of an acceptable reason for the suppression of all advertising by attorneys. . . .

In holding that advertising by attorneys may not be subjected to blanket suppression, and that the advertisement at issue is protected, we, of course, do not hold that advertising by attorneys may not be regulated in any way. We mention some of the clearly permissible limitations on advertising not foreclosed by our holding.

Advertising that is false, deceptive, or misleading of course is subject to restraint. *See Virginia Pharmacy Board v. Virginia Citizens Consumer Council*, 425 U.S., at 771–772, and n. 24, 96 S.Ct., at 1830–1831. . . . In fact, because the public lacks sophistication concerning legal services, misstatements that might be overlooked or deemed unimportant in other advertising may be found quite inappropriate in legal advertising. For example, advertising claims as to the quality of services a matter we do not address today are not susceptible of measurement or verification; accordingly, such claims may be so likely to be misleading as to warrant restriction. Similar objections might justify restraints on in-person solicitation. We do not foreclose the possibility that some limited supplementation, by way of warning or disclaimer or the like, might be required of even an advertisement of the kind ruled upon today so as to assure that the consumer is not misled. In sum, we recognize that many of the problems in defining the boundary between deceptive and nondeceptive advertising remain to be resolved, and we expect that the bar will have a special role to play in assuring that advertising by attorneys flows both freely and cleanly.

As with other varieties of speech, it follows as well that there may be reasonable restrictions on the time, place, and manner of advertising. . . . And the special problems of advertising on the electronic broadcast media will warrant special consideration.

The constitutional issue in this case is only whether the State may prevent the publication in a newspaper of appellants' truthful advertisement concerning the availability and terms of routine legal services. We rule simply that the flow of such information may not be restrained, and we therefore hold the present application of the disciplinary rule against appellants to be violative of the First Amendment.

The judgment of the Supreme Court of Arizona is therefore affirmed in part and reversed in part.

It is so ordered.

[There were some strong dissenting opinions that expressed the view that lawyer advertising was a demeaning and unfortunate practice and was not constitutionally protected speech, as intended by the meaning of the First Amendment. Also, one dissenting opinion expressed the view that there were too many lawyers in the country for the states' bar associations to effectively monitor lawyer advertising. It is suggested that readers with the desire for extra study read the entire *Bates case.*]

Case Questions

1. Which of the six arguments put forward by the State Bar of Arizona in support of their position that lawyer advertising should be prohibited seems to you to be the most persuasive?
2. Which of those six arguments seems to be the least persuasive?
3. Can you think of any arguments not presented by the State Bar of Arizona that could be made in support of a ban on lawyer advertising?
4. Can you think of any responses to the State Bar of Arizona not made by the Supreme Court that could be made in support of allowing of lawyer advertising?
5. How did the Court place some limits on its watershed decision?

AN OVERVIEW OF THE RULES ON ADVERTISING

Unlike the principles of client confidentiality, whose consequences may be controversial to the public but are not necessarily to the legal profession, the rules on advertising are more controversial within the legal profession than outside it. Many lawyers, including past presidents of the American Bar Association, still believe that lawyer advertising is unseemly and should be prohibited. And since lawyers are regulated at the state level, it is important that one become familiar with one's own jurisdiction's rules on lawyer advertising because those rules may differ significantly from the general rules created by the ABA.

Information about Legal Services Shall Not Be False or Misleading

ABA Model Rule 7.1 states, "A lawyer shall not make a false or misleading communication about the lawyer or the lawyer's services." This rule is broader than just advertising and encompasses any communication lawyers (or their employees) would make about their legal services, whether made to the public or to an individual. All communications made by the law firm, from a television commercial to a holiday greeting card, need to occur within the bounds of the governing ethics rules. The ABA Model Code stated that a "lawyer shall not . . . use . . . any form of public communication containing a false, fraudulent, misleading, deceptive, self-laudatory or unfair statement or claim." DR 2–101. It also allowed a lawyer to list certain kinds of information, such as memberships in bar associations or foreign language fluency, and it allowed lawyers to publish such information in the geographic areas in which "the lawyer resides or maintains offices or in which a significant part of the lawyer's clientele resides." DR 2–101(B). That rule also required that such information be "*presented in a dignified manner*" (emphasis added).

ABA Model Rule 7.1 categorizes three kinds of information that qualify as false or misleading: (a) fraudulent information: material misrepresentations of fact or law or equivalent omissions of fact; (b) inappropriate implications: statements that are likely to create unjustified expectations of success or that give the impression the lawyer can succeed by sidestepping the law; or (c) inappropriate comparisons: unsubstantiated statements that compare one lawyer's services to another's.

Fraudulent Information

Generally, fraud involves some material misrepresentation of fact designed to induce someone to act in reliance on the misrepresentation and resulting in harm to the person whose reliance was miscast. Misrepresentations of fact can also be made through silence, where one would have a duty to speak. For instance, if a statute requires car dealers to inform their customers about the dealers' cars whose engines have been rebuilt, then a car dealer could commit fraud two ways: lying about whether a car's engine was rebuilt, or simply saying nothing about a car whose engine was rebuilt.

Determining what makes a statement fraudulent is not always easy. In a Minnesota case, a lawyer placed an advertisement in the yellow pages that said, "we have an office near you" and then listed nine cities. Of those nine locations, seven of were simply office buildings where the lawyer rented space on an hourly basis whenever he would meet with clients in those areas. The state ethics committee concluded that such an advertisement was false and misleading and that it warranted discipline. The lawyer argued that his clients never complained about the advertisement and that some were grateful he made spaces available for them far from his primary office. The Minneapolis Supreme Court reversed the decision of the ethics committee, finding that, although the lawyer's advertisement was vague and not forthcoming, it was not a material misrepresentation as a matter of law. *In re Charges of Unprofessional Conduct against 95–30*, 550 N.W.2d 616 (Minn. 1996). However, when a lawyer advertised by using his name and the phrase "and Affiliates," he was reprimanded because there were, in fact, no affiliates. Instead, the attorney was a sole practitioner who had occasionally shared office space with other lawyers. *Medina County Bar Assn v. Grieselhuber*, 678 N.E.2d 535 (Ohio 1997).

Statements made about a lawyer's fees can be found to be material misrepresentations. Although Chapter 7 discusses legal fees, at this point is important to recognize that a prospective client's misunderstanding about what constitutes "fees" can be exacerbated by deceitful statements or advertisements made by lawyers. (Remember, since legal assistants are prohibited from establishing fees because that would constitute the unauthorized practice of law, misunderstandings about fees should rarely occur because of the legal assistant's misstatements.) A United States Supreme Court case is illustrative in that it involved a lawyer who was sanctioned for a variety of advertising violations, including an advertisement that included the statement, "if there is no recovery, no legal fees are owed by our clients." That statement was found to be misleading because it did not include any mention that the client would be liable for the costs and expenses of litigation. *Zauderer v. Office of Disciplinary Counsel*, 471 U.S. 626 (1985). In a California case, an attorney was disciplined for communication violations, including mailing letters to prospective bankruptcy clients that mentioned that only 60 dollars in cash was needed to apply for debt relief, but failed to mention that legal fees would reach ten times as much. *Leoni v. State Bar*, 704 P.2d 183 (Cal. 1985). Other courts have found that incomplete statements about fees or advertised fees that are lower than the charged fees are examples of misleading statements. *See People v. Roehl*, 655 P.2d 1381 (Colo. 1983); *Florida Bar v. Gudish*, 421 So. 2d 501 (Fla. 1982).

Inappropriate Implications

No lawyer in his or her right mind would say to a prospective client, "Choose me, but be advised that your chances of getting what you want are no greater than if you choose a lawyer by throwing a dart at the phone book." All marketing is designed to get the public to want the products or services being advertised. But statements made in connection with legal services, whether made for the mass media or communicated in person by the legal assistant, must avoid creating an unjustified expectation of success or giving the impression that success can be obtained through flouting the law.

Unjustified Expectations   Unjustified expectations are created when the client is led to believe that a favorable outcome is assured or that because of the lawyer's past performance, similar results will occur. As to the former, lawyers are generally not allowed to engage in a selling technique known as **puffing**, which involves making grand statements about a product or service but does not qualify as a **warranty**. For instance, the seller of a house can say, without getting in trouble, "This is the best house on the block," since no prospective buyer should expect to win a lawsuit arguing that the seller lied and that, in fact, the house was only the second best on the block. But lawyers and their employees may make no such grand statements. In an Arizona case, a lawyer was suspended for 30 days for, **inter alia**, running a television advertisement that showed a car accident, a couple in a hospital waiting room, the husband/father kissing his daughter goodbye for the last time, and then the lawyer arguing before a jury in a courtroom. Because the lawyer never took cases to trial as a matter of law firm policy and had never tried a personal

puffing—A real word, used in sales contexts to mean an opinion or belief that is not meant to be taken as a statement of fact or warranty.

warranty—A statement that amounts to a promise of quality or the assurance of certain facts.

inter alia—A Latin phrase that means "among other things."

injury case, the court found the commercial to be misleading. *Matter of Zang*, 741 P.2d 267 (Ariz. 1987).

Promoting one's track record can also create unjustified expectations. Such was the problem in an Indiana case where an attorney was disciplined for sending an improper solicitation letter to prospective clients that included detailing the attorney's track record in successfully **plea bargaining** drunk driving cases. *In re Frank*, 440 N.E.2d 676 (Ind. 1982). The problem associated with statements about a lawyer's track record is that, even if unstated, an implication might be sent that future clients can expect the lawyer to achieve the same results. Statements of fact, however, are not always held to be misleading, including stating that "thousands of successful claims have been brought against this particular manufacturer." D.C. Bar Comm. on Legal Ethics, Op. 188 (1987).

plea bargaining—Negotiating in a criminal case, resulting in the prosecutor and the defendant agreeing to dispose of the charges through a settlement in which the defendant pleads guilty to a lesser charge.

Testimonials can also lead to unjustified expectations. The Comment to MR 7.1 mentions advertisements containing client endorsements as something that would ordinarily be prohibited if they create unjustified expectations. Some states, including Connecticut, Florida, and Indiana, take a conservative approach to client testimonials or endorsements and expressly ban them. Other states, such as California and New York, allow limited use of testimonials. California requires the disclosure of impersonators and dramatizations in advertisements (Cal. Bus. & Prof. Code § 6157.2), and New York allows the use of client testimonials as long as they include a disclaimer stating that past results cannot guarantee or predict similar future outcomes (N.Y. State Bar Ass'n Comm. on Professional Ethics, Op. 614 [1990]).

Sidestepping the Law   Although it almost goes without saying, lawyers and their paralegals are not allowed to make any statements in connection with legal services that give the impression that favorable results can be obtained through means that are outside the scope of applicable ethics rules or other laws. Certain lawyers carry more influence than others, and many clients are more than willing to pay for such influence, but lawyers may not imply that they can represent legal matters through the use of impermissible influence. Suppose that a criminal defense lawyer states to a client that she (the lawyer) is a friend of the district attorney and so the chances of a favorable plea bargain are good. That kind of statement would violate MR 7.1(b). In a South Carolina case, a lawyer aired two television commercials involving automobile accidents. In one of the commercials, an actor playing a police officer called the lawyer to the accident scene in order to get the lawyer's opinion about who was at fault; in the other commercial, the lawyer was directing the police officer's on-scene activities. Both commercials were found to be in violation of South Carolina's version of MR 7.1(b), because they implied that the lawyer had influence over the police. *Matter of Pavilick*, 488 S.E.2d 309 (S.C.1997).

Inappropriate Comparisons

The third kind of misleading statements prohibited by MR 7.1 involve unsubstantiated comparisons of one lawyer's services to another. MR 7.1(c). Again, the distinction between lawyer advertising and other forms of business advertising needs to be made. No legitimate advertising can be **libelous**; sellers of products and services are allowed to say, "You'll like ours better than theirs." But lawyers are prohibited from making comparisons to other lawyers unless those comparisons are factually substantiated. Some bar associations have issued ethics opinions that provide specificity to this general prohibition. Alabama prohibited the use of a commercial that suggested viewers call a lawyer referral service, rather than "take a chance" on the phone book (Ala. State Bar Gen. Counsel, Op. 89–18 [1989]); Philadelphia prohibited the advertising phrase, "Big city experience, small town service," because it subjectively implied that the advertising lawyer's services were better than other lawyers' services (Philadelphia Bar Association Guidance Comm.; Op. 94–12 [1995]); and Virginia prohibited the use of an advertising letter to criminal defendants in which the lawyer stated that his fees were lower than others in the community (Va. State Bar Comm. on Legal Ethics, Informal Op. 862 [1986]). Grand statements and superlatives are not the only kind of inappropriate comparisons; any comparison that is unverified is inappropriate. Even words such as "experienced" and phrases such as "quickly becoming recognized as a premier personal injury law firm" have been found to be inappropriate because of the difficulty in verifying them. *See Spencer v. Honorable Justices of Superior Court*, 579 F. Supp. 880 (E.D. Pa. 1984); *In re Anonymous*, 637 N.E.2d 131 (Ind. 1994).

libelous—Libel is a false written statement that is published and made in order to harm the reputation of another. Slander is the spoken form of libel. Libel and slander are different forms of defamation.

Lawyer Advertising: The Nuts and Bolts

Although lawyers were allowed to advertise in phone books before *Bates*, that decision resulted in the expansion of lawyer advertising into other media. ABA Model Rule 7.2(a) expressly allows lawyers to advertise their "services through public media, such as a . . . newspaper or other periodical, outdoor advertising, radio or television, or through written or recorded communication." MR 7.2(b) requires lawyers to keep a copy of every recording of an advertisement or communication for two years, as well as a record of its use. MR 7.2(c) prohibits lawyers from paying anyone for recommending the lawyer's services, with three exceptions: (1) lawyers may pay for the costs associated with permissible advertising; (2) lawyers may make contributions to a not-for-profit legal lawyer referral service or legal service organization; and (3) lawyers may purchase a law firm (provided it comports with the rule on sales of law firms, MR 1.17). Last, any lawyer advertisement must "include the name of at least one lawyer responsible for its content." MR 7.2(d). Model Rule 7.2 is quite similar to the Model Code provisions on advertising in DR 2–101, except that the Model Code did not require that advertisements include the name of a lawyer responsible for the ad.

After Bates: *Can States Still Restrict Lawyer Advertising?*
The short answer is yes, state ethics rules can place certain restrictions on the methods by which lawyers advertise or promote their services. The restrictions can vary from jurisdiction to jurisdiction. For instance, South Carolina allows lawyers

to offer discount coupons for their services as part of the "Welcome Wagon" program for new community residents (S.C. Bar Ethics Advisory Comm.; Op. 96–27 [1997]); Alabama, however, does not, believing that participation in the Welcome Wagon gives the misleading impression that a third party is endorsing the lawyer's services (Ala. State Bar General Counsel, Op. 91–17 [1991]).

Whatever the limits placed on lawyer advertising, all restrictions must be constitutionally legitimate, which means that if commercial speech is to be restricted, it must be tied to a legitimate state interest. Two U.S. Supreme Court cases that followed *Bates* are instructive.

In re R.M.J.   In *In re R.M.J.*, 455 U.S. 191 (1982), Missouri's Supreme Court Advisory Committee moved to disbar a lawyer because he advertised in ways other than those listed as permissible in the Missouri rules. Two of his violations included the fact that he listed his areas of practice using words other than those allowed in the rules (he used "personal injury" and "real estate" instead of "tort law" and "property law") and he had sent announcement cards to persons other than lawyers, clients, former clients, personal friends, and relatives (as limited in the rules). The Missouri Supreme Court reprimanded him instead, and he appealed. The United States Supreme Court reversed, finding that because the attorney's advertisements were not misleading, they could not be prohibited since the state had failed to show any substantial interest in restricting the use of the words the lawyer had chosen to describe his areas of practice. Moreover, the Court ruled that the state had shown no evidence that an absolute ban on mailing announcement cards to anyone other than allowed in the state's rule was necessary.

Zauderer v. Office of Disciplinary Counsel   The Supreme Court dealt with the restrictions on illustrations used in lawyer advertising in *Zauderer v. Office of Disciplinary Counsel*, 471 U.S. 626 (1985). That case involved an Ohio lawyer who was reprimanded by the Ohio Supreme Court for placing an advertisement in 36 newspapers that sought clients who may have been harmed by an intrauterine contraceptive device (IUD) known as the Dalkon Shield. The advertisement included a line drawing of the Dalkon Shield, as well as the question, "Did you use this IUD?" The ad then proceeded to inform readers how they could contact the lawyer and included information on fees that said: "The cases are handled on a contingent fee basis of the amount recovered. If there is no recovery, no legal fees are owed by our clients." Over 200 women contacted the lawyer after seeing the advertisement. The Ohio Supreme Court found that the ad violated the advertising rules because those rules prohibited drawings or illustrations, required ads to be dignified, and required any mention of contingency fees to also disclose the distinction between fees and costs.

While acknowledging that jurisdictions have the authority to limit lawyer advertising, the U.S. Supreme Court focused its analysis on misleading or false advertising. The Court found that Ohio could not prohibit the advertisement under the general theory that it was seeking a particular class of client since the advertisement was not deceptive and did not amount to illegal solicitation.

Furthermore, the Court found that it was an unconstitutional infringement of free speech to prohibit drawings or illustrations in lawyer advertisements because of an assumed danger of viewer confusion when, as was the case here, the illustration of the Dalkon Shield was accurate. Concerning the state's interest in promoting dignified advertising, the Court noted that Ohio made no suggestion that the ad was undignified. And (more fundamentally) even if such a danger of undignified ads was palpable, that would still be insufficient to trigger an outright ban on ads with illustrations. The Court also decided that a general interest in promoting dignified communication does not allow for an abridgement of First Amendment rights. However, the Court did agree with the Ohio Supreme Court that the advertisement warranted a reprimand because the statements in the advertisement concerning fees was misleading: it failed to alert the viewer to the difference between contingency fees and litigation costs.

A Few Generalities about Lawyer Advertising

Beyond the larger concepts of the constitutionality and free speech aspects of lawyer advertising, there remain the specifics of such advertising. What follows are some explanations on a few advertising guidelines found in the ABA Model Rules and Model Code and their effects in certain jurisdictions.

Types of Truthful Information That Can Be Included in an Advertisement   The ABA Model Rules and Model Code provide a framework on advertising that the jurisdictions that regulate lawyers put in effect by specifying the kinds of information that are appropriate to be communicated in an advertisement. And, as previously stated, those rules vary considerably. Pennsylvania, for instance, prohibits the use of advertisements containing the endorsements of a celebrity or public figure. Pennsylvania Rules of Professional Conduct, 7.2(d). Some states, including Indiana, advise as to what factual information is appropriate in legal advertisements. The following excerpt from New York's ethics rules is an example of the kinds of information that can be communicated:

It is proper to include information, provided its dissemination does not violate the provisions of DR 2-101 [1200.6] (A), as to:

1. legal and nonlegal education, degrees and other scholastic distinctions, dates of admission to any bar; areas of the law in which the lawyer or law firm practices, as authorized by the Code of Professional Responsibility; public offices and teaching positions held; memberships in bar associations or other professional societies or organizations, including offices and committee assignments therein; foreign language fluency;

2. names of clients regularly represented, provided that the client has given prior written consent;

3. bank references; credit arrangements accepted; prepaid or group legal services programs in which the attorney or firm participates; and

4. legal fees for initial consultation; contingent fee rates in civil matters when accompanied by a statement disclosing the information required by

DR 2–101 [1200.6] (L); range of fees for services, provided that there be available to the public free of charge a written statement clearly describing the scope of each advertised service; hourly rates; and fixed fees for specified legal services. New York Code of Professional Responsibility DR 2–101(C).

Record Keeping   The Model Rules require that lawyers retain a copy of any advertisement for two years after it has been used. (The Model Code had no time limit.) Utah has modified its requirements on retaining advertisements to cover Internet advertising and mandates that firms retain every Web page from their Web sites. Although the ABA rules do not require that advertisements be approved before dissemination, some states require lawyers to submit a copy of their advertisements to the authority within the state's lawyer regulatory scheme: Florida (*Florida Bar v. Doe,* 634 So. 2d 160 [1994]); Indiana (*In re Anonymous,* 637 N.E. 2d 131 [1994]); Texas (*Texans Against Censorship, Inc. v. State Bar of Texas,* 888 F. Supp. 1328 [E.D. Tex. 1995]).

Advertising a Specialty   ABA Model Rule 7.4 has guidelines under which lawyers may advertise that they specialize in a particular area of the law. The general rule in many states is that lawyers may not state or imply that they specialize in a field of practice unless one of three exceptions apply: (a) lawyers may list themselves as a **patent** attorney (or something similar) if they have been admitted to practice before the United States Patent and Trademark Office; (b) lawyers who practice **admiralty** law may designate that fact; and (c) lawyers may advertise that they have been certified as a specialist if the certification was granted by an approved certification agency or, if the agency is not approved by the jurisdictions where the lawyers practice, that fact is listed in the advertisement. As shown by the case *In re Anonymous,* used in Chapter 1's "How to Brief a Case" section, lawyers can even be sanctioned if they use an advertisement that implies they are specialized, if they have not been certified according to their jurisdiction's certification prerequisites.

The Model Code had a stricter rule on specializations, as did the original version of the Model Rules, but the ABA amended Model Rule 7.4 after the Supreme Court's decision in *Peel v. Attorney Registration and Disciplinary Commission,* 496 U.S. 91 (1990). In *Peel,* the Court overturned an Illinois rule that prohibited all specialization listings except admiralty, patent, and trademark. Although Illinois argued that, since it had no certification or specialization programs of its own, it had the right to protect the public from misleading designations, the Court found that such a blanket prohibition was too broad. Therefore, Illinois could not prohibit Peel from identifying himself as "Certified Trial Specialist by the National Board of Trial Advocacy."

In light of *Peel,* many states have amended their specialization allowances, but Kansas has removed its prerequisites on specialization altogether. Its specialization rule simply says, "A lawyer may communicate the fact that the lawyer does or does not practice in particular fields of law." Kansas Rules of Professional Conduct, Rule 7.4. Regardless of a jurisdiction's specialization or certification rules, lawyers in that

patent—The grant of ownership in an invention, giving the owner exclusive rights over the invention for a certain number of years.

admiralty—Admiralty law involves the traditional rules and practices associated with the navigation of the sea or commercial transaction conducted on navigable waterways. Admiralty law is also known as maritime law.

jurisdiction may always advertise that their practice is limited to certain areas of practice (for instance, personal injury law). Such a statement is not the same as a statement concerning a specialization.

Paying for Advertisements   Obviously, lawyers not only have the right, but also the obligation, to pay for their advertisements. MR 7.2(c)(1). But both the Model Rules and the Model Code prohibit lawyers from giving anything of value to someone in exchange for a recommendation of the lawyer's services. This means that a lawyer may not pay someone a "finder's fee" for steering business their way. Lawyers have been sanctioned for paying money—or giving free legal services—to everyone, from other lawyers to business associates and even prison inmates, as a way to get more clients. Giving something of value to someone or some entity as part of a referral arrangement can also occur indirectly. For instance, lawyers can have business relationships that can lead to payments that ethics commissions view as referral fees. It has been found to be improper for a real estate company to market a lawyer's services to its clients and then charge a fee to the lawyer for such promotion. Ill. State Bar Association Comm. on Professional Ethics, Op. 96–04 (1996). It has also been found to be improper for a lawyer to speak at an estate-planning seminar if the financial planner conducting the seminar recommends the lawyer's services to the attendees. Cincinnati Bar Association Ethics Comm., Op. 95–05. The ABA has even taken the position that a law firm may not make a loan to another law firm when the method of repaying the loan is the debtor firm making referrals to the creditor firm. ABA Comm. on Ethics and Professional Responsibility, Formal Op. 94–388 (1995).

One of the exceptions to the general prohibition of paying for referrals is that lawyers may pay the usual charges of a not-for-profit lawyer referral service or legal services organization. MR 7.2(C)(2). Some examples of the kinds of organizations that would qualify are a public defender's office, a military legal assistance office, a legal aid society, and a referral agency sponsored by a bar association. A few states list the kinds of organizations that qualify. As an example, Indiana categorizes in its advertising rules the four kinds of qualified lawyer referral services that a lawyer may compensate. Indiana Rules of Professional Conduct, Rule 7.3(e)(1–4).

In a fascinating case that illustrates the uncertainty of determining if a payment is in violation of the finder's fee prohibition, a Washington, D.C., area lawyer was accused of illegally paying someone to refer his services after he hired another firm's paralegal and paid her a salary of $80,000 dollars a year. The paralegal had formerly worked at a high-volume personal injury firm and became disgruntled because the firm was going to drastically reduce her salary. Before starting employment at the new firm, she showed her new employer copies of many client information cards that she had accumulated while working at her former firm. Her new employment with the second firm was conditioned on that firm obtaining 100 personal injury files within a year of hiring her. Later, the lawyer who hired her sent cards announcing the opening of his new office to about 100 of his paralegal's former clients. The paralegal's former firm accused the lawyer of paying the paralegal to refer clients to him, and the disciplinary tribunal agreed. However, the Maryland

Court of Appeals dismissed the disciplinary charges, finding that there was no evidence that the salary to the paralegal constituted an inappropriate payment, particularly in light of the fact that the paralegal received a salary of over $87,000 dollars at her former firm! *Attorney Grievance Commission of Maryland v. Wills*, 705 A.2d 1121 (Md. 1998).

Lawyer Advertising beyond the Printed Page

Nothing in the U.S. Supreme Court's decisions on lawyer advertising prohibits lawyers from advertising on the radio or television; likewise, nothing in the Model Rules or Model Code prohibits such advertising. Many states allow such advertising, finding that if lawyer advertising was restricted to just the printed page, such a restriction would unconstitutionally deny information about legal services to those who are illiterate, handicapped, or financially disadvantaged—the kinds of people who would be in need of such advertising. *See Grievance Comm. for Hartford–New Britain Judicial Dist. v. Trantolo*, 470 A.2d 228 (Conn. 1984); *In re Petition for Rule of Court Governing Lawyer Advertising*, 564 S.W.2d 638 (Tenn. 1978). (However, in the Tennessee case, the Court banned the use of billboard advertising.)

A few states do place strict limitations on the use of television advertisements. Iowa's rule on advertising lists nineteen kinds of information that may be communicated and, as concerns television advertisements, states:

> The same information, in words and numbers only, articulated by a single non-dramatic voice, not that of the lawyer, and with no other background sound, may be communicated on television. No visual display shall be allowed except that allowed in print as articulated by the announcer. Iowa Code of Professional Responsibility, DR 2–101(B)(5).

A challenge was brought to that rule but the Iowa Supreme Court upheld the it, and the U.S. Supreme Court refused to hear the case. *Committee on Professional Ethics and Conduct v. Humphrey*, 377 N.W.2d 565 (Iowa 1985), appeal dismissed, 475 U.S. 1114, reh'g denied, 476 U.S. 1165 (1986). New Jersey modified its rule on advertising (N.J. Rules of Professional Conduct 7.2[a]) following a decision by the New Jersey Supreme Court that prohibited drawings, animations, dramatizations, music, or lyrics used in connection with televised advertising. *Petition of Felmeister and Isaacs*, 518 A.2d 188 (N.J. 1986).

One step beyond radio and television advertising is prerecorded telephone advertising. This kind of advertising involves a computer-generated phone call, placed to recipients (not necessarily seeking specific legal help) who, upon answering the phone, have the opportunity to listen to a taped lawyer advertisement. This kind of advertisement became allowed under the ABA Model Rules in 1989, after MR 7.2 was changed, adding "recorded" communication to the list of permissible communication.

Although this kind of communication is commonly called telephone solicitation—and rarely well received, for that matter—it is actually considered advertising and not solicitation, since the receiver of the phone simply needs to hang up in order to end the phone call. However, if the lawyer knows that the recipient does not want such phone calls, then placing a prerecorded phone call constitutes impermissible solicitation. More than a few state ethics opinions authorize the prerecorded telephone advertisement. Ill. State Bar Ass'n Comm. on Professional Ethics, Op. 97–6 (1988); Ind. State Bar Ass'n Legal Ethics Comm., Op. 3 of 1996; Iowa State Bar Ass'n Comm. on Professional Ethics and Conduct, Op. 86–6 (1986); Md. State Bar Ass'n Comm. on Ethics, Op. 88–61. However, Alabama does not allow such advertising (Ala. State Bar Gen. Counsel, Op. 87–43 [1987]); and neither does Ohio, a state whose rules are based on the ABA Model Code (Ohio Sup. Ct. Bd. of Comm'rs on Grievances and Discipline, Op. 90–2 [1990]).

Advertising on the Internet

Although the Internet boom of the late 1990s has been relabeled a bust since 2000, much of that downturn has been in the area of pure business-to-consumer Internet businesses, where profit margins were thin or nonexistent. As technology has advanced, however, the ability to advertise has expanded. As early as 1995, bar associations and legal scholars have considered the propriety of lawyer advertising on the Internet, with the consensus being that lawyers can do so as long as their advertising complies with applicable ethics rules.

A law firm Web page is a common form of advertising that is considered in the same category as telephone directory advertising, and is allowable. For instance, Florida expressly allows Internet advertising in its ethics rules and declares that "computer-accessed communications" are a permissible form of advertising. Florida Rules of Professional Conduct, Rule 4–7.1(a). Specific rules governing Internet advertising are also in place (Rule 4–7.6) and include allowing the sending of unsolicited e-mail advertisements to prospective clients within certain guidelines, such as requiring that all subject lines in e-mail advertising have the statement "legal advertising" (Rule 4–7.6[c][3]). Texas requires that a hard copy of the opening screen of a firm's Web site be sent to the Texas Advertising Review Committee, in compliance with the Texas Disciplinary Rules of Professional Conduct, Rule 7.07. Other states' ethics opinions have given approval to legal advertising on the Internet, subject to applicable advertising rules. State Bar of Ariz. Comm. on Rules of Professional Ethics and Conduct, Op. 96–1 (1996); Iowa State Bar Ass'n Comm. on Professional Ethics, Op. 96–10 (1997); State Bar of Mich. Comm. on Professional and Judicial Ethics, Op. RI–276 (1997); Tenn. Sup. Ct. Bd. of Professional Responsibility Ethics Comm., Op. 95–A–570 (1995).

Some law-related Web sites allow users to be linked to law firm Web sites. These third-party Web sites, once they are accessed by a prospective client seeking general legal information, categorize law firms and provide direct links to the firms' home pages. Some states do not allow law firms to participate in such linked Internet advertising if the firm must pay a fee to a for-profit Web site in order to provide such a link (see the previous section on referral fees). Ohio Supreme Court Board of Commissioners on Grievances and Discipline, Op. 2001–2 (2001); Ohio Supreme Court Board of Commissioners on Grievances and Discipline, 2000–5 (2000); Nebraska State Bar Association Adv. Op. 95–3 (1995). Iowa makes no distinction between for-profit and not-for-profit linked Web sites, and it prohibits its attorneys from using such on-line referral services. Iowa State Ass'n Comm. on Professional Ethics and Conduct, Op. 00-07 (2000). Other jurisdictions do allow attorneys to associate with for-profit Web sites in order to access clients, including class-action plaintiffs. Maine Board of Bar Overseers Professional Ethics Comm., Op. 174 (2000); District of Columbia Bar Legal Ethics Committee, Op. 302 (2000); Bar Association of Nassau County Committee on Professional Ethics, Op. 01–4 (2001).

Finally, it should be advised that the issues concerning legal advertising on the Internet are distinct from issues concerning practicing law on the Internet. Because a jurisdiction allows its lawyers to advertise on the Internet does not mean it also allows lawyers to practice law through such electronic means of communication.

Should Advertising Be Dignified?

At a speech in 1995, former U.S. Supreme Court Chief Justice Warren Burger referred to "huckster-shyster" advertising lawyers, who bring shame to the profession by the methods in which they advertise. He further stated the following:

> Unfortunately, the shyster conduct in solicitation and advertising is no longer limited to the "ambulance chasers." Today we see television ads, yellow pages ads, and (believe it or not) ads on billboards forty feet wide and fifteen feet high, touting a lawyer or law firm reaching out for clients. With such ads, lawyers usually emphasize that the "First Conference Is Free." Doesn't this have the ring of "Come into my parlor, said the spider to the fly?" It is sheer nonsense to say that the public needs lawyer advertising for people to have effective access to the judicial system. 63 Fordham Law Review 949 (1995).

The ABA Model Code of Professional Responsibility required that advertisements be presented in a "dignified manner." DR 2–101 (B). Even though the ABA Model Rules do not require dignified ads, an ABA Commission on Advertising put forward some nonbinding, aspirational goals, adopted in 1988, which included calling for dignified lawyer advertising. And some states, such as Indiana, which have adopted the ABA Model Rules, still retain a requirement that advertising be done in a "dignified manner." Ind. Rules of Prof. Conduct 7.1(b). Other states, such as New Jersey, removed the dignity requirement from their rules. *Petition of Felmeister and Isaacs*, 518 A.2d 188 (N.J. 1986).

Provocative Advertisements: Are There No Limits?   New York, which follows the ABA Model Code, also removed the dignity requirement from its advertising rule. One wonders, had New York not removed the dignity requirement, what it would have done with the case of Rosalie Osias, a real estate lawyer from Long Island who uses sexually suggestive poses and double entendre to advertise her legal services. Some of her ads, placed in banking trade magazines, have shown her sitting atop a Harley-Davidson motorcycle, in high heels, wearing a short leather skirt and a low-cut jacket, with the caption, "We will ride anything . . . to get to your closing on time." In other ads, she is similarly dressed and sprawled across a desk or is only wearing lingerie. One ad shows her in high heels, wearing a short skirt, with her leg propped up on a stack of law books with the attached caption, "Anywhere . . . Anytime . . . Anyhow . . . Anybody . . . ANY POSITION . . . We are Ready . . . [then, in a smaller type size] to close your loan."

Not surprisingly, other lawyers were less than thrilled with her methods of advertising. In fact, her county's bar association contemplated bringing charges against her, believing her ads were a disgrace, but eventually decided against it. Ms. Osias claimed victory—she says her practice increased 800 percent—and argued that her ads were a necessary means to help her break into the New York real estate market, something she says is run by an "old-boys network." She was even quoted in an *ABA Journal* article as saying, "I think female attorneys should market themselves visually. . . . They're not going to make money just being smart and having a J.D. in hand. It's OK as long as they deliver serious and good legal work." 83 A.B.A. Journal, at 14 (1997). However, one male lawyer, in the spirit of "if you can't beat them, join them," decided to compete with her by running an advertisement that showed him topless behind a shower curtain, with the caption, "I might not look as good in a bikini as other attorneys, but I do good loans."

ADVERTISING AND THE PARALEGAL

Whenever paralegals are speaking about their firms' legal services, they need to be especially careful that whatever they say could not reasonably be construed to be false or misleading. Because paralegals need to follow their jurisdictions' lawyer conduct rules, they should likewise be careful about statements that compare one lawyer's services to another or create unjustified expectations. Also, legal assistants who perform administrative tasks in smaller firms should be extra careful that, before placing any advertisement for the firm, the advertisement does not inappropriately state or imply any lawyer specializations.

The Paralegal as Part of the Law Firm's Advertising

Many jurisdictions allow paralegals to be listed on the firm's letterhead and other stationery, as well as to be included in the firm's advertising. Whether paralegals would be listed is another matter. Professional letterhead can be quite expensive, and since paralegals are not part of the more permanent structure of the firm (i.e., the partners), firms may decide to limit their letterhead listings. Similarly, paralegals may have business cards that list them as paralegals (or legal assistants) of the firm, including their educational degrees or certifications. This realization should come as no surprise since such listings, if true and clearly delineated, do not violate the principles against false or misleading communication. Usually, it is state ethics opinions that give such approval, sometimes overturning prior ethics opinions. For example, New Jersey and Texas issued ethics opinions expressly allowing paralegals to be listed on law firm letterhead, thus rescinding prior opinions that prohibited it. (New Jersey State Bar Committee on Attorney Advertising, Op. 16 [1994]); (Professional Ethics Committee of the Supreme Court of Texas, Op. 436 [1986]).

The following is a nonexclusive list of other jurisdictions that have issued ethics opinions or rules of court permitting the listing of paralegals on firm letterhead and/or on business cards: Alabama (1986); Cleveland, OH (1989); Colorado (1990); Connecticut (1985); Florida (1986); Hawaii (1984); Illinois (1989); Indiana (1984, and in the Guidelines for the Use of Legal Assistants, 1994); Kansas (1992); Massachusetts (1983); Michigan (1991, and in the Guidelines for the Utilization of Legal Assistants, 1993); Minnesota (1980); Mississippi (1984); Missouri (in the Guidelines for Practicing with Paralegals, 1987); New Hampshire (business cards only, 1987); New Mexico (business cards only, 1986); New York (1997, although in 1992 it prohibited the use of "paralegal coordinator" or any title that includes the word "advocate"); Oregon (1977); Rhode Island (business cards only, 1993); South Carolina (1988); South Dakota (in the Guidelines for the Utilization of Legal Assistants, 1992); Virginia (1989); Washington (in the Guidelines for the Utilization of Legal Assistant Services, 1994); and Wisconsin (1985).

Direct Advertising by Independent Paralegals: Be Careful

As was discussed in Chapters 2 and 3, some jurisdictions allow paralegals to operate as independent contractors. As entrepreneurs, those paralegals have a keen interest in getting the message out that they can provide legal assistant services. Then, for them, advertising becomes a means to an end. Although there is almost no direct authority on the subject, entrepreneurial paralegals should safely be able to advertise their services as long as they remember one important fact: since only lawyers or law firms can hire a freelance paralegal, the advertising can only be directed toward lawyers. Advertising that is directed toward the public is illegal, since only lawyers can represent the public. Advertisements placed by an independent contracting paralegal in the yellow pages, for instance, which give the impression that anyone in need of legal services should contact the paralegal are the kinds of misleading communications that can result in legal action against the paralegal.

A case discussed in Chapter 2, *State v. Robinson*, 468 S.E.2d 290 (S.C. 1996), is instructive on this point. There, a paralegal advertised his services in the yellow pages quite dramatically with the statement, "If your rights have been violated—call me," in an attempt to get prospective litigants as customers. He also distributed a business card that referred to him as a "paralegal consultant." In fact, he represented others in court sixteen times. Not surprisingly, the South Carolina Supreme Court issued an **injunction** against him, denying his claim that he had a First Amendment right of free speech to advertise the way he did. As to his business card, the phrase *paralegal consultant* should be avoided by all independent contracting paralegals because it is a misleading title.

injunction—A court order forbidding a party to do something or ordering them to start doing something.

SOLICITATION

Although advertising and solicitation have the same objective—getting clients—the rules that govern solicitation are the inverse of the rules that govern advertising. The ethics rules generally allow lawyers to advertise and then present exceptions that limit or prohibit certain kinds of advertising. However, the ethics rules generally prohibit lawyers from soliciting but then present limited exceptions that allow certain kinds of solicitation. So strict are the solicitation rules that some states actually make illegal solicitation a crime, usually under the label of barratry. (Georgia, in Ga. Code Ann. § 16–10–95[b], makes barratry a felony punishable by up to five years in prison; New Mexico, in N.M.Stat. Ann. § 30–27–3, makes barratry a misdemeanor.)

What makes solicitation of clients such a different activity from advertising? The means to achieve the objective is the difference. Advertising is intended toward no one specifically; it is directed toward the masses. Solicitation is more personal, occurring very often in face-to-face situations or toward targeted groups. Although one of the funniest scenes in the movie of John Grisham's book *The Rainmaker* involves Danny DeVito's character scrounging for clients in the rooms of the local hospital, his behavior is clearly illegal. Because it is quite difficult for courts to regulate such personal contact between lawyers and prospective clients and because of the belief that solicitation is highly susceptible to abuse, the U.S. Supreme Court has approved the banning of certain forms of solicitation (Exhibit 6–3).

There is an alternative view to the strict approach to solicitation taken by the U.S. Supreme Court and the states. A few legal ethics scholars believe that the abuses associated with client solicitation are overblown and that by continuing to prohibit or severely restrict solicitation, the bar perpetuates the unfortunate notion of lawyers as predators hunting financial gain. Furthermore, these scholars argue that the more information consumers have about legal services, the better off they are, particularly those in the general public who need low-cost legal services.

The Rules against Direct Contact with Prospective Clients

ABA Model Rule 7.3(a) provides, "A lawyer shall not by in-person or live telephone contact solicit professional employment from a prospective client with

Advertising	Solicitation
• is generally allowed, but has limitations and some restrictions	• is generally prohibited, but has limited exceptions
• is directed to the masses	• is targeted to individuals
• is passive, requiring the recipient to do nothing	• is confrontational, requiring the recipient to respond
• is considered less susceptible to abuse	• is considered highly susceptible to abuse

Exhibit 6–3   Advertising versus Solicitation

pecuniary—That which concerns money.

whom the lawyer has no family or prior professional relationship when a significant motive for the lawyer's doing so is the lawyer's **pecuniary** gain." ABA Model Code DR 2–104(A) was similar in scope, forbidding a lawyer from accepting employment that came as a result of unsolicited legal advice to a layperson who was not a "close friend, relative, former client (if the advice is germane to the former employment), or one whom the lawyer reasonably believes to be a client." Notice that the Model Rules's version is stricter since it makes no exception for soliciting the lawyer's friends.

In-Person Solicitation

While the exceptions will be discussed below, it is important to bear in mind that the strictest application of the anti-solicitation rules is in the area of direct contact: in-person or live telephone solicitation. The U.S. Supreme Court gave its express approval of such a prohibition in *Ohralik v. Ohio State Bar Association*, 436 U.S. 447 (1978).

While reading *Ohralik*, pay attention to the reasons given by the Court for allowing the ban on in-person solicitation.

Case Law

Ohralik v. Ohio State Bar Association, 436 U.S. 447 (1978)

Mr. Justice POWELL delivered the opinion of the Court.

In *Bates v. State Bar of Arizona*, 433 U.S. 350, 97 S.Ct. 2691, 53 L.Ed.2d 810 (1977), this Court held that truthful advertising of "routine" legal services is protected by the First and Fourteenth Amendments against blanket prohibition by a State. The Court expressly reserved the question of the permissible scope of regulation of "in-person solicitation of clients—at the hospital room or the accident site, or in any other situation that breeds undue influence—by attorneys or their agents or 'runners.'" *Id.*, at 366, 97 S.Ct., at 2700. Today we answer part of the question so reserved, and hold that the State—or the Bar acting with state authorization—constitutionally may discipline a lawyer for soliciting clients in person, for pecuniary gain, under circumstances likely to pose dangers that the State has a right to prevent.

Appellant, a member of the Ohio Bar, lives in Montville, Ohio. Until recently he practiced law in Montville and Cleveland. On February 13, 1974, while picking up his mail at the Montville Post Office, appellant learned from the postmaster's brother about an automobile accident that had taken place on February 2 in which Carol McClintock, a young woman with whom appellant was casually acquainted, had been injured. Appellant made a telephone call to Ms. McClintock's parents, who informed him that their daughter was in the hospital. Appellant suggested that he might visit Carol in the hospital. Mrs. McClintock assented to the idea, but requested that appellant first stop by at her home. During appellant's visit with the McClintocks, they explained that their daughter had been driving the family automobile on a local road when she was hit by an uninsured motorist. Both Carol and her passenger, Wanda Lou Holbert, were injured and hospitalized. In response to the McClintocks' expression of apprehension that they might be sued by Holbert, appellant explained that

Ohio's guest statute would preclude such a suit. When appellant suggested to the McClintocks that they hire a lawyer, Mrs. McClintock retorted that such a decision would be up to Carol, who was 18 years old and would be the beneficiary of a successful claim.

Appellant proceeded to the hospital, where he found Carol lying in traction in her room. After a brief conversation about her condition, appellant told Carol he would represent her and asked her to sign an agreement. Carol said she would have to discuss the matter with her parents. She did not sign the agreement, but asked appellant to have her parents come to see her. Appellant also attempted to see Wanda Lou Holbert, but learned that she had just been released from the hospital. He then departed for another visit with the McClintocks.

On his way appellant detoured to the scene of the accident, where he took a set of photographs. He also picked up a tape recorder, which he concealed under his raincoat before arriving at the McClintocks' residence. Once there, he re-examined their automobile insurance policy, discussed with them the law applicable to passengers, and explained the consequences of the fact that the driver who struck Carol's car was an uninsured motorist. Appellant discovered that the McClintocks' insurance policy would provide benefits of up to $12,500 each for Carol and Wanda Lou under an uninsured-motorist clause. Mrs. McClintock acknowledged that both Carol and Wanda Lou could sue for their injuries, but recounted to appellant that "Wanda swore up and down she would not do it." *Ibid.* The McClintocks also told appellant that Carol had phoned to say that appellant could "go ahead" with her representation. Two days later appellant returned to Carol's hospital room to have her sign a contract, which provided that he would receive one-third of her recovery.

In the meantime, appellant obtained Wanda Lou's name and address from the McClintocks after telling them he wanted to ask her some questions about the accident. He then visited Wanda Lou at her home, without having been invited. He again concealed his tape recorder and recorded most of the conversation with Wanda Lou. After a brief, unproductive inquiry about the facts of the accident, appellant told Wanda Lou that he was representing Carol and that he had a "little tip" for Wanda Lou: the McClintocks' insurance policy contained an uninsured-motorist clause which might provide her with a recovery of up to $12,500. The young woman, who was 18 years of age and not a high school graduate at the time, replied to appellant's query about whether she was going to file a claim by stating that she really did not understand what was going on. Appellant offered to represent her, also, for a contingent fee of one-third of any recovery, and Wanda Lou stated "O.K."

Wanda's mother attempted to repudiate her daughter's oral assent the following day, when appellant called on the telephone to speak to Wanda. Mrs. Holbert informed appellant that she and her daughter did not want to sue anyone or to have appellant represent them, and that if they decided to sue they would consult their own lawyer. Appellant insisted that Wanda had entered into a binding agreement. A month later Wanda confirmed in writing that she wanted neither to sue nor to be represented by appellant. She requested that appellant notify the insurance company that he was not her lawyer, as the company would not release a check to her until he did so. Carol also eventually discharged appellant. Although another lawyer represented her in concluding a settlement with the insurance company, she paid appellant one-third of her recovery in settlement of his lawsuit against her for breach of contract.

Both Carol McClintock and Wanda Lou Holbert filed complaints against appellant with the Grievance Committee of the Geauga County Bar Association. The County Bar Association referred the grievance to appellee, which filed a formal complaint with the Board of Commissioners on Grievances and Discipline of the Supreme Court of Ohio. After a hearing, the Board found that appellant had violated Disciplinary Rules (DR) 2–103(A) and 2–104(A) of the Ohio Code of Professional Responsibility. The Board rejected appellant's defense that his conduct was protected under the First and Fourteenth Amendments. The Supreme Court of Ohio adopted the findings of the Board, reiterated that appellant's conduct was not constitutionally protected, and increased the sanction of a public reprimand recommended by the Board to indefinite suspension. . . . We now affirm the judgment of the Supreme Court of Ohio.

The solicitation of business by a lawyer through direct, in-person communication with the prospective client has long been viewed as inconsistent with the profession's ideal of the attorney-client relationship and as posing a significant potential for harm to the prospective client. It has been proscribed by the organized Bar for many years. Last Term the Court ruled that the justifications for prohibiting truthful, "restrained" advertising concerning "the availability and terms of routine legal services" are insufficient to override society's interest, safeguarded by the First and Fourteenth Amendments, in assuring the free flow of commercial information. *Bates*, 433 U.S., at 384, 97 S.Ct., at 2709. The balance struck in *Bates* does not predetermine the outcome in this case. The entitlement of in-person solicitation of clients to the protection of the First Amendment differs from that of the kind of advertising approved in *Bates*, as does the strength of the State's countervailing interest in prohibition.

A

Appellant contends that his solicitation of the two young women as clients is indistinguishable, for purposes of constitutional analysis, from the advertisement in *Bates*. Like that advertisement, his meetings with the prospective clients apprised them of their legal rights and of the availability of a lawyer to pursue their claims.

. . . [T]he State does not lose its power to regulate commercial activity deemed harmful to the public whenever speech is a component of that activity. . . . In-person solicitation by a lawyer of remunerative

employment is a business transaction in which speech is an essential but subordinate component. While this does not remove the speech from the protection of the First Amendment, as was held in *Bates* and *Virginia Pharmacy*, it lowers the level of appropriate judicial scrutiny. Unlike a public advertisement, which simply provides information and leaves the recipient free to act upon it or not, in-person solicitation may exert pressure and often demands an immediate response, without providing an opportunity for comparison or reflection. The aim and effect of in-person solicitation may be to provide a one-sided presentation and to encourage speedy and perhaps uninformed decisionmaking; there is no opportunity for intervention or counter-education by agencies of the Bar, supervisory authorities, or persons close to the solicited individual. . . .

It also is argued that in-person solicitation may provide the solicited individual with information about his or her legal rights and remedies. In this case, appellant gave Wanda Lou a "tip" about the prospect of recovery based on the uninsured-motorist clause in the McClintocks' insurance policy, and he explained that clause and Ohio's guest statute to Carol McClintock's parents. But neither of the Disciplinary Rules here at issue prohibited appellant from communicating information to these young women about their legal rights and the prospects of obtaining a monetary recovery, or from recommending that they obtain counsel. DR 2–104(A) merely prohibited him from using the information as bait with which to obtain an agreement to represent them for a fee. The Rule does not prohibit a lawyer from giving unsolicited legal advice; it proscribes the acceptance of employment resulting from such advice. . . .

B

The state interests implicated in this case are particularly strong. In addition to its general interest in protecting consumers and regulating commercial transactions, the State bears a special responsibility for maintaining standards among members of the licensed professions. . . . The substantive evils of solicitation have been stated over the years in sweeping terms: stirring up litigation, assertion of fraudulent claims, debasing the legal profession, and potential harm to the solicited client in the form of overreaching, overcharging, underrepresentation, and misrepresentation. The American Bar Association, as *amicus curiae,* defends the rule against solicitation primarily on three broad grounds: It is said that the prohibitions embodied in DR2–103(A) and 2–104(A) serve to reduce the likelihood of overreaching and the exertion of undue influence on lay persons, to protect the privacy of individuals, and to avoid situations where the lawyer's exercise of judgment on behalf of the client will be clouded by his own pecuniary self-interest. We need not discuss or evaluate each of these interests in detail as appellant has conceded that the State has a legitimate and indeed "compelling" interest in preventing those aspects of solicitation that involve fraud, undue influence, intimidation, overreaching, and other forms of "vexatious conduct." Brief for Appellant 25. We agree that protection of the public from these aspects of solicitation is a legitimate and important state interest.

We agree that the appropriate focus is on appellant's conduct. And, as appellant urges, we must undertake an independent review of the record to determine whether that conduct was constitutionally protected. *Edwards v. South Carolina,* 372 U.S. 229, 235, 83 S.Ct. 680, 683, 9 L.Ed.2d 697 (1963). But appellant errs in assuming that the constitutional validity of the judgment below depends on proof that his conduct constituted actual overreaching or inflicted some specific injury on Wanda Holbert or Carol McClintock. His assumption flows from the premise that nothing less than actual proved harm to the solicited individual would be a sufficiently important state interest to justify disciplining the attorney who solicits employment in person for pecuniary gain. Appellant's argument misconceives the nature of the State's interest. The Rules prohibiting solicitation are prophylactic measures whose objective is the prevention of harm before it occurs. The Rules were applied in this case to discipline a lawyer for soliciting employment for pecuniary gain under circumstances likely to result in the adverse consequences the State seeks to avert. . . .

On the basis of the undisputed facts of record, we conclude that the Disciplinary Rules constitutionally could be applied to appellant. . . . The facts in this case present a striking example of the potential for overreaching that is inherent in a lawyer's in-person solicitation of professional employment. They also demonstrate the need for prophylactic regulation in furtherance of the State's interest in protecting the lay public. We hold that the application of DR2-103(A) and 2-104(A) to appellant does not offend the Constitution.

Accordingly, the judgment of the Supreme Court of Ohio is affirmed.

Case Questions

---

1. Attorney Ohralik argued that there was no evidence that anyone suffered harm as a result of his solicitation activities. Is that accurate?
2. What did you think was the key general distinction the Court made between advertising and solicitation?
3. What exactly did the Court decide with respect to solicitation?
4. Why was this case not decided simply on the basis of Ohralik's free-speech rights?
5. What arguments were put forth by the Court that supported its decision?
6. Ohralik did more than engage in improper solicitation. Reexamine the facts again and find other ethics violations in Ohralik's activities.

Legal Ethics

Solicitation Other Than in Person

Although it is seems obvious to think of solicitation as being a face-to-face endeavor, other forms of contact with prospective clients are also viewed as solicitation, rather than advertising. Three forms will be discussed: written solicitation, telephone solicitation, and Internet solicitation.

Written Solicitation   When does a written advertisement become a written solicitation? It does so when it is a targeted mailing. Although many jurisdictions had prohibited mailed solicitations, the U.S. Supreme Court ruled in a few cases that a total ban on such solicitation was unconstitutional. In *In re R.M.J.*, 455 U.S. 191 (1982) (previously discussed in this chapter), the Supreme Court ruled that Missouri could not prohibit lawyers from mailing announcement cards to classes of persons not listed in Missouri's rules (clients, former clients, lawyers, personal friends, and relatives). Although the Court recognized the state's interest in regulating commercial speech (solicitation), it found that such a broad prohibition was too restrictive.

Then, in *Shapero v. Kentucky Bar Association*, 486 U.S. 466 (1988), the Court reversed Kentucky's decision that prohibited a lawyer from sending advertisement letters to any prospective client whose home was subject to **foreclosure**. Even though the letters were targeted solicitations made for pecuniary gain, the Court found that such a total ban on targeted mailings was unconstitutional in light of the fact that the mailings were truthful. The Court distinguished written solicitation from in-person solicitation, finding less danger of coercion in solicitation letters.

In 1995, however, the U.S. Supreme Court upheld Florida's restriction on mailed advertisements in *Florida Bar v. Went For It, Inc.*, 515 U.S. 618. As you read the case, notice the Court's emphasis on the balance between free speech and the negative perception of lawyers.

foreclosure—The act of a creditor to take ownership and control of property that was used as collateral by the debtor.

Case Law

Florida Bar v. Went For It, Inc., 515 U.S. 618 (1995)

Justice O'CONNOR delivered the opinion of the Court.

Rules of the Florida Bar prohibit personal injury lawyers from sending targeted direct-mail solicitations to victims and their relatives for 30 days following an accident or disaster. This case asks us to consider whether such Rules violate the First and Fourteenth Amendments of the Constitution. We hold that in the circumstances presented here, they do not.

In 1989, the Florida Bar (Bar) completed a 2-year study of the effects of lawyer advertising on public opinion. After conducting hearings, commissioning surveys, and reviewing extensive public commentary, the Bar determined that several changes to its advertising rules were in order. In late 1990, the Florida Supreme Court adopted the Bar's proposed amendments with some modifications. *The Florida Bar: Petition to Amend the Rules Regulating the*

Florida Bar—Advertising Issues, 571 So.2d 451 (Fla.1990). Two of these amendments are at issue in this case. Rule 4–7.4(b)(1) provides that

> [a] lawyer shall not send, or knowingly permit to be sent, . . . a written communication to a prospective client for the purpose of obtaining professional employment if: (A) the written communication concerns an action for personal injury or wrongful death or otherwise relates to an accident or disaster involving the person to whom the communication is addressed or a relative of that person, unless the accident or disaster occurred more than 30 days prior to the mailing of the communication.

Rule 4–7.8(a) states that

> [a] lawyer shall not accept referrals from a lawyer referral service unless the service: (1) engages in no communication with the public and in no direct contact with prospective clients in a manner that would violate the Rules of Professional Conduct if the communication or contact were made by the lawyer.

Together, these Rules create a brief 30-day blackout period after an accident during which lawyers may not, directly or indirectly, single out accident victims or their relatives in order to solicit their business.

In March 1992, G. Stewart McHenry and his wholly owned lawyer referral service, Went For It, Inc., filed this action for declaratory and injunctive relief in the United States District Court for the Middle District of Florida challenging Rules 4–7.4(b)(1) and 4–7.8(a) as violative of the First and Fourteenth Amendments to the Constitution. McHenry alleged that he routinely sent targeted solicitations to accident victims or their survivors within 30 days after accidents and that he wished to continue doing so in the future. Went For It, Inc., represented that it wished to contact accident victims or their survivors within 30 days of accidents and to refer potential clients to participating Florida lawyers. In October 1992, McHenry was disbarred for reasons unrelated to this suit, *Florida Bar v. McHenry*, 605 So.2d 459 (Fla.1992). Another Florida lawyer, John T. Blakely, was substituted in his stead.

Constitutional protection for attorney advertising, and for commercial speech generally, is of recent vintage. . . . In *Bates v. State Bar of Arizona, supra*, the Court struck a ban on price advertising for what it deemed "routine" legal services. . . . Nearly two decades of cases have built upon the foundation laid by *Bates*. It is now well established that lawyer advertising is commercial speech and, as such, is accorded a measure of First Amendment protection.(Citations omitted.) Such First Amendment protection, of course, is not absolute. . . . Mindful of these concerns, we engage in "intermediate" scrutiny of restrictions on commercial speech, analyzing them under the framework set forth in *Central Hudson Gas & Elec. Corp. v. Public Serv. Comm'n of N.Y.*, 447 U.S. 557, 100 S.Ct. 2343, 65 L.Ed.2d 341 (1980). Under *Central Hudson*, the government may freely regulate commercial speech that concerns unlawful activity or is misleading. *Id.*, at 563–564, 100 S.Ct., at 2350. Commercial speech that falls into neither of those categories, like the advertising at issue here, may be regulated if the government satisfies a test consisting of three related prongs: First, the government must assert a substantial interest in support of its regulation; second, the government must demonstrate that the restriction on commercial speech directly and materially advances that interest; and third, the regulation must be "'narrowly drawn.'"

We have little trouble crediting the Bar's interest as substantial. On various occasions we have accepted the proposition that

> "States have a compelling interest in the practice of professions within their boundaries, and . . . as part of their power to protect the public health, safety, and other valid interests they have broad power to establish standards for licensing practitioners and regulating the practice of professions. *Goldfarb v. Virginia State Bar*, 421 U.S. 773 (1975).

. . . Under *Central Hudson*'s second prong, the State must demonstrate that the challenged regulation "advances the Government's interest 'in a direct and material way.'" . . . The Bar submitted a 106-page summary of its 2-year study of lawyer advertising and solicitation to the District Court. That summary contains data—both statistical and anecdotal—supporting the Bar's contentions that the Florida public views direct-mail solicitations in the immediate wake of accidents as an intrusion on privacy that reflects poorly upon the profession. As of June 1989, lawyers mailed 700,000 direct solicitations in Florida annually, 40% of which were aimed at accident victims or their survivors. Summary of the Record in No. 74,987 (Fla.) on Petition to Amend the Rules Regulating Lawyer Advertising (hereinafter Summary of Record), App. H, p. 2. A survey of Florida adults commissioned by the Bar indicated that Floridians "have negative feelings about those attorneys who use direct mail advertising." Magid Associates, Attitudes & Opinions Toward Direct Mail Advertising by Attorneys (Dec. 1987), Summary of Record, App. C(4), p. 6. Fifty-four percent of the general population surveyed said that contacting persons concerning accidents or similar events is a violation of privacy. *Id.*, at 7. A random sampling of persons who received direct-mail advertising from lawyers in 1987 revealed that 45% believed that direct-mail solicitation is "designed to take advantage of gullible or unstable people"; 34% found such tactics "annoying or irritating"; 26% found it "an invasion of your privacy"; and 24% reported that it "made you angry." *Ibid.* Significantly, 27% of direct-mail recipients reported that their regard for the legal profession and for the judicial process as a whole was "lower" as a result of receiving the direct mail. *Ibid.* The anecdotal record mustered by the Bar is noteworthy for its breadth and detail. With titles like "Scavenger Lawyers" (The Miami Herald, Sept. 29, 1987) and "Solicitors Out of Bounds" (St. Petersburg Times, Oct. 26, 1987), newspaper editorial pages in Florida have burgeoned with criticism of Florida lawyers who send targeted direct mail to victims shortly after accidents. See Summary of Record, App. B, pp. 1–8. . . .

The study summary also includes page upon page of excerpts from complaints of direct-mail recipients. For example, a Florida citizen described how he was "'appalled and angered by the brazen attempt'" of a law firm to solicit him by letter shortly after he was injured and his fiancee was killed in an auto accident. Summary of Record, App. I(1), p. 2. Another found it "'despicable and inexcusable'" that a Pensacola lawyer wrote to his mother three days after his father's funeral. *Ibid.* Another described how she was "'astounded'" and then "'very angry'" when she received a solicitation following a minor accident. *Id.*, at 3. Still another described as "'beyond comprehension'" a letter his nephew's family received the day of the nephew's funeral. *Ibid.* One citizen wrote, "'I consider the unsolicited contact from you after my child's accident to be of the rankest form of ambulance chasing and in incredibly poor taste. . . . I cannot begin to express with my limited vocabulary the utter contempt in which I hold you and your kind.'" *Ibid.*

In light of this showing—which respondents at no time refuted, save by the conclusory assertion that the Rule lacked "any factual basis," . . . we conclude that the Bar has satisfied the second prong of the *Central Hudson* test.

Passing to *Central Hudson*'s third prong, we examine the relationship between the Bar's interests and the means chosen to serve them. . . . "What our decisions require," . . . "is a 'fit' between the legislature's ends and the means chosen to accomplish those ends," a fit that is not necessarily perfect, but reasonable; that represents not necessarily the single best disposition but one whose scope is 'in proportion to the interest served,' that employs not necessarily the least restrictive means but . . . a means narrowly tailored to achieve the desired objective." *Ibid.* [citations omitted]. . . . We are not persuaded by respondents' allegations of constitutional infirmity. We find little deficiency in the ban's failure to distinguish among injured Floridians by the severity of their pain or the intensity of their grief. Indeed, it is hard to imagine the contours of a regulation that might satisfy respondents on this score. Rather than drawing difficult lines on the basis that some injuries are "severe" and some situations appropriate (and others, presumably, inappropriate) for grief, anger, or emotion, the Bar has crafted a ban applicable to all postaccident or disaster solicitations for a brief 30-day period. . . . The Bar's rule is reasonably well tailored to its stated objective of eliminating targeted mailings whose type and timing are a source of distress to Floridians, distress that has caused many of them to lose respect for the legal profession. . . .

We believe that the Bar's 30-day restriction on targeted direct-mail solicitation of accident victims and their relatives withstands scrutiny under the three-pronged *Central Hudson* test that we have devised for this context. The Bar has substantial interest both in protecting injured Floridians from invasive conduct by lawyers and in preventing the erosion of confidence in the profession that such repeated invasions have engendered. The Bar's proffered study, unrebutted by respondents below, provides evidence indicating that the harms it targets are far from illusory. The palliative devised by the Bar to address these harms is narrow both in scope and in duration. The Constitution, in our view, requires nothing more.

The judgment of the Court of Appeals, accordingly, is *Reversed.*

Case Questions

1. What exactly was the solicitation restriction that Florida instituted which precipitated this case?
2. What is the *Central Hudson* test for regulating commercial speech?
3. The Court categorized three kinds of information gathered by the Florida Bar Association that helped convince the Court that Florida's regulation advanced the "Government's interest in a direct and material way." What were those three categories of information?
4. Do you think this case would have been decided differently had not the Florida Bar collected such scathing rebukes from the public concerning accident victim solicitations?
5. Can you think of any reasons why the Court's decision could be considered wrong or too restrictive?

Florida is not alone in putting a time distance between accidents and the solicitation of accident victims by lawyers. Arkansas, Georgia, Kentucky, New Mexico, and Maryland also require lawyers to wait thirty days before soliciting the victims or family members of those who may have a personal injury of wrongful death lawsuit. Interestingly, Maryland's original, thirty-day ban (Md. Code Ann., Bus. Occup. & Prof. § 10–605.1) also applied to the solicitation of criminal or traffic defendants, but a federal court found that part of the statute to be unconstitutional. *Ficker v. Curran*, 119 F.3d 1150 (Fourth Cir. 1997).

Model Rule 7.3(c) also adds a condition to allowing written solicitations, requiring that the words "Advertising Material" be placed on the outside of the envelope. California, for instance, requires that mailed advertisements be labeled "Advertisement" or "Newsletter" in at least 12-point typeface on the first page. Ca. Professional Conduct Rule 1–400(E), Standard 5.

Telephone Solicitation   According to MR 7.3(a), live telephone contact made to a prospective client is prohibited if a significant motive for such contact is pecuniary gain. As was previously discussed in the section on advertising, pre-recorded telephone advertising is allowed in many jurisdictions, but when the lawyer knows that the recipient does not want to receive such an advertising phone call, then to do so would be constitute unlawful solicitation. And, according to the Comments in MR 7.3, since the contents of live telephone conversations between a lawyer and a prospective client are not subject to third-party scrutiny, the danger of misleading communication is heightened.

Internet Solicitation While many jurisdictions have drawn the parallel between yellow pages advertising and Internet advertising, they have also consistently drawn a parallel between in-person solicitation and Internet chatroom solicitation. Internet chat rooms, where people can gather (almost anonymously) and talk to each other in real time, would generally be considered off-limits for lawyers to use as an alternative to the in-person solicitation prohibition. Some jurisdictions have issued ethics opinions that expressly forbid lawyer solicitation in such chat rooms. Michigan State Bar Association Ethics Op. RI–276 (1996); Utah State Bar Ethics Advisory Commission, Op. 97–10 (1997); Virginia State Bar Advertising Committee's Op. A–0110 (1998); West Virginia Lawyer Disciplinary Board Op. 98–03 (1998).

The sending of e-mails to prospective clients does not fall within the above-mentioned prohibition but could still be unlawful if done outside the scope of the controlling jurisdiction's rules. An important quandary raised by Internet solicitation is the fact that the lawyer may be in violation of the solicitation rules of jurisdictions to which the lawyer's Internet communications are sent, if those jurisdictions have rules that differ from the jurisdiction where the lawyer is licensed. Moreover, discussions with prospective clients in chat rooms where the lawyer is not the initiating party would be, by definition, viewed as something other than prohibited solicitation. *See* Illinois State Bar Association Ethics Op. 96–10 (1996).

Permissible Solicitation

As a general principle, lawyers are prohibited from soliciting prospective clients in face-to-face situations or real-time electronic situations when the primary motive is financial gain and are allowed to solicit prospective clients through written mailings or pre-recorded telephone calls. Even where the prospective client can be solicited, lawyers may not engage in any solicitation where the prospective client communicates that he or she does not want to be solicited; nor may lawyers use solicitation that involves harassment or duress. MR 7.3(b)(1), (2).

Certain kinds of solicitation are permitted, however, either because they are expressly allowed by the rules or are not covered in the rules.

Prior Relationships
Both sets of rules allow a lawyer to solicit those with whom the lawyer has had a professional or family relationship. The Model Code also allows lawyers to solicit

close friends. The allowance for lawyers to solicit present or former clients, as well as family members (and friends), demonstrates that there is less a threat of abuse—which is at the heart of the strict solicitation rules—when those being solicited already know the lawyer.

Class Actions

The Comments to MR 7.2 state that "[n]either this Rule nor Rule 7.3 prohibits communications authorized by law, such as notice to members of a class in **class action** litigation." Moreover, in *Gulf Oil Co. v. Bernard*, 452 U.S. 89 (1981), the Supreme Court held that the Federal Rules of Civil Procedure allow for direct contact with those who may be potential plaintiffs in a class action lawsuit. That decision does not mean that such solicitation is automatically allowed in class actions brought in state courts, but some jurisdictions do allow the solicitation of members of a class, either by court decisions, ethics opinions, or through their advertising and solicitation rules.

class action—A lawsuit brought by a representative of a large group of plaintiffs (or prospective plaintiffs) on behalf of the group. Rule 23 of the Federal Rules of Civil Procedure governs class actions.

Not-for-Profit Solicitation

The same day the Supreme Court upheld the ban on in-person solicitation in *Ohralik v. Ohio State Bar Association*, 436 U.S. 447 (1978), it reached a different conclusion in *In re Primus*, 436 U.S. 412 (1978). There, the Court affirmed the right of a lawyer associated with the American Civil Liberties Union to send a solicitation letter to women who might have been harmed in connection with government-provided medical services, informing the women that free legal services were available. The Court distinguished *Primus* from *Ohralik* on the grounds that not-for-profit solicitation was a form of political expression and, therefore, protected under the First Amendment. Traditionally, solicitation is a commercial endeavor, which is why the solicitation restriction in MR 7.3(a) concerns solicitation, "when a significant motive for the lawyer's doing so is the lawyer's pecuniary gain." Such a different view toward not-for-profit solicitation can even be traced back to an ABA ethics opinion from 1935 that stated the anti-solicitation Canon was not aimed at lawyers who were willing to devote some of their time to representing indigent citizens whose constitutional rights may have been violated. ABA Comm. on Professional Ethics and Grievances, Formal Op. 148 (1935).

Solicitation and the Legal Assistant

Consistent with the theme of this text, paralegals and legal assistants can do nothing that lawyers cannot do. Therefore, all non-lawyer employees need to be acquainted with their jurisdictions' solicitation rules and follow them accordingly. Since lawyers pay the price for the misconduct of their employees, paralegals who demonstrate their knowledge of the nuances of the applicable solicitation rules can save their firms from unintended sanctions. Knowing whether one's jurisdiction allows for the solicitation of class action members, or puts a time buffer between accidents and the contacting of prospective clients, is as important as knowing what the unauthorized practice of law is.

Furthermore, Model Rule 8.4(a) states that it is professional misconduct for a lawyer to knowingly assist or induce someone else to violate the Rules of Professional Conduct, or use someone else to violate the Rules. While the scope of that rule is broad, it has been specifically applied in situations where lawyers have employed **accident runners**, or have paid fees to marketing firms that solicit business in ways that violate the rules. As well, there is too much case law involving lawyers who were caught using their non-lawyer employees—from their paralegals to their secretaries and investigators—to illegally solicit legal business.

accident runners—Persons hired by lawyers to find personal injury clients, usually by going to the scene of accidents or disasters. Accident runners are respected even less than ambulance chasers.

A Case Study in Illegal Solicitation

The following *Wall Street Journal* article is a tour de force in exposing the dark side of the solicitation of prospective clients who are the recent victims of tragedy.

Master of Disaster

by Max Boot, Assistant Features Editor

HOUSTON—A funny thing happened to John O'Quinn on his way to becoming the second-highest-paid lawyer in America: Some of his fellow attorneys tried to kick him out of the profession. In 1987 the State Bar of Texas brought a suit to have the flamboyant personal injury attorney disbarred for using "accident runners" to solicit clients after an airplane crash. Mr. O'Quinn pled "no contest" to the charges in 1989, but thanks to a high-powered defense team, he managed to keep his law license.

Today Mr. O'Quinn is famous around the country as one of the leading lawyers suing breast implant manufacturers. Not long ago, he and law partner Richard Laminack were even featured on the cover of Fortune magazine under the headline "Lawyers from Hell." Forbes magazine estimated that he earned $40 million last year (a number he denies), almost twice as much as basketball superstar Shaquille O'Neal. Yet even as Mr. O'Quinn reached the pinnacle of success, it appears that he and his

firm were up to their old tricks—representing clients whose cases were solicited in ways that were almost certainly unethical and quite possibly illegal.

Or so says Betty Edward. And she should know. She was an "accident runner" hired by Benton Musslewhite, an attorney who works in the same downtown office building as Mr. O'Quinn and has long served as a "pipeline" to the more famous lawyer. Ms. Edward has come forward to tell the extraordinary story—complete with boxes of supporting documents—of how she "hustled" cases last year for Messrs. Musslewhite and O'Quinn following an airplane crash. Her account, now under investigation by the South Carolina attorney general's office, provides a behind-the-scenes perspective on how modern-day "ambulance chasing" really works.

USAir Flight 1016 crashed near Charlotte, N.C., on July 2, 1994, killing 37 passengers and wounding 14 others (four crew members were also injured). Within days, according to Ms. Edward,

Benton Musslewhite was on the phone with her. He knew her as one of the most active plaintiffs he had represented in a suit against a hazardous waste site in Houston, and he now made her an intriguing offer: Go down to South Carolina, where more than half of the crash victims lived, and find clients for Messrs. Musslewhite and O'Quinn. In return, Mr. Musslewhite promised her $1,000 a day and all expenses paid, plus bonuses when the cases settled—a fabulous sum to be sure, but one that she never succeeded in collecting in full. Ms. Edward was 49 years old, unemployed, unmarried, dependent on Supplemental Security Income [SSI] and Medicaid. Beguiled by the cash waved in her face—"I'd never had that much money in my hands before"—she agreed to go.

She insists she didn't know that it's against the law in both South Carolina and Texas for lawyers or their representatives to personally solicit accident victims as clients (at the time, it was a misdemeanor in both states and a violation of State Bar rules; it's now a felony in Texas). At any rate, Mr. Musslewhite assured her that, since they already had one client from the crash, it was perfectly legal to send her down to South Carolina as an "investigator." Contacted by The Wall Street Journal, he reiterated that "we told Betty she was to gather information only," but if one of the family members "didn't have an attorney and was interested in getting representation, they could contact us." Mr. Musslewhite said "that's the appropriate way to do it," but when asked what "information" Ms. Edward gathered, he replied: "Oh golly! That's privileged work product."

The reality is that this high school dropout had neither a private investigator's license nor any experience in investigative work. "I was really being asked to hustle cases," she says. "I didn't know what I was getting into."

The clients that Ms. Edward would bring in went to both Mr. Musslewhite and Mr. O'Quinn, and Mr. Musslewhite says that "the cases were financed by Mr. O'Quinn." But Mr. O'Quinn doesn't hire accident runners personally. As his lawyer,

Thomas McDade, put it in a letter to the Journal, "She [Ms. Edward] was not hired by Mr. O'Quinn or sent by him or instructed by him." That chore is handled by less prominent attorneys like Mr. Musslewhite, who gets a percentage of the final settlement in return for soliciting cases and any other work he may do. That strategy was vindicated during the 1987 Texas State Bar investigation into an international case-running operation. While Mr. O'Quinn emerged relatively unscathed, Mr. Musslewhite (whose practice Mr. O'Quinn admitted to bankrolling in his 1989 settlement with the State Bar) wound up losing his license for three years. But Mr. Musslewhite wasn't able to insulate Mr. O'Quinn and his firm from the appearance of unethical conduct in the USAir case.

Betty Edward was sent down to Columbia, S.C., with a list of all the victims of the crash that was on the letterhead of O'Quinn, Kerensky, McAninch & Laminack, Mr. O'Quinn's law firm. She also carried preprinted forms authorizing "John M. O'Quinn, P.C." to represent accident victims on a contingency-fee basis; all she had to do was get family members to fill in their names and sign on the last page. To entice prospective clients, Ms. Edward was given a variety of materials: a generic letter from Mr. O'Quinn ("We are writing to let you know that you can join [crash survivor] Mr. [Dorian] Doucette in this suit, and that we would be honored to represent you"); a video plugging the O'Quinn law firm ("We provide the individual with the opportunity to fight large corporations for their rights on a level playing field"); and a booklet containing Mr. O'Quinn's resume and press clips (including an item from Forbes listing him among America's highest-paid lawyers). On one occasion, Ms. Edward ran out of promotional material and a woman in Mr. O'Quinn's office FedExed her some more (Ms. Edward still has the receipt).

Once down in Columbia, she worked closely with Carl Shaw, an attorney in Mr. O'Quinn's office, and Darlene Hopper, a registered nurse on Mr. O'Quinn's staff, both ostensibly there (in the words of Mr. O'Quinn's attorney) "to obtain information about the crash." And at one point Mr. O'Quinn himself flew down to Columbia, where he recalls a "casual meeting" with Ms. Edward in a hotel room.

To gain entree into victims' homes, the legal team still needed a local contact. So they recruited, of all people, a local minister, the Rev. Charles (Carlos) Williams Jr. of the Full Gospel Word & Worship Center. Mr. Williams told Ms. Edward in a telephone conversation she secretly tape-recorded that he was promised $1,000 a day plus bonuses, the same amount promised to Ms. Edward.

(Mr. Williams did not respond to numerous telephone messages from the Journal, but after being contacted by Mr. O'Quinn's attorney, he faxed the Journal a letter on Jan. 2 stating that as a former sheriff's deputy his only role was to "help investigate the facts relating to the plane crash" and that Betty Edward "was doing the same investigative work as me," an interesting assertion in light of Ms. Edward's professed inability to do any investigative work. In fact, during the tape-recorded conversation on Dec. 8, 1995, Ms. Edward told Mr. Williams, "We could go to the penitentiary for them [the lawyers] and they got money like that, millions of dollars, and us thinking we just working innocently, uh, honestly, y'know. Pitiful!" His reply? "That's right.")

Together, Ms. Edward and Mr. Williams went around to the funerals and homes of accident victims and their families, a fact confirmed by two of the victims' families. Ms. Edward later realized that she and Mr. Williams were sent because they're both black and so were most of the victims. Ms. Edward says that her skin color, combined with her bubbly personality—"I'm a people person"—allowed her to establish an easy rapport with family members. "They cried on my shoulder, we played with the babies, they took pictures," she recalls. "They were the sweetest people and they were grateful to me. I really enjoyed it." Others were less happy to see her. "Some of the family members were in so much grief they didn't accept their relatives were gone. Others had already signed up with other attorneys."

By early September 1994, Ms. Edward had helped snare several cases, giving Messrs. O'Quinn and Musslewhite a grand total of seven USAir clients—litigation worth millions of dollars. Mr. Musslewhite confirms paying Betty Edward roughly $39,000 for her services on the USAir cases, but he adds that it wasn't his money; he says Mr. O'Quinn paid all the case expenses. The payments were made in cash, because Ms. Edward was still getting SSI benefits, so she didn't want to report her outside income.

All of this is highly unethical, not to say illegal. The U.S. Supreme Court has ruled that attorneys may send letters to potential clients, but in-person solicitation, especially by non-attorneys, is still illegal in both Texas and South Carolina. Mr. O'Quinn tried to challenge the "barratry" statute as unconstitutional during his 1987 disciplinary case, but it was upheld by the Texas Supreme Court. Even the Texas Trial Lawyers Association, a group of plaintiffs' attorneys, filed a brief in that case arguing that the use of accident runners is a "cruel and shabby" practice. "For individuals who may already be at their wits' end because of the tragedy they have suffered, such conduct by 'runners' serves, at best, to compound their suffering," the trial lawyers' group wrote. "At worst, it impels them into making an important decision about legal representation when they are least equipped to do so."

The reason that Messrs. O'Quinn and Musslewhite's conduct has now come to light is the same reason it surfaced in 1987—disgruntled accident runners have decided to spill the beans. In this case, Betty Edward says she was never paid thousands of dollars promised her by the attorneys.

Benton Musslewhite, who has filed for Chapter 11 bankruptcy protection, says John O'Quinn is responsible for all case expenses, and the multimillionaire litigator hasn't been willing to pay the extra money to the runners. Mr. O'Quinn's attorney, for his part, insists that "there never was any relationship between Mr. O'Quinn and Betty Edward and he owes her no money. . . . She was retained by Mr. Musslewhite and worked solely for him."

Mr. Musslewhite told the Journal he's "frustrated" by Mr. O'Quinn's repeated refusals to "resolve" Ms. Edward's "legitimate claims." "I don't know why John won't do it, Betty," Mr. Musslewhite told Ms. Edward in a phone conversation she secretly tape-recorded. "We're talking peanuts here. I don't know why he puts me into a spot that puts hardship on y'all." Ms. Edward offers her own explanation: "They felt they could brush me off because I'm a small fry. They thought there was nothing I could do to them." Now, presumably, they know different.

The $40 million question is: What, if anything, will happen to John O'Quinn and Benton Musslewhite? The South Carolina attorney general's office has offered Ms. Edward limited immunity (technically, a "proffer" letter) to tell her story. But Mr. O'Quinn has been the Teflon trial lawyer so far. When Mary Klager, one of his breast implant plaintiffs, charged him with mixing up her tissues and needlessly leading her to get a double mastectomy, a

local judge dismissed the charges (see "A Tale of Silicone City," Nov. 29, 1995). When Mr. O'Quinn pleaded "no contest" to the earlier charges of accident running, he got off with a slap on the wrist—a "public reprimand," two years' probation, 100 hours of community service and $38,000 in court costs.

"The O'Quinn case gave the illusion that it was OK to use accident runners," says Larry Doherty, the former chairman of the Texas State Bar grievance committee that put together the 1987 charges against the high-profile litigator. "It sure took the wind out of our sails, and I don't know if the bar ever recovered. Texas is still a hotbed of ambulance-chasing, accident-running lawyers, and I don't know if anybody has done anything about it." Maybe South Carolina will act where Texas hasn't. . . .

Article Questions

1. What is an accident runner?
2. How did Ms. Edward come to be hired by Mr. Musslewhite?
3. What did Mr. Musslewhite tell the *Wall Street Journal* that Ms. Edward was hired to be? What makes that claim ludicrous?
4. If Mr. Musslewhite hired Ms. Edward, then why is Mr. O'Quinn the target of this article and the subsequent bar investigation?
5. Why would the crash victims and/or their families need to see Mr. O'Quinn's resume, as was the case when Ms. Edward was "visiting" with them?
6. What was the minister's role in this affair?
7. What evidence is there that Ms. Edward, like the lawyers, was also duplicitous?
8. How did this whole conspiracy get to the attention of the various authorities?
9. How has Mr. O'Quinn sailed through nearly unscathed in prior disciplinary matters?
10. What discipline would you give to the three major players in this solicitation scandal?

In April 1997, John O'Quinn, Charles Benton Musslewhite, and two other lawyers were indicted by the South Carolina attorney general and accused of conspiracy, the unauthorized practice of law, illegal solicitation of clients, and illegal fee splitting. The two other attorneys charged in the matter were Carl Shaw, a lawyer in O'Quinn's office, and Charles Benton Musslewhite, Jr. The reason the South

Carolina Attorney General brought criminal charges was that, since the South Carolina bar has no authority to bring disciplinary charges against out-of-state attorneys, criminal charges were the only viable option. O'Quinn's attorney, Thomas McDade, responded by describing the South Carolina anti-solicitation statute as archaic and unconstitutional. Continuing to rely on the argument that Musslewhite and others committed the transgressions, O'Quinn was quoted as saying: "I have done nothing wrong and am innocent of these charges. There are rules about soliciting clients, as there should be, and we followed every one of them."

By July 1997, South Carolina adopted a rule that requires out-of-state lawyers who promote their services or advertise in South Carolina to comply with its rules regarding solicitation and advertising. Failure to comply would subject out-of-state lawyers to a variety of sanctions, including having to refund all legal fees gained through the unlawful tactics. And as for John O'Quinn, his legal troubles in South Carolina came to a close when he agreed to plead guilty to practicing law without a license in South Carolina. Part of the plea bargain included the following punishment: he gave approximately $300,000 to South Carolina to fund legal ethics programs.

ETHICS 2000 AND ADVERTISING AND SOLICITATION

There have been more than a few changes made to the advertising and solicitation rules by the Ethics 2000 Commission, including eliminating certain parts of the advertising rules, as well as bringing the Internet within the scope of the solicitation rules.

MR 7.1 and Communications Concerning a Lawyer's Services

Proposal by the Ethics 2000 Commission
The newer version of MR 1.7 eliminates sections (b) and (c) because they were believed to be overly broad. However, the message of those two sections has been turned into two Comments. One Comment concerns how truthful statements can still be misleading if there is a "substantial likelihood that it will lead a reasonable person to formulate a specific conclusion about the lawyer or the lawyer's services for which there is no reasonable factual foundation." The other former rule is now a Comment concerning lawyers who create unjustified expectations based on unsubstantiated comparisons to other lawyers' services. That Comment also states that "the inclusion of appropriate disclaimer or qualifying language may preclude a finding that a statement is likely to create unjustified expectations. . . ."

Action Taken by the ABA House of Delegates
Approved.

MR 7.2 and Advertising

Proposal by the Ethics 2000 Commission
The language of the new MR 7.2 eliminates the specific kinds of advertising in favor of the phrase, "recorded or electronic communication, including public media." Such a broader phrase allows the rule to keep pace with current technology. The current Section (b), which requires lawyers to maintain a copy of their advertisements for two years, has been eliminated because the Committee found that such a requirement was too burdensome. The new version allows a lawyer to pay the usual charges of a for-profit legal services plan if the legal services plan is state-approved. The new version also allows a law firm, in addition to named lawyers within the firm, to be responsible for an advertisement's content. An addition to one of the Comments now discusses the Internet and mentions e-mail as permissible advertising.

Action Taken by the ABA House of Delegates
Approved.

MR 7.3 and Solicitation

Proposal by the Ethics 2000 Commission
Certain stylistic changes have been made to MR 7.3, but the most significant, substantive change is that Section (a) of the new version now lists "real-time electronic" as a contact method that is severely restricted. An Internet chatroom is an example of a real-time electronic contact under this rule. The exceptions to direct solicitation prohibitions now includes a lawyer contacting someone with whom the lawyer has a "close personal" relationship. This exception is similar to that which is given in the ABA Model Code of Professional Responsibility, and the Committee believed there to be no legitimate justification for prohibiting lawyers from offering their legal services to a close friend. There are also some minor additions to the Comments.

Action Taken by the ABA House of Delegates
Approved.

MR 7.4 and Communication of Fields of Practice

Proposal by the Ethics 2000 Commission
The title of MR 7.4 has been expanded to "Communication of Fields of Practice *and Specialization*" (emphasis added). The rule has been effectively rewritten such that the parts concerning specialization are in a Section distinct from the parts on patent attorneys and admiralty practice. Another change prohibits lawyers from claiming certification if the certifying organization is not approved by an

appropriate state authority, or accredited by the ABA, while requiring that when lawyers are allowed to claim a certification, the certifying organization be "clearly identified" in the advertisement. This allows the prospective client to investigate the claim of certification. Finally, the Comments that allowed for non-approved certifying organizations have been eliminated.

Action Taken by the ABA House of Delegates
Approved.

MR 7.5 and Firm Names and Letterheads

Proposal by the Ethics 2000 Commission
There are no significant changes to MR 7.5, but the Comments mention that a lawyer or law firm may be identified by a Web site address.

Action Taken by the ABA House of Delegates
Approved.

Summary

Although nothing explicitly prohibited lawyers from advertising before the first rules of ethics were created, most lawyers refrained from advertising their services because of the tradition against it. The first ABA set of ethics rules frowned on lawyer advertising. But by the 1950s, the ABA modified its rules to allow lawyers to advertise in phone books and legal directories.

Because advertising and solicitation qualify as commercial speech, they can be regulated more strictly than religious or political speech. And for much of the twentieth century, the U.S. Supreme Court upheld state laws that severely restricted lawyer advertising. The Supreme Court then changed its position in *Bates v. State Bar of Arizona*, finding that lawyers had a First Amendment right to truthfully advertise certain kinds of standardized information about their legal services. Following that decision, states could not prohibit all forms of advertising.

The rules on communication about a lawyer's services prohibit lawyers from making any false or misleading statements. Three types of information are usually considered false or misleading statements: fraudulent statements, or material misrepresentations of fact or law; statements that are likely to create unjustified expectations about the likelihood of success; and unsubstantiated comparisons of one lawyer's services to another's. Statements that concern legal fees have been found to be misleading when they do not accurately represent that the client will have to pay certain fees or costs. Some rules also prohibit statements that are self-laudatory.

The rules on lawyer advertising allow lawyers to advertise in print, on the radio, and on television. However, lawyers must retain copies of their advertisements, and in some jurisdictions, must obtain prior approval before placing advertisements. The Supreme Court struck down restrictions on the types of words used to describe a lawyer's practice, and prohibitions on illustrations in advertisements in decisions that followed *Bates*. Although lawyer advertising is allowed, the bar can still restrict certain types or methods of advertising, including prohibiting the use of celebrity endorsements or testimonials. All jurisdictions can require that advertisements be kept for a certain number of years, and can prescribe the manner in which lawyers advertise themselves to be specialists. While a lawyer is allowed to pay for lawful advertisements, the rules prohibit a lawyer from paying someone to recommend the lawyer's services. Such referral, or finder's, fees are allowed when the referral service is a not-for-profit service or legal aid society.

Although radio and televised advertisements are allowed, restrictions on such advertising can include prohibiting dramatizations or music. Some jurisdictions allow the use of pre-recorded telephone advertisements, unless the sending lawyer knows that the recipient does not want such phone calls. The newest form of lawyer advertising is Internet advertising. Most jurisdictions allow lawyers to advertise on the Internet, including maintaining a law firm Web site, but the rules on record keeping still apply.

The Model Code originally required that advertising be dignified, but eventually that requirement was removed. The Model Rules has no rule regarding dignified ads. Although this is an amorphous concept to enforce, some jurisdictions still maintain the dignified presentation requirement. But former Supreme Court justices and American Bar Association presidents have decried the degrading manner in which lawyers seek business.

When communicating to prospective clients, legal assistants need to be careful not to make false or misleading statements about their firm's services because, as agents for the firm, they can implicate their supervising lawyers in violation of the communication and advertising rules. Many jurisdictions allow paralegals to have their own business cards, and to be listed on firm letterhead. Paralegals who are self-employed as independent contractors can advertise in order to get business, but only to lawyers or law firms. A paralegal who advertises to the general public will be engaging in the unauthorized practice of law.

Solicitation is a different activity than advertising because solicitation is targeted towards individuals or specific groups. As opposed to advertising, solicitation is considered a suspect activity because of its susceptibility to abuse, and is only allowed under certain conditions. But, some legal scholars argue that the restrictions on solicitation are too severe and prevent the public from learning more information about their legal options. Both the Model Rules and Model Code prohibit face-to-face solicitation of prospective clients with whom the lawyer has no prior relationship and when financial gain is the primary reason for the solicitation. The Supreme Court affirmed the right of a state to prohibit in-person solicitation in *Ohralik v. Ohio State Bar Association*, finding that the potential for coercion and other forms of abuse allow for such a strict restriction.

Solicitation other than in-person solicitation, such as written solicitation, is also highly regulated, but not as strictly as the former. In a few Supreme Court cases, the Court ruled that states could not institute outright bans on mailed solicitations when those solicitations are truthful, but in *Florida Bar v. Went For It, Inc.,* the Supreme Court upheld the right of states to institute time restraints on the mailing of written solicitations. Telephone and Internet solicitation are also restricted, with some jurisdictions prohibiting lawyers from using Internet chat rooms for solicitation purposes.

Certain kinds of solicitation are allowed, however. Lawyers can solicit their relatives, and their present and former clients. The Model Code's solicitation rule also allows lawyers to solicit their friends. Lawyers can also solicit prospective clients in order to find members for a class action suit. Another exception to the anti-solicitation rules is not-for-profit solicitation, such as solicitation made in order to help prospective clients assert political, or other constitutional, rights.

Paralegals need to know the specific solicitation rules governing the jurisdiction where they work, since the solicitation rules vary from jurisdiction to jurisdiction. Beyond the need to protect the firm against unintended solicitation violations, paralegals also need to protect against engaging in the kind of unlawful solicitation known as accident running. Although paralegals could not be sanctioned by the bar for engaging in unlawful solicitation or for taking inappropriate fees for finding clients, such behavior reflects poorly on the paralegal profession.

The Ethics 2000 Commission made some changes to the Model Rules' advertising rules, all of which were accepted by the ABA House of Delegates. Some of the changes include dropping the part of the rule that requires lawyers to keep copies of their advertisements for stated periods of time, as well as expressly allowing the use of e-mail advertisements. The solicitation rules have been updated to include real-time electronic contact as impermissible solicitation, and they also, in a fashion similar to the Model Code, allow a lawyer to solicit those with whom the lawyer has a close, personal relationship. The specialization rules have been tightened to prohibit a lawyer from advertising a legal certification that does not come from an ABA- or state-approved certifying organization.

Points to Ponder

1. Why did lawyers originally refrain from advertising?
2. On what basis did the American Bar Association begin to prohibit lawyer advertising?
3. Advertising is considered commercial speech and, as such, is relatively easy to regulate. Why?
4. On what basis did the Supreme Court decide in *Bates* that the bar could not prohibit lawyer advertising?
5. How do the ABA rules on communication of a lawyer's services differ (slightly) from the rules on advertising?
6. What kinds of statements about the lawyer's services are prohibited?
7. What three kinds of information fall under those prohibitions?
8. When could a lawyer or his or her legal assistant make a comparative statement about another lawyer's services?
9. Does your jurisdiction's communication or advertising rules prohibit other categories of statements not mentioned in the ABA's rules?
10. What is the difference between lawfully paying for advertisements and unlawfully paying someone to refer clients to the firm?
11. Does your jurisdiction have any particular restrictions on the use of radio or television advertisements?
12. Does your jurisdiction have any rules that apply to Internet advertising?
13. Do you think lawyer advertising should be dignified? What would make an advertisement undignified?
14. Regardless of whether it is specifically allowed, why could it be said there is nothing wrong with a law firm letterhead that lists legal assistants or business cards that list legal assistants?
15. Does your jurisdiction have a legal assistant rule or guideline that allows legal assistants to be listed on letterheads or have their own business cards?
16. Can an independent contracting paralegal advertise?
17. How is solicitation distinguished from advertising?
18. Why is solicitation more strictly regulated than advertising?
19. What kind of solicitation is the most restricted?
20. What kind of solicitation is the least restricted?
21. Do you think the rules on solicitation are too severe? Why or why not?

22. Does your jurisdiction have any limitations on authorized solicitation, such as instituting a blackout period for solicitation following accidents or disasters?
23. What is the difference between telephone advertising and telephone solicitation?
24. What kind of activity on the Internet is generally considered to be impermissible solicitation?
25. Under what circumstances is solicitation not restricted?
26. What kinds of solicitation could qualify as not-for-profit solicitation?
27. Why is it critical that paralegals know their jurisdiction's solicitation rules?
28. Why is accident running considered to be so sleazy? Is it really as bad is the press makes it out to be?
29. Are there any rules of thumb a legal assistant should keep in mind that can help prevent the legal assistant from engaging in impermissible solicitation?
30. What noticeable changes did the Ethics 2000 Commission make to the ABA Model Rules on advertising and solicitation?

Key Concepts

Accident runner	Material misrepresentation
Advertising	Not-for-profit solicitation
Commercial speech	Referral service
Finder's fee	Solicitation
Inappropriate implications	Third-party advertising Web sites
Internet advertising	Unjustified expectations
Internet solicitation	Written solicitation

Key Terms

accident runners	foreclosure	pecuniary
admiralty	injunction	plea bargaining
circulars	inter alia	puffing
class action	libelous	warranty
commercial speech	patent	

Chapter 7

Fees and Fee Sharing

A lawyer's opinion is worth nothing unless paid for.

—**English proverb**

A lawyer with his briefcase can steal more than a hundred men with guns.

—**Don Corleone, in** *The Godfather,* **by Mario Puzo**

INTRODUCTION

As the cliché says, you get what you pay for. And when many clients pay for legal services, they get heartburn. Lawyers are not cheap unless they are free, in which case the client is most likely an indigent person accused of a crime. But why should lawyers be cheap? They go to college with one goal in mind: to get good enough grades to get into law school. Successful applicants then go to law school, which can be both extremely expensive and arduous. After a few years of the terror and tedium of law school, the graduates spend more money applying and studying to pass the bar exam, which is also both expensive and arduous. Failure means they must try again or seek other employment. Already having given up at least seven of their income-producing years, new attorneys seek their way in an ever more crowded and specialized field. And with experience and success come the fruits of their labors: wealth. That is the American way. At least those lawyers wise enough to hire and use legal assistants can earn more income while their clients receive less heartburn.

This chapter will examine the rules governing legal fees. Included in this chapter will be a discussion of the types of legal fees and the principles that help determine whether a legal fee is reasonable, as well as the distinction between fees and expenses. Also, ethics considerations concerning fees and the legal assistant will be discussed, including the rules that prohibit the splitting of legal fees between lawyers and legal assistants. Finally, there will be an examination of the rules and case law that allow legal assistant fees to be recovered from the opposing party in jurisdictions where the law already authorizes the recovery of lawyers' fees.

TYPES OF LEGAL FEES

Despite what people may garner from lawyer jokes, the principal options for paying a legal bill are not the client's future inheritance, firstborn, or soul. The common methods for paying for legal services are the hourly rate, the contingent fee, and the fixed fee.

Hourly Rate

Lawyers often bill their clients based on an hourly rate, which is then measured for billing purposes in fractions, such as one-tenth or one-sixth of an hour. Hourly rates can fluctuate drastically, with variables ranging from the experience and reputation of the lawyer to the type of practice and the lawyer's location, since lawyers in larger metropolitan areas generally charge more than their counterparts in smaller cities. For instance, it was reported that some of lawyers who represented President Bill Clinton in the 1998 **impeachment** proceedings charged $600 an hour. According to the 2001 Survey of Law Firm Economics (surveying 399 U.S. law firms), conducted by the law firm-consulting group Altman Weil, Inc., the average hourly rate for an **equity partner**/shareholder is $246; the average hourly rate for a **non-equity partner** is $219; and the average hourly rate for an associate lawyer is $164. And according to the same survey, the average hourly rate for a paralegal supervisor is $104; the average hourly rate for a senior paralegal is $88; and the average hourly rate for a legal assistant is $83.

It is easy an easy claim, and one often made, that lawyers charge too much. But no one is forced to hire any particular lawyer, and regardless of a lawyer's hourly rate, lawyers earn less than their stated rate because the overhead expenses of running a law firm (from the office rent to the coffee filters) are paid from their hourly rate. One method gaining in popularity for defraying the out-of-pocket costs incurred in hiring a lawyer is the use of prepaid legal insurance. Prepaid legal insurance operates similarly to other forms of insurance: the consumer pays a premium, sometimes called a membership fee, and is then entitled to either fully covered or discounted legal services in certain specified instances. Although prepaid legal services cannot cover a defendant accused of murder, more standardized legal needs, such as wills or real estate matters, are provided by lawyers within the legal service providers network. The ABA promotes the use of prepaid legal insurance plans through its American Prepaid Legal Services Institute, which provides consumers with information on those organizations or companies that offer group or prepaid legal services plans.

Contingent Fee

A **contingent fee**, also called a contingency fee, is a method of payment in which the lawyer's fee is dependent upon a recovery for the client and is a percentage of the client's recovery. The United States Supreme Court first recognized the legiti-

impeachment—The constitutionally authorized act of formally accusing a high government official of what the Constitution calls "high crimes and misdemeanors." Following impeachment, there is an impeachment trial for the accused, whose conviction results in removal from office.

equity partner—A partner in a law firm who is a shareholder, having voting rights.

non-equity partner—A partner in a law firm who receives a partnership share, but has no voting rights.

contingent fee—A fee paid to a lawyer that is only paid if the lawyer succeeds in recovering a settlement or judgment for the client. The contingent fee is a percentage of what the client obtains.

macy of the contingent fee contract in 1853, in *Wylie v. Coxe,* 56 U.S. 415, a case in which a plaintiff's attorney was to be paid 5 percent of whatever was recovered for the plaintiff in a claim against a foreign government. Usually, the lawyer's percentage of the client's recovery increases as the lawyer's efforts to obtain success increase. For instance, contingent fee percentages can range from 20 to 25 percent if the case settles to 30 to 35 percent if the case is won at trial and 40 to 45 percent if the judgment is successfully kept on appeal. Lawyers can also arrange to charge an hourly or flat fee, which is then translated into a contingent fee if they succeed in recovering a settlement or judgment. Lawyers who charge a contingent fee obviously have a financial stake in the outcome of the case, but a contingent fee is an American exception to laws against champerty. (Contingent fees are still prohibited in Great Britain and Canada because of their laws against champerty and barratry.)

Although the contingent fee is most often associated with the personal injury cases, it can be used in a variety of cases, including civil rights actions and real estate tax appeals. In order for a contingent fee to be legitimate, the outcome must be unknown. For instance, a lawyer could not charge a contingency fee for drafting someone's will and take 30 percent of whatever the testator's property he or she successfully brings under the will, since the property was already the client's. And although plaintiffs' lawyers most often use contingent fee arrangements, defense attorneys can use them as well. Such an arrangement, called a **reverse contingent fee**, involves the lawyer being paid a percentage of what he or she saves the client from losing.

The contingent fee has been historically promoted as a means to provide a low-income person access to justice, since the cash-poor client owes the lawyer no fee unless he or she succeeds. Three problems are associated with that premise. First, it may be inaccurate (see the section, "Fees in Excess of Statutory Allowances"). Second, some clients would prefer to pay a fixed fee rather than a contingent fee. Although the lawyer is obligated to offer the client reasonable alternatives to a contingency fee, some critics argue that the contingent fee is being overused. In his book *Litigation Explosion* (Truman Talley Books–Dutton, 1991), Walter K. Olson discusses contingent fees and states that a Federal Trade Commission report found that 97 percent of personal injury lawyers took cases only on a contingent basis, refusing to be paid on an hourly basis (Olson, 47). Third, regardless of the wealth or lack thereof of the client, contingent fees can be enormous, resulting in claims that lawyers are siphoning from the public welfare. For instance, the United States Chamber of Commerce was so irritated by the $11 billion in legal fees awarded to the plaintiffs' attorneys as a result of the 1998 class-action settlement involving twenty-one states and the tobacco industry that it called on the U.S. Congress to investigate the fees award. And *Time* magazine published a cover story in July 2000 on class actions and legal fees that asked the question, "Are lawyers running America?"

Fixed Fee

A **fixed fee**, also called a flat fee, involves the lawyer charging a predetermined amount for the legal services the client desires. The ABA has defined a fixed

reverse contingent fee—A type of contingent fee arrangement that involves the lawyer being paid a percentage of what the lawyer saves the client from losing, as opposed to a percentage of what the lawyer obtains for the client.

fixed fee—A predetermined fee that covers all of the lawyer's efforts in services rendered for a particular client matter. A fixed fee is distinguished from an hourly rate.

fee as a fee that "embraces all work to be done, whether it be relatively simple and of short duration, or complex and protracted." ABA Commission on Ethics and Professional Responsibility, Informal Op. 1389 (1977). Fixed fees can be commonplace for fairly routine and standardized legal services, such as drafting a simple will or a real estate document, representing a party in an uncontested divorce, or representing a debtor in a straight-forward, Chapter 7 bankruptcy petition. Fixed fees are thought of as being more consumer-friendly, since the client knows at the time of hiring the lawyer how much he or she is going to cost. And since the process of finding a lawyer is a consumer activity, the use of fixed fees for certain services allows the consumer to comparison shop.

THE RULES ON LEGAL FEES

There are at least three sources of rules that concern the lawyer's relationship to the client's money. First, there are the rules that directly concern legal fees, which are found in ABA Model Rule 1.5 and ABA Model Code DR 2–106. There are also rules concerning the safekeeping of the client's property, which includes the client's money, which are found in MR 1.15, and DR 9–102. And there are rules concerning the lawyer's duty to return the client's property, including unearned fees, when the lawyer and client relationship is terminated, which are found in MR 1.16 and DR 2–109.

A Lawyer's Fee Shall Be Reasonable

ABA MR 1.5(a) states, "A lawyer's fee shall be reasonable." ABA DR 2–106(A) states that a lawyer "shall not enter into an agreement for, charge, or collect an illegal or clearly excessive fee." DR 2–106(B) also states, "A fee is excessive when, after a review of the facts, a lawyer of ordinary prudence would be left with a definite and firm conviction that the fee is in excess of a reasonable fee." There is a difference, some scholars argue, between the Model Rules' emphasis on reasonableness and the Model Code's emphasis on excessiveness.

Nothing in the Model Rules or Model Code explicitly defines an unreasonable or clearly excessive fee, a fact that has caused some consternation from those who wish there were more specific guidelines on fees. Both versions, however, provide a nonexclusive list of factors to be taken into consideration when determining whether a fee is reasonable or excessive. Some of those factors include the following: the time and labor involved; the level of skill required to perform the services; the chance that other legal employment will be precluded by taking the client's case; the nature and length of the professional relationship with the client; the fee customarily charged in the locality for similar legal services; the experience and reputation of the lawyer performing the services; and whether the fee is fixed or contingent. MR 1.5(a); DR 2–106(B).

Certain Activities Are Nonbillable

Not everything lawyers or their non-lawyer employees do can be billed. Some activities are considered non-billable, which makes the act of billing the client, not the size of the bill, unreasonable. That means if a lawyer bills 40 hours a week, he or she must work anywhere from 5 to 15 percent more than 40 hours a week in order to account for activities that are not billable. And the same goes for the paralegal whose time is billable. Although it might seem too obvious for mention, courts have still needed to state that a lawyer may not bill a client for the time it takes him or her to respond to ethics charges made by that client. *In re Lawyers Responsibility Board Panel No. 94–17*, 546 N.W.2d 744 (Minn. 1996). And although proofreading one's work is a necessary activity, a court refused to honor a bill that included the time a lawyer spent proofreading an internal memorandum. *Wright v. U-Let-Us Skycap Services, Inc.*, 648 F.Supp. 1216 (D. Colo. 1986).

Generally, overhead costs are not billable to the client because they are recouped through the lawyer's fee. *See* ABA Commission on Ethics and Professional Responsibility, Formal Op. 93–379 (1993). Connecticut issued an ethics opinion that considered it inappropriate for a law firm to add to its clients' bills a flat "administrative expense" that covered expenses such as long-distance phone calls, photocopying, and postage. Connecticut State Bar Association Commission on Professional Ethics, Op. 94–24 (1994). Courts have also found that the typical office housekeeping activities associated with litigation may not be billed separately to the client. In a federal case where the plaintiff's attorney fees were recoverable under a federal statute, the court refused to award fees for over 102 hours claimed by the plaintiff's attorneys, paralegals, and secretaries for such things as copying and distributing memos, tagging exhibits, reviewing and organizing files, and reproducing documents. The court declared such clerical activity to be the kind of housekeeping expenses that the firm's hourly rate was meant to cover. *Keith v. Volpe*, 644 F. Supp. 1317 (C.D. Cal. 1986).

Fees in Excess of Statutory Allowances

Although the ethics rules place no limit on the percentage of a contingent fee, some statutes put limits on certain kinds of contingent fees. For instance, the Federal Torts Claim Act puts a cap on contingency fees at 25 percent and provides for fines and imprisonment for lawyers who violate the contingency fee limit. 28 U.S.C. § 2678. New York has a contingency fee cap for medical, dental, and podiatric malpractice cases. As the recovery increases, the contingency percentage decreases, capping out at 10 percent of any amount over $1,250,000 of the sum recovered. N.Y. Jud. Law § 474–a(2). Florida has a similar sliding scale for contingency fees in personal injury actions, but it is made part of the state's professional responsibility rule on legal fees. Fla. State Bar Rule 4–1.5(f)(4). And California has a cap on contingency fees for medical malpractice cases, which ranges from 40 percent on the first $50,000 recovered, and de-escalates to 15 percent on any recovery over $600,000. Cal. Bus. and Prof. Code § 6146.

When lawyers charge fees in violation of authorized caps, courts will not only reject the petitioned fees but may also issue sanctions for violating the limitations.

For instance, in a West Virginia case, a lawyer who represented worker's compensation claimants violated the state statute that capped attorneys' fees in permanent disability claims at 20 percent of the benefits to be received, instead charging some clients upward of 40 percent. During the disciplinary proceeding, the lawyer claimed that the clients had waived their rights to hold the lawyer within the statutory limits. However, the court decided that such a waiver may not be made under the statute's clear language. It suspended the lawyer for ninety-one days and required him to pay restitution to his clients. *Committee on Legal Ethics of West Virginia State Bar v. Burdette*, 445 S.E.2d 733 (W. Va. 1994).

Can a Fee Be Unreasonable Because It Is Too High?

One of the many ingenious aspects of a free-market economy is that the prices of goods and services are what they should be because the law of supply and demand sets the price. A car, whether a Saturn or a BMW, costs what it should—whatever the marketplace will bear. Absent fraud, no one purchasing a car would likely then sue the dealer by claiming the price was too high, since he or she agreed to the price in the first place. Such is not the case with purchasing legal services because legal fees can be too high, despite the client's original agreement to pay the fee. Because the lawyer-client relationship imposes fiduciary obligations on the lawyer, charging the client a fee is an act that is different than other commercial endeavors, such as selling someone a car. Even where there is a written fee agreement, courts always retain the power to review a legal fee for reasonableness. In a case that serves as a reminder why the public likes car dealers more than it likes lawyers, a lawyer represented a client in a personal injury action, resulting in a settlement of $1,000. After the case was settled, the client got to keep only $45. Once the matter came to the attention of the court, the lawyer argued that the fee agreement and the final bill were detailed in writing to the client and the client agreed to the charges. Nevertheless, the court found that the attorney had taken advantage of a client "with very limited understanding," and the lawyer was disbarred. *State ex rel. Oklahoma Bar Ass'n v. Hatcher*, 452 P.2d 150 (Okla. 1969).

A lawyer's fee can also be considered unreasonable or excessive when it was not earned. Where the lawyer does very little work to earn a sizable fee, the fact that the client agreed to the fee is secondary to the question of whether the fee should have been reduced. For example, in an Illinois case, an elderly woman in the hospital, who believed that some of her financial assets, such as **certificates of deposits (CDs)**, had been stolen, contacted a lawyer for help. The lawyer told her he would charge her $175 an hour, or a contingency fee of one-third of whatever he recovered for her. She opted for the contingency fee. The lawyer's work involved him discovering that her 23 CDs were safe and sound at the various banks where she had purchased them, a fact that the woman had, in the interim, discovered on her own. Then the lawyer registered the CDs in the name of a trust he created for the client and charged her a fee of $160,000, amounting to one-third of the value of her CDs. Not only did the court find that the lawyer wrongly used a contingency fee since he actually "recovered" nothing for the client, it also found that the fee was excessive in light of the minimal work required to do what the client needed. *In re*

certificates of deposit (CDs)—A type of conservative investment wherein someone gives money to a bank or other financial institution in exchange for promissory notes from the institutions detailing the interest to be paid on the money and the date on which the principal and interest will be paid to the investor.

Gerard, 548 N.E.2d 1051 (Ill. 1989). (And because the attorney, a Mr. Gerard, was also licensed in Indiana, Missouri, and Wisconsin, those jurisdictions, likewise, suspended him.)

Fees can also be considered unreasonable when a lawyer is inefficient. Because the rules require lawyers to act competently (MR 1.1; DR 6–101(A)), a lawyer who is inexperienced should not charge the client for the time it takes him or her to become competent to handle the client's case. *In re Estate of Larson*, 694 P.2d 1051 (Wash. 1985). And when a lawyer, charging an hourly rate, works really slowly, especially intentionally so, a court can order him or her to reduce or return the fee. For instance, a lawyer was disciplined for billing a client for, among other things, the six hours it took him to drive to a law library, when there was one fifteen minutes away from the lawyer. *In the Matter of Comstock*, 664 N.E.2d 1165 (Ind. 1996).

The ABA has stated that a lawyer may not bill for being "doubly efficient"— billing one client for working on a matter while at the same time billing another client for traveling on a different matter. ABA Commission on Ethics and Professional Responsibility, Formal Op. 94–389 (1994). **Double billing** (billing two clients at the same time) is different from **bill padding** (inflating one's billable hours for a particular client), but both are deceitful practices.

A lawyer may also not bill the client at the lawyer's hourly rate for work that he or she did that could have been done by the legal assistant or other support staff and then would have been billed at their lower, hourly rate. *Davis v. City and County of San Francisco*, 976 F.2d 1536 (9th Cir. 1992). To have qualified paralegals requires that they be used cost-effectively for clients.

double billing—A dishonest billing practice that involves one billing two clients at the same time.

bill padding—A dishonest billing practice that involves one exaggerating the time spent working on a client's case.

Legal Fees Need to Be Clearly Explained to the Client

ABA MR 1.5(b) provides: "When the lawyer has not regularly represented the client, the basis or rate of the fee shall be communicated to the client, preferably in writing, before or within a reasonable time after commencing the representation."

The ABA Model Code had no similar rule, but an Ethical Consideration did state that it is "usually beneficial to reduce to writing the understanding of the parties regarding the fee, particularly when it is contingent." EC 2–19. The Comments to MR 1.5 declare that a lawyer does not have to set forth all the factors that contribute to the fee; rather, stating whether the rate is an hourly charge, a fixed fee, or an estimated fee is sufficient. Confusion can occur due to the lawyer's inadequate explanation of the fee or the client's failure to understand the arrangement, the latter case still being the lawyer's responsibility. Although neither the Model Rules nor the Model Code requires written fee arrangements for all representation, such is not the case in Ethics 2000's proposal for MR 1.5(b). (See the section "Ethics 2000 and Fees.") Three areas of fees explanation will be discussed: the explanation the initial client should receive, the difference between fees and costs, and the difference between an advance and a retainer.

Explanation for the New Client

The first Comment to Model Rule 1.5 provides that when the lawyer is hired by a new client, "an understanding as to the fee should be promptly established." Again, such a maxim falls short of requiring that a written fee agreement be established for the new client, but there is a greater emphasis on the lawyer's responsibility to attend to the understanding of the new client. The rules are more relaxed when it comes to a client with whom the lawyer has a continuing professional relationship. However, the new client might have never before retained any lawyer—not just the lawyer about to be retained—and have no idea how the overall legal fee system works. Here, a careful initial interview of the prospective client, by the lawyer or the lawyer's paralegal, can alert the lawyer to the need to clearly explain the fee agreement. A few jurisdictions have altered the "preferably in writing" language from MR 1.5(b) and require that the fee agreement be put in writing if the lawyer has not regularly represented the client. *See* Conn. R.P.C. 1.5(b); D.C. R.P.C. 1.5(b); N.J. R.P.C. 1.5(b); Pa. R.P.C. 1.5(b). The ABA has, on a few occasions, issued ethics opinions that concern the need of the lawyer to fully explain the fee arrangement with a prospective client. *See* ABA Commission on Ethics and Professional Responsibility, Formal Op. 94–389 (1994); Formal Op. 93–379 (1993); Informal Op. 86–1521 (1986).

What Should Be in the Fee Agreement for the New Client?   The fee agreement should explain what the lawyer was hired to do and the extent of his or her services to the client. It should explain how the lawyer's fee is going to be calculated, including how any legal assistant time will be billed to the client; how certain items, such as travel time and expenses, will be billed; how often the client is going to be billed; and how the client is to pay the lawyer. Concerning methods of payment, the American Bar Association issued an ethics opinion in 2000 that approved of lawyers accepting credit card payments as a method for clients to pay their legal bills. ABA Commission on Ethics and Professional Responsibility, Formal Op. 00–419 (2000). That opinion invalidated prior opinions from the 1960s and 1970s that had opposed credit card payments for legal fees. Not all jurisdictions allow lawyers to accept credit card payments from clients, and some put limitations on their use. A majority decision by Texas's Committee on Professional Ethics, for instance, allowed lawyers to accept credit card payments, although the committee acknowledged the minority's dissent. But the committee unanimously opposed the advertisement of credit card emblems or decals in law offices, believing that such use would constitute unlawful solicitation. Texas State Bar Association Committee on Professional Ethics, Op. 349 (1969). Montana allows lawyers to accept credit card payments in all but bankruptcy cases. State Bar of Montana Ethics Committee, Op. 000003 (2000).

If there is a contingent fee arrangement, the agreement should cover how the lawyer's percentage will be calculated, including whether the contingent fee will be taken from the recovery before or after litigation expenses have been paid. And regardless of the type of fee arrangement, the agreement should also clearly provide procedures concerning how any future fee dispute will be handled, such as whether the agreement calls for mediation or arbitration mechanisms.

The Difference between Fees and Costs

"If you don't recover, we don't take a fee." How many times has that, or another, similar, phrase been stated on radio or television or put in print? More important, how many members of the public understand the meaning of such phrases? Part of the lawyer's duty in explaining the fee arrangements is to distinguish fees from costs for the client. Generally, fees are what the lawyer charges for his or her professional effort, be it hourly or contingent fees. Costs are different. Costs are general expenses, such as court filing fees or litigation expenses, including discovery costs. (Costs, however, are different than administrative overhead expenses, discussed in the section "Certain Activities Are Non-Billable.") That means that even in a contingent fee arrangement in which the plaintiff ultimately does not recover a judgment, the lawyer might still present a bill for the litigation costs.

When confusion arises over the meaning of the fee arrangements, courts will favor the client rather than the lawyer. For example, an Illinois lawyer billed a client a fixed fee of $10,000 in a divorce representation. A lawsuit ensued over the fee because the lawyer refused to provide an itemized bill to the client. Despite the lawyer's claim that a fixed fee need not be itemized, the court declared that the client is always entitled to an itemized bill, and remanded the case for a determination of whether the fee was reasonable. *In re Marriage of Pitulla*, 491 N.E.2d 90 (Ill. App. Ct. 1986). In a Colorado case, a client hired a lawyer for a matter and agreed to pay a contingent fee under the terms of a written agreement. The terms of the agreement required the client to pay the fee even if he or she fired the lawyer, regardless of success on the merits. During the representation, the lawyer was granted a motion to remove himself from the representation for "an irreconcilable conflict." Then, the lawyer billed the client, who refused to pay. The court found in favor of the client because nothing in the fee agreement mentioned whether the client had any financial responsibility to the lawyer under the facts presented in the case: the lawyer, and not the client, terminated the lawyer-client relationship. The court also rejected the lawyer's request for recovery under the theory of **quantum merit**, resolving the ambiguity in the contract in favor of the client. *Elliott v. Joyce*, 889 P.2d 43 (Colo. 1994).

Clearly Explaining the Legal Assistant's Contribution to the Bill   Generally, clients are not unhappy to pay fees associated with the time billed by the legal assistant because of the legal assistant's lower hourly rate. But part of the fees explanation to the client should include distinguishing the lawyer's billable time from the legal assistant's billable time. A South Carolina ethics opinion states that a lawyer may charge the client separately for the work of a paralegal or a secretary, provided the client agrees in advance to the arrangement and as long as the work performed by the lawyer's staff is not administrative or secretarial. South Carolina Bar Association, Ethics Op. 94–37 (1995).

In an Ohio case, a lawyer contracted with a client for a contingency fee of 33 percent if the case settled, plus "all necessary filing fees, court costs and

quantum merit—A Latin phrase that means "as much as he deserved." Quantum merit is an equitable principle used in contract cases by plaintiffs attempting to recover something for their efforts when courts have already determined that operative legal principles deny the validity of a contract.

other out of pocket expenses incurred in said litigation." The case settled for $30,000. The lawyer took $9,900 as his fee, but also billed the client for $2,982, which consisted of the billable hours of the lawyer's secretary and paralegal. The court ruled that in a contingency fee case, litigation costs do not include the billable hours of the lawyer's employees. *Columbus Bar Association v. Brooks*, 721 N.E.2d 23 (Ohio 1999). More significantly for Ohio lawyers, the court also stated that when a lawyer charges an hourly rate, secretarial costs may not be billed separately because such costs are "overhead" costs, but the court approved of paralegal hours being separately billed if the client agrees to that in writing. *Id.* at 25.

The Difference between an Advance and a Retainer

Lawyers can require that clients pay money up front; the Comments to MR 1.5 acknowledge that. Another reason why the fee agreement should be put in writing is to avoid confusion as to whether the money paid up front to the lawyer is in the form of an **advance** or a retainer. The difference between an advance and a retainer is significant. An advance is a prepayment of legal fees before they have been earned. That makes an advance a payment that is subject to being returned, at least in part, in the event that the lawyer-client relationship terminates before the lawyer's billable time has equaled the advance. Both MR 1.16(d) and DR 2–110(A)(2) and (3) require lawyers to return any unearned portion of an advance payment. If a lawyer fails to return the unearned portion of an advance fee, sanctions can range from suspension to disbarment. See *In re Baltimore*, 522 N.Y.S.2d 563 (N.Y. 1987), in which a lawyer was disbarred for repeated violations involving refusing to return unearned portions of advance fees.

A retainer, sometimes called a general retainer, is a payment made to secure the lawyer's availability, not a prepayment of the lawyer's future services. To put a lawyer "on retainer" is to pay the lawyer for the right to use him or her at a future date or for a future matter or to pay him or her so that another prospective client cannot retain the lawyer's services. (Think of a retainer like a down payment made on a car that the purchaser might never need or drive.) Because of the nature of a retainer, a lawyer actually earns the retainer upon its being paid. This makes the general retainer a nonrefundable payment. *Baranowski v. State Bar*, 593 P.2d 613 (Cal. 1979).

Because nonrefundable retainers are drastic, more and more jurisdictions require such a retainer agreement to be clearly explained to the client, while some jurisdictions are starting to reject them on public policy grounds. Alabama takes the position that lawyers may not call fees nonrefundable nor use any language in the fee agreement that suggests that any fee paid to the lawyer is not subject to an adjustment or refund. Alabama State Bar General Counsel, Op. R 93–21 (1993). Wisconsin, however, allows for the use of nonrefundable retainers. State Bar of Wisconsin Commission on Professional Ethics, Op. E–93–4 (1993).

Whatever form a retainer takes, it is still subject to the general doctrine of reasonableness. In a New York case, a client seeking a divorce signed a writ-

advance—A prepayment for future legal services made to an attorney at the beginning of the representation. As the lawyer works on the case, the advance is being earned.

ten fee agreement with her lawyer that called for the payment of a $15,000 retainer that was "not to be returned to the client, in whole or in part, under any circumstances." When the client reconciled with her husband, the divorce became unnecessary and she sought the return of her money. Despite the clear language in the agreement concerning the nonrefundability of the fee, the court found that the nonrefundable retainer was unconscionable for a variety of reasons. First, the court considered it grossly excessive and shocking of its conscience in light of the fact that the attorney only worked less than five hours for the client before she wanted to drop the divorce proceedings. Second, the court considered the retainer agreement to be in the form of an unreasonable liquidated damages provision. Furthermore, the court found that nonrefundable retainer agreements violate what it called "the universal contract principle which requires the non-breaching party to mitigate its damages." *Joel R. Brandes, P.C. v. Zingmond,* 573 N.Y.S.2d 579 (N.Y. Sup. 1991).

Where Is the Client's Money to Be Kept?

When a client pays a retainer or an advance to a lawyer, the money does not automatically become the property of the lawyer to do with as the lawyer wishes; and ABA MR 1.15 and DR 9-102 concern how the lawyer should keep the client's money. The rules also apply to situations where the lawyer receives funds for the client, such as when an insurance company settles a case with the plaintiff and sends a check to his or her lawyer.

Separate Accounts

The client's money must be kept in an account that is separate from the lawyer's personal bank account. The lawyer may also not use the funds as if they were part of the law firm's cash flow. When the client's money and the lawyer's money are in the same account, such **commingling** of funds violates MR 1.15(a) and DR 9-102(A). Commingling can also lead to a more serious transgression, **conversion**, which involves the lawyer using the client's money as if it were his or her own. In order to avoid such a violation, a law firm needs to establish trust accounts, putting its clients' money in those accounts, and maintain accurate records. Believe it or not, a lawyer who was given over $34,000 of his estate client's money put the money in a box and stuck it under a floorboard in his attic. Later, when asked about the money, the lawyer claimed it was safe and sound in his mother-in-law's safe deposit box, which, if true, would have still been the wrong place to keep the money. *Cuyahoga County Bar Association v. Petrancek,* 669 N.E.2d 828 (Ohio 1996).

In the following case, one of America's most famous lawyers became one of its most infamous lawyers, after being disbarred for mishandling client funds. Pay extra attention to the long and winding fact pattern and the novel arguments F. Lee Bailey made defending himself.

commingling—The unlawful mixing of one person's money with another person's money in the same account.

conversion—A tortuous act that involves one exercising authority over another's property, to the deprivation, and without the permission, of the innocent party.

Case Law

The Florida Bar v. Bailey, 803 So.2d 683 (Fla. 2001)

PER CURIAM.

F. Lee Bailey seeks review of a referee's report finding numerous, serious violations of the Rules Regulating the Florida Bar and recommending permanent disbarment. . . . For the reasons that follow, we approve the referee's findings of guilt and order that F. Lee Bailey be disbarred.

FACTS

The Florida Bar filed a complaint against Bailey alleging seven counts of misconduct in violation of various Rules Regulating the Florida Bar in the course of Bailey's representation of his client, Claude Duboc.[1] After a final hearing was held over a number of days in which witnesses testified and exhibits were introduced into evidence, the referee issued a detailed twenty-four page report containing her findings of fact and conclusions of law. The referee began the report with an overview of the factual setting that provided the framework for further findings as to all counts of charged misconduct:

In 1994, Bailey represented Duboc in a criminal case filed against Duboc by the United States alleging violations of Title 21 of the United States Code, which prohibits drug smuggling. The indictment also included forfeiture claims under Title 18 of the United States Code. Bailey worked out a deal with the United States Attorneys ("U.S. Attorneys") covering Duboc's plea, repatriation of assets, and payment of attorneys' fees. Under the agreement, Duboc would plead guilty and forfeit all of his assets to the United States Government. All of Duboc's cash accounts from around the world would be transferred to an account identified by the U.S. Attorney's Office. To deal with the forfeiture of Duboc's real and personal property, 602,000 shares of Biochem Pharma ("Biochem") stock, valued at $5,891,352.00, would be transferred into Bailey's Swiss account. Bailey would use these funds to market, maintain and liquidate Duboc's French properties and all other assets. In order to put this unusual arrangement in context, we set forth the specific factual findings surrounding this plea agreement and Bailey's role in it:

The ultimate strategy employed by Respondent [Bailey] was that Duboc would plead guilty and forfeit all assets to the United States Government in the hopes of a reduction of sentence based on what [Bailey] described as "extraordinary cooperation." First, Duboc would identify and transfer all cash accounts from around the world into an account identified by the United States Attorney's Office.

The forfeiture of the real and personal properties held in foreign countries presented some nettlesome problems. Duboc owned two large estates in France and valuable car collections, boats, furnishings and art works. Most of these properties were physically located in France. The two estates required substantial infusions of cash for maintenance.

The idea proposed by [Bailey] was to segregate an asset, a particular asset, one that would appreciate in value over time, so that when it came time for Duboc to be sentenced following entry of a plea of guilty, the United States Government would not argue in opposition to a defense claim that part of the appreciation in value was not forfeitable to the United States. Ultimately, the object was to sequester a fund which would not be entirely subject to forfeiture.

The identified asset was 602,000 shares of Biochem Pharma Stock. This would serve as a fund from which [Bailey] could serve as trustee and guardian of Duboc's French properties. Duboc's primary interest was to maximize the amount of forfeitures that would be turned over to the United States. This stock would provide a sufficient fund from which to market, maintain and liquidate the French properties and all other assets. [Bailey] explained that it would be prudent to hold the Biochem stock because the company was conducting promising research on a cure for AIDS, and the loss the government would suffer if large blocks of stock were dumped on the market.

Money was transferred immediately into a covert account identified by the United States Attorney's Office. Duboc provided written instructions to the various financial institutions and the orders were then faxed. On April 26, 1994, the Biochem stock certificates were transferred to [Bailey's] Swiss account at his direction. The Respondent provided the account number. On May 17, 1994, United States District Court Judge Maurice Paul held a pre-plea conference in his chambers. At the conference, the following arrangement as to attorneys' fees, including those for Bailey, was reached: "[T]he remainder value of the stock which was being segregated out would be returned to the court at the end of the day, and from that asset the Judge would be—a motion would be filed for a reasonable attorney's fee for Mr. Bailey." Later in the day on May 17, Duboc pled guilty to two counts in open court and professed his complete cooperation with the U.S. Attorney's Office. . . .

Count I of the Bar's complaint charged Bailey with commingling. Bailey was entrusted with liquidating stock that belonged to Duboc, referred to as "the Japanese Stock." Upon liquidation, Bailey was then to transmit the proceeds to the United States. Bailey sold the Japanese stock and deposited approximately $730,000 into his Credit Suisse account on or about July 6, 1994. Bailey then transferred the money into his Barnett Bank Money Market Account. The money was paid to the United States Marshal on or about August 15, 1994. The referee found that Bailey admitted that his money market account was not a lawyer's trust account, nor did Bailey create or maintain it as a separate account for the sole purpose of maintaining the stock proceeds. In concluding that Bailey had engaged in commingling, the referee rejected Bailey's claims that there were no personal funds in the Barnett Bank account at the time Bailey transferred the funds from the Japanese Stock into this account, and that Bailey's deposit of the proceeds into a non-

trust account was "inadvertent error." The referee concluded that Bailey violated Rule Regulating the Florida Bar 4–1.15(a) by failing to set up a separate account for these funds and also by commingling client funds with his personal funds.

Count II of the Bar's complaint charged Bailey with misappropriating trust funds and commingling. On or about May 9, 1994, the 602,000 shares of Biochem stock were transferred into Bailey's Credit Suisse Investment Account. Bailey sold shares of stock and borrowed against the stock, deriving over $4 million from these activities. Bailey then transferred $3,514,945 of Biochem proceeds from the Credit Suisse account into his Barnett Bank Money Market Account. Bailey had transferred all but $350,000 of these proceeds into his personal checking account by December 1995. From this account, Bailey wrote checks to his private business enterprises totaling $2,297,696 and another $1,277,433 for other personal expenses or purchases. Bailey further paid $138,946 out of his money market account toward the purchase of a residence. The referee rejected Bailey's two defenses to the Bar's charge of misappropriation: (1) he never held the stock in trust for Duboc or the United States; rather, it was transferred to him in fee simple absolute; and (2) this stock was not subject to forfeiture. The referee found Bailey guilty of violating Rules Regulating the Florida Bar 3–4.3 (lawyer shall not commit any act that is contrary to honesty and justice), 4–1.15(a) (commingling funds), 4–8.4(b) (lawyer shall not commit a criminal act that reflects adversely on the lawyer's honesty, trustworthiness, or fitness as a lawyer), 4–8.4(c) (lawyer shall not engage in conduct involving deceit, dishonesty, fraud or misrepresentation), and 5–1.1 (requiring money or other property entrusted to an attorney to be held in trust and applied only for a specific purpose).

Count III charged Bailey with continuing to expend Biochem funds in contravention of two federal court orders. In January 1996, Judge Paul issued two orders regarding the Duboc criminal case; one on the 12th and the other on the 25th. The January 12 order relieved Bailey as Duboc's counsel, substituting the

Coudert Brothers law firm. The order further required Bailey to give within 10 days "a full accounting of the monies and properties held in trust by him for the United States of America." The order froze all of the assets received by Bailey from Duboc and further prohibited their disbursement. The January 25 order directed Bailey to bring to a February 1, 1996, hearing all of the shares of Biochem stock that Duboc had turned over to Bailey. The referee found that Bailey continued to use the Biochem proceeds that he held in trust after service and knowledge of the January 12 and January 25, 1996, orders. . . .

The referee found Bailey guilty of violating Rules Regulating the Florida Bar 3–4.3 (lawyer shall not commit an act that is contrary to honesty and justice), rule 4–8.4(b) (lawyer shall not commit a criminal act that reflects adversely on the lawyer's honesty, trustworthiness, or fitness as a lawyer), rule 4-8.4(c) (lawyer shall not engage in conduct involving deceit, dishonesty, fraud or misrepresentation). . . .

Count IV of the Bar's complaint charged Bailey with giving false testimony. The referee found that Bailey testified falsely before Judge Paul and the U.S. Attorneys that he did not see the January 12 or January 25 orders until the morning of a civil contempt hearing held on February 2, 1996. The referee further found that Bailey was not being truthful when: (1) in his answer to the Bar's complaint, Bailey denied that he had received the orders and that he had testified falsely before Judge Paul; and (2) Bailey testified before the referee at the final hearing.

Specifically, the referee found numerous reasons why this testimony was false. First, Bailey had a conversation with the Assistant U.S. Attorney about the terms of the January 12 order following its entry. Indeed, on January 19, when Bailey met with the Assistant U.S. Attorneys, he accused them of obtaining the order from the judge ex parte. In addition, when Bailey returned to his Palm Beach office on January 18, he marshaled documents in support of the accounting that the January 12 order required him to provide. In the letter to Judge Paul dated January 21, 1996, Bailey "plainly concedes that he knew of the terms of the order as early as January 16, 1996." In that letter, he referred to the manner, mode and method by which Judge Paul entered the order. He complained in the letter that "Your Honor was persuaded to act on representations which are *at a minimum* subject to sharp challenge." As the referee notes, "these assertions could not have been made *unless* [Bailey] had seen the January 12 order." Further, as to the January 25, 1996, order, it was served upon Bailey by "fax transmission, United States mail, and personally by the U.S. Marshal's Service pursuant to the very terms of the order." Based on these factual findings, the referee found Bailey guilty of violating Rules Regulating the Florida Bar 3–4.3, 4–8.4(b), 4–8.4(c), and 4–3.3(a)(1) (lawyer shall not knowingly make a false statement of material fact or law to a tribunal).

Count V of the Bar's complaint charged Bailey with self-dealing in the course of his representation of Duboc. [The gist of this complaint was that, since Bailey argued he owned the Biochem stock outright, the more of the gains from the stock he kept, the less his client, Duboc, would be able to turn over to the government in an attempt to reduce his sentence, which obviously created a conflict of interest between Bailey and his client. Also, the referee concluded that Bailey procrastinated in selling one of Duboc's French estates, and that he did so for his own personal benefit. The referee concluded that these acts violated Florida's version of ABA Model Rule 1.7(b), 1.8(a), and 1.8(b).]

Count VII of the Bar's complaint charged Bailey with ex parte communications, self-dealing, and disclosure of confidential information. In connection with this count, the referee found that on May 17, 1994, Duboc appeared before Judge Paul and entered a plea and cooperation agreement. Duboc pled guilty to counts II and III of the indictment. The referee found that the only way Duboc would get a reduced sentence was if Judge Paul was convinced that Duboc had completely and totally cooperated and had forfeited all of his assets to the United States. On January 4, 1996, Bailey wrote a letter to Judge Paul stating, "*I have sent no copies of this letter to anyone,* since I believe its distribution is within Your Honor's sound discretion."

(Emphasis added.) This letter contains an express admission that it was ex parte. In this ex parte letter to Judge Paul, Bailey stated that: (1) Duboc pled guilty because he had no defense due to the strength of the case, (2) Duboc chose this course because it was his only option, not in a spirit of remorse or cooperation, (3) Duboc was a "multimillionaire druggie," (4) by consulting with other counsel, Duboc was no longer acting in the spirit of cooperation, and (5) Duboc's new defense team had interests contrary to those of his client and the court. Bailey sent a second letter to Judge Paul on January 21, 1996, a copy of which was sent to the U.S. Attorney's Office, threatening to seek an order to invade the attorney-client privilege in an attempt to defeat Duboc's position that the stock was held in trust.

The referee found that both of Bailey's letters were sent to compromise Duboc before the sentencing judge and to protect Bailey's interest and control of Duboc's and the U.S. Government's money. The referee recommended that Bailey be found guilty of violating Rules Regulating the Florida Bar 4–1.6(a) (lawyer shall not reveal information relating to representation of a client), 4–1.8(a), 4–1.8(b), 4–3.5(a) (lawyer shall not seek to influence a judge), 4–3.5(b) (in an adversary proceeding, lawyer shall not communicate as to the merits of the cause with a judge).

Having made the above findings of fact and recommendations as to guilt, the referee considered the appropriate discipline for Bailey's misconduct: . . .

Prior to considering any aggravating or mitigating factors, the referee stated that "any of the violations of the rules regulating the Florida Bar which have been proven by the Bar as set forth above, would singularly warrant [disbarment]. . . ." The referee then listed the following aggravating factors: dishonest or selfish motive, a pattern of misconduct, multiple offenses, submission of false statements, refusal to acknowledge the wrongful nature of the conduct, and substantial experience in the practice of law. Further, the referee considered that a federal judge recently found Bailey to be in civil contempt in another case. The referee noted that Bailey has two prior disciplinary actions; a censure in Massachusetts

in 1970 and a suspension for one year of the privilege of applying for permission to appear pro hac vice in New Jersey in 1971; however, these incidents were too remote in time to be considered in aggravation. The referee did not find any mitigation.

ANALYSIS

. . . Having reviewed the extensive record before us, we conclude that there is competent substantial evidence to support the referee's findings of fact and conclusions of guilt as to each count of misconduct. Although each of the rule violations is extremely serious, ranging from trust account violations to misappropriation of funds, lying to a federal judge, self-dealing and compromising the position of a client, we focus on Bailey's actions regarding the Biochem stock (count II) because the gist of his defense in this case was that the Bar never established the stock was to be held by Bailey in trust. In connection with this, we also review whether, regardless of Bailey's claim that the stock had been transferred to him in "fee simple," this claimed right to the stock would permit him to act in disregard of the judge's orders (count III).

The Biochem Pharma Stock (Count II)—The most contested issue in this case is whether a trust was created with the transfer of the Biochem stock from Duboc to Bailey. The Bar argued that the plea agreement with the U.S. Government provided that Bailey was to hold the stock in trust for the benefit of the U.S. Government. Bailey would use the stock to maintain and liquidate Duboc's properties. After this was accomplished, the stock or its replacement assets would be forfeited to the United States in order to maximize any benefit to Bailey's client for his cooperation. However, Bailey argued that the stock was transferred to him in fee simple. He agreed that he was required to utilize the Biochem stock to derive the funds necessary to maintain and liquidate the French properties. However, Bailey asserted that after the properties were sold, he was only accountable to the United States for the value of the stock on the date that Duboc transferred it to Bailey's Swiss account (which was approximately $6 million), and not for any appreciation—which, as of January 1996, amounted to over $10 million. In other words, Bailey claims that he was entitled to all of the Biochem stock and proceeds from the sale of the stock, minus the approximate $6 million for which he was accountable to the U.S. Government. As he wrote Judge Paul in his letter of January 21, 1996:

> I viewed [the value of the stock of $5,891,352.00 on May 9, 1994] as an account in which the United States had an interest to this extent: after the payment of costs associated with the case and fees approved by Your Honor, any balance of the $5,891,352.00 remaining would revert to the United States. Because of this view, I did not declare the funds to be income to myself. (Emphasis omitted.)

We conclude that regardless of the manner in which he was to hold the stock, Bailey is guilty of the most serious and basic trust account violations. The stock, by his own admission, was given to Bailey by his client neither as a gift, nor as an earned fee. Rather, the stock was given to Bailey to be used for the benefit of Duboc, and ultimately the U.S. Government. Bailey was required to use the stock to maximize Duboc's forfeitures to the U.S. Government in the hope that Duboc would receive a reduction of sentence for his cooperation. In his January 21, 1996, letter to Judge Paul, even Bailey recognized that the U.S. Government had an interest in the transfer value of the Biochem stock. Nevertheless, from the day it was transferred to him, Bailey treated the money as his own. . . .

A lawyer shall hold in trust, separate from the lawyer's own property, funds and property of clients or third persons that are in a lawyer's possession in connection with a representation. . . . *In no event may the lawyer commingle the client's funds with those of the lawyer or those of the lawyer's law firm. . . .*

Further and importantly, Bailey admits that Judge Paul would approve the amount of Bailey's fee for representing Duboc, and that his fee would be taken from the approximate $6 million value of the Biochem proceeds. Therefore, even if some of the initial $6 million corpus was to be used for payment of an attorneys' fee, Bailey was not entitled to the fee until it was approved by Judge Paul—a fact that Bailey admits in his January 21 letter to Judge Paul, and that he admits in this case. Indeed, in a letter written to his own client, Duboc, before a falling out occurred, Bailey explained that:

> You do not face the dilemma since I will be paid with Chief Judge Paul's approval—only that amount which is commensurate with the result achieved in your case, and the amount of work that went into it. Our interests are therefore in perfect alignment.

. . . Therefore, under Rule Regulating the Florida Bar 5-1.1, Bailey had a duty to safekeep this property and use it only for the aforementioned purposes. The transfer value of this stock or its proceeds could neither be commingled nor could it be withdrawn. The fact that a portion of this fund was to be used for payment of any attorneys' fees only serves to highlight this fact—that the monies were to be held in trust for a specific purpose. . . .

The January 12 and January 25 orders (Count III)—Judge Paul's January 12, 1996, order provides that "[a]ll monies, real and personal property and other assets received by Bailey from or on behalf of Duboc, including the aforementioned Biochem Pharma stock shall be frozen as of the date of this order and no further disbursement of any of these funds shall be made unless authorized by this Court." The January 25 order required Bailey to "bring with him all shares of stock of Biochem Pharma, Inc. held by him, or by others, which represent the stock turned over to him by the Defendant, Claude Duboc, or Duboc's representatives. If the Biochem Pharma, Inc. stock has been replaced by any other form of asset while in the possession of Mr. Bailey, then the replacement stock will be brought to this Court at the time of the above hearing." . . .

Even if Bailey felt that he was entitled to the stock proceeds in his personal account, this does not permit him to act in contravention of two federal court orders. . . . Therefore, we conclude that Bailey violated rules

3–4.3, 4–3.4(c), 4–8.4(a) and 4–8.4(d) by acting in contravention of Judge Paul's orders.

DISCIPLINE

Bailey has committed multiple counts of egregious misconduct, including offering false testimony, engaging in ex parte communications, violating a client's confidences, violating two federal court orders, and trust account violations, including commingling and misappropriation. Disbarment is the presumed discipline for many of these acts of misconduct. For example, as to Bailey's mishandling of the Biochem stock, Standard 4.11 of the Florida Standards for Imposing Lawyer Sanctions provides: "Disbarment is appropriate when a lawyer intentionally or knowingly converts client property regardless of injury or potential injury." As to Bailey's violation of the January 12 and 25 orders, Standard 6.21 provides that "[d]isbarment is appropriate when a lawyer knowingly violates a court order or rule with the intent to obtain a benefit for the lawyer or another, and causes . . . potentially serious interference with a legal proceeding." Regarding Bailey's ex parte communication with Judge Paul, Standard 6.31 provides that "[d]isbarment is appropriate when a lawyer: . . . (b) makes an unauthorized ex parte communication with a judge or juror with intent to affect the outcome of the proceeding."

Case law also supports disbarment for the types of misconduct committed by Bailey. . . . Bailey has committed some of the most egregious rules violations possible, evidencing a complete disregard for the rules governing attorneys. "[M]isuse of client funds is one of the most serious offenses a lawyer can commit. Upon a finding of misuse or misappropriation, there is a presumption that disbarment is the appropriate punishment." [*Florida Bar v.*] *Tillman,* 682 So.2d at 543.

Bailey's false testimony and disregard of Judge Paul's orders demonstrate a disturbing lack of respect for the justice system and how it operates. Bailey's self-dealing and willingness to compromise client confidences are especially disturbing. Not only did Bailey use assets that his client intended to forfeit to the U.S. Government for Bailey's own purposes, but Bailey also attempted to further his own interests by disparaging his client in an ex parte letter to the judge who would sentence his client. Bailey's self-dealing constitutes a complete abdication of his duty of loyalty to his client. His willingness to compromise his client for personal gain shows an open disregard for the relationship that must be maintained between attorney and client: one of trust, and one where both individuals work in the client's best interest. Such misconduct strikes at the very center of the professional ethic of an attorney and cannot be tolerated.

By this disbarment, Bailey's status as a member of The Florida Bar shall be terminated and he may not reapply for readmission for a period of five years, and then he may "only be admitted again upon full compliance with the rules and regulations governing admission to the bar." R. Regulating Fla. Bar 3-5.1(f). This includes retaking the Florida bar examination, complying with the rigorous background and character examination, and demonstrating knowledge of the rules of professional conduct required of all new admittees.[4]

CONCLUSION

Accordingly, F. Lee Bailey is hereby disbarred from the practice of law in the State of Florida. . . .

WELLS, C.J., and SHAW, HARDING, ANSTEAD, PARIENTE, LEWIS, and QUINCE, JJ., concur.

[In March 2002, Mr. Bailey was suspended from the U.S. Supreme Court, and then in April 2002, he was disbarred by the Massachusetts Supreme Judicial Court.]

The following case footnotes correspond to the portions of the case that are printed in the textbook. Although it may seem that other footnotes are missing, they are not presented because their corresponding portions of the court's opinion have been redacted.

[1]Count number six of the Bar's complaint was dismissed and is therefore not discussed further.

[4]Although we regard these rule violations as extremely serious and warranting disbarment, we do not accept the

referee's recommendation of permanent disbarment. Under the rules, the minimum period of disbarment is for five years (and thereafter until the attorney is readmitted to the practice of law). See R. Regulating Fla. Bar 3-5.1(f). In 1998, the Court amended the Rules Regulating the Florida Bar to specifically provide for permanent disbarment. See In re Amendments to Rules Regulating The Florida Bar, 718 So.2d 1179, 1181 (Fla.1998) (amending rule 3-5.1(f) "to authorize permanent disbarment as a disciplinary sanction").

Case Questions

1. Why did Mr. Bailey have possession of his client's stock?
2. How did the court conclude that Mr. Bailey went beyond commingling his client's property to converting his client's property?
3. What exactly was Mr. Bailey's defense to the charge that he misappropriated his client's property?
4. What facts caused the court to also conclude that Mr. Bailey engaged in acts that damaged his client's interests? What were his client's interests?
5. If Mr. Bailey's acts were so egregious (including lying to a federal judge) and there were no mitigating factors, why did the court refuse to uphold the referee's recommendation of permanent disbarment?

There is a wrinkle to the separate accounts situation, which involves retainers. If a retainer is viewed as a payment to secure the lawyer's availability (called a general or non-refundable retainer), then it is earned upon receipt, which would seem to make it the lawyer's money. However, not only are there some jurisdictions that refuse to accept the notion of the nonrefundable retainer, but there are also jurisdictions that state that all advance payments, be they "advances" or "retainers," must be placed in trust accounts. *See Iowa Supreme Court Bd. of Professional Ethics and Conduct v. Apland,* 577 N.W.2d 50 (Iowa 1998).

When the lawyer receives money on behalf of the client, such as a settlement check, the lawyer must notify the client promptly, and deliver the money promptly to the client. MR 1.15(b); DR 9-102(B). This also applies where a third party has an interest in the money, such as a case in which the plaintiff's insurance company has the right to **subrogation** for its costs in covering the plaintiff's medical bills. And if, at the end of the representation, the client disputes the lawyer's fee, MR 1.15(C) and DR 9–102(A) require that the funds that are the subject of the dispute remain in the trust account until the dispute is resolved.

subrogation—When someone who has made a payment on another's behalf has the legal or equitable right to be paid back from the party who was originally liable for the payment. Subrogation often occurs when an insurance company pays its insured party under the terms of the insurance contract, and then is subrogated in the insured party's lawsuit against the defendant.

Interest on Lawyers' Trust Accounts (IOLTA)

When client funds are placed in a bank account, does the client get any interest earned on those deposited funds or does the lawyer get to keep the money for setting up and administering the account? Neither does, because every state and the District of Columbia have in place an Interest on Lawyers' Trust Account (IOLTA) program. Such a program requires that any interest earned on client trust accounts that are nominal or of a short duration be turned over to the state bar association in order to promote charitable services, such as low-cost legal aid offices. Florida created the first IOLTA program in 1981, and the ABA issued an ethics opinion in 1982, finding it permissible for a lawyer to participate in an IOLTA program. ABA Commission on Ethics and Professional Responsibility, Formal Op. 348 (1982). Such programs are possible due to a 1980 change in the federal banking laws that allows banks to pay interest on any demand deposit accounts (sometimes called a **NOW account**). 12 U.S.C. § 1832.

NOW account—Negotiable order of withdrawal account. A NOW account is an account that allows the depositor to withdraw sums of money from the account at will. NOW accounts are also called demand deposit accounts.

States differ on how IOLTA programs are administered. For instance, the Virginia Legal Services Corporation has been administering Virginia's IOLTA program since 1995, using those funds to support its ten local Legal Services organizations, which help provide legal services to the poor. North Carolina's IOLTA program, in operation since 1984, provides grants in four categories: providing civil legal aid to indigents; enhancement and improvement of grievance and disciplinary procedures for lawyers; development and maintenance of a fund for student loans for legal education on the basis of need; and such other programs designed to improve the administration of justice as may be proposed by the IOLTA Board of Trustees and approved by the North Carolina Supreme Court. North Carolina claims that less than 10 percent of the IOLTA funds are used to administer the program, which leaves quite an impressive payout ratio.

Is an IOLTA Program Constitutional?   The United States Supreme Court rendered a controversial decision concerning IOLTA programs in 1998, in *Phillips v. Washington Legal Foundation*, 524 U.S. 156 (1998). In this case, a public interest group, an attorney, and a businessman who regularly used attorneys sued the Texas Supreme Court, arguing that Texas's IOLTA program (under the authority of the Texas Supreme Court) violated the Fifth Amendment's Takings Clause. The plaintiffs' theory was that the interest remitted for IOLTA purposes was client property because it was earned from money that belonged to the client, and therefore, the property could not be taken without "just compensation." The Supreme Court framed the issue on appeal as "whether the interest on an IOLTA account is 'private property' of the client for whom the principal is being held." And in a five-to-four decision written by Chief Justice William Rehnquist, the Court ruled that the interest earned in IOLTA accounts was the private property of the owner of the principal (i.e., the client). However, the Court did not express any opinion on whether IOLTA programs constituted a "taking" under the Fifth Amendment's Takings Clause. The Court then remanded the case back to the lower court to determine whether Texas's IOLTA program constituted a taking, in violation of the Fifth Amendment.

To the dismay of the American Bar Association and the Texas Supreme Court, in October 2001, the Fifth Circuit Court of Appeals reversed the district court and ruled that the Texas IOLTA program violated the Fifth Amendment. *Washington Legal Foundation v. Texas Equal Access to Justice Foundation*, 270 F.3d 180 (Fifth Cir. 2001).

A similar decision was reached in January 2001, when the Ninth Circuit Court of Appeals found that the state of Washington's IOLTA program constituted a taking of private property and remanded the case to the district court in order to determine whether any just compensation was due. *Washington Legal Foundation v. Legal Foundation of Washington*, 236 F.3rd 1097 (9th Cir. 2001). But in November 2001, on appeal from the remand to the District Court, the 9th Circuit Court of Appeals took a different view and ruled that Washington's IOLTA program does not violate the Fifth Amendment. 271 F.3d 835 (9th Cir. 2001).

Then, in June 2002, the U.S. Supreme Court agreed to take the appeal from the Ninth Circuit's most recent decision on IOLTA. 122 S.Ct. 2355 (2002). And on March 26, 2003, the U.S. Supreme Court rendered what seems to be the final word on the constitutionality of IOLTA programs, when it ruled in a 5–4 decision that the interest earned in IOLTA accounts may be used to fund charitable legal services. *Brown v. Legal Foundation of Washington,* No. 01-1325. Essentially, the court ruled that there was no 5th Amedment "takings" problem, concluding that clients suffer no real loss when interest earned in their trust accounts is used to fund legal services programs. Therefore, no "just compensation" was required.

Special Rules Regarding Contingent Fees

Because of the nature of a contingent fee arrangement and its susceptibility to misunderstanding by the client or overreaching by the lawyer, there are a few rules that apply specifically to contingent fees.

Contingent Fees Need to Be in Writing

As stated earlier in the chapter, neither the ABA Model Rules nor the ABA Model Code requires that all fees arrangements be put in writing for the client. However, the ABA Model Rules does require that

> a contingent fee agreement shall be in writing and shall state the method by which the fee is to be determined, including the percentage or percentages that shall accrue to the lawyer in the even of settlement, trial or appeal, litigation expenses to be deducted from the recovery, and whether such expenses are to be deducted before or after the contingent fee is calculated. MR 1.5(c).

This type of language requires not only a declaratory written fee agreement, but also an explanatory written fee agreement. For instance, which is the higher fee: (a) 25 percent of the net recovery at settlement or (b) 20 percent of the gross recovery at settlement? Even though that answer cannot be made unless one knows the settlement amount and the litigation costs, the fact that the Model Rules requires a delineation of how the contingent fee will be determined helps clients—especially new clients—get a better handle on what their lawyers expect to be paid. Notice that MR 1.5(c) does not require the client's signature on the written contingent fee agreement, but simply that contingent fee agreement be in writing. (See the section "Ethics 2000 and Fees," however, for the change proposed by the Ethics 2000 Commission.)

The ABA Model Code, however, does not require contingent fees to be in writing (DR 2–106), although the Ethical Consideration that expressed the preference that fee agreements be in writing particularly mentioned the contingent fee (EC

2–19). Of those states that still follow the Model Code format on legal fees, some states, such as New York, require a written contingency agreement, including requiring the signature of the client and the lawyer on the agreement. N.Y. C.P.R DR 2–106(C). Other states, such as Nebraska, Ohio, and Oregon, do not require written contingent fee agreements. Neb. C.P.R. DR 2–106(C); Oh. C.P.R. DR 2–106(C); Or. C.P.R. DR 2–106(C).

Lawyers in Model Rules jurisdictions are subject to discipline, not only for failing to put a contingent fee agreement in writing, but also for collecting fees that exceed the contingent fee agreement. In an Indiana case, a lawyer contracted with a client to take 33¹/₃ percent of any amount recovered in a personal injury suit against a nursing home. The case was settled for $27,500. The attorney kept $9,516.16 of the settlement, which was $300 more than 33¹/₃ percent. In addition to being sanctioned for taking more than provided in the fee agreement, the lawyer was also sanctioned for violating another aspect of MR 1.5(c), the requirement that at the conclusion of the matter, the lawyer provide the client with a written statement that details how the contingent fee came to be what the lawyer retained. *Matter of Brown*, 669 N.E.2d 989 (Ind. 1996).

Certain Kinds of Cases May Not Be Taken on a Contingent Basis

There are two prohibitions on contingent fees. First, both the Model Rules and the Model Code prohibit contingent fees in criminal cases. MR 1.5(d)(2); DR 2–106(C). Second, the Model Rules prohibits a lawyer from taking a contingent fee in a domestic relations case in which the lawyer's payment "is contingent upon the securing of a divorce or upon the amount of **alimony** or support, or property settlement." MR 1.5(d)(1). The Model Code has no similar prohibition, but it does have an Ethical Consideration that declares, "[c]ontingent fee arrangements in domestic relation cases are rarely justified." EC 2–20. However, some states, such as Iowa, New York, and Oregon, have added the domestic relations contingent-fee prohibition to their versions of the Model Code. Ia. C.P.R. DR 2–106(C); N.Y. C.P.R. DR 2–106(C)(1); Or. C.P.R. DR 2–106(C)(1).

As to the former, a contingent fee arrangement in a criminal case is considered to be an incurable conflict of interest for the lawyer under MR 1.7(b) and DR 5–101(A). Also, MR 1.8(j)(2) provides for an allowance of contingent fees only in civil cases. Because of the high stakes for the defendant accused of a crime, it is believed to be too dangerous a risk that the lawyer's judgment might be affected by having a financial stake in the outcome of a criminal case. As to the latter, domestic relations cases—divorce, property settlement, child support, paternity, and so on—can be highly emotional matters, and courts have taken the view that when a lawyer takes a contingency fee in a divorce case, for instance, such an arrangement goes against **public policy**. Not only does it hinder chances of reconciliation, but as one court put it many years ago:

> The sanctity of the marriage relation, the welfare of children, the good order of society, the regard for virtue, all of which the law seeks to foster and protect are ample reasons why such [a contingent fee] contract should be held to be contrary to public policy. *Opperud v. Bussey*, 46 P.2d 319 (Okla. 1935).

alimony—Payments made by one spouse to another spouse, following a divorce, that are made to support the other spouse. Some states have eliminated alimony as a general requirement in divorce.

public policy—Generalized views about the American culture or ideals upon which specific laws are made.

Some jurisdictions, however, do allow lawyers to take contingency fees in post-divorce actions where an attempt is made to collect property that was supposed to be transferred as part of the property distribution arrangement. *See* Illinois State Bar Association Commission on Professional Ethics, Op. 96–16 (1996); Kansas Bar Association Professional Ethics Commission, Op. 97–4 (1997).

Fee Sharing between Lawyers of Different Firms

While there is no restriction on how lawyers within a firm share their fees, there are restrictions on how lawyers of different firms may share fees. ABA Model Rule 1.5(e) states that lawyers from different firms who are working on the same case may share fees only if:

(1) the division is in proportion to the services performed by each lawyer or, by written agreement with the client, each lawyer assumes joint responsibility for the representation;

(2) the client is advised of and does not object to the participation of all the lawyers involved; and

(3) the total fee is reasonable.

The Model Code also allows for an almost identical type of fee sharing. DR 2–107(A). The key difference between the two versions is that the Model Code requires the shared fee to be proportionate to the work done by each lawyer, while the Model Rules allows for disproportionate sharing, provided that all involved lawyers assume joint responsibility for the work. Both schemes require the client's consent to the fee-sharing arrangement.

PROHIBITION AGAINST FEE SHARING BETWEEN LAWYERS AND NON-LAWYERS

Both the Model Rules and Model Code allow lawyers in different firms to share a fee provided the client consents to the fee sharing, but there is no similar allowance for the sharing of fees between a lawyer and a non-lawyer. In fact, the legal assistant exceptions to the fee-sharing prohibition seem more like exemptions, because they do not allow the sharing of client fees so much as they allow for the sharing of the lawyer's (or law firm's) income.

Why Is Sharing Fees with a Non-Lawyer Prohibited?

One of the strongest arguments in support of the increased use of paralegals is that clients get a smaller bill. Because a paralegal can do many tasks in place of a lawyer and because a paralegal's billing rate is considerably less than an associate's or partner's rate, the client gets high-quality legal services at a cheaper cost. Therefore, assuming that a paralegal, on behalf of the attorney and in support of the client's case, engages in substantive legal work but does not engage in the unauthorized practice of law, what would be wrong with allowing him or her to share in the fee? The answer lies in the title of ABA Model Rule 5.4, "Professional Independence of a Lawyer." MR 5.4(a) states that lawyers and law firms may not share legal fees with a non-lawyer. The Model Code has the same prohibition in DR 3–102(A). The interest promoted by such a prohibition is that the professional judgment of the lawyer—that for which the client is paying—could be at risk if a non-lawyer has direct rights to share in the fee.

Fee Sharing and Independent Contractors

This reasoning behind prohibiting fee sharing between lawyers and their independent contractors has been expressed in a number of national ethics opinions, one of which found that the prohibition protects against the unauthorized practice of law and the chance that the lawyer's independence will be at risk. ABA Commission on Ethics and Professional Responsibility, Formal Op. 86–1519 (1986). *See also* ABA Commission on Ethics and Professional Responsibility, Formal Op. 87–355 (1987). In a New Jersey case, a lawyer made an agreement with an investigator specializing in workers' compensation and personal injury litigation that stated: "I will give you 50 percent of everything you bring in. If you go into business with me, we will draw the same money. I consider us full and equal partners." However, not only did the court refuse to honor the contract, declaring it void as a matter of law because it violated the fee-sharing prohibition, but under the theory of quantum merit, it also refused to award the investigator any award for his efforts. *Infante v. Gottesman*, 558 A.2d 1338 (N.J. Super. 1989). In a Colorado case involving this prohibition, a lawyer representing sexual harassment plaintiffs was disciplined for attempting to make a contingent fee with a private investigator and a counselor working on the case for him. Rather than paying the investigator and the counselor an hourly fee for their services with respect to the sexual harassment cases, the lawyer wanted to pay them a percentage of whatever he recovered. *People v. Easley*, 956 P.2d 1257 (Colo. 1998). And in an Arizona case, a lawyer was disciplined for a fee arrangement he made with a debt collection agency that hired him, which involved him remitting his entire fee to the collection agency, whereupon the agency would pay him his share of the fee. *In re Struthers*, 877 P.2d 789 (Ariz. 1994). This prohibition has been found to apply even where a lawyer shares a fee with a suspended lawyer. *Attorney Grievance Commission of Maryland v. Brennan*, 714 A.2d 157 (Md. 1998).

Fee Sharing and Law Firm Employees

Despite the clear language of MR 5.4(a), lawyers are occasionally disciplined for sharing fees with their non-lawyer employees. Occasionally, these arrangements violate not only the fee-sharing prohibition, but also the prohibition of paying someone a finder's fee. A New Jersey case illustrates this kind of double-sided arrangement. In *Gallagher v. Weiner*, 1993 WL 460101 (U.S. Dist. N.J., 1993), Gallagher was hired as the office manager of Weiner's firm under a contract that called for him to be paid $15,000 of every $250,000 collected by the firm from clients he brought with him. Although the contractual arrangement was clear, the court found it to be unenforceable because it violated a New Jersey law that prohibited fee splitting and finder's fees.

Fee Sharing and Paralegals

How does this apply to the paralegal? If the danger of a lawyer sharing a fee with a non-lawyer is that the lawyer's professional independent judgment of the lawyer could be hindered when a non-lawyer has a financial stake in the case, does that danger apply to the paralegal? Assuming other applicable ethics rules are being followed—unauthorized practice of law, and illegal solicitation, for instance—is the lawyer's professional judgment going to be at risk by rewarding the paralegal directly from the lawyer's fee? Usually, employees have no ability to control the professional actions of their employers. Fascinatingly, the original version of MR 5.4 would have allowed a lawyer to share a legal fee with a non-lawyer if the compensation was reasonable and the non-lawyer used no solicitation in order to receive the compensation. That version, however, never made it out of the ABA House of Delegates. Thus we return back to the original premise: a paralegal may not directly share in the legal fees earned by a lawyer. In an Iowa fee-sharing case, a lawyer retained the services of a paralegal who had been recently released from prison, and the paralegal provided the lawyer with a client still behind bars. Upon taking the case, the lawyer required the client to pay a retainer to the lawyer and a retainer to the paralegal (who then proceeded to do unsupervised legal work for the client). The court found that such an arrangement was a violation of the prohibition of fee sharing and suspended the lawyer indefinitely. And by the time the disciplinary case made its way to the Iowa Supreme Court, the paralegal had made his way back to prison. *Committee on Professional Ethics and Conduct of Iowa State Bar Association v. Lawler,* 342 N.W.2d 486 (Iowa 1984).

Tying a legal assistant's compensation to the number of cases filed is also a violation of the fee-sharing rules. In a Michigan case, a firm that specialized in bankruptcy cases paid a base salary to its legal assistants who conducted initial interviews with prospective clients if the firm filed a minimum of fifteen bankruptcy cases per week. If the firm filed more than fifteen cases per week, those legal assistants would receive more pay, in increments that leveled off at $1,150 per week. Although the firm said that the lawyers and their clients, and not the legal assistants, made the decisions whether to file bankruptcy petitions, the court found that the compensation scheme created a vested financial interest in the legal assistants, which encouraged them to present their consultation information to the lawyers in ways that would promote the filing of bankruptcies. *In re Bass,* 227 B.R. 103 (Bkrtcy. E.D.Mich. 1998).

A variety of ethics opinions share the view that the compensation of legal assistants may not be directly tied to their work product. Maryland held that a lawyer may not pay non-lawyer employees compensation based on a percentage of the client's total recovery. Maryland State Bar Association Commission on Ethics, Op. 94–103 (1984). Ohio declared that a law firm may not pay non-lawyer employees compensation calculated as a percentage of their billable hours for work performed on behalf of a client. Ohio State Bar Association Ethics Op. 97–4 (1997). New York City's Bar Association also decided that firms may not pay commissions or bonuses to non-lawyer employees that are directly tied to specific fees, or for cases brought to the firm by those employees. New York City Bar Association, Ethics Op. 95–11 (1995). *See also* Pennsylvania Bar Association Formal Op. 98–75 (1998); Illinois State Bar Association Advisory Opinion on Professional Conduct, Op. 94–8 (1994); Dallas, Texas, Bar Association Ethics Op. 1991–03 (1991); Colorado State Bar Association Ethics Op. 97 (1991); Georgia Bar Association Advisory Op. 21 (1977).

Getting What Was Promised: Breach of Contract and Illegal Fee Sharing

Can legal assistants recover their promised compensation even if the arrangements violate the fee-sharing rules? Generally, the answer is no, because contracts that violate the law are usually considered to be void and, therefore, ineligible for breach of contract consideration. For instance, courts do not hear breach of contract suits over illegal gambling contracts.

An Indiana case, *Trotter v. Nelson*, 648 N.E 2d 1150 (Ind. 1997), serves as a blueprint demonstrating how many courts treat suits over illegal fee-sharing agreements. In the case, a non-lawyer employee (but something short of a legal assistant) sued her former employer, an attorney, over an alleged compensation promise. She claimed that the attorney promised her 5 percent of any fees from worker's compensation cases that she personally referred to the attorney. The attorney argued the agreement did not exist, and even if it did, it violated the referral fee rules and was unenforceable. The employee argued that the agreement was a permissible profit-sharing arrangement, which made it an enforceable contract. Because the agreement was not in writing, the legal analysis was made under an assumption that the agreement had actually been made. The Indiana Court of Appeals had held that even if the agreement violated the rules of professional conduct, it could still be enforced because a contract that violates the rules of professional responsibility is not the same as a contract that violates a statute. But the Indiana Supreme Court disagreed, declaring that the rules of professional conduct are a declaration of the state's public policy. As to the lawsuit, the court first found that the agreement, if it actually existed, was an impermissible profit-sharing agreement, as argued by the employer. Then, the court found that such an agreement was unenforceable because it violated "public policy." *Trotter,* at 1155.

Such a view is not the case everywhere, or at least not in Texas. In *Atkins v. Tinning,* 865 S.W.2d 533 (Tex. App. 1993), the Texas Court of Appeals reached an opposite conclusion on facts similar to *Trotter v. Nelson. Atkins* involved a private investigator who sued an attorney for failure to honor an oral agreement in which the private investigator was to receive one-third of the attorney's contingency fees from cases where he gathered evidence. When the attorney failed to pay the investigator a $300,000 fee, the investigator sued the him, whereupon the attorney had the investigator arrested and charged with barratry. Although the Court found that such an alleged contract between a lawyer and non-lawyer was in violation of the disciplinary rules—and could subject the attorney to professional sanction—it specifically refused to find that the disciplinary rules had any application to non-lawyers. Such a view distinguished the disciplinary rules from other kinds of law, such as statutes. Therefore, the Court said the agreement, if made, was not illegal, even though the agreement violated the disciplinary rules. *Atkins,* at 537.

When Is a Compensation Scheme Not Fee Sharing and What Is the Difference?

Model Rule 5.4(a) does have three exceptions. The first two do not apply to the paralegal. Those exceptions allow a lawyer or law firm to pay money to the estate (or other qualified representative) of a dead (or disabled) lawyer that the lawyer was owed in connection with earned fees or the sale of a law practice. MR 5.4(a)(1) and (2).

MR 5.4(a)(3) does apply to the paralegal, because it states, "A lawyer or law firm may include non-lawyer employees in a compensation or retirement plan, even though the plan is based in whole or in part on a profit-sharing arrangement." This exception allows a lawyer or law firm to fund retirement compensation programs, such as a **401k plan**, for their non-lawyer employees. It also allows paralegals to be paid bonuses or be included in profit-sharing plans. The predecessor Model Code has a similar exception in DR 3–102(A)(3).

If legal assistants cannot be paid directly from the legal fees earned by the lawyer or otherwise share in those fees, then how can they be paid bonuses or be part of a profit-sharing plan using contribution from the firm's legal fees? There are two differences between prohibited fee sharing and allowed compensation plans.

Extra Compensation Can Come from Net Proceeds

The first difference between prohibited fee sharing and allowed compensation plans is that an allowed retirement compensation program or profit-sharing plan is funded from the net proceeds of earned legal fees. Paid legal fees constitute **gross revenue**, which is what may not be shared with a legal assistant or any other non-lawyer. Retirement compensation programs and profit-sharing plans are funded from monies left over after expenses and overhead have been paid. Fee-sharing prohibitions involve gross revenues, but a lawyer or law firm can share whatever they want with whoever they want from what is left over after paying the bills.

Extra Compensation Can Come from General Success Rather Than Specific Success

The second difference is that compensation plans, such as bonuses, may not be made payable to a legal assistant contingent on the success of a specific matter. A general bonus, such as a quarterly bonus, may be paid to a legal assistant, but if he or she is paid a specific bonus for work on a particular case, that kind of transaction would be inappropriate because it vests in the legal assistant a direct, financial interest in the case and could affect his or her judgment. Although MR 5.4(a) concerns protecting the professional judgment of lawyers, legal assistants (as agents of their lawyers) also need to exercise their duties without having their judgment inappropriately clouded. Furthermore, specific bonuses can masquerade as finders' fees, in violation of the rules that prohibit a lawyer from compensating someone for recommending his or her services. MR 7.2(c); DR 2–103(B).

The American Bar Association issued an ethics opinion in 1979 that approved of the inclusion of non-lawyer employees in a law firm's profit-sharing plan. Although the opinion specifically concerned a firm's non-lawyer administrator, its

401k Plan—An employee retirement plan authorized by Section 401 of the Internal Revenue Code, sometimes called a salary reduction plan. In a 401k plan, an employee's pre-tax contributions are matched in some percentage by their employer's contributions.

gross revenue—Sometimes called gross income, this is the total revenue received before deductions, such as expenses.

reasoning is equally applicable to all non-lawyer employees, in that its approval of non-lawyer participation in profit-sharing plans is contingent on two factors: the profit-sharing method must be based on the firm's net profits; and the profit-sharing is not based on a percentage of specific client fees. ABA Commission on Ethics and Professional Responsibility, Informal Op. 1440 (1979). Some states have followed suit and issued opinions approving of profit-sharing plans. Virginia, for instance, issued three closely related opinions that approve of the following: law firms including non-lawyer employees in profit-sharing plans (Virginia State Bar Standing Comm. on Legal Ethics, Op. 767 (1986)); law firms paying bonuses to secretaries based on profits (Op. 806 (1986)); and collections firms compensating non-lawyer employees on a percentage of collections profits (Op. 885 (1987)).

Utah has issued two ethics opinions that are slightly different from the traditional view expressed by the ABA and many jurisdictions. Concerning the sources of finances that are used to fund extra compensation plans, Utah has stated that non-lawyer employees may be included in retirement plans, *regardless of whether the payments are based on the firm's gross or net income*, as long as there is nothing in the arrangement that would impair the lawyer's independence and the payment is not tied to a fee from a specific case. Utah State Bar Association, Ethics Advisory Committee Op. 139 (1994). And the same 2002 ethics opinion authorizing independent contracting paralegals (discussed in Chapter 3) prohibits lawyers from sharing fees with their independent contracting paralegals to the extent allowed for paralegals who are firm employees. Utah State Bar Association, Ethics Advisory Committee Op. 02–07 (2002). Although the opinion approves of firms compensating their employed paralegals based on a percentage of the firm's fees, it disapproves of the same compensation for independent contractors, reasoning that they are in a "less subordinate role" than their employed counterparts, which implicates the independent judgment policy behind a prohibition on sharing fees with non-lawyers.

RECOVERY OF LEGAL FEES FROM THE OPPOSING PARTY IN LITIGATION

There are occasions where successful litigants can keep more of their recovery because the other side has to pay the legal fees for both sides. Such a system, commonly known as "loser pays," is thought by some legal reformers to be a desirable way to minimize the filing of frivolous or otherwise wasteful litigation. Some statutes authorize trial courts to allow plaintiffs to recover their attorneys' fees in addition to their damages. At the federal level, 42 U.S.C. § 1988(b) grants trial courts the discretion to award "a reasonable attorney's fee" to successful plaintiffs suing under certain federal civil rights statutes. Such reform, though, is not without controversy in cases where the public perceives lawyers as being greedy. For example, when Rodney King was severely beaten by the Los Angeles Police Department in March 1991, his civil rights were severely violated. And as a result of the civil rights case settled between Mr. King and the city of Los Angeles, Mr.

King's legal fees were paid by the city. The settlement amount Mr. King received from the city was $3.8 million. But the legal bill his lawyers submitted to the city was $4.4 million, for 13,000 hours of work, which included the time his lawyers spent on talk shows.

Separate Recovery of Legal Assistant Fees in Federal Cases

One of the important moments in the history of legal assisting occurred in 1978, when a federal bankruptcy statute was amended to allow the bankruptcy court the discretion to also award the recovery of the fees of a paralegal (called a "paraprofessional") employed by an attorney. 11 U.S.C. § 330(a). An important, connected question is whether legal assistant fees also can be recovered where a statute authorizes the recovery of attorney's fees, but does not mention legal assistant fees.

The following case, which serves as a watershed moment in the history of the paralegal profession, answers that question affirmatively, at least where federal statutes authorize the recovery of an attorney's fee. While reading the case, notice how the Court gives its approval to the paralegal's role in a law firm. Notice also the focus of the dissenting opinion.

Case Law

Missouri v. Jenkins, 491 U.S. 274 (1989)

Justice BRENNAN delivered the opinion of the Court.

This is the attorney's fee aftermath of major school desegregation litigation in Kansas City, Missouri. We granted certiorari, 488 U.S. 888, 109 S.Ct. 218, 102 L.Ed.2d 209 (1988), to resolve two questions relating to fees litigation under 90 Stat. 2641, as amended, 42 U.S.C. § 1988. First, does the Eleventh Amendment prohibit enhancement of a fee award against a State to compensate for delay in payment? Second, should the fee award compensate the work of paralegals and law clerks by applying the market rate for their work?

I

This litigation began in 1977 as a suit by the Kansas City Missouri School District (KCMSD), the

school board, and the children of two school board members, against the State of Missouri and other defendants. The plaintiffs alleged that the State, surrounding school districts, and various federal agencies had caused and perpetuated a system of racial segregation in the schools of the Kansas City metropolitan area. They sought various desegregation remedies. KCMSD was subsequently realigned as a nominal defendant, and a class of present and future KCMSD students was certified as plaintiffs. After lengthy proceedings, including a trial that lasted 7 1/2 months during 1983 and 1984, the District Court found the State of Missouri and KCMSD liable, while dismissing the suburban school districts and the federal defendants. It ordered various intradistrict remedies, to be paid for by the State and KCMSD, including $260 million in capital improvements and a magnet-school plan costing over $200 million. . . .

The plaintiff class has been represented, since 1979, by Kansas City lawyer Arthur Benson and, since 1982, by the NAACP Legal Defense and Educational Fund, Inc. (LDF). Benson and the LDF requested attorney's fees under the Civil Rights Attorney's Fees Awards Act of 1976, 42 U.S.C. § 1988.[1] Benson and his associates had devoted 10,875 attorney hours to the litigation, as well as 8,108 hours of paralegal and law clerk time. For the LDF the corresponding figures were 10,854 hours for attorneys and 15,517 hours for paralegals and law clerks. Their fee applications deleted from these totals 3,628 attorney hours and 7,046 paralegal hours allocable to unsuccessful claims against the suburban school districts. With additions for post-judgment monitoring and for preparation of the fee application, the District Court awarded Benson a total of approximately $1.7 million and the LDF $2.3 million.

In calculating the hourly rate for Benson's fees the court noted that the market rate in Kansas City for attorneys of Benson's qualifications was in the range of $125 to $175 per hour, and found that "Mr. Benson's rate would fall at the higher end of this range based upon his expertise in the area of civil rights." It calculated his fees on the basis of an even higher hourly rate of $200, however, because of three additional factors: the preclusion of other employment, the undesirability of the case, and the delay in payment for Benson's services. The court also took account of the delay in payment in setting the rates for several of Benson's associates by using current market rates rather than those applicable at the time the services were rendered. For the same reason, it calculated the fees for the LDF attorneys at current market rates. Both Benson and the LDF employed numerous paralegals, law clerks (generally law students working part time), and recent law graduates in this litigation. The court awarded fees for their work based on Kansas City market rates for those categories. As in the case of the attorneys, it used current rather than historic market rates in order to compensate for the delay in payment. It therefore awarded fees based on hourly rates of $35 for law clerks, $40 for paralegals, and $50 for recent law graduates. The Court of Appeals affirmed in all respects.

II

[Here, the Court resolved the first issue, deciding that the Eleventh Amendment's principle of sovereign immunity does not prohibit an award against a state for attorney's fees to be enhanced because the state delayed in making the required payment to the plaintiff.]

III

Missouri's second contention is that the District Court erred in compensating the work of law clerks and paralegals (hereinafter collectively "paralegals") at the market rates for their services, rather than at their cost to the attorney. While Missouri agrees that compensation for the cost of these personnel should be included in the fee award, it suggests that an hourly rate of $15—which it argued below corresponded to their salaries, benefits, and overhead—would be appropriate, rather than the market rates of $35 to $50. According to Missouri, § 1988 does not authorize billing paralegals' hours at market rates, and doing so produces a "windfall" for the attorney.

We begin with the statutory language, which provides simply for "a reasonable attorney's fee as part of the costs." 42 U.S.C. § 1988. Clearly, a "reasonable attorney's fee" cannot have been meant to compensate only work performed personally by members of the bar. Rather, the term must refer to a reasonable fee for the work product of an attorney. Thus, the fee must take into account the work not only of attorneys, but also of secretaries, messengers, librarians, janitors, and others whose labor contributes to the work product for which an attorney bills her client; and it must also take account of other expenses and profit. The parties have suggested no reason why the work of paralegals should not be similarly compensated, nor can we think of any. We thus take as our starting point the self-evident proposition that the "reasonable attorney's fee" provided for by statute should compensate the work of paralegals, as well as that of attorneys. *The more difficult question is how the work of paralegals is to be valuated in calculating the overall attorney's fee* [emphasis added].

The statute specifies a "reasonable" fee for the attorney's work product. In determining how other elements of the attorney's fee are to be calculated, we have consistently looked to the marketplace as our guide to what is "reasonable." . . . A reasonable attorney's fee under § 1988 is one calculated on the basis of rates and practices prevailing in the relevant market, *i.e.,* "in line with those [rates] prevailing in the community for similar services by lawyers of reasonably comparable skill, experience, and reputation," and one that grants the successful civil rights plaintiff a "fully compensatory fee," *Hensley v. Eckerhart,* 461 U.S. 424, 435, 103 S.Ct. 1933, 1940, 76 L.Ed.2d 40 (1983), comparable to what "is traditional with attorneys compensated by a fee-paying client."

All else being equal, the hourly fee charged by an attorney whose rates include paralegal work in her hourly fee, or who bills separately for the work of paralegals at cost, will be higher than the hourly fee charged by an attorney competing in the same market who bills separately for the work of paralegals at "market rates." In other words, the prevailing "market rate" for attorney time is not independent of the manner in which paralegal time is accounted for.[8] Thus, if the prevailing practice in a given community were to bill paralegal time separately at market rates, fees awarded the attorney at market rates for attorney time would not be fully compensatory if the court refused to compensate hours billed by paralegals or did so only at "cost." Similarly, the fee awarded would be too high if the court accepted separate billing for paralegal hours in a market where that was not the custom.

We reject the argument that compensation for paralegals at rates above "cost" would yield a "windfall" for the prevailing attorney. Neither petitioners nor anyone else, to our knowledge, has ever suggested that the hourly rate applied to the work of an associate

attorney in a law firm creates a windfall for the firm's partners or is otherwise improper under § 1988, merely because it exceeds the cost of the attorney's services. If the fees are consistent with market rates and practices, the "windfall" argument has no more force with regard to paralegals than it does for associates. And it would hardly accord with Congress' intent to provide a "fully compensatory fee" if the prevailing plaintiff's attorney in a civil rights lawsuit were not permitted to bill separately for paralegals, while the defense attorney in the same litigation was able to take advantage of the prevailing practice and obtain market rates for such work. Yet that is precisely the result sought in this case by the State of Missouri, which appears to have paid its own outside counsel for the work of paralegals at the hourly rate of $35.[9]

Nothing in § 1988 requires that the work of paralegals invariably be billed separately. If it is the practice in the relevant market not to do so, or to bill the work of paralegals only at cost, that is all that § 1988 requires. Where, however, the prevailing practice is to bill paralegal work at market rates, treating civil rights lawyers' fee requests in the same way is not only permitted by § 1988, but also makes economic sense. By encouraging the use of lower cost paralegals rather than attorneys wherever possible, permitting market-rate billing of paralegal hours "encourages cost-effective delivery of legal services and, by reducing the spiraling cost of civil rights litigation, furthers the policies underlying civil rights statutes."[10]

Such separate billing appears to be the practice in most communities today.[11] In the present case, Missouri concedes that "the local market typically bills separately for paralegal services," (Tr. of Oral Arg. 14), and the District Court found that the requested hourly rates of $35 for law clerks, $40 for paralegals, and $50 for recent law graduates were the prevailing rates for such services in the Kansas City area. (App. to Pet. for Cert. A29, A31, A34.) Under these circumstances, the court's decision to award separate compensation at these rates was fully in accord with § 1988.

IV

The courts below correctly granted a fee enhancement to compensate for delay in payment and approved compensation of paralegals and law clerks at market rates. The judgment of the Court of Appeals is therefore *Affirmed*.

Justice MARSHALL took no part in the consideration or decision of this case. . . .

Chief Justice REHNQUIST, dissenting.

I agree with Justice O'CONNOR [who dissented in part] that the Eleventh Amendment does not permit an award of attorney's fees against a State which includes compensation for delay in payment. Unlike Justice O'CONNOR, however, I do not agree with the Court's approval of the award of law clerk and paralegal fees made here.

42 U.S.C. § 1988 gives the district courts discretion to allow the prevailing party in an action under 42 U.S.C. § 1983 "a reasonable attorney's fee as part of the costs." The Court reads this language as authorizing recovery of "a 'reasonable' fee for the attorney's work product," which, the Court concludes, may include separate compensation for the services of law clerks and paralegals. But the statute itself simply uses the very familiar term "a reasonable attorney's fee," which to those untutored in the Court's linguistic juggling means a fee charged for services rendered by an individual who has been licensed to practice law. Because law clerks and paralegals have not been licensed to practice law in Missouri, it is difficult to see how charges for their services may be separately billed as part of "attorney's fees." And since a prudent attorney customarily includes compensation for the cost of law clerk and paralegal services, like any other sort of office overhead—from secretarial staff, janitors, and librarians, to telephone service, stationery, and paper clips—in his own hourly billing rate, allowing the prevailing party to recover separate compensation for law clerk and paralegal services may result in "double recovery."

The Court finds justification for its ruling in the fact that the prevailing practice among attorneys in Kansas City is to bill clients separately for the services of law clerks and paralegals. But I do not think Congress intended the meaning of the statutory term "attorney's fee" to expand and contract with each and every vagary of local billing practice. Under the Court's logic, prevailing parties could recover at market rates for the cost of secretaries, private investigators, and other types of lay personnel who assist the attorney in preparing his case, so long as they could show that the prevailing practice in the local market was to bill separately for these services. Such a result would be a sufficiently drastic departure from the traditional concept of "attorney's fees" that I believe new statutory authorization should be required for it. That permitting separate billing of law clerk and paralegal hours at market rates might "'reduc[e] the spiraling cost of civil rights litigation'" by encouraging attorneys to delegate to these individuals tasks which they would otherwise perform themselves at higher cost, may be a persuasive reason for Congress to enact such additional legislation. It is not, however, a persuasive reason for us to rewrite the legislation which Congress has in fact enacted. . . .

I also disagree with the State's suggestion that law clerk and paralegal expenses incurred by a prevailing party, if not recoverable at market rates as "attorney's fees" under § 1988, are nonetheless recoverable at actual cost under that statute. The language of § 1988 expands the traditional definition of "costs" to include "a reasonable attorney's fee," but it cannot fairly be read to authorize the recovery of all other out-of-pocket expenses actually incurred by the prevailing party in the course of litigation. Absent specific statutory authorization for the recovery of such expenses, the prevailing party remains subject to the limitations on cost recovery imposed by Federal Rule of Civil Procedure 54(d) and 28 U.S.C. § 1920, which govern the taxation of costs in federal litigation where a cost-shifting statute is not applicable. Section 1920 gives the district court discretion to tax certain types of costs against the losing party in any federal litigation. The statute specifically enumerates six categories of expenses which may be taxed as costs: fees of the court clerk and marshal; fees of the court reporter; printing fees and witness fees; copying fees; certain docket fees; and fees of court-appointed experts and interpreters. We have held that this list is exclusive. *Crawford Fitting Co. v. J.T. Gibbons, Inc.*, 482 U.S. 437, 107 S.Ct. 2494, 96 L.Ed.2d 385 (1987). Since none of these categories can possibly be construed to include the fees of law clerks and paralegals, I would also hold that reimbursement for these expenses may not be separately awarded at actual cost.

I would therefore reverse the award of reimbursement for law clerk and paralegal expenses.

The following case footnotes correspond to the portions of the case that are printed in the textbook. Although it may seem that other footnotes are missing, they are not presented because their corresponding portions of the court's opinion have been redacted.

[1]Section 1988 provides in relevant part:

In any action or proceeding to enforce a provision of sections 1981, 1982, 1983, 1985, and 1986 of this title, title IX of Public Law 92-318 [20 U.S.C. § 1681 et seq.], or title VI of the Civil Rights Act of 1964 [42 U.S.C. § 2000d et seq.], the court, in its discretion, may allow the prevailing party, other than the United States, a reasonable attorney's fee as part of the costs.

[8]The attorney who bills separately for paralegal time is merely distributing her costs and profit margin among the hourly fees of other members of her staff, rather than concentrating them in the fee she sets for her own time.

[9]A variant of Missouri's "windfall" argument is the following: "If paralegal expense is reimbursed at a rate many times the actual cost, will attorneys next try to bill separately—and at a profit—for such items as secretarial time, paper clips, electricity, and other expenses?" Reply Brief for Petitioners 15–16. The answer to this question is, of course, that attorneys seeking fees under § 1988 would have no basis for requesting separate compensation of such expenses unless this were the prevailing practice in the local community. The safeguard against the billing at a profit of secretarial services and paper clips is the discipline of the market.

[10]It has frequently been recognized in the lower courts that paralegals are capable of carrying out many tasks, under the supervision of an attorney, that might otherwise be performed by a lawyer and billed at a higher rate. Such work might include, for example, factual investigation, including locating and interviewing witnesses; assistance with depositions, interrogatories, and document production; compilation of statistical and financial data; checking legal citations; and drafting correspondence. Much such work lies in a gray area of tasks that might appropriately be performed either by an attorney or a paralegal. To the extent that fee applicants under § 1988 are not permitted to bill for the work of paralegals at market rates, it would not be surprising to see a greater amount of such work performed by attorneys themselves, thus increasing the overall cost of litigation. Of course, purely clerical or secretarial tasks should not be billed at a paralegal rate, regardless of who performs them. What the court in Johnson v. Georgia Highway Express, Inc., 488 F.2d 714, 717 (CA5 1974), said in regard to the work of attorneys is applicable by analogy to paralegals:

"It is appropriate to distinguish between legal work, in the strict sense, and investigation, clerical work, compilation of facts and statistics and other work which can often be accomplished by non-lawyers but which a lawyer may do because he has no other help available. Such non-legal work may command a lesser rate. Its dollar value is not enhanced just because a lawyer does it."

[11]Amicus National Association of Legal Assistants reports that 77 percent of 1,800 legal assistants responding to a survey of the association's membership stated that their law firms charged clients for paralegal work on an hourly billing basis. Brief for National Association of Legal Assistants as Amicus Curiae 11.

Case Questions

1. How many hours of paralegal time were billed? Did the prevailing party bill to the state of Missouri?
2. Why did Missouri argue that it should not have to pay for what the Court collectively called paralegal fees?
3. Why did the Court include paralegal fees as an allowable recovery under the statute that allows for the recovery of "reasonable attorney's fees"?
4. Why did the Court determine that the paralegal market rate, rather than the actual cost of the paralegal time, would be the allowable recovery?

5. What is the difference between the market rate and the actual cost?
6. Under what conditions did the Court find that paralegal fees would be recoverable?
7. Why did Chief Justice Rehnquist disagree with the Court's decision?
8. If, as Justice Rehnquist stated, a prudent attorney will include the cost of paralegals in the attorney's hourly rate, then would there be any practical difference between the Court's decision and Justice Rehnquist's dissent?

Separate Recovery of Legal Assistant Fees in State Cases

Some states have avoided the dilemma of *Missouri v. Jenkins* by expressly stating, through legislation, that where the law allows for the recovery of attorney's fees, it also includes paralegal fees. For example, Ind. Code § 1–1–4–6(b) states, "A reference in the Indiana Code to attorney's fees includes paralegal's fees." Illinois's statute, following the line of reasoning in *Missouri v. Jenkins*, specifically allows for the recovery of paralegal fees at "market rates." 5 Ill. Comp. Stat. 70/1.35. Other states expressly provide for the recovery of legal assistant fees where attorney fees are recoverable. *See* Ala. R. Civ. Pro., Rule 79(g)(1)(C); Cal. Prob. Code §10811(b); Fla. Stat. ch. 57.104; N.J. R. Ct., Rule 4:42–9(b); N.Y. Sur. Ct. Proc. Law § 2110.4. In fact, New York reaffirmed its position on the recovery of legal assistant fees, extending it to a statute that allows for the recovery of legal fees for court-appointed defense attorneys in death penalty cases. *Mahoney v. Pataki*, 2002 WL 857412 (N.Y. May 7, 2002).

It is important to realize that *Missouri v. Jenkins* allows for the recovery of paralegal fees where the work done by the paralegal is substantive legal work, which an attorney would do if not for the paralegal's efforts. Clerical or secretarial work is not the kind of work that courts are likely to allow as recoverable, even if done by a paralegal and even where a statute allows for the recovery of paralegal fees. In a case that predates *Missouri v. Jenkins,* a federal court refused to allow the recovery of paralegal costs, not because the statute failed to mention paralegals but because there was insufficient evidence that the employee in question, who was called a paralegal, was, in fact, a paralegal. Not only did the employee have no paralegal training, but also she mostly performed clerical duties. *Jones v. Armstrong Cork Co.*, 630 F.2d 324 (11th Cir. 1980). Interestingly, Florida's statute on the recovery of attorney's fees allows the trial court to consider the work of "any legal assistants who contributed nonclerical, meaningful legal support to the matter involved and are working under the supervision of an attorney." Fla. Stat. ch. 57.104.

The following state case involves a request for the recovery of legal assistant fees under a state statute that only mentions the recovery of attorney fees. Notice the logical progression of the court's analysis concerning the recovery of legal assistant fees.

Case Law

Absher Const. Co. v. Kent School Dist. No. 415, 917 P.2d 1086 (Wash. App. 1995)

PER CURIAM.

Kent School No. 415 (Kent) has requested an attorney fee award which includes payment for the time of non-lawyer personnel. We hold that such time may be compensable as part of an attorney fee award and set out guidelines for determining when such fees are appropriate. We find, however, that the total amount requested by Kent is not reasonable under the circumstances of this case and therefore award a lesser amount.

The appellants sued Kent for amounts they claimed were owing under a public works contract, approximately $205,000. Kent won on summary judgment and was awarded $34,648.86 in fees and costs. Kent also prevailed on appeal and now seeks an additional $36,911.54 in fees and costs. The basis for the award is RCW 39.04.240.

The fee request includes time for the following individuals:

(1) A partner in practice for 20 years billed 104.2 hours at $225.00 per hour ($23,445);

(2) A fourth-year associate billed 53.1 hours at $130.00 per hour ($6,903);

(3) A sixth-year associate billed 4.5 hours at $155.00 per hour ($697.50);

(4) A legal assistant billed 39.5 hours at $67.00 per hour ($2,646.50);

(5) A legal editor billed 4 hours at $62.00 per hour ($248); and

(6) A legal clerk billed 8.5 hours at $35.00 per hour ($297.50).

The latter three are not attorneys. No case in Washington specifically addresses whether the time of non-lawyer personnel may be included in an attorney fee award.

We find persuasive the reasoning of the Arizona court in *Continental Townhouses East Unit One Ass'n v. Brockbank*, 152 Ariz. 537, 733 P.2d 1120, 73 A.L.R.4th 921 (1986). Properly employed and supervised non-lawyer personnel can decrease litigation expense. Lawyers should not be forced to perform legal tasks solely so that their time may be compensable in an attorney fee award. The question then becomes what sort of work performed by non-lawyer personnel is compensable. Regardless of the name given to the category of person who performs the work, we believe, as did the Arizona court, that the definition of legal assistant formulated by the American Bar Association Standing Committee on Legal Assistants provides appropriate guidance. Under that definition:

> A legal assistant is a person, qualified through education, training, or work experience, who is employed or retained by a lawyer, law office, governmental agency, or other entity in a capacity or function which involves a performance, under the ultimate direction and supervision of an attorney, of specifically delegated substantive legal work, which work, for the most part, requires a sufficient knowledge of legal concepts that, absent such assistant, the attorney would perform the task.

The following criteria will be relevant in determining whether such services should be compensated: (1) the services performed by the non-lawyer personnel must be legal in nature; (2) the performance of these services must be supervised by an attorney; (3) the qualifications of the person performing the services must be specified in the request for fees in sufficient detail to demonstrate that the person is qualified by virtue of education, training, or work experience to perform substantive legal work; (4) the nature of the services performed must be specified in the request for fees in order to allow the reviewing court to determine that the services performed were legal rather than clerical; (5) as with attorney time, the amount of time expended must be set forth and must be reasonable; and (6) the amount charged must reflect reasonable community standards for charges by that category of personnel.

Employing these criteria, we allow only part of the fees requested for the legal assistant's services. He has requested compensation for preparing pleadings for duplication, preparing and delivering copies, requesting copies, and obtaining and delivering a docket sheet. We do not view this time as work which falls within these guidelines. We do allow an award for time spent preparing the briefs and related work. In computing the time we allow for him, we will assume, absent any other evidence in the record, that the hourly rate of $67.00 is reasonable for this

type of work. We allow an award of $2,110.50 for 31.5 hours. We allow the recovery of fees for the time claimed by the legal editor for verifying citations and quotations. We disallow the time claimed for the legal clerk, which appears to consist primarily of obtaining copies of pleadings and organizing working copies of the pleadings. . . .

[The portion of the opinion dealing with the review of the attorneys' fees has been deleted.]

In sum, we conclude that the fees of non-lawyer personnel may be properly requested as part of an attorney fee award. In this case, applying the factors and considerations listed above, we award $23,055.50 plus $1,633.74 as a reasonable attorney fee on appeal, together with $134.65 costs on appeal.

Case Questions

1. What is the general theory put forward supporting the notion that legal assistant time can be recovered under a statute that does not specifically authorize it?
2. What specific qualifications would a legal assistant have to possess in order to meet the Court's test?
3. Why did the Court refuse certain portions of the bill that were allocated to the work of legal assistants?
4. How did the community standards come into play in this case?

promissory estoppel—An exception to the requirement of "consideration," which is a required element to a valid contract. Generally, promissory estoppel allows a party who relied upon the promise of another party to recover what was promised, even though the relying party would be unable to recover under contract law.

A more traditional approach to awarding legal assistant fees when the authorizing statute only mentions attorney's fees is the following case, which involved a suit for breach of contract, innocent misrepresentation, and **promissory estoppel** (a doctrine from the law of equity that allows one who relied on a promise of another to recover what was promised even though no enforceable contract existed under contract law). Although the court reached the opposite decision to that made in *Absher Const. Co. v. Kent School Dist. No. 415*, it did so with misgivings.

Case Law

Joerger v. Gordon Food Service, Inc., 568 N.W.2d 365 (Mich. App. 1997)

[The lawsuit involved Joerger suing Gordon Food Service for breach of contract, innocent mis-

representation, and promissory estoppel. Although Joerger won at trial, the jury awarded plaintiff no damages, and then the trial court granted Gordon Food Service's motion to award it attorney's fees as a sanction against Joerger for failing to settle the case following a mediation evaluation. State law allowed such a sanction, and the trial judge granted Gordon Food Service's request of $131,540 in attorney fees and also $7,348.95 in costs. Joerger appealed the verdict as well as the mediation sanction. The appellate court ruled against Joerger on almost all the issues presented in the appeal; these are not featured here in the text. The remaining issue, as the excerpts show, dealt with paralegal fees.]

. . . Plaintiffs also challenge the billings attributable to two individuals identified only by the initials "NAS" and "LAD." Plaintiffs argue that the individuals were not identified and no billing rate was provided for these individuals. Contrary to plaintiffs' assertions, the record reveals that these individuals were identified, by name, as two paralegals employed by defense counsel. Defendant also informed plaintiffs and the court that their hourly rate was $75. Accordingly, these arguments are without merit.

We do find merit, however, in plaintiffs' argument that the independent expenses attributable to the use of paralegals is not recoverable as costs. For purposes of mediation sanctions, "actual costs" include "those costs taxable in any civil action." MCR 2.403(O)(6). Chapter 24 of the Revised Judicature Act, M.C.L. § 600.2401 *et seq.*; M.S.A. § 27A.2401 *et seq.,* governs costs. *Taylor v. Anesthesia Associates of Muskegon, PC,* 179 Mich.App. 384, 387, 445 N.W.2d 525 (1989). M.C.L. § 600.2405; M.S.A. § 27A.2405 provides that the following items may be taxed and awarded unless otherwise directed:

(1) Any of the fees of officers, witnesses, or other persons mentioned in this chapter or [M.C.L. § 600.2501 *et seq.*; M.S.A. § 27A.2501 *et seq.*] unless a contrary intention is stated.
(2) Matters specially made taxable elsewhere in the statutes or rules.
(3) The legal fees for any newspaper publication required by law.

(4) The reasonable expense of printing any required brief and appendix in the supreme court, including any brief on motion for leave to appeal.
(5) The reasonable costs of any bond required by law, including any stay of proceeding or appeal bond.
(6) Any attorney fees authorized by statute or by court rule.

Our review of the provisions of the statute indicates nothing supporting an award of costs for expenses generated by paralegals. In the absence of statutory authorization, costs may not be awarded to recompense for a claimed litigation expense. *Taylor, supra* at 387–388, 445 N.W.2d 525.

Expenses generated by paralegals are also not recoverable as a separate component of mediation sanctions. Both MCR 2.403(O)(6) and M.C.L. § 600.2405; M.S.A. § 27A.2405 use the phrases "attorney fee" and "attorney fees." . . .

Clearly, attorney fees are not meant to compensate only work performed personally by members of the bar. Rather, the term must refer to a reasonable fee for the work product of an attorney that necessarily includes support staff. The rule allowing an award of attorney fees has traditionally anticipated the allowance of a fee sufficient to cover the office overhead of an attorney together with a reasonable profit. The inclusion of factor 5, *the expenses incurred,* reflects the traditional understanding that attorney fees should be sufficient to recoup at least a portion of overhead costs. *Johnston v. Detroit Hoist & Crane Co.,* 142 Mich.App. 597, 601, 370 N.W.2d 1 (1985); *Detroit Bank & Trust Co. v. Coopes,* 93 Mich.App. 459, 468, 287 N.W.2d 266 (1979). Fixed overhead costs include such items as employee wages, rent, equipment rental, and so forth. *Id.* Thus, until a statute or a court rule specifies otherwise, the attorney fees must take into account the work not only of attorneys, but also of secretaries, messengers, *paralegals,* and others whose labor contributes to the work product for which an attorney bills a client, and it must also take account of other expenses and profit.

We therefore must rule, albeit reluctantly, that the reasonable "attorney fees" should already include the work of paralegals, as well as that of attorneys and other factors underlying the fee. Accordingly, we remand in order for the trial court to reduce the award of attorney fees by the amount attributable to the independent paralegal billings.

We, however, find it noteworthy that a growing number of our sister states have allowed an independent recovery of paralegal or legal assistant time in attorney fee awards under statute, rules of court, or decisional law authorizing awards of attorney fees. In most cases, with respect to paralegals and legal assistants, recovery is available "if a legal assistant performs work that has traditionally been done by any attorney." See, e.g., *Gill Savings Ass'n v. Int'l Supply Co., Inc.,* 759 S.W.2d 697, 702 (Tex.App., 1988). To qualify for such recovery, the evidence must establish: (1) that the legal assistant is qualified through education, training, or work experience to perform substantive legal work; (2) that substantive legal work was performed under the direction and supervision of an attorney; (3) the nature of the legal work that was performed; (4) the hourly rate being charged for the legal assistant; and (5) the number of hours expended by the legal assistant. *Id.*

We find that the increasing practice of allowing an independent recovery of paralegal or legal assistant time in attorney's fee awards has merit. We recognize that the day-to-day duties of a legal assistant will vary from law firm to law firm. If, however, the paralegal performs work that has traditionally been done by an attorney, we believe that it follows that a separate expense should be allowable. Neither statute nor court rule, however, currently allow such expenses as separate billable items. It is not our task to rewrite statutes. We therefore encourage the Legislature to change the statute or the Supreme Court to change the court rule to provide for appropriate billing for paralegal fees.

Affirmed in part, reversed in part, and remanded.

TAYLOR, Presiding Judge (concurring in part and dissenting in part).

I concur with the majority opinion except for that portion of part IV that holds that independent expenses attributable to the use of paralegals are not recoverable as mediation sanctions. Thus I would affirm the trial court's award of mediation sanctions that included costs attributable to paralegals.

The majority remands this case to the trial court with instructions that it reduce the award of attorney fees by the amount attributable to the independent paralegal billings because "attorney fees" must take into account the work not only of attorneys, but also of secretaries, messengers, paralegals, and others whose labor contributes to the work product for which an attorney bills a client. . . .

The flaw in the majority opinion is that its holding is dependent on how a law firm prepares its bills for the court. As I understand the holding, if the firm billed its client separately for paralegals or any other cost, such as secretaries or messengers, but, pursuant to prior agreed-to arrangements with the client, when submitting the billings to the trial court for mediation sanctions, folded those into "attorney fees," they would not run afoul of the majority's holding. Presumably, all sophisticated firms who anticipate possible mediation sanctions will now adopt that procedure. We have, then, another puzzling fiction in a field where there are far too many now. . . .

Case Questions

---

1. Why did the court refuse to award paralegal fees even though it appeared to want to?
2. Why did the presiding judge disagree with the court's reasoning?
3. Which of the two preceding opinions do you find more legally persuasive?

On October 24, 2000, the Michigan Supreme Court amended Court Rule 2.626, which concerns attorney fees, so that it states the following:

An award of attorney fees may include an award for the time and labor of any legal assistant who contributed nonclerical, legal support under the supervision of an attorney, provided the legal assistant meets the criteria set forth in Article 1, § 6 of the Bylaws of the State Bar of Michigan.

The Staff Comment to the new rule states that the change was made in response to *Joerger v. Gordon Food Service, Inc.*

ETHICAL CONSIDERATIONS FOR THE LEGAL ASSISTANT

When it comes to fees, the legal assistant needs to keep two key thoughts in mind: do not set—or appear to set—legal fees, and be sure to accurately report billable time. Although the source of these directives is the operable lawyer ethics rules, the legal assistant ethics codes also speak to these concerns.

The Legal Assistant May Not Establish Fees

As discussed in Chapter 3, one of the acts commonly agreed to constitute the unauthorized practice of law is the establishment of legal fees. Almost all the national organizations that have created codes of ethics for legal assistants or paralegals specifically mention the prohibition against establishing fees. ABA Model Guidelines for the Utilization of Legal Assistant Services, Guideline 3(b); NALA Code of Ethics and Professional Responsibility, Canon 3(b); NALA Model Standards and Guidelines for Utilization of Legal Assistants, Guideline 2; NFPA Model Disciplinary Rules and Ethical Considerations, Rule 1.8. (This Rule is a general prohibition of the unauthorized practice of law.)

For those paralegals who engage in initial client interviews or who have regular client contact, it is especially critical that questions about legal fees or about the bill be directed to the supervising attorney. If a firm charges a fixed fee for certain kinds of work, some would say that a legal assistant is not establishing fees by answering a general question related to the amount of a fixed fee (or, for that matter, responding to a question about a particular lawyer's hourly rate). Nevertheless, erring on the side of caution is a safer way to deal with the billing questions of a client or prospective client. Concerning the preparation of the client's bill, at least one ethics opinion has stated that a firm may delegate to a non-lawyer the final authority for preparing the client's bill, but that the firm remains responsible for the ethics compliance of the bill (such as ensuring it is reasonable) and should supervise the non-lawyer accordingly. New York City Bar Association, Ethics Op. 94–9 (1994).

The Legal Assistant Must Report Accurate Hours

It is a fact of economics that profits increase as worker productivity increases and that productivity increases through speed and efficiency. The hamburger joint that can serve twice as many customers in a day as its competitor can serve will make twice as much money, assuming it does not employ twice as many employees as its competitor. Efficient employees are the key because efficiency increases productivity, which in turn increases profits.

The cloud in the silver lining to increased productivity is that one can only work so fast. Average billable hours for lawyers has increased dramatically in the last forty years, and it is not uncommon for associates in large firms to bill more than two thousand hours a year. Along with that increase comes an increasing demand on paralegals to bill more hours. That demand can cause legal assistants to do what lawyers sometimes do: pad their billable hours or double bill. Such unethical activity is a two-headed monster. Not only is it illegal and wrong in and of itself, but it also can result in sanctions against the firm since lawyers are responsible for the misconduct of their non-lawyer employees.

The NFPA Model Disciplinary Rules and Ethical Considerations specifically discusses honesty in billing in EC–1.2(c), which says, "A paralegal shall ensure that all timekeeping and billing records prepared by the paralegal are thorough, accurate, and honest." Also, EC–1.2(d) states:

> A paralegal shall not knowingly engage in fraudulent billing practices. Such practices may include, but are not limited to: inflation of hours billed to a client or employer; misrepresentation of the nature of tasks performed; and/or submission of fraudulent expense and disbursement documentation.

When legal assistants have been caught engaging in dishonest billing practices, the result is the same as when lawyers get caught—the client gets a reduced bill or a refund. But because legal assistants are unlicensed, they cannot be subject to professional discipline unless issued by legal assistant or paralegal organizations. Regarding the pressure on paralegals to maintain their billable hours, Ohio does not allow law firms to pay its non-lawyer employees based on a percentage of their billable hours. Ohio State Bar Association, Ethics Op. 97–4 (1997).

Unbelievable Dedication to One's Job

A curious example of overeager diligence is the bankruptcy case, *In re Maruko Inc.*, 160 B.R. 633 (S.D. Cal. 1993). The case involved the bankruptcy judge's review of almost $2 million in requested attorneys' fees and costs. The fees were attributed to thirteen attorneys, three paralegals, and a few courier services. While the court reduced some portion of the fees for all of the lawyers and paralegals due to inappropriate or double billing, the first paralegal discussed in the case really caught the attention of the judge. After attempting to make sense of all the handwritten notes, arrows, and circles added to that paralegal's original time sheets, the judge compared the mess to a diagram for a football play. Furthermore, the judge took note of the fact that the paralegal billed in excess of 24 hours a day *three times*. Needless to say, the judge reduced that paralegal's portion of the bill in the amount of $20,700. *Id.* at 643. Fortunately for the paralegal, her name was withheld. One wonders if she was a member of a paralegal or legal assistant organization and, if so, whether she was sanctioned for her considerable deceitfulness.

ETHICS 2000 AND FEES

The Ethics 2000 committee proposed certain changes to the rules on fees, most notably the requirement that fee agreements be in writing, that contingent fee agreements be signed by the client and that expenses also be reasonable.

MR 1.5 and Fees

Proposal by the Ethics 2000 Commission

The new MR 1.5(a) states that "A lawyer shall not make an agreement for, charge, or collect an unreasonable fee," rather than stating the fee shall be reasonable. This change is similar to the Model Code's prohibition of excessive fees. Also, the new MR 1.5(a) now prohibits a lawyer from charging "an unreasonable amount for expenses." This change incorporates what is expressed in ethics opinions: excessive expenses are as bad as excessive fees.

The new MR 1.5(b) requires that the lawyer put in writing the scope of the representation, the basis for the fee, and expenses the client will have to pay. This change is designed to promote the client's understanding of any future obligations to the lawyer. An exception is provided where the lawyer will charge the same fee to a regularly represented client, or where the total fee will be $500 or less.

The new MR 1.5(c) has two noticeable changes. First, it requires that the contingent fee agreement be signed by the client (instead of simply being in writing). Second, it requires that the contingent fee agreement "clearly notify the client of any expenses for which the client will be liable whether or not the client is the prevailing party." This change is in concert with MR 1.8(e), which allows a lawyer to advance litigation expenses, but which the client may eventually have to pay.

There are some new Comments to the new MR 1.5 that discuss the reasonableness of legal expenses, as well as the reasonableness of contingent fees.

Action Taken by the Ethics 2000 Commission

The House of Delegates accepted 1.5, but not before amending the proposal by eliminating the requirement in 1.5(b) that all fee agreements be in writing, as well as the corresponding $500 exception (and the Comments that concern requiring written fee agreements).

MR 5.4 and the Sharing of Fees with Non-Lawyers

Proposal by the Ethics 2000 Commission

The only change to the new MR 5.4 is an allowance for lawyers to share court-awarded fees with a non-profit organization that was directly involved in the case. This change is in concert with an ABA ethics opinion (93–374) that found that sharing fees with a non-profit organization does not threaten the independent judgment of a lawyer, which is the danger that is avoided by prohibiting the sharing of fees between a lawyer and a non-lawyer.

Action Taken by the ABA House of Delegates

Approved.

Summary

There are three prevalent kinds of legal fees. An hourly rate is charged for the lawyer's time, measured in increments. Hourly rates vary throughout the country, but more experienced attorneys and partners charge more per hour than associates. A contingency fee is a percentage of whatever the lawyer recovers for the client or, in certain situations, saves for the client. Contingency fee percentages increase as the lawyer's efforts for the client increase, with percentages ranging from 20 percent at settlement to 45 percent after appeal. Contingency fees are controversial when they are thought of as exploiting the client or harming the general welfare of the country because of their sheer size. A fixed fee is a predetermined amount that is charged for the lawyer's services. Fixed fees are more common for routine legal services, such as the preparation of basic wills.

The key rules that govern legal fees are the Model Rules' Rule 1.5 and the Model Code's Rule DR 2–106. MR 1.5 prohibits unreasonable fees, while DR 2–106 prohibits fees that are clearly excessive. Both versions list eight nonexclusive variables that factor into the equation of what makes a fee reasonable, and some of those factors include the following: the time and labor involved; whether the lawyer will be precluded from taking other cases while working on the client's case; the results obtained; and the experience, reputation, and ability of the lawyer involved. Not everything a lawyer does can be billed to the client, and overhead expenses of running a law office are usually not billable. Where statutes place caps on legal fees, a lawyer may not exceed those limits, even if the client agrees to the higher fee.

Despite the fee agreement reached between the lawyer and client, courts always have jurisdiction to review the fee for reasonableness. Courts generally find fees to be unreasonable or excessive if the lawyer has taken advantage of the client. Such instances of overreaching involve the lawyer failing to reduce the bill if it turns out that very little effort is needed to obtain the client's objectives or if the lawyer works exceptionally slowly in order to increase the bill. A lawyer also may not bill the client for his or her own incompetence or for acts that could have been done by the lawyer's legal assistant, but instead were done by the lawyer him- or herself in order to be billed at a higher hourly rate.

Legal fees need to be clearly explained to the client, although neither the Model Rules nor the Model Code require that all legal fees be explained to the client in writing. Three critical areas of explanation the client should receive concerning fees involve the explanation the new client should receive, the difference between fees and costs, and the difference between an advance and a retainer. The rules require that the fee agreement be promptly explained to the new client, although, again, there is no requirement that the fees be explained in writing. Fees are what the lawyer is expecting to be paid for the representation, while costs are expenses incurred during the representation that the client is usually expected to pay. Courts favor the client when confusion arises over his or her understanding about fees versus costs. If the paralegal's time is billed on an hourly rate, the lawyer needs to explain to the client the paralegal's contribution to the bill. If the client is expected to pay any money up front, the lawyer also needs to clearly explain to the client the difference between an advance and a retainer. An advance is a prepayment of the lawyer's fee. Since a prepayment is yet to be earned, an advance is subject to being returned. A retainer, often called a general retainer, is a payment made to secure the lawyer's availability. Because of the nature of a retainer, it is earned upon payment, which makes it a nonrefundable payment, although jurisdictions are starting to oppose nonrefundable payments made to lawyers.

MR 1.15 and DR 9–102 concern the keeping of the client's money and require that it be kept separately from the lawyer's money. Such commingling can lead to conversion of the client's property. Therefore, lawyers set up client trust accounts in order to keep the client's money separate. The rules on keeping the client's money separate apply whenever the lawyer possesses property in which the client has an interest, including cases where the lawyer and client dispute the lawyer's bill. Every jurisdiction has in place an IOLTA program that requires the interest earned on client trust accounts that are nominal or of a short duration to be turned over to the bar association, where the funds are used for low-cost legal services.

There are specific rules, found in MR 1.5, that concern contingent fees. First, contingent fee agreements are required to be in writing. The Model Code, however, does not require that contingent fee agreements be in writing, but certain jurisdictions that operate under the Model Code do require written contingent fee agreements. Contingent fee agreements also need to clearly detail how the fee is to be determined. Both the Model Rules and the Model Code prohibit contingent fee agreements in criminal cases, and the Model Rules also prohibit contingency fees in domestic relations cases.

Lawyers in different firms are allowed to share legal fees under certain circumstances, including when the client agrees to the fee sharing. The rules, however, prohibit lawyers from sharing legal fees with non-lawyers. The policy behind such a prohibition—whether the non-lawyer is an independent contractor, paralegal, or any other non-lawyer employee—is the protection of the lawyer's professional judgment and independence. Illegal fee-sharing contracts between a lawyer and a non-lawyer are generally considered to be void. An exception is made for the non-lawyer employee, allowing them to be compensated with bonuses or retirement plans, as long as the extra compensation comes from the net proceeds of legal fees and no bonus is given with respect to a specific case.

Legal assistant fees can be recovered under statutes that provide for lawyer fees to be recovered by the opposing party. At the federal level, the U.S. Supreme Court declared, in *Missouri v. Jenkins*, that legal assistant fees could be recovered at the market rate in federal lawsuits, even though the statute only mentions the recovery of lawyer fees. At the state level, many jurisdictions also allow for the recovery of paralegal fees through statutes or case law. In cases where paralegal fees are recoverable, they are generally only recoverable if the efforts of the paralegal are substantive, rather than clerical.

As mentioned in the Model Rules and the Model Code, as well as the national rules of ethics for paralegals and legal assistants, non-lawyer employees may not establish legal fees. Those paralegals who have client contact need to be careful to avoid discussing a client's bill in ways that violate that prohibition. Furthermore, all paralegals who engage in hourly billing need to report accurate and honest time sheets and must not engage in double billing or padding the bill.

The Ethics 2000 Commission proposed a few changes to Model Rule 1.5, not all of which were accepted by the ABA House of Delegates. An addition to the rule now prohibits the charging of unreasonable expenses. The ABA House of Delegates, however, rejected the specific requirement that all fee agreements be in writing. The new version of MR 1.5 now requires that the client sign the contingent fee agreement and that the agreement have an explanation regarding expenses.

Points to Ponder

1. Do you think the idea of prepaid legal insurance makes sense?
2. What is a contingent fee?
3. Do you think the government should place limits on all contingency fees or eliminate them altogether? Why or why not?
4. What goes into determining whether a lawyer's fee is reasonable? Which of the eight factors listed in MR 1.5(a) or DR 2–106(B) do you think is the most relevant?
5. Why is it that a lawyer cannot bill the client for everything the lawyer does? What kinds of acts would qualify as being non-billable?
6. Does your jurisdiction place caps on fees collected in certain kinds of cases? Are statutory limits on fees a violation of someone's freedom to make a contract?
7. What would make a lawyer's fee unreasonable or excessive simply because it is too high?
8. Assuming a fee agreement was put in writing, what kinds of information should it include, particularly if the client was new?
9. What is the difference between legal fees and costs? Why is it important that the distinction be made?
10. What is the difference between an advance and a retainer, and why does it matter?
11. When a client makes an advance payment to their lawyer, where should the money go?
12. What is an IOLTA program, and how does it work? What is your view on the constitutionality of an IOLTA?
13. Why is it that the Model Rules requires contingency fee agreements to be in writing? If you are in a Model Code jurisdiction, does your set of rules still require written contingent fee agreements? What information should a contingent fee agreement contain?
14. What kinds of cases are generally prohibited from being taken on a contingent fee, and why? What kind of domestic relations case could be taken on a contingent fee?
15. Why do you think the client needs to consent to fee sharing between lawyers of different firms?
16. How could the lawyer's judgment be negatively affected if the lawyer was allowed to share fees with a non-lawyer?
17. What exceptions to the fee-sharing rules apply to the non-lawyer employee? What parameters determine whether such exceptions are appropriate?
18. At the end of the film *Erin Brockovich* (as in the real-life case the film was based on), Erin's lawyer made her a millionaire. Was that an appropriate payment?
19. Do you think a lawyer should be required to honor a fee-sharing agreement made with a paralegal even if it violates the rules on fee sharing?

20. Does your jurisdiction have a court rule or statute that expressly allows for the recovery of paralegal fees where the law allows for the recovery of attorney fees?
21. Given that the U.S. Supreme Court decided *Missouri v. Jenkins*, then why could a court still refuse to award paralegal fees?
22. What kind of statements, if any, could the legal assistant make to the prospective client concerning the lawyer's fee while still avoiding the establishment of fees?
23. Do you think paralegals should not work under a billable hours format, so as to protect against the pressure to engage in some of the false billing practices that lawyers engage in occasionally?
24. What significant proposals for changing the rules on fees were made by the Ethics 2000 Commission? What proposals did the ABA House of Delegates reject?
25. Is there anything not covered by the rules on fees that you think should be addressed?

Key Concepts

Advance

Bill padding

Commingling

Contingent fee

Double billing

Fixed fee

Hourly rate

Interest on lawyers' trust account

Litigation costs

Non-billable activities

Non-lawyer fee sharing

Prepaid legal insurance

Reasonable fee

Recovery of paralegal/legal assistant fees

Reverse contingent fee

Statutorily limited fees

Key Terms

advance	double billing	NOW account
alimony	equity partner	promissory estoppel
bill padding	fixed fee	public policy
certificates of deposit (CDs)	401k plan	quantum merit
commingling	gross revenue	reverse contingent fee
contingent fee	impeachment	subrogation
conversion	non-equity partner	

Miscellaneous Ethics Issues

Chapter

8

> *After twenty-five years' observation, I can give it as the condensed history of most, if not all, good lawyers, that they lived well and died poor.*
>
> —Daniel Webster, nineteenth-century lawyer and statesman extraordinaire

> *I have watched with great sadness the decline in esteem held by our society of lawyers.*
>
> —Sandra Day O'Connor, United States Supreme Court justice, 1981–

INTRODUCTION

There are some rules of ethics, as well as corresponding ethics opinions and cases, that are beyond the scope of this book because they do not closely relate to paralegals and legal assistants. There are also rules of ethics that should be of concern to legal assistants but are not neatly organized in discrete fashion, as are the confidentiality rules or the conflicts of interest rules. This chapter will explore a variety of those miscellaneous ethics rules, many of which concern litigation. First, there will be an analysis of the legal team's duty to provide the client with competent representation, including the need to adequately communicate with the client. Next, there will be an examination of ethics rules that concern the legal team's duty to be truthful with courts, clients, represented persons, and unrepresented persons. There will also be an inquiry into whether there are any circumstances under which a non-lawyer could be held liable for legal malpractice. Finally, this chapter will close by looking at the duty of lawyers and legal assistants to reach out to their communities by providing pro bono services. Because this chapter focuses on a variety of different ethics issues (and their corresponding ethics rules), a discussion of the Ethics 2000 changes will be included throughout the chapter rather than as a separate section at the chapter's end.

COMPETENCE

The very first rule of the ABA Model Rules of Professional Conduct is not about confidentiality or conflicts of interest, but rather concerns competence. ABA Model Rule 1.1 states; "A lawyer shall provide competent representation to a client. Competent representation requires the legal knowledge, skill, thoroughness and preparation reasonably necessary for the representation." The ABA Model Code of Professional Responsibility has a similar provision; ABA DR 6–101(A) prohibits a lawyer from taking a case that "he knows or should know that he is not competent to handle, without associating himself with a lawyer who is competent to handle it." The Ethics 2000 Commission proposed no changes to MR 1.1 except for a few additions to the Comments, which were accepted by the ABA House of Delegates.

Preparation

estate plan—A legal structure designed to pass on one's assets to others in life and at death and to minimize estate taxes and probate costs.

forms books—Books that have samples of various kinds of complaints, answers, and other litigation documents.

Ultimately, a lawyer must be prepared to handle the client's case, be it a transaction (such as creating an **estate plan**) or litigation. And as the Rules and Comments attest, a lawyer must possess the legal knowledge and skills needed to be competent. The legal knowledge necessary to adequately represent a client involves more than knowing the substantive law of the underlying matter (for instance, knowing the difference between a partnership and a limited partnership), but also knowing the procedural minutiae of the jurisdiction, including the state and local court rules. **Forms books** that help lawyers draft pleadings or motions and professional practice series volumes that help lawyers apply statutes and court rules to specific areas of practice can be valuable tools in bringing one up to speed. Remember from Chapter 7, however, that the client should not be billed for the time it takes a practitioner to reach a stage of competence.

For the new lawyer, as with anyone who is attempting something new, there is the dreaded learning curve. If one's first day on the job is one's worst day on the job, then things can only get better with experience. Unfortunately, however, the new lawyer is bound by the same competency requirement that affects the most experienced lawyer in the jurisdiction. That leaves new lawyers with a disproportionate competency burden, for which courts will still hold them accountable. (See *Lewis v. State Bar*, 621 P.2d 258 [Cal. 1981], where, in a concurring opinion, a Justice stated that law schools should do more to prepare students for law practice.) Even in a firm where the new lawyer is expected to sink or swim, it is incumbent on him or her to ask for help. In an Indiana case, a new lawyer was severely disciplined for a web of deceit created to cause his clients—who were contesting a will—to think he was proceeding with their case. His ever-escalating, three-year sham included taking his clients to the statehouse, telling them he had an appointment concerning their case with the supreme court, and then telling them, after entering and reentering different doors of the statehouse, that the appointment had been postponed. And, as he eventually acknowledged, his troubles stemmed not just from the fact that he lacked the skills to handle the litigation, but because he was afraid to ask others in his firm for help. *In re Deardorff*, 426 N.E. 2d 689 (Ind. 1981).

Diligence

Connected to the duty of competence is diligence, and ABA MR 1.3 states, "A lawyer shall act with reasonable diligence and promptness in representing a client." The Model Code's DR 6–101(A)(3) mandates that a lawyer should not "[n]eglect a legal matter entrusted to him." And Ethical Consideration 6–4 states that a lawyer needs to "give appropriate attention to his legal work." The Ethics 2000 Commission made no changes to MR 1.3 but proposed a few more Comments to the rule, which were accepted by the House of Delegates.

Diligence is a necessary component of competence because, regardless of a lawyer's superior legal knowledge and skill, the duty of competence would be violated if a lawyer neglects the client's matter, fails to meet deadlines, or seeks unreasonable delays. One of the Comments to Model Rule 1.3 puts it plainly: "Perhaps no professional shortcoming is more widely resented than procrastination."

Reasonable diligence applies throughout all stages of the client's case, from investigating the facts and law sufficiently to know the applicable statute of limitations, to staying abreast of discovery timetables and court dates and completing tasks necessary to protect the client's interests in the event of a positive or negative judgment. In a case that would make a dead turtle look fast by comparison, a New York lawyer, having timely filed a personal injury complaint on behalf of his client, then neglected the case for fourteen years. Upon being investigated for his dilatory tactics, the lawyer claimed that it was his litigation strategy to delay the case until the opposing party's best witness was no longer available. The court took the view that such a strange strategy would have been impossible for the lawyer to devise, since he never investigated the client's case after filing the complaint, and so could not have known who that witness was. *In re Kovitz*, 504 N.Y.S.2d 400 (App. Div. 1986).

A lawyer's duty to be diligent also extends to the ending of the lawyer-client relationship, requiring that he or she inform the client if intending to withdraw from the case. Failure to do so subjects a lawyer to sanction. An extreme example of this failure is a Colorado case in which a lawyer was disbarred in absentia for leaving sixty clients in the lurch after he abandoned his law practice and left the state. *People v. Crist*, 948 P.2d 1020 (Colo. 1997).

Communication

How long will it be before there is a "Lawyers Are from Mars, Clients . . ." book on communication for legal professionals? It would seem that if one were to read all the books on improving one's communication skills, there would be no time left over to actually talk to anyone. But in fact poor communication is a significant cause of client grievances filed with bar associations or disciplinary committees. In Indiana, for example, the state supreme court's disciplinary commission reports that over 35 percent of the grievances filed against lawyers involve allegations of lack of client communication (which includes nondiligence in the representation). (The upside may be that it is better that more client complaints against lawyers concern communication and diligence failures than misdeeds such as fraud or illegal conduct.)

The duty to communicate with clients is expressly covered in ABA Model Rule 1.4, which states,

> (a) A lawyer shall keep a client reasonably informed about the status of a matter and promptly comply with reasonable requests for information.
> (b) A lawyer shall explain a matter to the extent reasonably necessary to permit the client to make informed decisions regarding the representation.

The ABA Model Code has no singular counterpart, although a variety of Disciplinary Rules and Ethical Considerations discuss the lawyer's duty to not neglect a client's case, and to promptly inform a client about material developments. *See* DR 6–101(A)3; EC 7–8; EC 9–2.

The duty to communicate with the client becomes more difficult to honor as a lawyer's caseload increases, but nonetheless, he or she must maintain open lines of communication with the client through all stages of the case. There are many disciplinary cases with instances of lawyers being sanctioned for inadequate client communication, from failing to inform the client of the legal proceedings undertaken or material changes in the case and failing to respond to the client's requests for information about the status of the case in a timely manner to failing to inform the client of mistakes made or about the conclusion of the case, and even failing to inform the client that the lawyer has withdrawn from the case or left the law firm.

Often in litigation, settlement negotiations take place in the absence of the parties as the lawyers haggle over settlement offers or the language of the settlement agreement. Nevertheless, the Rules, the Comments, and the case law make it clear that a lawyer must communicate all settlement offers with the client unless he or she knows the client will reject the offer. And because the client is the decision maker concerning the substance of his or her case, the lawyer needs to keep him or her reasonably well informed so that he or she can make informed decisions.

Competence and the Legal Assistant

As a member of the legal team, the legal assistant has a corresponding duty to provide competent and diligent services. As discussed in Chapter 2, ABA Model Rule 5.3, which is operative in most jurisdictions, requires partners and supervising lawyers to make reasonable efforts to ensure that their non-lawyer employees comport themselves with the same professional obligations as if they were lawyers.

What Makes a Legal Assistant Competent?

Canon 6 of the NALA Code of Ethics and Professional Responsibility requires a legal assistant to "maintain integrity and a high degree of competency through education and training . . . and through continuing education." The NALA Model Standards and Guidelines for Utilization of Legal Assistants discusses competency in its Section on Standards and lists seven different standards, many of them education related, that help determine a legal assistant's minimum qualifications. The NFPA Model Disciplinary Rules and Ethical Considerations speaks to the issue of competence in Rule 1.1, where it states, "A paralegal shall achieve and maintain a high level of competence." Three Ethical Considerations amplify the above maxim. EC–1.1(a) states that competency is achieved through education, training, and work experience; EC–1.1(b) requires a paralegal to participate in continuing education; and EC–1.1(c) concerns diligence, requiring a paralegal to "perform all assignments promptly and efficiently."

The law has such a broad horizon that the **West Digest System®**, a research tool every paralegal should know how to use, is organized under 414 separate topics and has thousands of subdivisions. There are federal and state statutes, federal and state administrative rules, and federal and state rules of court, not to mention local versions of the above-described kinds of primary authority. Since an overwhelming majority of jurisdictions in America do not require certain prerequisites in order for one to work as a legal assistant or to use the titles "paralegal" or "legal assistant," competence may be in the eye of the beholder—the employer. There are, however, certain competency factors about which all paralegal and legal assistant organizations are in agreement. First, one should get a high-quality education from an accredited college whose legal program is a member of the American Association for Paralegal Education and is either ABA approved or in compliance with ABA curriculum standards. Second, all those who work in a legal environment need to take **continuing legal education (CLE)** courses. Lawyers must earn a minimum number of CLE credits annually in order to maintain their law licenses. Legal assistants should try to do the same, although it can be difficult for them to earn annual CLE credits if their employers will not subsidize the cost of those courses. Considering that a half-day seminar can cost upward of several hundred dollars, it takes considerable commitment to stay current, even if required to maintain one's certification with either the NALA or NFPA.

The Legal Assistant and Client Communication

Because the economics of legal assistant–client contact are favorable, legal assistants often communicate with clients on behalf of lawyers. Interviewing clients, assisting clients in discovery matters, taking client phone calls, and writing correspondence to clients are just some of the ways in which the use of legal assistants is beneficial to both clients and law firms. Little things, such as returning client phone calls in a timely way and sending the client courtesy copies of all documents prepared on his or her behalf, can go a long way to prevent him or her from becoming disgruntled and in the mood to file a grievance against the lawyer.

West Digest System®—A method for researching case law, designed by the West Publishing Co., in which the law is divided into 414 topics, which are then divided into thousands of subtopics. When matched together, each topic and subtopic is known by its title and "key number" and corresponds to the key numbers of the headnotes for the cases, which are found by using a West digest.

continuing legal education (CLE)—A lawyer must earn certain annual CLE credits, as determined by the jurisdiction in which he or she is licensed. CLE credits, commonly called CLEs, are earned by attending bar-sponsored or -approved seminars that concern different practice areas of the law. Lawyers must also earn continuing legal ethics credits as part of their annual CLE requirements.

Nevertheless, a lawyer's duty to communicate with clients cannot be completely delegated to non-lawyer employees because the responsibility for honoring the communication duty rests with the lawyer. For example, in a Kansas case, a lawyer with a high-volume bankruptcy practice ran his law firm through hiring over a dozen paralegals but giving them very little training. Judges repeatedly cautioned the lawyer about his shoddy law practice, to which he responded by repeatedly blaming his employees. Eventually, three of those former employees contacted the state bar's disciplinary administrator, telling him of their former employer's practices. The evidence showed the lawyer's complete lack of supervision of his paralegals and failure to communicate with his clients. In fact, on one occasion the lawyer divided thirty days' worth of past phone messages among his employees, telling them to find out what the callers wanted. He was suspended from the practice of law indefinitely. *In re Farmer*, 950 P.2d 713 (Kan. 1997).

In the following case, a lawyer was held responsible for failing to communicate with his client and allowing his non-lawyer employees to commit the unauthorized practice of law because of his failure to supervise them and his sole reliance on their contact with his client.

Case Law

Mays v. Neal, 938 S.W.2d 830 (Ark. 1997)

GLAZE, Justice

This dispute arose after Mays's law firm, Mays & Crutcher, P.A., undertook to represent Vanessa Conley, who on July 18, 1994, was involved in a motor vehicle accident in Little Rock. The other vehicle involved in the accident was a rental car, which was insured by Empire Insurance Company. At the scene of the accident, a man, later known to be Tim Mason, approached Conley, asking her who caused the accident. Conley said that Mason identified himself as an investigator, and suggested Conley needed legal representation. This interchange resulted in Conley signing a contract employing Mays as her attorney. Mason gave Conley a business card bearing the name of Catherine Stevens and instructed Conley that Stevens was the person Conley should call.[1] Stevens later sent a copy of Conley's contract to Empire, along with her business card.

Conley said that, on July 19, 1994, Stevens called Conley's home and spoke with her husband, and Conley says she returned the call on July 20, 1994. Conley claims that, during her conversation with Stevens, Stevens referred her to the Price Chiropractic Clinic. Conley was subsequently treated by the Price Clinic from about July 25, 1994, to October 21, 1994. In November 1994, negotiations to settle Conley's claim took place between Stevens and Chuck Traylor, who was the claims adjuster with Empire Insurance Co. Some confusion and differences occurred between Stevens and Conley over the method and amount of payment Conley would approve before reaching any settlement. Conley also expressed that, although she had been released by the Price Clinic, she was still having pain and needed to see another doctor. Conley became dissatisfied with the manner in which her case was being handled, and on November 30, 1994, she went to Mays's office to retrieve her file. While Stevens retained possession of Conley's file because Mays was not present, it is clear the Mays-Conley relationship had been severed by December 6, 1994—the date Stevens had notified Empire Insurance by letter (with a copy to Conley) that Mays no longer represented Conley. The letter also reflected that Conley had rejected Empire's $9,000.00 offer to settle, but Mays had retained an attorney's lien on any proceeds to be paid Conley in the future. Conley later claimed she had been unaware of any $9,000.00 offer until she received a copy of the December 6 letter.

Conley subsequently pursued her claim without the assistance of an attorney, and sought information from Empire Insurance by writing that Company on March 26, 1995. Empire's adjuster, Traylor, responded, indicating that he had not received the December 6 letter written by Mays, that he had already settled Conley's claim by having spoken with "Jim," who was with Mays's firm, and that Conley would have to obtain a letter reflecting Mays no longer represented her. In May of 1995, Conley forwarded to Traylor a copy of Mays's earlier December 6 letter, and informed Traylor that she had since contacted the Supreme Court Professional Conduct Committee and complained about Mays's representation. She further asked Traylor for a copy of the $9,000.00 check dated November 30, 1994, which purportedly had been sent to Mays in settlement of her claim. Upon receipt of Conley's May 1995 letter, Traylor sent Conley another letter, wherein he forwarded her a copy of the $9,000.00 check. The check had never been cashed. In August of 1995, Conley filed her formal complaint against Mays with the Professional Conduct Committee, alleging eight violations of the Model Rules of Professional Conduct, two of which the Committee eventually found meritorious. Besides complaining to the Committee about her initial confusion concerning the manner in which Mays established his contractual relationship with Conley, she also complained he failed to communicate and keep her informed concerning the law firm's negotiations with Empire Insurance Company in her

behalf. . . .

We first address the Committee's decision that Mays violated Rule 1.4(b) by failing to communicate properly with his client, Conley. Rule 1.4(b) provides, "[A] lawyer shall explain a matter to the extent reasonably necessary to permit the client to make informed decisions regarding the representation." Adequacy of communication depends in part on the kind of advice or assistance involved. *See* Comment to Rule 1.4(b). The Comment further offers the example that, in negotiations where there is time to explain a proposal, the lawyer should review all important provisions with the client before proceeding to an agreement.

In the present case, such a review did not happen. In fact, from the beginning, there is proof that Mays's law firm failed to explain its contract with Conley or make clear early in the employment relationship the objectives of that legal representation. While Mays testified that he initially tries to make contact with his clients, he conceded that he never met with Conley or spoke to her by telephone. Mays further conceded that Conley's only contact with his firm was through his staff, and Stevens admitted that she had worked on Conley's case before Mays knew Conley was a client. In addition, Conley averred that her only contact with the firm was through Stevens even though, on several occasions, Conley had asked for an appointment with Mays. Each time Conley was told she should communicate with Stevens. In sum, although Mays and Stevens both related that Mays had instructed Stevens how Conley's case should be settled, the evidence is undisputed that Conley was afforded no opportunity to communicate directly with Mays and to ask him questions about her case. Obviously, the record supports the view that Mays had relied entirely upon his non-lawyer staff member to communicate with Conley even though Conley had posed questions concerning her legal representation, and was denied the opportunity to resolve those questions by meeting with him. . . .

[The portion of the opinion dealing with the lawyer's violation of MR 5.3 and 5.5, assisting others in the unauthorized practice of law, has been deleted.]

From the foregoing rules and principles, it is clear that, while a lawyer may delegate certain tasks to his assistants, he or she, as supervising attorney, has the ultimate responsibility for compliance by the non-lawyer with the applicable provisions of the Model Rules. In reviewing the record, we conclude Mays failed in this respect both in his firm's initial contracting with Conley and when negotiating her claim.

We again review in more detail the events leading to the signing of Conley as a client. In fact, Conley's testimony reflects she was confused and dissatisfied with her legal representation beginning when she signed Mays's contract at the scene of her accident on July 18, 1994. She said that she did not know who Mason was or what she had signed. She thought the paper she signed was for Mason to investigate the accident and to authorize him to get information. Mays testified that he did not employ, nor did he know Tim Mason, even though Mason possessed Stevens's business card and the law firm's employment contract which Conley signed. Ray Keech, an investigator and process server hired by the Committee, testified that in his attempts to locate Mason he was given a phone number, which turned out to be that for Mays & Crutcher. When Keech called the number, the person answering indicated that Mason only came into the office about once a month. . . .

We also note that there was substantial evidence that Mays had provided inadequate supervision over the manner in which his assistants negotiated Conley's claim. Mays testified that he monitored Conley's personal injury claim and evaluated it after receiving medical reports, bills, and wage-loss statements. He stated that he met with Stevens and Morris, and established a high and low range within which to settle. Mays said that Jimmy Morris had most of the contacts with Empire Insurance, and Stevens mostly dealt with Conley. Because Conley's injury was a "soft-tissue" injury and she had incurred medical expenses of $2,700.00 to $2,800.00, Mays said he set a settlement range between $6,500.00 and $10,500.00.

Contrary to Stevens's version, Conley testified that she had never told Stevens how much she wished to net and never authorized a settlement in any amount. Nonetheless, Mays stated that he had authorized settlement for $9,000.00 because he could make some money and satisfy Conley as well. Without obtaining Conley's approval, Morris called Traylor at Empire Insurance, and the Company sent Mays a check for $9,000.00. While Conley had advised Stevens she would not settle for the Company's offer, Conley was unaware the Company had sent a $9,000.00 check until months after she had terminated Mays's firm.

Also adding to Conley's confusion was that, while Conley knew of Stevens, she was wholly unaware of the role Morris played in the negotiations with Empire Insurance, and only learned of Morris's existence after the insurance company later told her it had settled Conley's claim with "Jim." Unlike with Stevens, Morris's name was never disclosed as an assistant on the law firm stationery.

In sum, we must conclude, as did the Committee, that Mays failed to properly delegate his legal work and responsibilities and failed to properly supervise work delegated to his assistants. If he had, he would have been in the position at the least to have tried to resolve the questions that continued to resurface during his legal representation of Conley. For these reasons, we affirm the Committee's decisions.

The following case footnote corresponds to the portion of the case that is printed in the textbook. Although it may seem that other footnotes are missing, they are not presented because their corresponding portions of the court's opinion have been redacted.

[1]The business card reflected the Mays & Crutcher Law Offices and showed Catherine Stevens as "Senior Claims Manager."

Case Questions

1. What solicitation and other violations were committed by Tim Mason?
2. What violations were committed by Catherine Stevens?
3. Empire Insurance believed it had settled the case with "Jim." Who was he?
4. How could attorney Mays contend he did not know who Tim Mason was, when Mason was the one who signed up Conley as a client for Mays?
5. Mays settled a claim on behalf of a client he had never met (who had requested to talk with him) and then Mays placed a lien on his client's future settlement. In light of that and the other activities of his agents, explain how it was that he was only reprimanded.

Protecting Yourself against Charges of Incompetence

Because competence is expected, and not simply encouraged, those who want to be competent must be willing to do whatever is necessary to achieve it. Often, that requires legal assistants to spend, personal time learning about the nuances of the area of the law in which they work, brushing up on legal software, perusing forms books, and scanning legal periodicals for practice-specific updates or changes. Another important item to bear in mind is that asking someone for assistance is a sign of competence, not inadequacy; a legal assistant who fails to ask for help could later be the reason a lawyer's representation is found to be incompetent. And because language is the tool used by legal professionals, every legal assistant should know how to use the English language effectively, including punctuation.

Paying attention to detail is, perhaps, the most important component of competent work. More legal assistants work in litigation than do not, and litigation is rife with competence pitfalls. Although trials are so often the sole focus of fictionalized accounts of litigation, in reality the trial is the tip, while the discovery process is the iceberg. The volumes of papers that need to be date-stamped, processed, and indexed can be mind-boggling. Much of that work, including summarizing depositions, drafting pleadings, researching and drafting motions, working with accountants and other litigation consultants, and maintaining contact with the client and with opposing counsels or their employees, falls on the desks of paralegals. Throughout what can seem to be an endless process, legal assistants must manage those details, remembering that failure to sufficiently follow the procedural rules can result in a negative judgment for the client, not to mention a negative employee review.

When lawyers formally defend against disciplinary charges of incompetence by blaming their non-lawyer employees, courts turn away their collective ears for two reasons: (a) MR.5.3 makes lawyers responsible for the conduct of their non-lawyer employees; and (b) even if such a defense was factually accurate, non-lawyers cannot be professionally disciplined by a court. If it is true that the duty of competence imposes a disproportionate burden to the new lawyer, it could be said that the burden is even greater to the legal assistant. Here is why: although the lawyer is formally responsible to the client, it is possible that when explaining an error to the client, the lawyer might place the brunt of the blame on the legal assistant, regardless of whether the legal assistant is at fault. As unfair as it may be, for the sake of saving face, blame is often passed down the hierarchy. Therefore, it is critical that non-lawyer employees, through vigilant efforts of professional work, protect themselves as much as is possible against accusations of incompetent handling of client affairs.

Two Perspectives on Competence and Professionalism

High-ranking officials from the NALA and the NFPA have each written an essay for this chapter on the following topic: What makes a legal assistant or paralegal competent and professional?

Vicki J. Kunz, President of the National Association of Legal Assistants   [Vicki J. Kunz, CLAS, is a certified legal assistant specialist and is employed by MDU Resources Group, Inc., Bismarck, North Dakota, as a Risk Management Specialist II. Ms. Kunz has been with MDU Resources Group for four years and has worked in both the corporate legal department and risk management departments. She has been a paralegal since 1984 and has been deeply involved, in leadership roles, in the National Association of Legal Assistants, Inc., since 1986. She was recently installed as NALA president and has completed terms as first vice president, second vice president, treasurer, and secretary. She has chaired many committees, including the National Certifying Board for the CLA Program. Ms. Kunz obtained her CLA designation in 1987 and her Civil Litigation Specialist designation in 1990, both from the National Association of Legal Assistants. She is a charter member of the Western Dakota Association of Legal Assistants, founded in 1986, and has been a legal assistant member of Big Muddy Bar Association since 1991. She is also a board member for the Missouri Slope Areawide United Way, a past president of the Bismarck Business and Professional Women's Club, and a member of Toastmasters International, in which she holds the Competent Toastmaster (CTM) designation.]

It goes without saying that the number one quality of any paralegal is that of having high moral and ethical standards. Throw in the desire to continuously learn and the special characteristic of compassion for others, and you will find a true professional paralegal.

A legal assistant's ethical conduct should be of utmost integrity. There is no question that legal assistants must adhere to the same professional rules and responsibility of lawyers and they must live by the profession's code of ethics. These factors contribute to the professional strength and trust a paralegal develops with their employer and their employer's clients.

To possess a balanced relationship with employers, it is important to recognize that paralegals maintain the same level of professionalism as their employers in order to earn the same level of respect. Professionalism is about being trustworthy and living by high ethical standards. In addition, professional development also plays a significant part in being a true professional.

Continue to grow in your profession and take on new challenges—seek out continuing legal education opportunities such as seminars, on-line courses, and workshops. Pursue training in a new area such as technology or a specialized area of law. Or even better, set yourself apart from others in your field by seeking certification, a proven, measurable, and respected credential.

Advice I have shared over the years with many paralegals, and the basis of my theme as NALA President, is *Professionalism is a choice.* You must commit to your own professional growth—no one is going to do it for you. One of the best opportunities you have in making that commitment is by getting actively involved in your local or national professional organization. You can only prosper and benefit by surrounding yourself with other professionals. The continual investment you make in your professional organization will keep you on track in developing your own career.

Lesley G. Cox, Vice President on Positions and Issues, National Federation of Paralegal Associations   [Lesley G. Cox, RP, is a Senior Paralegal at Church Church Hittle & Antrim in Noblesville, Indiana, where she has been a litigation paralegal for over twelve years. She attended the State University of New York at Plattsburgh and received her paralegal education at Indiana University in Indianapolis, Indiana. She became a Paralegal Advanced Competency Exam (PACE) Registered Paralegal in 1999. Ms. Cox is serving her second term as the vice president of positions and issues of the National Federation of Paralegal Associations. The following areas come under her purview: bar associations, case law, ethics, legislation, multidisciplinary practice, regulation review, special research, and unauthorized practice of law. Prior to her election she served as NFPA's Multidisciplinary Practice Coordinator and also served on the Regulation Review and PACE Liaison committees. She is the Immediate Past-President of the Indiana Paralegal Association (IPA) where she also served as for several years as IPA's Secondary representative to NFPA. She is a member of the Indiana State Bar Association's paralegal task force, which was instrumental in gaining paralegal membership in that association. She is also a member of the Indianapolis Bar Association and is on its paralegal executive and professional responsibility committees. She is a past chair of the Hamilton County Paralegal Association and an ATLA paralegal affiliate. Lesley was awarded the 2000 NFPA Dyncorp Outstanding Local Leadership Award.]

What makes a paralegal competent and professional? The answer to this question has several layers—professional, professionalism, and profession.

Each profession has its own standards and criteria. Through the representation of national associations, [we] paralegals have largely self-directed our profession and have set many of these standards and criteria for ourselves. Paralegals have become an integral part of the legal team, and the effective utilization of paralegals is essential to providing the highest quality and most cost-effective legal services. It is the recognition by attorneys and the endorsement of courts across the country and around the world that have given validity to paralegals and the paralegal profession.

Professionalism is the conduct or qualities that characterize a professional person. I include competence in this area as it is one of those qualities, and it is through the criteria below that we gain competence.

What are the criteria and standards that need to be established for recognition of a profession? Education is the first key. It is only through education and training that we gain the competence to be able to perform substantive legal tasks. It is this substance that courts are looking for when they award paralegal fees. Another key is the need for continuing that legal education. It is vital that we maintain our level of skills, increase our knowledge and stay current with the law. Many states and jurisdictions have adopted paralegal definitions and rules or guidelines regarding paralegals. These are the first steps in regulating paralegals and another key in establishing this field as a profession. It is vital that paralegals be regulated in some fashion, whether through licensing, certification or some other means, with established criteria, rules to follow, and a mechanism to enforce those rules. Pro bono service is another factor. Paralegals can benefit the community, the private bar, the judiciary, and the paralegal profession by volunteering their time, abilities, and skills as trained legal professionals. Testing is another important step. NFPA developed PACE (Paralegal Advanced Competency Exam) as a means to test the competency of experienced paralegals. Paralegals can use PACE to validate experience and job skills; establish credentials; and increase their value to their organization and clients. Finally, and perhaps most importantly, one of the most significant criteria for competence and professionalism is our adherence to ethical guidelines and rules of professional responsibility. NFPA recognizes not only an attorney's ethical obligations with respect to the utilization of paralegal services but also recognizes those obligations as they apply to paralegals individually. NFPA members supported that premise when they created and adopted the NPFA Model Code of Ethics and Professional Responsibilities, delineating the principles for ethics and conduct to which every paralegal should aspire.

Paralegals, an integral part of the legal profession, are professionals in the truest sense of the word.

TRUTHFULNESS

More than a few rules of ethics concern the lawyer's—and by extension, the paralegal's—duty to be truthful. Although it might go without saying that a lawyer should be truthful, the rules formalize the appropriate conduct of the lawyer in certain situations, much of which has to do with litigation. Also, the comments to the rules help explain what it means to be untruthful.

The General Rule on Truth

ABA Model Rule 4.1 clearly states the following:

In the course of representing a client a lawyer shall not knowingly:
(a) make a false statement of material fact or law to a third person; or

(b) fail to disclose a material fact to a third person when disclosure is necessary to avoid assisting a criminal or fraudulent act by a client, unless disclosure is prohibited by Rule 1.6

That language is identical to the language in MR 3.3(a)(1) and (2), which concerns truthfulness to a tribunal. MR 4.1 is nearly identical to two provisions in DR 7–102(A) in the ABA Model Code. DR 7–102(A)(3) states that a lawyer shall not "[c]onceal or knowingly fail to disclose that which he is required by law to reveal." And DR 7–102(A)(5) states, "In his representation of a client, a lawyer shall not . . . [k]nowingly make a false statement of law or fact." The Ethics 2000 version of MR 4.1 is the same as the present version, although the Committee added some new Comments to MR 4.1, which were accepted by the ABA House of Delegates.

The basic rule on truthfulness has a multitude of layers of interpretation. Of those, legal assistants should remember three important concepts associated with the truthfulness duty. First, it is only a "knowing" **misrepresentation** that is in violation of the ethics rules. While negligent misrepresentations may be the cause of other legal problems, intentional misrepresentations are the kinds that the professional responsibility rules consider untruthful. Second, an intentional misrepresentation must be "material" in order to be unethical. Without splitting hairs unnecessarily, not all falsehoods are created equal, and a material misrepresentation is one that is significant in proportion to the statement in full. Third, failure to disclose what should be disclosed is as much a misrepresentation as stating something falsely. This concept is a delicate one. Although a legal assistant may not use silence to help a client commit a crime or fraudulent act, a legal assistant may also not disclose anything that would violate the lawyer-client confidentiality rule.

misrepresentation—A false or untruthful statement. Silence can be considered misrepresentation when there is a duty to speak. Misrepresentation can be negligent, as well as intentional.

Clients and Truthfulness

Zealous representation of the client is mentioned in Canon 7 of the ABA Model Code and also discussed in the Comments to ABA Model Rule 1.3, but zealousness must be tempered by fairness to the other side and its legal team, as well as fidelity to the administration of justice. Two areas of violations with respect to clients will be discussed: bringing frivolous claims and putting forth false evidence.

Frivolous Claims
After a twenty-seven-year-old man was found in his underwear and dead, having drowned in the tank of a killer whale at Sea World Orlando, his parents sued Sea World, arguing that the park was to blame because it portrayed the killer whale as safe and huggable. Is that a frivolous lawsuit? What about Stella Liebeck, who suffered third degree burns on her thighs and genitals after spilling the McDonald's coffee that was resting between her legs as she sat in a car? Was her lawsuit against McDonald's frivolous? After the trial judge reduced the jury verdict, Ms. Liebeck was awarded $640,000, but the parties eventually reached a confidential settlement. In the minds of many Americans, her case was ridiculous. However, not as

many of those who cast aspersions on her were aware that McDonald's had been the recipient of over 700 complaints in the ten-year period before the infamous lawsuit about her severe coffee burns. Nor did many know that McDonald's held its coffee at a temperature between 180° and 190° F., about 40 degrees hotter than coffee made at home. Almost everyone bearing an axe to grind with the American legal system starts their argument with a favorite story about a frivolous lawsuit that wastes court resources and is filed by a money-hungry lawyer with no hint of ethics. Even Ann Landers got involved recounting as true the story of a mythical case—a so-called urban legend. A column of hers included a harangue on the legal system by discussing a case in which a woman sued a pharmacy for negligence because she purchased a tube of contraceptive jelly at the pharmacy, went home and made some toast, put the jelly on the toast and ate it, had sex, and got pregnant. As the story goes, her lawsuit proceeded along the line that the pharmacy should have done more to alert her to the fact that contraceptive jelly is not to be eaten.

ABA Model Rule 3.1 does not define what constitutes a frivolous claim, but it does state that a lawyer should not bring or defend a frivolous claim. MR 3.1 also states that in criminal cases, a lawyer may defend a client (including one who has committed acts that constitute the crime) so as to force the prosecution to prove every element of the charges. DR 7–102(A)(1) of the ABA Model Code states that a lawyer may not "[f]ile a suit, assert a position, conduct a defense, delay a trial, or take other action on behalf of his client when he knows or when it is obvious that such action would serve merely to harass or maliciously injure another." The Ethics 2000 proposal for MR 3.1 includes a slight change that prohibits a lawyer from taking a case, "unless there is a basis *in law and fact* for doing so that is not frivolous," and that proposal was accepted by the House of Delegates (emphasis added).

Frivolousness is a highly subjective concept because there is little specific instruction on what makes a case frivolous. Part of the confusion is due to the fact that chance of success is considered an inadequate litmus test, since even a long-shot case has a right to be filed. But there are two types of claims that courts will find lacking in merit. First, claims made in **bad faith** are considered frivolous. A bad faith claim includes one that is made for no other purpose than to harass or embarrass someone else. An example of a bad faith case comes from North Dakota, where a lawyer was publicly reprimanded for harassing his ex-wife by groundlessly suing her for invasion of privacy and slander. *In re Bard*, 519 N.W.2d 286 (N.D. 1994).

Second, claims are considered frivolous if they are so devoid of substance that there could be no legitimate basis for relief or remedy. Often, courts refer to these types of cases as having no basis in law or facts. Such was the case in an example from New York, where a lawyer was sanctioned with a $1,500 fine for what the appellate court called leveling a "frontal assault" against a trial judge. This frontal assault involved the lawyer seeking a **writ of mandamus** against a newly assigned trial judge for not responding to the lawyer's trial motions quickly enough to suit his tastes. Ironically, the lawyer was nailed for maliciously attempting to sanction a judge for moving slowly in a case the lawyer had been handling for nineteen years. *Public Administrator of County of New York v. Cohen*, N.Y.S.2d 106 (App. Div. 1995).

bad faith—Something done in bad faith is done dishonestly, or with ulterior motives.

writ of mandamus—An order issued by a court, ordering some official to do a particular act that was requested by the party seeking the writ of mandamus.

Consider Caesar Barber, the New York resident who filed a suit in July 2002, claiming that fast food was the "legal" cause of his obesity and related health problems. Is he responsible for his own health and showing his true gluttony by trying to reap millions from the four largest fast food chains by claiming they should have told him that items like triple cheeseburgers with bacon and large orders of french fries contribute to health problems? Or does he have a legitimate lawsuit when he blames the provider of his favorite foods for enticing him to eat their food but failing to inform him of the actual fat content in it? His lawsuit is seeking other plaintiffs so it can be certified as a class action, and the way one views that kind of lawsuit—frivolous or legitimate—might have as much to do with one's political views as one's legal opinions.

Distinct from the professional responsibility rules, sanctions can be issued against lawyers who file frivolous claims because of Civil Procedure Rule 11, operative in the federal and state civil procedure rules. That rule requires that the attorney of record (i.e., the one who signs the pleadings, motions, or other litigation filings) be responsible to ensure that the filings are well grounded in fact and not made for any improper purpose. Sanctions are also available under Civil Procedure Rule 37 against lawyers who are found to have abused the discovery process. Furthermore, Rule 38 of the Federal Rules of Appellate Procedure provides, "If a court of appeals shall determine that an appeal is frivolous, it may award just damages and single or double costs to the appellee."

A federal statute provides for sanctions against an attorney, or other person permitted to conduct cases in federal court, who "multiplies the proceedings in any case unreasonably and vexatiously." 28 U.S.C. § 1927. California has a statute designed to prevent vexatious litigation. It defines a such a litigant in different categories, including one who has in a seven-year period brought at least five non–small claims actions that have ended in negative judgments or have not been brought to adjudication within two years. Cal. Code of Civil Proc. § 391(b)(1). Once the determination is made that someone is a vexatious litigant, that person must obtain court approval before bringing another suit or else be found in contempt of court. Cal. Code of Civil Proc. § 391.7. Legislation that restricts one's right to sue is controversial, but California's vexatious litigation statute has been upheld on appeal against claims that it is unconstitutional. *Wolfgram v. Wells Fargo Bank*, 61 Cal.Rptr.2d 694 (Cal. App. 1997).

False Evidence
ABA Model Rule 3.3(a)(1)(2), and (4) prohibit a lawyer from making material misrepresentations to a tribunal, failing to disclose material facts when disclosure is necessary to prevent assisting the client in committing a criminal or fraudulent act, and offering evidence the lawyer knows is false. The Model Code has nearly identical prohibitions in DR 7–102(A)(5), DR 7–102(A)(3), and DR 7–102(A)(4). The Ethics 2000 version of MR 3.3 has been revised and reorganized. Included in this revision is the removal of the word "material" from MR 3.3(a)(1), as well as expanding the lawyer's duty to take remedial action if he or she becomes aware that someone is engaging, or has engaged, in fraudulent activity with respect to the case. The ABA House of Delegates accepted the new MR 3.3.

Problems in this area can occur when the lawyer knows the client wants to testify falsely. If the case is a civil matter, the lawyer may not allow the client to testify falsely, preventing this by going so far as to inform the judge about the intended perjury if, after discussing the matter with the client, it is clear that the latter still insists on testifying falsely.

The answer is not so easy in a criminal matter, however, because of a criminal defendant's constitutional rights. Although a lawyer may not put a criminal defendant on the stand and assist him or her in committing perjury, there is a line of thinking that says that a lawyer may "cut the baby in two" by allowing the defendant to take the stand to present his or her testimony in a narrative. This approach involves the defendant talking from the witness stand, but without any direct examination by the defense lawyer. During the closing argument, the lawyer will also avoid referring to the defendant's testimony. Courts have given their approval to this narrative approach to perjured testimony because, as one court put it, "the narrative approach best accommodates the competing interests of the defendant's constitutional right to testify and the attorney's ethical obligations." *People v. Johnson*, 72 Cal.Rptr.2d 805, 818 (Cal.App. 1998) (Also in the case, the court cited other jurisdictions that approved of the narrative approach.)

Not all jurisdictions agree with the narrative approach to perjured testimony in criminal cases. The Comments to MR 3.3 criticize the narrative approach, and the ABA reaffirmed its opposition in an ethics opinion that states that if all attempts at dissuading the client from lying on the stand fail, the lawyer must disclose the intended perjury to the court. ABA Commission on Ethics and Professional Responsibility, Formal Op. 87–353 (1987). Also, the United States Supreme Court took a case on perjured testimony in *Nix v. Whiteside*, 475 U.S. 157 (1986). In *Nix*, a murder defendant planned on testifying falsely about whether the victim was holding a gun at the time of the attack, and the defendant's lawyer explained that he would have to inform the trial court of the defendant's actions if the latter insisted on testifying falsely. The defendant testified truthfully and then, after being convicted, appealed on the grounds that he was denied effective assistance of counsel because his counsel prevented his intended testimony. The Supreme Court affirmed the conviction, finding that, although the constitutional right to testify is certain, "it is elementary that such a right does not extend to testifying falsely." *Nix*, at 173. However, *Nix v. Whiteside* does not mean that a jurisdiction is prohibited from adopting the narrative approach; it does mean that a defendant cannot cry foul in those jurisdictions that refuse to allow for the narrative approach.

Other problems can arise when working with clients in discovery matters or helping them gather information in transactional matters, such as estate planning. There will be occasions when clients will express or imply a desire to hide information or assets or bend the truth. Although clients are allowed to seek every lawful advantage possible, they may not use the legal process for fraudulent purposes or as a refuge against the truth. For example, in a social security case, a lawyer was sanctioned for submitting a doctor's report that the lawyer knew had been changed in parts that concerned the extent of her client's injuries, as well as the dates of treatments. *In re Watkins*, 656 So.2d 984 (La. 1995). Therefore, when a paralegal has a reasonable suspicion that the client is being deceitful, it is imperative that those suspicions be reported to the supervising lawyer, because the lawyer is responsible for the paralegal's conduct, including any failure to take preventative or remedial action. Remember, if the client's presentation of fraudulent information is discovered, the lawyer, despite being unaware of the fraud, could be sanctioned for failing to adequately supervise the paralegal who was aware of it and failed to report it to the lawyer.

Unfortunately, there are occasions where lawyers violate the rules, not by allowing their clients to present false information, but by altering their clients' information. In an Arizona case, a lawyer changed the draft answers of his client's interrogatories before turning the final answers over to the opposing party, who had submitted the interrogatory questions. The client did not become aware of the changes until over a year later and, in the disciplinary proceedings, the lawyer argued that he did not violate MR 3.3 since the reason he had changed his client's draft answers was because they were originally incorrect. The court, in sanctioning the lawyer, stated that it was troubled by the lawyer's novel argument. *In re Shannon*, 876 P.2d 548 (Ariz. 1994). And in another case, a lawyer representing the **personal representative** of an **intestate estate** submitted a final account to the estate (which now had a different personal representative), which included attorney's fees. The new personal representative verified the account and mailed it back to the attorney for filing with the probate court. Upon receiving the verified account, the lawyer realized that she had underestimated her legal fees, so she instructed her legal assistant to alter the document by changing the legal fees portion. The legal assistant questioned the lawyer about the appropriateness of that and was told that the lawyer would contact the personal representative to get permission. That was not done, however. The legal assistant did change the document as instructed, but mailed it to the personal representative with a cover letter stating that changes had been made to the final account. Unfortunately, the representative never read the letter or altered account, which postponed the inevitable controversy by three months. In the disciplinary proceedings, the court considered the lawyer's actions a violation of several rules on honesty and suspended her for 120 days, but it offered no view on the complicity of the legal assistant. *In re Morris*, 953 P.2d 387 (Or. 1998).

personal representative— Someone appointed to manage the legal affairs of another person, or of an estate.

intestate estate—The personal and real property of a person who died without leaving a valid will to direct the transfer of that property.

Represented Persons and Truthfulness

ABA Model Rule 4.2 concerns under what circumstances a member of a legal team may contact a person represented by a lawyer, and states, "In representing a client, a lawyer shall not communicate about the subject of the representation with a person the lawyer knows to be represented by another lawyer in the matter, unless the lawyer has the consent of the other lawyer or is authorized by law to do so." This rule, which is known as the anticontact rule, is designed to protect against a lawyer taking unfair advantage of someone outside the presence of that person's lawyer. As stated in ABA Commission on Ethics and Professional Responsibility, Formal Op. 95–396 (1995), one of the purposes of this type of rule is to protect a represented person from unwittingly divulging privileged or harmful information that would not have been disclosed if the other lawyer were present.

This rule has a broader application beyond lawsuits and also applies when a lawyer knows the person to be contacted is represented by a lawyer in connection with the reason why the first lawyer wants to make contact. For instance, a lawyer could not directly contact a person from whom the lawyer's client wants to purchase a piece of property *if* the other person has retained a lawyer for the purposes of assisting in the sale of the property. The Ethics 2000 proposal for MR 4.2 has an addition to its exceptions that allows a lawyer to directly contact a represented person if the lawyer is authorized by a court order, and it was accepted by the ABA House of Delegates (along with some new Comments).

The ABA Model Code's anticontact rule is nearly identical, but the difference is significant. Not only does DR 7–104(A)(1) prohibit a lawyer from making inappropriate contact, but it also prohibits a lawyer from causing another person to make inappropriate contact. That language expressly covers the conduct of legal assistants. More important, DR 7–104(A)(1) uses the word "party" instead of "person." That distinction is significant because in jurisdictions that operate under the Model Code, a lawyer or legal assistant would only be prohibited from directly contacting the other party (which might require that there be formal legal proceedings underway), not others related to the legal matter, such as the party's family members or employees who have retained lawyers concerning the legal matter. Moreover, some jurisdictions that have adopted the Model Rules still use the word *party* in the language of MR 4.2 (which was used in the original ABA version of MR 4.2, prior to 1995), even though the title of MR 4.2 uses the word *person*. Some of the Model Rules jurisdictions whose version of MR 4.2 concerns parties rather than persons include: Alaska (which concerns "a party or person" in its rule), Arizona, Colorado, Connecticut, Illinois, Indiana, Kansas, Michigan, and Pennsylvania. California, which uses a set of ethics rules that are not modeled formally after either the Model Rules or Model Code, also has an anticontact rule that applies to parties, instead of persons. Therefore, legal assistants should be careful to learn whether their jurisdiction prohibits direct contact with represented persons or represented parties.

The Legal Assistant and the Anticontact Rules

When a lawyer is prohibited from making direct contact with a represented person, then so is the non-lawyer agent or employee of the lawyer, since neither can do what the principal is prohibited from doing. In a California case, a lawyer attempted to contact another attorney's clients in connection with a legal matter involving both lawyers' clients. After being warned by the other lawyer not to do so, the first lawyer sent a threatening letter to the other party and then, after being caught, claimed that his legal assistant sent the letter, despite the fact that the letter purported to bear the lawyer's signature. Without disputing the lawyer's claim that his employee sent the letter, the court found him in violation of the anticontact rule, regardless of who sent the letter. *Crane v. State Bar*, 635 P.2d 163 (Cal. 1981).

Exceptions to the Anticontact Rules

Despite whether one's jurisdiction prohibits direct contact with represented persons or parties, there are some common exceptions that apply. One exception not mentioned in the text of MR 4.2, but mentioned in the comments, is that parties (or persons) are allowed to have direct contact with one another outside the presence of their lawyers, but only if the client making contact is not, in essence, reading from a script devised by his or her lawyer. In an Ohio case, an attorney had his personal injury client, who was the plaintiff, call the defendant three days before the trial in order to tell the defendant what the plaintiff planned to testify. To make matters worse, during the conversation the plaintiff handed the phone to his lawyer who, forgetting that the defendant was represented, discussed the case with the defendant. Fortunately, for the sake of his law license, the lawyer withdrew from the case. *Trumball County Bar Association v. Makridis*, 671 N.E. 2d 31 (Ohio 1996).

When lawyers represent themselves pro se, they are wearing two hats: lawyer and party. Because the rules allow represented parties or persons to have direct contact with each other, it might seem that a self-represented lawyer would fall under that anticontact exception. That is not necessarily the case, and some jurisdictions, such as Idaho, Oregon, and Wyoming, have concluded that a self-represented lawyer may not make direct contact with a represented person since it would impossible to take off the lawyer hat. *See Runsvold v. Idaho State Bar*, 925 P.2d 1118 (Idaho 1996); *Sandstrom v. Sandstrom*, 880 P.2d 103 (Wyo. 1994); and *In re Conduct of Smith*, 861 P.2d 1013 (Or. 1993). Oregon, in fact, amended its anticontact rule to expressly cover a "lawyer representing a lawyer's own interest." Or. R. CPR DR 7–104(A)(1). Even in those jurisdictions that forbid pro se lawyers from making direct contact with any represented party or person, such a prohibition would not apply to any non-lawyer who was pro se in a case and wanted to communicate directly with the other party, even if the other party was represented.

Members of one legal team can also make direct contact with a represented person if the purpose of the communication is outside the scope of the representation. For instance, a lawyer representing a client suing a city government in a zoning permit matter may directly contact a representative of the city to discuss the quality of the city's snow removal system. Members of one legal team may also make direct contact with intended witnesses to the legal matter, such as doctors or other experts. ABA Commission of Ethics and Professional Responsibility, Formal Op. 93–378 (1993). And, as stated in MR 4.2, members of one legal team may make direct contact with a represented person if the other lawyer gives consent or if the contact is authorized by law. Those contacts that are authorized by law include cases in which statutes or rules of court provide permission, such as court rules that authorize for service of process on a party. ABA Commission and Professional Responsibility, Formal Op. 95–396 (1995).

In the criminal litigation context, the anticontact rules get very confusing when juxtaposed with criminal procedure law, both in the investigative phase and the adjudicative phase. For instance, in 1989, Attorney General Richard Thornburgh issued a controversial memorandum that stated federal prosecutors were not bound by state anticontact rules and could not be sanctioned for violating them. That position then became part of the Code of Federal Regulations in 1994 in 29 C.F.R. §77 et seq. After much friction between the Justice Department, the ABA, and the states, the U.S. Congress got involved in 1998 and passed a statute that expressly makes federal prosecutors subject to the ethics rules of the states wherein they work. It then ordered the attorney general (then Janet Reno) to amend the Department of Justice Rules in accordance with the statute. 28 U.S.C. §503B(a) and (b). Those changes were then made to 29 C.F.R. §77.3.

Unrepresented Persons and Truthfulness

During the course of representing a client, the lawyer and the lawyer's staff will have contact with those who are, or might be, connected to the case. Often those persons will be unrepresented, such as someone who worked with the client or who may have witnessed an accident that is the cause of the litigation. A variety of ethical issues are involved when contact is made with those persons who do not have legal representation. Foremost of those considerations is the requirement that those contacting unrepresented persons may not state or imply neutrality.

ABA Model Rule 4.3 requires that a lawyer making contact with an unrepresented person clearly explain to that person that he or she is not disinterested. Furthermore, the rule requires that the lawyer make a reasonable effort to clear up any misunderstanding the unrepresented person may have about the purpose of his or her contact. The ABA Model Code has no similar rule, although DR 7–104(A)(2) prohibits a lawyer from giving "advice to a person who is not represented by a lawyer, other than the advice to secure counsel." The Ethics 2000 version of MR 4.3 proposed a new sentence that is reminiscent of the Model Code and the Comment to MR 4.3, in that it says, "The lawyer shall not give legal advice to an unrepresented person, other than the advice to secure counsel, if the lawyer knows or reasonably should know that the interests of such a person are or have a reasonable possibility of being in conflict with the interests of the client." The House of Delegates accepted the new MR 4.3.

Not only is it misleading to imply neutrality to an unrepresented party, it also could be unfair since the information gleaned from the unrepresented party might actually turn it into an adverse party who unwittingly helped give information to the other side. For example, such a veiled projection of neutrality would be inappropriate if the person being contacted is known by the lawyer or legal assistant to be someone who will be served a complaint soon, once enough information is gathered. False impressions of disinterest in the litigation can also be made when the legal team contacts employees of the other party. In a lawsuit involving an airline crash, a consultant of the plaintiff's lawyer sent a deceptive letter and questionnaire to the pilots of the airline (the defendant), the stated purpose being to identify the training and experience of the pilots. What the pilots were not told was that the questionnaire was sent to gather information that might be used against the airline in the pending litigation. Upon learning of the tactic, the trial court sanctioned the plaintiff's attorney for violating MR 4.3 by excluding from evidence the information learned from the questionnaires. *In re Air Crash Disaster,* 909 F. Supp. 1116 (N.D. Ill. 1995).

The codes of conduct drafted by paralegal organizations also require their members to be forthright when communicating with unrepresented persons. Guideline 1 of the NALA Model Standards and Guidelines for Utilization of Legal Assistants states, "Legal assistants should: 1. Disclose their status as legal assistants at the outset of any professional relationship with a client, other attorneys, a court or administrative agency or personnel thereof, *or members of the general public*" (emphasis added). Furthermore, Canon 1 of the NALA Code of Ethics and Professional Responsibility provides that "A legal assistant . . . [may not] take any actions that attorneys may not take," while Canon 5 restates Guideline 1 of the NALA Model Standards. EC–1.7(a) of the NFPA Model Disciplinary Rules and Ethical Considerations states, "A paralegal's title shall clearly indicate the individual's status and shall be disclosed in all business and professional communications *to avoid misunderstandings and misconceptions about the paralegal's role and responsibilities*" (emphasis added).

When communicating with witnesses who are unrepresented, legal assistants need to keep two important maxims in mind: (a) do not give legal advice, and (b) do not tell witnesses what to do or say. Refraining from giving legal advice is hard to do when in contact with unrepresented witnesses because once they know the interviewer works for a lawyer, they are likely to ask, "What should I do?" Lawyers need to be careful that their information gathering does not cross the line into causing the witness to think that the lawyer-client relationship has been created. Paralegals also need to be especially careful when communicating with unrepresented witnesses, not only in identifying their role and status, but also in how they deal with the witness's questions.

In addition to previously cited rules on honesty, Model Rule 3.4(a) prohibits a lawyer from unlawfully obstructing another party's access to evidence or unlawfully destroying or hiding things that have evidentiary value. MR 3.4(b) and (f) also prohibit a lawyer from assisting a witness in testifying falsely or counseling someone, including a prospective witness, to refuse to give relevant information to the other side. That prohibition also would include advising a prospective witness person to leave the jurisdiction. Witness preparation is an acknowledged part of trial preparation, but not much is stated in the rules about what would cross the line from appropriate preparation into inappropriate coaching, other than to say that lawyers may not assist witnesses in offering perjured testimony. When interviewing witnesses or assisting them in preparing for deposition or trial testimony, paralegals must not tell witnesses—including clients—what to say or what the legal impact of their testimony would be.

Advising a witness to leave the jurisdiction is considered to be an obstruction of justice, even if the lawyer claims a good faith reason for such advice. An Ohio lawyer, after completing the direct examination of his client, advised his client (during a recess) to leave the courthouse and not go directly home, so that the client, by his absence, could not be subject to cross-examination. To the trial court's astonishment, the lawyer claimed the advice was given because the lawyer believed that, after the recess was over, the unfinished case was barred by operation of a statutory timetable and, therefore, the court no longer had jurisdiction over the case. Neither the trial court nor the disciplinary panel was impressed by the tactic, and the lawyer was sanctioned. *Office of Disciplinary Counsel v. Slodov*, 660 N.E.2d 1164 (Ohio 1996).

Ex Parte Communication and Truthfulness

Although lawyers are duty bound to zealously represent their clients, all actions done on their clients' behalf must be within the bounds of fairness. Included in this notion of fairness is the prohibition on lawyers having **ex parte communication** (i.e., private or outside the presence of opposing counsel) with judges or jury members. ABA Model Rules 3.5(a) and (b) state, "A lawyer shall not: (a) seek to influence a judge, juror, prospective juror or other official by means prohibited by law; (b) communicate ex parte with such a person except as permitted by law." The Model Code has a similar prohibition. DR 7–108(A) states, "Before the trial of a case a lawyer . . . shall not communicate with . . . anyone he knows to be a member of the **venire**," and DR 7–108(B) prohibits a lawyer from communicating with "any member of the jury" during the trial of a case; and DR 7-110(B) prohibits a lawyer from "communicat[ing] . . . as to the merits of the cause with a judge or an official before whom the proceeding is pending, except . . . upon adequate notice to opposing counsel" unless "otherwise authorized by law."

Contacting a judge without the knowledge of the opposing counsel is wrong, even if the contact is not made for the purposes of trying to influence the judge. Recall from Chapter 7 that one of the violations that contributed to F. Lee Bailey's disbarment was his ex parte letter to the trial judge overseeing the plea bargain and sentence of Bailey's drug-dealing client. In fact, the court acknowledged that Bailey's ex parte communication with the judge was, by itself, sufficient to warrant disbarment.

The rules on juror-communication are even stricter than those concerning judges because, although many jurisdictions allow a lawyer to communicate with a judge during a case if the contact is unrelated to the case (such as a social contact), contact with a juror, even in a social setting, can result in a mistrial. In an Iowa case, a trial verdict in favor of the defendant was overturned because two of the defendant's lawyers had shared a drink with the jury foreman before the trial was over, after coincidentally meeting in a restaurant on a Friday night. Despite the fact that the juror was the one who initiated the contact and a lack of evidence that the trial was discussed during the social contact, the appellate court found such contact projected an appearance of impropriety that cast doubt on the jury system. *Omaha Bank for Cooperatives v. Siouxland Cattle Cooperative*, 305 N.W.2d 458 (Iowa 1981). Beyond that, some jurisdictions prohibit lawyers or their employees from contacting jurors even after the trial is complete (*L.S. Mississippi Bar*, 649 So. 2d 810 (Miss. 1995)), or require court permission before making post-trial contact with jurors (*Florida Bar v. Newhouse*, 489 So. 2d 935 (Fla. 1986)). Some ethics

ex parte communication— Communication made to the court during litigation in the absence of the other party or the other party's attorney.

venire—A member of the legal process, including the jury.

opinions, however, do allow for post-trial juror contact, including one ethics opinion allowing a firm to assign a paralegal the responsibility of contacting the jurors, as long as the contact involves no harassment or intimidation. Pa. State Bar Association, Ethics Op. 91–52 (1991).

The Ethics 2000 Commission proposed a few changes to MR 3.5, including rephrasing MR 3.5(b) to limit its application to "during the proceeding." Also, the juror communication prohibition was moved to a new MR 3.5(c), and the prohibition was rephrased so as to allow post-verdict communications with jurors unless prohibited by court order or the juror declares a desire not to communicate or if the communication involves deceit, duress, or harassment. This relaxing of the prohibition against juror communication was prompted by the fact that some courts have ruled that the present MR 3.5(b) was unconstitutionally overbroad because it applied to all juror communications, including even after the trial was over. These proposals were accepted by the House of Delegates.

The NFPA Model Disciplinary Rules and Ethical Considerations clearly states in EC 1.2(a): "A paralegal shall not engage in any ex parte communications involving the courts or any other adjudicatory body in an attempt to exert undue influence or to obtain advantage or the benefit of only one party." Because paralegals can be valuable members of the trial team, the opportunity for inappropriate contact is equally available to them. From **voir dire** through the trial, paralegals need to do more than avoid discussing the case with the jurors; they must stay away from them. Furthermore, a legal assistant needs to speak up if he or she knows anyone in the jury pool or on the jury. An extreme example of lawyer misconduct involved a prospective juror who was married to the legal secretary of one of the parties' lawyers. Not only did the prospective juror lie about his wife's employment, but the lawyer was also complicit in the fraud, failing to truthfully question the prospective juror about his relationships with any of the parties. When the fraud was discovered, the lawyer was suspended for six months. *Matter of Roberts*, 442 N.E.2d 986 (Ind. 1982).

Although lawyers can use jury consultants to help identify favorable prospective jurors, lawyers and their employees cross the line when trying to make contact with prospective jurors. Courts even sanction lawyers when their associates have made intentional contact with the relatives of prospective jurors or jurors in order to determine the jurors' views on matters related to the litigation. *See In re Two Anonymous Members of the South Carolina Bar*, 298 S.E.2d 450 (S.C. 1982). In a federal case, the district court sanctioned a lawyer who employed a private investigator to investigate jurors on the lawyer's trial. The private investigator used a telephone survey as the pretext to contact the jurors. Although the investigator concocted the telephone survey scheme, the lawyer's culpability was attributed to the fact that he delegated to his "poorly trained" paralegal the responsibility to contact the investigator. Interestingly, part of the sanctions included a requirement that the law firm formulate a seminar to train its paralegals about the ethical pitfalls of litigation. *Hill-Rom Co. v. Kinetic Concepts* (S.C. Jan. 14, 1999).

Contact with jurors can go beyond the stupid to the criminal and become jury tampering. All states and the federal government have jury-tampering statutes. For instance, federal law criminalizes the threatening or intimidation of jurors as well as

voir dire—The process of picking jurors by questioning prospective jurors on matters related to the case, including biases and prejudices.

attempts to influence them, including in writing, and provides for punishments that can include many years in prison. 18 U.S.C. § 1503 and § 1504.

Legal Research and Truthfulness

Both the ABA Model Rules and Model Code make it clear that, when citing legal authority to a court, either orally or in writing, a lawyer must disclose authority that is directly adverse to the lawyer's client when the authority comes from the court's jurisdiction and the other lawyer fails to cite it. MR 3.3(a)(3); DR 7–106(B)(1). At first blush, it seems antithetical to the competitive nature of litigation to require one lawyer to do what might be described as the other lawyer's work. If, during the course of representing a client, a lawyer fails to discover a statute or case that is directly helpful, how unhappy would the other lawyer's client be to find out that his or her advocate shared that helpful statute or case with the judge? It seems evident that if such directly adverse authority were found by the lawyer whose client would be hurt by its discovery, then the lawyer whose client would be helped by such a discovery should have been able to find it.

    This ethical dilemma is a conflict of duties, but because lawyers are officers of the court, their duty to the administration of justice is paramount to their duty to their clients. Courts make decisions based on the applicable law, and lawyers are expected to provide courts with all applicable law. In fact, the Comment to MR 3.3 that concerns this duty to provide directly adverse authority says, "The underlying concept is that legal argument is a discussion seeking to determine the legal premises properly applicable to the case." Because legal research is one of the authorized tasks that legal assistants can perform, it is incumbent on those legal researchers to make their supervising attorneys aware of directly adverse, controlling authority. In order to qualify, such primary authority would: (1) have to come from the same jurisdiction of the court who has authority over the litigation (i.e., a Kansas Supreme Court case being contemplated for litigation occurring in a Kansas court), and (2) be directly adverse (i.e., a holding that is specifically negative to the client's position). Even if the legal researcher is unsure whether the discovered authority is directly adverse, it is better to err on the side of caution and show the research to the supervising attorney. The substance of MR 3.3(a)(3) remains the same in Ethics 2000, although its location has been moved to MR 3.3(a)(2).

    Some critics argue that such a rule is much ado about nothing because in order to sanction a lawyer for failing to disclose directly adverse controlling authority, a court would first have to establish that the lawyer knew of the directly adverse authority, not simply that the lawyer did not cite it. For example, in a case from Texas, a lawyer representing a defendant convicted of murder cited to the appellate court one case that had become moot due to a change in an operative statute and, at the oral arguments, supported his argument by citing a case that had been expressly overruled six years earlier by a controlling case. Although the court advised the lawyer to do better research in the future, no sanction was given because there was no evidence that the lawyer knowingly violated Texas's rule on citing directly adverse authority. *Geter v. State* 1996 WL 459767 (Tex.App.-Dallas 1996). Others argue that it is an almost irrelevant rule because there are few cases where lawyers have been professionally disciplined for violating MR 3.3(a)(3). However, there are more than a few cases, particularly federal cases, where lawyers have been sanctioned under civil procedure Rule 11 for failing to cite directly adverse authority.

Not every jurisdiction expresses concern about whether its lawyers are failing to cite directly adverse, controlling authority. Alabama, the first state to have a code of lawyer ethics, has dispensed altogether with the requirement that its lawyers cite to the court directly adverse authority, as has Kentucky. Ala. R.P.C. 3.3(a)(3); Ky. R.P.C. 3.3(a)(3).

In the following case, the appellate court has little difficulty concluding that the lawyers in question *knowingly* failed to cite directly adverse authority that was controlling in the jurisdiction.

Case Law

Jorgenson v. Volusia County, 846 F.2d 1350 (11th Cir. 1988)

PER CURIAM

The appellants, attorneys Eric Latinsky and Fred Fendt, were sanctioned by the district court pursuant to Fed.R.Civ.P. 11 for failing to cite adverse, controlling precedent in a memorandum filed in support of an application for a temporary restraining order and a preliminary injunction. In the appellants' initial appeal to this court, the case was remanded to the district court because the court had failed to notify the attorneys in advance that it was considering sanctions, and did not give them an opportunity to respond. *Jorgenson v. County of Volusia*, 824 F.2d 973 (11th Cir.1987) (unpublished opinion). On remand, the district court reaffirmed the imposition of sanctions, and the attorneys appeal. We affirm.

Appellants filed an application in the district court for a temporary restraining order and a preliminary injunction on behalf of their clients, who own and operate a lounge known as "Porky's." In support of the application, appellants filed a memorandum of law which challenged the validity of a Volusia County ordinance prohibiting nude or semi-nude entertainment in commercial establishments at which alcoholic beverages are offered for sale or consumption. The memorandum failed to discuss or cite two clearly relevant cases: *City of Daytona Beach v. Del Percio*, 476 So.2d 197 (Fla.1985) and *New York State Liquor Authority v. Bellanca*, 452 U.S. 714, 101 S.Ct. 2599, 69 L.Ed.2d 357 (1981). We find that this failure supports the imposition of Rule 11 sanctions in the circumstances of this case.

The field of law concerning the regulation of the sale and consumption of alcohol in connection with nude entertainment is a narrow and somewhat specialized field. Prior to the opinion of the Supreme Court of Florida in *Del Percio*, the critical question of whether the state of Florida had delegated its powers under the Twenty-First Amendment to counties and municipalities had gone unanswered. In some circles, that decision was long-awaited. If the state had delegated the authority, local ordinances regulating the sale or consumption of alcohol would be entitled to a presumption in favor of their validity which is conferred by the Twenty-First Amendment. *See Bellanca,* 452 U.S. at 718, 101 S.Ct. at 2601. If the state had not delegated the authority, the ordinances would be subject to the stricter review applicable to exercises of the general police power. *See Krueger v. City of Pensacola,* 759 F.2d 851, 852 (11th Cir.1985).

The question regarding Florida's delegation of its powers under the Twenty-First Amendment was answered by the Supreme Court of Florida in *Del Percio,* a case in which one of the appellants, Latinsky, participated. The court held that the powers had been delegated. Less than one year later, on or about January 13, 1986, Latinsky and an associate brought the instant suit seeking a declaration that a similar ordinance was unconstitutional and requesting a temporary restraining order and a preliminary injunction. In their presentation to the court, the appellants cited a number of cases describing the limits on the exercise of the general police power. However, they did not advise the court in any way that *Del Percio* had been decided, despite the fact that *Del Percio* required that the validity of the ordinance be judged in light of powers retained under the Twenty-First Amendment rather than the general police power.

The appellants purported to describe the law to the district court in the hope that the description would guide and inform the court's decision. With apparently studied care, however, they withheld the fact that the long-awaited decision by the Supreme Court of Florida had been handed down. This will not do. The appellants are not redeemed by the fact that opposing counsel *subsequently* cited the controlling precedent. The appellants had a duty to refrain from affirmatively misleading the court as to the state of the law. They were not relieved of this duty by the possibility that opposing counsel might find and cite the controlling precedent, particularly where, as here, a temporary restraining order might have been issued *ex parte.*

In this court, appellants argue that the cases were not cited because they are not controlling. We certainly acknowledge that attorneys are legitimately entitled to press their own interpretations of precedent, including interpretations which render particular cases inapplicable. It is clear, however, that appellants' attempts to show that *Del Percio* and *Bellanca* are not controlling are simply post hoc efforts to evade the imposition of sanctions. Neither the original complaint nor the memorandum of law filed by appellants in the district court reflect or support the arguments they now raise. Indeed, it is likely that the arguments were not raised previously because they are completely without merit. In the circumstances of this case, the imposition of Rule 11 sanctions by the district court was warranted. The judgment of the district court is AFFIRMED.

Case Questions

1. How could the court safely conclude that the sanctioned lawyers knowingly failed to cite controlling authority?
2. Why would the *Del Percio* case be controlling in a federal court if that case came from a state appellate court?
3. If the opposing counsel cited both key cases to the District Court, why would the District Court and the Eleventh Circuit of Appeals bother to take the time to sanction the lawyers who failed to do so?

MALPRACTICE LIABILITY FOR THE NON-LAWYER

Malpractice is the bane of doctors and lawyers, the threat of which causes the purchase and careful renewal of malpractice liability insurance. Can a non-lawyer be held liable for legal malpractice? The short answer is Yes—although there are few cases that discuss the issue, and even fewer that involve paralegals. Logically, one might think that, since non-lawyers are unlicensed, they could not be held liable for malpractice, because malpractice is generally defined as the improper or negligent conduct of a professional in the performance of his or her profession. There are occasions, however, where courts have found non-lawyers liable for malpractice, despite their status.

malpractice—Improper or harmful conduct committed by a professional in the course of their profession.

What Constitutes Malpractice?

The cause of action for legal malpractice based on negligence has four elements: (1) a duty owed by the defendant to the plaintiff; (2) a breach of that duty, shown through a failure to exercise reasonable care; (3) losses suffered by the plaintiff; and (4) **proximate cause** between the defendant's negligent conduct and the plaintiff's losses. Concerning Element 2, a failure to exercise reasonable care involves determining whether the lawyer's conduct was less than what a similarly situated, reasonable lawyer would have done. And, as is the case with any claim of negligence, there must be proximate cause: a direct link between the unreasonable act and the alleged harm. As a general rule, making a mistake, even a big mistake, would not result in malpractice if the plaintiff could not prove that the loss suffered was caused by the lawyer's misconduct. For instance, if a lawyer were to incompetently draft a will for a client who ended up spending every last penny before dying, there would be no malpractice case since a correctly drafted will would have resulted in the same outcome for the heirs (no inheritance).

proximate cause—In the context of what would make one liable, proximate cause is that which shows a sufficient connection to the defendant's conduct and the plaintiff's injury.

Sometimes, clients sue their lawyers for malpractice after a litigation loss, but the fact that a client lost a lawsuit does not necessarily mean that the lawyer was negligent. And even if the lawyer acted negligently, that does not mean there will be a finding of malpractice. In order to win such a malpractice claim, the client is generally required to show that the outcome would have been different "but for" the lawyer's blunder. Such a standard is akin to the client retrying the case in a "what if?" world (what if a different lawyer had done things differently?). If a court finds that a case would have been unwinnable in any lawyer's hands, then the client's malpractice claim is thwarted.

In a case from Kansas illustrating that principle—as well as an example of a non-lawyer's liability for legal malpractice—a couple sued a lawyer and his brother for malpractice. It seems that the Webbs, fearing losing their house and fifty-six acres to a foreclosure, transferred their property to some friends who put up the money to prevent the foreclosure. The Webbs used the services of Charles Pomeroy (the person who did their taxes) to draft the documents transferring title to the "buyers." However, Charles failed to draft a written repurchase agreement so that the Webbs could get their property back when they had the money. The friends, in an unfriendly move, decided to sell the property, and the Webbs, now using E. Pomeroy, the lawyer-brother of Charles, lost the eventual lawsuit. The Webbs sued both brothers for malpractice. The Kansas Court of Appeals ruled in favor of E. Pomeroy in the malpractice lawsuit because the suit was lost due to the lack of any written evidence of the repurchase agreement and would have been lost regardless of E. Pomeroy's tactics at trial. However, the court reversed the trial court's directed verdict in favor of Charles Pomeroy. Upon holding Charles to the same standard as if he were a lawyer (because he wrongfully engaged in legal transactions), the court declared that he could be liable for his negligence in failing to secure a written repurchase agreement. *Webb v. Pomeroy*, 655 P.2d 465 (Kan. App. 1982).

The Theory behind Non-Lawyer Malpractice

If non-lawyer members of the legal team, such as paralegals, are so unregulated as to be unlicensed in their own field—much less unlicensed to practice law—how could they be held liable as professionals for their misdeeds? The answer lies in the fact that malpractice is a tort; it is a particular kind of negligence. A court will not refuse to hold someone liable for negligence simply because the defendant had no legal right to do what he or she did incompetently. A license entitles one to engage in a profession, but it does not insulate the professional against professional negligence. Likewise, the lack of a license does not prevent the tortfeasor from being accountable for performing improper acts. Remember from Chapter 3 that a jurisdiction's highest court cannot sanction a non-lawyer for engaging in the unauthorized practice of law because the non-lawyer is not a member of the bar and, therefore, not subject to professional discipline. It can, however, issue a cease and desist order to the non-lawyer practicing law without a license and then hold him or her in contempt of court for a violation of the court's order.

Despite the lack of a regulating court's ability to discipline a non-lawyer, a jury could still find that his or her incompetent, unauthorized practice of law constituted negligence. In a Washington State case, property owners sold a piece of real estate with the assistance of a non-lawyer escrow agent who drafted the closing documents. Those documents failed to make the property a security interest in the transaction, and when the buyer eventually filed for bankruptcy and disappeared, the sellers lost $35,000. After finding that the escrow agent had engaged in the unauthorized practice of law, the Washington Supreme Court declared that the escrow agent's failure to explain to the sellers the significance of an unsecured real estate sale constituted legal negligence for which the escrow agent was liable. *Bowers v. Transamerica Title Ins. Co.*, 675 P.2d 193 (Wash. 1983).

The following landmark case involving a non-lawyer sued for malpractice has been cited in scores of cases, many of those concerning whether a beneficiary of a contract between a lawyer and a client can sue the lawyer for negligence.

Case Law

Biakanja v. Irving, 320 P.2d 16 (Cal. 1958)

GIBSON, Chief Justice.

Plaintiff's brother, John Maroevich, died, leaving a will which devised and bequeathed all of his property to plaintiff. The will, which was prepared by defendant, a notary public, was denied probate for lack of sufficient attestation. Plaintiff, by intestate succession, received only one-eighth of the estate, and she recovered a judgment against defendant for the difference between the amount which she would have received had the will been valid and the amount distributed to her.

Defendant, who is not an attorney, had for several years written letters and prepared income tax returns for Maroevich. The will was typed in defendant's office and "subscribed and sworn to" by Maroevich in the presence of defendant, who affixed his signature and notarial seal to the instrument. Sometime later Maroevich obtained the signatures of two witnesses to the will neither of whom was present when Maroevich signed it. These witnesses did not sign in the presence of each other, and Maroevich did not acknowledge his signature in their presence.

An attorney who represented Maroevich's stepson in the probate proceedings testified that he had a telephone conversation with defendant shortly after Maroevich's death, in which defendant said he prepared the will and notarized it. According to the attorney, defendant, in discussing how the will was witnessed, "admonished me to the effect that I was a young lawyer, I'd better go back and study my law books some more, that anybody knew a will which bore a notarial seal was a valid will, didn't have to be witnessed by any witnesses." The court found that defendant agreed and undertook to prepare a valid will and that it was invalid because defendant negligently failed to have it properly attested. The findings are supported by the evidence.

The principal question is whether defendant was under a duty to exercise due care to protect plaintiff from injury and was liable for damage caused plaintiff by his negligence even though they were not in privity of contract. In *Buckley v. Gray*, 1895, 110 Cal. 339, 42 P. 900, 31 L.R.A. 862, it was held that a person who was named as a beneficiary under a will could not recover damages from an attorney who negligently drafted and directed the execution of the will with the result that the intended beneficiary was deprived of substantial benefits. The court based its decision on the ground that the attorney owed no duty to the beneficiary because there was no privity of contract between them. *Mickel v. Murphy*, 147 Cal.App.2d 718, 305 P.2d 993, relying on *Buckley v. Gray*, supra, held that a notary public who prepared a will was not liable to the beneficiary for failing to have it properly executed. When *Buckley v. Gray*, supra, was decided in 1895, it was generally accepted that, with the few exceptions noted in the opinion in that case, there was no liability for negligence committed in the performance of a contract in the absence of privity. Since that time the rule has been greatly liberalized, and the courts have permitted a plaintiff not in privity to recover damages in many situations for the negligent performance of a contract.

Liability has been imposed, in the absence of privity, upon suppliers of goods and services which, if negligently made or rendered, are "reasonably certain to place life and limb in peril." [citations omitted] . . . Prosser, Torts (2d ed. 1955), ss 84–85, p. 497 et seq. There is also authority for the imposition of liability where there is no privity and where the only foreseeable risk is of damage to tangible property [citations omitted]. . . . [S]ee Prosser, supra, s 84, pp. 501–502. . . .

The determination whether in a specific case the defendant will be held liable to a third person not in privity is a matter of policy and involves the balancing of various factors, among which are the extent to which the transaction was intended to affect the plaintiff, the foreseeability of harm to him, the degree of certainty that the plaintiff suffered injury, the closeness of the connection between the defendant's conduct and the injury suffered, the moral blame attached to the defendant's conduct, and the policy of preventing future harm. Cf. Prosser, Torts (2d ed. 1955), ss 36, 88, 107, pp. 168, 172, 544–545, 747; 2 Harper and James, Torts (1956), s 18.6, p. 1052. Here, the "end and aim" of the transaction was to provide for the passing of Maroevich's estate to plaintiff. See *Glanzer v. Shepard*, 233 N.Y. 236, 135 N.E. 275, 23 A.L.R. 1425. Defendant must have been aware from the terms of the will itself that, if faulty solemnization caused the will to be invalid, plaintiff would suffer the very loss which occurred. As Maroevich died without revoking his will, plaintiff, but for defendant's negligence, would have received all of the Maroevich estate, and the fact that she received only one-eighth of the estate was directly caused by defendant's conduct.

Defendant undertook to provide for the formal disposition of Maroevich's estate by drafting and supervising the execution of a will. This was an important transaction requiring specialized skill, and defendant clearly was not qualified to undertake it. His conduct was not only negligent but was also highly improper. He engaged in the unauthorized practice of the law (Bus. & Prof.Code, s 6125; cf. *People v. Merchants' Protective Corp.*, 189 Cal. 531, 535, 209 P. 363; *People v. Sipper*, 61 Cal.App.2d Supp. 844, 848, 142 P.2d 960; *Grand Rapids Bar Ass'n v. Denkema*, 290 Mich. 56, 287 N.W. 377, 380; *State ex rel. Wyoming State Bar v. Hardy*, 61 Wyo. 172, 156 P.2d 309, 313, which is a misdemeanor in violation of section 6126 of the Business and Professions Code. Such conduct should be discouraged and not protected by immunity from civil liability, as would be the case if plaintiff, the only person who suffered a loss, were denied a right of action.

We have concluded that plaintiff should be allowed recovery despite the absence of privity, and the cases of *Buckley v. Gray*, 110 Cal. 339, 42 P. 900, 31 L.R.A. 862, and *Mickel v. Murphy*, 147 Cal.App.2d 718, 305 P.2d 993, are disapproved insofar as they are in conflict with this decision.

The judgment is affirmed.

Case Questions

1. Aside from the fact that the notary should not have drafted and executed someone's will, what did he or she do that was negligent?
2. What is privity of contract and why would it matter that the plaintiff lacked it?
3. Of the factors the court listed as decisive on whether someone should be liable to another without there being privity of contract, which factor do you think applied most directly here?
4. In addition to the negligence, what else convinced the court that the notary should be liable to the plaintiff for the loss of seven-eighths of the plaintiff's inheritance?
5. Does your jurisdiction allow non-lawyers to draft and execute wills or trusts?

When a court allows a law office employee to be held liable for legal malpractice, such an allowance flows first from a finding that the non-lawyer was engaging in the unauthorized practice of law, especially where the client is unaware of the non-lawyer's status. Then, if the client suffers from the incompetent acts of the non-lawyer's unauthorized performance, a court will hold the non-lawyer to the same standards of conduct to which a lawyer is held. Therefore, a legal assistant *who is working under the supervision of a lawyer and in furtherance of lawyer's representation of the client* and commits a negligent act would generally not be liable for malpractice, but the lawyer still would be.

In the following case, a law clerk was sued for malpractice by a client who believed that the law clerk was a lawyer. While reading it, notice the dissenting opinion's different view on the facts in the case.

Case Law

Busch v. Flangas, 837 P.2d 438 (Nev.1992)

PER CURIAM

Appellant Mary Busch is the former owner of the Busch Bavarian Pastry Shop. In 1984, Busch agreed to sell the shop. A customer suggested that Busch contact respondent Delwin Potter, who worked for respondent Peter Flangas, to help draw up documents pertaining to the sale of the bakery. Believing Potter to be a lawyer, Busch contacted Flangas' law office and made an appointment with Potter. Potter was in fact a law clerk employed by Flangas. The necessary documents for the sale of the bakery were prepared, but a UCC-1 financing statement necessary to the perfecting of Busch's security interest in the bakery equipment pending final payment was never filed. The buyers failed to satisfy their financial obligation to Busch and eventually filed bankruptcy. Busch, as an unsecured creditor, lost her interest in the bakery equipment. Busch instituted a malpractice action against Potter and Flangas, alleging that Potter's negligence caused her to lose her security interest in the bakery equipment. Busch claimed that Flangas was also liable for his employee's negligence. Potter and Flangas claimed that another attorney had supervised Potter's work, thus relieving both of them of any liability. The district court granted summary judgment in favor of Potter and Flangas, and Busch appealed. We reverse. . . .

Even though both parties moved for summary judgment, this did not relieve the district court of its

responsibility to determine whether genuine issues of fact existed. *Ardmore Leasing Corp. v. State Farm Mut. Auto. Ins. Co.,* 106 Nev. 513, 796 P.2d 232 (1990). Our review of the record reveals the existence of disputed material facts concerning the issue of Potter's and Flangas' liability. Summary judgment was therefore improper.

[The court first determined that the district court erred in concluding that Busch's bakery had been leased, instead of sold, and was, therefore, outside the scope of the Uniform Commercial Code.]

Busch presented substantial evidence indicating that the transaction required a UCC-1 financing statement, which Potter failed to file, to secure her interest in the bakery equipment. Although Potter is not an attorney, he can be subject to a legal malpractice claim if he attempts to provide legal services. *See Bowers v. Transamerica Title Ins. Co.,* 100 Wash.2d 581, 675 P.2d 193 (1983). Therefore, summary judgment was improperly granted as to Potter.

Flangas contends that he cannot be liable for malpractice because he never met Busch nor attempted to provide legal services for her. Clearly, this contention is without merit. Busch's claim against Flangas states a cause of action on a *respondeat superior* theory. Thus, Flangas may be liable for Potter's negligence if Potter was acting within the scope of his employment when he performed services for Busch. *Molino v. Asher*, 96 Nev. 814, 618 P.2d 878 (1980). Respondents concede that Potter was employed by Flangas, but claim that on this occasion Potter was supervised by another attorney[1] who maintains a separate practice, but who nevertheless occasionally utilized the services of Potter or Flangas' secretaries.

Busch claims that Flangas was responsible for supervising Potter's work, and attached to her opposition to the motions for summary judgment copies of Potter's paychecks from Flangas covering the period of time when Potter performed services for Busch. At a minimum, Busch raised a genuine issue below as to Flangas' liability. Therefore, summary judgment was improperly granted as to Flangas. NRCP 56(c).

After careful consideration, we have determined that the other issues raised by the parties are without merit. The summary judgment in favor of respondents is reversed, and the case is remanded to the district court for a trial on the merits.

SPRINGER, Justice, with whom LEAVITT, District Judge, agrees, dissenting:

I conclude that the trial court was correct in granting summary judgment; therefore, I respectfully dissent.

The Flangas Judgment

The case against Flangas is based on actual negligence on his part and not on vicarious liability. An employer is liable for an employee's acts which the employer authorized or ratified, upon familiar principles of negligence and agency. Vicarious liability, on the other hand, is based on conduct which is not the conduct of the employer but which extends to any and all *tortious* conduct which an agent performs within the "scope of employment." Busch does not plead a case for vicarious liability nor does she aver that all of Potter's tortious acts were done in the scope of his employment for Flangas. Rather than trying to impute Potter's negligence to Flangas under the doctrine of *respondeat superior*, Busch's complaint charges specific and independent negligence on the part of Flangas. According to the complaint,

"Flangas knew that Defendant Potter was representing himself as an attorney and performing legal services on behalf of Defendant Flangas." In other words, Flangas knowingly let a non-lawyer work in his office *as* a lawyer. There is no evidence that this charge is true.

Busch argues in her "Opposition to Motion for Summary Judgment" that Potter is guilty of "malpractice per se." This may be true, but absent an allegation that such untoward and outrageous action by Potter was done in the scope and power of his employment by Flangas, no vicarious liability can exist.[1] Because there is no claim for vicarious liability and because there is no evidence to support actual negligence on the part of Flangas, I would affirm the trial court's summary judgment in his favor.

The Potter Judgment

The gist of Busch's claim against Potter is that Potter "represented himself to Plaintiff as an attorney and further represented that he was competent and able to prepare all documents . . . and . . . to protect the Plaintiff's [legal] interests," and that Potter was then guilty of legal malpractice when he "negligently failed and omitted to cause the UCC-1 Financing Statement to be filed with the appropriate agency."

If, as is clearly the case, Potter had not "represented himself to Plaintiff as an attorney," he could not, of course, have undertaken the duty "to prepare all documents" nor "to fully protect the Plaintiff's [legal] interests." By Busch's own testimony, neither Flangas nor Potter ever represented that Potter was a lawyer. Busch "assumed" that Potter was a lawyer because one of her customers at the bakery told her so. There is no evidence that Potter was either acting as a lawyer or representing himself to be a lawyer. According to Potter's affidavit, he prepared the documents in question at the behest of and *under* the supervision of another attorney, John Stone. I believe that the trial court was correct in concluding that there was no evidence to support the allegation that Potter "represented himself to Plaintiff as an attorney" or that as a non-attorney working for attorney

Stone, Potter owed a duty to Busch relative to the preparation and filing of the UCC documents. I

would affirm the trial court's summary judgment in favor of Potter.

The following case footnotes correspond to the portions of the case that are printed in the textbook. Although it may seem that other footnotes are missing, they are not presented because their corresponding portions of the court's opinion have been redacted.

[1] The statute of limitations has run against this other attorney, precluding a claim against him.

[1] In the mentioned Opposition papers, Busch tardily mentions "the theory of respondeat superior," but neither the complaint nor the motion documents support this kind of claim of liability.

Case Questions

1. If Potter worked for attorney Flangas, why did the court say that Potter could be separately liable for malpractice?
2. What evidence showed that Potter worked for Flangas?
3. Why does the dissent believe that the summary judgment in favor of Flangas should be affirmed?
4. Why does the dissent believe that the summary judgment in favor of Potter should be affirmed?
5. Do you think Potter held himself out as a lawyer to Busch?

Non-Lawyer Malpractice Is Not a Universal View

Not all jurisdictions subscribe to the view that a non-lawyer can be found liable for legal malpractice. For instance, Ohio does not allow a paralegal to be sued for malpractice. In an Ohio case, the president of a corporation sued the corporation's attorney and the attorney's paralegal for malpractice, and the case was dismissed on summary judgment. While affirming the trial court's summary judgment, the Ohio Court of Appeals noted that since the paralegal was not an attorney, "she could not be charged with malpractice." *Palmer v. Westmeyer*, 549 N.E.2d 1202,1209 (Ohio App. 1988).

Similarly, in *In re Estate of Divine*, 635 N.E.2d 581 (Ill. App. 1994), discussed in Chapter 5 on conflicts of interest, the Illinois Court of Appeals refused to adopt the view that a paralegal has a fiduciary duty to the client because the paralegal works for the lawyer who does have a fiduciary duty to the client. In that case, the court refused to hold the paralegal liable to the heirs of an elderly client with whom that paralegal had become quite close, including being named a co-owner of the client's extremely large bank accounts and inheriting money under the client's will. And in Alabama, the Supreme Court ruled in a case with a similar, non-lawyer-malpractice issue that there was no state right to sue a union for legal malpractice. The case involved disgruntled union members who sued their union for legal malpractice after the union inadequately represented the members in a discrimination suit. *United Steelworkers of America, AFL-CIO v. Craig*, 571 So.2d 1101 (Ala. 1990). (Although that case did not involve a paralegal, it did involve a non-lawyer being sued for malpractice.)

Even in California, where *Biakanja v. Irving* held that a non-lawyer could be liable for legal malpractice, there is a different view concerning negligent legal representation by non-lawyers in administrative adjudications. The case taking this position involved a steelworker who was injured on the job and was awarded over $8,000 by the state Industrial Accident Commission. The steelworker (whose name was Bland) sued a fellow union member (whose name was Reed), claiming that Reed's advice negligently caused Bland to miss out on suing an industrial company that Bland believed caused his injuries. The California Court of Appeals acknowledged that non-lawyers were engaging in legal practice when appearing before the Industrial Accident Commission, but it was authorized since state law allowed it. Nevertheless, the court ruled it was improper to hold a non-lawyer practicing before the commission to the same standard of care as that of a lawyer. *Bland v. Reed*, 67 Cal.Rptr. 859 (Cal. Ct. App. 1968).

PRO BONO SERVICES

Sharing is a virtue, and although *virtuous* is an adjective the public might rarely use when thinking about lawyers, the legal profession has a history of sharing its legal services with the less fortunate. In fact, one could make the argument that the indigent have more access to lawyers than does the middle class, at least as it concerns the right to state-provided representation in criminal cases and entrée to state-sponsored legal aid. Within the lawyer culture, the idea of serving the public good is expressed formally in the rules concerning pro bono services. *Pro bono* is the short version of *pro bono publico*, which is Latin, meaning *for the public good or welfare*.

The Evolution of the Pro Bono Rules

The ABA Model Code (the predecessor to the ABA Model Rules) has no Disciplinary Rules on pro bono services, but there are a few Ethical Considerations that discussed them. EC 2–25, following Canon 2, titled "A Lawyer Should Assist the Legal Profession in Fulfilling Its Duty to Make Legal Counsel Available," states:

> The basic responsibility for providing legal services for those unable to pay ultimately rests upon the individual lawyer, and personal involvement in the problems of the disadvantaged can be one of the most rewarding experiences in the life of a lawyer. Every lawyer, regardless of professional prominence or professional workload, should find time to participate in serving the disadvantaged.

And EC 8–3, following Canon 8, titled "A Lawyer Should Assist in Improving the Legal System," declares, "Those persons unable to pay for legal services should be provided needed services."

The original version of the ABA Model Rules took a more definite position than did the Model Code by stating:

> A lawyer should render public interest legal service. A lawyer may discharge this responsibility by providing professional services at no fee or a reduced fee to persons of limited means or to public service or charitable groups or organizations by service in activities for improving the law, the legal system, or the legal profession, and by financial support for organizations that provide legal services to persons of limited means. ABA MR 6.1 (1983 version).

The current version of MR 6.1 is more specific than the original version and states, "A lawyer should aspire to render at least (50) hours of pro bono publico legal services per year." MR 6.1 then lists ways in which a lawyer can fulfill that responsibility, including providing free or substantially discounted legal services to charitable or similar organizations, or persons of limited means. The Ethics 2000 version of MR 6.1, which was accepted by the House of Delegates, has added a beginning sentence to the rule that states, "Every lawyer has a professional responsibility to provide legal services to those unable to pay."

Despite the changes made to the original version of MR 6.1, many jurisdictions that have adopted the Model Rules still retain the language of the original MR 6.1. New York, a jurisdiction that follows the Model Code, has replaced the language of EC 2–25 with the language of the original MR 6.1. Oregon, another Model Code jurisdiction, has an Aspirational Standard 15.100 (not found in the Oregon Rules of Professional Conduct but in the Board of Bar Governors Policies) stating that every Oregon attorney should endeavor to annually provide eighty hours of pro bono services, including twenty to forty hours of free representation to the poor.

Should Lawyers Be Required to Perform Pro Bono Services?

If one is not obligated to follow a rule, then there is no rule. Although MR 6.1 is part of the Model Rules, it is not mandatory since both versions use the word *should*. However, the original draft of the first version of MR 1.6 used the word *shall*, instead of should. That language did not survive the ABA legislative process because of a concern that requiring pro bono work was unconstitutional and unworkable. In fact, even the members of the Ethics 2000 Commission invited comments on whether its version of MR 6.1 should be changed to require lawyers to engage in pro bono activities, but such a significant change was not made. States, of course, are free to mandate pro bono services, just as states have mandated that interest on lawyer trust accounts be transferred to bar associations to help fund legal aid services (discussed in Chapter 7).

Although lawyers are not required to perform pro bono services, the trend has been moving toward that direction since the advent of the ABA Model Code. In fact, the State Bar of Nevada Board of Governors unanimously voted in 1994 to implement a mandatory pro bono requirement, with the failure to comply subjecting an attorney to discipline, including license revocation. However, the reaction by some of the rank and file of the Nevada bar was so hostile that the plan was dropped in 1995.

Florida's version of MR 6.1 comes close to requiring pro bono services, and it has some interesting parts. MR 6.1(a) includes a statement in favor of pro bono services that is different from the Model Rules, one that specifically exempts judges and other members of the bar who cannot practice law. MR 6.1(b) states that pro bono is not mandatory, but then goes on to list two ways in which lawyers can fulfill their pro bono responsibility: (1) annually providing at least twenty hours of pro bono legal service to the poor, or (2) annually giving at least $350 to a legal aid organization. MR 6.1(d) then increases the mandatory nature of pro bono by requiring every Florida lawyer to complete a form (at the time of paying one's yearly bar fees) that certifies whether the lawyer has or has not fulfilled their annual pro bono responsibility. The form also provides room for the lawyer to describe how the pro bono responsibility was met in ways other than those listed in 6.1(b). And MR 6.1(e) allows a lawyer to bank for future years' fulfillments any pro bono hours in excess of the annual twenty hours. Although MR 6.1(b) states that failure to fulfill one's responsibilities does not subject a lawyer to discipline, MR 6.1(d) states that failure to complete and return the form does subject a lawyer to discipline.

Those opposed to mandatory pro bono argue that such a requirement is unconstitutional in that requiring lawyers to work free of charge violates the equal protection clause of the Fourteenth Amendment, since no other occupation or profession is required to give away their labor or services. Furthermore, it is argued that a pro bono requirement violates the Fifth Amendment's Takings Clause because the government (courts that regulate the bar) cannot take private property (a lawyer's time and skill) without "just compensation." Another argument made against mandatory pro bono is that it is un-American to force anyone, lawyer or otherwise, to do good, not to mention that it is presumptuous to think that all lawyers can afford—after paying their law school bills, bar fees, overhead, and taxes—to provide a unilaterally determined number of free hours.

Those in favor of mandatory pro bono service point to the fact since the practice of law is a monopoly, those who make up part of the monopoly should appropriately handle such power by providing some services that benefit the common good without expectation of compensation. Another supporting argument is that mandatory pro bono service is the best way to combat the growing legal needs of the poor. There is also the argument that the practice of law is a profession and not purely a business, so that a comparison of lawyers to plumbers, for instance, for the purposes of anti-mandatory pro bono arguments, is miscast. Finally, one could argue that mandatory pro bono programs could do a great deal to combat the general disdain the public has for lawyers.

Although lawyers are not required to provide pro bono services, more than a few law schools require pro bono service as a prerequisite to graduation. Tulane University School of Law became the first law school to adopt a mandatory program in 1987 and, according to the American Association of Law Schools, since Tulane instituted its program, thirteen other law schools instituted mandatory programs. The University of Pennsylvania Law School, one of the mandatory pro bono schools, has a public service program that requires students to perform seventy hours of law-related services as a condition of graduation eligibility. Penn law students can fulfill their requirements in a variety of ways, including providing services at legal aid offices, government legal departments, and political action committee offices. Students can also provide assistance to professors, as well as lawyers in private practice who are working on pro bono cases.

Pro Bono and the Paralegal

As the phrase goes, what is good for the goose is good for the gander. All the national ethics codes designed specifically for paralegals and legal assistants mention pro bono services. Guideline 10 of the ABA Model Guidelines for the Utilization of Legal Assistant Services states, "A lawyer who employs a legal assistant should facilitate the legal assistant's participation in appropriate continuing education and pro bono publico activities." It is interesting that the Comment to Guideline 10 discusses the benefits that will accrue to the lawyer who includes the legal assistant in the pro bono legal services the lawyer is obligated to provide under MR 6.1, and then states, "*where appropriate, the legal assistant is encouraged to provide such services independently*" (emphasis added). Furthermore, the ABA's Standing Committee on Legal Assistants created a brochure in 1995 entitled "How to Use Legal Assistants in Pro Bono Publico Programs." This brochure discusses the advantages of legal assistants engaging in pro bono activities and lists ways in which legal assistants across the country are participating, including serving as intake interviewers and screeners at government-funded legal services programs and local bar association pro bono programs, as well as participating as client advocates in court approved special advocacy (CASA) programs. The brochure acknowledges that any legal assistant pro bono program needs to include attorney supervision of the work being done and should carry professional liability insurance.

Paralegal pro bono activities are also encouraged through the rules of court or statutes that formally approve of the use of paralegals and legal assistants, since those guidelines borrow heavily from any of the above mentioned paralegal or legal assistant codes of ethics. *See* Indiana Rules of Professional Conduct, Use of Legal Assistants, Guideline 9.9; Michigan Guidelines for the Utilization of Legal Assistant Services, Guideline 8; State Bar of Montana, Paralegal Rules of Professional Responsibility, Rule 3; Nebraska Guidelines for the Utilization of Legal Assistants, Article II (P)(5); and Washington State Bar Association Guidelines for the Utilization of Legal Assistant Services, Guideline 10.

The NFPA Model Disciplinary Rules and Ethical Considerations encourages pro bono activities in Rule 1.4, by stating, "A paralegal shall serve the public interest by contributing to the delivery of quality legal services and the improvement of the legal system." Following Rule 1.4 is EC–1.4(b), which states, "A paralegal shall support **bona fide** efforts to meet the need for legal services by those unable to pay reasonable or customary fees; for example, participation in pro bono projects and

bona fide—Genuine, or good faith.

volunteer work." Furthermore, the NFPA added to Rule 1.4 a new ethical consideration, EC–1.4(d), which calls for paralegals to contribute twenty-four hours annually to properly supervised pro bono activities. All NFPA members are annually asked to complete the NFPA Pro Bono Reporting Form, certifying that they contributed twenty-four hours of service. The NFPA also has a pro bono committee to coordinate NFPA's pro bono vision, has a national pro bono conference, and gives a national award to an NFPA member association that has made significant contributions to community pro bono efforts.

The NALA also is a formal supporter of pro bono services, and has held forums on promoting pro bono activities. Guideline 4 of The NALA Model Standards and Guidelines for Utilization of Legal Assistants states, "In the supervision of a legal assistant, consideration should be given to: . . . 5. Encouraging and supporting memberships and active participation in professional organizations." The Comment to Guideline 4 discusses the working relationship between lawyers and legal assistants extending to cooperative efforts on public services activities, and also makes reference to the pro bono encouragement in Guideline 10 of the ABA Model Guidelines.

Many state and local paralegal associations take an active role in promoting pro bono activities. For instance, the Legal Assistant Division of the State Bar of Texas and the Texas State Bar Standing Committee of Legal Assistants have sponsored a joint project called Pro Bono Partners. Funded by a grant from the Texas Bar Foundation, Pro Bono Partners teams a legal assistant with a lawyer on either an ad hoc or continuing basis so that both can work together on pro bono services. The team with greatest number of pro bono hours is recognized at the annual state bar convention, while the Legal Assistant Division has an Exceptional Pro Bono Service Award, given to one of its members who has provided extraordinary pro bono services. In light of the fact that legal assistants make less money than lawyers, it speaks highly of those legal assistants who volunteer their time in helping those who could not otherwise afford it.

Summary

Lawyers are required to provide competent representation. Competency is defined by having the legal knowledge and skill necessary to represent the client's interests. Even the new lawyer is held to the same competency standard that applies to the experienced lawyer. Connected to the duty of competence is the requirement that lawyers act with reasonable diligence on behalf of their clients. Despite the fact that the rules of ethics also require that lawyers keep their clients reasonably informed about their cases, lack of communication is the significant cause of client complaints against lawyers. The communication duty includes the need to pass along to the client settlement offers made by the opposing party, because the client is the one with the right to accept or reject such offers.

As a member of the legal team, the legal assistant has a corresponding duty to provide competent and diligent services. Competence requires that legal assistants be prepared to handle the matters assigned to them, and all the national paralegal ethics codes speak to the issue of competence and diligence. Meeting the requirement of competence and professionalism involves legal assistants being properly educated and trained, as well as regularly earning Continuing Legal Education (CLE) credits. Because legal assistants often have a lot of client contact, they need to be especially careful to communicate effectively, which includes promptly returning phone calls and possessing effective writing skills. However, a lawyer's duty to communicate with clients cannot be completely delegated to non-lawyer employees since the responsibility for honoring the communication duty rests with the lawyer. Legal assistants, particularly those who work in litigation firms, must strive to maintain a standard that is as competent as possible to protect themselves against being blamed for incompetent representation.

More than a few rules of ethics concern the lawyer's—and by extension, the paralegal's—duty to be truthful. The rules make it clear that a lawyer may not make a material misrepresentation in the course of representing a client. Failure to disclose what is needed to prevent the commission of a fraud or crime would also be a violation of the ethics rules. In order to commit a violation, the lawyer or legal assistant would first have to know of the misrepresentation and the misrepresentation would have to be material.

Lawyers are prohibited from bringing frivolous claims on behalf of their clients. A frivolous claim is not one that has a slim chance of winning; rather, it is a claim (or defense) that has no basis in law or fact. Also, claims are considered frivolous when they are made in bad faith or for the purpose of harassing the other party. Not only do the ethics rules prohibit frivolous claims, but a variety of civil and appellate procedure rules and statutes prohibit them as well.

Lawyers are prohibited from putting forth false evidence. The most extreme example of this is false testimony, and the rules require lawyers to do everything possible to prevent their clients from testifying falsely. Even in criminal cases, clients do not have a constitutional right to testify falsely. Paralegals need to consult with their supervising attorneys whenever there is a reasonable suspicion that clients are not being forthcoming, such as in discovery matters, since even if lawyers are unaware of their clients' deceit, they could still be subject to discipline for failing to adequately supervise their employees.

Members of the legal team should avoid directly communicating with persons who are represented by counsel, unless permission has been given or the law authorized the contact. This type of rule is designed to protect a person from being taken advantage of by the other side's lawyer when the contacted person is without the assistance of his or her own lawyer. However, some jurisdictions still use the language from either the anticontact rule of the Model Code or that of the Model Rules and only prohibit the direct contact of represented parties. There are exceptions to the anticontact rule, including the right of parties to directly communicate with one another and the right to make direct contact with the intended witnesses of a party. Because the anticontact rule applies equally to all members of the legal team, paralegals need to be careful about contacting represented persons.

A variety of ethical issues are involved when contact is made with those persons who do not have legal representation. Foremost of those considerations is the requirement in jurisdictions that operate under a version of the Model Rules that those contacting unrepresented persons may not state or imply neutrality. The rules require that a member of the legal team making contact with an unrepresented person clearly explain to that person that the lawyer is not disinterested and clear up any misunderstanding the unrepresented person may have about the neutrality of the person contacting them. The purpose behind such a rule is fairness to those who, unless they are lawyers, are at a disadvantage when discussing matters related to a case with a lawyer or another member of the legal team. The Model Code has no similar prohibition other than requiring that the only advice a lawyer should give to an unrepresented person is to get a lawyer. All of the paralegal ethics codes require that paralegals disclose their status at the outset of any professional communication. Paralegals should also make sure not to give legal advice—or imply it—to unrepresented persons or advise them to leave the jurisdiction.

Because the interests of fairness in litigation are so important, the rules prohibit lawyers from having any ex parte communication with any judge or jury member involved in the litigation. While attempts at inappropriately influencing a judge or jury member are clearly wrong (and are very often criminalized), the simple act of having inappropriate contact with a judge or jury member could be the cause of professional discipline. The paralegal codes of ethics, likewise, prohibit ex parte communication, and those paralegals that go to court with their attorneys must have no contact with members of the jury during the course of the legal proceedings.

An area of litigation fairness that may seem a bit odd is the requirement that lawyers are required to cite directly controlling adverse authority to the court when the opposing party has failed to cite it. In order to be sanctioned for such a legal research violation, it would need to be established that the lawyer was aware the adverse legal authority existed. Some argue that such a rule is much ado about nothing, and two jurisdictions have abandoned the requirement altogether. Nevertheless, legal assistants conducting legal research need to make their supervising attorneys aware of any negative legal authority.

Malpractice is the failure of a lawyer to exercise reasonable care with respect to the client's case, and a resulting harm to the client caused by the lawyer's negligence. While it is clear that lawyers can be found liable for their own negligence and for the negligence of their non-lawyer employees, it is also possible for a non-lawyer to be the subject of a legal malpractice lawsuit since malpractice is a tort and is distinct from professional discipline. The starting point for any case of non-lawyer malpractice starts with the unauthorized practice of law because, despite the lack of a regulating court's ability to discipline a non-lawyer, a jury could still find that the non-lawyer's incompetent, unauthorized practice of law constituted negligence. Not all jurisdictions, however, agree that a legal assistant or other non-lawyer can be liable for malpractice, particularly when the one suing for malpractice was not deceived about the non-lawyer's status.

Although nothing in the Model Code or Model Rules requires a lawyer to provide pro bono services, lawyers, as a group, have a history of providing pro bono services to the public. The most recent version of the Model Rules encourages lawyers to provide a minimum of fifty annual pro bono hours, and some jurisdictions' pro bono rules suggest up to eighty annual hours. Some law schools do make pro bono services a prerequisite to graduation.

Despite being a relatively young profession, paralegalism has a strong history of involving itself in pro bono services. Starting with the ABA Model Guidelines for the Utilization of Legal Assistant Services, all paralegal codes of conduct and many state legal assistant organizations specifically mention and sponsor pro bono activities. Legal assistants engage in a variety of pro bono activities, including assisting at legal aid offices and volunteering in court appointed special advocacy programs. In most situations, legal assistants need to perform their pro bono activities under the supervision of lawyers, so as not to engage in a charitable form of the unauthorized practice of law.

Points to Ponder

1. What does it mean to say that a lawyer must be competent?
2. In addition to the substantive law, what else must a lawyer know in order to be competent?
3. What kinds of activities would qualify as satisfying the lawyer's duty to communicate with the client?
4. What can legal assistants do to improve the lines of communication between lawyers and clients?
5. What determines whether a legal assistant is competent?

6. Lawyers are required to obtain Continuing Legal Education credits. Do you think that paralegals should also be required to do the same?
7. What different rules concern the legal team's duty to be truthful?
8. Can you think of an example of an untruth that would not have to be disclosed because it is not a material misrepresentation?
9. How do you think one can balance the duty of confidentiality with the duty to be honest to opposing parties and courts?
10. What makes a claim a frivolous one? Do you think the Sea World drowning case and/or the McDonald's coffee spill case are examples of frivolous suits?
11. Does your jurisdiction have a statute that concerns vexatious litigation?
12. What steps should be followed when a member of the legal team believes that the client wants to testify falsely? Other than in a litigation context, what might a client do that could qualify as false and, therefore, require lawyer intervention?
13. Do you think the narrative approach for putting on false testimony in criminal cases is more fair to the defendant or more unfair to the legal system?
14. What is the general rule on dealing with represented persons?
15. What are some of the exceptions to the rule in (14)?
16. What is the significance to distinguishing between represented persons and represented parties in an anticontact rule?
17. Does your jurisdiction cover represented persons?
18. What is expected of one making contact with an unrepresented person?
19. What is ex parte communication and why is it not allowed?
20. What is wrong with a paralegal talking to a member of the jury during the lunch break, as long as the case is not discussed?
21. What changes did the Ethics 2000 Commission propose to the ex parte rule?
22. Do you think that lawyers should be sanctioned for failing to cite directly adverse, controlling legal authority? Why or why not?
23. What is legal malpractice? Why is it that a negative result for a client does not necessarily mean that the lawyer will be found to have committed malpractice?
24. How can non-lawyers be liable for legal malpractice if they are unlicensed to practice law?
25. Can a legal assistant who works under the supervision of a lawyer be found liable for malpractice?
26. In what different ways can a lawyer fulfill pro bono obligations?
27. Do you think that pro bono activities or contributions should be mandatory for lawyers?
28. Do you think that pro bono services should be mandatory for legal assistants? Should pro bono activities be required for students as a condition to graduating?

Key Concepts

Anticontact rule

Competence and client representation

Diligence and client representation

Directly adverse authority

Ex parte communication

Frivolous lawsuits

Malpractice

Narrative approach to perjured testimony

Non-lawyer malpractice

Preparation and client representation

Pro bono

Truthfulness and client representation

Vexatious litigant

Key Terms

bad faith	forms books	proximate cause
bona fide	intestate estate	venire
continuing legal education (CLE)	malpractice	voir dire
estate plan	misrepresentation	West Digest System®
ex parte communication	personal representative	writ of mandamus

ABA Model Guidelines for the Utilization of Legal Assistant Services

Appendix

A

PREAMBLE

State courts, bar associations, or bar committees in at least seventeen states have prepared recommendations[1] for the utilization of legal assistant services.[2] While their content varied, their purpose appears uniform: to provide lawyers with a reliable basis for delegating responsibility for performing a portion of the lawyer's tasks to legal assistants. The purpose of preparing model guidelines is not to contradict the guidelines already adopted or to suggest that other guidelines may be more appropriate in a particular jurisdiction. It is the view of the Standing Committee on Legal Assistants of the American Bar Association, however, that a model set of guidelines for the utilization of legal assistant services may assist many states in adopting or revising such guidelines. The Standing Committee is of the view that guidelines will encourage lawyers to utilize legal assistant services effectively and promote the growth of the legal assistant profession.[3] In undertaking this project, the Standing Committee has attempted to state guidelines that conform with the American Bar Association's Model Rules of Professional Conduct, decided authority, and contemporary practice. Lawyers, or course, are to be first directed by Rule 5.3 of the Model Rules in the utilization of legal assistant services, and nothing contained in these guidelines is intended to be inconsistent with that rule. Specific ethical considerations in particular states, however, may require modification of these guidelines before their adoption. In the commentary after each guideline, we have attempted to identify the basis for the guideline and any issues of which we are aware that the guideline may present: those drafting such guidelines may wish to take them into account.

> *Guideline 1*: A lawyer is responsible for all of the professional actions of a legal assistant performing legal assistant services at the lawyer's direction and should take reasonable measures to ensure that the legal assistant's conduct is consistent with the lawyer's obligations under the ABA Model Rules of Professional Conduct.

Comment to Guideline 1: An attorney who utilizes a legal assistant's services is responsible for determining that the legal assistant is competent to perform the tasks assigned, based on the legal assistant's education, training, and experience, and for ensuring that the legal assistant is familiar with the responsibilities of attorneys and legal assistants under the applicable rules governing professional conduct.[4]

Under principles of agency law and rules governing the conduct of attorneys, lawyers are responsible for the actions and the work product of the nonlawyers they employ. Rule 5.3 of the Model Rules[5] requires that partners and supervising attorneys ensure that the conduct of nonlawyer assistants is compatible with the lawyer's professional obligations. Several state guidelines have adopted this language. *E.g.,* Commentary to Illinois Recommendation (A), Kansas Guideline III(a), New Hampshire Rule 35, Sub-Rule 9, and North Carolina Guideline 4. Ethical Consideration 3–6 of the Model Code encouraged lawyers to delegate tasks to legal assistants provided the lawyer maintained a direct relationship with the client, supervised appropriately, and had complete responsibility for the work product. The adoption of Rule 5.3, which incorporates these principles, implicitly reaffirms this encouragement.

Several states have addressed the issue of the lawyer's ultimate responsibility for work performed by subordinates. For example, Colorado Guideline 1.c, Kentucky Supreme Court Rule 3.700, Sub-Rule 2.c, and Michigan Guideline I provide: "The lawyer remains responsible for the actions of the legal assistant to the same extent as if such representation had been furnished entirely by the lawyer and such actions were those of the lawyer." New Mexico Guideline X states "[the] lawyer maintains ultimate responsibility for and has an ongoing duty to actively supervise the legal assistant's work performance, conduct, and product." Connecticut Recommendation 2 and Rhode Island Guideline III state specifically that lawyers are liable for malpractice for the mistakes and omissions of their legal assistants.

Finally, the lawyer should ensure that legal assistants supervised by the lawyer are familiar with the rules governing attorney conduct and that they follow those rules. *See* Comment to Model Rule 5.3; Illinois Recommendation (A) (5), New Hampshire Supreme Court Rule 35, Sub-Rule 9, and New Mexico, Statement of Purpose; *see also* NALA's Model Standards and Guidelines for the Utilization of Legal Assistants, guidelines IV, V, and VIII (1985, revised 1990) (hereafter "NALA Guidelines.").

The Standing Committee and several of those who have commented upon these Guidelines regard Guideline 1 as a comprehensive statement of general principle governing lawyers who utilize legal assistant services in the practice of law. As such it, in effect, is a part of each of the remaining Guidelines.

Guideline 2: **Provided the lawyer maintains responsibility for the work product, a lawyer may delegate to a legal assistant any task normally performed by the lawyer except those tasks proscribed to one not licensed as a lawyer by statute, court rule, administrative rule or regulation, controlling authority, the ABA Model Rules of Professional Conduct, or the Guidelines.**

Comment to Guideline 2: The essence of the definition of the term legal assistant adopted by the ABA Board of Governors in 1986 is that, so long as appropriate supervision is maintained, many tasks normally performed by lawyers may be delegated to legal assistants. Of course, Rule 5.5 of the Model Rules, DR 3–101 of the Model Code, and most states specifically prohibit lawyers from assisting or aiding a nonlawyer in the unauthorized practice of law. Thus, while appropriate delegation of tasks to legal assistants is encouraged, the lawyer may not permit the legal assistant to engage in the "practice of law." EC 3–5 under the Model Code gave some guidance by equating the practice of law to the application of the professional judgment of the lawyer in solving clients' legal problems. Further, ABA Opinions 316 (1967) states:

A lawyer can employ lay secretaries, lay investigators, lay detectives, lay researchers, accountants, lay scriveners, nonlawyer draftsmen, or nonlawyer researchers. In fact, he may employ nonlawyers to do any task for him except counsel clients about law matters, engage directly in the practice of law, appear in court, or appear in formal proceedings as part of the judicial process, so long as it is he who takes the work and vouches for it to the client and becomes responsible for it to the client.

Most state guidelines specify that legal assistants may not appear before courts, administrative tribunals, or other adjudicatory bodies unless their rules authorize such appearances; may not conduct depositions; and may not give legal advice to clients. *E.g.,* Connecticut Recommendation 4; Fla. EC 3-6 (327 So.2d at 16); and Michigan Guideline II. *Also see* NALA Guidelines IV and VI. But it is also important to note that, as some guidelines have recognized, pursuant to federal or state statute legal assistants are permitted to provide direct client representation in certain administrative proceedings. *E.g.,* South Carolina Guideline II. While this does not obviate the attorney's responsibility for the legal assistant's work, it does change the nature of the attorney supervision of the legal assistant. The opportunity to use such legal assistant services has particular benefits to legal services programs and does not violate Guideline 2. *See generally ABA Standards for Providers of Civil Legal Services to the Poor.* Std. 6.3, at 6.17–6.18 (1986).

The Model Rules emphasize the importance of appropriate delegation. The key to appropriate delegation is proper supervision, which includes adequate instruction when assigning projects, monitoring of the project, and review of the completed project. The Supreme Court of Virginia upheld a malpractice verdict against a lawyer based in part on negligent actions of a legal assistant in performing tasks that evidently were properly delegable. *Musselman v. Willoughby Corp.*, 230 Va. 337, 337 S.E.2d 724 (1985). *See also* C. Wolfram, *Modern Legal Ethics* (1986), at 236, 896. All state guidelines refer to the requirement that the lawyer "supervise" legal assistants in the performance of their duties. Lawyers should also take care in hiring and choosing a legal assistant to work on a specific project to ensure that legal assistant has the education, knowledge, and ability necessary to perform the delegated tasks competently. *See* Connecticut Recommendation 14, Kansas Standards I, II, and III, and New Mexico Guideline VIII. Finally, some states describe appropriate delegation and review in terms of the delegated work losing its identity and becoming "merged" into the work product of the attorney. *See* Florida EC 3–6 (327 So.2d at 16).

Legal Assistants often play an important role in improving communication between the attorney and the client. EC 3–6 under the Model Code mentioned three specific kinds of tasks that legal assistants may perform under appropriate lawyer supervision: factual investigation and research, legal research, and the preparation of legal documents. Some states delineate more specific tasks in their guidelines, such as attending client conferences, corresponding with and obtaining information from clients, handling witness execution of documents, preparing transmittal letters, maintaining estate/guardianship trust accounts, etc. *See, e.g.,* Colorado (lists of specialized functions in several areas follow guidelines); Michigan, Comment to Definition of Legal Assistant; New York, Specialized Skills of Legal Assistants; Rhode Island Guideline II; and NALA Guideline IX. The two-volume *Working with Legal Assistants*, published by the Standing Committee in 1982, attempted to provide a general description of the types of tasks that may be delegated to legal assistants in various practice areas.

There are tasks that have been specifically prohibited in some states, but that may be delegated in others. For example, legal assistants may not supervise will executions or represent clients at real estate closings in some jurisdictions, but may in others. *Compare* Connecticut Recommendation 7 and Illinois State Bar Association Position Paper on Use of Attorney Assistants in Real Estate Transactions (May 16, 1984) *with* Georgia "real estate job description," Florida Professional Ethics Committee Advisory Opinion 89–5 (1989), and Missouri, Comment to Guideline I, which permit legal assistants to conduct real estate closings. *Also compare* Connecticut Recommendation 8 (prohibiting attorneys from authorizing legal assistants to supervise will executions) *with* Colorado "estate planning job description," Georgia "estate, trusts, and wills job description," Missouri, Comment to Guideline I, and Rhode Island Guideline II (suggesting that legal assistants may supervise the execution of wills, trusts, and other documents).

Guideline 3: A lawyer may not delegate to a legal assistant:
(a) Responsibility for establishing an attorney-client relationship.
(b) Responsibility for establishing the amount of a fee to be charged for a legal service.
(c) Responsibility for a legal opinion rendered to a client.

Comment to Guideline 3: The Model Rules and most state codes require that lawyers communicate with their clients in order for clients to make well-informed decisions about their representation and resolution of legal issues. Model Rule 1.4. Ethical Consideration 3–6 under the Model Code emphasized that "delegation [of legal tasks to nonlawyers] is proper if the lawyer *maintains a direct relationship with his client,* supervises the delegated work, and has complete professional responsibility for the work product." (Emphasis added.) Accordingly, most state guidelines also stress the importance of a direct attorney-client relationship. *See* Colorado Guideline 1, Florida EC 3–6, Illinois Recommendation (A)(1), Iowa EC 3–6(2), and New Mexico Guideline IV. The direct personal relationship between client and lawyer is necessary to the exercise of the lawyer's trained professional judgment.

An essential aspect of the lawyer-client relationship is the agreement to undertake representation and the related fee arrangement. The Model Rules and most states require that fee arrangements be agreed upon early on and be communicated to the client by the lawyer, in some circumstances in writing. Model Rule 1.5 and Comments. Many state guidelines prohibit legal assistants from "setting fees" or "accepting cases." *See, e.g.,* Colorado Guideline 1 and NALA Guideline VI. Connecticut recommends that legal assistants be prohibited from accepting or rejecting cases or setting fees "if these tasks entail any discretion on the part of the paralegal." Connecticut Recommendation 9.

EC 3–5 states:

[T]he essence of the professional judgment of the lawyer is his educated ability to relate the general body and philosophy of law to a specific legal problem of a client; and thus, the public interest will be better served if only lawyers are permitted to act in matters involving professional judgment.

Clients are entitled to their lawyers' professional judgment and opinion. Legal assistants may, however, be authorized to communicate legal advice so long as they do not interpret or expand on that advice. Typically, state guidelines phrase this prohibition in terms of legal assistants being forbidden from "giving legal advice or counseling clients about legal matter." *See, e.g.,* Colorado Guideline 2, Connecticut Recommendation 6, Florida DR 3–104; Iowa EC 3–6(3), Kansas Guideline I, Kentucky Sub-Rule 2, New Hampshire Rule 35, Sub-Rule 1, Texas Guideline I, and NALA Guideline VI. Some states have more expansive wording that prohibits legal assistants from engaging in any activity that would require the exercise of independent judgment. Nevertheless, it is clear that all states, as well as the Model Rules, encourage direct communication between clients and a legal assistant insofar as the legal assistant is performing a task properly delegated by a lawyer. It should be noted that a lawyer who permits a legal assistant to assist in establishing the attorney-client relationship, communicating a fee, or preparing a legal opinion is not delegating responsibility for those matters and, therefore, may be complying with this guideline.

Guideline 4: **It is the lawyer's responsibility to take reasonable measures to ensure that clients, courts, and other lawyers are aware that a legal assistant, whose services are utilized by the lawyer in performing legal services, is not licensed to practice law.**

Comment to Guideline 4: Since, in most instances, a legal assistant is not licensed as a lawyer, it is important that those with whom the legal assistant deals are aware of that fact. Several state guidelines impose on the lawyer responsibility for instructing a legal assistant whose services are utilized by the lawyer to disclose the legal assistant's status in any dealings with a third party. *See, e.g.,* Michigan Guideline III, part 5, New Hampshire Rule 35, Sub-Rule 8, and NALA Guideline V. While requiring the legal assistant to make such disclosure is one way in which the attorney's responsibility to third parties may be discharged, the Standing Committee is of the view that it is desirable to emphasize the lawyer's responsibility for the disclosure and leave to the lawyer the discretion to decide whether the lawyer will discharge that responsibility by direct communication with the client, by requiring the legal assistant to make the disclosure, by a written memorandum, or by some other means. Although in most initial engagements by a client it may be prudent for the attorney to discharge this responsibility with a writing, the guideline requires only that the lawyer recognize the responsibility and ensure that it is discharged. Clearly, when a client has been adequately informed of the lawyer's utilization of legal assistant services, it is unnecessary to make additional formalistic disclosures as the client retains the lawyer for other services.

Most state guidelines specifically endorse legal assistants signing correspondence so long as their status as legal assistant is indicated by an appropriate title. *E.g.,* Colorado Guideline 2; Kansas, Comment to Guideline IX; and North Carolina Guideline 9; *also see* ABA Informal Opinion 1367 (1976). The comment to New Mexico Guideline XI warns against the use of the title "associate" since it may be construed to mean associate-attorney.

Guideline 5: **A lawyer may identify legal assistants by name and title on the lawyer's letterhead and on business cards identifying the lawyer's firm.**

Comment to Guideline 5: Under Guideline 4, above, an attorney who employs a legal assistant has an obligation to ensure that the status of the legal assistant has an obligation to ensure that the status of the legal assistant as a nonlawyer is fully disclosed. The primary purpose of this disclosure is to avoid confusion that might lead someone to believe that the legal assistant is a lawyer. The identification suggested by this guideline is consistent with that objective, while also affording the legal assistant recognition as an important part of the legal services team.

Recent ABA informal Opinion 1527 (1989) provides that nonlawyer support personnel, including legal assistants, may be listed on a law firm's letterhead and reiterates previous opinions that approve of legal assistants having business cards. *See also* ABA Informal Opinion 1185 (1971). The listing must not be false or misleading and "must make it clear that the support personnel who are listed are not lawyers."

Nearly all state guidelines approve of business cards for legal assistants, but some prescribe the contents and format of the card. *E.g.,* Iowa Guideline 4 and Texas Guidelines VIII. All agree the legal assistant's status must be clearly indicated and the card may not be used in a deceptive way. New Hampshire Supreme Court Rule 7 approves the use of business cards so long as the card is not used for unethical solicitations.

Some states do not permit attorneys to list legal assistants on their letterhead. *E.g.,* Kansas Guideline VIII, Michigan Guideline III, New Hampshire Rule 35, Sub-Rule 7, New Mexico Guideline XI, and North Carolina Guideline 9. Several of these states rely on earlier ABA Informal Opinions 619 (1962), 845 (1965), and 1000 (1977), all of which were expressly withdrawn by ABA Informal Opinion 1527. These earlier opinions interpreted the predecessor Model Code and DR 2-102 (A), which, prior to *Bates v. State Bar of Arizona,* 433 U.S. 350 (1977), had strict limitations on the information that could be listed on letterheads. States which do permit attorneys to list names of legal assistants on their stationery, if the listing is not deceptive and the legal assistant's status is clearly identified, include: Arizona Committee on Rules of Professional Conduct Formal Opinion 3/90 (1990); Connecticut Recommendation 12; Florida Professional Ethics Committee Advisory Opinion 86–4 (1986); Hawaii, Formal Opinion 78–8–19 (1978, as revised 1984); Illinois State Bar Association Advisory Opinion 87–1 (1987); Kentucky Sub-Rule 6; Mississippi State Bar Ethics Committee Opinion No. 93 (1984); Missouri Guideline IV; New York State Bar Association Committee on Professional Ethics Opinion 500 (1978); Oregon Ethical Opinion No. 349 (1977); and Texas, Ethics Committee Opinion No. 406 (1983). In light of the United States Supreme Court opinion in *Peel v. Attorney Registration and Disciplinary Commission of Illinois,* __ U.S. __, 110 S. Ct. 2281 (1990), it may be that a restriction on letterhead identification of legal assistants that is not deceptive and clearly identifies the legal assistant's status violates the First Amendment rights of the lawyer.

Guideline 6: **It is the responsibility of a lawyer to take reasonable measures to ensure that all client confidences are preserved by a legal assistant.**

Comment to Guideline 6: A fundamental principle underlying the free exchange of information in a lawyer-client relationship is that the lawyer maintain the confidentiality of information relating to representation.

It is a matter of common knowledge that the normal operation of a law office exposes confidential professional information to nonlawyer employees of the office. This obligates a lawyer to exercise care in selecting and training his employees so that the sanctity of all confidences and secrets of his clients may be preserved. EC 4–2, Model Code.

Rule 5.3 of the Model Rules requires "a lawyer who has direct supervisory authority over the nonlawyer [to] make reasonable efforts to ensure that the person's conduct is compatible with the professional obligations of the lawyer." The Comment to Rule 5.3 makes it clear that lawyers should give legal assistants "appropriate instruction and supervision concerning the ethical aspects of their employment, particularly regarding the obligation not to disclose information relating to the representation of the client." DR 4–101 (D) under the Model Code provides that: "A lawyer shall exercise reasonable care to prevent his employees, associates, and others whose services are utilized by him from discharging or using confidences or secrets of a client. . . ."

It is particularly important that the lawyer ensure that the legal assistant understands that *all* information concerning the client, even the mere fact that a person is a client of the firm, may be strictly confidential. Rule 1.6 of the Model Rules expanded the definition of confidential information ". . . not merely to matters communicated in confidence by the client but also to all information relating to the representation, whatever its source."[6] It is therefore the lawyer's obligation to instruct clearly and to take reasonable steps to ensure the legal assistant's preservation of client confidences. Nearly all states that have guidelines for the utilization of legal assistants require the lawyer "to instruct legal assistants concerning client confidences" and "to exercise care to ensure that legal assistants comply" with the Code in this regard. Even if the client consents to divulging information, this information must not be used to the disadvantage of the client. *See, e.g.,* Connecticut Recommendation 3; New Hampshire Rule 35, Sub-Rule 4; NALA Guideline V.

Guideline 7: **A lawyer should take reasonable measures to prevent conflicts of interest resulting from a legal assistant's other employment or interests insofar as such other employment or interests would present a conflict of interest if it were that of the lawyer.**

Comment to Guideline 7: A lawyer must make "reasonable efforts to ensure that [a] legal assistant's conduct is compatible with the professional obligations of the lawyer." Model Rule 5.3. These professional obligations include the duty to exercise independent professional judgment on behalf of a client, "free of compromising influences and loyalties." ABA Model Rules 1.7 through 1.13. Therefore, legal assistants should be instructed to inform the supervising attorney of any interest that could result in a conflict of interest or even give the appearance of a conflict. The guideline intentionally speaks to other employment rather than only past employment, since there are instances where legal assistants are employed by more than one law firm at the same time. The guideline's reference to "other interests" is intended to include personal relationships as well as instances where a legal assistant may have a financial interest (i.e., as stockholder, trust, beneficiary, or trustee, etc.) that would conflict with the client in the matter in which the lawyer has been employed.

"Imputed Disqualification Arising from Change in Employment by Nonlawyer Employee." ABA Informal Opinion 1526 (1988), defines the duties of both the present and former employing lawyers and reasons that the restrictions on legal assistants' employment should be kept to "the minimum necessary to protect confidentiality" in order to prevent legal assistants from being forced to leave their careers, which "would disserve clients as well as the legal profession." The Opinion describes the attorney's obligations (1) to caution the legal assistant not to disclose any information and (2) to prevent the legal assistant from working on any matter on which the legal assistant worked for a prior employer or respecting which the employee has confidential information.

If a conflict is discovered, it may be possible to "wall" the legal assistant from the conflict area so that the entire firm need not to be disqualified and the legal assistant is effectively screened from information concerning the matter. The American Bar Association has taken the position that what historically been described as a "Chinese wall" will allow nonlawyer personnel (including legal assistants) who are in possession of confidential client information to accept employment with a law firm opposing the former client so long as the wall is observed and effectively screens the nonlawyer from confidential information. ABA Informal Opinion 1526 (1988). *See also* Tennessee Formal Ethics Opinion 89–F–118 (March 10, 1989). The implication of this Informal Opinion is that if a wall is not in place, the employer may be disqualified from representing either party to the controversy. One court has so held. *In re: Complex Asbestos Litigation,* No. 828684 (San Francisco Superior Court, September 19, 1989).

It is not clear that a wall will prevent disqualification in the case of a lawyer employed to work for a law firm representing a client with an adverse interest to a client of the lawyer's former employer. Under Model Rule 1.10, when a lawyer moves to a firm that represents an adverse party in a matter in which the lawyer's former firm was involved, absent a waiver by the client, the new firm's representation may continue only if the newly employed lawyer acquired no protected information and did not work directly on the matter in former employment. The new Rules of Professional Conduct in Kentucky and Texas (both effective on January 1, 1990) specifically provide for disqualification. Rule 1.10(b) in the District of Columbia, which became effective January 1, 1991, does so as well. The Sixth Circuit, however, has held that the wall will effectively insulate the new firm from disqualification if it prevents the new lawyer-employee from access to information concerning the client with the adverse interest. *Manning v. Waring, Cox, James, Sklar & Allen,* 894 F.2d 222 (Sixth Cir. 1988). [As a result of the Sixth Circuit opinion, Tennessee revised its formal ethics opinion, which is cited above, and now applies the same rule to lawyers, legal assistants, law clerks, and legal secretaries.] *See generally,* NFPA, "The Chinese Wall—Its Application to Paralegals" (1990).

The states that have guidelines that address the legal assistant conflict of interest issue refer to the lawyer's responsibility to ensure against personal, business, or social interests of the legal assistant that would conflict with the representation of the client or impinge on the services rendered to the client. *E.g.,* Kansas Guideline X, New Mexico Guideline VI, and North Carolina Guideline 7. Florida Professional Ethics Opinion 86–5 (1986) discusses a legal assistant's move from one firm to another and the obligations of each not to disclose confidences. *See also* Vermont Ethics Opinion 85-8 (1985) (a legal assistant is not bound by the Code of Professional Responsibility and, absent an absolute waiver by the client, the new firm should not represent client if legal assistant possessed confidential information from old firm).

Guideline 8: **A lawyer may include a charge for the work performed by a legal assistant in setting a charge for legal services.**

Comment to Guideline 8: The U.S. Supreme Court in *Missouri v. Jenkins,* 491 U.S. 274 (1989), held that in setting a reasonable attorney's fee under 28 U.S.C. Sec. 1988, a legal fee may include a charge for legal assistant services at "market rates" rather than "actual cost" to the attorneys. This decision should resolve any question concerning the propriety of setting a charge for legal services based on work performed by a legal assistant. Its rationale favors setting a charge based on the "market" rate for such services, rather than their direct cost to the lawyer. This result was recognized by Connecticut Recommendation 11, Illinois recommendation D, and Texas Guideline V prior to the Supreme Court decision. *See also* Fla. Stat. Ann. Sec. 57.104 (1991 Supp.) (adopted in 1987 and permitting consideration of legal assistant services in computing attorneys' fees) and Fla. Stat. Ann. Ss 744.108 (1991 Supp.) (adopted in 1989 and permitting recovery of "customary and reasonable charges for work performed by legal assistants" as fees for legal services in guardianship matters.)

It is important to note, however, that *Missouri v. Jenkins* does not abrogate the attorney's responsibilities under Model Rule 1.5 to set a reasonable fee for legal services, and it follows that those considerations apply to a fee that includes a fee for legal assistant services. Accordingly, the effect of combining a market rate charge for the services of lawyers and legal assistants should, in most instances, result in a lower total cost for the legal service than if the lawyer had performed the service alone.

Guideline 9: **A lawyer may not split legal fees with a legal assistant nor pay a legal assistant for the referral of legal business. A lawyer may compensate a legal assistant based on the quantity and quality of the legal assistant's work and the value of that work to a law practice, but the legal assistant's compensation may not be contingent, by advance agreement, upon the profitability of the lawyer's practice.**

Comment to Guideline 9: Model Rule 5.4 and DR 3–102(A) and 3–103(A) under the Model Code clearly prohibit fee "splitting" with legal assistants, whether characterized as splitting of contingent fees, "forwarding" fees, or other sharing of legal fee. Virtually all guidelines adopted by state bar associations have continued this prohibition in one form or another.[7] It appears clear that a legal assistant may not be compensated on a contingent basis for a particular case or paid for "signing up" clients for a legal practice.

Having stated this prohibition, however, the guideline attempts to deal with the practical consideration of how a legal assistant properly may be compensated by an attorney or law firm. The linchpin of the prohibition seems to be the advance agreement of the lawyer to "split" a fee based on a preexisting contingent arrangement.[8] There is no general prohibition against a lawyer who enjoys a particularly profitable period recognizing the contribution of the legal assistant to that profitability with a discretionary bonus. Likewise, a lawyer engaged in a particularly profitable specialty of legal practice is not prohibited from compensating the legal assistant who aids materially in that practice more handsomely than the compensation generally awarded to legal assistants in that geographic area who work in law practices that are less lucrative. Indeed, any effort to fix a compensation level for legal assistants and prohibit greater compensation would appear to violate the federal antitrust laws. *See, e.g., Goldfarb v. Virginia State Bar*, 421 U.S. 773 (1975).

Guideline 10: **A lawyer who employs a legal assistant should facilitate the legal assistant's participation in appropriate continuing education and pro bono publico activities.**

Comment to Guideline 10: While Guideline 10 does not appear to have been adopted in the guidelines of any state bar association, the Standing Committee on Legal Assistants believes that its adoption would be appropriate.[9] For many years the Standing Committee on Legal Assistants has advocated that the improvement of formal legal assistant education will generally improve the legal services rendered by lawyers employing legal assistants and provide a more satisfying professional atmosphere in which legal assistants may work. *See, e.g.,* ABA Board of Governors, Policy on Legal Assistant Licensure and/or Certification, Statement 4 (February 6, 1986); ABA Standing Committee on Legal Assistants, "Position Paper on the Question of Legal Assistant Licensure or Certification" (December 10, 1985), at 6 and Conclusion 3. Recognition of the employing lawyer's obligation to facilitate the legal assistant's continuing professional education is, therefore, appropriate because of the benefits to both the law practice and the legal assistants and is consistent with the lawyer's own responsibility to maintain competence under Model Rule 1.1. *See also* EC 6–2 of the Model Code.

The Standing Committee is of the view that similar benefits will accrue to the lawyer and legal assistant if the legal assistant is included in the pro bono publico legal services that a lawyer has a clear obligation to provide under Model 6.1 and, where appropriate, the legal assistant is encouraged to provide such services independently. The ability of a law firm to provide more pro bono publico services will be enhanced if legal assistants are included. Recognition of the legal assistant's role in such services is consistent with the role of the legal assistant in the contemporary delivery of legal services generally and is consistent with the lawyer's duty to the legal profession under Canon 2 of the Model Code.

THE STANDING COMMITTEE ON LEGAL ASSISTANTS
OF THE AMERICAN BAR ASSOCIATION
May 1991

NOTES

[1]An appendix identifies the guidelines, court rules, and recommendations that were reviewed in drafting these Model Guidelines.

[2]On February 6, 1986, the ABA Board of Governors approved the following definition of the term "legal assistant":

A legal assistant is a person, qualified through education, training, or work experience, who is employed or retained by a lawyer, law office, governmental agency, or other entity in a capacity or function which involves the performance, under the ultimate direction and supervision of an attorney, of specifically delegated substantive legal work, which work, for the most part, requires a sufficient knowledge of legal concepts that, absent such assistant, the attorney would perform the talk.

[In some contexts, the term "paralegal" is used interchangeably with the term legal assistant.

[3]While necessarily mentioning legal assistant conduct, lawyers are the intended audience of these Guidelines. The Guidelines, therefore, are addressed to lawyer conduct and not directly to the conduct of the legal assistant. Both the National Association of Legal Assistants (NALA) and the National Federation of Paralegal Associations (NFPA) have adopted guidelines of conduct that are directed to legal assistants. *See* NALA, "Code of Ethics and Professional Responsibility of the National Association of Legal Assistants, Inc." (adopted May 1975, revised November 1979, and September 1988); NFPA "Affirmation of Responsibility" (adopted 1977, revised 1981).

[4]Attorneys, of course, are not liable for violations of the ABA Model Rules of Professional Conduct ("Model Rules") unless the Model Rules have been adopted as the code of professional conduct in a jurisdiction in which the lawyer practices. They are referenced in this model guideline for illustrative purposes: if the guideline is to be adopted, the reference should be modified to the jurisdiction's rules of professional conduct.

[5]The Model Rules were first adopted by the ABA House of Delegates in August of 1983. Since that time many states have adopted the Model Rules to govern the professional conduct of lawyers licensed in those states. Since a number of states still utilize a version of the Model Code of Professional Responsibility ("Model Code"), which was adopted by the House of Delegates in August of 1969, however, these comments will refer to both the Model Rules and the predecessor Model Code (and the Ethical Considerations and Disciplinary Rules found under the canons in the Model Code).

[6]Rule 1.05 of the Texas Disciplinary Rules of Professional Conduct (1990) provides a different formulation, which is equally expansive:

"Confidential Information" includes both "privileged information" and "unprivileged client information." "Privileged information" refers to the information of a client protected by the lawyer-client privilege of Rule 503 of the Texas Rules of Evidence or of Rule 503 of the Texas Rules of Texas Rules of Criminal Evidence or by the principles of attorney-client privilege governed by Rule 501 of the Federal Rules of Evidence for the United States Courts and Magistrates. "Unprivileged client information" means all information relating to a client or furnished by the client, other than privileged information, acquired by the lawyer during the course of or by reason of the representation of the client.

[7]Connecticut recommendation 10: Illinois recommendation D; Kansas Guideline VI; Kentucky Supreme Court Rule 3.700, Sub-rule 5; Michigan Guideline III, part 2; Missouri Guidelines II; New Hampshire Rule 35, Sub-Rules 5 and 6; New Mexico Guideline IX; Rhode Island Guideline VIII and IX; South Carolina Guideline V; Texas Guideline V.

[8]In its Rule 5.4, which will become effective on January 1, 1991, the District of Columbia will permit lawyers to form legal services partnerships that include nonlawyer participants. Comments 5 and 6 to that rule, however, state that the term "nonlawyer participants" should not be confused with the term "nonlawyer assistants" and that "[n]onlawyer assistants under Rule 5.3 do not have managerial authority or financial interests in the organization."

[9]While no state has apparently adopted a guideline similar to Model Guideline 10, parts 4 and 5 of NALA Guideline VIII suggest similar requirements. Sections III and V of NFPA's "Affirmation of Professional Responsibility" recognize a legal assistant's obligation to "maintain a high level of competence" (which is achieved through continuing education . . .") and to "serve the public interest." NFPA has also published a guide to assist legal assistant groups in developing public service projects. *See* NFPA, "Pro Bono Publico (For the Good of the People)" (1987).

NFPA Model Code of Ethics and Professional Responsibility and Guidelines for Enforcement

PREAMBLE

The National Federation of Paralegal Associations, Inc. ("NFPA") is a professional organization comprised of paralegal associations and individual paralegals throughout the United States and Canada. Members of NFPA have varying backgrounds, experiences, education and job responsibilities that reflect the diversity of the paralegal profession. NFPA promotes the growth, development and recognition of the paralegal profession as an integral partner in the delivery of legal services.

In May 1993 NFPA adopted its Model Code of Ethics and Professional Responsibility ("Model Code") to delineate the principles for ethics and conduct to which every paralegal should aspire. Many paralegal associations throughout the United States have endorsed the concept and content of NFPA's Model Code through the adoption of their own ethical codes. In doing so, paralegals have confirmed the profession's commitment to increase the quality and efficiency of legal services, as well as recognized its responsibilities to the public, the legal community, and colleagues.

Paralegals have recognized, and will continue to recognize, that the profession must continue to evolve to enhance their roles in the delivery of legal services. With increased levels of responsibility comes the need to define and enforce mandatory rules of professional conduct. Enforcement of codes of paralegal conduct is a logical and necessary step to enhance and ensure the confidence of the legal community and the public in the integrity and professional responsibility of paralegals.

In April 1997 NFPA adopted the Model Disciplinary Rules ("Model Rules") to make possible the enforcement of the Canons and Ethical Considerations contained in the NFPA Model Code. A concurrent determination was made that the Model Code of Ethics and Professional Responsibility, formerly aspirational in nature, should be recognized as setting forth the enforceable obligations of all paralegals.

The Model Code and Model Rules offer a framework for professional discipline, either voluntarily or through formal regulatory programs.

NFPA MODEL DISCIPLINARY RULES AND ETHICAL CONSIDERATIONS

1.1   A Paralegal Shall Achieve and Maintain a High Level of Competence

Ethical Considerations

EC–1.1(a)   A paralegal shall achieve competency through education, training, and work experience.

EC–1.1(b)   A paralegal shall participate in continuing education in order to keep informed of current legal, technical, and general developments.

EC–1.1(c)   A paralegal shall perform all assignments promptly and efficiently.

1.2   A Paralegal Shall Maintain a High Level of Personal and Professional Integrity

Ethical Considerations

EC–1.2(a)   A paralegal shall not engage in any ex parte communications involving the courts or any other adjudicatory body in an attempt to exert undue influence or to obtain advantage or the benefit of only one party.

EC–1.2(b)   A paralegal shall not communicate, or cause another to communicate, with a party the paralegal knows to be represented by a lawyer in a pending matter without the prior consent of the lawyer representing such other party.

EC–1.2(c)   A paralegal shall ensure that all timekeeping and billing records prepared by the paralegal are thorough, accurate, honest, and complete.

EC–1.2(d)   A paralegal shall not knowingly engage in fraudulent billing practices. Such practices may include, but are not limited to: inflation of hours billed to a client or employer; misrepresentation of the nature of tasks performed; and/or submission of fraudulent expense and disbursement documentation.

EC–1.2(e)   A paralegal shall be scrupulous, thorough, and honest in the identification and maintenance of all funds, securities, and other assets of a client and shall provide accurate accounting as appropriate.

EC–1.2(f)   A paralegal shall advise the proper authority of non-confidential knowledge of any dishonest or fraudulent acts by any person pertaining to the handling of the funds, securities, or other assets of a client. The authority to whom the report is made shall depend on the nature and circumstances of the possible misconduct (e.g., ethics committees of law firms, corporations and/or paralegal associations, local or state bar associations, local prosecutors, administrative agencies, etc.). Failure to report such knowledge is in itself misconduct and shall be treated as such under these rules.

1.3   A Paralegal Shall Maintain a High Standard of Professional Conduct

Ethical Considerations

EC–1.3(a)   A paralegal shall refrain from engaging in any conduct that offends the dignity and decorum of proceedings before a court or other adjudicatory body and shall be respectful of all rules and procedures.

EC–1.3(b)   A paralegal shall avoid impropriety and the appearance of impropriety and shall not engage in any conduct that would adversely affect his/her fitness to practice. Such conduct may include, but is not limited to: violence, dishonesty, interference with the administration of justice, and/or abuse of a professional position or public office.

EC–1.3(c)   Should a paralegal's fitness to practice be compromised by physical or mental illness, causing that paralegal to commit an act that is in direct violation of the Model Code/Model Rules and/or laws governing the jurisdiction in which the paralegal practices, that paralegal may be protected from sanction upon review of the nature and circumstances of that illness.

EC–1.3(d)   A paralegal shall advise the proper authority of non-confidential knowledge of any action of another legal professional that clearly demonstrates fraud, deceit, dishonesty, or misrepresentation. The authority to whom the report is made shall depend on the nature and circumstances of the possible misconduct (e.g., ethics committees of law firms, corporations and/or paralegal associations, local or state bar associations, local prosecutors, administrative agencies, etc.). failure to report such knowledge is in itself misconduct and shall be treated as such under these rules.

EC–1.3(e)   A paralegal shall not knowingly assist any individual with the commission of an act that is in direct violation of the Model Code/Model Rules and/or the rules and/or laws governing the jurisdiction in which the paralegal practices.

EC–1.3(f)   If a paralegal possesses knowledge of future criminal activity, that knowledge must be reported to the appropriate authority immediately.

1.4   A Paralegal Shall Serve the Public Interest by Contributing to the Delivery of Quality Legal Services and the Improvement of the Legal System

Ethical Considerations

EC–1.4(a)   A paralegal shall be sensitive to the legal needs of the public and shall promote the development and implementation of programs that address those needs.

EC–1.4(b)   A paralegal shall support efforts to improve the legal system and access thereto and shall assist in making changes.

EC–1.4(c)   A paralegal shall support and participate in the delivery of Pro Bono Publico services directed toward implementing and improving access to justice, the law, the legal system or the paralegal and legal professions.

EC–1.4(d)   A paralegal should aspire annually to contribute twenty-four (24) hours of Pro Bono Publico services under the supervision of an attorney or as authorized by administrative, statutory or court authority to:

1. persons of limited means; or
2. charitable, religious, civic, community, governmental and educational organizations in matters that are designed primarily to address the legal needs of persons with limited means; or
3. individuals, groups or organizations seeking to secure or protect civil rights, civil liberties or public rights.

1.5   A Paralegal Shall Preserve All Confidential Information Provided by the Client or Acquired from Other Sources before, during, and after the Course of the Professional Relationship

Ethical Considerations

EC–1.5(a)   A paralegal shall be aware of and abide by all legal authority governing confidential information in the jurisdiction in which the paralegal practices.

EC–1.5(b) A paralegal shall not use confidential information to the disadvantage of the client.

EC–1.5(c) A paralegal shall not use confidential information to the advantage of the paralegal or of a third person.

EC–1.5(d) A paralegal may reveal confidential information only after full disclosure and with the client's written consent; or, when required by law or court order; or, when necessary to prevent the client from committing an act that could result in death or serious bodily harm.

EC–1.5(e) A paralegal shall keep those individuals responsible for the legal representation of a client fully informed of any confidential information the paralegal may have pertaining to that client.

EC–1.5(f) A paralegal shall not engage in any indiscreet communications concerning clients.

1.6 A Paralegal Shall Avoid Conflicts of Interest and Shall Disclose Any Possible Conflict to the Employer or Client, as Well as to the Prospective Employers or Clients

Ethical Considerations

EC–1.6(a) A paralegal shall act within the bounds of the law, solely for the benefit of the client, and shall be free of compromising influences and loyalties. Neither the paralegal's personal or business interest, nor those of other clients or third persons, should compromise the paralegal's professional judgment and loyalty to the client.

EC–1.6(b) A paralegal shall avoid conflicts of interest that may arise from previous assignments, whether for a present or past employer or client.

EC–1.6(c) A paralegal shall avoid conflicts of interest that may arise from family relationships and from personal and business interests.

EC–1.6(d) In order to be able to determine whether an actual or potential conflict of interest exists a paralegal shall create and maintain an effective recordkeeping system that identifies clients, matters, and parties with which the paralegal has worked.

EC–1.6(e) A paralegal shall reveal sufficient non-confidential information about a client or former client to reasonably ascertain if an actual or potential conflict of interest exists.

EC–1.6(f) A paralegal shall not participate in or conduct work on any matter where a conflict of interest has been identified.

EC–1.6(g) In matters where a conflict of interest has been identified and the client consents to continued representation, a paralegal shall comply fully with the implementation and maintenance of an Ethical Wall.

1.7 A Paralegal's Title Shall Be Fully Disclosed

Ethical Considerations

EC–1.7(a) A paralegal's title shall clearly indicate the individual's status and shall be disclosed in all business and professional communications to avoid misunderstandings and misconceptions about the paralegal's role and responsibilities.

EC–1.7(b) A paralegal's title shall be included if the paralegal's name appears on business cards, letterhead, brochures, directories, and advertisements.

EC–1.7(c) A paralegal shall not use letterhead, business cards, or other promotional materials to create a fraudulent impression of his/her status or ability to practice in the jurisdiction in which the paralegal practices.

EC–1.7(d)   A paralegal shall not practice under color of any record, diploma, or certificate that has been illegally or fraudulently obtained or issued or which is misrepresentative in any way.

EC–1.7(e)   A paralegal shall not participate in the creation, issuance, or dissemination of fraudulent records, diplomas, or certificates.

1.8   A Paralegal Shall Not Engage in the Unauthorized Practice of Law

Ethical Considerations

EC–1.8(a)   A paralegal shall comply with the applicable legal authority governing the unauthorized practice of law in the jurisdiction in which the paralegal practices.

NFPA GUIDELINES FOR THE ENFORCEMENT OF THE MODEL CODE OF ETHICS AND PROFESSIONAL RESPONSIBILITY

2.1   Basis for Discipline

2.1(a)   Disciplinary investigations and proceedings brought under authority of the Rules shall be conducted in accord with obligations imposed on the paralegal professional by the Model Code of Ethics and Professional Responsibility.

2.2   Structure of Disciplinary Committee

2.2(a)   The Disciplinary Committee ("Committee") shall be made up of nine (9) members including the Chair.

2.2(b)   Each member of the Committee, including any temporary replacement members, shall have demonstrated working knowledge of ethics/professional responsibility-related issues and activities.

2.2(c)   The Committee shall represent a cross-section of practice areas and work experience. The following recommendations are made regarding the members of the Committee.

1. At least one paralegal with one to three years of law-related work experience.
2. At least one paralegal with five to seven years of law-related experience.
3. At least one paralegal with over ten years of law-related experience.
4. One paralegal educator with five to seven years of work experience; preferably in the area of ethics/professional responsibility.
5. One paralegal manager.
6. One lawyer with five to seven years of law-related work experience.
7. One lay member.

2.2(d)   The Chair of the Committee shall be appointed within thirty (30) days of its members' induction. The Chair shall have no fewer than ten (10) years of law-related work experience.

2.2(e)   The terms of all members of the Committee shall be staggered. Of those members initially appointed, a simple majority plus one shall be appointed to a term of one year, and the remaining members shall be appointed to a term of two years. Thereafter, all members of the Committee shall be appointed to terms of two years.

2.2(f)   If for any reason the terms of a majority of the Committee will expire at the same time, members may be appointed to terms of one year to maintain continuity of the Committee.

2.2(g)   The Committee shall organize from its members a three-tiered structure to investigate, prosecute, and/or adjudicate charges of misconduct. The members shall be rotated among the tiers.

2.3   Operation of Committee

2.3(a)   The Committee shall meet on an as-needed basis to discuss, investigate, and/or adjudicate alleged violations of the Model Code/Model Rules.

2.3(b)   A majority of the members of the Committee present at a meeting shall constitute a quorum.

2.3(c)   A Recording Secretary shall be designated to maintain complete and accurate minutes of all Committee meetings. All such minutes shall be kept confidential until a decision has been made that the matter will be set for hearing as set forth in Section 6.1 below.

2.3(d)   If any member of the Committee has a conflict of interest with the Charging Party, the Responding Party, or the allegations of misconduct, that member shall not take part in any hearing or deliberations concerning those allegations. If the absence of that member creates a lack of a quorum for the Committee, then a temporary replacement for the member shall be appointed.

2.3(e)   Either the Charging Party or the Responding Party may request that, for good cause shown, any member of the Committee not participate in a hearing or deliberation. All such requests shall be honored. If the absence of a Committee member under those circumstances creates a lack of a quorum for the Committee, then a temporary replacement for that member shall be appointed.

2.3(f)   All discussions and correspondence of the Committee shall be kept confidential until a decision has been made that the matter will be set for hearing as set forth in Section 6.1 below.

2.3(g)   All correspondence from the Committee to the Responding Party regarding any charge of misconduct and any decisions made regarding the charge shall be mailed certified mail, return receipt requested, to the Responding Party's last known address and shall be clearly marked with a "Confidential" designation.

2.4   Procedure for the Reporting of Alleged Violations of the Model Code/ Disciplinary Rules

2.4(a)   An individual or entity in possession of non-confidential knowledge or information concerning possible instances of misconduct shall make a confidential written report to the Committee within thirty (30) days of obtaining same. This report shall include all details of the alleged misconduct.

2.4(b)   The Committee so notified shall inform the Responding Party of the allegation(s) of misconduct no later than ten (10) business days after receiving the confidential written report from the Charging Party.

2.4(c)   Notification to the Responding Party shall include the identity of the Charging Party, unless, for good cause shown, the Charging Party requests anonymity.

2.4(d)   The Responding Party shall reply to the allegations within (10) business days of notification.

2.5   Procedure for the Investigation of a Charge of Misconduct

2.5(a)   Upon receipt of a Charge of Misconduct ("Charge"), or on its own initiative, the Committee shall initiate an investigation.

2.5(b)   If, upon initial or preliminary review, the Committee makes a determination that the charges are either without basis in fact or, if proven, would not constitute professional misconduct, the Committee shall dismiss the allegations of misconduct. If such determination of dismissal cannot be made, a formal investigation shall be initiated.

2.5(c)   Upon the decision to conduct a formal investigation, the Committee shall:

1. mail to the Charging and responding Parties within three (3) business days of that decision notice of the commencement of a formal investigation. That notification shall be in writing and shall contain a complete explanation of all Charge(s), as well as the reasons for a formal investigation and shall cite the applicable codes and rules;

2. allow the Responding Party thirty (30) days to prepare and submit a confidential response to the Committee, which response shall address each charge specifically and shall be in writing; and

3. upon receipt of the response to the notification, have thirty (30) days to investigate the Charge(s). If an extension of time is deemed necessary, that extension shall not exceed ninety (90) days.

2.5(d)   Upon conclusion of the investigation, the Committee may:

1. dismiss the Charge upon the finding that it has no basis in fact;

2. dismiss the Charge upon the finding that, if proven, the Charge would not constitute Misconduct;

3. refer the matter for hearing by the Tribunal; or

4. in the case of criminal activity, refer the Charge(s) and all investigation results to the appropriate authority.

2.6   Procedure for a Misconduct Hearing before a Tribunal

2.6(a)   Upon the decision by the Committee that a matter should be heard, all parties shall be notified and a hearing date shall be set. The hearing shall take place no more than thirty (30) days from the conclusion of the formal investigation.

2.6(b)   The Responding Party shall have the right to counsel. The parties and the Tribunal shall have the right to call any witnesses and introduce any documentation that they believe will lead to the fair and reasonable resolution of the matter.

2.6(c)   Upon completion of the hearing, the Tribunal shall deliberate and present a written decision to the parties in accordance with procedures as set forth by the Tribunal.

2.6(d)   Notice of the decision of the Tribunal shall be appropriately published.

2.7   Sanctions

2.7(a)   Upon a finding of the Tribunal that misconduct has occurred, any of the following sanctions, or others as may be deemed appropriate, may be imposed upon the Responding Party, either singularly or in combination:

1. letter of reprimand to the Responding Party; counseling;

2. attendance at an ethics course approved by the Tribunal; probation;

3. suspension of the license/authority to practice; revocation of license/authority to practice;

4. imposition of a fine; assessment of costs; or

5. in the instance of criminal activity, referral to the appropriate authority.

2.7(b)   Upon the expiration of any period of probation, suspension, or revocation, the Responding Party may make application of reinstatement. With the application for reinstatement, the Responding Party must show proof of having complied with all aspects of the sanctions imposed by the Tribunal.

2.8   Appellate Procedures

2.8(a)   The parties shall have the right to appeal the decision of the Tribunal in accordance with the procedure as set forth by the Tribunal.

DEFINITIONS

Appellate Body means a body established to adjudicate an appeal to any decision made by a Tribunal or other decision-making body with respect to formally-heard Charges of Misconduct.

Charge of Misconduct means a written submission by any individual or entity to an ethics committee, paralegal association, bar association, law enforcement agency, judicial body, government agency, or other appropriate body or entity, that sets forth non-confidential information regarding any instance of alleged misconduct by an individual paralegal or paralegal entity.

Charging Party means any individual or entity who submits a Charge of Misconduct against an individual paralegal or paralegal entity.

Competency means the demonstration of: diligence, education, skill, and mental, emotional, and physical fitness reasonably necessary for the performance of paralegal services.

Confidential Information means information relating to a client, whatever its source, that is not public knowledge nor available to the public. ("Non-Confidential Information" would generally include the name of the client and the identity of the matter for which the paralegal provided services.)

Disciplinary Committee means any committee that has been established by an entity such as a paralegal association, bar association, judicial body, or government agency to: (a) identify, define and investigate general ethical considerations and concerns with respect to paralegal practice; (b) administer and enforce the Model Code and Model Rules and; (c) discipline any individual paralegal or paralegal entity found to be in violation of same.

Disciplinary Hearing means the confidential proceeding conducted by a committee or other designated body or entity concerning any instance of alleged misconduct by an individual paralegal or paralegal entity.

Disclose means communication of information reasonably sufficient to permit identification of the significance of the matter in question.

Ethical Wall means the screening method implemented in order to protect a client from a conflict of interest. An Ethical Wall generally includes, but is not limited to, the following elements: (1) prohibit the paralegal from having any connection with the matter; (2) ban discussions with or the transfer of documents to or from the paralegal; (3) restrict access to files; and (4) educate all members of the firm, corporation, or entity as to the separation of the paralegal (both organizationally and physically) from the pending matter. For more information regarding the Ethical Wall, see the NFPA publication entitled "The Ethical Wall—Its Application to Paralegals."

Ex parte means actions or communications conducted at the instance and for the benefit of one party only, and without notice to, or contestation by, any person adversely interested.

Investigation means the investigation of any charge(s) of misconduct filed against an individual paralegal or paralegal entity by a Committee.

Letter of Reprimand means a written notice of formal censure or severe reproof administered to an individual paralegal or paralegal entity for unethical or improper conduct.

Misconduct means the knowing or unknowing commission of an act that is in direct violation of those Canons and Ethical Considerations of any and all applicable codes and/or rules of conduct.

Paralegal is synonymous with "Legal Assistant" and is defined as a person qualified through education, training, or work experience to perform substantive legal work that requires knowledge of legal concepts and is customarily, but not exclusively, performed by a lawyer. This person may be retained or employed by a lawyer, law office, governmental agency, or other entity or may be authorized by administrative, statutory, or court authority to perform this work.

Pro Bono Publico means providing or assisting to provide quality legal services in order to enhance access to justice for persons of limited means; charitable, religious, civic, community, governmental and educational organizations in matters that are designed primarily to address the legal needs of persons with limited means; or individuals, groups or organizations seeking to secure or protect civil rights, civil liberties or public rights.

Proper Authority means the local paralegal association, the local or state bar association, Committee(s) of the local paralegal or bar association(s), local prosecutor, administrative agency, or other tribunal empowered to investigate or act upon an instance of alleged misconduct.

Responding Party means an individual paralegal or paralegal entity against whom a Charge of Misconduct has been submitted.

Revocation means the recision of the license, certificate or other authority to practice of an individual paralegal or paralegal entity found in violation of those Canons and Ethical Considerations of any and all applicable codes and/or rules of conduct.

Suspension means the suspension of the license, certificate or other authority to practice of an individual paralegal or paralegal entity found in violation of those Canons and Ethical Considerations of any and all applicable codes and/or rules of conduct.

Tribunal means the body designated to adjudicate allegations of misconduct.

Appendix C

NALA Model Standards and Guidelines for Utilization of Legal Assistants

INTRODUCTION

The purpose of this annotated version of the National Association of Legal Assistants, Inc. Model Standards and Guidelines for the Utilization of Legal Assistants (the "Model," "Standards" and/or the "Guidelines") is to provide references to the existing case law and other authorities where the underlying issues have been considered. The authorities cited will serve as a basis upon which conduct of a legal assistant may be analyzed as proper or improper.

The Guidelines represent a statement of how the legal assistant may function. The Guidelines are not intended to be a comprehensive or exhaustive list of the proper duties of a legal assistant. Rather, they are designed as guides to what may or may not be proper conduct for the legal assistant. In formulating the Guidelines, the reasoning and rules of law in many reported decisions of disciplinary cases and unauthorized practice of law cases have been analyzed and considered. In addition, the provisions of the American Bar Association's Model Rules of Professional Conduct, as well as the ethical promulgations of various state courts and bar associations have been considered in the development of the Guidelines.

These Guidelines form a sound basis for the legal assistant and the supervising attorney to follow. This Model will serve as a comprehensive resource document and as a definitive, well-reasoned guide to those considering voluntary standards and guidelines for legal assistants.

I

Preamble

Proper utilization of the services of legal assistants contributes to the delivery of cost-effective, high-quality legal services. Legal assistants and the legal profession should be assured that measures exist for identifying legal assistants and their role in assisting attorneys in the delivery of legal services. Therefore, the National Association of Legal Assistants, Inc., hereby adopts these Standards and Guidelines as an educational document for the benefit of legal assistants and the legal profession.

Comment

The three most frequently raised questions concerning legal assistants are (1) How do you define a legal assistant; (2) Who is qualified to be identified as a legal assistant; and (3) What duties may a legal assistant perform? The definition adopted in 1984 by the National Association of Legal Assistants answers the first question. The Model sets forth minimum education, training and experience through standards which will assure that an individual utilizing the title "legal assistant" has the qualifications to be held out to the legal community and the public in that capacity. The Guidelines identify those acts which the reported cases hold to be proscribed and give examples of services which the legal assistant may perform under the supervision of a licensed attorney.

These Guidelines constitute a statement relating to services performed by legal assistants, as defined herein, as approved by court decisions and other sources of authority. The purpose of the Guidelines is not to place limitations or restrictions on the legal assistant profession. Rather, the Guidelines are intended to outline for the legal profession an acceptable course of conduct. Voluntary recognition and utilization of the Standards and Guidelines will benefit the entire legal profession and the public it serves.

II

Definition

The National Association of Legal Assistants adopted the following definition in 1984:

> Legal assistants, also known as paralegals, are a distinguishable group of persons who assist attorneys in the delivery of legal services. Through formal education, training, and experience, legal assistants have knowledge and expertise regarding the legal system and substantive and procedural law which qualify them to do work of a legal nature under the supervision of an attorney.

Comment

This definition emphasizes the knowledge and expertise of legal assistants in substantive and procedural law obtained through education and work experience. It further defines the legal assistant or paralegal as a professional working under the supervision of an attorney as distinguished from a non-lawyer who delivers services directly to the public without any intervention or review of work product by an attorney. Statutes, court rules, case law and bar associations are additional sources for legal assistant or paralegal definitions. In applying the Standards and Guidelines, it is important to remember that they were developed to apply to the legal assistant as defined herein.

Lawyers should refrain from labeling those who do not meet the criteria set forth in this definition, such as secretaries and other administrative staff, as legal assistants.

For billing purposes, the services of a legal secretary are considered part of overhead costs and are not recoverable in fee awards. However, the courts have held that fees for paralegal services are recoverable as long as they are not clerical functions, such as organizing files, copying documents, checking docket, updating files, checking court dates and delivering papers. As established in *Missouri v. Jenkins*, 491 U.S.274, 109 S.Ct. 2463, 2471, n.10 (1989) tasks performed by legal assistants must be substantive in nature which, absent the legal assistant, the attorney would perform.

There are also case law and Supreme Court Rules addressing the issue of a disbarred attorney serving in the capacity of a legal assistant.

III

Standards

A legal assistant should meet certain minimum qualifications. The following standards may be used to determine an individual's qualifications as a legal assistant:

1. Successful completion of the Certified Legal Assistant ("CLA") certifying examination of the National Association of Legal Assistants, Inc.;
2. Graduation from an ABA approved program of study for legal assistants;
3. Graduation from a course of study for legal assistants which is institutionally accredited but not ABA approved, and which requires not less than the equivalent of 60 semester hours of classroom study;
4. Graduation from a course of study for legal assistants, other than those set forth in (2) and (3) above, plus not less than six months of in-house training as a legal assistant;
5. A baccalaureate degree in any field, plus not less than six months in-house training as a legal assistant;
6. A minimum of three years of law-related experience under the supervision of an attorney, including at least six months of in-house training as a legal assistant; or
7. Two years of in-house training as a legal assistant.

For purposes of these Standards, "in-house training as a legal assistant" means attorney education of the employee concerning legal assistant duties and these Guidelines. In addition to review and analysis of assignments, the legal assistant should receive a reasonable amount of instruction directly related to the duties and obligations of the legal assistant.

Comment

The Standards set forth suggest minimum qualifications for a legal assistant. These minimum qualifications, as adopted, recognize legal related work backgrounds and formal education backgrounds, both of which provide the legal assistant with a broad base in exposure to and knowledge of the legal profession. This background is necessary to assure the public and the legal profession that the employee identified as a legal assistant is qualified.

The Certified Legal Assistant ("CLA") examination established by NALA in 1976 is a voluntary nationwide certification program for legal assistants. The CLA designation is a statement to the legal profession and the public that the legal assistant has met the high levels of knowledge and professionalism required by NALA's certification program. Continuing education requirements, which all certified legal assistants must meet, assure that high standards are maintained. The CLA designation has been recognized as a means of establishing the qualifications of a legal assistant in supreme court rules, state court and bar association standards and utilization guidelines.

Certification through NALA is available to all legal assistants meeting the educational and experience requirements. Certified Legal Assistants may also pursue advanced specialty certification ("CLAS") in the areas of bankruptcy, civil litigation, probate and estate planning, corporate and business law, criminal law and procedure, real estate, intellectual property, and may also pursue state certification based on state laws and procedures in California, Florida, Louisiana and Texas.

IV

Guidelines

These Guidelines relating to standards of performance and professional responsibility are intended to aid legal assistants and attorneys. The ultimate responsibility rests with an attorney who employs legal assistants to educate them with respect to the duties they are assigned and to supervise the manner in which such duties are accomplished.

Comment

In general, a legal assistant is allowed to perform any task which is properly delegated and supervised by an attorney, as long as the attorney is ultimately responsible to the client and assumes complete professional responsibility for the work product.

ABA Model Rules of Professional Conduct, Rule 5.3 provides:

With respect to a non-lawyer employed or retained by or associated with a lawyer:
(a) a partner in a law firm shall make reasonable efforts to ensure that the firm has in effect measures giving reasonable assurance that the person's conduct is compatible with the professional obligations of the lawyer;
(b) a lawyer having direct supervisory authority over the non-lawyer shall make reasonable efforts to ensure that the person's conduct is compatible with the professional obligations of the lawyer; and
(c) a lawyer shall be responsible for conduct of such a person that would be a violation of the rules of professional conduct if engaged in by a lawyer if:
(1) the lawyer orders or, with the knowledge of the specific conduct ratifies the conduct involved; or
(2) the lawyer is a partner in the law firm in which the person is employed, or has direct supervisory authority over the person, and knows of the conduct at a time when its consequences can be avoided or mitigated but fails to take remedial action.

There are many interesting and complex issues involving the use of legal assistants. In any discussion of the proper role of a legal assistant, attention must be directed to what constitutes the practice of law. Proper delegation to legal assistants is further complicated and confused by the lack of an adequate definition of the practice of law.

Kentucky became the first state to adopt a Paralegal Code by Supreme Court Rule. This Code sets forth certain exclusions to the unauthorized practice of law:

For purposes of this rule, the unauthorized practice of law shall not include any service rendered involving legal knowledge or advice, whether representation, counsel or advocacy, in or out of court, rendered in respect to the acts, duties, obligations, liabilities or business relations of the one requiring services where:
A. The client understands that the paralegal is not a lawyer;
B. The lawyer supervises the paralegal in the performance of his or her duties; and
C. The lawyer remains fully responsible for such representation including all actions taken or not taken in connection therewith by the paralegal to the same extent as if such representation had been furnished entirely by the lawyer and all such actions had been taken or not taken directly by the attorney. Paralegal Code, Ky.S.Ct.R3.700, Sub-Rule 2.

South Dakota Supreme Court Rule 97–25 Utilization Rule a(4) states: " The attorney remains responsible for the services performed by the legal assistant to the same extent as though such services had been furnished entirely by the attorney and such actions were those of the attorney."

Guideline 1

Legal assistants should:

1. Disclose their status as legal assistants at the outset of any professional relationship with a client, other attorneys, a court or administrative agency or personnel thereof, or members of the general public;
2. Preserve the confidences and secrets of all clients; and
3. Understand the attorney's Rules of Professional Responsibility and these Guidelines in order to avoid any action which would involve the attorney in a violation of the Rules, or give the appearance of professional impropriety.

Comment

Routine early disclosure of the legal assistant's status when dealing with persons outside the attorney's office is necessary to assure that there will be no misunderstanding as to the responsibilities and role of the legal assistant. Disclosure may be made in any way that avoids confusion. If the person dealing with the legal assistant already knows of his/her status, further disclosure is unnecessary. If at any time in written or oral communication the legal assistant becomes aware that the other person may believe the legal assistant is an attorney, immediate disclosure should be made as to the legal assistant's status.

The attorney should exercise care that the legal assistant preserves and refrains from using any confidence or secrets of a client, and should instruct the legal assistant not to disclose or use any such confidences or secrets.

The legal assistant must take any and all steps necessary to prevent conflicts of interest and fully disclose such conflicts to the supervising attorney. Failure to do so may jeopardize both the attorney's representation of the client and the case itself.

Guidelines for the Utilization of Legal Assistant Services adopted December 3, 1994 by the Washington State Bar Association Board of Governors states:

Guideline 7: A lawyer shall take reasonable measures to prevent conflicts of interest resulting from a legal assistant's other employment or interest insofar as such other employment or interests would present a conflict of interest if it were that of the lawyer.

In Re Complex Asbestos Litigation, 232 Cal. App. 3d 572 (Cal. 1991), addresses the issue wherein a law firm was disqualified due to possession of attorney-client confidences by a legal assistant employee resulting from previous employment by opposing counsel.

The ultimate responsibility for compliance with approved standards of professional conduct rests with the supervising attorney. The burden rests upon the attorney who employs a legal assistant to educate the latter with respect to the duties which may be assigned and then to supervise the manner in which the legal assistant carries out such duties. However, this does not relieve the legal assistant from an independent obligation to refrain from illegal conduct. Additionally, and notwithstanding that the Rules are not binding upon non-lawyers, the very nature of a legal assistant's employment imposes an obligation not to engage in conduct which would involve the supervising attorney in a violation of the Rules.

The attorney must make sufficient background investigation of the prior activities and character and integrity of his or her legal assistants.

Further, the attorney must take all measures necessary to avoid and fully disclose conflicts of interest due to other employment or interests. Failure to do so may jeopardize both the attorney's representation of the client and the case itself.

Legal assistant associations strive to maintain the high level of integrity and competence expected of the legal profession and, further, strive to uphold the high standards of ethics.

NALA's Code of Ethics and Professional Responsibility states, "A legal assistant's conduct is guided by bar associations' codes of professional responsibility and rules of professional conduct."

Guideline 2

Legal assistants should not:

1. Establish attorney-client relationships; set legal fees; give legal opinions or advice; or represent a client before a court, unless authorized to do so by said court; nor
2. Engage in, encourage, or contribute to any act which could constitute the unauthorized practice law.

Comment

Case law, court rules, codes of ethics and professional responsibilities, as well as bar ethics opinions now hold which acts can and cannot be performed by a legal assistant. Generally, the determination of what acts constitute the unauthorized practice of law is made by State Supreme Courts.

Numerous cases exist relating to the unauthorized practice of law. Courts have gone so far as to prohibit the legal assistant from preparation of divorce kits and assisting in preparation of bankruptcy forms and, more specifically, from providing basic information about procedures and requirements, deciding where information should be placed on forms, and responding to questions from debtors regarding the interpretation or definition of terms.

Cases have identified certain areas in which an attorney has a duty to act, but it is interesting to note that none of these cases state that it is improper for an attorney to have the initial work performed by the legal assistant. This again points out the importance of adequate supervision by the employing attorney.

An attorney can be found to have aided in the unauthorized practice of law when delegating acts which cannot be performed by a legal assistant.

Guideline 3

Legal assistants may perform services for an attorney in the representation of a client, provided:

1. The services performed by the legal assistant do not require the exercise of independent professional legal judgment;
2. The attorney maintains a direct relationship with the client and maintains control of all client matters;
3. The attorney supervises the legal assistant;
4. The attorney remains professionally responsible for all work on behalf of the client, including any actions taken or not taken by the legal assistant in connection therewith; and
5. The services performed supplement, merge with and become the attorney's work product.

Comment

Legal assistants, whether employees or independent contractors, perform services for the attorney in the representation of a client. Attorneys should delegate work to legal assistants commensurate with their knowledge and experience and provide appropriate instruction and supervision concerning the delegated work, as well as ethical acts of their employment. Ultimate responsibility for the work product of a legal assistant rests with the attorney. However, a legal assistant must use discretion and professional judgment and must not render independent legal judgment in place of an attorney.

The work product of a legal assistant is subject to civil rules governing discovery of materials prepared in anticipation of litigation, whether the legal assistant is viewed as an extension of the attorney or as another representative of the party itself. Fed. R. Civ. P. 26 (b)(2).

Guideline 4

In the supervision of a legal assistant, consideration should be given to:

1. Designating work assignments that correspond to the legal assistant's abilities, knowledge, training and experience;
2. Educating and training the legal assistant with respect to professional responsibility, local rules and practices, and firm policies;
3. Monitoring the work and professional conduct of the legal assistant to ensure that the work is substantively correct and timely performed;
4. Providing continuing education for the legal assistant in substantive matters through courses, institutes, workshops, seminars and in-house training; and
5. Encouraging and supporting membership and active participation in professional organizations.

Comment

Attorneys are responsible for the actions of their employees in both malpractice and disciplinary proceedings. In the vast majority of cases, the courts have not censured attorneys for a particular act delegated to the legal assistant, but rather, have been critical of and imposed sanctions against attorneys for failure to adequately supervise the legal assistant. The attorney's responsibility for supervision of his or her legal assistant must be more than a willingness to accept responsibility and liability for the legal assistant's work. Supervision of a legal assistant must be offered in both the procedural and substantive legal areas. The attorney must delegate work based upon the education, knowledge and abilities of the legal assistant and must monitor the work product and conduct of the legal assistant to insure that the work performed is substantively correct and competently performed in a professional manner.

Michigan State Board of Commissioners has adopted Guidelines for the Utilization of Legal Assistants (April 23, 1993). These guidelines, in part, encourage employers to support legal assistant participation in continuing education programs to ensure that the legal assistant remains competent in the fields of practice in which the legal assistant is assigned.

The working relationship between the lawyer and the legal assistant should extend to cooperative efforts on public service activities wherever possible. Participation in pro bono activities is encouraged in ABA Guideline 10.

Guideline 5

Except as otherwise provided by statute, court rule or decision, administrative rule or regulation, or the attorney's rules of professional responsibility, and within the preceding parameters and proscriptions, a legal assistant may perform any function delegated by an attorney, including, but not limited to the following:

1. Conduct client interviews and maintain general contact with the client after the establishment of the attorney-client relationship, so long as the client is aware of the status and function of the legal assistant, and the client contact is under the supervision of the attorney.
2. Locate and interview witnesses, so long as the witnesses are aware of the status and function of the legal assistant.
3. Conduct investigations and statistical and documentary research for review by the attorney.
4. Conduct legal research for review by the attorney.
5. Draft legal documents for review by the attorney.
6. Draft correspondence and pleadings for review by and signature of the attorney.
7. Summarize depositions, interrogatories and testimony for review by the attorney.
8. Attend executions of wills, real estate closings, depositions, court or administrative hearings and trials with the attorney.
9. Author and sign letters providing the legal assistant's status is clearly indicated and the correspondence does not contain independent legal opinions or legal advice.

Comment

The United States Supreme Court has recognized the variety of tasks being performed by legal assistants and has noted that use of legal assistants encourages cost-effective delivery of legal services, *Missouri v. Jenkins*, 491 U.S.274, 109 S.Ct. 2463, 2471, n.10 (1989). In *Jenkins*, the court further held that legal assistant time should be included in compensation for attorney fee awards at the rate in the relevant community to bill legal assistant time.

Courts have held that legal assistant fees are not a part of the overall overhead of a law firm. Legal assistant services are billed separately by attorneys, and decrease litigation expenses. Tasks performed by legal assistants must contain substantive legal work under the direction or supervision of an attorney, such that if the legal assistant were not present, the work would be performed by the attorney.

In *Taylor v. Chubb*, 874 P.2d 806 (Okla. 1994), the Court ruled that attorney fees awarded should include fees for services performed by legal assistants and, further, defined tasks which may be performed by the legal assistant under the supervision of an attorney including, among others: interview clients; draft pleadings and other documents; carry on legal research, both conventional and computer aided; research public records; prepare discovery requests and responses; schedule depositions and prepare notices and subpoenas; summarize depositions and other discovery responses; coordinate and manage document production; locate and interview witnesses; organize pleadings, trial exhibits and other documents; prepare witness and exhibit lists; prepare trial notebooks; prepare for the attendance of witnesses at trial; and assist lawyers at trials.

Except for the specific proscription contained in Guideline 1, the reported cases do not limit the duties which may be performed by a legal assistant under the supervision of the attorney.

An attorney may not split legal fees with a legal assistant, nor pay a legal assistant for the referral of legal business. An attorney may compensate a legal assistant based on the quantity and quality of the legal assistant's work and value of that work to a law practice.

CONCLUSION

These Standards and Guidelines were developed from generally accepted practices. Each supervising attorney must be aware of the specific rules, decisions and statutes applicable to legal assistants within his/her jurisdiction.

© Copyright 1997; Adopted 1984; Revised 1991, 1997; National Association of Legal Assistants, Inc. Reprinted with permission of National Association of Legal Assistants, 1516 S. Boston, #200, Tulsa, OK 74119. http://www.nala.org

Appendix D

NALA Code of Ethics and Professional Responsibility

A legal assistant must adhere strictly to the accepted standards of legal ethics and to the general principles of proper conduct. The performance of the duties of the legal assistant shall be governed by specific canons as defined herein so that justice will be served and goals of the profession attained. (See Model Standards and Guidelines for Utilization of Legal Assistants, [Appendix C.])

The canons of ethics set forth hereafter are adopted by the National Association of Legal Assistants, Inc., as a general guide intended to aid legal assistants and attorneys. The enumeration of these rules does not mean there are not others of equal importance although not specifically mentioned. Court rules, agency rules and statutes must be taken into consideration when interpreting the canons.

> *Definition:* Legal assistants, also known as paralegals, are a distinguishable group of persons who assist attorneys in the delivery of legal services. Through formal education, training and experience, legal assistants have knowledge and expertise regarding the legal system and substantive and procedural law which qualify them to do work of a legal nature under the supervision of an attorney.

CANON 1

A legal assistant must not perform any of the duties that attorneys only may perform nor take any actions that attorneys may not take.

CANON 2

A legal assistant may perform any task which is properly delegated and supervised by an attorney, as long as the attorney is ultimately responsible to the client, maintains a direct relationship with the client, and assumes professional responsibility for the work product.

CANON 3

A legal assistant must not: (a) engage in, encourage, or contribute to any act which could constitute the unauthorized practice of law; and (b) establish attorney-client relationships, set fees, give legal opinions or advice or represent a client before a court or agency unless so authorized by that court or agency; and (c) engage in conduct or take any action which would assist or involve the attorney in a violation of professional ethics or give the appearance of professional impropriety.

CANON 4

A legal assistant must use discretion and professional judgment commensurate with knowledge and experience but must not render independent legal judgment in place of an attorney. The services of an attorney are essential in the public interest whenever such legal judgment is required.

CANON 5

A legal assistant must disclose his or her status as a legal assistant at the outset of any professional relationship with a client, attorney, a court or administrative agency or personnel thereof, or a member of the general public. A legal assistant must act prudently in determining the extent to which a client may be assisted without the presence of an attorney.

CANON 6

A legal assistant must strive to maintain integrity and a high degree of competency through education and training with respect to professional responsibility, local rules and practice, and through continuing education in substantive areas of law to better assist the legal profession in fulfilling its duty to provide legal service.

CANON 7

A legal assistant must protect the confidences of a client and must not violate any rule or statute now in effect or hereafter enacted controlling the doctrine of privileged communications between a client and an attorney.

CANON 8

A legal assistant must do all other things incidental, necessary, or expedient for the attainment of the ethics and responsibilities as defined by statute or rule of court.

CANON 9

A legal assistant's conduct is guided by bar associations' codes of professional responsibility and rules of professional conduct.

Adopted: May 1, 1975; Revised, 1979, 1988 and 1995; ©National Association of Legal Assistants, Inc. Reprinted with permission of the National Association of Legal Assistants, 1516 S. Boston, #200, Tulsa, OK 74119. http://www.nala.org

Legal Ethics and Related Web Sites

SPECIFIC LEGAL ETHICS WEBSITES

ABA Center for Professional Responsibility	http://www.abanet.org/cpr/home.html
American Legal Ethics Library	http://www.law.cornell.edu/ethics
Georgetown Journal of Legal Ethics	http://www.law.georgetown.edu/journals/ethics/
Legalethics.com	http://www.legalethics.com
Net Ethics	http://www.computerbar.org/netethics/
Texas Ethics Reporter	http://www.law.uh.edu/ethics/

STATE BAR ASSOCIATIONS (SOME POST THEIR ETHICS OPINIONS ON-LINE)

Alabama State Bar Association	http://www.alabar.org/
Alaska State Bar Association	http://www.alaskabar.org/
Arizona State Bar Association	http://www.azbar.org/
Arkansas Bar Association	http://www.arkbar.com/
California State Bar Association	http://www.calbar.org/
Connecticut State Bar Association	http://www.ctbar.org/
Delaware State Bar Association	http://www.dsba.org/

District of Columbia Bar	http://www.dcbar.org/
Florida State Bar Association	http://www.flabar.org/
Georgia State Bar Association	http://www.gabar.org/
Hawaii State Bar Association	http://www.hsba.org/
Idaho State Bar Association	www2.state.id.us/isb/
Illinois State Bar Association	http://www.illinoisbar.org/
Indiana State Bar Association	http://www.inbar.org/
Iowa State Bar Association	http://www.iowabar.org/main.nsf
Kansas Bar Association	http://www.ksbar.org/
Kentucky Bar Association	http://www.kybar.org/
Louisiana State Bar Association	http://www.lsba.org/
Maine State Bar Association	http://www.mainebar.org/
Maryland State Bar Association	http://www.msba.org/index.htm
Massachusetts State Bar Association	http://www.massbar.org/
State Bar of Michigan	http://www.michbar.org/
Minnesota State Bar Association	http://www.mnbar.org/
Mississippi State Bar Association	http://www.msbar.org/
Missouri Bar Association	http://www.mobar.org/
State Bar of Montana	http://www.montanabar.org/
Nebraska State Bar Association	http://www.nebar.com/
Nevada State Bar Association	http://www.nvbar.org/
New Hampshire State Bar Association	http://www.nhbar.org/
New Jersey State Bar Association	http://www.njsba.com/
State Bar of New Mexico	http://www.nmbar.org/
New York State Bar Association	http://www.nysba.org/index.shtml
North Carolina State Bar Association	http://www.ncbar.com/index.asp
State Bar Association of North Dakota	http://www.sband.org/
Ohio State Bar Association	http://www.ohiobar.org/
Oklahoma State Bar Association	http://www.okbar.org/
Oregon State Bar Association	http://www.osbar.org/
Pennsylvania State Bar Association	http://www.pa-bar.org/
Colegio de Abogados de Puerto Rico	http://www.capr.org/
Rhode Island State Bar Association	http://www.ribar.com/
South Carolina Bar Association	http://www.scbar.org/
South Dakota State Bar Association	http://www.sdbar.org/
Tennessee Bar Association	http://www.tba.org/
Texas State Bar Association	http://www.sbot.org/
Utah State Bar Association	http://www.utahbar.org/
Vermont State Bar Association	http://www.vtbar.org/
Virgin Islands Bar Association	http://www.vibar.org/
Virginia State Bar Association	http://www.vsb.org/
Washington State Bar Association	http://www.wsba.org/
West Virginia State Bar Association	http://www.wvbar.org/
Wisconsin State Bar Association	http://www.wisbar.org/
Wyoming State Bar Association	http://www.wyomingbar.org/

LEGAL ASSISTANT/PARALEGAL AND RELATED WEB SITES

ABA Standing Committee on Legal Assistants	http://www.abanet.org/legalassts/home.html
American Association for Paralegal Education	http://www.aafpe.org
Law and Politics: Paralegal Section	http://www.geocities.com/CapitolHill/Lobby/5011 /paralegal.html
Legal Assistant Division of the State Bar of Texas	http://www.lad.org
Legal Assistant Management Association	http://www.lamanet.org
National Association of Legal Assistants	http://www.nala.org
National Federation of Paralegal Associations	http://www.paralegals.org

MISCELLANEOUS LEGAL WEB SITES THAT CAN AID IN ETHICS RESEARCH

CrossingtheBar.Com	http://www.crossingthebar.com
FindLaw	http://www.findlaw.com/
HierosGamos	http://www.hg.org/
Law and Politics: Internet Guide	http://www.geocities.com/CapitolHill/Lobby/5011 /lpig.html
LawIDEA	http://www.lawidea.com/
Lawyers.com	http://www.lawyers.com/default.asp
LegaldotNet	http://www.legal.net/
Lexis/Nexis	http://www.lexis-nexis.com/default.asp
Loislaw	http://www.loislaw.com/
NOLO	http://www.nolo.com
Palidan Legal Resources	http://www.palidan.com
The 'Lectric Law Library	http://www.lectlaw.com/
Versus Law	http://www.versuslaw.com
Westlaw	http://www.westlaw.com/about/

Legal Ethics Movie Guide

This guide is neither exhaustive nor definitive. It is just for fun. I am a movie fan, and thought it would be interesting to include in the textbook a list of certain movies whose themes are connected, even if peripherally, to the subject of legal ethics. What follows is a quick description of a few great, and not so great, movies in which legal ethical dilemmas are a part of the story. But, be advised: movies about the legal system and its members are no more accurate than war movies or more realistic than musicals; they may be, but that is unlikely. The reader is advised not to judge these movies solely on their real life, legal accuracy. For example, if the Ashley Judd film, *Double Jeopardy*, were supposed to be a legally authentic interpretation of the Fifth Amendment's protection, it wouldn't have been entertaining to watch on a Friday night. The fact that *Jaws* presented a far-fetched depiction of a shark bearing grudges in no way lessens its greatness as a film. Finally, although many of these movies are derivatives of books, they are placed on this list without consideration of their book version.

AND JUSTICE FOR ALL (R, 1979)

What does it say about a legal movie when the characters who are the oddest and most loathsome are the judges and the members of the ethics committee? This is not to say the lawyers in this movie are normal or above reproach; it is just that they are more normal by comparison. Even though this film was less than favorably reviewed by the professional movie critics, I love it. Al Pacino does a devil of a job advocating for his clients in a Baltimore criminal justice system that is as bleak and broken down as a metaphor for legal and political cancer could ever be. Without giving away the pivotal points in the plot, what you find in *And Justice for All* is a month or so in the life of a gritty, idealistic, but not naive, defense lawyer who is not above going to jail to make a point. As he confronts the injustice in the system, while trying to comfort his panicked clients, Pacino is forced by the blackmail of an ethics charge to defend a client whom he despises. While watching Pacino emote his ever-mounting frustration at what he is facing, you forget that he played mafioso Michael Corleone, the master of steely composure. And for sheer visceral satisfaction, few scenes in a movie compare to the end of this one.

A CIVIL ACTION (R, 1998)

This thoroughly sad movie is not a legal thriller as advertised when it was released, but is a well-crafted story about a litigation nightmare. This is not a John Grisham story in more ways than one, starting with the fact that it is based on a true story. When hot-shot attorney Jan Schlictmann, played by John Travolta, agrees to take the collective cases of some Massachusetts families who believe their children have been poisoned from water polluted by some large industrial companies, he makes two critical decisions, on which the movie hinges. First, he and his firm front the litigation costs; and second, since he wants to put the families on the witness stand, he refuses millions of settlement dollars, believing the trial will provide a greater yield. Robert Duvall is superb as a Harvard Law School professor who brilliantly represents one of the defendant conglomerates. This movie raises thoughtful questions about how justice is affected by the discovery process and trial judges.

CLASS ACTION (PG-13 1991)

This overlooked movie is interesting on many levels. First, it involves a famous tort lawyer, played by Gene Hackman, suing a car company for what can best be called "the Ford Pinto problem." Second, the car company is defended by a firm that, curiously, has working on the case a lawyer, played by Mary Elizabeth Mastrantonio, who happens to be Hackman's character's daughter. And the two do not get along. Mastrantonio, an associate, is having a relationship with a more senior lawyer, whose prior actions have affected the car company's problem. As Mastrantonio comes to believe her value to the firm is for reasons other than her talent, she devises quite a solution. This film has family tensions, office romances, discovery abuses, courtroom histrionics, and the most stunning senior partner law office one could imagine.

ERIN BROCKOVICH (R, 2000)

Julia Roberts plays Ms. Brockovich in a compelling, true story about how one courageous paralegal took on a toxic utility company in California. As a struggling single mother starting a new job at a small law firm that represented her during a personal injury claim, Erin stumbles onto a major environmental case involving a polluting utility company, which will put her and her personal relationships at risk. Julia Roberts won an Academy Award poignantly capturing the desperation and ingenuity of a woman who fights demographic prejudice to keep such an unwinnable case alive. It is certainly intriguing to think of this paralegal being so powerful as to intimidate her own supervising lawyer, as well as other lawyers brought in to assist in the litigation. Here's a question: is Erin's door-to-door solicitation of prospective clients appropriate under your own jurisdiction's rules? What about the check she receives from her boss at the end? Look for the cameo appearance of the real Erin Brockovich early in the movie. But be advised: there are those, including journalists and even some of the plaintiffs, who believe the movie is less than accurate with respect to the facts of the Hinkley lawsuit.

A FEW GOOD MEN (R, 1992)

I considered leaving this movie off the list since it concerns, not the American legal system, but the American military justice system, something I know almost nothing about. But, taking my own advice about the purpose of this legal movie guide, I decided not to worry about what I did not know. Tom Cruise and Demi Moore star in this legal drama as young navy lawyers appointed to defend two marines accused of killing another in a hazing incident at a Marine base in Guantanamo Bay, Cuba. Since Tom Cruise settles cases, rather than litigates them, we are supposed to get the hint that he was given the case for just that reason. Things are strictly business between Cruise and Moore, who do not like each other, as they investigate Moore's theory that there is more to the story, namely, that someone (Jack Nicholson to Kiefer Sutherland) ordered the hazing incident that went awry. The movie is too obvious a preparation for the inevitable courtroom fireworks between Cruise and Nicholson, but the fireworks are still bright and loud. On an ethics level, a point is made in the movie about whether Cruise will be charged with a crime by the prosecutor (Kevin Bacon) if Cruise, without evidence and in cross-examination, accuses the much higher ranking Nicholson of lying. This Rob Reiner film is good but approaches propaganda (unlike his following film, *The American President,* which is good and clearly is propaganda).

THE FIRM (R, 1993)

One of the first John Grisham novels to be made into a movie, *The Firm* is outstanding. Tom Cruise plays eager law school grad Mitch McDeere, seduced by a rich offer from a Memphis firm that seems to have family values. This would be wonderful except for the fact that the family they value is the Mafia. This firm loses lawyers to accidental deaths like the "rock band" Spinal Tap loses drummers. Poor Mitch and his lovely wife, played by Jeanne Tripplehorn, come to realize they are pawns in this chess game between the firm and the government. With a huge supporting cast punctuated by Gene Hackman (this time a diabolical lawyer), Holly Hunter (a private investigator's girlfriend/secretary), and Ed Harris (the FBI agent working on Mitch), this long film travels from the idyllic to the horrific. Can Mitch catch the bad guys, save his life, and keep his law license? If you have not seen the movie, let us just say that the principles of fair billing and confidentiality have never been so fascinating.

THE GINGERBREAD MAN (R, 1998)

An oddly titled film from a John Grisham script that went to video quickly, this thriller involves the law simply because its protagonist is a Savannah attorney, played by Kenneth Branagh. This maelstrom, occurring during a hurricane, asks the question: how bad can things get when a lawyer sleeps with someone he barely knows who then becomes his client, who happens to have a sterotyped, Pentecostal-crazy father, eerily played by Robert Duvall? The answer to the above question is: things can get really bad. While watching this film, I wondered why, if Branagh's character would risk his career, and more, for the pleasure of dating his client, then why didn't he just date the character played by Daryl Hannah, who worked in his firm? Such a movie is a guilty pleasure for those who like films reminiscent of Alfred Hitchcock.

JAGGED EDGE (R, 1985)

A few years before terrorizing Michael Douglas in *Fatal Attraction*, Glenn Close co-starred in this movie as a lawyer who agrees to represent a super-rich newspaper publisher, played by Jeff Bridges, who is accused of brutally murdering his wife (her death is the reason why he became rich). Having left the criminal law due to guilt over a past case, Close's character only begrudgingly gives in to her senior partner's wishes that she represent the publisher if she can be convinced that he didn't do it. Imagine that. Adding to the movie's tension, Close goes up against a politically minded district attorney, someone with whom she committed a serious ethics violation years ago, who is the reason why she stopped practicing criminal law. Set in San Francisco, this courtroom thriller is both a whodunit and a love story—that is, if a lawyer falling in love with her murder-defendant client, who might be a sociopath, is your kind of a love story. And along with the murderous clues, the film happens to be sprinkled with a few gaffes, including one where Close wears two different suits in the same courtroom scene.

LIAR LIAR (PG-13, 1997)

How do you know when a lawyer is lying? His mouth starts moving. That joke essentially sets up the premise for this fairy tale about Fletcher Reede, a lawyer played bombastically by Jim Carrey, who has no choice but to be absolutely honest for twenty-four hours. *Liar Liar* shows us we might not always want to learn the truth, especially if it involves sharing an elevator with Fletcher. Fletcher's life as a lawyer is seamless only because it is stitched with constant fabrications. But his life as an ex-husband and sort-of-father is becoming increasingly disappointing to his former wife and five-year-old son. After his little boy's birthday wish comes true, Fletcher soon comes to discover he can only speak the truth, the whole truth, and nothing but the truth. While attempting to represent a sleazy spouse involved in a divorce and to become a partner in his law firm—and at the same time avoid the former object of his affection (his boss), Fletcher is losing valuable time with his son. Can Fletcher win an ugly case without telling any lies? Can he even keep his job without telling any lies? Can anyone deny that Jim Carrey is so much more than a one-note performer? Be honest.

MY COUSIN VINNY (R, 1992)

When a character played by Ralph Macchio, and his friend, get wrongly arrested for murder while traveling through the Deep South, Cousin Vinny, played by Joe Pesci, gets their phone call and drives down from Brooklyn with his fiancé, played by Marisa Tomei, to save the day. There's just one problem. Vinny has only just passed the bar after many attempts and is no more capable of defending the two against murder charges than he is of being comfortable spending time in the hayseed town where his clients await their trial. Although this movie pokes a little fun at the southern culture, it does not shy away from also lampooning the northerners. Not only does Vinny lie about his identity to the judge, but he puts his fiancé on the stand—as a tire track expert. (It worked so well that Tomei won an Oscar.) The dignified trial judge is warmly played by Fred Gwynne, who was TV's Herman Munster. Remember, this is a comedy; so don't critique the courtroom scenes too harshly.

PHILADELPHIA (R, 1994)

Tom Hanks won an Academy Award for this movie, playing Andrew Beckett, a rising associate in a blue-blood, downtown law firm, who sues the firm after he is fired, purportedly for incompetence and attitude problems. Beckett rightly believes his termination was arranged after the partners discovered he is gay (a fact Beckett had kept to himself) and suffering from the complications of AIDS. As other firms give Beckett the cold shoulder—not because he has AIDS, but because he wants to sue a powerful law firm, which is yet another ethics issue—Beckett turns to another attorney, excellently played by Denzel Washington. He is the opposite of Beckett, not because of race, but because he is a television-advertising ambulance chaser who also initially discriminates against Beckett because of his illness. *Philadelphia* is as much about Denzel Washington's personal journey as it is about the case. The movie would have been more poignant had it been made five or ten years earlier, but nevertheless, it raises important issues. With a strong supporting cast including Antonio Banderas, Mary Steenburgen, and Jason Robards, the movie follows a predictable path that many "wronged versus wrong" trial stories take. It is nice to see Beckett using a paralegal for substantive work, as he does early in the movie. Having attended college in the city of brotherly love, I wish the movie had been entitled "Boston" or "New York" instead.

PRESUMED INNOCENT (R, 1990)

Before there was John Grisham, there was Scott Turow, and if you like your legal movies dark and emotionally painful, this one is for you. This gripping mystery stars Harrison Ford, in one of his few non-heroic roles, as Rusty Sabich, the assistant district attorney given the unfortunate assignment of solving the vicious murder of a woman with whom he had been involved and obsessed, who also worked in his office. As the evidence points to Rusty, he is thrown overboard by his friend, the district attorney, who is in a tight re-election campaign against a former assistant district attorney. As his strangely loyal wife stands by her man, Rusty seeks the help of a superstar defense attorney, played marvelously by Raul Julia. This plot thickens like a roux; everyone seems to have something to hide. Is the prosecution cheating? Is the defense cheating? Is the judge cheating? Is the—you get the picture. And if you do get this picture, keep the children away, since *Presumed Innocent* has some racy moments. Part of the pleasure of watching this excellent movie is seeing Harrison Ford in such a dark role, something we rarely see.

THE RAINMAKER (PG-13, 1997)

My personal favorite for a classroom setting, this David versus Goliath story is rich with professional responsibility quandaries. Fresh, and broke, from law school, Rudy Baylor, played by Matt Damon, cannot avoid working for a lawyer named Bruiser, located in a strip mall, whose cases are scrounged up by a self-proclaimed "paralawyer" who has flunked the bar six times, delightfully played by Danny DeVito. In a plot that is straightforward but still compelling, Rudy represents a poor young man dying of leukemia, whose insurance company repeatedly denied his request for medical treatment coverage. Right before Bruiser's firm is raided by the Feds, Rudy and his paralawyer set up their own firm, while taking on the evil insurance company, represented by an even more vile law firm. In the meantime, Rudy rents an apartment from an odd widow for whom he has written a will and falls in love with a young, abused married woman who becomes his client. If the ends do justify the means, then try to ignore the legal ethics violations committed by the heroic team of Damon and DeVito as they fight an evil insurance company, an unethical litigator, and (for a little while) a corrupt trial judge. Danny Glover's understated, father-like performance as the second judge makes the movie even more satisfying.

SUSPECT (R, 1987)

This movie starts tragically with a bang, which then becomes part of the backdrop to this legal thriller starring Cher as an overworked, underpaid, Washington, D.C., public defender, who is desperately in need of a vacation. Instead, a mean judge, played by John Mahoney (the lovable Dad on *Frazier*), appoints her to represent a deaf-mute homeless man (excellently portrayed by Liam Neeson), who is accused of murdering a legal secretary. Not expected to do much with her client or his case, Cher starts to prepare a defense that seems, in some odd way, to lead to political intrigue and treachery. Thankfully, this is not one of those movies where the lawyer gets romantically involved with her client. She gets involved with a member of the jury instead. Dennis Quaid plays that juror, a slick lobbyist who begins to act like one of the Hardy Boys while in cahoots with Cher, who frets over all the ethics violations she is committing. Sure the plot has holes in it, and the ending seems forced, but the movie is well acted and fun to watch.

A TIME TO KILL (R, 1996)

One of the more difficult movies on this list to watch, *A Time to Kill* tells the story of Carl Lee Haley, a poor black man portrayed by Samuel L. Jackson, who shoots and kills two white men who brutally raped and almost murdered his little daughter. Since the slayings are vigilantism, Carl Lee is charged with first-degree murder. He is defended by Jake Bergantz, played by Matthew McConaughey. The question in the film is not whether Carl Lee did it, but whether he can get a fair trial in his small Mississippi hometown, which is deeply racially divided. As much as I tried and after multiple viewings, I cannot say I like this movie because it is so over-the-top that it seems like a caricature. Even after the rape and courthouse killings, there are Ku Klux Klan attacks, police abuses, a race riot, a fire-bombing, a sniper attack, a bomb planting, a house burning, cheating prosecutors, cheating defense lawyers, cheating jurors, a kidnapping, and more. There is, early in the film, an interesting ethical dilemma involving whether Bergantz is somehow responsible for the killings since Carl Lee discusses with Bergantz the prospect of killing the rapists before he kills them. Concerning the trial, ask yourself whether Bergantz is violating the rules of ethics by putting his client on the stand to support a defense (insanity) that both he and his client know is inapplicable.

TO KILL A MOCKINGBIRD (UNRATED, 1962)

To state the obvious, this is a thoroughly rewarding film to watch and is much more than a courtroom drama. It is also the only film on this list to be part of the American Film Institute's "100 Greatest American Movies" (at number 34). Gregory Peck won an Oscar playing Atticus Finch, a widowed southern lawyer in a Depression-era small town, raising two adventurous children—a daughter named Scout, and a son named Jem—who call their father by his first name. Atticus is appointed to defend a black man, Tom Robinson (played with such distinction by Brock Peters), wrongfully accused of raping a white woman, while, at the same time, his children are on a hunt to get a good look at the supposedly scary man down the street, Boo Radley (one of Robert Duvall's first roles). This compelling story, both tragic and uplifting, is told by Scout, and the movie focuses more on the children than their lawyer father. While Atticus and his family endure the hatred of some of the racist folks in town because he is representing Tom Robinson, Atticus never wavers in showing his children how to live a dignified life through quiet courage. The courtroom scenes and Atticus's closing argument are quite compelling, particularly since Atticus's children are watching the trial from the balcony, seated with the black members of the community who welcome them in the "Negroes Only" section. If you have not seen this movie, watch it. If you have seen it, watch it again.

12 ANGRY MEN (UNRATED, 1957)

This is a must-see movie. Henry Fonda stars as a member of a jury deliberating after the murder trial of a Puerto Rican boy accused of patricide. This black-and-white film, shot like a play and consisting of frank dialogue in a steamy, New York City jury room, forces the viewer to confront obvious guilt with the nuances of reasonable doubt raised by one dissenting juror. This movie has an all-star cast with many recognizable faces, including Jack Klugman and Jack Warden. It is no more a coincidence that Henry Fonda's suit is white than it is predictable what the film's conclusion will be. However, it is the journey that makes this film so enjoyable. It is a good thing that justice is blind, or else the hero's own unethical sleight of hand would have been noticed.

THE VERDICT (R, 1982)

Unlike a law library and its keeping of case law, video rental stores thin the ranks by getting rid of older movies. Here is a movie that may, unfortunately, be hard to locate, but do what it takes to find it. Before *The Rainmaker* and *A Civil Action*, there was *The Verdict*, a thoroughly compelling, Oscar-nominated movie. Paul Newman's performance is so outstanding that it is a shame he was not awarded the Oscar for which he was nominated. In the film, Newman plays Frank Galvin, a pathetic, alcoholic, nearly disbarred lawyer who goes to funerals handing his business card to the bereaved. Why Galvin was nearly disbarred helps to explain the alcoholism, which in turn helps to explain why he only has one client, a woman left brain-dead after a medical procedure in a Catholic hospital in Boston. Galvin has one chance for redemption while facing a huge law firm with all the resources necessary to destroy his case in the press and the courtroom. While it is easy to notice the nasty tricks pulled by the defense counsel (headed by James Mason of Hitchcock movie fame), one must also realize that Galvin could be disbarred for the many ethics violations he commits: miscommunication with the client's guardian (her sister) regarding a settlement offer, wrongful solicitations, lying, deceit with unrepresented persons, and more. However, considering all Galvin has been through, we almost have to accept it, like stealing to feed one's starving family. Unlike many movies today, which spoon-feed key plot lines to the audience in preparation for a predictable and tidy ending, this film requires you to pay attention to dialogue, character development, and innuendo. Although criticized by lawyers at the time of its release for being unfairly unrealistic, this movie truly succeeds at being a magnificent legal drama.

Glossary

Accident runners: Persons hired by lawyers to find personal injury clients, usually by going to the scene of accidents or disasters. Accident runners are respected even less than ambulance chasers.

Adjudication: The process of formally resolving a controversy, based on evidence presented.

Admiralty: Admiralty law involves the traditional rules and practices associated with the navigation of the sea, or commercial transaction conducted on navigable waterways. Admiralty law is also known as maritime law.

Advance: A prepayment for future legal services made to an attorney at the beginning of the representation. As the lawyer works on the case, the advance is being earned.

Affidavit: A written statement of declaration made under oath and very often in the course of litigation.

Affirm: The decision of an appellate court that maintains the status quo and keeps the lower court's decision in place.

Aggregate settlement: A settlement made by all parties on the same side of a case. Sometimes called a joint settlement.

Alimony: Payments made by one spouse to another spouse, following a divorce, that are made to support the other spouse. Some states have eliminated alimony as a general requirement in divorce.

Alternative dispute resolution (ADR): Methods of resolving conflict outside the traditional method of litigation and a trial. Forms of ADR include negotiation, mediation, and arbitration.

Amicus curiae: A Latin phrase that means "friend of the court." An amicus curiae brief is a brief filed by one who is not a party to the lawsuit, but who believes the court needs to read the legal perspective presented in the amicus brief in order to make a correct decision.

Annotated: When a rule of court or statute is annotated, that means it is privately published, and comes with research material in addition to the statute or rule.

Antifederalist: A founding father who opposed the design of the Constitution because it provided for an unlimited federal government.

Appearance of impropriety: A standard of ethical conduct, found in the Model Code of Professional Responsibility, in which lawyers are advised to avoid certain activities because those activities look bad, rather than actually being bad.

Arbitration: An alternative dispute resolution mechanism where parties agree to submit their dispute to a neutral third party, called an arbitrator, who renders a decision, which is usually binding. Arbitration, usually a creature of contract, is quicker and, therefore, less expensive than traditional litigation.

Associate: A lawyer in a law firm who has not reached partnership status, but may be on a partnership track. Associates report to their supervising partner or partnership mentor.

Bad faith: Something done in bad faith is done dishonestly or with ulterior motives.

Barratry: Historically, barratry was the crime of stirring up frivolous, or groundless, litigation.

Bill padding: A dishonest billing practice that involves one exaggerating the time spent working on a client's case.

Black letter law: Legal principles that have become so accepted and unequivocal that they are cited as truisms.

Bona fide: Genuine, or good faith.

Cause of action: Facts that are sufficient to entitle a party to claim a legal wrong, entitling the claimant to a remedy. Lawsuits are based upon causes of action and can be dismissed if they fail to state a claim of action.

Certificates of deposit (CDs): A type of conservative investment wherein someone gives money to a bank or other financial institution in exchange for promissory notes from the institutions detailing the interest to be paid on the money and the date on which the principal and interest will be paid to the investor.

Champerty: An agreement between the lawyer and client where the lawyer agrees to pay the costs of the litigation in exchange for the client transferring to the lawyer the client's ownership in any future judgment. The historical prohibition of champerty has been relaxed by the allowances of contingency fees.

Circulars: Notices or advertisements sent to certain groups of people.

Class action: A lawsuit brought by a representative of a large group of plaintiffs (or prospective plaintiffs) on behalf of the group. Rule 23 of the Federal Rules of Civil Procedure governs class actions.

Comments: In this context, a comment is the official commentary of the rules committee that follows specific rules of court. They are designed to give meaning to the specific rules.

Commercial speech: Communications made for business purposes. Speech made in the pursuit of capitalism is commercial speech, and it is less protected under free speech doctrines than religious or political speech.

Commingling: The unlawful mixing of one person's money with another person's money in the same account.

Common law: This phrase has three related definitions. In this context, common law refers judge made law, or the process whereby appellate courts make precedent that lower courts must follow. Because of our colonial history with England, America is known as a common law country.

Companion cases: Two or more appellate cases that are connected because they involve the same parties in similar legal situations, or different parties with the same legal issue.

Constituent: A part of something else that is a distinct entity.

Contempt: Also known as contempt of court, an act or omission that tends to obstruct the administration of justice or shows disrespect for the court, and can include disobeying the instructions or orders of the court.

Contingent fee: A fee paid to a lawyer that is only paid if the lawyer succeeds in recovering a settlement or judgment for the client. The contingent fee is a percentage of what the client obtains.

Continuing legal education (CLE): A lawyer must earn certain annual CLE credits, as determined by the jurisdiction in which he or she is licensed. CLE credits, commonly called CLEs, are earned by attending bar-sponsored or -approved seminars that concern different practice areas of the law. Lawyers must also earn continuing legal ethics credits as part of their annual CLE requirements.

Conversion: A tortuous act that involves one exercising authority over another's property, to the deprivation, and without the permission, of the innocent party.

Deposition: A litigation discovery device, similar to testifying at trial, whereby the deponent is put under oath and subject to lawyer questioning. Depositions occur in law offices or conference room, but not in courtrooms.

Disciplinary commission: A panel consisting mostly of lawyers and authorized by a state supreme court to investigate and prosecute lawyer misconduct.

Discovery: A pre-trial procedure used in litigation where parties gain information from each other. Discovery is designed to promote open disclosure of relevant evidence and is supposed to operate without court involvement.

Double billing: A dishonest billing practice that involves one billing two clients at the same time.

Engagement letter: A letter from a lawyer to a client that formally acknowledges that the firm has accepted the client's case and sets forth the terms of the representation.

Equity partner: A partner in a law firm who is a shareholder, having voting rights.

Estate plan: A legal structure designed to pass on one's assets to others in life and at death and to minimize estate taxes and probate costs.

Ex parte communication: Communication made in litigation in the absence of the other party or the other party's attorney.

Federalist: A founding father who believed in the need for the federal government to have unlimited power, as designed in the Constitution.

Fiduciary: One who has a legal duty to act in the best interests of another. Lawyers are fiduciaries to their clients, as parents are to their minor children.

Fixed fee: A predetermined fee that covers all of the lawyer's efforts in services rendered for a particular client matter. A fixed fee is distinguished from an hourly rate.

Foreclosure: The act of a creditor to take ownership and control of property that was used as collateral by the debtor.

Forms books: Books that have samples of various kinds of complaints, answers, and other litigation documents.

401k plan: An employee retirement plan authorized by Section 401 of the Internal Revenue Code, sometimes called a salary reduction plan. In a 401k plan, an employee's pre-tax contributions are matched in some percentage by their employer's contributions.

Fraud: An intentional deception that results in a legal injury to another. Fraud usually involves a material misrepresentation (which can include silence), made to deceive the other party, reliance by the other party on the misrepresentation, and resulting harm.

Gross revenue: Sometimes called gross income, this is the total revenue received before deductions, such as expenses.

Impeachment: The constitutionally authorized act of formally accusing a high government official of what the Constitution calls "high crimes and misdemeanors." Following impeachment, there is an impeachment trial for the accused, whose conviction results in removal from office.

Independent contractor: One who is self-employed, but hired to work for others as needed, such as an attorney, an accountant, or a caterer.

Independent counsel: A special prosecutor, authorized by specific statute with a broad scope of authority to investigate and, if necessary, criminally prosecute high government officials.

Indigent: Poor, determined to be incapable of paying for a lawyer's services.

Informed consent: Giving one's agreement to take a certain action, including doing nothing, after having had the possible ramifications and consequences of taking that action fully explained.

Injunction: A court order forbidding a party to do something or ordering them to start doing something.

Insider trading: The buying or selling of a company's stock, by the company's insiders, based on information the insiders know, and before that information is released to the public. Insiders are usually defined as executive officers, directors, or shareholders of a corporation owning at least 10 percent of the corporation's stock.

Inter alia: A Latin phrase that means "among other things."

Interrogatories: An interrogatory is discovery device that involves one party sending to the other party a set, or sets, of questions that are to be answered under oath and in writing.

Intestate estate: The personal and real property of a person who died without leaving a valid will to direct the transfer of that property.

Judicial review: The doctrine from *Marbury v. Madison* that gives appellate courts the right to review the constitutionality of the acts of the legislative and executive branches, in addition to reviewing the decision of lower courts.

Jurisdiction: In this context, jurisdiction means a particular place over which a court has authority, and usually means a state.

Libelous: Libel is a false written statement that is published and made in order to harm the reputation of another. Slander is the spoken form of libel. Libel and slander are different forms of defamation.

Liquidated damages clause: A part of a contract that predetermines the monetary damages one party would owe the other in the event of breach of contract. Liquidated damages need to be a reasonable estimate of the damages suffered in order to be valid.

Malfeasance: A wrongful or unlawful act.

Malpractice: Improper or harmful conduct committed by a professional in the course of their profession.

Mediation: A form of ADR in which a third party, known as a neutral, assists the opposing parties in the process of trying to reach a settlement.

Memorandum of law: An internal memorandum of law is legal analysis of the merits of a client's case. An external memorandum of law is an advocacy document, similar to a brief, presented to a court.

Misdemeanor: Generally, a lower classified crime, in comparison to a felony.

Misrepresentation: A false or untruthful statement. Silence can be considered misrepresentation when there is a duty to speak. Misrepresentation can be negligent, as well as intentional.

Motions: Formal applications to a court (such as a motion for summary judgment), requesting the court to issue an order.

Multi-state bar exam: A bar exam that allows the successful applicant to be licensed in more than one jurisdiction. Such an exam is a result of a reciprocity agreement between the jurisdictions.

Non-equity partner: A partner in a law firm who receives a partnership share, but has no voting rights.

NOW account: Negotiable order of withdrawal account. A NOW account is an account that allows the depositor to withdraw sums of money from the account at will. NOW accounts are also called demand deposit accounts.

Office of Independent Counsel (OIC): A statutorily created special legal office, empowered to investigate and prosecute misconduct by members of the executive branch of government and other high-ranking government officials.

Original jurisdiction: The authority an appellate court has to hear a case directly, before the case proceeds through the trial court and then is appealed.

Partner: A lawyer who has been granted ownership status in a firm, having been voted in as a partner by the other partners. Partners generally share in the firm's profits.

Patent: The grant of ownership in an invention, giving the owner exclusive rights over the invention for a certain number of years.

Pecuniary: That which concerns money.

Personal representative: Someone appointed to manage the legal affairs of another person, or of an estate.

Plea bargaining: Negotiating in a criminal case, resulting in the prosecutor and the defendant agreeing to dispose of the charges through a settlement in which the defendant pleads guilty to a lesser charge.

Pleadings: Formal allegations of facts that consist of the plaintiff's claim (the complaint) or the defendant's denial (the answer).

Positive law: A phrase that is used to refer to law made through political means.

Prenuptial agreement: A contract entered into by two people intending to marry each other, in which the people agree in writing to their respective property rights in the event of divorce or death.

Prima facie: On its face, or on the surface.

Pro bono: Legal services provided to a client free of charge, or at a reduced rate. The original Latin form was pro bono publico, which means for the public good or welfare.

Promissory estoppel: An exception to the requirement of "consideration," which is a required element to a valid contract. Generally, promissory estoppel allows a party who relied upon the promise of another party to recover what was promised, even though the relying party would be unable to recover under contract law.

Pro se: A Latin phrase that refers to one representing oneself in a legal matter.

Proximate cause: In the context of what would make one liable, proximate cause is that which shows a natural connection to the defendant's conduct and the plaintiff's injury.

Public policy: Generalized views about the national culture or ideals upon which specific laws are made.

Puffing: A real word, used in sales contexts to mean an opinion or belief that is not meant to be taken as a statement of fact or warranty.

Quantum merit: A Latin phrase that means "as much as he deserved." Quantum merit is an equitable principle used in contract cases by plaintiffs attempting to recover something for their efforts when courts have already determined that operative legal principles deny the validity of a contract.

Real estate closing: The formal consummation of a sale of real estate, which usually involves the signing of many documents, payment of the real estate, and delivery of the deed or title.

Recuse: When someone, such as a judge or other person of influence, removes him- or herself from participation in a matter, because of a conflict of interest.

Remand: A remand occurs when an appellate court sends at least part of an appeal back to a lower court in order to reexamine the evidence or damages in light of the higher court's decision.

Respondeat superior: A Latin phrase that means "let the superior reply." This is a legal doctrine that makes employers (or principals) liable for the misconduct of their employees (or agents) that is committed within the scope of the employment.

Restatement: Unified, systematic statements on the common law, created by the American Law Institute. There are many restatements, including the Restatement of Contracts, the Restatement of Agency, and the Restatement of Torts.

Retainer: A payment, similar to an advance, made to an attorney, which is made to secure the lawyer's availability. When a retainer is called a general retainer, it is usually nonrefundable because the lawyer has earned the retainer upon payment. When a retainer is called a special retainer, it is usually a refundable payment, much like an advance. See Chapter 7.

Reverse: The opposite of affirm.

Reverse contingent fee: A type of contingent fee arrangement that involves the lawyer being paid a per-centage of what the lawyer saves the client from losing, as opposed to a percentage of what the lawyer obtains for the client.

Rules of court: Sets of rules that are adopted by the highest appellate court of a jurisdiction and apply to the practice of law, unlike statutes, which are passed by a legislature and apply to all.

Security interest: Where a creditor secures the repayment of a loan by taking legal title to certain property of the debtor, known as collateral. In the event of default, the creditor has rights to the collateral. A mortgage is an example of a security interest.

Shareholder's derivative lawsuit: A lawsuit in which a shareholder of a corporation, on behalf of the corporation, sues the corporation's board of directors, alleging that their actions have harmed the corporation. Any benefits from the derivative lawsuit flow to the corporation, not personally to the shareholder.

Solicitor general: The third ranking member of the U.S. Justice Department. The solicitor general represents the federal government before the U.S. Supreme Court.

Subrogation: When someone who has made a payment on another's behalf has the legal or equitable right to be paid back from the party who was originally liable for the payment. Subrogation often occurs when an insurance company pays its insured party under the terms of the insurance contract, and then is subrogated in the insured party's lawsuit against the defendant.

Summary judgment: A litigation strategy in which a trial is prevented because the judge dismisses the case due to two prerequisites: (a) there are no material facts concerning the case that are in disagreement by both parties; and (b) the law applying to the case is on the side of the party who has asked the judge for a summary judgment.

Surety bond: A written instrument filed with a court in which one promises to be liable up to the amount stated in the bond in the event that of negligence or failure to perform.

Trust: A legal mechanism where property is held by one party for the benefit of another. A trust is created when the Donor transfers the property into the trust, where the Trustee holds the legal title to the property, while the Beneficiary of the trust has the equitable title in the property, which means the benefits (income) of the trust are provided to the beneficiary.

Trust account: A special bank account where the property of the client is held and maintained by the attorney.

Undue influence: Where one party, in a position of strength over another party who is in a position of weakness, causes that party to enter into a contractual relationship with the superior party, or causes that party to give a gift to the superior party. Undue influence takes away the free will of the weaker party because of the unfair influence of the superior party.

Unified bar association: A bar association whose members must join upon being admitted to practice to law in the jurisdiction of the bar association. A unified bar association is also known as an integrated bar association.

Vacate: Similar to a remand, but sometimes a higher court vacates a lower court's decision to temporarily set it aside with instructions that the lower court rewrite its opinion in light of the higher court's opinion.

Venire: A member of the legal process, including the jury.

Voir dire: The process of picking jurors by questioning prospective jurors on matters related to the case, including biases and prejudices.

Waived: To waive a right or prerogative is to give it up. A waiver can be implied.

Warranty: A statement that amounts to a promise of quality or the assurance of certain facts.

West Digest System®: A method for researching case law, designed by the West Publishing Co., in which the law is divided into 414 topics, which are then divided into thousands of subtopics. When matched together, each topic and subtopic is known by its title and "key number" and corresponds to the key numbers of the headnotes for the cases, which are found by using a West digest.

Writ of mandamus: An order issued by a court, ordering some official to do a particular act that was requested by the party seeking the writ of mandamus.

Index

Locators in **bold** indicate exhibits.

A

AAfPE (American Association for
  Paralegal Education),
  25–26
ABA (American Bar Association)
  about, 3–4
  conflict of interest ethics
    opinions, 161
  definition of paralegals/legal assistants,
    30, 101
  paralegals/legal assistants as members,
    55–56
  rules of ethics and professional
    conduct, 3–5, **6**, 20
  suits against nonlawyers providing
    public legal service, 94–99
  Web sites for paralegals/legal
    assistants, 25, 371–373
ABA Canons of Professional Ethics,
  4, 212
ABA Commission on Nonlawyer
  Practice, 94
*ABA Compendium of Professional
  Responsibility Rules and Standards*
  (2001), 5

ABA Ethics 2000 Commission
  about, 4
  advertising and solicitation,
    248–250
  anticontact rules, 316, 318
  confidentiality, 130–131
  conflicts of interest, 204–207
  ex parte communication, 320–321
  fees, 260, 293–294
  pro bono rules, 332, 333
  supervision of paralegals/legal
    assistants, 56
  truthfulness, basic rule for, 311
  unauthorized practice of law (UPL),
    106–107
  on UPL, 106–107
ABA House of Delegates, 4. *See also*
    ABA Ethics 2000 Commission
ABA Litigation Section, 1
ABA Model Code of Professional
    Responsibility
  adoption of, 4
  advertising, 220, 225–228, 230
  anticontact rules, 315–316
  competence, 302

  on confidentiality, 111–114, **112**,
    115, 117
  on confidentiality exceptions,
    123–127
  conflicts of interest, 155, 156–157,
    177–184
  contingency fees, 273–274
  ethics opinions of, 20
  legal fee rules, 257, 260–261
  legal research and truthfulness, 322
  for paralegal independent
    contractors, 100
  for paralegals/legal assistants, 31
  pro bono rules, 332, 333
  prohibited transactions and conflicts
    of interest, 184
  and respondeat superior principle, 38
  solicitation, 234, 241–243
  state rules of court, 5, **6**
  truthfulness, 310–313, 315, 318,
    320–322
  and UPL, 71–72
ABA Model Guidelines for Utilization
    of the Legal Assistant Service,
    341–350

conflicts of interest rules, 203
duty of confidentiality, 116
for paralegal independent
    contractors, 100
permitted activities, 83
SCOLA issuance of, 25
statement of, 241–250
and UPL, 63–64, 72–73, 74
ABA Model Rules of Professional
    Conduct
adoption of, 4
advertising, 219–220, 222–223,
    225–228
anticontact rules, 315–316
competence, 300–302, 307
on confidentiality, 111–114, **112,**
    115, 117
confidentiality, exceptions to,
    123–127
conflicts of interest, 155, 156,
    174–184
contingent fees, 273–274
corporation/organization conflict of
    interest, 184–187, 207
ethics opinions of, 20
ex parte communication, 320
fee-sharing, 275–279
illegal activity and corporation/
    organization conflict of
    interest, 186
imputed disqualification, 187–190
legal fee rules, 257, 260–261, 264
legal research and truthfulness,
    322–323
for paralegal independent
    contractors, 100
for paralegals/legal assistants, 31,
    37–38, 45–46
pro bono rules, 332–334
and SCOLA Model Guidelines, 25
solicitation, 233–234, 241–244,
    248–250
state rules of court, 5, **6**
truthfulness, 310–313, 315–322
and UPL, 71–72
ABA Special Committee on Lay
    Assistants for Lawyers, 24
ABA Special Committee on Legal
    Assistants, 24
"The ABA Standards for Imposing
    Lawyer Sanctions"
    (ABA), 20
ABA Standing Committee on Legal
    Assistants (SCOLA). *See* SCOLA

(Standing Committee on Legal
    Assistants)
*Absher Const. Co. v. Kent School Dist. No.
    415,* 287–288
accident runners, 244
Adams, John, 8, 9, 154–155, 167
adjudication, 62
administrative agency adjudication
    case law/study: *Florida Bar re Advisory
        Opinion on Nonlawyer
        Representation in Securities
        Arbitration,* 89–92
    federal agencies, and paralegal/legal
        assistant permitted activity,
        86–87
    as paralegal/legal assistant permitted
        activity, 85–92
    and UPL, 62, 82
Administrative Procedures Act, 86
admiralty law, 226
adoption of a child, and joint
    representation, 167
ADR (alternative dispute resolution),
    78–79
advance, 263–264
advertising, 211–253. *See also*
    solicitation
    ABA Ethics 2000 Commission,
        248–250
    case law/studies
        Bates v. State Bar of Arizona, 213,
            215–219
        *Peel v. Attorney Registration and
            Disciplinary Commission,* 226
        In re R.M.J., 224, 238
        *Zauderer v. Office of Disciplinary
            Counsel,* 224–225
    as dignified, 230–231
    false or misleading, 219–223
    history of, 211–213, **214**
    independent paralegals/legal assistants
        direct, 232
    Internet, 229–231
    non-print media, 228–229
    paralegals/legal assistants in firm,
        231–232
    payment for, 227–228
    record keeping, 226
    rules overview, 219–231
    specialization rules, 223, 226–227
    state restrictions on, 223–225
    truthful information in, 225–226
    vs. solicitation, 233, **233**
affidavit, 14

affirm, defined, 10
aggregate settlement, 182
Alabama Bar Association Code of Ethics
    (1887), 4, 212
alimony, 274
alternative dispute resolution (ADR),
    78–79
Altman Weil, Inc., 29, 255
AMA Model Task Force on the Model
    Definition of the Practice of
    Law, 64
American Association for Paralegal
    Education (AAfPE), 25–26
American Bar Association. *See* ABA
    (American Bar Association)
American Law Institute, 115
American Prepaid Legal Services
    Institute, 255
*American Terrorist: Timothy McVeigh and
    the Oklahoma City Bombing*
    (McVeigh and Jones),
    122–123
amicus curiae, 193
And Justice for All (film), 374–375
annotated, defined, 5
annotated rules of court, 5
anticontact rules, 315–319
antifederalism, 8
APA State Legislative Clearinghouse, 61
appearance of impropriety, 188
arbitration
    as alternative dispute resolution, 64,
        65, 78, 87
    case law/study: *Florida Bar re Advisory
        Opinion on Nonlawyer
        Representation in Securities
        Arbitration,* 89–92
    defined, 182
Arkansas Supreme Court Committee on
    Professional Conduct, 14–15, 16
Arons, Marilyn, 94
Arthur Anderson, 185
associate, 24
Atkins v. Tinning, 278
attorney-client privilege, 131–147. *See
    also* client representation
    defined, 131
    disclosures after waiving, 122–123
    discovery, basic rules of,
        135–136, 150
    as discovery/evidentiary doctrine,
        131, **132**
    inadvertent disclosure, 138–147
    paralegals/legal assistants, 148–150

relationship establishment, 73, 76, 176

work product rule, basics of, 136–138

Attorney Grievance Commission of Maryland v. Ficker, 43–45

attorney opinion work product rule, 136–137. *See also* work product rule

Attucks, Crispus, 154

Auletta, Ken, 128

B

bad faith, 312

Bailey, F. Lee, 180

bankruptcy courts, 99

bar associations, state

definition of paralegals/legal assistants, 32, 101

paralegals/legal assistants as members, 55–56

regulation of legal profession, 3

bar exam, multi-state, 3

Barber, Caesar, 313

barratry, 183, 256

Bates v. State Bar of Arizona, 213, 215–219

Belli, Melvin, 211

Biakanja v. Irving, 327–328

bill padding, 260, 292

billable hours. *See* fees

black letter law, defined, 10

Boies, David, 128

bona fide, 335

Boot, Max, 244–247

Boston Massacre, 154–155

breach of contract and illegal fee sharing, 278

briefing a case. *See* case brief, process of creating

Brill, Howard, 15

Bureau of Labor Statistics, 28, 29

Busch v. Flangas, 329–331

business transactions with clients, and conflicts of interest, 168, 177–178

Butterfield, L. H., 155

C

canons, 4, 74. *See also* NALA Code of Ethics and Professional Responsibility

cap on contingency fees, 258–259

case brief, process of creating, 9–13

about, 9

case law/study: *In the Matter of Anonymous,* 11–13

decision section, 10–11

dissenting opinion, 9

elements of, 9–11

facts section, 9–10

holding section, 10

issue section, 10

reasoning section, 10

case law/studies

advertising

Bates v. State Bar of Arizona, 213, 215–219

Peel v. Attorney Registration and Disciplinary Commission, 226

In re R.M.J., 224, 238

Zauderer v. Office of Disciplinary Counsel, 224–225

case brief creation

In the Matter of Anonymous, 11–13

competence

Mays v. Neal, 304–307

confidentiality

Corey v. Norman, Hanson & DeTroy, 139–141

Goldsborough v. Eagle Crest Partners, Ltd., 145–147

Lipin v. Bender, 142–144

Mayberry v. State, 132–135

Palomba v. Sullivan, 120–121

People v. Harris, 118–120

In re Anonymous, 112–113

In re Grand Jury Investigation of Ocean Transportation, 145

Samaritan Foundation v. Superior Court, 148–149

United States v. Microsoft, 127–128

conflicts of interest

Ciaffone v. District Court, 199–201

Florida Bar v. Clark, 166–167

Florida Bar v. Mastrilli, 164–165

Hayes v. Central States Orthopedic Specialists, Inc., 192–193

In re Complex Asbestos Litigation, 193–198

In re DiSandro, 170–174

Wheat v. United States, 162–163

disbarment

Clinton disbarment proceedings, 13–20

In the Matter of Hein, 17–20

In re Elkins, 53–54

disciplinary actions

Attorney Grievance Commission of Maryland v. Ficker, 43–45

Clinton disbarment proceedings, 13–20

In the Matter of Hein, 17–20

Musselman v. Willoughby Corporation, 39–42

In re Elkins, 53–54

State v. Robinson, 47–49, 232

fees

Absher Const. Co. v. Kent School Dist. No. 415, 287–288

Atkins v. Tinning, 278

Florida Bar v. Bailey, 265–271

Joerger v. Gordon Food Service, Inc., 287–290

Missouri v. Jenkins, 281–286

In re Maruko Inc., 292–293

Trotter v. Nelson, 278

malpractice

Biakanja v. Irving, 326–328

Busch v. Flangas, 329–331

Webb v. Pomeroy, 325

solicitation

Florida Bar v. Went For It, Inc., 238–241

Gulf Oil Co. v. Bernard, 243

Ohralik v. Ohio State Bar Association, 234–237, 243

O'Quinn's techniques, 244–248

In re Primus, 243

Shapero v. Kentucky Bar Association, 238

truthfulness

Jorgenson v. Volusia County, 323–324

Nix v. Whiteside, 314

unauthorized practice of law (UPL)

Florida Bar re Advisory Opinion on Nonlawyer Representation in Securities Arbitration, 89–92

Florida Bar v. Catarcio, 95–98

In re Ethics Opinion No. 24 of the Committee on the Unauthorized Practice of Law, 102–106

In re Flint, 62

In re Thonert, 65–70

cause of action, 45

CD (certificates of deposit), 259

cell phones and client confidentiality, 129–130, 150

certificates of deposit (CD), 259

certification of paralegals/legal assistants, 29–33, 34–35, **35**
Certified Legal Assistant (CLA) Program, NALA, 27–28, 37, 308
champerty, 183, 256
Chinese wall doctrine, 190, 191, 192
Church Church Hittle & Antrim, IN, 309
Ciaffone v. District Court, 199–201
circulars, 212
A Civil Action (film), 375
civil cases, joint representation in, 163
CLA (Certified Legal Assistant) Program, NALA, 27–28, 37, 308
Class Action (film), 375
class actions, 181–182, 243
CLE (continuing legal education), 303
client representation
    confidentiality, 117–123
    conflicts of interest, 157–177, **158,** 178, 203–204
    consent of, and imputed disqualification, 189–190
    diligence and, 301
    establishing attorney-client relationship, 73, 76, 176
    fee explanation, 260–264
    former client conflict, 175–176, 187, 204
    interviews of, 84
    preparation and, 300–301, 319
    prior relationships and solicitation, 242–243
    truthfulness and (*See* truthfulness and client representation)
Clinton, Hillary, 137–138
Clinton, William Jefferson, 13–20, 255
co-plaintiffs, and joint representation, 163
combined claims, settlement of, 182
comments, ABA Model Rules of Professional Conduct, 4
commercial speech, 213
commingling funds, 264
common law, 9
communication
    client, with paralegals/legal assistants, 303–307
    and competence, 301–302
    ex parte, 320–321
    mobile phones and client confidentiality, 129–130, 150

companion cases, 170
compensation. *See* fees
competence and client representation
    case law/study: *Mays v. Neal,* 304–307
    communication, 301–302
    diligence, 301
    and paralegals/legal assistants, 302–310
    preparation, 300–301
cone of silence doctrine, 190
confidentiality, 110–153
    ABA Ethics 2000 Commission, 130–131
    ABA Model Codes and Rules on, 111–114
    about, 110–111
    as an ethical doctrine, 131, **132**
    application to lawyer's employees, 115–116
    attorney-client privilege, 131–147
    case law/studies
        Corey v. Norman, Hanson & DeTroy, 139–141
        Goldsborough v. Eagle Crest Partners, Ltd., 145–147
        Lipin v. Bender, 142–144
        Mayberry v. State, 132–135
        Palomba v. Sullivan, 120–121
        People v. Harris, 118–120
        In re Anonymous, 112–113
    duty of, 111–123
    exceptions to, 123–127
    invocation of, 114–115
    length of, 115
    non-confidential client information, 117–123
    organization as client, 116–117
    paralegal/legal assistant and, 148–150
    technology and client confidentiality, 127–130
confidentiality, exceptions to, 123–127
    collection of fees, 126–127
    defense of claim against lawyer, 125–126
    implied authorization, 123–124
    prevention of client criminal conduct/fraud, 124–125
conflicts of interest, 154–210
    ABA Ethics 2000 Commission, 204–207
    ABA Model Codes and Rules on, 155, 156–157
    John Adams as example, 154–156, 167

avoiding, 203–204
    case law/studies
        Ciaffone v. District Court, 199–201
        Florida Bar v. Clark, 166–167
        Florida Bar v. Mastrilli, 164–165
        Hayes v. Central States Orthopedic Specialists, Inc., 192–193
        In re Complex Asbestos Litigation, 193–198
        In re DiSandro, 170–174
        Wheat v. United States, 162–163
    common, 157–177, **158**
    corporations/organizations as clients, 184–187, 207
    financial interests of lawyer and, 168, 180–181
    imputed disqualification, 187–202
    prohibited transactions, 177–184
    rules for paralegals/legal assistants, 203
conflicts of interest, common
    ABA Ethics 2000 Commission, 204–205, 206
    about, 157, **158**
    case law/studies
        Florida Bar v. Clark, 166–167
        Florida Bar v. Mastrilli, 164–165
        In re DiSandro, 170–174
    caused by lawyer's interests, 167–170
    double representation, 157–159
    joint representation, 162–167
    between present and former clients, 174–177, 187
    simultaneous representation in different, unrelated matters, 160
    suing an existing client in unrelated lawsuit, 160–162
conflicts of interest, prohibited transactions, 177–184
    ABA Ethics 2000 Commission, 205–206
    ABA Model Code, 184
    agreements limiting lawyer liability, 182–183
    business transactions with clients, 177–178
    financial assistance to client, 180–181
    gifts from clients, 178–180, 187
    lawyers ownership of client's case, 183–184
    media rights for client's story, 180
    related lawyers opposing each other, 183
    settlement of combined claims, 182

third-party payment of legal expenses, 181–182

using client information to client detriment, 178

constituents

  corporation/organization conflict of interest, 184–187, 207

  defined, 116

contempt, 14

contingency (contingent) fee

  cases not allowed to be taken with, 274

  defined, 255

  rules for, 273–275

  vs. ownership fee, 183–184

  in writing, 273–274

continuing legal education (CLE), 303

conversion, 264

Corey v. Norman, Hanson & DeTroy, 139–141

corporate constituents, 116–117

corporation/organization as client

  conflict of interests, 184–187, 207

  duty of confidentiality, 116–117

costs. *See also* fees

  explanation of fees to client, 262–263

  of lawyer vs. paralegals/legal assistants, 24

  of litigation, 262, 263, 273

  overhead, and legal fees, 258

court representation and UPL, 62, 77–78

court sanctions of paralegals/legal assistants, 45–47, 49

Cox, Lesley G., 309–310

credit cards for legal fees, 261

criminal activity,

  corporation/organization conflict of interest, **185,** 185–187

criminal cases

  anticontact rules, 317–318

  contingent fees prohibited, 274

  joint representation in, 162–163

criminal conduct/fraud by client, 124–125

curriculum and education of paralegals/legal assistants, 25–26, 30–36, **35**

D

Dalkon shield advertising, 224–225

Darrow, Clarence, 110

decision section in case brief, 10–11

defendant, double representation of, 157–159, **158**

defense of claim against lawyer and confidentiality, 125–126

depositions, 13, 14, 78

The Diary and Autobiography of John Adams, 155

dignified manner of advertising, 230–231

diligence and client representation, 303

direct adverse authority, 322–323

direct contact, solicitation by, 234

disbarment

  case law/studies

    Clinton disbarment proceedings, 13–20

    In the Matter of Hein, 17–20

    In re Elkins, 53–54

  as disciplinary sanction, 6–7

  lawyers as paralegals/legal assistants, 51–54

disciplinary actions

  association sanctions, 37

  case law/studies

    Attorney Grievance Commission of Maryland v. Ficker, 43–45

    Clinton disbarment proceedings, 13–20

    In the Matter of Hein, 17–20

    Musselman v. Willoughby Corporation, 39–42

    In re Elkins, 53–54

    State v. Robinson, 47–49, 232

  court sanctions, 45–47, 49

  for lawyers, 6–7

  lawyer's duty of supervision, 37–38, 42–43

  for paralegals/legal assistants, 36–49

disciplinary commission, 6–7

Disciplinary Rules in ABA Model Code of Professional Responsibility, 4, 187

discovery

  assisting, as paralegal/legal assistant permitted activity, 85

  and attorney-client privilege, 131, **132**

  basic rules of, 135–136, 150

  defined, 111

disqualification. *See also* imputed disqualification and conflicts of interest

  avoidance by paralegals/legal assistants, 201–202, **202**

  general policy on, 187–188

dissenting opinion in case brief, 9

divorce, 165, 274

double billing, 260, 292

double representation as conflict of interest, 157–159, **158**

E

e-mail and client confidentiality, 127–129, 150

education of paralegals/legal assistants, 25–26, 30–36, **35**

employee screens, and imputed disqualification, 189–203

encrypted e-mail, 127, 128, 129, 150

engagement letter, 176

Enron, 185

equity partner, 255

Erin Brockovich (film), 375

establishing fees, 73

establishing the attorney-client relationship, 73, 76, 176

estate plan, 300

ethical issues. *See specific topics*

ethical wall doctrine, 190

Ethics 2000 Commission. *See* ABA Ethics 2000 Commission

ethics opinions, 20

ex parte communication, 320

examinations and tests, legal professionals, 3, 27–28

exceptions to confidentiality. *See* confidentiality, exceptions to

exempt employee, 49–51

experience, paralegals/legal assistant requirements, 32–33

explanation of fees to client, 260–264

extra compensation, 279–280

F

facsimile machines and client confidentiality, 129

Facts and Findings (NALA), 27

facts section in case brief, 9–10

false evidence, 313–315

family law and contingent fees, 274

family-related lawyers opposing each other as conflict of interest, 183

fast food obesity, 313

fax machines and client confidentiality, 129

federal agencies and paralegal/legal assistant permitted activity, 86–87

federal cases, recovery of legal fees from opposing party in litigation, 281

Federal Tort Claim Act, 258
Federal Trade Commission (FTC),
   64, 256
federalist, defined, 8
fees, 254–298. *See also* contingency
   (contingent) fee
   ABA Ethics 2000 Commission, 260,
      292–293
   advance, 263–264
   agreement for new client, 261
   case law/studies
      *Absher Const. Co. v. Kent School
         Dist. No. 415*, 287–288
      Atkins v. Tinning, 278
      Florida Bar v. Bailey, 265–271
      Joerger v. Gordon Food Service, Inc.,
         287–291
      Missouri v. Jenkins, 281–285
      In re Maruko Inc., 291–292
      Trotter v. Nelson, 278
   confidentiality and confidentiality
      exceptions, 122, 127–127
   and conflicts of interest, 168,
      180–181
   costs of lawyer vs. paralegals/legal
      assistants, 24
   establishment and UPL, 73, 76
   ethical considerations for
      paralegals/legal assistants,
      291–293
   explanation of fees to client, 260–264
   fee sharing between lawyers and non-
      lawyers, 275–280, 294
   fixed rate, 256–257
   hourly rate, 255
   lawyer's ownership of client's case,
      183–184
   litigation costs, 262, 263, 273
   and overhead costs, 258
   of paralegals, 28–29, 49–51
   plan vs. fee sharing, 278–280
   recovery from opposing party in
      litigation, 280–291
   retainer, 114, 263–264
   rules on, 257–275
   salary of paralegals/legal assistants,
      28–29, 49–51
   third-party payment of legal expenses,
      conflicts of interest, 181–182
   types of, 255–257
fees, rules on legal, 257–275
   clearly explained to client, 260–264
   client's money kept separate,
      264–273

contingent fee rules, 273–274
fee sharing between lawyers of
   different firms, 275
reasonableness, 257–260
fees, sharing
   breach of contract and illegal fee
      sharing, 278
   independent contractors, 276
   law firm employees, 276
   between lawyers and non-lawyers,
      275–280, 294
   between lawyers of different
      firms, 275
   paralegals/legal assistants, 277–278
   vs. compensation plan, 279–281
A Few Good Men (film), 375–376
fiduciary, 114, 115
films for legal ethics, 374–380
financial issues. *See* fees
finder's fee, 279
The Firm (film), 114, 376
Fiske, Robert B., Jr., 137
fixed fee, 256–257, 256–275, 291
flat fee, 256–275, 291
*Florida Bar re Advisory Opinion on
   Nonlawyer Representation in
   Securities Arbitration*, 89–92
Florida Bar v. Bailey, 265–271
Florida Bar v. Catarcio, 95–98
Florida Bar v. Clark, 166–167
Florida Bar v. Mastrilli, 164–165
Florida Bar v. Went For It, Inc., 238–241
Ford Motor Company, 185
foreclosure, 238
formal ethical opinions, 20
former client conflict, 175–176,
   187, 204
forms books, 300
401k plan, 279
fraud
   false evidence, 313–315
   fraudulent information and
      advertising, 220–221
   prevention, as confidentiality
      exception, 125
frivolous lawsuits, 311–313
FTC (Federal Trade Commission),
   64, 256

G
Gates, Bill, 127–128
gifts from clients, 178–180, 187
The Gingerbread Man (film), 376
Gingrich, Newt, 129

Goldsborough v. Eagle Crest Partners, Ltd.,
   145–147
Grisham, John, 233, 375, 376
gross revenue, 279
guidelines, as term in professional
   conduct, 31
Gulf Oil Co. v. Bernard, 243

H
Harris, Jean, 118–121
*Hayes v. Central States Orthopedic
   Specialists, Inc.*, 192–193
Hearst, Patty, 180
Hearst, William Randolph, 180
holding section in case brief, 10
Holmes, Oliver Wendell, Jr., 23
hot potato client, 175–176
hourly rate, 255
hours, reporting by paralegals/legal
   assistants, 292–293

I
identity of client, confidentiality of,
   121–122
illegal activity, corporation/organization
   conflict of interest, **185**,
   185–187
impeachment, 255
implied authorization and
   confidentiality, 123–124
impropriety, appearance of, 188
imputed disqualification and conflicts of
   interest, 187–202
   ABA Ethics 2000 Commission, 206
   case law/studies
      Ciaffone v. District Court, 199–201
      In re Complex Asbestos Litigation,
         193–198
   client consent, 189–190
   formerly associated lawyers, 188–189
   general policy of disqualification,
      187–188
   presumption of shared
      confidences, 189
   screens for non-lawyer employees,
      191–203
   screens for paralegal/legal assistants,
      192–203, **202**
   screens for tainted lawyers,
      190–191, 207
in-person solicitation, 234
In re Anonymous, 112–113
In re Complex Asbestos Litigation,
   193–198

In re DiSandro, 170–174
In re Elkins, 53–54
In re Ethics Opinion No. 24 of the Committee on the Unauthorized Practice of Law, 102–106
In re Flint, 62
In re Grand Jury Investigation of Ocean Transportation, 145
In re Grand Jury Subpoena Duces Tecum, 137–138
In re Maruko Inc., 292–293
In re Primus, 243
In re R.M.J., 224, 238
In re Thonert, 65–70
In the Matter of Anonymous, 11–13
In the Matter of Hein, 17–20
inadvertent disclosure of confidential material, 138–147
　case law/studies
　　Corey v. Norman, Hanson & DeTroy, 139–141
　　Goldsborough v. Eagle Crest Partners, Ltd., 145–147
　　Lipin v. Bender, 142–144
　privileged status retained, 138–139, 141
　waiver of privilege, 144–145
inappropriate comparisons and advertising, 222–223
inappropriate implications and advertising, 221–222
independent contractors, 99–106, 276
independent counsel, 13
independent paralegal practices
　case law/studies
　　Florida Bar v. Catarcio, 95–98
　　In re Ethics Opinion No. 24 of the Committee on the Unauthorized Practice of Law, 102–106
　independent contractors, paralegal/legal assistant, 99–106
　public legal service by nonlawyers, 94–95, 98–99
　regulation of, 93–94
　and UPL, 93–106
indigent, 181
informal ethical opinions, 20
informed consent, 130
injunction, 46–47, 232
insider trading, 190
insurance, prepaid legal, 255
intentionally created conflict, 176–177
inter alia, 221

Interest on Lawyers' Trust Accounts (IOLTA), 271–273
Internet advertising, 229–231
Internet solicitation, 242
interrogatory, 135
intestate estate, 315
IOLTA (Interest on Lawyers' Trust Accounts), 271–273
issue conflict, 161–162
issue section in case brief, creating, 10

J
Jagged Edge (film), 376–377
jailhouse lawyers and UPL, 75–76
Jefferson, Thomas, 8, 62
Joerger v. Gordon Food Service, Inc., 287–291
joint representation, conflict of interest, 162–167
　case law/studies
　　Florida Bar v. Clark, 166–167
　　Florida Bar v. Mastrilli, 164–165
　in civil cases, 163
　in criminal cases, 162–163
　in nonlitigation setting, 163, 165–167
　overview, **158**
Jones, Paula, 13–14, 16
Jones, Stephen, 122–123
Jorgenson v. Volusia County, 323–324
judges, ex parte communication with, 320
judicial review, 7–9
juries, ex parte communication with, 320–321
jurisdiction
　defined, 4
　state supreme court over legal professionals, 4–5, **6**

K
Kendall, David, 14, 16
King, Rodney, 280
Kunz, Vicki J., 308–309

L
LAMA/Altman Weil *2002 Annual Compensation Survey,* 29
LAMA (Legal Assistant Management Association), 26, 50
The LAMA Manager (journal), 26
last link doctrine, 122
lawyers. *See specific topics*
lawyer's interests, conflicts of interest caused by, **158**, 167–174

about, 167
business interests, 168
case law/study: *In re DiSandro,* 170–174
financial interests, 168
intentionally created conflict, 176–177
lawyer-client relationship establishment, 176
sexual relationships with clients, 168–170
legal advice. *See* opinions, legal
legal assistance, history of, 24–26
Legal Assistant Management Association (LAMA), 26, 50
legal assistants. *See* paralegals/legal assistants
legal correspondence, drafting, 84–85
legal documents
　drafting, 84
　sale of, and UPL, 62–63, 80–81
legal ethics exam, 3
legal fees. *See* fees
legal insurance, prepaid, 255
legal research
　as paralegal/legal assistant permitted activity, 84
　and truthfulness, 321–324
legislative regulation. *See* state regulation by statute
Leo J. Shapiro & Associates, 1
letterhead and advertising, 231–232, 250
Lewinsky, Monica, 14, 16, 137
Liar, Liar (film), 377
libel, 223
licensure of paralegals/legal assistants, 29–30, 33–36, **35**
Liebeck, Stella, 311
Lincoln, Abraham, 62, 211, **212**
linked third-party advertising Web sites, 229–230
Lipin v. Bender, 142–144
liquidated damages clause, 165
litigation costs, 262, 263, 273
Litigation Explosion (Olson), 256
location of client, confidentiality of, 122
Louis XII, King of France, 60

M
malfeasance, 37
malpractice, defined, 324

malpractice liability for non-lawyers,
    325–331
  case law/studies
    Biakanja v. Irving, 327–328
    Busch v. Flangas, 329–331
    Webb v. Pomeroy, 325
  cause of action elements, 325
  legal theory behind, 326–331
  not universal, 331
Marbury, William, 8
Marbury v. Madison, 7–9
Marshall, John, 9
"Master of Disaster" in *Wall Street
    Journal* (Boot), 244–247
material misrepresentation, 220–221
Mayberry v. State, 132–135
Mays v. Neal, 304–307
McDade, Thomas, 248
McDermott, Jim, 129
McDonald's coffee lawsuit, 311
McDougal, James and Susan, 137
McVeigh, Timothy, 122–123
MDU Resources Group, 308
media rights for client's story, conflicts
    of interest, 180
mediation, 79
memorandum of law, 84
Microsoft, United States v., 127–128
misdemeanor, 61
misrepresentation, 311, 314
Missouri v. Jenkins, 281–285
mobile phones and client confidentiality,
    129–130, 150
money. *See* fees
motions, 63
movies for legal ethics, 374–380
multi-state bar exam, 3
Musselman v. Willoughby Corporation,
    39–42
My Cousin Vinny (film), 377

N
NALA Code of Ethics and Professional
    Responsibility, 368–370
  competence, 303
  conflicts of interest rules, 203
  duty of confidentiality, 116
  issuance, 27
  and UPL, 74
NALA Model Standards and Guidelines
    for Utilization of Legal
    Assistants, 360–367
  anticontact rules and unrepresented
    persons, 318–319

competence, 308–309
conflicts of interest rules, 203
issuance, 27
permitted activities, 84–85
pro bono service, 335
statement of, 360–367
and UPL, 74
NALA (National Association of Legal
    Assistants)
  Certified Legal Assistant (CLA)
    Program, 27–28, 37
  compensation and overtime, 51
  on licensure of paralegals/legal
    assistants, 33–34
  as professional organization, 27–28
*NALA National Utilization and
    Compensation Report (2002),* 29
NALA Net Files, 27
NALA Rules for Disciplinary
    Proceedings, 37
narrative approach to perjured
    testimony, 314
National Association of Legal Assistants
    (NALA). *See* NALA (National
    Association of Legal Assistants)
*National Occupational Employment and
    Wage Estimates, 2000* (Bureau of
    Labor Statistics), 29
The National Paralegal Reporter (NFPA
    journal), 26
negative stereotypes and ethics, 1–2
negligence, malpractice based on, 325
negotiable order of withdrawal (NOW)
    account, 272
negotiation on behalf of someone's legal
    rights, and UPL, 63
new lawyers, and competency, 300–301
NFPA Affirmation of Professional
    Responsibility, 26
NFPA Guidelines for the Enforcement
    of the Model Code of Ethics and
    Professional Responsibility, 37
NFPA Informal Ethics and Disciplinary
    Opinions, 27
NFPA Model Code of Ethics and
    Professional Responsibility and
    Guidelines for Enforcement,
    351–359
  issuance, 26
  permitted activities, 83–84
  sanctioning, 37
  and UPL, 74
NFPA Model Disciplinary Rules and
    Ethical Considerations

accurate billing, 291
competence, 303
conflicts of interest rules, 203
duty of confidentiality, 116
ex parte communication, 321
pro bono service, 335
and UPL, 73–74
NFPA (National Federation of Paralegal
    Associations)
  compensation and overtime, 51
  competence, 309–310
  disbarred/suspended lawyers as
    paralegals/legal assistants, 52
  on licensure of paralegals/legal
    assistants, 34
  as professional association, 26–27
  salary survey, 29
NFPA Paralegal Advanced Competency
    Exam (PACE), 27
Nix v. Whiteside, 314
Nixon, Richard, 15, 154
non-billable activities, 258
non-equity partner, 255
non-lawyer fee sharing, 275–280, 293
non-lawyer malpractice. *See* malpractice
    liability for non-lawyers
nonlitigation setting, joint
    representation in, 163, 165–167
nonrefundable retainers, 263–264
not-for-profit solicitation, 243
NOW (negotiable order of withdrawal)
    account, 272

O
O'Connor, Sandra Day, 299
Office of Independent Counsel (OIC),
    137–138
Ohralik v. Ohio State Bar Association,
    234–237, 243
OIC (Office of Independent Counsel),
    137–138
Olson, Walter K., 256
opinions, legal
  attorney opinion work product rule,
    136–137
  dissenting opinion in case brief, 9
  ethics opinions, 20
  giving, and UPL, 62, 74–76
opposing party in litigation, fee recovery
    from, 280–290
O'Quinn, John, 244–248
organizations as clients. *See*
    corporation/organization as
    client

original jurisdiction, 81
outsourcing, 100
overhead costs, and legal fees, 258
overtime for paralegals/legal assistants,
    49–51
ownership fee, 183–184

P

Pace (Paralegal Advanced Competency
    Exam), 27, 310
PACE-Registered Paralegal (R-P) title,
    27
Palomba v. Sullivan, 120–121
Paralegal Advanced Competency Exam
    (PACE), 27, 310
The Paralegal Educator (AAfPE
    journal), 26
paralegals/legal assistants, 23–59
    ABA definition of, 30, 101
    ABA Ethics 2000 Commission, on
        supervision, 56
    and administrative agencies, 85–88
    advertising, 231–232
    anticontact rules, 315–316
    authorized activities, 83–85
    case law/studies
        Ciaffone v. District Court, 199–201
        Florida Bar v. Catarcio, 95–98
        *Hayes v. Central States Orthopedic
            Specialists, Inc.,* 192–193
        In re Complex Asbestos Litigation,
            193–198
        *In re Ethics Opinion No. 24 of the
            Committee on the Unauthorized
            Practice of Law,* 102–106
    case law/study: *Florida Bar re Advisory
        Opinion on Nonlawyer
        Representation in Securities
        Arbitration,* 89–92
    certification of, 29–33, 34–35, **35**
    client communication, 303–307
    compensation, 28–29, 49–51
    competence, 303, 307–308
    confidentiality, 148–150
    conflicts of interest rules, 203
    contribution to legal fee, 262–263
    definitions of, 27, 30–33
    disbarred/suspended lawyers as,
        51–54
    discipline and sanctioning of, 36–49
    duty of confidentiality, 115–116
    education, 25–26, 30–36, **35**
    fees, ethical considerations for,
        290–292

gifts from clients, and conflicts of
    interest, 179–180, 187
history of, 24–26
illegal activity and
    corporation/organization conflict
    of interest, 186–187
legal assistance, history of, 24–26
licensure of, 29–30, 33–36, **35**
local rules of court, 92–93
membership in state bar associations,
    55–56
non-lawyer fee sharing, 275–280, 293
permitted practices, 83–93
place in practice of law, 63–65
pro bono services by, 310, 334–336
professional associations, 26–28
on professionalism, 308–310
protecting self when changing
    jobs, 204
qualifications and prerequisites for, 32
In re Elkins, 53–54
roles and ethical/legal obligations, 2
rules of court, 5
salary, 28–29, 49–51
salary vs. overtime, 49–51
screens for, 192–202, 192–203,
    193, 202
solicitation, 243–244
partner, 24
patent, 226
pecuniary, 234
*Peel v. Attorney Registration and
    Disciplinary Commission,* 226
People v. Harris, 118–120
perjury in narrative testimony, 314
personal representative, 315
Philadelphia (film), 377–378
plaintiffs
    class action claim settlement conflicts
        of interests, 181–182
    co-plaintiffs, and joint
        representation, 163
    double representation, 157–159, **158**
plea bargaining, 222
pleadings, 63, 82, 85
positive law, 61
practice of law, description, 61–70. *See
    also specific topics*
prenuptial agreement, 165
prepaid legal insurance, 255
preparation and client representation,
    300–301, 319
prerecorded telephone advertising,
    228–229

present and former clients, conflicts of
    interest between, 174–177
    disqualification, 187
    former client, defined, 175–176
    intentionally created conflict,
        176–177
    overview, **158,** 174–175
    protecting interests of, 203
    relationship establishment, 176
Presumed Innocent (film), 378
presumption of shared confidences,
    189, 202
prevention of client criminal
    conduct/fraud and
    confidentiality, 124–125
prima facie, 122
prior relationships and solicitation,
    242–243
privileged materials, 141–147, 150
pro bono, defined, 180
pro bono services, 332–336
    evolution of rules, 332–333
    and paralegal/legal assistant, 334–336
    as required activity, 333–334
pro se representation, 77, 317
professional association for lawyers. *See*
    ABA (American Bar Association)
professional associations for
    paralegals/legal assistants, 26–28.
    See also specific organizations
professional conduct. *See* rules of ethics
    and professional conduct
Professional Ethics (Sharswood), 4
promissory estoppel, 287
prospective clients and
    confidentiality, 114
provocative advertising, 230–231
proximate cause, 325
public policy, defined, 274
public regard for lawyers, 1–2
puffing, 221
Puzo, Mario, 254

Q

quantum merit, 262
quasi-judicial agencies. *See*
    administrative agency
    adjudication

R

R-P (PACE-Registered Paralegal) title, 27
radio advertising, 228
The Rainmaker (film), 378
The Rainmaker (Grisham book), 233

Ray, Robert, 13
real estate law
    closing the transaction, 81–82
    and joint representation, 165–166
reasonable fees, 257–260
    about, 257
    fees in excess of statutory allowances,
        258–259
    nonbillable activities, 258
    unreasonableness, 259–260
reasoning section in case brief, 10
record keeping for advertising, 223, 226
recovery of legal fees
    paralegal/legal assistant fees, 277,
        281–290
recovery of legal fees from opposing
        party in litigation
    case law/studies
        *Absher Const. Co. v. Kent School
            Dist. No. 415,* 287–288
        Joerger v. Gordon Food Service, Inc.,
            287–290
        Missouri v. Jenkins, 281–285
        in federal cases, 281
        in state cases, 285–287, 290
recuse, 163
referral service, 223, 227, 230
referrals, prohibition against payment
        for, 227–228
regulation of legal profession, 1–22
    ABA role in, 3–5, **6**, 20
    by bar associations, 3
    briefing a case, process of, 9–13
    case law/study: Clinton disbarment
        proceedings, 13–20
    disciplinary process summary, 6–7
    negative stereotypes and ethics, 1–2
    of paralegals/legal assistants, 23
    reasons for lack of legislative
        regulation, 7–9
Rehnquist, William H., 23
related lawyers opposing each other,
        conflicts of interest, 183
remand, 10
represented persons, anticontact rules,
        315–316
research, legal
    as paralegal/legal assistant permitted
        activity, 84
    and truthfulness, 321–324
respondeat superior, 37–38, 42–43
restatement, 115
retainer, 114, 263–264
reverse, as appellate court decision, 10

reverse contingent fee, 256
Rogers, Will, 110
Roosevelt, Theodore "Teddy," 154
rules of court
    defined, 5
    disbarred/suspended lawyers as
        paralegals/legal assistants, 52–53
    paralegal/legal assistant permitted
        activity in, 92–93
rules of ethics and professional conduct.
    *See also specific codes, rules and
    guidelines*
    ABA on, 3–5, **6**
    prohibition of UPL, 62–63, 71–74
    and rule of court, 5

S

salary, paralegals/legal assistants, 28–29,
        49–51
Samaritan Foundation v. Superior Court,
        148–149
sanctions. *See also* disciplinary actions
    association, 37
    of paralegals/legal assistants, 45–47, 49
The Scarsdale Diet (Tarnower), 118
SCOLA (Standing Committee on Legal
        Assistants)
    on ABA Model Guidelines for the
        Utilization of the Legal Assistant
        Service, 25, 241–250
    definition of paralegals/legal
        assistants, 30–32
    founding of, 24
    on licensure of paralegals/legal
        assistants, 33, 35, 36
scope of employment doctrine, 37, 42
screens for paralegals/legal assistants,
        191–202
    case law/studies
        Ciaffone v. District Court, 199–201
        *Hayes v. Central States Orthopedic
            Specialists, Inc.,* 192–193
        In re Complex Asbestos Litigation,
            193–198
    court approved, 192–193, **193**
    disqualification avoidance,
        201–202, **202**
    elements of effective, **193**
    lack of court approval, 198–199
    for non-lawyer employees, 191–192
screens for tainted lawyers, 190–191,
        207
secretary vs. paralegals/legal
        assistants, 24, 27

Securities and Exchange Commission
        (SEC), 190
security interest, 177
self-help legal service, 77, 80–81
separate accounts for legal fees, 264–273
    case law/study: *Florida Bar v. Bailey,*
        265–271
    commingling or conversion, 264
    Interest on Lawyers' Trust Accounts
        (IOLTA), 271–273
    retainers, 271
settlement, aggregate, 182
settlement of combined claims, conflicts
        of interest, 182
sexual relationships, client-lawyer,
        168–170
Shakespeare, William, 1, 2
Shapero v. Kentucky Bar Association, 238
shared confidences, presumption of,
        189, 202
shareholder's derivative lawsuit, 163
Sharswood, George, 4
Shaw, Carl, 247
sidestepping the law and
        advertising, 222
simultaneous representation in different,
        unrelated matters, conflict of
        interest, **158**, 160
small claims court representation, and
        UPL, 62, 77
solicitation, 233–248. *See also*
        advertising
    ABA Ethics 2000 Commission,
        248–250
    case law/studies
        Florida Bar v. Went For It, Inc.,
            238–241
        Gulf Oil Co. v. Bernard, 243
        *Ohralik v. Ohio State Bar
            Association,* 234–237, 243
        O'Quinn's techniques, 244–248
        In re Primus, 243
    direct contact, rules against, 233–242
    and paralegals/legal assistants,
        243–244
    permitted, 242–243
    vs. advertising, 233, **233**
solicitor general, 137
specialization, legal, and advertising,
        223, 226–227, 249–250
Standing Committee on Legal Assistants
        (SCOLA). *See* SCOLA
        (Standing Committee on Legal
        Assistants)

Starr, Kenneth, 13, 137

state agencies, paralegal/legal assistant permitted activity, 87–88

state bar associations
definition of paralegals/legal assistants, 32, 101
paralegals/legal assistants as members, 55–56
regulation of legal profession, 3

state regulation by statute
advertising restrictions, 223–225
practice of law defined by positive law, 61–63, 70–71
prohibition of UPL, 61–63, 70–71
reasons for lack of, 7–9
recovery of legal fees from opposing party in litigation, 285–287, 290
rules of court, 5

state-specific considerations. *See specific topics*

state supreme courts
adoption of ABA rules of ethics, 4–5, **6**
definition of paralegals/legal assistants, 31–33, 101
legal profession regulation, 7
paralegal regulation, 31

State v. Robinson, 47–49, 232

statute, regulation by. *See* state regulation by statute

statutorily limited fees, 257, 258–259

subrogation, 271

suing an existing client in unrelated lawsuit, conflict of interest, **158**, 160–162

summary judgement, 14

supreme courts. *See* state supreme courts; U.S. Supreme Court

surety bond, 80

Survey of Law Firm Economics (2001), 255

Suspect (film), 378

suspended lawyers, 51–54

T

tainted persons
employee screen, 191–203, **202**
lawyer screen, 190–191, 207

Tarnower, Herman, 118–121

technology and client confidentiality, 127–130
case law/studies
Corey v. Norman, Hanson & DeTroy, 139–141

Goldsborough v. Eagle Crest Partners, Ltd., 145–147
Lipin v. Bender, 142–144
Mayberry v. State, 132–135
e-mail, 127–129, 150
fax machines, 129
mobile phones, 129–130, 150

telephone solicitation, 234, 241–242

television advertising, 228

testimonial advertising and unjustified expectations, 222

tests and examinations, legal professionals, 3, 27–28

third parties
confidentiality in presence of, 117–121
payment of legal expenses, conflicts of interest, 181–182
Web site advertising, 229–230

Thornburgh, Richard, 317

A Time to Kill (film), 379

To Kill a Mockingbird (film), 379

tobacco class-action lawsuit settlement contingency fees, 256

transactional document execution and UPL, 62–63, 80–81

Trotter v. Nelson, 278

trust, 161

trust account, 83

truthfulness and client representation, 310–324
anticontact rules, 315–318
case law/studies
Jorgenson v. Volusia County, 323–324
Nix v. Whiteside, 314
ex parte communication, 320–321
false evidence, 313–315
frivolous claims, 311–313
general rule on, 310–311
legal research, 321–324
represented persons and, 315–316
unrepresented persons and, 318–319

12 Angry Men (film), 379

2000 National Occupational Employment and Wage Estimates (Bureau of Labor Statistics), 29

U

unauthorized practice of law (UPL), 60–109
ABA Ethics 2000 Commission, 106–107
about, 60

attorney rules of professional conduct, prohibition by, 71–72
case law/studies
Florida Bar re Advisory Opinion on Nonlawyer Representation in Securities Arbitration, 89–92
Florida Bar v. Catarcio, 95–98
In re Ethics Opinion No. 24 of the Committee on the Unauthorized Practice of Law, 102–106
In re Flint, 62
In re Thonert, 65–70
and independent paralegal practices, 93–106
paralegal codes of conduct, prohibition by, 72–74
permitted paralegal practices, 83–93
practice of law, defined, 61–70
prohibited paralegal practices, 74–82
statute, prohibition by, 70–71

undue influence, 178

unified bar association, 3

United States v. Microsoft, 127–128

unjustified expectations and advertising, 221–222

unrepresented persons and truthfulness, 318–319

UPL. *See* unauthorized practice of law (UPL)

U.S. Chamber of Commerce, 256

U.S. Constitution, *Marbury v. Madison,* 8

U.S. Department of Labor, 28, 29, 50

U.S. Justice Department, 64, 318

U.S. Patent and Trademark Office, 226

U.S. Supreme Court
Clinton's resignation from Supreme Court bar, 14, 16
confidentiality and corporation/organization as client, 117
on contingency fees, 255–256
doctrine of judicial review, 7–9
Interest on Lawyers' Trust Accounts (IOLTA), 272–273
jailhouse lawyers and UPL, 75–76
joint representation in criminal cases, 162–163
on lawyer advertising, 213–219, 224–225, 231
Marbury v. Madison, 7–9
representation decisions and lawyer financial interests, 168
solicitation, 233, 234–241, 243

V

vacate, 10

Vallinoto v. DiSandro. See In re DiSandro

venire, 320

The Verdict (film), 380

vexatious litigant, 313

voir dire, 321

von Bismarck, Otto, 61

W

waiver, and inadvertent disclosure,
 144–145

Wall Street Journal, 244, 247

warranty, 221

Web sites

 law firms, 229–231

 NALA Net Files, 27

 for paralegals/legal assistants, 25, 373

 state bar associations, 371–372

Webb v. Pomeroy, 325

Weber Wright, Susan, 13, 14, 16

Webster, Daniel, 299

West Digest System, 303

Wheat v. United States, 162–163

Whitewater investigation, 13,
 137–138

wills, execution of, and UPL, 62–63,
 80–81

witness competency statutes, 131, **132**

work product rule, 131, **132,** 136–138

World War 3.0: Microsoft and Its Enemies
 (Auletta), 128

writ of mandamus, 312

written solicitation, 238–241

Wythe, George, 62

Z

Zauderer v. Office of Disciplinary Counsel,
 224–225